WW2

Readings on Critical Issues

WW2

Readings on Critical Issues

Edited by

Theodore A. Wilson
Associate Professor of History
The University of Kansas

Charles Scribner's Sons   **New York**

Acknowledgments

This book is intended to be an introduction to certain important problems in the history of the Second World War. It offers a sampling of the rich and varied historical sources deriving from that tragic, tempestuous period. Other issues and certainly other documents might accomplish these purposes equally well. Indeed, the range of controversial and challenging questions—historical, philosophical, and moral—about the Second World War seems virtually limitless. The problems dealt with here are of particular interest to me, and I hope that my selections will intrigue and provoke others.

I welcome this opportunity to acknowledge my debt to a colleague at the University of Kansas, Professor Lynn Nelson, who first persuaded me to "teach" the Second World War. Clayton Koppes and Sally Bruce of the K.U. Extramural Independent Study Center suffered my editorial apprenticeship with remarkable patience. Elsie Kearns and Barbara Wood of Scribners College Department have offered both patience and much-needed encouragement. The sound advice and tolerance of these people, as well as the assistance of Gregory D. Black and Roberta A. Spires, is deeply appreciated. As always, Judith Wilson performed splendidly as proofreader and psychiatrist.

Lawrence, Kansas
March 20, 1974

Theodore A. Wilson

Contents

Unit III: The Sort of War It Was

Unit IV: Dimensions of Grand Strategy

Unit V: Death from the Skies

Unit VI: Of War Crimes and Operational Necessity

Unit VII: The Nature of Wartime Diplomacy

Unit VIII: Legacies of the Second World War

Unit I

Why They Fought

Is man innately aggressive? Are wars an inevitable product of organized social activity? Of particular types of economic and political organization? Can any good result from the slaughter of human beings by other human beings? These and a multitude of other questions may be and have been asked about war, the social invention that *Homo sapiens* alone can claim.

To ask why men fight wars is to pose the central and as yet unsolved question of the ages. Elaborate philosophical systems have been created to explain this behavior; equally complex political systems have been devised to abolish it. Thus far, neither philosophers nor international-relations experts have done very well. The related though less ambitious question, why did men fight the Second World War, raises painfully difficult moral and historical issues. Is war ever justifiable? Many intelligent and sincere people who had suffered through the First World War came to believe that nothing justified armed force and, in the 1920's and 30's, they preached absolute pacifism. Yet some, and perhaps most, of these same people accepted the Second World War as both necessary and just. What makes a "just war" just? Can such questions ever be usefully asked or answered?

The selections that follow are intended to serve as stimuli for consideration of such questions. The documents survey various explanations among those offered by participants in the Second World War. Although they perhaps reveal more about the rationalizations that individuals and governments adopted to justify their participation in the conflict, these excerpts do express some of the actual motives for this particular war. They also demonstrate that "guilt," and "justice," and "aggression" had become relative matters by 1939. The essays offer several "classic" statements on the nature of war—and thus on the nature of man. The insights they provide, if not very appealing, enable us to view the Second World War in a broader perspective—an opportunity that was not available to those who fought it.

Documents

1 From War to War: The Tragedy of Munich

Winston S. Churchill

For Winston Churchill the issue was simple: the Second World War was but another episode in the eternal struggle between Good and Evil. The Allies were under divine protection; Hitler and his cohorts were the devil's spawn. Churchill professed hatred of war as an institution, and that may be so. He certainly despised the impersonal, mechanical activity that modern warfare had become. However, the man who had served as a dashing young officer in India, who had proven his courage in a daring escape from the Boers and in cavalry charges against the dervishes in the Sudan, also believed that war was a necessary evil and that it called forth the best as well as the worst qualities of mankind. The following excerpt from Churchill's memoirs, The Second World War, *concludes the first volume of his monumental work. By describing the coming of war between "Hitlerite Germany" and the Allies, Churchill expresses the viewpoint of a generation, of a class, and of a man for whom this war was a magnificent opportunity for personal vindication.*

It may be well here to set down some principles of morals and action which may be a guide in the future. No case of this kind can be judged apart from its circumstances. The facts may be unknown at the time, and estimates of them must be largely guesswork, coloured by the general feelings and aims of whoever is trying to pronounce. Those who are prone by temperament and character to seek sharp and clear-cut solutions to difficult and obscure problems, who are ready to fight whenever some challenge comes from a foreign Power, have not always been right. On the other hand, those whose inclination is to bow their heads, to seek patiently and faithfully for peaceful compromise, are not always wrong. On the contrary, in the majority of instances they may be right, not only

From **The Gathering Storm**, vol. I of **The Second World War** by Winston S. Churchill, pp. 319–21. Copyright 1948 by Houghton Mifflin Company. Reprinted by permission of the publisher, Houghton Mifflin Company.

morally but from a practical standpoint. How many wars have been averted by patience and persisting good will! Religion and virtue alike lend their sanctions to meekness and humility, not only between men but between nations. How many wars have been precipitated by firebrands! How many misunderstandings which led to wars could have been removed by temporising! How often have countries fought cruel wars and then after a few years of peace found themselves not only friends but allies!

The Sermon on the Mount is the last word in Christian ethics. Everyone respects the Quakers. Still, it is not on these terms that Ministers assume their responsibilities of guiding states. Their duty is first so to deal with other nations as to avoid strife and war and to eschew aggression in all its forms, whether for nationalistic or ideological objects. But the safety of the State, the lives and freedom of their own fellow countrymen, to whom they owe their position, make it right and imperative in the last resort, or when a final and definite conviction has been reached, that the use of force should not be excluded. If the circumstances are such as to warrant it, force may be used. And if this be so, it should be used under the conditions which are most favourable. There is no merit in putting off a war for a year if, when it comes, it is a far worse war or one much harder to win. These are the tormenting dilemmas upon which mankind has throughout its history been so frequently impaled. Final judgment upon them can only be recorded by history in relation to the facts of the case as known to the parties at the time, and also as subsequently proved.

There is, however, one helpful guide, namely, for a nation to keep its word and to act in accordance with its treaty obligations to allies. This guide is called *honour*. It is baffling to reflect that what men call honour does not correspond always to Christian ethics. Honour is often influenced by that element of pride which plays so large a part in its inspiration. An exaggerated code of honour leading to the performance of utterly vain and unreasonable deeds could not be defended, however fine it might look. Here, however, the moment came when Honour pointed the path of Duty, and when also the right judgment of the facts at that time would have reinforced its dictates.

2   The Virtues of War

Adolf Hitler

Adolf Hitler believed that war was man's most enabling and beneficial activity. His pronouncements on the subject, vast in number, were highly consistent. As the following brief excerpt from Hitler's Secret Conversations *shows, the* Fuehrer *was a proponent of Social Darwinism, a brutal philosophical system derived from the biological principle of "survival of the fittest." Hitler assumed that Germany had to be the "fittest" nation because it was successful in war, and it would be successful in war because it was most fit. It is doubtful whether, even in his crumbling* Fuehrerbunker *in ruined Berlin, Hitler recognized the circularness—and therefore the speciousness—of this argument.*

For the good of the German people, we must wish for a war every fifteen or twenty years. An army whose sole purpose is to preserve peace leads only to playing at soldiers—compare Sweden and Switzerland. Or else it constitutes a revolutionary danger to its own country.

If I am reproached with having sacrificed a hundred or two thousand men by reason of the war, I can answer that, thanks to what I have done, the German nation has gained, up to the present, more than two million five hundred thousand human beings. If I demand a tenth of this as a sacrifice, nevertheless I have given 90 per cent. I hope that in ten years there will be from ten to fifteen millions more of us Germans in the world. Whether they are men or women, it matters little: I am creating conditions favourable to growth.

Many great men were the sixth or seventh children of their family. When such-and-such a man, whom one knows, dies, one knows that one has lost. But does one know what one loses by the limitation of births? The man killed before he is born—that remains the enigma.

Wars drive the people to proliferation, they teach us not to fall into the error of being content with a single child in each family.

* * *

War has returned to its primitive form. The war of people against people is giving place to another war—a war for the possession of the great spaces.

Originally war was nothing but a struggle for pasturegrounds. To-day war is nothing but a struggle for the riches of nature. By virtue of an inherent law, these riches belong to him who conquers them.

The great migrations set out from the East. With us begins the ebb, from West to East.

That's in accordance with the laws of nature. By means of the struggle, the élites are continually renewed.

The law of selection justifies this incessant struggle, by allowing the survival of the fittest.

Christianity is a rebellion against natural law, a protest against nature. Taken to its logical extreme, Christianity would mean the systematic cultivation of the human failure.

3   THE RISE AND FALL
OF THE THIRD REICH

William L. Shirer

The noted journalist and broadcaster William L. Shirer was in Berlin when word came of the German invasion of Poland. Nine months later Shirer witnessed the surrender, in the Forest of Compiegne, of the French army and nation to a victorious Germany. His descriptions of these events add further insights toward an understanding of Hitler's motives and his limitless capacity for revenge and personal glorification.

The Launching of World War II

At daybreak on September 1, 1939, the very date which Hitler had set in his first directive for "Case White" back on April 3, the German armies poured across the Polish frontier and converged on Warsaw from the north, south and west.

Overhead German warplanes roared toward their targets: Polish troop columns and ammunition dumps, bridges, railroads and open cities. Within a few minutes they were giving the Poles, soldiers and civilians alike, the first taste of sudden death and destruction from the skies ever experienced on any great scale on the earth and thereby inaugurating a terror which would become dreadfully familiar to hundreds of millions of men, women and children in Europe and Asia during the next six years, and whose shadow, after the nuclear bombs came, would haunt all mankind with the threat of utter extinction.

It was a gray, somewhat sultry morning in Berlin, with clouds hanging low over the city, giving it some protection from hostile bombers, which were feared but never came.

The people in the streets, I noticed, were apathetic despite the immensity of the news which had greeted them from their radios and from the extra editions of the morning newspapers. Across the street from the Adlon Hotel the morning shift of laborers had gone to work on the new I. G. Farben building just as if nothing had happened, and when newsboys came by shouting their extras no one laid down his tools to buy one. Perhaps, it occurred to me, the German people were simply dazed at waking up on this first morning of September to find themselves in a war which they had been sure the Fuehrer somehow would avoid. They could not quite believe it, now that it had come.

What a contrast, one could not help thinking, between this gray apathy and the way the Germans had gone to war in 1914. Then there had been a wild enthusiasm. The crowds in the streets had staged delirious demonstrations, tossed flowers at the marching troops and frantically cheered the Kaiser and Supreme Warlord, Wilhelm II.

There were no such demonstrations this time for the troops or for the Nazi warlord, who shortly before 10 A.M. drove from the Chancellery to the Reichstag through empty streets to address the nation on the momentous happenings which he himself, deliberately and cold-bloodedly, had just provoked. Even the robot members of the Reichstag, party hacks, for the most part, whom Hitler had appointed, failed to respond with much enthusiasm as the dictator launched into his explanation of why Germany found itself on this morning engaged in war. There was far less cheering than on previous and less important occasions when the Leader had declaimed from this tribune in the ornate hall of the Kroll Opera House.

Though truculent at times he seemed strangely on the defensive, and throughout the speech, I thought as I listened, ran a curious strain, as though he himself were dazed at the fix he had got himself into and felt a little desperate about it. . . .

Having lied so often on his way to power and in his consolidation of power, Hitler could not refrain at this serious moment in history from thundering a few more lies to the gullible German people in justification of his wanton act.

You know the endless attempts I made for a peaceful clarification and understanding of the problem of Austria, and later of the problem of the Sudetenland, Bohemia and Moravia. It was all in vain . . .

In my talks with Polish statesmen . . . I formulated at last the German proposals and . . . there is nothing more modest or loyal than these proposals. I should like to say this to the world. I alone was in the position to make such proposals, for I know very well that in doing so I brought myself into opposition to millions of Germans. These proposals have been refused. . . .

For two whole days I sat with my Government and waited to see whether it was convenient for the Polish Government to send a plenipotentiary or not . . . But I am wrongly judged if my love of peace and my patience are mistaken for weakness or even cowardice . . . I can no longer find any willingness on the part of the Polish Government to conduct serious negotiations with us . . . I have therefore resolved to speak to Poland in the same language that Poland for months past has used toward us . . .

This night for the first time Polish regular soldiers fired on our own territory. Since 5:45 A.M. we have been returning the fire, and from now on bombs will be met with bombs.

Thus was the faked German attack on the German radio station at Gleiwitz, which, as we have seen, was carried out by S.S. men in Polish uniforms under the direction of Naujocks, used by the Chancellor of Germany as justification of his cold-blooded aggression against Poland. And indeed in its first communiqués the German High Command referred to its military operations as a "counterattack." Even Weizsaecker did his best to perpetrate this shabby swindle. During the day he got off a circular telegram from the Foreign Office to all German diplomatic missions abroad advising them on the line they were to take.

In defense against Polish attacks, German troops moved into action against Poland at dawn today. This action is for the present not to be described as war, but merely as engagements which have been brought about by Polish attacks.

Even the German soldiers, who could see for themselves who had done the attacking on the Polish border, were bombarded with Hitler's lie. In a grandiose proclamation to the German Army on September 1, the Fuehrer said:

The Polish State has refused the peaceful settlement of relations which I desired, and has appealed to arms . . . A series of violations of the frontier, intolerable to a great Power, prove that Poland is no longer willing to respect the frontier of the Reich.

In order to put an end to this lunacy, I have no other choice than to meet force with force from now on.

Only once that day did Hitler utter the truth.

I am asking of no German man [he told the Reichstag] more than I myself was ready throughout four years to do . . . I am from now on just the first soldier of the German Reich. I have once more put on that coat that was most sacred and dear to me. I will not take it off again until victory is secured, or I will not survive the outcome.

In the end, this once, he would prove as good as his word. But no German I met in Berlin that day noticed that what the Leader was saying quite bluntly was that he could not face, not take, defeat should it come. . . .

* * *

Victory in the West

I followed the German Army into Paris that June, always the loveliest of months in the majestic capital, which was now stricken, and on June 19 got wind of where Hitler was going to lay down his terms for the armistice which Pétain had requested two days before. It was to be on the same spot where the German Empire had capitulated to France and her allies on November 11, 1918: in the little clearing in the woods at Compiègne. There the Nazi warlord would get his revenge, and the place itself would add to the sweetness of it for him. On May 20, a bare ten days after the great offensive in the West had started and on the day the German tanks reached Abbeville, the idea had come to him. Jodl noted it in his diary that day: "Fuehrer is working on the peace treaty . . . First negotiations in the Forest of Compiègne." Late on the afternoon of June 19 I drove out there and found German Army engineers demolishing the wall of the museum where the old *wagon-lit* of Marshal Foch, in which the 1918 armistice was signed, had been preserved. By the time I left, the engineers, working with pneumatic drills, had torn the wall down and were pulling the car out to the tracks in the center of the clearing on the exact spot, they said, where it had stood at 5 A.M. on November 11, 1918, when at the dictation of Foch the German emissaries put their signatures to the armistice.

And so it was that on the afternoon of June 21 I stood by the edge of the forest at Compiègne to observe the latest and greatest of Hitler's triumphs, of which, in the course of my work, I had seen so many over the last turbulent years. It was one of the loveliest summer days I ever remember in France. A warm June sun beat down on the stately trees—elms, oaks, cypresses and pines—casting pleasant shadows on the wooded avenues leading to the little circular clearing. At 3:15 P.M. precisely, Hitler arrived in his big Mercedes, accompanied by Goering, Brauchitsch, Keitel, Raeder, Ribbentrop and Hess, all in their various uniforms, and Goering, the lone Field Marshal of the Reich, fiddling with his field marshal's baton. They alighted from their automobiles some two hundred yards away, in front of the Alsace-Lorraine statue, which was draped with German war flags so that the Fuehrer could not see (though I remembered from previous visits in happier days) the large sword, the sword of the victorious Allies of 1918, sticking through a limp eagle representing the German Empire of the Hohenzollerns. Hitler glanced at the monument and strode on.

I observed his face [I wrote in my diary]. It was grave, solemn, yet brimming with revenge. There was also in it, as in his springy step, a note of the triumphant conqueror, the defier of the world. There was something else . . . a sort of scornful, inner joy at being present at this great reversal of fate—a reversal he himself had wrought.

When he reached the little opening in the forest and his personal standard had been run up in the center of it, his attention was attracted by a great granite block which stood some three feet above the ground.

Hitler, followed by the others, walks slowly over to it [I am quoting my diary], steps up, and reads the inscription engraved (in French) in great high letters:

"Here on the Eleventh of November 1918 Succumbed the Criminal Pride of the German Empire—Vanquished by the Free Peoples Which It Tried to Enslave."

Hitler reads it and Goering reads it. They all read it, standing there in the June sun and the silence. I look for the expression in Hitler's face. I am but fifty yards from him and see him through my glasses as though he were directly in front of me. I have seen that face many times at the great moments of his life. But today! It is afire with scorn, anger, hate, revenge, triumph.

He steps off the monument and contrives to make even this gesture a masterpiece of contempt. He glances back at it, contemptuous, angry—angry, you almost feel, because he cannot wipe out the awful, provoking lettering with one sweep of his high Prussian boot. He glances slowly around the clearing, and now, as his eyes meet ours, you grasp the depth of his hatred. But there is triumph there too—revengeful, triumphant hate. Suddenly, as though his face were not giving complete expression to his feelings, he throws his whole body into harmony with his mood. He swiftly snaps his hands on his hips, arches his shoulders, plants his feet wide apart. It is a magnificent gesture of defiance, of burning contempt for this place now and all that it has stood for in the twenty-two years since it witnessed the humbling of the German Empire.

4   What Are the Real Causes?

Harold Nicolson

In a pamphlet issued by the British government, Harold Nicolson, a gifted historian and biographer, set forth in condensed form the official justification of England's decision for war. Why Britain Is at War *was, therefore, propaganda for the British point of view. Nicolson's treatment is, nonetheless, of interest because he was aiming at a broad popular audience and because he dealt with basic questions about the necessity and morality of Great Britain's involvement in this conflict.*

The British people are by nature peaceful and kindly. They desire nothing on earth except to retain their liberties, to enjoy their pleasures, and to go about their business in a tranquil frame of mind. They have no ambition for honour and glory, and they regard wars, and even victories, as silly, ugly, wasteful things. They are not either warriors or heroes until they are forced to become so; they are sensible and gentle women and men.

In common with other branches of the Anglo-Saxon race they are a mixture of realism and idealism. Being somewhat indolent by temperament, it is only by dire necessity that they can be stirred to do unpleasant things. Yet when this necessity arises they like to make a virtue of it. This leads them at times to render unto God the things which are Caesar's and has earned them the reputation of hypocrisy. In many ways, this reputation is unfair. No Englishman feels really happy unless both his practical and his moral instincts are engaged.

This sleepy, decent and most pacific race can only be roused to violent action by two emotions: the first is fear; the second is anger. Before he agrees to make war the Briton must have (a) a sense of personal danger and (b) a sense of personal outrage. His deep instinct of self-preservation, and his long moral tradition must simultaneously be aroused. Ever since 1933 Adolf Hitler has titivated one or other of these two emotions but, until March 15th, 1939, he did not provoke them both simultaneously. Until that vital date, half the people of Great Britain were frightened without being angry and the other half were angry without being frightened. The combination of menace and humiliation which Herr Hitler contrived on March 15th united these two halves.

Let me begin with the menace, since it aroused our practical side, the instinct for self-preservation. Why did the whole British people, on that March 15th, 1939, feel that the rape of Prague was a menace to our own existence?

During the previous six years the thought of "national security" had seldom been absent from our minds. A sense of impending and imponderable

From **Why Britain Is at War** by Harold Nicolson (London: Penguin Books Ltd., 1940), pp. 128–41. Copyright 1940 by Harold Nicolson. Reprinted by permission of Nigel Nicolson.

danger hung over us night and day. Each one of us responded to the acute discomfort of such anxiety in different ways. Some tried to find ease of mind by dismissing the danger as imaginary and by repeating as some mystic incantation the formula: "There will be no war." Others sought relief in believing that it might be possible for us to withdraw from the dangerous infections of Europe and to seek isolation in our Empire overseas. Others again urged that the cancer was rapidly increasing and that only by early and drastic operation could it be removed. While others believed in all sincerity that the menace was not as malignant as some supposed and that by a little patience, a little tact, a little conciliation the wild animal which threatened us might be satisfied and tamed.

It was this latter school of thought which produced and directed the policy of appeasement. It is easy to condemn that policy. It is all too easy to be wise after the event and to contend that if we had risked a little for the League of Nations in 1935 we should not be risking our all to-day. It is easy to argue that had we and France taken a strong line in 1936, Germany would not have fortified the Rhineland and thus provided herself with a barrier behind which she could increase her power and her depredations in the East. It is easy to condemn our Government for not having intervened in Austria or Czechoslovakia, for not having introduced conscription earlier, for not having rushed in 1933 into a vast programme of armament in the air. It is impossible to deny that the Nazis have been able to delude and trick us at every turn. It is impossible to deny that we were too slow to realise the nature of their ambition or the extreme cunning of their method. Their technique has been, as I have tried to show, consistent throughout.

I am conscious that as this story has been unfolded the British Government have been made to seem amazingly optimistic, gullible and blind. We must remember, however, that at each stage Herr Hitler knew exactly what he wanted, could guard his own secrets, could operate with the utmost speed and discipline, and was deterred by no considerations of consistency or honour. The British Government were throughout blinded by their fierce detestation of war. Even had they realised earlier, that Herr Hitler's ambition was unlimited and that he would never be satisfied with minor gains, they could not have taken preventive action without the approval of the British public. Until Herr Hitler made the gross error of tearing up the Munich agreement and thereby humiliating Great Britain in the person of her Prime Minister, such approval would not have been given.

It is easy also to criticise Mr. Chamberlain for the rigidity with which, until March 15, 1939, he pursued a policy which has since been proved mistaken. Yet we must remember that throughout the period he was reflecting the ideas and wishes of a great mass, perhaps even a great majority, of British opinion. The Prime Minister is representative of those great civic virtues which have rendered our mercantile community the backbone of the country; he was throughout honourable, patient and sincere. By sacrificing so much in the cause of appeasement he may not perhaps have rendered peace more certain, but he assuredly showed the country and the world that war, if it came, would not be of our contrivance; that we should enter upon it with loathing but with resolution; and that our hands were clean.

What has all this to do with the instinct of self-preservation? It has this to do. The motive of self-preservation operated throughout the period from 1933-1939. Until March 15th last it was believed by the Prime Minister and his intimate advisers that if we could only avoid a head-on collision our own life might be preserved. After March 15th they cherished no such illusions. The tiger was not merely attacking the native huts down in the village; he was fixing lustful eyes upon our own large bungalow. Hitler was out for loot. And since the British and French Empires offered the richest loot in the world, it was probable, it was even certain, that in the end we also should be attacked. It is this realisation which accounts for the sudden reversal of policy after March 15th. In a single night the British people found that their instinct of self-preservation had been aroused. It had been aroused, if I may repeat myself, by the realisation that Herr Hitler was not out to defend his own rights but to violate the rights of others. It was then at last that we saw that he was a menace to the world.

The British people have never been accustomed to formulate their instincts in logical terms. They possess the most sensitive antennae, and when danger threatens these antennae convey warnings to the whole ant-heap or hive. Such warning was conveyed on March 15th. For 250 years and more the British people have known instinctively that their safety depended upon preventing the continent of Europe and therefore their sea communications from falling under the domination of a single Power. It was this instinct which prompted them (at great cost to themselves) to fight Spain, Holland, Louis XIV, Napoleon and Wilhelm II. They called this instinct by varying names. Sometimes they called it "The Balance of Power"; at other, and more sentimental moments, they called it "The protection of the smaller Nations." Yet whatever names they may have given to the instinct it was there as a durable, firm and recurrent element in their national destiny. It is a sound biological instinct; it is the instinct of self-preservation.

It is conditioned by hard and inescapable facts. Great Britain is a small island containing a large population dependent for their food supplies upon imports from overseas. She is also a small island situated but twenty-five miles from the European peninsula, and connected with her vast Empire, and its sources of food and raw materials, by tenuous and exposed arteries of communication. She is thus one of the most vulnerable countries upon earth. If once these slim arteries were severed then she would lose her very life-blood. Germany might be invaded and conquered, but she would still remain Germany. France might be invaded and conquered and would still remain France. If once Great Britain lost control over her own communications, she would not only cease to be a Great Power, but would cease to be a Power at all. She would become a parasite living upon the good-will of other organisms. She would not only lose her authority, her riches and her possessions; she would also lose her independence. It is for this reason that, once any European Power arouses our instinct of self-preservation, we become unanimously alarmed. We know that any fight into which we enter is a fight for life. Herr Hitler (stupidly from his point of view) has managed to arouse this instinct.

"But why," you may ask, "should Germany's seizure of a distant city in Central Europe constitute a menace to the British Empire?" For this reason. Because he thereby disclosed that his true ambition was one of conquest. Until then he had always had some plausible excuse for his depredations. There was no excuse at all for the seizure of Prague. It was conquest, naked and undisguised. There was no reason why, if he seized Prague, he might not also seize Copenhagen, Amsterdam, Brussels, Berne and Stockholm. A tiger had been let loose on Europe and the little countries were not strong enough to resist. It was not because Prague had been seized, or Danzig threatened, that we were alarmed: Miss Mundy might just as well have been Miss Jones or Miss Smith; what frightened us was that murder was abroad. It was not so much Poland that we guaranteed thereafter; it was our help in catching the murderer.

The motive of self-preservation is not an unselfish motive; it is a selfish motive. We knew that if these murders continued, if the tiger remained at large, all the small States of Europe might succumb to his might and ambition. He would attain to such gigantic power that even the British Fleet might be unable to restrain him. German armies might reach Istanbul and push on to the very confines of India. German submarines might be based in Rotterdam. German air forces might be congregated twenty-five miles from Dover. The danger was personal and immediate. The beacons flared a warning.

There are many people in England who believe that war is in itself such an evil thing that it would be better to surrender without resisting. If we were at war with a civilisation, such as that of the United States, which is of a standard equal, if not superior, to our own, I should not question that argument. I should willingly see Great Britain revert to the position of a smaller Power rather than sacrifice the lives of her people. Yet we are not fighting against a civilisation which is equal to our own. We are fighting against a civilisation which is lower than that which we, through centuries of trial and error, have ourselves been able to evolve. It is at this stage that the motive of fear, or self-preservation, shades off into the moral motive, which expresses itself in anger. Why should our lovely Christian code of honour surrender to this pagan brutality? Why should the fine culture of France be wrecked by barbarian invasion? It is to prevent such surrenders that we are prepared to fight.

Let me now consider the moral motive.

We must be careful to avoid self-righteousness. The main motive governing the actions of any country, or any animal, must be the motive of self-preservation. I contend however that the Anglo-Saxon race cannot be fired to the extremes of sacrifice and effort unless a moral motive is also present. We know that to-day we are fighting for our lives. We also want to know that we are fighting for something more important than our lives. We are certainly fighting for something more important.

Were it mere selfishness that directs our motives, would it be conceivable that a Government which represents the propertied classes of this country would embark on war? Whatever may be the outcome of this struggle we can be certain that the rich will lose. Herr von Ribbentrop has consistently assured his Führer that never will a Conservative Government make war for a principle, since their only principle is the maintenance of their own privileges and fortunes. Whatever happens, these will go. If the instinct of self-preservation were the sole guiding instinct, then the British propertied classes would have allowed Hitler to possess all the world provided he left them with their own incomes and privileges. Quite deliberately, knowing full well the consequences of their actions, they are prepared to sacrifice all their possessions rather than to allow this evil to triumph. Is this selfishness? Seldom has a whole class committed suicide in so great a cause.

This is a national, and not a class, struggle. Herr von Ribbentrop (as all those who take a low view of human nature) has proved to be wrong. But is it true, as the German says, that the whole nation is in fact guided solely by the instinct of self-preservation and has no higher aim in mind? It is completely untrue. We entered this war to defend ourselves. We shall continue to, to its most bitter end, in order to save humanity.

I am well aware that this assertion will bring a smile to many lips and, if read by the Führer, will cause him to scream with rage. I am not, I think, self-righteous upon the subject. We have often, as during the South African War, departed from these ideals. We have often pretended that we were pursuing moral or unselfish purposes when we were in fact pursuing predatory and selfish purposes. We have in this manner acquired a great Empire and a very general reputation for hypocrisy. Yet it could scarcely be denied that the conception of "decency" and "fairness" is a peculiarly Anglo-Saxon conception and that we have constantly endeavoured in our home and foreign policy to apply those conceptions to our conduct. We have not always succeeded; we have often failed; but assuredly we have tried.

I should ask those who regard this assertion as an instance of British cant to consider the following proposition. From 1815 to 1914 Great Britain was the strongest Power in the world. Her command of the seas, her vast financial resources, enabled her to have the decisive voice in almost any dispute which might arise between other nations. She possessed this overwhelming power for almost a century. Of late years that power, owing to the invention of the bombing aeroplane and other causes, has declined. Yet is there a single small State in Europe that has not regretted our loss of power? Is there a single small State in Europe to-day who would not rejoice if, owing to some amazing invention, we were again to become the arbiter of world affairs? Conversely, is there a single State in Europe which welcomes the tremendous power which Germany has amassed, or which does not regard with terror the ruthless nihilism of the Nazi system? Surely this is a true, and even a moderate, statement? Surely it is true that if between 1815 and 1914 Germany had been possessed of similar supremacy, she would not have exercised it, as we exercised it, in such a manner as to identify her own predominance with the freedom and self-development of the smaller European peoples? And if this be true, then surely the conclusion is also true, namely that we do in fact endeavour to exercise power in a more humane and progressive manner than do the rulers of Germany. And that therefore what is all too vaguely known as "The Anglo-Saxon Ideal" does in fact represent for mankind something higher than the ideals of the rubber truncheon and the concentration camp. Assuredly, as Mr. Chamberlain has said, we are fighting evil things.

The evolution of the human race, from the savage to the civilised man, has been marked by certain stages of advancement. The Greeks discovered the beauty of the liberated mind; the Nazis deny that the mind of the individual should ever be free. The Romans established the rule of law and the sanctity of Treaties; the Nazis have only their own Nazi law and have violated every treaty which they have signed. Christ taught us the lessons of gentleness, of tolerance, of loving kindness; the Nazis deny Christ as a Jew and despise human charity as a decadent virtue. The age of chivalry taught us that we should not kick in the stomach those who are weaker than ourselves; Herr Hitler proclaims that the weak have "no right to live." The French eighteenth century evolved the elegance of taste and the balance of reason; Herr Hitler has reduced taste to the level of a cheap picture post-card and has declared reason to be the enemy of the State. We in England have evolved the conception of "decency" and "fairness"; the Nazis regard these conceptions as hypocritical and debased. "Remember," said Herr Hitler, when addressing school children recently, "Remember to be hard." Their little faces blinked obediently into an expression of brutality.

Are we aware even now of the actual cruelty of the Nazi system?

I do not wish to indulge in atrocity stories. Any German of intelligence and courage, any neutral resident in Germany, will tell you how the Nazi Gauleiters have taken the soul of that magnificent people in their hands and twisted it until it has assumed the crooked, tortured, combative shape of the swastika. We know how family life in Germany has been poisoned by fear and delation, and how the children are taught in their schools to betray their parents to the local Nazi leaders. We know how scholars and men of letters have been deprived of their posts and driven from their country solely because they refused to teach or tell the lies which Dr. Goebbels demanded. We know how the great Nazi machine has taken the boys of Germany and stamped them into uniform shapes as if they were but buttons in a factory. We know that the whole energy of the system has devised the slogan: "Hear nothing that we do not wish you to hear. See nothing that we do not wish you to see. Believe nothing that we do not wish you to believe. Think nothing that we do not wish you to think." We know that all those who do not bow the knee to Baal, such as Pastor Niemöller and Cardinal Faulhaber, are imprisoned or persecuted. We know that all gaiety and laughter has been hushed. We know that they have taught their people not to think.

Do we always remember and realise the actual physical side? I have met a man who was sent to a German concentration camp and thereafter released. He managed to escape into Switzerland and I saw him later in Paris. He was an elderly man of short stature and great girth. On arrival at the camp he was made to take off all his clothes and to creep on all fours around the room. The youths of the S.S. who were in control of the camp amused themselves by flicking with wet towels at his naked frame. They then told him to urinate into the mouth of an elderly Jew, who was also stripped naked. When he refused to do so, they were both flogged until they were unconscious. I did not believe this story at the time. Since then I have heard other stories which confirm it in every detail. I cannot conceive that, in any circumstances which could possibly arise, could youths of my own race either wish, or be allowed by their elders, to behave with such obscenity. Even animals do not expose each other to such humiliations. We have all in our experience met boys who are capable of sadistic cruelty. Yet never in the history of civilised man have such boys been told that what they did was right.

"Yes," you will answer, "that is all very shocking and painful, but what has it to do with us?"

It has this to do. If England surrenders, the whole of Europe will surrender. Our responsibility is magnificent and terrible. I should not be willing to sacrifice my life or the lives of my sons for any material victory. I shall willingly sacrifice everything I possess to prevent the victory of this foul and ghoulish idea.

"Yes," you may murmur, "all that is very noble. But will it profit the world if in seeking to destroy Hitler we succeed only in destroying ourselves? Is it not possible that the Führer, having now obtained his Lebensraum in Poland, may this time be sincere in his assurances and may rest in peace?"

It is possible, but it is not probable. The risk is too great to take. For if indeed Herr Hitler were allowed undisturbed to digest and organise the vast territories that he has conquered; if he be allowed, owing to our surrender, to dominate indirectly the other small countries of Europe; then he will say to us at his good pleasure: "I am anxious, as I have always been anxious, to place the relations between Germany and the British Empire upon a permanently peaceful basis. All I ask of you is that you should hand over to me your African colonies and the Malay States; that you should transfer to me the sum of £500,000,000 in gold and foreign credits; and that you should give me the *Hood*, the *Nelson*, and the *Rodney* in addition to naval tonnage equal to those ships which were surrendered at Scapa Flow."

We shall then not be in a position to refuse this request. We shall thereafter become a vassal State.

I conclude with a sentence written by one who was, in his time, a personal friend of Hitler and a high Nazi official, and who left his leader and his country in honourable disgust. "Hitler," writes Dr. Rauschning, "is not a man with whom a reasonable being concludes an agreement: He is a phenomenon which one slays or is slain by."

We shall not be slain.

5   WHY I FIGHT

The American soldier was generally inarticulate about and disinterested in such abstract questions as war aims, mankind's innate aggressiveness, or the evils perpetrated by totalitarian regimes. As delineated by Bill Mauldin's cartoon characters, Willy and Joe, the average GI apparently gave little thought to the "whys" of the war because he was so concerned with concrete issues—getting warm food and dry socks, and returning home as soon as possible and in one piece. When asked to define their stakes in the war, American soldiers usually resorted to motherhood and apple-pie rhetoric, substituting lofty phrases for conviction. There is a good deal of this awkwardness and diffidence about war aims in the following selection, taken from a volume of prize-winning essays submitted for a contest in North Africa in 1943. The three essays are, however, representative of important aspects of the American attitude toward the war.

"I Fight to Remain Free"

by Cpl. Jack J. Zurofsky

This is why I fight:

I fight because it's my fight.

I fight because my eyes are unafraid to look into other eyes; because they have seen happiness and because they have seen suffering; because they are curious and searching; because they are free.

I fight because my ears can listen to both sides of a question; because they can hear the groanings of a tormented people as well as the laughter of free people; because they are a channel for information, not a route for repetition; because, *if I hear and do not think, I am deaf.*

I fight because my mouth does not fear to utter my opinions; because, though I am only one, my voice helps forge my destiny; because I can speak from a soap-box, or from a letter to the newspapers, or from a question that I may ask my representatives in Congress; because when my mouth speaks and can only say what everyone is forced to say it is gagged.

I fight because my feet can go where they please, because they need no passport to go from New York to New Jersey and back again; because if I want to leave my country I can go without being forced and without bribing and without the loss of my savings; because I can plant my feet in farm soil or city concrete without anybody's by your leave; because when my feet walk only the way they are forced to walk they are hobbled.

From United States Army, **Why I Fight** (Washington, D.C.: U.S. Government Printing Office), pp. 3–14.

I fight because of all of these and because I have a mind, a mind which has been trained in a free school to accept or reject, to ponder and to weigh—a mind which knows the flowing stream of thought, not the stagnant swamp of blind obedience; a mind schooled to think for itself, to be curious, skeptical, to analyze, to formulate, and to express its opinions; a mind capable of digesting the intellectual food it receives from a free press—because if a mind does not think it is the brain of a slave.

I fight because I think I am as good as anybody else; because of what other people have said better than ever I could, *"Certain inalienable rights"*, *"right to life, liberty, and the pursuit of happiness"*, *"government of the people, and for the people"*, *"give me liberty or give me death."*

I fight because of my memories—the laughter and play of my childhood, the ball games I was in and the better ones I watched, my mother telling me why my father and she came to America at the turn of the century, my sisters marrying, my high school graduation, the first time I saw a cow, the first year we could afford a vacation, the crib at Camp Surprise Lake after the crowded, polluted Coney Island waters, hikes in the fall with the many-colored leaves falling, weenie and marshmallow roasts over a hot fire, the first time I voted, my first date and the slap in the face I got instead of the kiss I attempted, the way the nostrum quack would alternate with political orators on our street corner, *seeing the changes for the better in my neighborhood*—the El going down, streets being widened to let the sun in, new tenements replacing the old slums—the crowd applauding the time I came through with the hit that won us the borough championship; the memories, which if people like me do not fight, our children will never have.

I fight because I have something to fight for.

I fight because of the life I hope to live when the fighting is finished, because that life offers opportunity and security and the freedom to read and write and listen and think and talk, because, as before, my home will be my castle with the drawbridge down only to those that I invite, because if I do not fight life itself will be death.

I fight because I believe in progress—not reaction, because—despite our fault, there is hope in our manner of life, because if we lose there is no hope.

I fight because some day I want to get married and I want my children to be born into a free world, because my forefathers left me a heritage of freedom which it is my duty to pass on, because if we lost it would be a crime to have children.

I fight because it is an obligation, because free people must fight to remain free, because when the freedom of one nation or one person are taken away the rights of all nations and all people are threatened, because—through our elected representatives—I had the choice—to fight or not to fight.

I fight not so much because of Pearl Harbor *but because of what Pearl Harbor meant*. Because, finally after skirmishes with the Ethiopians, the Manchurians, the Chinese, the Austrians, the Czechoslovakians, the Danes, the Spaniards, and the Norwegians, *fascism was menacing us as we had never before been menaced*, because only the craven will not defend themselves.

I fight because *"it is better to die than live on one's knees"*.

I fight because only by fighting today will there be peace tomorrow.

I fight because I am thankful that I am not on the other side; because, but for the Grace of God or an accident of Nature, the brutalized Nazi could have been me and, but for my fighting, will be my child.

I fight in the fervent hope that those that follow me will not have to fight again but in the knowledge that, if they have to, they will not be found wanting in the crisis.

I fight to remain free.

* * *

"We Did Not Pant for War"

by Pvt. Clarence Weinstock

Some weeks ago I was at a hospital to which sick and wounded men are sent from the front. Every evening those of us who were well enough to be up went to the dayroom to read, work jigsaw puzzles, or listen to the guitar players. We sat around in the handsome maroon bathrobes of the Medical Department of the Army. The robes were initialed MDUSA and the boys, with the wry humor of men who live dangerously, claimed this meant *Many die U shall also.*

One night we sang. Old American songs, souvenirs of other times of crisis, *"John Brown's Body"*, *"There's a Long, Long Trail Awinding"*, songs of the land, *"Red River Valley"*, *"Shenandoah"*, songs of cities, *"East Side, West Side"*, *"St. Louis Blues"*.

We stopped for a moment and the man with the guitar said, *"Ever hear this one?"* He hit the strings and sang. We knew the tune—everyone does—but here were the words:

> *There's no one on the skyline,*
> *That's sure a pretty good sign*
> *Those Eighty Eights are breakin' up*
> *That old gang of mine.*
>
> *Gee, you get that lonesome feelin'*
> *When you hear that shrapnel whine,*
> *Those Eighty Eights are breakin' up*
> *That old gang of mine.*

Many of the boys laughed, but not as you do at a good joke. They grinned because they could still make fun of death, because brave men kid when there is really nothing to laugh about.

Afterward, lying on my cot, I kept thinking, *"Do these boys who are so good in a fight, and so gentle and thoughtful toward each other here, have to be asked what they are fighting for?"* Isn't that one of those questions you cannot grasp because the answer seems so obvious? *"Why do you want to live?" "Is happiness good or bad for one?"*

I heard the question put another way in the same dayroom. The boys were talking about going home, where there were no C rations, no shells, bombs, booby traps and machine pistols. *"Sure, everybody wants to get out of this,"* someone said, *"but which one of us, one man alone, would take a personal trip ticket to the States and wish the others good luck in their foxholes?"*

It was in the song of the 88's and through the dayroom speaker that I began to find my answer.

No man stands alone. In war you leave your family and peacetime friends and the comrades of your company lessen your fears and your loneliness. In them you rediscover your country, the men of all states, the people who made America, with their hundred ways of speaking, their tall stories and their fast answers, their clever repair-job hands and their clear making-something minds, their easy giving and willingness to be shown, their big laughter at false fronts and their quick comeback for injustice. You hear their songs of longing and battle, of loneliness and solidarity, the songs of the whole history of your country. And then you know why you fight on the cold Italian beaches and hills: *If you failed these men it would be like walking out of your own house and never coming back again.*

Yet that isn't all you fight for. You can live in a house and not know who built it; but you have got to remember the thoughts and blood that made our house, America, if you value your freedom. I'm not thinking of the school textbooks where you see pictures of noble gentlemen in lacy shirts and velvet breeches signing the Declaration of Independence. I mean Franklin when he joked like the men in the hospital—*"We must all hang together or we will all hang separately."* I mean Tom Paine writing on a drum in a snowy field by the light of his fellow soldiers' lamps: *"These are the times that try men's souls. The summer soldier and the sunshine patriot will, in this crisis, shrink from the service of their country; but he that stands it now deserves the love and thanks of man and woman. Tyranny, like hell, is not easily conquered; yet we have this consolation with us, that the harder the conflict the more glorious the triumph. What we obtain too cheap we esteem too lightly; it is dearness only that gives everything its value. Heaven knows how to put a proper price upon its goods; and it would be strange indeed if so celestial an article as freedom should not be highly rated."*

It took us some time to remember Tom Paine, to learn that we couldn't buy our freedom with other men's effort. Few of us knew that we were threatened and mocked in Manchuria, Ethiopia, and Spain. The men who died there, our brothers, fell unhelped and unmourned by America. Our neighbor, Mr. Chamberlain, could even say that the citizens of Czechoslovakia were a people *"of whom we know nothing"*, and whose affairs did not concern him. Mr. Chamberlain also did not know Tom Paine, who said, *"Where freedom is not there is my country."* Not until Pearl Harbor did we, as a nation, learn that liberty, like peace, is indivisible, that oppression anywhere on this earth menaces our happiness and security. If we fight today to free the countries overrun by

Fascism, we also fight against our own enslavement. Others' war of liberation is just as much our war of survival. Even if war had not been declared or waged against us, we, a free people, could not exist in a conquered world. We would be destroyed by a tyranny which our indifference had fed. We would have to yield to power because we had given up our heritage of liberty, keeping quiet when it was time to take up arms, crying peace when there was no peace.

What else do we fight for? We are an Army fighting for happiness. The pursuit of happiness was our idea and we fought for it in 1776. Because we won, the great French revolutionist, Saint Just was able to say, *Happiness is a new idea in Europe."* He meant that for thousands of years people may have desired and reached out for simple pleasures, but it didn't occur to them that they had a *right* to be happy. They fought wars because they were ordered to, or to make money, like the Hessians whom Washington defeated at Trenton. It took our forefathers, with their inalienable rights of man, to give men something truly their own to fight for.

Today we are at war with powerful industrial nations whose social structures are viciously antiquated. These countries never achieved a democratic revolution. Their rulers regard them as feudal domains from the boundaries of which raids are made on highways and neighboring lands. For them there are no citizens, only serfs whose value lies in their eagerness to sacrifice themselves for their *"betters"*. The Nazi knights rant about *"duty"* and *"sacrifice"*, and every soldier in Italy has seen, painted on walls and latrines, the favorite Fascist slogan, *"Credere, Obbedire, Combattere"*—believe, obey, fight. Our enemies used to like to call us effete democracies. Why effete? Because we desired happiness for ourselves and our fellow citizens? Now we know they are afraid of our great democratic happiness. For our idea of happiness is indissoluble with liberty and equality. It excludes no human being because of his color, the country he was born in, what he believes or doesn't believe. It knows no elite, no restricted, no privileged blood. It made us a great nation and as long as we hold to it we shall be united against our enemies.

What of my own personal happiness then? How does the great American dream, the pursuit of happiness, jibe with my present life? The answer is simple. I know how liberty had to be achieved in America and how it must be saved today. I know what price liberty. I could have no happiness if, knowing what I do know, I found myself unwilling or reluctant to pay. We cannot live the dream created by our fathers for us unless we give it new existence and reality—for ourselves and our children. *If freedom is imperilled by my comfort, I must give up my comfort.* My happiness now can only spring from the fight to preserve my freedom on a plane compatible with human dignity, on terms which do not involve its denial to millions of my brothers.

I fight to return to my native land, and to help make its future. I want every man and woman who fought or worked for victory to enjoy the riches they helped defend—the soldier, the sailor, the miner and millworker, the weaver and the typist. I want an America that will say to Anglo-Saxon and Slovak, Chinese and Porto Rican, Negro and Jews, *"I am your country, for which you stood watch with your guns and before the mast, at furnaces and in the fields,*

like this: *"To get back home again, to what we know and love; our families, our old jobs, our churches and our theaters, and our books and our little pleasures.* A fire in the grate, an easy chair, pipe and slippers, and maybe a glass of beer, and a friend to share it. A picnic in Oak Grove on a holiday, a fishing trip or a game of golf on a Sunday. The chance to fraternize with fellow Americans, to cheer for the Dodgers; to vote for your man and beef about him once he's in. The right to look your neighbor in the eye, and, if need be, tell him to go to blazes. . ." Home! Yes, that's a fair summing-up of what we all yearn to go back to, and so, in a sense, it is what we are fighting for.

But, O America, there is so much more! And O Americans, don't mistake by-products for the things that make them possible!

What am I fighting for?

Well, it goes a long way back.

It goes back into the taproots of America. Back beyond the World War, with its simple slogan of fighting to make the world safe for democracy. Back beyond '98, when we fought to set Cuba free. Back beyond the Civil War when we fought to make and keep America a nation of freemen. Back beyond 1812, when our cry was the freedom of the seas. Back even beyond the Revolution that saw our forefathers pledge *"their lives, their fortunes, and their sacred honor"* that the colonies might be freed from the yoke of the Hanoverian king. Back to the Bill of Rights, back, back to Magna Carta seven hundred years ago—that first great landmark of man's history-long effort to be politically free. And shining all down through the struggle, a golden thread spun and woven in English history and flung, gleaming, across the whole warp and woof of our American Dream, is that shining, lustrous thing—Freedom! Freedom of the individual to rule himself, to make his laws, to have his say in council, to set his course and follow his star!

Fine words, you say; but what have they to do with fighting a Germany whose chief concern perhaps was Europe, a Japan whose ambitions were—perhaps—only Oriental?

I say they have a lot to do with Japan and Germany. I say, in fact, that they have everything to do with them. Everything—and nothing. Nothing, in the obvious sense that our two ideologies are as far apart as the poles; but everything, because the two could not exist side by side in the world. They could not exist together, beyond a little space of time, because each denies the validity of the other and seeks to destroy it, and the incompatibility is so great that sooner or later they must clash bloodily. You ask, "Why couldn't we just go on as before and deal with the Continent through Germany?"

"Why *can't* we do business with Hitler?" and I answer that there are two reasons. First, Hitler would only want us to do business on his terms—which we, if we kept our honor, would find unpalatable. But the second reason is by far the more important, and at the same time it is the less demonstrable, because less tangible. It is the fact—and I am so sure of it that I label it a fact rather than a promise—that Nazism successful and dominant in Europe and Asia would result, as surely as the proverbial death and taxes, in the emergence and ultimate *dominance of the Nazi principle in American life.* America—the Americas—seeing

Nazism triumphant all over the globe—would Nazify itself, even if Germany made no attempt to Nazify us through military action. Not intentionally would we do so—perhaps even unwillingly. But a force so all-powerful, so obviously the successful governmental principle, would soon gain its proponents in America, and then its converts, and then its willing-to-try-anything-once followers, and finally its half-convinced acquiescers and dubious go-along-with-the-crowd straddlers and timid ones; and, first thing we know, we should have the German story all over again. *Fantastic?* Yes—and so are the workings of human nature and the vagaries of the democratic but *politically unoriented* minds of the people. We must realize that America is no longer a band of colonials united against a greedy and unjust king; no longer a land with great frontiers to absorb poverty and the restless drive of men's spirit, with huge territories to quell, even if but temporarily, a slavery question with a Missouri Compromise. America's era of territorial expansion is over; our frontiers now are those of sociology and economics and political philosophy. These abstractions are our borders; we must defend them.

These are our twentieth century counterparts of *"Fifty-four forty or fight!"* and we must extend them. These are territories of the mind and spirit, and wars for or against them will first be wars of the mind and spirit, just as Nazism first warred in the minds of the German people, *working up fury and hate* before there were any overt acts of aggression. Yield an inch anywhere along the borders, and the enemy has a foothold, a bridgehead from which to carry on his insidious work. And had we not gone into the struggle, and Nazism had stood triumphantly and mockingly over the graves of European democracy, there would have been the foothold, the opening wedge. Men *(some, not all—but alas! enough)* would have looked at each other in confusion and alarm and doubt. They would have said, fearingly, *"Democracy has failed in Europe. We thought it was the best way, but how can it be, if it is so weak? Maybe the Nazis have something. Maybe . . . maybe . . . "* So the whispers would have started, and run along gathering weight and hysterical conviction as they ran; and so the dike is penetrated, the trickle grows into a breach, the enemy is across and the border is lost. Men, searching for a new challenge, a new panacea, a new Way, a new answer to old problems, would seize on this ready-to-hand answer—and we are swept away.

That's why I'm fighting, somewhere in that welter of words. I'm fighting because of tortured certainty that we *must* fight, or write ignominy and defeat on the page of our generation. I'm fighting to kill Fascism *now*, before it has a chance to eat its ugly way into American vitals. I'm fighting because I hate Nazism and all its works, and Nazism leaves me no other way of damning it but by the sword. I'm fighting because I don't want any hint of a *"maybe"* in American thinking. I'm fighting because the world, like our own America, *"cannot exist half slave and half free."* I'm fighting because I think China has a right to live as a nation, not exist as a vast puppet state. I'm fighting because I just can't see a Lidice die unavenged—not just because Lidice is a crime for all history, but because Lidice stands for all the helpless people who have been ground under the Nazi heel. I'm fighting because America, my beloved America is threatened with mortal danger—and far too many of her people have not sensed it.

I'm fighting because I want to be able to look my children in the face some day and say to them that America wasn't afraid to fight once again for ideal, the ideals that have made America great. I love peace, and I hate war for the shocking waste of everything that it is; *but even war is preferable to supine acquiescence in international murder*, not merely of the body, but of the spirit. I'm not ready, at the behest of a pseudo-super race, to yield without a struggle those priceless things which are at once our tradition and the future hope of the world. It is a trite phrase, but *America has a rendezvous with destiny*. She must meet it with honor and courage, proudly, as befits a queen among nations. I am fighting for the Christian future of the world, the dignity of the individual, the whole concept of democracy. I don't want to see them all swept away, a birthright sold for a mess of Nazi pottage.

That's why I'm fighting!

6   THE VOICE OF FIGHTING RUSSIA

The following selections are from The Voice of Fighting Russia, *a collection of speeches, essays, and testimonial letters issued by the Russian government. This English-language publication was designed to inform Russia's allies of the heroic struggle being carried on by the Soviet armed forces and the Russian people. Both in the essay "What We Are Defending" by Alexei Tolstoy, son of the great novelist Leo Tolstoy, and in the "typical" letters to the front, the dominant theme is of sacrifice for Mother Russia. The need to protect the Soviet regime, the beacon of world communism, is subdued.*

What We Are Defending

by Alexei Tolstoy

The program of the National Socialists has not been exhausted in Hitler's book. This contains only that which could be confessed. The further development of their program harbors within itself such delirious, sadistic, bloody aims that to confess them would be disadvantageous. But the Nazis' conduct in the occupied

From **The Voice of Fighting Russia,** edited by Lucien Zacharoff (New York: Alliance Book Corporation, 1942), pp. 19–25, 195–98.

countries somewhat reveals the "secret," the hints are all too obvious—slavery, starvation and brutalization await all who do not say in good time and firmly: "Death is better than Nazi victory."

The Nazis are self-assured to the point of hysteria. After conquering Poland and France, essentially through bribery and diversionist decomposition of the military might of the enemy, after conquering other, smaller lands that fell with honor before an immeasurably stronger adversary, the Nazis hastily began to materialize the further development of their platform. Thus, in Poland, in concentration camps which confine Polish workingmen and Polish intellectuals, as early as the spring of this year mortality reached seventy per cent; today it is wholesale. Poland's population is being exterminated. In Norway, the Nazis picked several thousand citizens, put them aboard barges, and "without helm and sails" let them drift on the ocean. During the offensive in France, with a particularly sadistic relish the Nazis bombarded small undefended towns filled with refugees, "combed" them in a strafing flight, crushed with tanks all that could be crushed. Then came their infantry—out of the shelters the Nazis dragged half-dead children, distributed chocolate among them, and posed for the photographers with them, in order to be able to distribute, where they would do the trick, such documents testifying to German "humaneness." By the time they reached Serbia, they no longer gave away chocolate nor posed with children for the cameras.

All these deeds flow out of the general National Socialist program, namely, the conquest of Europe, Asia, the Americas, all continents and islands. Exterminated are all the defiant, who are unwilling to reconcile themselves to the loss of their independence. In the legal and material sense all peoples are being converted into speech-endowed animals and are working on terms dictated to them. If the Nazis find population numbers in one country or another excessive, they reduce them by extermination in the concentration camps or by some other less cumbrous method. Then, having arranged all this, like the Lord, in six days, on the seventh day the Nazis, as behooves the premier race with blond elongated heads, begin to live well, eating sausages to repletion, clinking beer mugs, yelling stein songs about their superman origin. . . .

All this is not out of a fantastic novel in the style of H.G. Wells—it is precisely so that they are determined soberly to develop their program in the Reich Chancery in Berlin. It is for this that they are spilling rivers of blood and tears, for this cities are burning, thousands of ships are blown up and sunk, and scores of millions of peaceful populations are dying from hunger.

To smash up the armies of the Third Empire, to sweep off the face of the earth all Nazis with their barbarously bloody designs, to give our country peace, repose, eternal freedom, prosperity, every opportunity of continued development on the road of the higher human freedom—such is the lofty and noble mission that must be carried out by the Russian and all other peoples of the Soviet Union.

The Germans calculated on breaking into the U.S.S.R. with their tanks and bombers, as they did in Poland, France, and other states, where victory was secured in advance by their preliminary undermining work. On the frontiers of the U.S.S.R. they hit against a wall of steel and their blood has spurted far and wide. The German armies, driven into battle by the red-hot iron of terror and madness, have encountered the powerful strength of an intelligent, courageous, freedom-loving people which in the course of its thousand-year-old history has many times expelled by sword and bayonet the invaders of the spacious expanses of its native soil—the Khazars, Polovtzi and Pechenegi, the Tartar hordes and Teutonic Knights, the Poles, Swedes, Napoleon's Frenchmen and Wilhelm's Germans. . . . "They all have flashed before us."

Previously, the people of my country rose to the struggle, understanding full well that they would receive no thanks from either the Tsar, the whipper-in, or the boyar. But ardent was their love for their land, for their untender fatherland. Inextinguishably there burned in their minds the faith in the coming of the day of justice when they would cast off their hunched backs all parasites, when Russian soil would be their soil and they would plow it up for the golden harvest from ocean to ocean.

In the War for the Fatherland in 1918-20, the White armies pressed our country from all sides and she—prostrated, famished, dying out from the typhus epidemic—after two years of a bloody and seemingly unequal struggle, broke the encirclement, drove out and exterminated the foe, and began to build a new life. The nation drew strength in toil illuminated by a great ideal, in its faith in happiness, in the love of the native land where sweet is the smoke and sweet is the bread.

So, on what mercy from the Soviet side can the Nazis reckon now as they drive the German people to face the Soviet steel fortresses hurtling into battle like a hurricane, the belts of Soviet fortifications roaring with their monstrous muzzles, the numberless warplanes, the Red Army bayonets?

> *Or are there not enough of us? Perhaps from*
> *Perm to Taurus;*
> *From Finland's chilly cliffs to fiery Colchis,*
> *Or from the shaken-up Kremlin*
> *To the immobile Cathay's walls,*
> *The Land of Russia will not arise,*
> *Its shield of steel all sparkling?*

The Russian has this characteristic—in life's difficult moments, in the years of trial, he easily renounces all that he has become accustomed to, that by which he has lived day by day. Behold, here was a man—so-so; suddenly it was demanded of him to become a hero, and he is a hero. . . . And how can it be otherwise? In the olden times of the recruit impressment, the boy destined for head-shaving had his fun for three days, he danced and, leaning his head on his palm, sang heart-rending songs; he bade farewell to his father and mother, and there he was, a different man—austere and fearless, guarding the honor of the fatherland. He followed Suvoroff's charger across the glaciers of the Alps as he kept his precarious foothold by digging his bayonet into the ice; at Moscow he repulsed the attacks of Murat's cuirassiers; in a clean undershirt, shouldering his musket under the deadly bullet fire at Plevna, he stood awaiting the order to storm the inaccessible heights.

Three fellows came together from different villages to serve in the Red Army. Whether they were good or bad before this, no one knows. They were assigned to the tank corps and sent into battle. Their tank lunged far ahead into the midst of the enemy infantry, was crippled, expended all its ammunition. When the enemies had crept quite close to the disabled tank to take its crew prisoners, the three chaps came out of the machine. Each of the three had one last cartridge left, each raised his weapon to his temple; they had not surrendered. Glory to them, the proud fighters, cherishing the honor of the fatherland and the army.

A pursuit pilot related to me: "The enemy planes swirled about me like a swarm of bees. My neck hurt from turning my head so much. So great was the excitement that I was shouting at the top of my voice. I knocked down three and tried to get into a clinch with the fourth one. Above—sometimes the sky and sometimes the ground, the sun—now on the right of me, then on the left. I was somersaulting, diving, climbing up. So, I took aim at one enemy, and suddenly from under me an interceptor plane shot up, hung for a split second before my nose, I saw a man's face—strong, bearded, in his eyes hatred and a plea for mercy. . . . The interceptor turned upside down and smoke began to pour from it. Suddenly I could not move my leg, as though I had sat on it too long; this meant I was wounded. Then something hit my shoulder. My machine-gun cartridge ribbon gave out, I had nothing to fire with. I started away; my left arm hung lifelessly. The airdrome was far away. If only everything does not go dark before my eyes from loss of blood, I was thinking; yet, a dizzy film spread over my eyes, but I was already sitting down upon the airdrome, without my landing gear, on the ship's belly."

For more than half a century now I have watched my native land in its struggles for freedom, in its surprising changes. I recall the deathly quiet of Alexander III; the impoverished village with its wasteland, thatched roofs, and willows on the shore of a steppe river. I peer into the past and in my memory there arise the clever, clean-cut, unhurried people preserving their dignity. . . . Here is the father of my childhood playmate—Alexander Sizoff, very handsome with his curly blond beard, a powerful athlete. When of a holiday in the village the mighty Russian tug-of-war got under way in the deep snowdrifts, Sizoff's merry eyes watched through a small window; by and by he would come out, stand in the gate, and when entreaties for help addressed to him became particularly insistent, he pulled on his gloves and effortlessly felled the whole human wall. In a threadbare, undressed-sheepskin coat, his neck wrapped in a scarf, he trod a hundred versts in a blizzard behind a cart of corn, taking to the city his entire year's meager yield. Today his grandson, most certainly, throws himself like an angry falcon at the German bombers.

I remember how in a hut with a warm stove, where a young housewife sat at the loom, where a calf slumbered on a pile of straw in a corner, we children gathered on benches around the table, listening to a tall one-eyed old man resembling a horse and telling us fairy tales. He was an itinerant beggar, moving from village to village, spending the night wherever allowed. The young housewife behind the loom whispered to him: "What for are you telling them terrible and more terrible things all the time? Tell them something happy." He replied, "I know no happy tale, my dear; never heard it, never saw it." With his one terrible eye fixed on us, he continued, "They, mayhap, will see and hear something happy. . . ."

I remember the year 1914 when millions of people had received weapons into their hands. The intelligent people understood that its foremost and sacred duty was to drive the enemy from its soil. Straight out of their railroad trains the Siberian corps leaped to the bayonet attack, and there was nothing fiercer in that war than the Russian bayonet charges. It was only because of the ignorance, stupidity, utmost mediocrity of the Tsarist high command, because of the general looting and thievery, speculation and treason, that the Russian people failed to win that war.

Twenty-five years passed. From ocean to ocean rustled the golden collective-farm fields, orchards bloomed, cotton fluffed up where but a short time before there only drifted sterile sand. Streams of smoke ascended from scores of thousands of shops and factories. Perhaps the same grandson of Alexander Sizoff, the same kind of noble athlete, went underground to stir, titanlike, singlehanded, hundreds of tons of coal per shift. Thousand-ton hammers, shaking the earth, began to forge arms for the Red Army, the army of a liberated people, the army of freedom, the army which is a defender of this world's peace, of higher culture, of flowering and happiness.

This is my birthplace, my native soil, my fatherland—there is not in life a more ardent, deeper, and holier feeling than my love for you.

* * *

On the Battleline

Letters to the Front

A Letter to Six Sons

Major A.G. Legedzovsky one day received a letter from his parents. We quote this letter:

"My dear children! You, my six sons, are in the valorous Red Army. I give you a behest from your mother and myself: multiply tenfold the mortal blow at the Hitlerite hordes, in comparison with the blow which we, old Russian soldiers, gave the German armies in the First World War.

"Our motherland has equipped you, my dear sons, with a first-class military technique. The Party of Lenin and Stalin has taught and reared you. You have as your leaders the hard-hitting Stalinist hero generals, who are unreservedly devoted to us, workers and peasants. We are all behind you. The whole rear of the country, from young to old, will work, without a letup, in the War for the Fatherland, in the name of victory for the Red Army over the Nazi aggressors.

"Don't worry about us old people. We are working on our native collective farm, like all the rest of the collective farmers, and we will do all right in spite of the departure of the best, most advanced farmers to the War of the Fatherland, for the defense of our country.

"So, my dear oldest son, Anton Gordeyevich, lead your steeled tank detachment for the fatherland, for Stalin, for the Soviet people to a crushing blow on the Nazis!

"You, my dear son, Andrei Gordeyevich, following the example of your older brother, Anton, strike the German Fascists with your unit, as he struck them in 1918, as he struck the White Guard Finns in his time, so you too strike the German monsters a hundred times harder than I struck them in 1916. For freedom, for the honor of the Soviet people, spare neither your strength, nor blood, nor life!

"You, my dear son, Ivan Gordeyevich, Stalinist falcon, naval airman, sink the Fascist enemy's surface vessels and submarines!

"You, my dear son, Grigory Gordeyevich, with rifle and grenade in hand, clear the way on the battlefield of German-Nazi curs.

"You, my little boy, Nikolai Gordeyevich, in your Soviet land plane take vengeance on the Hitlerite carrion birds for their raids on our peaceful Soviet towns; beat them and then still more—on their own soil.

"And you, my dear youngest son, Vitaly, lieutenant of the Tank Corps, lead your menacing machines to storm the brutal enemy, dispatch your shells accurately and well into the maw of the monster; strike at the mad, insolent enemy.

"Our cause is just, we will conquer!

"Your parents,
"Gordey and Sofya Legedzovsky."

Hit the Enemy Harder, Sonny!

When Alexandra Matveyevna returned from the "Dzerzhinsky" textile factory, a letter was waiting for her on the table. Surely it is my son writing from the border, she thought joyously and hastily opened the envelope. "Mom! I am stationed in camp. I live well. I spend much time in studying. I am preparing to become a lieutenant in the reserves . . ."

"It's always like that: I wish he would write more, what he is doing and how he is. Always no time," the mother grumbled good-naturedly.

On the next day Matveyevna heard alarming news.

War! The faithless enemy had made a highwayman's raid on our land.

Her first thought was of her son. Her thoughts involuntarily turned toward the border.

In the evening a family council was held in the Fadeyevs' household. The second son, Alexey, returned from the Defense Commissariat.

"Mamma! They did not take me yet, until a special order. But many are volunteering. I also wish to leave for the front."

Tender, motherly eyes looked lovingly at her son.

"Decide for yourself, sonny, what's best. I will not hold you back. Don't worry about me; while I have the strength, I shall work. And if need be, the government will help. If I were younger, I would go along with you myself. But now my age won't let me, I'll soon be seventy. But I can be useful here. I'll go to the hospital to take care of the wounded. Mother's heart is big, there's much love in it," said Matveyevna, controlling her excitement.

And afterwards, grasping the pencil firmly in her gnarled fingers, she carefully scrawled:

"Senya! I have received your letter for which I send you a mother's thanks. And I also send you this behest: don't spare the enemy! Defend our sacred land to the last drop of blood. If necessary, give even your life without fear for our just cause."

The same evening another letter was sent to the front.

"Dear little son! I heard today over the radio how the knavish Nazis have made war on us. The bandits wish to deprive us of our happy life. A thief always acts like a thief. Only this time he will not escape with his head. Strike the enemy harder, my little son. Carry out honestly any order of our own Stalin. Don't shame my old age and the honor of the family."

Such a behest Alexandra Ivanovna Arefyeva, an old weaver of the "Dzerzhinsky" factory, gave not only to her Nikolai, formerly a machinist on the water front. Not far from Nikolai's bench stood other machinists' benches, including one of his brother, Georgy. The brothers worked together in the port. Together they had smashed up the Finnish White Guards in the bitterest cold. Now the fatherland called on them for new deeds.

"Don't you get upset, Mother. Brother and I will make it hot for the enemy. And before you know it, Lesha will come to help."

"Absolutely; I will come. Though they did not take me last year, now no one can hold me back. I am already nineteen. They'll find somebody at the Kiroff factory to whom I can turn over my press."

The old weaver stealthily wipes away a tear and talks excitedly:

"Go . . . go, my children, to the just and holy war. My mother's heart feels that you will return with victory."

A Father to His Son

Nikolai Alexandrovich Kamensky, a foreman of the "Krasny Proletary" factory, sent this letter to his son Alexander, who is in the Red Army:

"My dear son Alexander:

"I didn't think that I would be writing on the day after the Hitlerite gang had dared to make an attack on our country. I am certain that as an antiaircraft gunner you have given a good answer to these black curs. You have always dreamed of becoming an artillery man. Well, here you have the chance at last to shoot at a real target; yes, and it seems not only once.

"War! How often we have spoken of its inevitability, and here it is, brought on us by the Fascists. Now every one of us is a soldier: you and I and all our family. This evening as I came·from the factory, I didn't even have time to wash my hands, they sat upon me: questions without end. Vanya was especially insistent. As he is near the draft age, he'll soon be in the army. He wishes to go to the military committee in order to be called ahead of time. I tell him: in the

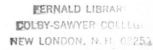

military committee there are plenty of people without you—we have innumerable people. And until they call you, you better work at the bench. You are a turner standing at the bench in the repair shop in place of your brother, so your job is to increase production.

"Your grandfather also grumbles. Recently he reached the age of seventy-seven. He says: 'Write to Shurka, to work at his antiaircraft gun without a miss. Write that the whole nation is stirring. We will choke them, but we will not give up our land.'

"You are serving near the city of Leningrad; I do not exactly know what the country is like there. But some of our folk came from near Ramenskoye, from Ostrovtzi; they say that the countryside is blossoming everywhere—in the fields and in the gardens a flourishing harvest is seen. Nowhere else is there such rich soil as our Russian soil, and now the Fascist scum covet it. But it won't turn out their way. Russia has for centuries stood like a wall against anyone who wanted to subjugate it.

"Every day we raise production. In every factory work hustles on a war footing. We grudge neither strength nor time. We will fill the gullet of that greedy snake Hitler with molten metal. Watch out, Alexander, don't disgrace the old Muscovite proletarian name of Kamensky. Don't let the Hitlerites near, stand at your post. Shoot straight, so that none of your shells misses. Mamma has gone away with the children to a resort. Grandfather received a ticket for the rest home. Your wife, Ekaterina Vasilevna, is in full health, as also is your daughter Tamara, who is in the kindergarten; she is improving and growing up in the fresh air.

"Your sister Katya works like a real Stakhanoffite and is strengthening national defense at the factory. Greetings from the neighbors. Well, take care and fulfill your duty. Defend your country and party, and conquer in the name of Stalin. We stay-at-homes will all work for the Red Army and give it whatever it requires. The Soviet land has risen like one man. We'll cut off the head of the bloodthirsty reptile, that's a fact. However hard it may be, we'll cut it off.

"Behind you stands the country—an immense nation, in all its incalculable strength. But if it should be necessary, your grandfather and I and Vanya and Katya, all of us will take up rifles, but we will win.

"Your father,
"N. Kamensky."

7 READ THIS ALONE—
AND THE WAR CAN BE WON

In preparation for its campaign to conquer Indochina, the Japanese army produced a pamphlet for the information of all soldiers, officers, and other ranks in the invasion force. Along with suggestions about personal hygiene, information regarding the special conditions of tropical warfare, instructions on shipboard routine, and descriptions of the flora and fauna found in the battle zone, this little book discussed the reasons for Japan's southward advance. Read This Alone—And the War Can Be Won *spells out in simple language the rationale for Japan's involvement in the global conflict.*

The Campaign Area in South Asia—What Is It Like?

The remarkable exploits of Yamada Nagamasa in Siam (the present Thailand) took place more than three hundred years ago, but in the years between then and the 1868 Restoration all overseas expansion by the Japanese was brought to a stop by the rigidly enforced seclusion policy of the Tokugawa shotguns, and in that intervening period the English, the French, the Americans, the Dutch, the Portuguese and others sailed into the Far East as if it were theirs by natural right, terrorized and subjugated the culturally backward natives, and colonized every country in the area. India and the Malay Peninsula were seized by the British, Annam by the French, Java and Sumatra by the Dutch, the Philippines by the Americans. These territories, the richest in natural resources in the Far East, were taken by a handful of white men, and their tens of millions of Asian inhabitants have for centuries, down to our own day, suffered constant exploitation and persecution at their hands.

We Japanese have been born in a country of no mean blessings, and thanks to the august power and influence of His Majesty the Emperor our land has never once, to this day, experienced invasion and occupation by a foreign power. The other peoples of the Far East look with envy upon Japan; they trust and honour the Japanese; and deep in their hearts they are hoping that, with the help of the Japanese people, they may themselves achieve national independence and happiness.

Three hundred and fifty million Indians are ruled by five hundred thousand British, sixty million South-east Asians by two hundred thousand Dutch, twenty-three million Indo-Chinese by twenty thousand Frenchmen, six million Malayans by a few ten thousand British, and thirteen million Filipinos by a few ten thousand Americans. In short, four hundred and fifty million natives of the

From **Singapore: The Japanese Version** by Masanobu Tsuji (Sydney, Australia: Ure Smith Proprietory Ltd., 1960), pp. 300–2, 304–5, 308, 347–49, Appendix 1. Reprinted by permission of the publisher.

Far East live under the domination of less than eight hundred thousand whites. If we exclude India, one hundred million are oppressed by less than three hundred thousand. Once you set foot on the enemy's territories you will see for yourselves, only too clearly, just what this oppression by the white man means. Imposing, splendid buildings look down from the summits of mountains or hills onto the tiny thatched huts of natives. Money squeezed from the blood of Asians maintains these small white minorities in their luxurious mode of life—or disappears to the respective home-countries.

These white people may expect, from the moment they issue from their mothers' wombs, to be allotted a score or so of natives as their personal slaves. Is this really God's will?

The reason why so many peoples of the Far East have been so completely crushed by so few white men is, fundamentally, that they have exhausted their strength in private quarrels, and that they are lacking in any awareness of themselves as a group, as peoples of Asia.

Without oil neither planes, warships nor cars can move. Britain and America, controlling the greater part of the world's oil and having far more than they can use for their own purposes, have nevertheless forbidden the export of oil to Japan, which is desperately short of it. More than that, they even obstruct Japan from buying oil in South Asia.

Rubber and tin are likewise indispensable for military operations, and the countries of South Asia are the richest sources in the whole of the Far East for these valuable commodities too. Although our country has sought to purchase them by fair methods, the Anglo-Americans have interfered even in this. And in the unscrupulous behaviour of these two countries in these matters lies one of the reasons why the present campaign has been forced upon us. The Dutch East Indies and French Indo-China are clearly in no position by themselves to oppose Japan, but they too, with Anglo-American bolstering, and under intimidation, are maintaining a hostile attitude. If shortage of oil and steel is Japan's weak point, the greatest weakness in America's economy is shortage of rubber, tin and tungsten, and these are supplied to America from South Asia and southern China. If Japan can master these areas not only will she gain control of the oil and steel which she needs for herself, but she will strike at America where it hurts most. And herein lies the reason for America's extreme dislike of Japan's southward advance, and the malicious manner in which she has striven to obstruct it. . . .

Why Must We Fight? How Should We Fight?

The 1868 Restoration, by the abolition of feudal clans and the establishment of prefectures, returned Japan to its ancient system of beneficent government by His Majesty the Emperor, and thereby rescued the country from grave peril—for the black ships of the foreigners which had come to Nagasaki and Uraga were ready to annex Japan on the slightest pretext. The New Restoration of the thirties has come about in response to the Imperial desire for peace in the Far East. Its task is the rescue of Asia from white aggression, the restoration of

Asia to the Asians, and—when peace in Asia has been won—the firm establishment of peace throughout the whole world.

The wire-pullers giving aid to Chaing Kai-shek and moving him to make war on Japan are the British and the Americans. The rise of Japan being to these people like a sore spot on the eye, they have tried by every means in their power to obstruct our development, and they are inciting the regime at Chungking, the French Indo-Chinese, and the Dutch East Indians to regard Japan as their enemy. Their great hope is for the destruction of the Asian peoples by mutual strife, and their greatest fear is that, with the help of a powerful Japan, the peoples of Asia will work together for independence. If the peoples of Asia, representing more than half of the world's population, were to make a united stand it would indeed be a sore blow to British, Americans, French and Dutch alike, who for centuries have battened and waxed fat on the blood of Asians.

Already Japan, the pioneer in this movement in the Far East, has rescued Manchuria from the ambitions of the Soviets, and set China free from the extortions of the Anglo-Americans. Her next great mission is to assist towards the independence of the Thais, the Annamese, and the Filipinos, and to bring the blessing of freedom to the natives of South Asia and the Indian people. In this we shall be fulfilling the essential spirit of "one world to the eight corners of the earth".

The aim of the present war is the realization, first in the Far East, of His Majesty's august will and ideal that the peoples of the world should each be granted possession of their rightful homelands. To this end the countries of the Far East must plan a great coalition of East Asia, uniting their military resources, administering economically to each other's wants on the principle of co-existence to the common good, and mutually respecting each other's political independence. Through the combined strength of such a coalition we shall liberate East Asia from white invasion and oppression.

The significance of the present struggle, as we have shown, is immense, and the peril which Japan has drawn upon herself as the central and leading force in this movement is greater than anything she has ever faced since the foundation of the country. The peoples of South Asia deeply respect the Japanese and place high hopes upon our success. It is vital, above all, that we should not betray this respect and these hopes. . . .

Conclusion

At stake in the present war, without a doubt, is the future prosperity or decline of the Empire. Slowly, little by little, like a man strangling his victim with a soft cord of silken floss, America has been prohibiting the export to Japan of oil and steel. Why such cautious methods? The reason, perhaps, is a fear that to deny all supplies at one stroke might drive Japan, in desperation, to invade South Asia. And if the rubber and tin of the South were to be seized by Japan, it would create a situation far more intolerable to America than even the present lack of steel and oil is to Japan. America's policy so far has been one of weakening Japan without rousing her to violent indignation.

We have already, perhaps, left things too late. If we remain patient a moment longer Japan's aircraft, warships and road transport may be forced to a standstill. Five years have passed since the outbreak of the China Incident. More than a hundred thousand of your comrades have perished on the mainland; and the greater part of the armaments with which Chiang Kai-shek killed those men was sold to him by England and America. England and America, whose desire it is to hold the Far East in a permanent state of subjugation and colonization, dread the thought of any solidarity between Asian peoples, and for some time all their policies have been directed towards the instigation of war between Japan and China. Our allies, Germany and Italy, are engaged in a life-and-death struggle with England, America and the Soviet Union on the European continent; America, having given full support to England, is already virtually a participant in that war. For the sake of Japan's own existence, and because of our moral obligations as members of the Tripartite Alliance, it is impossible for us to endure the present situation a moment longer. We embark now upon that great mission which calls upon Japan, as the representative of all the peoples of the Far East, to deal a resolute and final blow to centuries of European aggression in these lands. Our peerless Navy is prepared, and ready to strike with its full strength. The formula indicating its numerical strength in relation to the fleets of England and America is 3:5:5, but if you include in the calculation its superiority in equipment and morale that ratio becomes 7:5:5. Half the British fleet, moreover, has been destroyed by Germany. As far as our Navy is concerned, now is the great opportunity. The umbilical cord of the Chungking regime runs to England and America. If this is not speedily cut the Sino-Japanese war will drag on endlessly. The final reckoning of our holy crusade will come on the battlefields ahead. Hundreds of thousands of the heroic dead will be watching over us. The supreme offering for which the souls of your departed comrades long is victory in this battle. To show our heartfelt gratitude to the Navy, which is dominating a thousand miles of ocean, sweeping the seas clear of enemy obstacles, and protecting us day and night with tireless devotion, we must requite such labours with comparable fruits of battle. We Japanese, heirs to two thousand six hundred years of a glorious past, have now, in response to the trust placed in us by His Majesty the Commander-in-Chief, risen in the cause of the peoples of Asia, and embarked upon a noble and solemn undertaking which will change the course of world history. Officers and men, the eyes of the whole world will be upon you in this campaign, and, working together in community of spirit, you must demonstrate to the world the true worth of Japanese manhood. The implementation of the task of the Showa Restoration, which is to realize His Imperial Majesty's desire for peace in the Far East, and to set Asia free, rests squarely on our shoulders.

> Corpses drifting swollen in the sea-depths,
> Corpses rotting in the mountain-grass—
> We shall die, by the side of our lord we shall die
> We shall not look back.

Essays

8   What Is War?

Carl von Clausewitz

Carl von Clausewitz (1780-1831) is generally considered to be one of the great military thinkers of all time. His treatise On War *is a classic analysis of the theory and practice of warfare. His observations transcend the state of the art as it was known during his lifetime, and for that reason an excerpt from his introductory book, "On the Nature of War," has been included here. Clausewitz applied to his subject rigorous logic stripped of all emotional and ethical considerations. He was, in fact, almost entirely disinterested in questions of morality, except when such concerns affected the existing or potential balance of power. Nevertheless, the Clausewitzian perspective is vitally important for understanding the evolution of strategic thought. It has been said that only in the Second World War was Clausewitz fully understood and his arguments completely accepted.*

We shall not enter into any of the abstruse definitions of War used by publicists. We shall keep to the element of the thing itself, to a duel. War is nothing but a duel on an extensive scale. If we would conceive as a unit the countless number of duels which make up a War, we shall do so best by supposing to ourselves two wrestlers. Each strives by physical force to compel the other to submit to his will: each endeavours to throw his adversary, and thus render him incapable of further resistance.

War therefore is an act of violence intended to compel our opponent to fulfil our will.

Violence arms itself with the inventions of Art and Science in order to contend against violence. Self-imposed restrictions, almost imperceptible and hardly worth mentioning, termed usages of International Law, accompany it

Adapted from **On War** by Carl von Clausewitz, I (New York: Barnes & Noble, Inc., 1966), pp. 1–4. Reprinted by permission of Routledge & Kegan Paul Ltd.

without essentially impairing its power. Violence, that is to say, physical force (for there is no moral force without the conception of States and Law), is therefore the *means*; the compulsory submission of the enemy to our will is the ultimate *object*. In order to attain this object fully, the enemy must be disarmed, and disarmament becomes therefore the immediate object of hostilities in theory. It takes the place of the final object, and puts it aside as something we can eliminate from our calculations.

Now, philanthropists may easily imagine there is a skilful method of disarming and overcoming an enemy without causing great bloodshed, and that this is the proper tendency of the Art of War. However plausible this may appear, still it is an error which must be extirpated; for in such dangerous things as War, the errors which proceed from a spirit of benevolence are the worst. As the use of physical power to the utmost extent by no means excludes the co-operation of the intelligence, it follows that he who uses force unsparingly, without reference to the bloodshed involved, must obtain a superiority if his adversary uses less vigour in its application. The former then dictates the law to the latter, and both proceed to extremities to which the only limitations are those imposed by the amount of counteracting force on each side.

This is the way in which the matter must be viewed and it is to no purpose, it is even against one's own interest, to turn away from the consideration of the real nature of the affair because the horror of its elements excites repugnance.

If the Wars of civilised people are less cruel and destructive than those of savages, the difference arises from the social condition both of States in themselves and in their relations to each other. Out of this social condition and its relations War arises, and by it War is subjected to conditions, is controlled and modified. But these things do not belong to War itself; they are only given conditions; and to introduce into the philosophy of War itself a principle of moderation would be an absurdity.

Two motives lead men to War: instinctive hostility and hostile intention. In our definition of War, we have chosen as its characteristic the latter of these elements, because it is the most general. It is impossible to conceive the passion of hatred of the wildest description, bordering on mere instinct, without combining with it the idea of a hostile intention. On the other hand, hostile intentions may often exist without being accompanied by any, or at all events by any extreme, hostility of feeling. Amongst savages views emanating from the feelings, amongst civilised nations those emanating from the understanding, have the predominance; but this difference arises from attendant circumstances, existing institutions, etc., and, therefore, is not to be found necessarily in all cases, although it prevails in the majority. In short, even the most civilised nations may burn with passionate hatred of each other.

We may see from this what a fallacy it would be to refer the War of a civilised nation entirely to an intelligent act on the part of the Government, and to imagine it as continually freeing itself more and more from all feeling of passion in such a way that at last the physical masses of combatants would no longer be required; in reality, their mere relations would suffice—a kind of algebraic action.

Theory was beginning to drift in this direction until the facts of the last War taught it better. If War is an *act* of force, it belongs necessarily also to the feelings. If it does not originate in the feelings, it *reacts*, more or less, upon them, and the extent of this reaction depends not on the degree of civilisation, but upon the importance and duration of the interests involved.

Therefore, if we find civilised nations do not put their prisoners to death, do not devastate towns and countries, this is because their intelligence exercises greater influence on their mode of carrying on War, and has taught them more effectual means of applying force than these rude acts of mere instinct. The invention of gunpowder, the constant progress of improvements in the construction of firearms, are sufficient proofs that the tendency to destroy the adversary which lies at the bottom of the conception of War is in no way changed or modified through the progress of civilisation.

We therefore repeat our proposition, that War is an act of violence pushed to its utmost bounds; as one side dictates the law to the other, there arises a sort of reciprocal action, which logically must lead to an extreme. This is the first reciprocal action, and the first extreme with which we meet (*first reciprocal action*).

9   The Moral Equivalent of War

William James

The essay that follows was written in 1910 for the Association for International Conciliation, one of the most influential among the numerous organizations striving for the abolition of war in the years before the First World War. It is perhaps ironic that the essay is still read by people interested in the nature of war—so many years and so many wars later. The author, William James, was a pioneer in such fields as psychology and sociology and was one of the most highly respected men of his time. James brought to his analysis of the role of warfare in human society the guiding assumption that war could be made obsolete. He also believed, however, that war had brought large benefits to humanity. James's challenging essay seems as fresh and relevant to present problems as it was sixty years ago.

"The Moral Equivalent of War" by William James. From **Memories and Studies** (New York: David McKay Co., 1911), pp. 267–96. Reprinted by permission of Alexander R. James.

The war against war is going to be no holiday excursion or camping party. The military feelings are too deeply grounded to abdicate their place among our ideals until better substitutes are offered than the glory and shame that come to nations as well as to individuals from the ups and downs of politics and the vicissitudes of trade. There is something highly paradoxical in the modern man's relation to war. Ask all our millions, north and south, whether they would vote now (were such a thing possible) to have our war for the Union expunged from history and the record of a peaceful transition to the present time substituted for that of its marches and battles, and probably hardly a handful of eccentrics would say yes. Those ancestors, those efforts, those memories and legends, are the most ideal part of what we now own together, a sacred spiritual possession worth more than all the blood poured out. Yet ask those same people whether they would be willing in cold blood to start another civil war now to gain another similar possession, and not one man or woman would vote for the proposition. In modern eyes, precious though wars may be, they must not be waged solely for the sake of the ideal harvest. Only when forced upon one, only when an enemy's injustice leaves us no alternative, is a war now thought permissible.

It was not thus in ancient times. The earlier men were hunting men, and to hunt a neighboring tribe, kill the males, loot the village, and possess the females was the most profitable, as well as the most exciting, way of living. Thus were the more martial tribes selected, and in chiefs and peoples a pure pugnacity and love of glory came to mingle with the more fundamental appetite for plunder.

Modern war is so expensive that we feel trade to be a better avenue to plunder, but modern man inherits all the innate pugnacity and all the love of glory of his ancestors. Showing war's irrationality and horror is of no effect upon him. The horrors make the fascination. War is the *strong* life; it is life *in extremis*; war taxes are the only ones men never hesitate to pay, as the budgets of all nations show us.

History is a bath of blood. The *Iliad* is one long recital of how Diomedes and Ajax, Sarpedon and Hector, *killed*. No detail of the wounds they made is spared us, and the Greek mind fed upon the story. Greek history is a panorama of jingoism and imperialism—war for war's sake, all the citizens being warriors. It is horrible reading, because of the irrationality of it all—save for the purpose of making history—and the history is that of the utter ruin of a civilization in intellectual respects perhaps the highest the earth has ever seen.

Those wars were purely piratical. Pride, gold, women, slaves, excitement were their only motives. In the Peloponnesian War for example, the Athenians ask the inhabitants of Melos (the island where the "Venus of Milo" was found), hitherto neutral, to own their lordship. The envoys meet, and hold a debate which Thucydides gives in full and which, for sweet reasonableness of form, would have satisfied Matthew Arnold. "The powerful exact what they can," said the Athenians, "and the weak grant what they must." When the Meleans say that, sooner than be slaves, they will appeal to the gods, the Athenians reply:

Of the gods we believe and of men we know that, by a law of their nature, wherever they can rule they will. This law was not made by us, and we are not the first to have acted upon it; we did but inherit it, and we know that you and all mankind, if you were as strong as we are, would do as we do. So much for the gods; we have told you why we expect to stand as high in their good opinion as you.

Well, the Meleans still refused, and their town was taken. "The Athenians," Thucydides quietly says, "thereupon put to death all who were of military age and made slaves of the women and children. They then colonized the island, sending thither five hundred settlers of their own."

Alexander's career was piracy pure and simple, nothing but an orgy of power and plunder made romantic by the character of the hero. There was no rational principle in it, and the moment he died his generals and governors attacked one another. The cruelty of those times is incredible. When Rome finally conquered Greece, Paulus Aemilius was told by the Roman Senate to reward his soldiers for their toil by "giving" them the old kingdom of Epirus. They sacked seventy cities and carried off one hundred and fifty thousand inhabitants as slaves. How many they killed I know not, but in Aetolia they killed all the senators, five hundred and fifty in number. Brutus was "the noblest Roman of them all," but, to reanimate his soldiers on the eve of Philippi, he similarly promises to give them the cities of Sparta and Thessalonica to ravage if they win the fight.

Such was the gory nurse that trained societies to cohesiveness. We inherit the warlike type, and, for most of the capacities of heroism that the human race is full of, we have to thank this cruel history. Dead men tell no tales, and, if there were any tribes of other type than this, they have left no survivors. Our ancestors have bred pugnacity into our bone and marrow, and thousands of years of peace won't breed it out of us. The popular imagination fairly fattens on the thought of wars. Let public opinion once reach a certain fighting pitch, and no ruler can withstand it. In the Boer War both governments began with bluff but couldn't stay there; the military tension was too much for them. In 1898 our people had read the word "war" in letters three inches high for three months in every newspaper. The pliant politician McKinley was swept away by their eagerness, and our squalid war with Spain became a necessity.

At the present day, civilized opinion is a curious mental mixture. The military instincts and ideals are as strong as ever, but are confronted by reflective criticisms which sorely curb their ancient freedom. Innumerable writers are showing up the bestial side of military service. Pure loot and mastery seem no longer morally avowable motives, and pretexts must be found for attributing them solely to the enemy. England and we, our army and navy authorities repeat without ceasing, arm solely for "peace"; Germany and Japan it is who are bent on loot and glory. "Peace" in military mouths today is a synonym for "war expected." The word has become a pure provocative, and no government wishing peace sincerely should allow it ever to be printed in a newspaper. Every up-to-date dictionary should say that "peace" and "war" mean the same thing, now *in posse*, now *in actu*. It may even reasonably be said that the intensely sharp competitive *preparation* for war by the nations *is the real war*, permanent, unceasing, and that the battles are only a sort of public verification of the mastery gained during the "peace" interval.

It is plain that on this subject civilized man has developed a sort of double personality. If we take European nations, no legitimate interest of any one of them would seem to justify the tremendous destructions which a war to compass it would necessarily entail. It would seem as though common sense and reason ought to find a way to reach agreement in every conflict of honest interests. I myself think it our bounden duty to believe in such international rationality as possible. But, as things stand, I see how desperately hard it is to bring the peace party and the war party together, and I believe that the difficulty is due to certain deficiencies in the program of pacificism which set the militarist imagination strongly, and, to a certain extent, justifiably, against it. In the whole discussion both sides are on imaginative and sentimental ground. It is but one Utopia against another, and everything one says must be abstract and hypothetical. Subject to this criticism and caution, I will try to characterize in abstract strokes the opposite imaginative forces and point out what to my own very fallible mind seems the best utopian hypothesis, the most promising line of conciliation.

In my remarks, pacificist though I am, I will refuse to speak of the bestial side of the war regime (already done justice to by many writers) and consider only the higher aspects of militaristic sentiment. Patriotism no one thinks discreditable, nor does anyone deny that war is the romance of history. But inordinate ambitions are the soul of every patriotism, and the possibility of violent death the soul of all romance. The militarily patriotic and romantic-minded everywhere, and especially the professional military class, refuse to admit for a moment that war may be a transitory phenomenon in social evolution. The notion of a sheep's paradise like that revolts, they say, our higher imagination. Where then would be the steeps of life? If war had ever stopped, we should have to reinvent it, on this view, to redeem life from flat degeneration.

Reflective apologists for war at the present day all take it religiously. It is a sort of sacrament. Its profits are to the vanquished as well as to the victor, and, quite apart from any question of profit, it is an absolute good, we are told, for it is human nature at its highest dynamic. Its "horrors" are a cheap price to pay for rescue from the only alternative supposed, of a world of clerks and teachers, of coeducation and zoophily, of consumer's leagues and associated charities, of industrialism unlimited, and femininism unabashed. No scorn, no hardness, no valor any more! Fie upon such a cattleyard of a planet!

So far as the central essence of this feeling goes, no healthy-minded person, it seems to me, can help to some degree partaking of it. Militarism is the great preserver of our ideals of hardihood, and human life with no use for hardihood would be contemptible. Without risks or prizes for the darer, history would be insipid indeed, and there is a type of military character which everyone feels that the race should never cease to breed, for everyone is sensitive to its superiority. The duty is incumbent on mankind of keeping military characters in stock—of keeping them, if not for use, then as ends in themselves and as pure pieces of perfection—so that Roosevelt's weaklings and mollycoddles may not end by making everything else disappear from the face of nature.

This natural sort of feeling forms, I think, the innermost soul of army writings. Without any exception known to me, militarist authors take a highly mystical view of their subject and regard war as a biological or sociological necessity, uncontrolled by ordinary psychological checks and motives. When the time of development is ripe, the war must come, reason or no reason, for the justifications pleaded are invariably fictitious. War is, in short, a permanent human *obligation*. Gen. Homer Lea, in his recent book, *The Valor of Ignorance*, plants himself squarely on this ground. Readiness for war is for him the essence of nationality, and ability in it the supreme measure of the health of nations.

Nations, General Lea says, are never stationary—they must necessarily expand or shrink, according to their vitality or decrepitude. Japan now is culminating; and, by the fatal law in question, it is impossible that her statesmen should not long since have entered, with extraordinary foresight, upon a vast policy of conquest—the game in which the first moves were her wars with China and Russia and her treaty with England and of which the final objective is the capture of the Philippines, the Hawaiian Islands, Alaska, and the whole of our coast west of the Sierra passes. This will give Japan what her ineluctable vocation as a state absolutely forces her to claim, the possession of the entire Pacific Ocean; and, to oppose these deep designs, we Americans have, according to our author, nothing but our conceit, our ignorance, our commercialism, our corruption, and our femininism. General Lea makes a minute technical comparison of the military strength which we at present could oppose to the strength of Japan and concludes that the islands, Alaska, Oregon, and Southern California would fall almost without resistance, that San Francisco must surrender in a fortnight to a Japanese investment, that in three or four months the war would be over, and our republic, unable to regain what it had heedlessly neglected to protect sufficiently, would then disintegrate, until, perhaps, some Caesar should arise to weld us again into a nation.

A dismal forecast indeed! Yet not unplausible if the mentality of Japan's statesmen be of the Caesarian type of which history shows so many examples and which is all that General Lea seems able to imagine. But there is no reason to think that women can no longer be the mothers of Napoleonic or Alexandrian characters; and, if these come in Japan and find their opportunity, just such surprises as *The Valor of Ignorance* paints may lurk in ambush for us. Ignorant as we still are of the innermost recesses of Japanese mentality, we may be foolhardy to disregard such possibilities.

Other militarists are more complex and more moral in their considerations. The *Philosophie des Krieges* by S.R. Steinmetz is a good example. War, according to this author, is an ordeal instituted by God, who weights the nations in its balance. It is the essential form of the state and the only function in which peoples can employ all their powers at once and convergently. No victory is possible save as the resultant of a totality of virtues, no defeat for which some vice or weakness is not responsible. Fidelity, cohesiveness, tenacity, heroism, conscience, education, inventiveness, economy, wealth, physical health, and vigor—there isn't a moral or intellectual point of superiority that doesn't tell when God holds his assizes and hurls the peoples upon one another. *Die Weltgeschichte ist das Weltgericht*, and Dr. Steinmetz does not believe that in the long run chance and luck play any part in apportioning the issues.

The virtues that prevail, it must be noted, are virtues anyhow, superiorities that count in peaceful as well as in military competition; but the strain on them, being infinitely intenser in the latter case, makes war infinitely more searching as a trial. No ordeal is comparable to its winnowings. Its dread hammer is the welder of men into cohesive states, and nowhere but in such states can human nature adequately develop its capacity. The only alternative is degeneration.

Dr. Steinmetz is a conscientious thinker, and his book, short as it is, takes much into account. Its upshot can, it seems to me, be summed up in Simon Patten's word, that mankind was nursed in pain and fear and that the transition to a pleasure economy may be fatal to a being wielding no powers of defense against its disintegrative influences. If we speak of the *fear of emancipation from the fear regime*, we put the whole situation into a single phrase, fear regarding ourselves now taking the place of the ancient fear of the enemy.

Turn the fear over as I will in my mind, it all seems to lead back to two unwillingnesses of the imagination, one aesthetic and the other moral; unwillingness, first, to envisage a future in which army life, with its many elements of charm, shall be forever impossible and in which the destinies of peoples shall nevermore be decided quickly, thrillingly, and tragically by force, but only gradually and insipidly by evolution; and, second, unwillingness to see the supreme theater of human strenuousness closed and the splendid military aptitudes of men doomed to keep always in a state of latency and never show themselves in action. These insistent unwillingnesses, no less than other aesthetic and ethical insistencies, have, it seems to me, to be listened to and respected. One cannot meet them effectively by mere counterinsistency on war's expensiveness and horror. The horror makes the thrill, and, when the question is of getting the extremest and supremest out of human nature, talk of expense sounds ignominious. The weakness of so much merely negative criticism is evident—pacificism makes no converts from the military party. The military partly denies neither the bestiality nor the horror nor the expense; it only says that these things tell but half the story. It only says that war is *worth* them; that, taking human nature as a whole, its wars are its best protection against its weaker and more cowardly self and that mankind cannot *afford* to adopt a peace economy.

Pacificists ought to enter more deeply into the aesthetical and ethical point of view of their opponents. Do that first in any controversy, says J.J. Chapman, *then move the point*, and your opponent will follow. So long as antimilitarists propose no substitute for war's disciplinary function, no *moral equivalent* of war, analogous, as one might say, to the mechanical equivalent of heat, so long they fail to realize the full inwardness of the situation. And as a rule they do fail. The duties, penalties, and sanctions pictured in the Utopias they paint are all too weak and tame to touch the military-minded. Tolstoi's pacificism is the only exception to this rule, for it is profoundly pessimistic as regards all this world's values and makes the fear of the Lord furnish the moral spur provided elsewhere by the fear of the enemy. But our socialistic peace advocates all believe absolutely in this world's values, and, instead of the fear of the Lord and the fear of the enemy, the only fear they reckon with is the fear of poverty if one be lazy. This weakness pervades all the socialistic literature with which I am acquainted. Even in Lowes Dickinson's exquisite dialogue, high wages and short hours are the only forces invoked for overcoming man's distaste for repulsive kinds of labor. Meanwhile men at large still live as they always have lived, under a pain-and-fear economy—for those of us who live in an ease economy are but an island in the stormy ocean—and the whole atmosphere of present-day Utopian literature tastes mawkish and dishwatery to people who still keep a sense for life's more bitter flavors. It suggests, in truth, ubiquitous inferiority.

Inferiority is always with us, and merciless scorn of it is the keynote of the military temper. "Dogs, would you live forever?" shouted Frederick the Great. "Yes," say our Utopians, "let us live forever and raise our level gradually." The best thing about our "inferiors" today is that they are as tough as nails and physically and morally almost as insensitive. Utopianism would see them soft and squeamish, while militarism would keep their callousness, but transfigure it into a meritorious characteristic, needed by "the service" and redeemed by that from the suspicion of inferiority. All the qualities of a man acquire dignity when he knows that the service of the collectivity that owns him needs them. If proud of the collectivity, his own pride rises in proportion. No collectivity is like an army for nourishing such pride, but it has to be confessed that the only sentiment which the image of pacific cosmopolitan industrialism is capable of arousing in countless worthy breasts is shame at the idea of belonging to *such* a collectivity. It is obvious that the United States of America as they exist today impress a mind like General Lea's as so much human blubber. Where is the sharpness and precipitousness, the contempt for life, whether one's own, or another's? Where is the savage yes and no, the unconditional duty? Where is the conscription? Where is the blood tax? Where is anything that one feels honored by belonging to?

Having said thus much in preparation, I will now confess my own Utopia. I devoutly believe in the reign of peace and in the gradual advent of some sort of a socialistic equilibrium. The fatalistic view of the war function is to me nonsense, for I know that war-making is due to definite motives and subject to prudential checks and reasonable criticisms, just like any other form of enterprise. And when whole nations are the armies and the science of destruction vies in intellectual refinement with the sciences of production, I see that war becomes absurd and impossible from its own monstrosity. Extravagant ambitions will have to be replaced by reasonable claims, and nations must make common cause against them. I see no reason that all this should not apply to yellow as well as to white countries, and I look forward to a future when acts of war shall be formally outlawed between civilized peoples.

All these beliefs of mine put me squarely into the antimilitarist party. But I do not believe that peace either ought to be or will be permanent on this globe, unless the states pacifically organized preserve some of the old elements of army discipline. A permanently successful peace economy cannot be a simple pleasure economy. In the more-or-less socialistic future toward which mankind seems drifting, we must still subject ourselves collectively to those severities which answer to our real position upon this only partly hospitable globe. We must make new energies and hardihoods continue the manliness to which the military mind so faithfully clings. Martial virtues must be the enduring cement; intrepidity, contempt of softness, surrender of private interest, obedience to command must still remain the rock upon which states are built—unless, indeed, we wish for dangerous reactions against commonwealths fit only for contempt and liable to invite attack whenever a center of crystallization for military-minded enterprise gets formed anywhere in their neighborhood. .

The war party is assuredly right in affirming and reaffirming that the martial virtues, although originally gained by the race through war, are absolute and permanent human goods. Patriotic pride and amibition in their military form are, after all, only specifications of a more general competitive passion. They are its first form, but that is no reason for supposing them to be its last form. Men now are proud of belonging to a conquering nation, and without a murmur they lay down their persons and their wealth, if by so doing they may fend off subjection. But who can be sure that *other aspects of one's country* may not, with time and education and suggestion enough, come to be regarded with similarly effective feelings of pride and shame? Why should men not someday feel that it is worth a blood tax to belong to a collectivity superior in *any* ideal aspect? Why should they not blush with indignant shame if the community that owns them is vile in any way whatsoever? Individuals, daily more numerous, now feel this civic passion. It is only a question of blowing on the spark until the whole population gets incandescent and, on the ruins of the old morals of military honor, a stable system of morals of civic honor builds itself up. What the whole community comes to believe in grasps the individual as in a vise. The war function has grasped us so far, but constructive interests may someday seem no less imperative and impose on the individual a hardly lighter burden.

Let me illustrate my idea more concretely. There is nothing to make one indignant in the mere fact that life is hard, that men should toil and suffer pain. The planetary conditions once and for all are such, and we can stand it. But that so many men, by mere accidents of birth and opportunity, should have a life of *nothing else* but toil and pain and hardness and inferiority imposed upon them, should have *no* vacation, while others natively no more deserving never get any taste of this campaigning life at all—*this* is capable of arousing indignation in reflective minds. It may end by seeming shameful to all of us that some of us have nothing but campaigning and others nothing but unmanly ease. If now—and this is my idea—there were, instead of military conscription, a conscription of the whole youthful population to form for a certain number of years a part of the army enlisted against nature, the injustice would tend to be evened out, and numerous other goods to the commonwealth would follow. The military ideals of hardihood and discipline would be wrought into the growing fiber of the people; no one would remain blind, as the luxurious classes now are blind, to man's relations to the globe he lives on and to the permanently sour and hard foundations of his higher life. To coal and iron mines, to freight trains, to fishing fleets in December, to dish-washing, clothes-washing, and window-washing, to road-building and tunnel-making, to foundries and stokeholes, and to the frames of skyscrapers, would our gilded youths be drafted off, according to their choice, to get the childishness knocked out of them and to come back into society with healthier sympathies and soberer ideas. They would have paid their blood tax, done their own part in the immemorial human warfare against nature; they would tread the earth more proudly, the women would value them more highly, they would be better fathers and teachers of the following generation.

Such a conscription, with the state of public opinion that would have required it and the many moral fruits it would bear, would preserve in the midst of a pacific civilization the manly virtues which the military party is so afraid of seeing disappear in peace. We should get toughness without callousness, authority with as little criminal cruelty as possible, and painful work done cheerily because the duty is temporary and threatens not, as now, to degrade the whole remainder of one's life. I spoke of the moral equivalent of war. So far, war has been the only force that can discipline a whole community, and, until an equivalent discipline is organized, I believe that war must have its way. But I have no serious doubt that the ordinary prides and shames of social man, once developed to a certain intensity, are capable of organizing such a moral equivalent as I have sketched or some other just as effective for preserving manliness of type. It is but a question of time, of skillful propagandism, and of opinion-making men seizing historic opportunities.

The martial type of character can be bred without war. Strenuous honor and disinterestedness abound elsewhere. Priests and medical men are in a fashion educated to it, and we should all feel some degree of it imperative if we were conscious of our work as an obligatory service to the state. We should be *owned*, as soldiers are by the army, and our pride would rise accordingly. We could be poor, then, without humiliation, as army officers now are. The only thing needed henceforward is to inflame the civic temper as past history has inflamed the military temper. H.G. Wells, as usual, sees the center of the situation.

In many ways [he says], military organization is the most peaceful of activities. When the contemporary man steps from the street, of clamorous insincere advertisement, push, adulteration, underselling and intermittent employment into the barrack-yard, he steps on to a higher social plane, into an atmosphere of service and cooperation and of infinitely more honorable emulations. Here at least men are not flung out of employment to degenerate because there is no immediate work for them to do. They are fed and drilled and trained for better services. Here at least a man is supposed to win promotion by self-forgetfulness and not by self-seeking. And beside the feeble and irregular endowment of research by commercialism, its little shortsighted snatches at profit by innovation and scientific economy, see how remarkable is the steady and rapid development of method and appliances in naval and military affairs! Nothing is more striking than to compare the progress of civil conveniences which has been left almost entirely to the trader, to the progress in military apparatus during the last few decades. The house-appliances of today for example, are little better than they were fifty years ago. A house of today is still almost as ill-ventilated, badly heated by wasteful fires, clumsily arranged and furnished as the house of 1858. Houses a couple of hundred years old are still satisfactory places of residence, so little have our standards risen. But the rifle or battleship of fifty years ago was beyond all comparison inferior to those we possess; in power, in speed, in convenience alike. No one has a use now for such superannuated things.

Wells adds that he thinks that the conceptions of order and discipline, the tradition of service and devotion, of physical fitness, unstinted exertion, and universal responsibility, which universal military duty is now teaching European nations, will remain a permanent acquisition when the last ammunition has been used in the fireworks that celebrate the final peace. I believe as he does. It would be simply preposterous if the only force that could work ideals of honor and standards of efficiency into English or American natures should be the fear of being killed by the Germans or the Japanese. Great indeed is fear, but it is not, as our military enthusiasts believe and try to make us believe, the only stimulus known for awakening the higher ranges of men's spiritual energy. The amount of alteration in public opinion which my Utopia postulates is vastly less than the difference between the mentality of those black warriors who pursued Stanley's party on the Congo with their cannibal war cry of "Meat! Meat!" and that of the general staff of any civilized nation. History has seen the latter interval bridged over; the former one can be bridged over much more easily.

Unit II

Total War

The concept of "total war" is of particular value for understanding the Second World War. By almost any standard of comparison, this conflict affected more people in more ways—and to greater degrees—than any previous war. Total war is, of course, a relative concept. While a thermonuclear holocaust may be the only method guaranteed to bring total annihilation, any war is total to the individuals it destroys. Does it matter, then, that World War II was more "total" than earlier ones? Yes—if historical understanding of human behavior in times of crisis is important, because this war was one of the most intensive crises suffered by mankind. Whether they were or not, people believed they were engaged in a total stuggle, and they acted on that belief.

Some of the readings here suggest that the Second World War brought about "total" economic mobilization. This was true primarily in the highly industrialized nations. The war propelled those countries to unprecedented levels of government intervention in private economic life—as evidenced by ration books, work permits, and myriad other devices for controlling the "getting and spending" of citizens. The readings also suggest that, for a variety of reasons, the democracies were more successful than the authoritarian states in accomplishing the goal of full, efficient use of natural and human resources.

The totality of this war was underscored by the general belief that each and every inhabitant of the belligerent countries was fair game to the enemy. The slaughter of noncombatants was no new invention. Passages in the Bible, Greek and Roman accounts of such events as the siege of Athens and the utter destruction of Carthage, the practice of warfare in the Middle Ages, indicate that organized violence against all inhabitants of the enemy state is among the most ancient of human traditions. Beginning in the sixteenth century, however, there had been a determined and amazingly successful effort to codify the rules of war, by defining what were "proper" military activities and by extending the protection of international law to all persons who did not directly participate in those activities.

The Second World War brought a dramatic reversal of this trend; for all practical purposes, the idea of a "noncombatant" disappeared. That war was a struggle between peoples and not just a competition between professional armies had been accepted in principle since the Napoleonic Wars. However, World War II was perhaps the first modern conflict in which the populations of the belligerent powers understood and acted on this theory. A tinsmith, aircraft-factory worker, or farmer might be behind the battle lines, but his contribution to his nation's war effort was as important as that of the soldier bearing arms. Civilians became "legitimate" targets, as survivors of Cologne, Coventry, and Hiroshima are bitterly aware.

But did the factory workers and farmers really believe they were part of the front lines? Did the victims of saturation bombing face the horrors visited upon them in the same way soldiers faced combat? If the answers to such questions are in some measure affirmative, other questions can be asked. Did the degree of popular participation influence the outcome of the war? If so, how and why? Were the "democracies" more successful in mobilizing popular support than the so-called totalitarian states? If so, what does this suggest about the nature of these political systems in times of crisis?

Documents

1 War

Theodore H. White and Annalee Jacoby

Theodore White and Annalee Jacoby were members of an exclusive group of foreign correspondents who lived in China all through the war and its aftermath; they were, therefore, uniquely qualified to chronicle China's agony and to assess its future. The following excerpt from White and Jacoby's influential book Thunder out of China *describes the effects of the Japanese invasion. It is a tale of appalling brutality and suffering, but in the course of their narrative the authors also relate another story—how the impetus of total war caused the Chinese people to begin to make a nation out of chaos.*

The winter of '37-'38 worked a miracle in China. The seat of government was transferred to the upriver port of Hankow, 800 miles from the sea, and the most complete unity of spirit and motive that China had ever known existed there for a few months. The Hankow spirit could never be quite precisely defined by those who experienced it there and then. All China was on the move—drifting back from the coast into the interior and swirling in confusion about the temporary capital. War-lord armies from the south and southwest were marching to join the battle. The Communists were speeding their partisans deeper into the tangled communications that supported Japan's front. In Hankow the government and the Communists sat in common council, made common plans for the prosecution of the war. The government authorized the creation of a second Communist army—the New Fourth—on the lower Yangtze behind the Japanese lines; the Communists participated in the meetings of the Military Council.

The elite of China's writers, engineers, and journalists converged on Hankow to sew together the frayed strands of resistance. By spring of 1938,

From **Thunder Out of China** by Theodore H. White and Annalee Jacoby, pp. 53–67. Copyright 1946 by William Sloane Associates. Renewed, © 1974 by Theodore H. White and Annalee Jacoby. Reprinted by permission of William Morrow & Company, Inc.

when the Japanese resumed the campaign, with Hankow as their ultimate objective, the new armies and the new spirit had crystallized. In April 1938, for the first time in the history of Japan, her armies suffered a frontal defeat at the battle of Taierchwang. The setback was only temporary. Moving in two great arms, the Japanese forces closed on Hankow from the north and the east to pinch it off in the following fall. Almost simultaneously their landing parties seized Canton, the great port city of the south, and the Japanese rested on their arms a second time.

On paper the Japanese strategy was perfect. China falls into a simple geographical pattern. Western China is a rocky, mountainous land; eastern China is flat and alluvial, with scarcely a hill to break the paddies for miles on end. Both western and eastern China are drained by three great rivers that flow down from the mountains across the flatlands to the Pacific Ocean. The Japanese army now controlled the entire coast and all the centers of industry. It also controlled the outlets of the three great rivers. In the north it held the Peking-Tientsin area and the outlet of the Yellow River. In central China it garrisoned both banks of the Yangtze, from Shanghai through Nanking to Hankow. In southern China it held Canton and dominated the West River. With the cities, railways, and rivers under control, the Japanese felt that they could wait until a paralysis of all economic and transport functions brought Chinese resistance to a halt, and they waited. They were still waiting seven years later, when the Japanese army surrendered a ruined homeland to the Allies.

The Japanese blundered in China. Why they blundered was best explained later by one of the shrewder statesmen of the Chungking government, General Wu Te-chen, who said, "The Japanese think they know China too much." Japanese political and military intelligence in China was far and away the finest in the world, but it had concentrated on schisms and rifts, on personalities and feuds, on guns and factories. Its dossiers on each province, each general, each army, contained so much of the wickedness and corruption of China that the accumulated knowledge was blinding. The one fact that was obscure to them was that China was a nation. They had seen a revolution proceeding in China for thirteen years, but only its scum, its abortions, its internal tensions; they had not measured its results. They were fighting more than a coalition of armies; they were fighting an entire people. They had watched the infant growth of Chinese industries on the coast, had marked the new railways on the map. But the strength of the Chinese was not in their cities; it was in the hearts of the people. China was primitive, so primitive that the destruction of her industries and cities, her railways and machinery, did not upset her as similar disaster disrupted Europe in later days. China was rooted in the soil. As long as the rain fell and the sun shone, the crops would grow; no blockade of the Japanese navy could interpose itself between the peasant and his land. China had just emerged from chaos, but she was still so close to it that the disruption of war could be fitted into the normal routine of her life; if, for example, it was necessary to move government, industry, people, and army into the interior, it could be done. There was an enormous elasticity in the system that Japan meant to wreck—when it was struck, it yielded, but it did not break.

Through the long months of 1938, as the Chinese armies were pressed slowly back toward the interior, they found their way clogged by moving people. The breathing space of winter had given hundreds of thousands time to make their decision, and China was on the move in one of the greatest mass migrations in human history. It is curious that such a spectacle has not been adequately recorded by any Chinese writer or novelist. Certainly the long files of gaunt people who moved west across the roads and mountains must have presented a sight unmatched since the days of nomad hordes; yet no record tells how many made the trek, where they came from, where they settled anew. The government and the journals of China have recorded mainly those things that were important to the war, the movement of the armies, the officials, the universities, and the factories.

The government began evacuation of factories and industry almost immediately on the outbreak of the war. The entire operation was in the hands of one of the most brilliant and lovable men in China—her Minister of Economic Affairs, Dr. Wong Wen-hao. Wong was a tiny man, a scholarly doodler. He had a deep cleft in his forehead that made him oddly attractive, and his smile was unfailing. Through all the later years of the war he was one of the few senior officials in the cabinet who were never accused of corruption by anyone—his shining integrity lifted him above ordinary politics. China's prewar industry was a lopsided growth; it was concentrated at the coast and in a few great river cities. Chinese private capital had invested overwhelmingly in textiles and consumer goods. Heavy industry, dominated by the government, was a diminutive tail attached to the body of the economy; steel production was never more than 100,000 tons annually. The swiftness of the war in the north and the ferocity of the fighting at Shanghai threatened to consume almost overnight all the industry there was. Government records show now that in all some 400 factories, with something over 200,000 tons of equipment, were moved in the retreat. These seem modest figures in the light of Russia's later accomplishments; only by breaking them down can their significance be exposed. Wong abandoned almost all China's textile mills and consumer industries to the enemy and concentrated on moving heavy industries and arsenals inland. China salvaged less than 10 per cent of her textile capacity, with perhaps 40 per cent of her machine shops and heavy industry, but she saved more than 80 per cent of the capacity of her eleven obsolescent arsenals. This meant that the Chinese would be threadbare during the following years, but that the army's minimum needs might be met.

The early stages of the industrial hegira carried little glory. The removal from Shanghai started late; businessmen were reluctant to let their plants be moved; the government was slow in making its decisions. The first plant to go, the Shanghai Machine Works, one of the finest mechanical shops in the country, did not start up Soochow Creek till two weeks after the fighting began. Soochow Creek runs through the heart of Shanghai and skirted the battlefront. The machinery was loaded in rowboats, covered with leaves and branches for camouflage, and poled slowly upriver to the Yangtze; when air raids threatened, the rowboats sheltered in reeds by the side of the river. It was followed by other shops till the Japanese drive cut the city off from the Yangtze in early December. Because it was delayed too long, the Shanghai evacuation succeeded in moving only 14,000 tons of equipment before the enemy advance ended it.

Shanghai, however, had proved the thing could be done, and by the spring of 1938 dozens of movable plants in northern and central China were being taken down, repacked, and transhipped to the far interior. A major engineering operation was being performed while the national organism continued to function and resist. From the Yellow River one of the greatest textile mills in China, the Yufeng, set out on its trek to Szechwan, a province 1000 miles away and without a single railway. In February it packed its 8000 tons of machinery and bundled them off down the railway to Hankow. In May it kissed the railhead good-bye and set off by steamer upriver to the gorge mouth. In August it was repackaged again to fit on some 380 native junks, which took it up the tumbling gorges to Szechwan; 120 of the boats sank in the gorges, but the junkmen raised all but 21 and carried on. The convoy arrived in Chungking in April 1939; a patch of hilly ground had been cleared for its arrival, and by spring the company was busily training timid Szechwanese peasant women to tend the rusting spindles.

An industrial wilderness stretched from Hankow on into the west. Whatever went inland had to be moved by hand. Coolies by hundreds and thousands hauled at blocks of steel weighing up to 20 tons. By the last week of Hankow's resistance removals had hit a stupendous pace. The Hankow power plant had been operating up to the very last days, for it was essential to the functions of life, but it was impossible to leave behind in Hankow the enormous 18-ton turbine, which would be irreplaceable after retreat to Szechwan. The dismantling process reached the power plant early in October, but the turbine could not be inched aboard a steamer until October 23, just two days before the Japanese entered the city. The removal of such massive machinery presented problems that the tiny river steamers could not handle; no steamer that could thread the gorges had a crane capable of lifting more than 16 tons. The Chinese settled the problem by lashing heavy machinery to pontoons, floating the pontoons, tying the pontoons to the steamers, and sending the whole through the rapids in tow.

The new industries, resettled in Szechwan, were a Rube Goldberg paradise. Steel factories were built with bamboo beams; blast furnaces were supplied with coal carried in hand baskets. Copper refineries consumed copper coins collected from the peasantry, converted them into pure copper by the most modern electrolytic methods, then shipped the metal to arsenals buried deep in caves.

The migration of China's universities paralleled almost precisely the movement of her industries. Like industry China's system of higher education had grown in thirty years of chaos; it too had concentrated along the coast and in the great cities, and it too was one of the elements of the new China that Japan most feared. Every major turning point in modern Chinese history has been signalized by student uprisings and intellectual discontent. Students had generated the anti-Manchu uprisings. Their riots and demonstrations touched off the national uproar of 1919, when even corrupt war lords were forced to repudiate the Treaty of Versailles. Student-led riots struck some of the most important notes in the rising crescendo of revolution of the 1920's. Finally, the students and their professors were the most enthusiastic and vociferous demonstrators against Japan, outside of the Communist Party.

The four great universities of northern China—Peking National, Tsinghua, Yenching, and Nankai—were particularly loathed by the Japanese. They singled out Tsinghua, which had been built with American money, for special treatment. They smashed its laboratories or removed its equipment to Japan and used the student gymnasium to stable Japanese horses. Nankai University was almost completely destroyed. In the basement of Peking University, the seat of China's intellectual renaissance, Japanese special police set up examination headquarters for their political and military inquisition.

When the Japanese attacked in the summer of 1937, most of the students were away on summer vacation. The Ministry of Education sent out a call for them to appear at two rendezvous. One was to be at Sian in the north, on the inner bank of the Yellow River, the other at Changsha, south of the Yangtze. From Sian the students of two colleges were told to move to southern Shensi. When they arrived at the end of the railway, they set out on the tail end of their journey for a 180-mile march over the rugged Tsingling mountain range. The deans of the university were the general staff of the march, and they divided their 1500-odd men and women into sections of 500 each. Each unit was preceded by a police section, a foraging squad, and a communications squad; its rear was brought up by pack animals carrying rice and wheat cakes and by a few wheezing trucks crawling over unimproved roads. The foraging squads descended on villages, bought all the fresh vegetables they could find, and had enough greens on hand to start a meal when the rest of the students arrived with their cooking pots. The road they followed runs over some of the most primitive terrain in China. Local authorities quartered students in stables and farmhouses. Engineering students set up receiving stations to catch the evening broadcasts; next morning they hung up posters as news bulletins for the students farther back to read. For the villagers these bulletins were a first exposure to the phenomenon of current news.

As the Japanese drove farther inland, university after university packed up and moved away. Some evacuated their campuses within a few days of the Japanese entry; the students of Sun Yat-sen University were still poling boats bearing the college library out of the northern suburbs of Canton when the Japanese entered from the south. The agriculture department of National Central University decided that its prize herd of blooded cattle was too valuable to leave behind, and all through the summer of 1938 the cattle grazed their way inland just a few weeks ahead of the Japanese spearheads; not till the summer of 1939 did they finally reach the quiet interior, where the bulls settled down to bring joy to the scrawny, inbred cows of Szechwan. Of China's 108 institutions of higher learning, 94 were either forced to move inland or close down entirely. And yet the entire educational system had been re-established by the fall of 1939, and 40,000 students were enrolled in the refugee colleges, as against 32,000 who had been registered in the last academic year before the war.

The transferred institutions of learning clustered mainly in three centers. One was near Chungking, another near Chengtu in western China, the third at Kunming, capital of Yunnan. Each of these centers differed in texture and quality. The universities in the Chungking suburbs, under strict government control, were always infected by the capital's prevailing mood. The universities about Chengtu took refuge on the beautiful campus of the missionary West China Union University, where they were sheltered in relatively adequate quarters and, under the protection of Canadian and American missionaries, preserved their academic integrity almost inviolate; their scholastic standards remained consistently the highest throughout the war. The most important universities of northern China, however, all trekked on to the far southwest, where they combined at Kunming for the duration of the war as the National Southwest University. The northern universities had been noted before the war for their brilliant intellectual life, their advanced and sparkling political alertness; arriving in Kunming, they established themselves in squalor. The students were camped four, six, and eight to a room, some of them domiciled in a rat-ridden, cobwebbed abandoned theater; they ate rice and vegetables and not enough of these. The government, always suspicious of the advanced political views of the northern universities, watched these refuge institutions like a hawk, tightening the net of surveillance closer about them with each passing year. In the beginning it did not matter—the universities were too happy at having escaped the Japanese to care. If the students lived hard, they knew that all China, too, was suffering. As the years wore on and teachers hungered, as budgets were made a mockery by inflation, the National Southwest University began to re-assert itself politically and by the close of the war had become the principal seat of political discontent in southern China.

The migrations of factories and universities were the most spectacular. How many more millions of peasants and city folk were set adrift by the Japanese invasion no one can guess—estimates run all the way from three to twenty-five million. The peasants fled from the Japanese; they fled from the great flood of the Yellow River, whose dikes had been opened to halt the Japanese armies; they fled out of fear of the unknown. The workers who accompanied the factories numbered perhaps no more than 10,000; they came because without them the machines would be useless. The restaurant keepers, singsong girls, adventurers, the little merchants who packed their cartons of cigarettes or folded their bolts of cloth to come on the march, probably numbered hundreds of thousands. The little people who accompanied the great organized movements traveled by foot, sampan, junk, railway, and ricksha. Thousands crusted the junks moving through the gorges; hundreds of thousands strung out over the mountain roads like files of ants winding endlessly westward. There is no estimate of the number who died of disease, exposure, or hunger on the way; their bones are still whitening on the routes of march.

The war in China had settled into new molds by the summer of 1939. The trek was over; the wheels of what little industry had been salvaged were turning again in new homes; the universities were drawing up their fall curricula. The shattered armies were digging in on the hill lines. The front now ran in squiggly lines along the foothills of the west and along the rims of all the great river valleys. In the north the Communists began to dig deeper and deeper into the sleepy consciousness of the villagers; cut off from Chungking, they fashioned new tools of government and grew wiser and stronger each year. In central and southern China the loose federation of the Central Government and the war lords began to run in familiar ruts; only in Chungking, where the bombs fell from spring to autumn, the old spirit persisted for a few more years.

China did not realize for some time longer that it had arrived at a dead end. Meanwhile the Japanese hailed each of their new campaigns as a climactic thrust at Chungking, and the Chinese armies fought desperately to ward them off. These campaigns were small but bitter, part of a new pattern of war that the Japanese high command had settled on. The new pattern was to keep the fronts in a constant state of imbalance; new divisions and cadres were blooded in combat, then removed to reserve areas for use in future campaigns. The Japanese erected new industries along the coast in their rear and tied what remained of the Chinese economy into Japan's conveyor system.

The trouble with almost all the writing that war correspondents did in China was that it was built on press conferences and communiqués. We used phrases the world understood to describe a war that was incomprehensible to the West. Chinese communiqués, written by obscure men who had never smelled gunpowder or heard a shot fired in anger, spoke of thousands of men engaged, of bloody operations, of desperate attacks and counterattacks. The Chinese put out such communiqués for years, in the beginning because they themselves believed that the Japanese were still intent on smashing through the mountains to the heartland beyond. Long after they had ceased to believe their own statements, Chinese wordsmiths were still glossing the grimy, squalid contests at the front with the polished rhetoric of earlier days. There were no real fronts, no barrages, no breakthroughs, anywhere on the China front, but men wrote of them—of supply trains, logistics, encirclements. The Chinese newspapers themselves did not believe the reported claims of thousands on thousands of Japanese being trapped or encircled, but they printed them just the same. The foreign press became cynical. Sometimes the exaggerations were too difficult to take straight. Once American Army intelligence found there were only 30,000 Japanese engaged in an action; the Chinese military spokesman reported 80,000 in action, but the communiqués recorded enemy casualties totaling 120,000.

The campaigns the Japanese fought between 1938 and 1944 were foraging expeditions rather than battles. They had no greater strategic objective than to keep the countryside in terror, to sack the fields and towns, to keep the Chinese troops at the front off balance, and to train their own green recruits under fire. Most of them were known as rice-bowl campaigns, because they occurred most frequently in central China, the rice bowl of the land. The Japanese would concentrate several divisions, plunge deep into the front, ravage the countryside, and then turn back. The Chinese would counter by envelopment; their units would fall back before the thrusts, then close in on the flanks and rear to pinch off the garrison supply posts that the Japanese set up to feed their advance. The

Chinese could never do more than pinch off the Japanese salients and force them back into their dug-in bases; to do more than that would have required a weight of metal and equipment that Wong Wen-hao's transplanted industry could not hope to provide. The result was the permanent exhausting stalemate known as the China war.

This China war was fought along a flexible belt of no man's land, 50 to 100 miles deep, all up and down the middle of China. In this belt of devastation the Chinese had destroyed every road, bridge, railway, or ferry that might aid the Japanese in one of their periodic thrusts; the only Chinese defense was to reduce the country to immobility. Japanese and Chinese troops chased each other across the belt for six years; the peasants died of starvation, the troops bled, the villages were burned to the ground, towns changed hands as many as six or seven times, and yet for six years the front remained stable with few significant changes.

One of the typical campaigns of this period was proceeding in southeastern Shansi in the summer of 1939. Shansi is an important province—it is laden with coal and has the most considerable iron ores in China south of the Great Wall. It nestles into the elbow of the Yellow River, and its rugged mountains dominate the plains of northern China. By early 1939 the main Chinese positions in the province were cut into the slopes of the Chungtiao Mountains, which lie on the southern boundary, just north of the Yellow River. The guerrilla areas of the Communist Eighth Route Army were behind the Japanese strong points and around them; in front were Central Government troops.

I [White] went up to see this campaign in the fall of 1939—the first time I had visited the Chinese army at the front. In the next six years I saw the same sights over and over again, each year more drab, each year less inspiring.

I started out with a column of Chinese troop reinforcements, marching north to the line from the railhead on the Lunghai line. The troops were strung out over the hills in long files, trudging along without discipline or fixed pace. The padding of their straw-sandaled feet made the dust lift knee-high about them, and for miles away eyes in the hills saw an army marching by serpentines of dust in the sky. The commander of each unit rode at its head on his bony horse. Behind him were the foot soldiers, and behind them came the baggage train—coolie soldiers carrying ammunition boxes slung from staves on their shoulders; men burdened with sacks of rice; the company kitchen, consisting of a single soot-blackened cauldron carried by two men, bringing up the rear. This column had several serviceable pack guns slung on mules. At that time the whole Chinese army had about 1400 pieces of artillery all told for a front of 2000 miles. A single pack howitzer loaded on muleback looked heavier, more powerful, more important, than an entire battery of Long Toms. Later in the war animal-drawn baggage trains became a rarity, but this was 1939, and the column I accompanied had one—it crawled along even more slowly than the slogging foot soldiers. It was loaded high with sacks of rice and with military gear. On the sacks of rice one or two soldiers would be stretched dozing in the sun; the driver cracked his whip smartly over the animals, and the wheels screamed for lack of greasing, but no matter how the cart pitched in the rutted road, the soldiers stayed sleeping on their sacks. There was no hurry, for the war had lasted a long time already and would last years more. On wet days the march was a column of agony, the soldiers soaked through and through, their feet encased in balls of clay and mud.

Traffic to the front was two-way. There was the insistent beat of the marching men plodding forward, and in the opposite direction came the derelicts of the battlefield. The sick and the wounded usually made their way back to the rear on foot, on their own. A serious head wound or a bad abdominal wound meant death at the front, for the medical service could never move these men to operating stations in time for help. Those who could walk but who obviously were no longer of military usefulness were given passes that permitted them to make their way back by themselves. These were pitiful men, limping along over the mountain passes, dragging themselves up by clutching rocks or trees, leaning on staves. You met them at the saddle of each pass as they sat resting from the long climb and looking out over the next valley and next hill with glazed eyes. More rarely you saw sick or wounded carried by stretcher to the rear. They smelled horribly of wounds and filth, and flies formed a cloud about them or even made a crust over their pus-filled eyes or dirty wounds.

We crossed the Yellow River in dirty flatboats and then moved up over thinner passes to the front. We followed hard on the heels of the Japanese army retreating through the Hsin River valley. It was fall, the season of the millet harvest, and the kaoliang too was ripe. Chinese valleys are beautiful to look at from the outside, before you know the burden of sorrow and superstition within each village wall. When the road was in the clear on the ridge, you could see clouds of chaff puffing into the air from threshing floors where the peasants were flailing the grain from the husks. The persimmons were ripe and red, glowing from the thin branches of trees from which the leaves had long been blown. The earth was being plowed for winter wheat, and it smelled good; in some of the fields the thin blades of the new crop colored the soil with green, while in the next patch the heavy pink-and-brown kaoliang ears hung down from tall stalks to brush our heads as we rode past.

The Japanese had just left, but they had blazed a black, scarred trail of devastation across the countryside. You might ride for a day through a series of burned villages that were simply huddles of ruins. In some places the roads were so torn that not even Chinese mountain ponies could carry you down the ditches cut across them. You had to pick your way down on foot and lead your horse after you or ride for hours on the crest of a barren ridge looking out into the hills beyond. Then there would be a single hut standing by itself in the vastness of the hills; with roof fallen in and timbers burned black, it would stand as a symbol of the desolation that ran from end to end of no man's land.

The stories the villagers told were such tales as I heard repeated later after every Japanese sortie. The peasants had fled before the Japanese advance. When they did not flee voluntarily, they were forced to leave by government edict, and they took with them everything from seed grain to furniture. They bundled their pigs and cattle off into the hills, hid their clothes and valuables in the ground, and retired to the mountains to build mat sheds and wait for the armies to force a decision. The Japanese entered a barren wasteland. They had been held up by floods, and when they reached their key objectives they had two weeks' growth of beard; caked with mud, they were exhausted and furious.

In some of the districts through which I passed, every woman caught by the Japanese had been raped without exception. The tales of rape were so sickeningly alike that they were monotonous unless they were relieved by some particular device of fiendishness. Japanese soldiers had been seen copulating with sows in some districts. In places where the villagers had not had time to hide themselves effectively, the Japanese rode cavalry through the high grain to trample the women into showing themselves. The Japanese officers brought their own concubines with them from the large garrison cities—women of Chinese, Russian, Korean, or Japanese nationality—but the men had to be serviced by the countryside. When the Japanese transport system broke down in the mud, peasants were stripped naked, lashed to carts, and driven forward by the imperial army as beasts of burden. Japanese horses and mules were beaten to death in the muck; on any road and all the hills you could see the carcasses of their animals rotting and the bones of their horses whitening in the sun. The Chinese peasants who were impressed to take their places were driven with the same pitiless fury' till they too collapsed or were driven mad.

It took two weeks of riding and walking to get to the front. From a regimental command post I was led up the bank of a hill to the crest covered with stalks of tall wheat. With a soldier, I ran silently, crouching behind the wheat, and then dropped in convenient position. The man parted the wheat carefully and pointed down into the valley. There were whitewashed houses in the distance and the vague outline of a walled town. "Those are the Japanese," he whispered, pointing vaguely. I stared harder. Then I noticed something moving in the grain fields not far from us. "What's that?" I asked. The soldier did not even turn to follow my finger. "Those are the peasants," he said, "they have to harvest the grain, you know—it is the harvest season." Even the Japanese could understand that; they were peasants themselves. Except in the savagery of their raids they too could be neutral to the people who worked in the fields.

I traveled the front in Shansi for 30 or 40 miles that week; in later years I traveled it for many more miles in many provinces. It was always anticlimax. I saw nothing anywhere but detached clusters of men in foxholes who were guarding rusting machine guns or cleaning old rifles. Chinese outposts were clusters of twenty or thirty men linked to their battalion headquarters by runner, from battalion headquarters to division command by telephone. The Japanese were usually disposed in villages with concentrations of two or three hundred men supported by light field artillery. You could look down on the Japanese from the hills for over a thousand miles; at any point there would be five times as many Chinese soldiers as Japanese. Yet always the Japanese had heavy machine guns and field artillery; before any armed Chinese could move across the open mile or two to get at the Japanese, he would be cut down by enemy fire, which no support in his army's possession could neutralize.

It was all quiet on the China front in 1939. It was to be all quiet in the same way, for the same reasons, for five more long years.

2   Speech by the Reich Minister

Albert Speer

On December 1, 1944, Reich Minister Speer, the Third Reich's youthful wizard of production, spoke to an audience of munitions makers and top-level bureaucrats at the Luftwaffe *Research Center. Speer's remarks on this occasion attest to the complex, interrelated facets of what was known in every industrial nation as "the battle of production." Germany was very late in applying the concept of total war to economic life. As Speer's remarks suggest, the wastefulness of the first years of the war had been shocking, but under his direction remarkable strides were made in tapping previously unexploited resources. The outcome might have been vastly different had Germany put into effect a program of total mobilization at the beginning of the war.*

Colleagues! For the next few months our anxieties are governed by the transport situation which has deteriorated to an extraordinary extent in the West and South West of the Reich during recent months. Our production is to a great extent dependent on how far it will be possible to put transport back into some sort of order. Although transport is the responsibility of the Ministry of Transport and not ours, I want to point out and to make it clear on this occasion that it is the duty of all of us to help as far as possible to overcome at least part of the difficulties caused by daily air raids. Every few days I meet Secretary of State (*Staatssekretaer*) Ganzenmueller to discuss the necessary measures and I ask you too to make the closest possible contact in your district with the competent local authorities, since certainly in many cases more help could be given than was expected.

My last journey to the Ruhr, made together with Secretary of State Ganzenmueller, has shown that in various districts, owing to the lack of 300, 400 or 500 workers, the damage to the transport system at various very important junctions could not be repaired in the shortest possible time. When you look further to the Ruhr, where millions of people are working, and when again you look towards the rest of the Reich, cut off from the Ruhr, where also an enormous number of people are working, you will say it would really be a shame if this problem could not be solved and if the few hundred people needed to put a traffic centre in order in 3 or 4 days could not be found. You must not think that everything is alright, just because the officials concerned tell you the Reichsbahn has obtained everything it needs. If you look into the matter on the

From **The Strategic Air Offensive Against Germany, 1939–1945** by Charles Webster and Noble Frankland, IV (London: Her Majesty's Stationery Office, 1961), pp. 357–70. Reprinted by permission of the Controller of Her Britannic Majesty's Stationery Office.

spot and ask the man on the job what is still missing, you will get quite another picture of the possibilities for help. We need every available hand in the Ruhr.

Sitting at your desks you cannot judge what difficulties are to be overcome and what problems are to be solved. You can only judge what can be remedied, sometimes by relatively easy measures, when you see the work on the spot and become acquainted with the difficulties to be overcome. Therefore I ask you to co-operate closely with the men responsible for transport. They will gladly accept our initiative too. There will be no red tape either from Secretary of State Ganzenmueller or from myself. In many cases a traffic junction could be restored perhaps one or two days earlier. For this purpose it is necessary to bring an abundance of labour into action. It may happen in the Ruhr that perhaps at such a site no work at all needs to be done for several hours and the workers idle about until the next job can be started.

For the next few months the transport situation will become decisive for the armament output. The inspection of the Ruhr has shown the possibility of repairing transport damage much more quickly than was ever expected, when once the repair squads have been trained. It was the same in armament production, where after the heavy air raids on our factories we were at first very much afraid of the effects and after the first raids on Hamburg never thought it possible to maintain armament production at all, if these raids were to continue. Nobody who has witnessed the collapse of the works in Hamburg would then have believed that a multitude of these attacks could be directed, and very well directed, against our arms production and that we nevertheless would be able to maintain production. Everybody would have said that it was impossible.

Fortunately, in armaments production we had enough time at our disposal and the enemy did not increase his attacks step by step so that we were able to try to keep in step with our counter-measures to some extent. But it is another thing with the transport. The main difficulty is that the heavy raids on the transport system have started from 'one day to the next' so that the position differs from the armament industry, where naturally we have already tried everything in air raid damage repair work. Therefore it is necessary for everybody to help, and to exploit all possible means, putting our experiences at the disposal of the works so that we can speed up matters.

Owing to the crisis in transport, which, in itself, could easily be overcome (I must underline that) if only the air raids would stop for a short time, owing to this crisis quite a lot of circumstances have combined to cause us extraordinary difficulties in armament and war production. In the first place, the enemy is trying to cut off the Ruhr from the rest of the Reich. He has two reasons for this. Firstly to dislocate supplies to our front in the West, and secondly, as he openly admits, to deal a blow at the same time to our armament potential. You must realize that those people of the enemy who work out the plans for the economic bombing attacks know German industry very well and that there is here a clever and far-reaching planning in contrast to our earlier air raids on England. We have been lucky in that the enemy did not make methodical use of this detailed planning until the last half or three-quarters of this year and that before that he gave us enough time. This in fact has been a blunder from his point of view. At the moment, however, he is going all out to attack again and again our bottlenecks which are vitally important to us. He has destroyed both the Weser-Ems Canal and the Mittelland canal just when they had been repaired, and thereby deprives us of the possibility of relieving the transport by rail from the Ruhr by transfer to inland water transport. He declares openly that by these methods Salzgitter, the Peiner rolling mill and the other steel plants in Central Germany will come to a standstill and he is trying to seal the Ruhr from the remaining Reich by systematically destroying Hamm, Osnabrueck, Bielefeld, Muenster etc. When we previously tried to rebuild the bombed hydrogenation plants, raided again and again 4 or 5 or 6 times, I was blamed by many people (not only of the Party but also by others) for doing something that was senseless because when the repairs were finished a new attack would be made. They told me: why on earth have you done it, you cannot help it, the odds are so heavy against us that there is no sense in rebuilding. At that time we fought hard against that frame of mind. Herr Geilenberg has taken up the fight against all this opposition, some of which came from the works managements themselves. We have been able to produce a relatively respectable quantity of aviation fuel every month and about a week ago we again reached half of the fuel production we achieved before the bombing. You will see from this example the absolute necessity of trying again and again and of building up again and again even if the enemy returns the next day and smashes things up again. You must not think that the enemy, during half or three-quarters of a year, will obstinately attack the same target again and again. It is quite possible that he will change his targets so that by a sudden cessation of the raids a place which was hitherto always believed to be the object of the attack will be given a rest, and that we will then again be able to benefit by our constant reconstruction work.

The transport situation in the Ruhr is the cause of our inability to send to the rest of the Reich more than a fraction of the quantity of coal which we have previously dispatched. Previously about 20,000 waggons daily were provided for coal transport in the Ruhr. That was the minimum demand we could make and in fact far less than we have demanded of the Reichsbahn based on the daily coal output figures. The figure of 20,000 waggons daily has decreased on account of the raids to 6,000. That means we are already one third below the figure previously considered absolutely essential for the needs of our armament and war production. Unfortunately many consumers must be supplied in priority by these few waggons, all of them coming before armament production. Under no circumstances for instance, can we neglect the supply to the Reichsbahn. It has already occasionally happened that the Regional Executive of the Reichsbahn in Berlin and two other Regional Executives had a supply of coal sufficient for two days only and had to rely on stocks. If such cases occur again they are more than likely to result in the whole industry in the district concerned coming to a standstill, and cause a transport catastrophe which it will be impossible to stop. This would lead to enormous difficulties owing to the limited means available today and possibly to further catastrophes. Everybody who knows how extremely difficult it is to make good a break-down in the electric power supply and to restore the electricity supply of the grid system, will understand that coal for the use of the Reichsbahn must have first priority and that this first claim decreases the small number of waggons available in the Ruhr. The remaining quantities for our armament and war production, for the power plants etc., show a much more unfavourable balance than previously. The ratio was formerly 2 to 3 but today it is 1 to 6 or 7. We obtain from the Ruhr only one-sixth of what we previously obtained and the possibilities of obtaining compensation from Upper Silesia have long since been exhausted, as a long time ago already we tried to extend the limit for the dispatch of coal from Upper Silesia as far westward as possible because the Ruhr has always given us cause for worry in regard to the coal supply of the Reich.

It is, however, a fact that a pause in raids on the Ruhr of 3 days only has raised the figure of waggons provided from 6,000 back to 12,000. You can see from this the quick reaction, and I am convinced that the possibilities of restoring destroyed targets are not yet by a long way exhausted; if there are any pauses we will always quickly come to an increase enabling us to help here and there.

With regard to this lack of coal it is quite evident that we have in any case to restrict ourselves to a minimum in the armament industry if we are still to obtain useful results in this sphere. It is no use indulging in any illusions if the result is that we, by these illusions, would be able to produce on the largest basis in all sectors only fractional productions amounting to 20% or 30% or 40%. We must therefore have a clear idea of the result. In this connection it is particularly important to point out that both the authorities responsible for the distribution of coal and the Party authorities will save any quantity of coal which can possibly be saved, even if the population is faced with privations, and that for such privations the Party must accept responsibility. When for instance the gas situation in Berlin begins to reach a critical stage, it will be necessary first of all to switch off the gas supply for the population, at least to a considerable extent. It must not happen that in such a case armament production is cut off first for reasons of political convenience and that only afterwards is the much more difficult problem of switching off the supply for the population tackled. The local load distribution officers (*Bezirkslastverteiler*) will on my orders adopt a much more stringent policy. At the first instance I cannot help the fact that these people will be heavily blamed, but they must above all show enough backbone and must simply realize as distribution officers that these principles must be put into practice. If the Party authorities are unwilling to act on these principles then at least a conflict would arise, giving me the opportunity to decide the matter or to let the Fuehrer decide. If, however, in the beginning, not this stringent policy but an easier line is followed by the intermediate authorities (*Mittelinstanz*), we in the Head Office would not be able to help the armament industry at all, because we would not obtain any knowledge of these matters. I, therefore, ask the distribution officers for gas and electricity to act accordingly and to try to maintain war production as long as possible even if the population has to endure extreme shortages.

You have only to go to the towns of the Ruhr to see what calamities the population is able to endure. All would be futile if we could not manage to maintain our war production. Otherwise the enemy front would be pushed mile after mile into our territory and the privations which at present people refuse to put up with, would in a few months be forced upon the population in a much more terrible manner.

The Ruhr needs special help which is only starting now. We have to give up something from the rest of the Reich because we must not give up the Ruhr. The Ruhr is the vital base for at least half of the war production, enabling us to maintain our production for a long time ahead. It is, therefore, necessary, apart from the present drive for 30,000 auxiliary workers, to find another 450,000 skilled workers, which will be an additional help for the Ruhr. I have now ordered that the Ruhr is to obtain an additional monthly supply of 100,000 shoes out of the shoe production, which quantities naturally will be lost for the population of the other districts of the Reich. It is, however, necessary that these people who in the Ruhr not only have to suffer non-stop air raids but have been for some time already without gas and electricity and, therefore, without light, and who are compelled to live in the most primitive conditions, that these people are aware that the rest of the Reich is fully aware of its moral duty to help them generously. That will doubtless necessitate cuts in many sectors of the Reich which, however, must be put up with.

We have in preparation a so-called emergency or supplementary programme for the whole armament industry. This programme is based on the following facts:

Our programmes hitherto drawn up and ordered for all important branches of armament and war production have not been achieved in the last few months, as you know. The supply of basic materials for these programmes has however continued for many production processes in the required quantities. If you go to the factory yards you will see huge stocks of components (*Vorlieferungen*), sometimes sufficient for 3 to 6 months of the current production. For the transitional stage the transformation of these components into finished equipment must be managed, i.e. the necessary complements must be provided and we estimate that with about 20% of the total long-term quotas (*Kontingentsmengen*) a 100% completion can be obtained for some months. This may, of course, cause a corresponding gap in armament production, when the supplementary programme has been carried out. That, however, does not interest us at all. We want to finish what we can finish in the next few months. Think for instance of the U-boats: thanks to the efficiency of Herr Merker of the Stahlbau we have been able to finish enough *Stahlschuesse* (steel sections) to last us until May next year. The problem is, therefore, to carry out the necessary completion of these sections, i.e. to provide the interior installations, and this problem must be pressed forward accordingly. How that is to be carried out in detail is the subject of detailed discussions and plans. The committees (*Ausschuesse*) and rings (*Ringe*) which have been tackling this problem energetically for about a fortnight have to solve these problems. I want, however, to ask you, of the intermediate grades (*Mittelinstanz*), also to support all these efforts to the utmost in such a way that you utilize the huge stocks, stored by the various firms, to straighten matters out. We must make it possible to fight on under the present conditions for a long time by thawing these stocks.

Nevertheless we need not worry too much about future production; the last few months have shown what an immense toughness we possess in the arms industry and to what an astonishing extent we have kept production going, in spite of all the difficulties daily showered upon us. All planning estimates made by us (in some cases we are no longer making them to such an extent, as the results are mostly much more favourable than we in the Head Office could expect on the basis of our calculations), all these estimates have been greatly exceeded and we will, therefore, take care not to restrict anyone in his programme.

The emergency and supplementary programme is not intended to restrict the initiative of the works managers in any way, but guarantees that we obtain the parts required under all circumstances. As the supply of these parts comes from the Ruhr, it is mainly a question of transport. Since in the first place coal must be dispatched from the Ruhr, the products of the iron producing industry must remain in the background at first. Our most important task is to transport the last ton of coal we can get. We have arranged with the Reichsbahn to introduce a special voucher system (*Markensystem*) for products needed for finishing work. This voucher system will pass through the main committees and rings to the firms on a long-term basis and it will be possible to cover with these vouchers the way-bills for products from the Ruhr or from the other districts of Western Germany or South-West Germany which must at all costs reach the firms for the finishing processes. At the same time these vouchers should give us a hint as to where the most important bottlenecks are in the filling up of existing stocks. Big mistakes are quite possible, if we establish this programme on a purely theoretical basis. Therefore we, in the Head Office, will watch, through the Main Committees and Rings, which items we obtain by these transport quotas from the firms and we will be able by a compilation of these items to discover that for instance in the Ruhr this or that department of the *Mannesmann Roehren Werke* (Tube Works) is receiving extraordinarily high demands and that therefore in the Ruhr such and such sizes of Mannesmann tubes must be produced as long as possible; that, however, all the other departments apparently are unimportant for the supply and, therefore, have to take only second or third place. We can see in this way that for instance the firm Bosch in Stuttgart repeatedly obtains orders for a third or quarter of its production capacity for any particular item so that it may possibly be necessary, if there is no other way, to bring coal from Upper Silesia in a few waggons across Germany to Stuttgart, to maintain the production of the necessary supplies there under any circumstances. Thus we hope by this regulation of transport, not only to obtain a survey, entirely lacking as yet, of the traffic with the Ruhr and to prevent bottlenecks, but we think on top of this that this transport quota system will enable us to tackle the present real bottlenecks. I believe this the most important part of the problem. It is, however, important to deal most economically with these quotas so that only those products will be covered by quotas which are really essential complements.

On top of this we intend (this is also in agreement with the other Regional Executives) to delegate to each Regional Executive of the Reichsbahn a Transport Commissioner (*Verkehrsbevollmaechtigter*) from industry. These commissioners will on principle be appointed and assigned to their posts by me as Minister of Armament and War Production. They have to discuss in close contact with the heads of the Reichsbahn Regional Executives (*Reichsbahndirektionspraesident*) and their colleagues what is to have priority in dispatch. The selection of these personalities for which the Presidents of the Armaments Commission (*Ruestungskommissionen*) are still to make recommendations must be well considered, since, as I may point out, for the next six months certainly, the distribution of the transport capacities still available is more important than everything at the moment, more even than the distribution of coal and electric power. The better the selection is, the better will be the result for you. You must not choose anybody but take a person who possesses the necessary knowledge of industry and of whom you are convinced that he is able, owing to his special knowledge, to adapt himself to his work in the Reichsbahn and to establish his authority.

As for the Head Office (*Zentrale*), in the Central Waggon Office (*Zentralwagenamt*) a man will also be selected from industry to co-ordinate these representatives and to discuss the collective results daily with the Central Waggon Office.

An especially difficult problem is what has to be done with the districts situated directly behind the front line. I am thinking of the Saar, the district left of the Rhine, of Cologne and the industrial districts of Baden too. On my last journey to the Ruhr and the Rhine-Westphalian industrial district I found that left of the Rhine, especially in the Cologne-Aachen area, the idea already prevailed of dismantling the industrial plants ruthlessly and dispersing them to the area right of the Rhine. Two reasons argue against such a dispersal:

(1) Everybody who loses confidence in himself in this war sufficiently to disperse his industry will never get on in the world after the war. If for instance the city of Cologne were to give up all its industrial plants to-day, it would probably cease to be of any importance in the future, for in the eyes of the population its steadfastness in the war will also be judged.

(2) (and that is much more important) that these front line towns which have doubtless to suffer heavily, that these cities have to fulfill an extraordinarily important task. They have constantly to take care that the daily rhythm of supply for the troops at the front line is maintained. That is an immense problem and has to be tackled in the right way. It is indeed possible to help the troops to such an enormous extent and perhaps by such measures to increase the overall effect of our production at the front by 30% or 40%.

You know that the monthly figures for repair of motor vehicles, for instance of tanks etc., constitute about 30% to 40% of our total monthly output. If industry were to abandon these towns and no longer exist, the armed forces themselves with their repair squads would have to keep things in order. We all know, however, that industry is able to tackle this work with quite different means than those at the disposal of the armed forces. Therefore it is at all costs necessary to have in the districts near the front line some production of essential spares so that the necessary supply will be guaranteed. Therefore we have to try to organize this type of production on the largest possible scale and with the skilled workers available. The troops are extremely grateful for such action and will for their part see to it again and again and with all their strength, not only out of thankfulness but also in their own vital interest, that a city like Cologne, a city like München-Gladbach etc. will be kept going somehow.

An ideal solution for this type of co-operation with the troops has been found in the Saar. There, Herr Kelchner and Herr Roechling have organized a real customers' service with the troops. Roechling, who is already an old man, goes every day to the front from division to division and writes down what, as he says, his customers need. Then he delivers the goods. You would not believe to what extent the troops can be encouraged by such measures, against, as I must, however, point out, the fierce resistance of all bureaucrats in all branches of the armed forces who do not like this direct contact and believe that such proceedings are to their disadvantage. That is not so. For the pressure on these people near the front is immense and efficiency would decrease considerably, if, as hitherto, any order from the *Heereswaffenamt* (Army Weapons Office) were dropped onto the desk of the works manager and circulated in a routine manner by him after indifferent perusal. If the population knows that from this or that tank division, stationed 10 or 20 Km. distant, anybody may come with an order, industry would be keyed up and especially the masses will, out of anxiety for their homeland, achieve results which, otherwise, if we have the system of anonymous orders, could not be obtained at all, as they exceed their physical power. Therefore we must not care what these army bureaucrats say, but must carry out these methods. The assaults from outside directed against you will be stopped in Berlin and we will protect you. We must produce as much as possible in the districts near the front line directly for the troops, in order also to overcome the transport difficulties. We will, therefore, demand more and more from many presidents of Armaments Commissions (*Ruestungskommissionen*), who have moved up nearer to the front line, that their districts must manufacture completely as many things as possible; i.e. if we continue to produce in the Ruhr cases for all different calibres, send them from the Ruhr to the East, add the fuses from the Black Forest and then dispatch powder and explosive charge from another district and transport the finished product back again to bring the ammunition through the Ruhr to the front line, that would today be pure nonsense. We must see to it that, for example, what can be completely manufactured in the Ruhr must be made there. In other words, in these areas near the front we must see to it that we do not as hitherto move the complete gun to a small optical instrument, rather do we move the small box with the optical instrument to the Ruhr and try to complete the gun there. We will not worry if the *Muna* (ammunition establishment) is now in danger or if a house close by could perhaps be destroyed if the Muna blows up. Such obstructions have to be removed with the help of the front line troops. It is understood that in this case you must have close contact with the front line troops and also with the commanders of the army troops, with whose help any difficulties which may then arise can be removed. Naturally you have to consider carefully what you may be able to complete in your districts and to dispatch directly to the troops to ease the transport difficulties. The same applies to Italy; there the Brenner will doubtless become such an obstacle for us one day that we will not be able to bring back to the Reich what we have in Italy and that we had better organize things beforehand so as to produce there everything that can be completed there. The same applies to the Saar, to Upper Silesia, Upper Danube etc.

It is understood that these problems of completion of equipment for the troops must be co-ordinated with the main committees and in the last instance with Herr Saur. Herr Saur will within the next few days delegate someone exclusively for this task, and this man will see to it that these matters, so far seldom put into practice, will actually be put to the practical test.

You have obtained today a small insight into the various new developments of recent date. You have seen, however, that we have no miracle weapon at our disposal and probably never will have. We of the technical branch have always made it clear to everybody who wanted to know, that in the technical sphere miracles such as the layman expects are hardly possible. We are doubtless able to maintain our advantage, our technical advantage, in many directions, and, where this advantage has been lost, to gain the lead again in a great bound. One has, however, to point out to the layman that this would be possible only if the fighting spirit is there. My inspections of the front have shown again and again that the divisional commanders and regimental commanders are worried because the troops cling more and more to the belief in miracles. I think this is disastrous and quite unnecessary and that the slogan given by Churchill after Dunkirk, when he promised the population blood, sweat and tears, that this is a slogan suitable for every Teutonic people. I am therefore thankful that the propaganda line has recently been changed and now points out that such a miracle weapon will not come. The engineers, in particular, however, must underline again and again: technical progress is possible and we can doubtless achieve this progress if we can work undisturbed, but there are no miracles. What you have seen today is only a small sector and we have shown you things which are really already or about to be in serial production. The tanks you have seen, the Jagdtiger and Jagdpanther, are doubtless tanks which will be treated by the enemy with some respect. The fact is that first the Russians and now the English have themselves named the so-called Tiger II which they know from its previous use, the 'Royal Tiger' (*Koenigstiger*) and we have adopted this title, since it is really a 'royal' tank. A short time ago it was written in the 'Times' that a duel had taken place between their heaviest PAK, the 9.2 cm., very respectable indeed, the Sherman-tank and our Koenigstiger and that by a hair's breadth a catastrophe for the Americans had been avoided and that our tank's superiority has been clearly shown. On this occasion they described ours as the best tank in the world. I personally have, in the battle of Aachen, visited a tank repair shop near Julich of tank detachment 506 (a detachment equipped with Tiger II only) and have seen that the Tiger II could easily deflect a shell of the 9.2 cm. PAK fired at short range. What you see today, Jagdtiger and Jagdpanther, are types which surpass even the Tiger II as regards armour. The troops and we ourselves are not quite sure what would be the best: a light mobile tank or a super-heavy tank. Both of them have advantages and great disadvantages, but we think that we have found in our long-term tank programme, on the one hand with the fast, very mobile 38 to., which is almost exclusively the work of our Colonel Schaede, and, as a light tank, will be produced in maximum numbers of, we hope, some thousands per month, and on the other hand with the heavy tank types of the Panther, Tiger II, Panther Jaeger, Jagdpanther and Jagdtiger, that we have found with these types the right mixture for our tank forces and for our infantry divisions.

I know many of you are groaning under the many changes we have to make, gentlemen! We too would prefer to come out with huge figures and we know very well that, if we were now to stick stubbornly to the Panzer IV or if we had stuck to the Panzer III or originally to the Panzer II, that we would have production figures at least 50% or 60% higher than the present figures, and we know that the continuous changes which we are obliged to impose on all branches of industry reduce our production figures enormously. Since we, however, have not the slightest chance of reaching the production figures of the enemy, we have in any case to utilize any possibility of technical progress even if the production figures were to decrease somewhat. One Tiger II has certainly the same effect as 25 to 30 Shermans (as the troops—for instance General Manteuffel at Aachen a short time ago—have confirmed). He thinks he can join battle with 10 Tiger II against 200 Shermans because the penetration of the Sherman gun is not sufficient and that he can open the engagement with the Sherman at a much longer range, the penetration of his gun being that sufficient to knock out the Sherman. You will see from this example that it would be of no use to produce, let us say, the same number or double the number of Panzer IV as of the Tiger II, for the former stands in the ratio of 1 to 1 only to the Sherman. The Panzer IV has its advantages and disadvantages as compared with the Sherman, we have therefore to enter the field with an equal number to have corresponding successes. You see by this example that the Tiger II with three times the weight of the Panzer IV has about 20 times the fighting value. This means that, if we replace the Tiger II by the Panzer IV, we put into action 7 times the fighting value. For this reason we must always make allowance for these technical changes in design.

You, as the pioneers of our technical ideas, must, however, not forget outside that you are not engineers only, but must have a techno-political point of view (*Techno-Politische Auffassung*), i.e. you must apply your technical ability to the political sphere. You must prepare the soil for these technical doctrines, for these facts resulting from practical experience, that technical progress must always be for us the only guide in dealing with the enemy and that many difficulties must be put up with.

The figures reached in November are again a wonderful result for us, and one can in no way compare them with the results which we could justifiably have expected as the result of our efforts at the Central Office. We ourselves are surprised at the November results, just as we were in the previous months. And even the Fuehrer, when these figures were phoned through to him, emphasized his astonishment in view of the situation which we made clear to him in an objective manner, perhaps rather more objectively than was really necessary. I will to-day for the first time announce the figures really reached by us. I will do it for the reason that percentages figures are no longer any great help to you. After speaking too often of percentages it is necessary to divulge the real figures to you and these will confirm to you, too, our opinion that the figures are really grand. I ask for your discretion. Nobody will, as I must point out, believe our figures and now you are going to hear them you will say: where on earth does all this material go to? I have to reply: We had one withdrawal after another and each withdrawal has cost us nearly the whole equipment of the army group concerned. When I, after the withdrawal in those critical days, when our 'Marne-miracle' happened and the enemy did not advance further, when I in those days went to the front, I was informed by the troops of the Army's stocks of weapons and equipment. That was an alarming picture. One army had no more than 3 to 4 tanks, 80,000 machine guns, 30, 40 or 50 LFH (light field howitzers). That was all that was available. 4 weeks later, when I visited the same army again, the equipment of these armies had again reached 30% to 40% of their normal strength. You must not, however, believe that this completion came from stores, prepared in anticipation of these events, in fact it was the current production which came to the front. If your current production had not been so high, it would not have been possible, since the catastrophe which happened to the army groups Centre and North in South Russia last winter and to the army groups in France, for them to build new resistance lines again and again.

I have once had, worked out weapon by weapon, how many divisions could be re-established by the production of one year, in order to compare our total production of armaments with the number of men in the army, which is of course limited by the total population figure. This calculation has shown that we are able to re-equip by our armaments production 3.6 million soldiers, i.e. in practice we are able to re-equip the total regular field army in one year. Unfortunately we have actually had to do this in the past few years. Since, however, there is no longer any possibility of making further great withdrawals, it can be supposed that future losses will not be on the same scale. The losses in such battles as that of Aachen are insignificant as compared with the previous losses. They are slight for us and can be made good with a fraction of about 10% only of the production, i.e. if we continue to produce as before it would be a very easy matter (that is not exaggerated) to equip fully all front line forces with about 80% to 90% of their required strength in 4 to 5 months, not including new formations. That is in itself a fact which illustrates the results we have achieved in the armaments industry. The argument, made again and again, that the figures given by Speer and his people must be wrong, can best be refuted by pointing out that in every case the acceptance of weapons by a branch of the armed forces is based on the examination of the weapon, i.e. the declaration of its suitability for combat use will not be given by us (though we too are an authority of the Reich) but by the branch of the forces itself. For these reasons inspection by the army as well as by the air force and the navy has remained independent and we have by this arrangement a partner who accepts the weapons and declares independently that the weapon is suitable for combat use. Only when the partner has taken over the weapons are they counted as delivered. The figures, therefore, are figures for weapons actually taken over by the armed forces. At the end of the month sometimes 40 or 50 Flak or tanks are available. They are, however, not included in the figures and not acknowledged, if for any reason there is no possibility of obtaining a train for transporting these guns somewhere for testing. It goes so far that at present we have 700 completely finished aircraft which could not make their inspection flight solely because of bad weather. They could not be included in our figures, but have so far only been counted as accepted by industry. The figures are, therefore, indeed real figures, not propaganda figures; we need no propaganda figures because our figures are the best propaganda for us. . . .

These figures give a survey of the American and of our own production. The Americans are attacking in the West at present with a superiority of 10:1. The ratio of artillery fire on the fronts which are relatively quiet and without special actions is about 1:5 according to the reports of the divisions, i.e. they fire 5 times the quantities we are able to fire. When the Americans attack with 500 tanks we can oppose them with 50 tanks only. When they appear somewhere with 1,000 fighters we have only 100, whilst we actually reckon with a ratio of at most 1:2, adding England and the Russian front and subtracting on the enemy side his commitments against Japan.

America and England, [un] like ourselves, had no battles to fight from 1941 onward and could use their production of 1941, 42 and 43 and half that of 1944 almost exclusively to bring the combined totals into undivided use. We too had in 1939, as you know, a ridiculously low production compared with the present figures and were nevertheless able to carry out two campaigns in the years 1939 and 1940, because we had the output of the years 1937/38 which the enemy lacked at that time. If the enemy was compelled in 1939/40 to throw into the front its month-by-month output of a fully stepped-up armament production, while we were able to bring to bear the full weight of 2 or 3 years' production, to-day the position is reversed. He faces us with the weight of 2 to 3 years' rearmament.

One thing is clear: in a technical war carried out with technical weapons, the wear and tear of these weapons is enormous. You know that an aircraft engine must be replaced after 100 to 150 flying hours. You know, as everybody knows who has to deal with tanks, that the life of a tank generally does not exceed, for various reasons, ½ to ¾ of a year.

So far as powder and explosives are concerned, the strain on the enemy also exceeds by far his monthly capacity as we wish to examine still more exactly. In May he dropped on the Reich alone more than 89,000 to. of bombs with an explosives production of roughly 45,000 to 50,000 to. He has, however, dropped bombs on other fronts too. He must transport all his supplies, he must continuously supplement his ammunition stocks which are on the same level as ours and, therefore, amount to at least 35,000 to., he must drop bombs on Japan and bring up his explosives, he must put mines at the disposal of the navy. We believe that the Americans are at present using 2 to 2½ times as much as they produce each month. We cannot anticipate how long their reserves will last and when they will reach the state in which we unfortunately, have already been for 2 years. It is, however, certain that one day the moment will come when the Americans can no longer live on their 3 years' reserves, when these reserves must be exhausted and when they will be compelled to base their tactical plans on their monthly production. You see by this that doubtless they too are worried about this problem. At present the enemy (Eisenhower, Churchill, Roosevelt) is making pessimistic statements, not so much because he is really pessimistic but in order to step up his armaments production. He must do this, because he faces the same difficulties as we did after the campaign in France, when our whole industry was worrying about the coming postwar production and when everybody believed in a speedy end of the war and the start of a boom. The enemy is in a similar condition to-day and the supply difficulties of the Americans will be considerable in a quarter or half a year. It is, therefore, necessary for us to force them to commit as much of their material as possible for as long as we can.

The quality of our troops would make this possible but only on the condition, and this is the main point, that we obtain a new air force which will enable us to fight the final battle. This condition will be fulfilled in the not too distant future, as you have seen, based on the figures as they stand. In aviation, he who is still engaged in development and builds fighters with a fraction of expenditure of material, men and fuel as compared with the bombers has an advantage once he has turned out more than a certain number. The most important problem, therefore, is to increase the production of fighters again and again and especially that of the planes you have seen to-day, the superfast planes with a speed of 850 to 900 Km. per hour.

Furthermore, it is our duty to increase the output of Flak because in danger zones like the Ruhr the Flak can give us some sort of protection at least for the most important centres and factories.

Besides the things you have seen, we have some others in preparation which we believe will go into action as early as next spring. We believe that by then we will be able to produce the self-steering anti-aircraft rocket (*Flakrakete, die sich selbst auf das Flugzeug Steuert*) still in development, and go over to mass production of A4, the present V2.

If you hear of this development anywhere and are in the position to help somehow, please do it as it is most important for us to obtain a weapon which can be used against the enemy through cloud cover in bad weather. The enemy is enabled by his radio technical equipment to fly even in bad weather. The development, therefore, of air rockets (*Flugraketen*) reaching a height of 11 to 12,000 m. is a most important problem which must have special priority.

I have given you a survey of the achievements of our armaments industry in November and you will admit that these achievements are extraordinary. The figures of the next few months will reach the same level, if the Ruhr remains, at least to some extent, intact. We have throttled the supply of things which are not directly connected with armament production, the so-called indirect needs of the war industry, though we know that this throttling cannot be carried out in the long run but only for 1½ years without a far-reaching effect for the whole war industry. With this throttling of the indirect requirements we are able, if we can maintain the Ruhr at its previous production, to increase the armament programme. In the next few months we cannot expect to have the full Ruhr production at our disposal, nevertheless we must meet this situation by carrying out our production on the previous level by means of our supplementary programme.

I ask you to be optimistic for the future too just as we are always optimistic in spite of all difficulties. None of us would have believed that we could reach this production level at all, considering the difficulties showered on us in October and November and even in September. Everybody would have thought it absolutely foolish, if we had made such demands under present conditions. Nevertheless they have been fulfilled because we always started with immense optimism. That must go on. Because without optimism, by cold calculation only, we would probably have reached to-day only half the figures we have in fact reached. Therefore, we must always in this difficult period be conscious, based on these experiences, that much more can be achieved with German toughness, than anybody could ever do through sober reflection alone.

3   Assaying the Record

The United States at War, prepared by the War Records Section of the Bureau of the Budget, is an analysis of the organization and administration of American mobilization during the Second World War. The following selection from the book presents a persuasive argument for the superiority of democratic over authoritarian systems in times of crisis. A comparison of the success enjoyed by the respective sides in organizing and administering their war efforts demonstrated to the Bureau researchers that Germany and Japan were decidedly less able to cope with the complex task of waging modern war. Unanswered by this study is the question of significance: could Allied success and Axis

From Bureau of the Budget, **The United States at War** (Washington, D.C.: U.S. Government Printing Office), pp. 503–19.

failure be explained by reasons other than the ideological differences between the contending nations?

The principal purpose of this account has been to report on the nation's experience in World War II from the point of view of the Government's discharge of its administrative and managerial responsibilities. The American nation faced its greatest challenge; those who were selected to manage and administer its affairs faced a most severe test. The fighting men we trained, the goods we produced, the battles we won, measure the magnitude of the problems that were faced and the degree of success attained.

This volume has dealt with only a small part of the whole field of our wartime experience and cannot speak conclusively even on that portion. Like any attempt to capture the facts on a period of highly complex, swiftly moving events, immediately after their occurrence, this volume must suffer from a lack of perspective. Nor is it possible here to probe deeply into the meaning and significance of the many aspects of our war years. Constructive evaluation of our management of the war, like evaluation of the effects of war in the physical science as of the atomic bomb, in industrial technology, international relationships and social and economic changes, must await the factual and analytical contributions of many observers with widely divergent points of view enjoying the advantages of the perspective that time alone can give. It is hoped that this volume will stimulate numerous analysts to explore both more deeply and more broadly the many aspects of our society at war.

Even if evaluation of the events described in the preceding chapters is premature, it is nevertheless desirable to highlight certain aspects of our war administration. A particularly interesting method of doing this is by comparing the United States experience with the methods employed and the successes attained by our two major enemies, Germany and Japan. While much work remains to be done before the full story of the war activities of Germany and Japan will be available, sufficient information has already become accessible to permit the development of some highly important contrasts. The following discussion is based largely on the results of the expert examination of the German and Japanese war efforts by the United States Strategic Bombing Survey.

The friends of authoritarian government (i.e., government without a broad base of public participation) have in the past made much of its supposed administrative efficiency in arriving at decisions and in executing them without the hurdles that a democratic system faces in operating through the unregimented processes of public discussion and consent. Such apologists have urged that the exposure of governmental problems to public analysis and decision is a source of delay and weakness and that dictatorship over governmental administration eliminates problems such as this country faced in the planning and coordination of its war effort. These considerations were sufficiently influential in the minds of the leaders of the Nazis and the Japanese expansionists to lead them to the conclusion that democracies could not successfully thwart their designs. It was a fundamental assumption in their plans that the democracies would be so immobilized as to be unable even to accept the challenge in meaningful fashion.

The speed with which the democracies did accept the challenge and the manner in which they overwhelmed those who sought gain through war suggests that there is need to reexamine the claims to administrative superiority of authoritarian governments. In making these comparisons, it must be noted that it is somewhat easier to analyze the factors that contributed to defeat than it is to ferret out the failures and weaknesses of the victor. Careful technical analysis may well indicate that both of our enemies programmed and executed in certain areas in a manner superior to ours. This may, for example, prove to be the case in certain phases of the German tank production program and in Japanese production of aircraft. Though we won the war, we cannot afford to close our eyes to the possible lessons we may learn from the experience of our enemy. This is a highly important task that technicians and scholars must perform if the full significance of the war experience is to be exploited.

In many ways our task was far greater—from the administrative point of view—than that of either of our enemies. With a long antimilitaristic tradition, we were suddenly faced in late 1941 with war against the two most militaristic nations on earth. Both enjoyed the advantage of long preliminary planning and preparations. We faced the task of preparing simultaneously for two wars—one largely a land-air operation with naval support; the other primarily a naval-air operation with land support. In both cases the battlefronts were several thousands of miles distant imposing severe logistical problems. A third task was also thrust upon us: that of producing the supplies needed by our Allies and building a fleet of ships to carry these products to our Allies. The support of our Allies was invaluable to us but their pressing needs meant that we could not take time for long preparations since delay might deprive us of their support. Time, moreover, permitted our enemies to gain further strength from the exploitation of their conquests. To carry out simultaneously such complicated operations and to devote to each the proper proportion of our resources while avoiding the deadening effects of conflicts between those interested in one or another of these programs was an administrative achievement not to be disparaged.

The German leaders knew well that her productive potential was no match for a group of opponents which included the United States, and the Japanese were not unaware of the very great inferiority of their productive capacity. Both relied upon what they believed to be the "decadence" of our way of life and government to assure them that our superior resources would not be adequately employed to prevent the success of their challenge. Both relied further upon the strengthening of their economic potential by exploiting the resources of conquered territories. By the time we entered the war, Germany had brought all Western Europe into her economic orbit and Japan was in the process of vastly expanding the territory which she controlled in Asia. Both probably underestimated the time required to overcome the difficulties of such exploitation. While such conquests strengthened the German economy in certain critical areas, the aggregate contribution they made to her fighting potential was not great (see chart 60). The Japanese were probably even less successful.

CHART 60

Combat Munitions Production of Major Belligerents

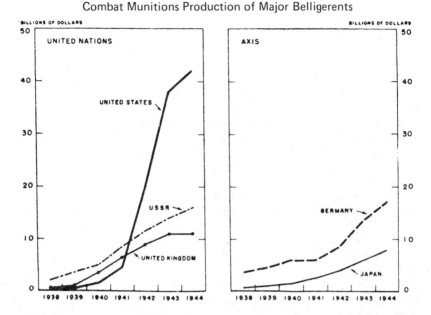

Our possession of vast resources would have meant little or nothing if the administrative abilities of this Nation had not been equal to the task of converting those resources into an adequate supply of the things needed by our Armed Forces and our Allies. Military victory was possible for the United States because of our resources; it was achieved because our political structure and our administrative capacities were such that we obtained a speedy mobilization adequate to the tasks of war imposed upon us.

The Nation's management of its war tasks was not, as the preceding pages have shown, a smooth, uninterrupted, undeviating progress toward unchanging objectives. Our ultimate goal—of forcing the unconditional surrender of those who had declared war on us—was clear. Likewise, there was little uncertainty about the program in its broadest view.

The intermediate objectives were, however, highly flexible and the execution of the program was changeable, at times hesitant and uncertain. This had to be. The tasks were unique, the problems not well understood, the resources not well inventoried, the necessary objectives not always clearly visualized, the methods to attain them untried. The whole intricate machinery had to be modified as goals were approached in one area, as problems appeared in another, or as military requirements shifted. All of these problems had to be met and solved through the democratic processes of government: the democratic tradition of free discussion, Congressional control of major policy, party government, and the continued recognition of the basic rights and status of the individual.

It is useful for this purpose to divide our observations into those relating to the three major administrative aspects of war administration: the development of over-all war policy; the determination of a program adequate to secure victory, once war has been declared; and the execution of the program with maximum effectiveness.

Development of Policy

On the matter of policy toward war, it need be said only that a truly democratic government with an intelligent well-informed electorate free to express its views is surely the best guarantee against aggressive military action. Certainly no one can read the first part of this volume and fail to be impressed by the reluctance of this nation to think of the possibility of armed conflict. The manner in which Germany and Japan went to war was possible only in governments in which such fundamental decisions were in the hands of a very few individuals who, controlling a propaganda machine, could cloak their decisions in plausibility and could impress their will upon an impotent public.

With war thrust upon us our reaction was to determine a program adequate to bring to a speedy conclusion the complete defeat of those who attacked us. The Government's executive branch established goals measured in such terms as scores of trained divisions, hundreds of ships, thousands of aircraft, thousands of tons of supplies to our Allies, objectives with which the legislative branch concurred and to which it gave full support. Military operations were planned by military men, the needed supplies were provided by free men and women working in independent industries guided and coordinated to a common end by a vast system of nonmilitary controls. Though there were times when we seemed to move at a snail's pace, our performance does not suffer from comparison with that of the Axis.

It is now perfectly clear that the Axis countries had not planned adequately beyond their initial aggressive thrusts. Their objectives in beginning wars on either side of the world were limited; the German attacks on Austria, then Czechoslovakia, then Poland were limited, distinct actions, as were those of Japan in her attacks first on Manchuria, then on China. Their decisions to undertake aggressive military actions were arrived at without the careful weighing of possible reprisals or of alternative courses of action that free debate, both within the Government and among a freely speaking public, would certainly have prompted. Had such possibilities been carefully considered, had the decision been for war even after their publics had the opportunity to express their views, it is highly probable that all-out munitions production would have been immediately planned to take care of any eventuality that might arise. German war production in 1939, 1940, and 1941 was surprisingly low as measured not only by later achievements but also as compared with that of her principal opponents, Great Britain and Russia (chart 61). Japanese production was likewise low. In both countries the limiting factor was not potential but the estimates of the war leaders as to what was required to accomplish the immediate aims. In both countries the planners of war assumed that short, quick

CHART 61 GNP of United States, Germany, and Japan

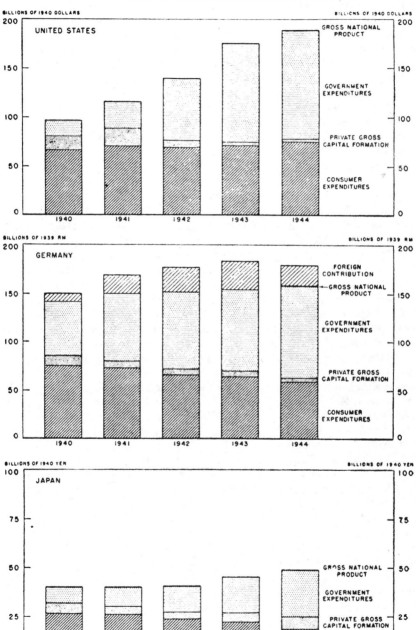

military campaigns would accomplish their objectives. They moved in a series of separate thrusts at nations even less prepared than they. No prolonged war against superior resources effectively mobilized was contemplated. The superior economic potentials of the countries attacked were not considered significant factors. Victory was to be won by strategic moves based on accumulated munition stocks, executed with a speed which would throw the democracies completely off balance.

The Czechoslovakian settlement at Munich seemed to confirm Germany's analysis of the decadence, blindness, and inertia of the democracies; the Polish, French, and Norwegian campaigns strengthened her confidence in the blitzkrieg. Germany achieved control of the Western European continent with an expenditure of armaments that only slightly exceeded current production. Her stocks were not significantly depleted.

The failure of England to capitulate after the fall of France forced Hitler to consider invasion. Nazi strategy and possibly her planning and programming also failed for the first time. Though her armament production was fast approaching that of Germany, England was not considered an immediate threat. Hitler turned upon Russia as a more promising victim for his military strategy. The attack began in the confident expectation that the experience of earlier campaigns was to be repeated; Russia was to be completely subjugated in 3 or 4 months.

No plans appear to have been made to cover the possibility that Russia's preparedness had been underestimated. Moreover, the strength that was to destroy Russian resistance was little more than that which had been thrown against France. Application against Russia of the strategy that had been employed against France would have required preparations on a far greater scale since Russian space, war potential, and armed strength was far greater. In the 9 months that elapsed from the time the decision was made to invade Russia to the actual beginning of the campaign, such preparations could probably have been made in large measure. They were not. Instead, the munitions production program was cut back in the fall of 1940. The German leaders were apparently blind to the possibility that the Russian venture would produce anything but another battle of France.

The defeat at Moscow brought Germany to the realization that she was involved in a long war against formidable opposition which was gaining time to mobilize its strength. Even so, Germany did not yet take extreme measures to concentrate its strength. Germany prepared a second blitzkrieg. Only after it had burned itself out at Stalingrad did Nazism begin to plan in terms which called for full mobilization.

Japan came to war seeking to extricate herself from entanglements from which she had gained no significant success. Her attempt to secure economic domination of China was frustrated, yet her ruling cliques were politically unable to approve of withdrawal. Japanese expansionists were thus driven to seek a solution to their dilemma in the muddy back waters of the European conflict. Such a solution called for expansion southward which was in any case part of the aims of the more extreme influences in her government. The sharp American reaction to the invasion of Indo-China—the embargoes clamped on capital and certain raw materials—was unexpected. In the ensuing crisis in her domestic political affairs, no compromise could be reached between the various groups who shared political power. As a result, the extremists who considered Germany's victory a certainty came into power determined to secure their share of the spoils. The strategy they envisioned assumed that Britain and Russia would be defeated, that one or two blows could crush American power in the Pacific; that a defense line could then be established which would be held against American attacks. These, it was assumed, would come slowly and in little strength. The Japanese assumed that after such attacks had been repulsed, the United States would be willing to negotiate peace.

The first step in this strategy, the attack on Pearl Harbor, was spectacularly successful. It immobilized the American naval power to a degree that could hardly have been planned upon. The Japanese had won what should have been adequate time to conquer and exploit the southern seas if administrative insight and capacity had been adequate. Conquer she did, probably more than she had originally planned. But once her initial conquests were completed, Japan failed to correctly analyze the problems she faced, found herself unable or unprepared to consolidate her position, to exploit her new resources to the strengthening of her military position, or to ward off attack. She met disaster at Midway but it was the defeat at Guadalcanal in late 1942 that brought to the Japanese a realization of the bankruptcy of their strategy, less than a year after Pearl Harbor.

The parallel between the two aggressor nations continued. Both found themselves in late 1942 and 1943 with the task of recasting their strategy, building new administrative machinery, and beginning a thorough mobilization.

Programming for War

If the popular concept of autocratic governments had been correct we would have expected to find that after such a government had decided upon conquest, it would have laid down a precise program for achieving its objectives, a program that would comprise evaluations of all the requisites for certain success in definite terms, and at something more than minimum levels. We would have expected that adequate governmental machinery would be established or at least provided for to guarantee the required mobilization of the nation's resources to the assumed task.

In the case of the democratic United States, once a definite goal was laid before us in December 1941, the programming of mobilization went forward steadily, and by contrast with Japan and Germany, rapidly. Steps were taken to lay the foundations for the necessary administrative and economic organization. Our program and our organization remained flexible, changing as circumstances demanded. But the story of the preceding chapters is one of movement—sometimes hesitant and uncertain but from the long point of view, definitely, constantly, and successfully—towards fuller and fuller devotion to our military objectives. We did not know how much victory might require; we found it difficult to learn to think in the magnitudes involved, but over the long run as a Nation we were not inclined to underestimate.

Long before they entered the war, both Germany and Japan had developed administrative machinery designed to expand their economic capacity, particularly that which was useful in war. Such machinery was established within the framework of sharply limited objectives as well as available resources. In the case of Germany, it is clear that the organizational and administrative problems of war were underestimated. No thought was given to the possibility that the existing machinery might prove inadequate. As the requirements of the war mounted beyond the ability of the established governmental machinery to handle, it displayed marked inflexibility and resistance to change—the typical marks of senile bureaucracy. The situation in Japan was perhaps even worse. The task of war preparations was thrown upon the existing administrative establishment, only very slightly modified to meet new demands. The Japanese government found it even more difficult to secure the adaptability of administrative arrangements and policies required by war. Both nations entered upon war with the United States with few adjustments in administrative organization. When military reverses forced upon them consideration of tighter mobilization, both were forced to improvisation. They experienced sharp internecine conflicts from which they suffered damaging delays.

Within a matter of months after Pearl Harbor, a civilian administrative branch of the American Government was charged with the responsibility of coordinating the demands of the military branches, Lend-Lease, and the civilian economy upon the Nation's industrial capacity. Its progress in securing such coordination was slow, hesitant and beset with obstacles. But the problem to be solved had been foreseen and the preliminary steps in developing a program that was to prove adequate had been taken with speed and dispatch. The difficulties and delays that were overcome, and the methods of executing the program and the results attained have been described in preceding chapters.

Prior to February 1942, Germany had no similar organization. Each of the three military branches was independently pressing its claims upon the nation's productive resources; protection of the civilian economy was a function of a fourth agency. The result was overlapping of orders, constant shifting of emphasis from one item to another, leakage of scarce materials into less essential uses, lack of interchangeability of products between the services, an inability to assure the production of most needed commodities first. These were wastes and inefficiencies that could not be tolerated when absolute capacity production became essential to the continued existence of the regime.

To correct such difficulties and to secure maximum volume of output of munitions finally seen as urgently needed, an Armaments Ministry was established early in 1943. Under the direction of Albert Speer, munitions output was substantially increased in 1943 and 1944. Since many segments of German industry were backward in the art of mass production, technical rationalization, such as simplification of design and standardization of products, was the source of much of the increase. Speer's method was that of expediting now one and then another program; now tanks, then aircraft, and at another time, artillery.

The total gain was thus concentrated in particular items. No over-all or comprehensive program was ever developed. In fact not until 1944 was aircraft, the largest single segment of the German munitions program, brought under the control of the Armaments Ministry. In consequence, component shortages and imbalance in supplies continually plagued the Nazi war effort.

The failure to prepare military clothing supplies against the possibility of delay in the timetable in Russia in 1940 is well known. Such failures plagued the Nazis throughout the war. Thus, a very large tank program undertaken in 1943 failed of its objective because of the failure to synchronize it with the over-all program and the consequent lack of components. There was persistent confusion as to the relative needs for fighter as compared with bomber aircraft. The lack of programming became clearly evident in the middle of 1944 when substantial resources continued to go into aircraft production despite the rapidly increasing shortage in petroleum fuels. Among other failures in programming were those in ammunition which after the battle of Moscow were in the aggregate very short.

The expansion of armaments production which followed from the efforts of the Armaments Ministry after 1942 were very largely a measure of the previously relatively low level of production of individual industries rather than a measure of the nation's fully mobilized industrial potential. Aside from the lack of foresight an_/ the programming defects, two of the more important causes for the failure of German production to reach higher levels may be cited. Long after it was apparent that steel supplies were short relative to the total need for munitions, the Government failed adequately to allocate this basic material. Until late 1942, steel allocation machinery was very primitive and it never was sufficiently well developed to prevent steel from going into less essential items or to restrict the accumulation of large inventories in the hands of private industrial firms. Of the same nature was the failure of the Nazis efficiently to utilize manpower. Labor and production controls were never integrated in the German war economy. There was at no time a synchronization of the activities of the three principal claimants on the available labor—the military, the munitions industries, and the civilian industries. The indiscriminate drafting of skilled and specialized labor into the armed services was a particularly damaging factor.

In the case of Japan, the measures that had been employed to make Pearl Harbor and the South Pacific conquests possible were relied upon until the end of 1942. During this time there was no expansion in the scale of economic planning and no significant shift in administrative organization. War responsibilities were exercised by the individual ministries of the Government, particularly by the Army and the Navy Ministries. No adequate coordinating function was performed, either within the Cabinet or elsewhere. The execution of production programs was the responsibility of the Industry Control Association which was headed by the executives of the great Japanese monopolies and cartels. The looseness of this organization and its inability to direct full efforts to the expanded war needs was recognized in late 1942. Almost a year passed, however, before Japan succeeded in establishing administrative machinery intended to coordinate demands and to secure full mobilization. But the great monopolies retained their positions, the Army and Navy remained to a large degree independent, and no single effective authority controlling the allocation of materials was ever established.

The programming deficiencies were equally, if not even more, striking. The economic life of the home islands of Japan was entirely dependent upon shipping not only for supplies of industrial raw materials but also for a significant portion of the nation's food supplies. Any benefit the expansionists could hope to derive from conquest, especially in strengthening her war potential, depended upon adequate shipping. Control of the seas was the cornerstone of her policies and programs. Even before the war, Japan did not possess under her own flag an adequate merchant fleet. Despite this obvious vulnerability, no adequate shipbuilding program was prepared. Although shipbuilding was on a relatively large scale during the latter thirties, new tonnage in 1941 was lower than in any year since 1935 while in 1942 it was well below 1940. Though the Japanese Navy was utterly dependent upon overseas sources of oil and though the nation was particularly deficient in tankers, there was no tanker-building program prior to 1943.

Other areas of deficient programming may be mentioned, particularly the failure—in what was otherwise an elaborate stockpiling program—to accumulate certain raw materials. It proved necessary in 1944 to reserve rubber for aircraft use while steel alloy metals were in inadequate supply. The failure of Japan to develop a synthetic oil industry or an aluminum-shale industry was not a deficiency in her programming as much as it was evidence of the fact that she staked everything on her control of overseas resources and that she was unable to provide reserve sources of supply.

These broad illustrations, which can be multiplied in detail, suggest a fundamental generalization: that programming in a democracy such as that of the United States, while it may seem slower and more argumentative, results in a sounder course of action. There was within the Axis countries no effective public check on the soundness of the analysis of the problems that were faced or the programs that were required. The principle of dictatorial or oligarchical rule provided no legitimate opportunity to attain the ultimate advantages that come from a thorough thrashing out of problems. In the United States the resistance of self-interested groups to the sacrifices entailed in war mobilization could be fairly quickly broken down by publicity. There was constant, step-by-step discussion of programs and their execution. In this continuing examination, Congress and the public as well as administrative officials participated. While errors were made, they were neither so numerous nor so long maintained, and hence, not as serious, as the errors made by the Axis Governments.

Execution of the Program

If programming must be balanced, flexible, effective, adequate, and coordinated, execution must be equally so. In an operation as complicated as modern war, the whole business breaks down if an important element in plan, program, or execution fails of proper performance.

No direct comparison between the execution of our mobilization program and that of Germany or Japan is possible. Germany failed to see the necessity of maximum mobilization until early in 1943. When she did undertake to secure all-out production, her plans were inadequate, and bomb damage proved a major handicap in carrying out her program. Like Germany, Japan saw no need for full mobilization until late—until after Guadalcanal in late 1942. Guadalcanal meant that her outer defensive zone had been penetrated and from that time on our submarine and aircraft attacks on her shipping were so successful as seriously to interfere with her efforts to expand production. It is nevertheless possible to point out some significant Axis shortcomings.

When in late 1942 and early 1943 the Axis countries were forced to a realization of their needs, they programmed sharp increases in production and sought administrative reorganization and economic tightening to attain it. Both countries pushed production upwards to reach peaks in 1944, peaks which were about three times their 1941 rate of output. In the case of the United States, we programmed production to the maximum possible beginning early in 1942. We achieved a fourfold increase in 1942 and reached in 1944 a peak ten times our 1941 level. The significant comparison is not so much the higher level reached by the United States, but the sustained speed with which we moved to it. We could have programmed for even higher levels in succeeding years had there been the need.

There is no support in such data for any argument for the superiority of autocratic methods of programming or executing a war plan. What military superiority the Axis possessed lay in their established semimobilized organizations and in their stocks. It was a superiority as limited as those inventories. Their production record clearly reflects the delay in their analysis of their needs; examination of their programming and execution will suggest that they were far from full efficiency in such matters also.

Once a program was established, the task of execution was that of maximizing a balanced flow of military products by efficient utilization of all available capital equipment, manpower, and raw materials. It is important to remember that the relative utilization of resources which obtains in the normal production of civilian-type commodities does not necessarily apply to the production of military necessities. A brief examination of comparative experiences with these factors is of interest.

Germany apparently enjoyed a general abundance of capital facilities, and suffered no stringency in this respect. There were a few notable exceptions to the generally easy situation, particularly in the synthetic oil and chemical industries, which were bottlenecks from the beginning, and the electric power system which was strained throughout most of the war. The German munitions industries generally, however, worked on a single shift throughout the war even after the all-out drive for production began in 1943. This compared with the United States where double- and triple-shift operations of facilities were very common. The German aircraft engine industry worked double shifts though the airframe capacity was sufficiently large to permit one-shift operation.

In the case of manpower, it is of interest to note that women were not mobilized, domestic service was reduced but slightly, and employment in civilian industries was largely maintained until late in the war. In each case the opposite was true in the United States. Hours worked per day were little greater than in this country. German civilian employment actually declined by 3.5 million, the result of withdrawals into the armed forces not sufficiently offset by the introduction of 7 million foreign laborers and prisoners of war.

The German situation was somewhat tighter in the case of raw materials. From their own point of view, steel supplies formed the basis for all war programming and were believed to be the limiting factor in their armament program. The fact was, however, that even in the peak production year of 1944 the steel supply was entirely adequate. This resulted, however, from the lack of a comprehensive over-all production program and also from a loose allocation system and not from an abundance of steel or lack of demand. By way of contrast, steel supply in the United States was always tight. Though large quantities of steel found their way to the civilian economy in Germany, the quantity available to the American civilian economy was throughout the war period at bed-rock minimum figures.

The German situation in other commodities was generally favorable, partly as a result of captured stocks and sources of supply, partly because of excellent execution of her conservation program. Her most vulnerable spot, as has been noted, lay in her supplies of liquid fuels. But her military strategy was adjusted to the available supply and these plans worked well until the debacle at Moscow.

The relatively easy situation of the German economy indicates that the Government failed in its efforts to achieve a balanced maximum mobilization either in plan or in execution. Many factors contributed to this result. Fundamental was the analysis of the needs of the military ventures. The inadequacy of those plans was reflected also in a lack of concern with the necessity of securing all possible production from the economy and this in turn led to an unwillingness of special groups to relinquish advantageous positions to the common good. In consequence of the absence of over-all programming, execution of the German war program followed the method of expediting now one item, then another. The situation was one of constant imbalance and hence of a smaller total then might have proven possible.

The Japanese situation is not easily subjected to evaluation in this manner. The nation had not had before the war any extensive volume of excess or underutilized capacity, and a large volume of new facility construction was undertaken. Yet while facilities in some areas remained inadequate, stocks of scarce materials were wasted expanding industries in which there was already excess capacity. Even after aircraft production was ostensibly unified under the Munitions Ministry in 1943, the controls were ineffective and branches of the Army and Navy continued to requisition materials, tools, and plants from manufacturers to whom they had been assigned. Accounting practices were so poor that control agencies were never able properly to regulate the distribution of materials. Scarce commodities leaked into the black market throughout the war.

Materials were sometimes channeled into low priority industries because the only way to keep peace between the Army and Navy was to give each half of available supplies; real power rested in the hands of committees which seldom agreed to take definite action. The fact that Japan from an early date was forced to resort to conscription to staff her munitions industries indicates that she suffered from a labor shortage which was particularly acute in the case of skilled labor. Here again, the lack of planning was costly and the training program which was undertaken began at too late a date to constitute an important contribution. But it was the narrow raw material base upon which the Japanese economy was built that was the crucial element. Efforts to broaden that base by the development of synthetic processes and the exploitation of low-grade resources were considered but not pushed. The Japanese economy in preparing for war could not afford to develop either the synthetic production of petroleum or the exploitation of low-grade sources of aluminum. In view of this fact, the failure to protect adequately overseas sources of supply, to secure maximum production of such material and maximum movement to the home islands were the key factors in Japanese failure. Perhaps nothing is more illustrative of the Japanese approach to the war than the fact that the manufacture of submarine locating devices was given only a very low production priority in 1941 and 1942; not until 1943 was their importance recognized. The Japanese war production peak in 1944 was attained by severe curtailment of the already low civilian standard of living, by the elimination of virtually all plant maintenance, and was well beyond the level which the raw material base could continue to supply.

One thing that a dictatorial government should be able to do better than a democracy—and this theory stimulated considerable demand in this country for a production or war czar—is to eliminate the pressures from different parts of the Government or the Nation for special advantages for their interests. Here again the theory failed to work. Nazi Germany constantly suffered from internal conflicts. Among these may be mentioned the unwillingness of the German Air Forces to accept an over-all, integrated production program, the conflicts over manpower, and then over production of civilian goods. In Japan the conflict between the Army and Navy over resources, and the failure of these two organizations to share stocks or facilities were serious deterrents to maximum effort. In both countries, the governments were unable to secure the full subservience of business efforts to their war efforts. Both were forced to work through and compromise with the great business cartels. These organizations remained special interest groups, never wholeheartedly devoted to the war effort but always concerned with maintaining relative advantage.

These comparisons are obviously not complete or conclusive. They cannot be. Even this evidence shows, however, how the organization and leadership of a free people operated in comparison with that of the dictatorships. The record dispels the notion that government in a time of stress is best conducted by autocrats. Our superiority in resources would have been of little significance without a parallel superiority in the ability to organize our efforts for the exploitation of these resources. Administrative personnel brought to the war agencies from business, from the colleges and universities, and from the permanent civil service demonstrated the existence of a reservoir of organizing talent superior to that of the dictatorships.

In the determination of our goals, free discussion occasionally brought delays—even dangerous delays—yet open debate operated to bring error into the open where it could be seen and corrected. The continuation in time of war of the politics of democracy occasionally enabled the advocates of private group advantage to threaten the general good, yet the give-and-take of the democratic process provided ways in which these tensions could be resolved before the war effort was seriously crippled. Our reluctance to establish even the semblance of autocratic rule may have been partly responsible for our constant struggle to coordinate or harmonize a mobilization effort made up of many separately operating parts, but problems of coordination do not disappear even in an autocratic administration and we developed methods that produced effective end results. Finally, freedom of expression and the absence of severe restraints on civil liberties aided mightily in enlisting the energies and loyalties of the people in the creation and supplying of a great war machine.

The record is one in which the American people can take pride. It was not without error, and while it contains much experience in administration that can profitably be studied, it does not contain a finished blueprint for governmental arrangements for future crises. It suggests, primarily, the strength of a free people, able and disposed to adjust their institutions and methods quickly to meet threats to their security.

4   The Soul of Russia

Ilya Ehrenbourg

"The Soul of Russia" is taken from An Army of Heroes, *a collection of sketches dealing with important aspects of the war on the Eastern Front in 1943. Ilya Ehrenbourg had an international reputation and was perhaps the best-known Soviet journalist in the English-speaking world. He felt that the Nazi invasion had set aflame the abiding love of country that every Russian harbored. Though the Germans might enjoy*

From **An Army of Heroes** by Ilya Ehrenbourg (Moscow), pp. 166–72.

temporary superiority in some things, Ehrenbourg asserted, the Russian people's willing sacrifice and total commitment to the war effort ensured eventual victory.

Two years ago I wrote: "We must set our jaws still more tightly. The Germans are in Kiev. This thought feeds our hatred. We shall pay them back, in full measure, so that their children's children will shiver with superstitious dread at the mere sound of the word 'Kiev.' We shall free Kiev. The blood of the enemy will wash out the traces of the enemy. Like the phoenix of old, Kiev shall rise again from the ashes."

Long and bitter months passed. The Germans advanced still deeper into Russia. They reached Nalchik, Elista, Stalingrad. Military observers of various countries speculated as to where the conquerors would go next, to Iraq or to India. A hotel owner in Bad-Kissingen sent out announcements about the sanatorium he was to open in Borzhom. In Kassel courses were given to train Sonderführers for Bashkiria. The financial sections of German newspapers stated that "the Azov works of F. Krupp" would be operating by 1945 and gladden the hearts of shareholders. In those days a great civil grief lay on our hearts like a stone. Amidst the salutes of victory we do not forget what we have lived through, nor shall we forget it. For us this experience is both grief and wisdom and the key to spiritual courage.

During the nights radio waves surge over the earth—long, medium, short. They have long forgotten their twittering of peaceful days. Now they beat like a pulse; over and over they carry the very same words: counterattack, pockets of resistance, lateral roads, crossings. Now in forty languages they are speaking about one and the same thing: the Germans are retreating. Military observers make no further mention of Iraq. Their eyes are fixed on the Dniester, the Bug, the Niemen. The Sonderführers who were trained to strike fear into the hearts of the Bashkirs are enrolled in route battalions. The Mariupol shares have become worthless scraps of paper. The hotel owner in Bad-Kissingen has taken complete leave of his senses and shouts at his wife: "You'll see, they'll come here. . . ." Over the southern steppes German divisions are fleeing. The phoenix Kiev has risen from the ashes. Hitler is trying to console the Germans: "The enemy is more than a thousand kilometres from the German border." His calculations are faulty: it is much less from Vitebsk to Eastern Prussia. Hitler is shrieking: "My nerves will stand it." But matters are coming to a head now, and Hitler's neck will not be able to stand it.

How did all this come about, asks an astonished world.

We ourselves were in the very thick of events, we lived from communique to communique, we fought and worked, we had no time to meditate. We know now how the 6th German Army was surrounded. We know what the German offensive on Kursk ended in. We know that we are routing the recent conquerors. But still we did not ponder over the question of how all this happened. We know that we have pulled through. We know that before us are the green shores of victory. But let us endeavour for a moment to stand aside, to look at ourselves with the eyes of history.

We frequently speak and write about the weakening of the German army. We know that Hitler's reserves are waning, that bomber aircraft are working havoc in his rear, that the two years of the fierce fighting in Russia have broken the back of his infantry. We know also that there are no genuine ideals in the German army of marauders and chicken snatchers, that discipline alone cannot replace spiritual ardour when things are hard, that the German soldier has grown weaker spiritually and that he is ripe for destruction. But then is it all a question of the Germans alone? Let us think of something else, of the growing might of our army.

The war is as labyrinthian, dark and dense as an impenetrable forest. It does not resemble the descriptions that are made of it—it is both simpler and more complicated. It is felt but not always understood by those who take part in it. It is understood but not felt by its latest analysers. Very probably the historian who has quite correctly appraised the full import of the forcing of the Dnieper pictures this crossing differently from what it was in reality, involuntarily bringing it into some kind of order. He smartens up the men, shaves the exhausted sergeants, brushes the dust from the officers' tunics. He most likely does not see the men around the campfire dreaming hazily about their homes and remarking that the cook keeps harping on mush and that it would be a good idea to bake some potatoes. The future generation will be even less able to imagine that it was these men who pushed across to the right bank of one of the widest rivers in Europe without pontoons. As for those who took part in the war, they know what war looks like. They know that four hundred kilometres, fighting every inch of the way, is no parade. They know that not only companies, battalions and regiments fight, but people with varying biographies, warm as a ball of wool, that each soldier is bound to his country by a separate thread. But it is not easy for those who participate in the war to grasp the historical significance of what is taking place. The great emotions of the given day are enough for them.

People of other countries frequently wonder how it is that our country held out in the tragic days of '41 and '42. Everyone knows how strong the German army was, how thoroughly Germany prepared for its predatory onslaught. The fate of France, with its military traditions and the indisputable courage of its freedom-loving and militant population, is remembered by all. Hitler enslaved Europe. Not the British Isles, of course. But we were not separated from Germany by a sea, nor did we have mountains. We stemmed the aggressors with our breasts, and now these people of other countries are disputing wherein the secret lies. Some say in the nature of Russian courage, in the traditional stamina of the Russian soldier, in the size and natural wealth of Russia, in the fact that Russia has never been conquered. Others object that times have changed. Bayonets, even those of the Russians, are impotent against "Tigers." In an epoch of motive power, space alone cannot save a people. They say that if Russia held out it is thanks to its structure, to the extraordinary patriotism of its peoples, to the fact that every citizen takes a vital interest in the fate of the state. They add to the word "Russia" another word, "Soviet."

Both are right. In the first years after the October Revolution, the Revolution seemed to us all important, frequently overshadowing history. In the course of the war the past arose and joined hands with the present and the future. We fully grasped the organic connection between Russia and the October Revolution. We realized that the Revolution had twice saved Russia: in 1917 and in 1941. If not for the Revolution, Russia might have lost her sovereign independence, might have betrayed her historical mission. But it was not by chance that the October Revolution was born in Russia. It sprang from all the aspirations of the Russian people. Its importance goes beyond state boundaries, and it is with good reason that it is called the greatest event of the twentieth century, but its roots go down deep into Russian history and it cannot be separated from the Russian character, even from the Russian landscape.

The men around the campfire on the right bank of the Dnieper are, of course, the sons of the Russian soldiers of ancient times. They have retained the love for their native land, the valour, the pluck and the staying power of their forefathers. But there is also something new in them, something born of the Revolution: they are not only soldiers, they are citizens.

Before me I have a confidential report of Lieutenant General Dettling, commander of a Sudeten division. This memorandum is headed: "Sentiments of the Local Population." Here is what the German general writes:

"The overwhelming majority of the population does not believe that the Germans will be victorious.... In some populated places attempts have been noticed on the part of many local inhabitants to establish contact with adherents of the Soviet system who have remained.... The young people of both sexes who have received an education are almost without exception pro-Soviet minded. They have a sceptical attitude towards our propaganda. These young people with a seven-year school education or higher ask questions after lectures that enable one to judge of their high mental level. As a blind they usually try to make out that they are simpletons. It is extremely difficult to influence them. They read any Soviet literature which is still around. This youth loves Russia above all else, and fears that Germany will convert their country into a German colony.... With the inception of German occupation the young people feel that they are deprived of a future. They are always pointing out that in the Soviet Union things were very good for the youth, since everything possible was done for them and they were ensured of a great future."

Lieutenant General Dettling would scarcely have drawn up such a memorandum in 1916. Patriotism existed then as well. Valour also existed before. But the young men and women, the peasants of the Smolensk Gubernia in the time of the Tsar, in the time of the estate system and castes, could not dream of a "great future." A certain Napoleonic officer called a partisan of 1812 "the confused soul of the Russian soil." It was not reason but their hearts that showed the serfs of that period the correct path, and they went after the aggressors with pitchforks. Their feats have been justified by history. The descendants of these serfs have become the masters of one of the greatest powers in the world. And the heroes of the *Molodaya Gvardia* (Young Guard) were led not by instinct but by the light of reason. They looked down on the German officers. Oleg Koshevoy knew that he was a representative of a lofty human society which was fighting against armed beasts. Such is the part played by the October Revolution.

The Soviet Union is being defended not only as a great state, but as a genuine democracy. The war is being waged by the people, to whom the state is as their own hearth and home. I have seen no few German generals. I think it is possible to recognize them in a bathhouse. They are a caste, just like the caste of Krupp factory owners, or the Junkers of Eastern Prussia. Such generals are bred, they are a race within the Aryan race. Who is it that is thrashing them? At Kiev Lieutenant General Dettling was routed by Lieutenant General Chenyakhovsky. The latter is thirty-six years old. He is the son of a railway clerk from Uman. Ever since childhood he has been burrowing into science as into rock. He is a man of tremendous culture, and what distinguishes him is his mind, his knowledge and his talent, not caste. He is only one of the many generals of a free and democratic state. I can think of colonels who at the beginning of the war were lieutenants; teachers, agronomists and mechanics on whose chests I saw the Suvorov Order. We may say that the German army is now being routed by an army enriched by military experience and led by capable officers, and we may also say that the Germans are being routed by a people who twenty-six years ago took the reins of their country into their own hands.

Everyone knows that one of the reasons for our victories is the extraordinary work of our war industry. Let us recall all the difficulties. Stalingrad, Kharkov, Dniepropetrovsk, Voronezh, Rostov and the Donbas were occupied by the enemy. Factories sprang up in the midst of wasteland. The steppes of Eastern Russia are not Detroit. Our workers bore all the deprivations, went without sufficient food, without enough sleep, but they gave the army tanks, aircraft, arms. The factories were born overnight, but the workers were not born overnight. They are the people created by the Soviet State, they are not the slaves of Krupp. They are creators, and it was their creative spirit that helped them in the terrible months.

What explains the fact that the Armenian Petrosyan, who was caught by the Germans, found in himself the strength despite the ebbing of his lifeblood to vanquish his would-be executioners and make his way back to his own lines? What helped the Georgian Gakhokidze wipe out the enemy on the last patch of Sevastopol soil? Why is it that the Uzbek Kayum Rakhmanov did not grudge his life in defence of Leningrad? Why did the Jew Papernik give his life at the approaches to Moscow? There was such a thing as the October Revolution. In its purifying flames was born a new Russia, a mother to all the peoples. Yesterday's "aliens" became citizens, state builders, and when the Germans attacked their native land they went into battle, all speaking in different tongues, all different in appearance, but all with the same emotion in their hearts.

I do not wish to say that before the war we achieved everything. In a certain Chasidic legend the wise man is asked: "What is heaven like?" And the wise man replied: "Every man creates his own heaven." A quarter of a century is but a brief hour for history. There is much that we did not manage to do as yet. In our society were not only all our best aspirations but also our shortcomings. In the course of the war we changed a great deal as we went along. We saw that we frequently lacked sufficient discipline, organization, personal initiative and sense of personal responsibility. We realized that our children need stronger moral foundations, that they must be more deeply imbued with the spirit of human dignity, patriotism, loyalty, chivalry, respect for old age and solicitude for the weak. But having realized our shortcomings, we saw in the fire of trials how lofty was our life, built as it was on equality and labour. The war has not only brought devastation to our country, it has steeled people and elevated them spiritually. When they return to peacetime labour, they will not forget what they have thought over and felt. They will bring the wisdom and heroics of the war years into their everyday life. They will help to create that heaven which will reflect the thoughts and sentiments of the much-tried Soviet people.

Labour and life will be made easier to us by the historical perspective that has now become the property of all. Without renouncing the ideals of the future, we have learned at the same time to derive strength from the past. We have grasped the full significance of the heritage left us by our forefathers. We have no desire either to renounce the past without discrimination or to accept it as something infallible. It is possible to receive as a heritage a house or a barren lot, a fortune or a debt. We shall learn from the military genius of Suvorov but not from the sovereign conceit of Paul. The German fascists are fond of speaking about traditions. But what have they taken from the past of the German people? Schiller's love of liberty? Goethe's wisdom? No, the tortures of the Nuremberg hangmen, the superstitious rigmarole of alchemists, the atrocities of the savage Huns and the barrack drill discipline of Friedrich's feldwebels. Every nation takes from its past whatever accords with its spiritual level, its life, its ideals. For us the past means Pushkin and not Benkendorf, Kutuzov and not Arakcheyev, the Decembrists and not Saltychikha, Plekhanov and Gorky and not Purishkevich and the shopkeepers of Okhotny Ryad. The October Revolution has helped us to understand the history of Russia, to make of the distant past a source of inspiration.

The victories of the Red Army already enable us to make out in the dim haze before the dawn the outlines of the great celebration of victory, of which the head of our state spoke to us even in the gravest hours.

What will the world be like after the war? This thought is already beginning to occur to us in the rare minutes of respite between battles, marches and war work. The fascists have wrought so much evil against us and all of Europe, have caused such devastation, so much suffering, that it sometimes plunges one's heart into the slough of despond. We see that schools, nurseries, museums, bright spacious residential houses, all built by our generation with such effort, have been burned to the ground. We see cows replacing the tractors stolen by the Germans. We see how our cherished ideals of brotherhood, human dignity, and liberty have been flouted, see letters from the slaves in Germany, the photographs of German atrocities, the savagery of the dark ages. The imagination easily continues the picture: the desert zone includes Paris, the vineyards of Greece, the lovely villages of Denmark, the factories of Belgium—all Europe. Everywhere are the same ashes in which the earth has clothed itself, the weeds, which our peasants call the "German harvest," torture, the humiliation of man, the flouting of reason, justice, humaneness. How can the earth rise from the dead? And sometimes the thought creeps into the heart of the low-spirited: has not the barbarism of fascism thrown humanity far back?

I do not wish to gloss over anything. I know how difficult it will be to rehabilitate both the ruined cities and the spiritual equilibrium of the people who have spent years under the rule of monsters. And yet I look ahead boldly to the future. Right will conquer on the field of battle. It will conquer also on the scaffolds of human construction. We have learned to value liberty even more dearly after the despotism of the Hitlerites, after the Gestapo, after the Burgomeisters, the spying and all the sins against human dignity which the Germans brought with them. The only bounds to liberty are the liberty of the next man and the happiness of one's country. The self-restraint of the Soviet fighting man is a guarantee that liberty will triumph.

We know the magical power of labour, and it is with good reason that we pay homage to it in our most sacred pledges. The labour of a free citizen is not a curse, is not a yoke, it is creation of a high order. It will be hard to raise cities and villages from nothingness, but the people who did not grudge their blood in defence of their native land will not grudge the sweat of their brow. In the villages that the Germans razed by fire I saw old men helping our soldiers' wives rebuild the houses. This is the pledge of our coming happiness. We know how to put egoism to shame, it has no place beside the graves of heroes.

It would seem that the idea of fraternity had gone up in smoke, but that is not so. It will arise with new force. I make bold to say this while the German hordes are still perpetrating their nefarious crimes. The Germans have proclaimed themselves the "herrensvolk." In reply the national dignity of all the peoples of the world has been roused. This should not bury the idea of fraternity but revive it, give it flesh and blood. By their crimes the Germans have excluded themselves from the family of nations. Stern retribution awaits them. We know that it is not individuals but millions who are to blame for the atrocities committed by the German army. We shall not be sentimental with the Hitlerites nor shall we attempt to teach snakes to kiss birds. But in our sufferings we have seen the sufferings of other peoples. The Siberian understands the sorrow of Greece. The Ukrainian knows what France is experiencing, and the Byelorussian peasant feels with the Norwegian fisherman in his anguish. The idea of fraternity has become tangible, has taken on flesh. The Red Army has become an army of liberty in the eyes of all peoples. Both in enslaved France and in distant America, people speak of its brave deeds with hope. By repulsing the blows of vulture Germany it has saved not only the freedom of our country but the freedom of the world. This is what guarantees that the idea of fraternity and humanism shall triumph, and I see in the distance a world made brighter by suffering, in which good is refulgent. Our people have shown their military virtues. Now all peoples know that the Soviet Union and its army will bring peace to a tortured world. We speak of this amidst the ashes of the Ukraine and Byelorussia with anguished hearts: who of us has not lost a brother, a son, or a friend? We speak of this inspired by the knowledge that we are strong and that ours is a just cause.

5 The American Way in War

D.W. Brogan

Many observers believed that the single most significant phenomenon of the conflict was the United States' manner and method of waging global war. The nationals of other countries were astonished by the rapidity and size of the United States' response to the war, and they were more than a little appalled by its contradictions—the fantastic wastefulness linked with the business-as-usual character of the American war effort. D.W. Brogan, a British essayist, took exception to the general European reaction in a brilliant wartime analysis, The American Character. Brogan was neither shocked nor surprised by the American response to World War II, for it was exactly typical, he claimed, of the American reaction to every war in which the nation had taken part.

Most American towns, big and little, are well provided with public statuary. There are the usual frock-coated philanthropists and politicians; there are monuments to record-breaking cows; to long-dead and therefore safely admired Indian chiefs; there is even a monument to the boll-weevil, which by killing the cotton crop forced one southern region into diversified farming. But the typical monument of an American town, north of the Mason and Dixon line and east of the Missouri, is a cast-iron statue to some hero of the Civil War, the most American of American wars. There they stand, with their little French képis over their ears, with their muskets or sabers, products of the main industry of a small New England town that made a corner in the business. In bigger cities generals ride on bronze horses, even generals whose public and private record was far from brilliant are thus honored. And in Washington, city of monuments, there

From **The American Character** by Denis W. Brogan, pp. 149–65. Copyright 1944, © 1956 by Denis Brogan. Reprinted by permission of Alfred A. Knopf, Inc.

are enough statues to soldiers, more or less distinguished, to make a Prussian paradise.

But there is one American soldier who has few monuments and little popular fame. Nevertheless it is George Brinton McClellan—at thirty-four General in Chief of the Union armies, and a year later unemployed, in personal and political disgrace—who is the typical American *successful* soldier; his way of war is the American way of war, and, even if he did not win the Civil War, it was won in his spirit and by his methods.

And that way of war was General Washington's way of war, was the way in which the American continent was conquered and held, the way taught to Americans by their own history, imposed on them by their own needs, and suggested by their own resources. It is a war of lines of communication, of supply, of material. Long before the term "logistics" became fashionable, the science was practiced by the organizers of little expeditions against the Indians, by the leaders of expeditions, peaceful in intent, across the plains to California, down to Santa Fe. *Space* determined the American way in war, space and the means to conquer space. Into empty land the pioneers moved, feeling their way slowly, carefully, timidly if you like. The reckless lost their scalps; the careful, the prudent, the rationally courageous survived and by logistics, by superiority in resources, in tenacity, in numbers. Americans who did not learn these lessons were not much use in the conquest of the West.

For from the beginning of their settlement, the colonists were faced with enemies who, once they had got guns and gunpowder, knew the million square miles of forest better than did the white newcomers. They knew all its possibilities and dangers, its trails, its swamps, its snakes, its poison oak and its poison ivy, its salt licks, its portages on the rivers, its passes in the mountains—knew them as well as a good German staff officer knows the country behind the West Wall. Some of these tribes, above all the Iroquois, were as militarized, were as much an army possessing a state, as modern Prussia or Paraguay or ancient Sparta. They could be fought, they could be conquered, only by patience, prudence, the massing of superior resources, the ignoring of opportunities for brilliant action till the time came. As Frontenac broke the threat of the Iroquois to the existence of New France, so, nearly a century later, General Sullivan cleared upstate New York for the settlement which has given that state Rome and Syracuse and Troy, Cato and Utica, where the Six Nations once ruled like the Spartiates or Chaka's Zulus. But it was not only General Sullivan who learned, for the young George Washington began his military career with the humiliating experience of being forced to surrender *by starvation* to more forest-wise French; and he saw, with his own eyes, the limitations of British military methods when that admirable parade-ground general, Braddock, marched straight ahead into the French and Indian country to death and the practical annihilation of his army. Other British generals have done the same; courage can work wonders, but not all wonders, and the Virginians were not so much won to respect by the courage as to horror or irony at the irrelevance of parade-ground virtues. For Americans, then and now, the battle is *always* the pay-off, to borrow Major Ingersoll's phrase. Victory is the aim, and the elegance of the means is a European irrelevance, recalling the days when war was the sport of kings. To Americans, war is not the sport of kings but the most serious national and personal concern which they like to fight in their own way and which, when they do fight it in their own way, they win.

This, of course, is concealed from Americans as well as from us by schoolboy romanticism. It is far more encouraging to daydreams to think of the West as having been won by a handful of totally reckless scouts and pioneers, hoping for an Indian war rather than fearing it, and ready to plunge into the trackless wilderness at the drop of the hat. There *were* people like that, reckless of their own and their fellows' lives. But they are not heroes to be remembered but horrible examples to be digested and then forgotten. Even the great romantic figures—Daniel Boone, Simon Kenton, even Bridger and Frémont—were heroes because they were *pathfinders*, men who did not get lost, did not venture into trackless places with no knowledge of where they were going. They were pathfinders for the solid, sober, cautious, anxious-to-live pioneers. Without the maps, without the oral or written instructions that those men provided, more parties of western-moving settlers would have suffered the fate of the Donner party: starvation, cannibalism, death, in the High Sierra or, like many less famous victims, on the High Plains or the grassy sea of the prairie. And behind the Boones and Kentons, the Bridgers and Frémonts, were the businessmen, George Washington and Leland Stanford. Matter-of-fact men, some of them rascals; all of them men with a clear head for bookkeeping. They wanted to settle men and women and cattle peacefully; they wanted to do it cheaply; they knew that distance was the enemy, the great weapon of the Indian and of his allies, hunger and thirst. So trails and roads, rivers that would float rafts and canoes and keel boats, salt licks where the cattle could restore their health, malaria-free ground where camps could be made—these were the elements of the problem of opening up the perpetual second front of the West. These provided for, the Indians could be conquered, perhaps without fighting. So the commander of Virginian riflemen under General Washington who had won the name of Mad Anthony Wayne was the general who, under President Washington, carefully prepared to avenge the defeats of his predecessor, defeats caused by bad and inadequate preparation. General Wayne did not rush on the Indians as if they had been British regulars of the old school; he prepared, with unsporting thoroughness, to move, safely and in overwhelming force. Long before he won the Battle of Fallen Timbers, Wayne had won the war and the prize of war, the Ohio country—won it from the Indians and from their British backers in the old French fort of Detroit.

As mad (in the American sense) as Anthony Wayne was that passionate pioneer, Andrew Jackson, favorite hero of his successor in the White House and in the leadership of the Democratic party, Mr. Roosevelt. But when Jackson fought the Cherokees he was as prudent up to the final decisive and morally-testing moment of battle as Wayne or Washington. He was as cautious then, he the duelist and political gambler, as he was ten months later, waiting for the Peninsular veterans of General Pakenham to march up to his breastworks outside New Orleans and be shot down in rows, as if they had been confronting German machine guns and not merely the rifles of well-hidden and practically safe frontiersmen.

The instances could be multiplied almost indefinitely. American history has some equivalents of the charge of the Light Brigade, or of the French cavalry at Reichshofen, or the German cavalry at Mars la Tour. But not many; and even the few there are illustrate the American way in war. Pickett's charge at Gettysburg, the destruction of the "flower of Virginia," is very famous, but it was very futile; it was a gesture regretted by Lee and condemned by Longstreet, that unamiable, overcautious, selfish soldier, more trusted by the rank and file of the Army of Northern Virginia than was either of the great twin brethren of brilliant battle, Lee and Jackson. The real American charge into the deadly breach was exemplified a few months later at Chattanooga when Philip Sheridan led his men racing up the mountain (waving them on, so one tradition has it, with a whisky bottle for a sword) and swept away the army of Braxton Bragg. And that dramatic "battle above the clouds" was a mere finale to a long play whose dénouement had been decided weeks before when the drab figure of General Grant appeared to take over from the brilliant Rosecrans—and Grant got a line of supplies opened into Chattanooga, a line down which poured the endless resources of the North to be launched suddenly, when the issue was beyond all doubt, like an avalanche pouring uphill on the gallant, outnumbered, under-equipped Southern army. Once the way was opened for the fields and factories of the North to supply Chattanooga, the campaign was over. The South could not exploit its victories; it could pick up tricks but not win a rubber. It had defeated Rosecrans, but it could not break that tenacious Virginian serving the North, George Thomas. He was the Rock of Chickamauga on which Grant built. And Thomas, a year later, waited even more patiently than Washington and Wayne while the brilliant thruster, Hood, fought and maneuvered and displayed initiative and fighting spirit. Thomas, indeed, waited so long that the impatient civilian Secretary of War, Stanton, wanted to remove him; but when the due time came, Thomas struck, and on December 15-16, 1864, in the battle of Nashville, he destroyed forever the Southern army in a victory "without a morrow" as complete as Cannae or Sedan. But that victory had been made easy more than a year before, when Thomas had held the railway and river nodal point of Chattanooga. It was a problem in statistics, in organization, in patience, an engineering problem. It is fitting that one of the greatest dams of the Tennessee Valley Authority should bear the name of Chickamauga, the name of one of those battles which decided that for twenty-five hundred miles the Mississippi should "flow unvexed to the sea" through a nation united by arms.

But, as has been said, there is in America, as elsewhere, the legend of campaigns much more like sporting events than these drab accumulations of overwhelming material resources. There are such campaigns. While General Nathan Bedford Forrest did not say that his scheme of war consisted in "getting there fustest with mostest," some such policy was imposed on the South. They could have force only in terms of time. The North could have force in terms of space which they could command as no one can command time. So Lee was forced to attempt miracles of movement, miracles that, with his inferior resources in men, railways, transport, even food, he did not always work. He asked far too much of his troops, of his staff, of his second-in-command, in the campaign of the Seven Days, where he had, facing Jackson and himself, the cautious, the fearful, the egoistic, the neurotic, the beloved and trusted and competent maker and leader of the Army of the Potomac, General McClellan. He asked too much in the concentration before Gettysburg; he did not ask too much when he exploited the fears of Hooker and the unknown trails of the Wilderness, or when in that scrub country he used all the arts of a great defensive general who had been trained as a tamer of the Mississippi, maker of locks and dams, to force General Grant to "fight it out on that line if it took all summer." Grant lost more men in that campaign than there were in Lee's whole army, but he was stronger at the end of it than he was at the beginning. He was strong enough *not* to continue to fight it out on that line, except morally, strong enough to shift his whole army to new bases, supplied by sea, invulnerable to Southern attack, shift it to the position chosen two years before by General McClellan. And from that position he was able to send out Sheridan to destroy the Valley of Virginia as thoroughly and as ruthlessly as the R.A.F. and the American Air Force are destroying the power of movement and of supply of the Reichswehr. Sheridan had to gallop twenty miles to rally his suprised troops, but a defeat at Winchester would have been only a minor inconvenience. A few months later, when Lee's army was desperately lunging south to find food and space to move in, Sheridan by his brilliant improvisation ended the war; but he ended it only a few days sooner than it would have ended anyhow. The decision that it would end—and end one way—was made when Sherman seized and burned the great railroad center of Atlanta and left Thomas to deal with the Southern army while he marched to the sea, almost unopposed, but breaking the will and the power of the South to resist. This march through Georgia of the young men of Sherman's army was, for them, a kind of picnic. They ran hardly more risk (except from an occasional Scarlett O'Hara) than did the young men of the Luftwaffe in the pleasant early summer of 1940 in the empty skies of France. But Sherman's army had waiting for them, on the coast, the new Northern fleet created out of next to nothing in two or three years—waiting with food and supplies and news and security. They were not like the unfortunate British and German soldiers of Gentleman Johnny Burgoyne marching to a new Saratoga. They were serving not George III and Lord George Germain, but a patient Illinois lawyer, Lincoln, who knew the West; a detestable railway lawyer, Stanton, who knew business; and that unromantic, imperturbable, undignified commander, General Grant.

That fleet itself was a highly rational, functional creation. Its boldest technical innovation in the war was the *Monitor*, the "cheesebox on a raft," the ancestor of the modern heavily armored, turreted gun platform that is the battleship. The Confederate *Virginia* (née *Merrimac*) was a plated man-of-war of the old type, far nearer to Nelson's *Victory* than to a modern battleship. But the real Union navy, created out of nothing, was the utilitarian fleet of gunboats and fast, light-draft cruisers that caught the blockade runners, the equivalent of

Coastal Command. That fleet went wherever the ground was a little damp—as Lincoln put it. It learned all the arts of amphibious operations on the high seas and in the great rivers. How many Americans who in the fall of 1943 were anxious over Salerno, for a day or two, remembered Pittsburg Landing, better known as Shiloh? It was an operation of the Salerno type, bloody and bitterly fought but on a greater scale. Admiral Samuel Du Pont (of the great munitions family) off Charleston, Admiral David Porter in the Mississippi—these are not such dramatic figures as the Great Catalan-American sailor, Farragut, forcing the mined and fortified approaches of New Orleans or Mobile, having himself tied to his mainmast like a new Ulysses and giving the famous order, "Damn the torpedoes!" (i.e., mines); but they are all representative officers of a service which, though until 1942 it had never fought a really great sea battle, not only had to its credit a brilliant series of single-ship actions, but also had learned to work with an army over four long and grim years, and had helped to secure for the North the time to turn one of the least armed and most pacific nations of modern times into the greatest military power on the globe. For even more in 1861 than in 1917 or 1941, the United States entered a great war in a state of non-preparation that recalls the inadequacy of Irish military methods when the Danes came, or of Mexican military methods when Cortes came armed with the apparently divine weapons of gunpowder and horses.

Americans have long been accustomed to jest at this repeated state of military nakedness. "God looks after children, drunkards, and the United States." There is a truth in that; space, remoteness, have given a little time to prepare—and the American people needs very little time. Hitherto it has had just enough, provided by accident, distance, or allies.

So we return to General McClellan, the brilliant product of West Point who had been sent to the Crimea to see how the great European nations made war and who had learned, at least, what not to do. He reported; he secured the adoption of a new saddle (still, I am told, an excellent saddle); and he retired to run great railroads. It was an excellent and typical training. Here were the problems of planning, of personnel management, of technical adaptation, of improvisation, for an American railroad in those days required as much elasticity in making and operating as an army on the march in hostile country. He learned to know the West, the growing, precedent-free, elastic country where anything was possible—if you knew how. It was a world very different from the narrow coastal plain, long settled, thickly peopled; a country where it was natural to try to imitate such brilliant maneuvers, such magnificent achievements of the pre-machine age, as Marlborough's march to the Danube in 1704 or Napoleon's march to the Danube in 1805.

But before he could succumb to or resist the temptation to imitate the pre-railway art of war, he had to get an army. The army of the United States in 1861 when the Civil War broke out was 16,000 strong, scattered in tiny posts all over the Indian country. Few officers (apart from those who had served in the Mexican War) had ever seen a thousand soldiers together. The new armies had to be created out of nothing; they were created. A few years before, McClellan had seen in the Crimea the slow and moderately effective creation of an efficient British army helping the French to besiege Sebastopol. Within six months of taking over the command of the Army of the Potomac (an army whose first martial experience had been Bull Run—a disastrous defeat followed by a humiliating rout), an admirably equipped, well-disciplined, coherent army of one hundred and fifty thousand men was learning how to fight, the hard way, in desperate drawn or lost battles. What was done in the East was being done in the West, too. Yet the political head of the War Department was a most representative Pennsylvania politician of an age when, even more than now, Philadelphia was "corrupt and contented." The military head of the army at the beginning of the war was a venerable, corpulent, almost immovable veteran who had been a brilliant success in the War of 1812 and, as an elderly general, had captured Mexico City fourteen years before. Hardly anybody in the United States had taken military matters seriously except the more energetic members of the tiny corps of professional officers—whose ablest leaders, Lee, Joe Johnston, and Albert Sidney Johnston, had gone over to the other side. Yet there were no breakdowns in supply such as made the British army in the Crimea almost unusable for months. Lincoln can hardly be described as stamping on the ground, but armies sprang out of it all the same and the task of conquering eight hundred thousand square miles was undertaken. Brilliant short-cut plans, straight marches on the Southern capital, raids and flanking maneuvers were attempted, with pretty uniformly disastrous results. The war was fought for four years by accumulating slowly but inexorably every kind of material resource, by laboriously teaching troops the very elements of their trade—the pupils being all ranks of officers as well as men.

The American soldier was as critical as the civilian. He despised a good many of his generals, for pretty good reasons. When Grant obstinately renewed futile attacks, his troops pinned letters to their tunics to their kinsfolk since they knew that many would fall outside the Confederate entrenchments but none would cross them. When "Uncle Billy" Sherman sternly rebuked a plundering soldier, he was told: "You can't expect all the cardinal virtues for thirteen dollars a month."

Behind the front there was profiteering; there was the evasion of military service through the purchase of substitutes who, in turn, often earned more than one bounty by enlisting over and over again—deserting as soon as they could. There was bitter dispute about the higher conduct of the war, complaints that the West was being neglected in favor of an equivalent of the modern "island-hopping" strategy in the East. But by 1865, with an army two million strong, the United States was the greatest military power in the world and one of the most formidable naval powers. Within fifteen years of the end of the war, she had again barely enough troops to keep the Indians in order and was reasonably doubtful of her ability to fight a successful naval war with Chile.

The Spanish War of 1898 lasted too short a time and the Spaniards were so feeble that nothing more was learned than that the American army was ill and the Navy well prepared to fight. When the next testing time came, many of the lessons of the Civil War had been learned—on paper. But in 1917, the army of little more than one hundred thousand men, short in all modern equipment, tanks, airplanes, and modern artillery, had to be turned—and was turned—in a year or so into an army of millions. It was sent overseas in numbers unprecedented in the history of the world, and those fresh, raw troops broke the heart of the Germans. The very reverses shook the temporary victors. As the Confederate army lived off captured Union stores and then sank into nakedness and weariness as that source failed with the cessation of victories, so the Germans were profoundly depressed by the lavish equipment of the Americans and the Allies they supplied. With resources far beyond the dreams of 1861, the United States of 1917-18 swamped the victorious armies of the Second Reich and broke their spirit.

Today, the same process is under way. The professional leaders of the American army are men trained to work in obscurity and often for basically civilian objects. They learn to make great dams, to build and operate civil projects like the Panama Canal, to organize the unemployed. They enter West Point as the necessary preparation for what, in all probability, will be an obscure and dull life. Their promotion in all the higher ranks depends on the good will of the Senate, which has the right to refuse confirmation of presidential nominations. So the professional soldier learns either to avoid politics like the plague or, in rarer cases, to play that dangerous game. Whether he enters the army at all often depends on a political accident, for the candidates for the entrance examination are nominated by Congressmen, and a would-be soldier whose family is Democratic but who lives in a Republican district is usually out of luck, his military dreams shattered forever—unless, like General Marshall, he has the tenacity to enter from one of the semi-official military schools, in General Marshall's case the Virginia Military Institute. And inside this officer corps recruited from men who won commissions in the last war or entered from VMI or the Citadel of Charleston, the West Pointers, wearing their rings, are an inner caste, cut off from the outside world. They do not even have that training in dealing with civilians that a high British officer gets from his War Office experience, since there are (the political chiefs apart) no high civilian officials in the American War Department; all senior officers get a turn of duty in purely administrative jobs.

And this small, almost anonymous body, serving in widely scattered posts kept up for political reasons where once the threat of Indian war provided real justification, have to deal with the elected representatives of a profoundly unmilitary people that becomes warlike only under great provocation. In peacetime they have to prepare elaborate plans for calling on the immense untapped resources of the United States in a future wartime for which no spiritual preparation can be made. They know that they can never be ready for war; that they must always have time given them that they may use space and the resources of space. They know, too, that their countrymen, brought up like all peoples to believe in a gilded version of their own history, forget that all American wars have, like this one, begun with disasters, not victories. They know that their countrymen are temperamental and versatile, easily bored with theory and all of them having to be shown, not simply told.

The American officer, then, must think in terms of material resources, existing but not organized in peacetime and taking much time and thought and experiment by trial and error to make available in wartime. He finds that his best peacetime plans are inadequate for one basic reason: that *any* plan which in peacetime really tried to draw adequately on American resources would cause its author to be written off as a madman; and in wartime, it would prove to have been inadequate, pessimistic, not allowing enough for the practically limitless resources of the American people—limitless once the American people get ready to let them be used. And only war can get them ready for that. The American soldiers can draw, then, but not before, on an experience in economic improvisation and in technical adaptation which no other country can equal. They can draw, too, on a healthily unprofessional attitude. Men will think, with their civilian and very unmilitary ways of doing things, of new and efficient ways of doing military things. They will build air fields in a week and ford rivers under fire in tractors and bulldozers as part of their new day's work—all the more efficiently that it was not their old day's work. So they used and made and unmade railways in the Civil War, the only modern war until 1914. They improvised railway bridges like that "beanpole and cornstalk" bridge that was built in nine days over Potomac Run and took the rail traffic of an army. So they created the great rail and shipping organization in France in 1918 which would have enabled Foch, in 1919, to deliver that "blow that cannot be parried" of which he had dreamed for forty years and which the Americans gave him the means to deliver. But, like the Negro playing possum in the American story, the Germans surrendered—"Don't shoot, Colonel, I'll come down!"

Wars are not won by generals or by plans alone; they are won by men. And the tradition of the American soldier is a practical one—almost overhumorously practical. He has never had much use or perhaps any use for the virtues of the parade ground. When the victorious Northern armies paraded through the streets of the long-beleaguered city of Washington in 1865, the spectators saw, with a natural special affection, the much enduring Army of the Potomac, veterans of so many unsuccessful, bloody, exhausting campaigns fought over the short hundred miles between Washington and Richmond. These were their own men, finally victorious. But the real curiosity was Sherman's western army. They had not driven to and fro through the Virginia Wilderness or bogged in the swamps of the James River. They had fought and marched and fought and marched down the Mississippi, across Tennessee, "from Atlanta to the sea" and up to the rear of Lee's army. And what the spectators saw was an army of boys—not boys in the modern American sense, i.e., men just short of middle age, but boys in their teens and young men in their early twenties. Grant's army was hardly more dressy than its shabby Commander, but Sherman's army loping along, with open necks and hardly any standard equipment, hardened and lithe, confident and brash, this was an American army, formidable, enterprising, humane, and ribald. Nothing could have been less like the armies of Europe than that, and the world was not to see a comparable sight again till the (British) Eighth Army emerged from the desert, clad as its fancy and its resources dictated, living by its own battle-learned discipline, and—if any of the Americans in Tunis had had the necessary historical imagination to see it—spiritual descendant of the American armies that in four years had fought through from the great central valley to the Atlantic coast.

But the American troops in Tunis were like the American troops in any war, needing to learn, ready to learn—after the need had been brought home to them. As Sheridan was told in 1870 by a philosophical Prussian general who saw his troops running away under murderous French fire, all troops "need to be a little shooted." So it was in 1776 and 1812 and 1861 and 1918. But the adjustment will be made, has been made, though in an American way. The heirs of Morgan's riflemen cannot be turned into the equivalent of the Brigade of Guards—at any rate not without great risk of losing what Morgan's riflemen had, which the Guards found was plenty. The American who, in peacetime, is a national figure if he is ready to walk a mile (for anything but a Camel) is, in wartime, fond of riding to the front in a jeep. But it was already said of eighteenth-century Virginia that its poor people would walk five miles to steal a horse to ride one. In a friendly country like the United States, it is impossible to breed soldiers who will automatically forget that an officer is a human being. And in a ribald and irreverent country, it is hard to get officers to insist, with British self-confidence, on their superiority to human weakness. There must be more give-and-take, more ignoring of unessentials, more confidence that in the hour of battle human virtues and common sense will do as much as automatic discipline of the old eighteenth-century type as exemplified at Bunker's Hill and New Orleans.

A country has the kind of army its total ethos, its institutions, resources, habits of peaceful life, make possible to it. The American army is the army of a country which is law-respecting without being law-abiding. It is the army of a country which, having lavish natural wealth provided for it and lavish artificial wealth created by its own efforts, is extravagant and wasteful. It is the army of a country in which melodramatic pessimism is often on the surface but below it is the permanent optimism of a people that has licked a more formidable enemy than Germany or Japan, primitive North America. It is the army of a country whose national motto has been "root, hog, or die." When convinced that death *is* the alternative, the hog roots. It is the army of an untidy country which has neither the time, the temperament, nor the need for economy. It is the army of a country in which great economic power is often piled up for sudden use; a final decisive military blow is merely a special variety of "corner." It is the army of a country of gamblers who are more or less phlegmatic in taking and calculating their losses, but who feel with all their instincts that they can never go wrong over a reasonable period of time in refusing to sell America short.

So the American way of war is bound to be like the American way of life. It is bound to be mechanized like the American farm and kitchen (the farms and kitchens of a lazy people who want washing machines and bulldozers to do the job for them). It is the army of a nation of colossal business enterprises, often wastefully run in detail, but winning by their mere scale and by their ability to wait until that scale tells. It is the army of a country where less attention is paid than in any other society to formal dignity, either of persons or of occupations, where results count, where being a good loser is not thought nearly so important as being a winner, good or bad. It is the country where you try anything once, *especially* if it has not been tried before. It is a country that naturally infuriates the Germans with their pedantry and their pathological conception of "honor." It is a country that irritates the English with their passion for surface fidelity to tradition and good form. It is the country of such gadget-minded originals as Franklin and Ford. It is a country whose navy, fighting its first great battles a century and a half after it could boast of Paul Jones, recovered from a great initial disaster and taught the heirs of Togo with what speed the heirs of Decatur and Farragut could back out of their corners, fighting. The Coral Sea, Midway, these are dates for the world to remember along with the new Thermopylae of the Marines at Wake Island or the new Bloody Angle of Tarawa. It is a country—and so an army—used to long periods of incubation of great railroads and great victories. It is the army of a people that took a long time to get from the Atlantic to the Pacific and that found the French and the Spaniards and the Russians before them. But they got there and stayed. The two hundred and fifty years from Virginia to California, like the four years from Washington to Richmond, must be remembered by us—and the Germans. That General Washington, after six years of barely holding his own, combined with the French fleet to capture a British army as easily as taking a rabbit in a snare—that is to be remembered too, for it was a matter not of fighting but of careful timing, of logistics.

That typical western soldier and adventurer, Sam Houston, waiting patiently until the Mexicans had rushed on to deliver themselves into his hands at San Jacinto—that is to be remembered. It is not Custer foolhardy and dramatic with his long hair and his beard who is the typical Indian fighter, but great soldiers like Sherman and Sheridan planning from St. Louis or Chicago the supplying of frontier posts, the concentration of adequate force. The Indian chiefs Joseph and Rain-in-the-Face were often artists in war at least on a level with Rommel. But to the Americans war is a business, not an art; they are not interested in moral victories, but in victory. No great corporation ever successfully excused itself on moral grounds to its stockholders for being in the red; the United States is a great, a very great, corporation whose stockholders expect (with all their history to justify the expectation) that it will be in the black. Other countries, less fortunate in position and resources, more burdened with feudal and gentlemanly traditions, richer in national reverence and discipline, can and must wage war in a very different spirit. But look again at the cast-iron soldier of the Civil War memorial. A few years before, he was a civilian in an overwhelmingly civil society; a few years later he was a civilian again in a society as civilian as ever, a society in which it was possible to live for many years without ever seeing a professional soldier at all, in which 25,000 soldiers, mainly in the Indian country, were invisible among fifty million people minding their own business. Such a nation cannot "get there fustest with mostest." It must wait and plan till it can get there with mostest. This recipe has never yet failed, and Berlin and Tokyo realize, belatedly, that it is not going to fail this time—that in a war of machines it is the height of imprudence to have provoked the great makers and users of machines and, in a war of passions, to have awakened, slowly but more and more effectively, the passions of a people who hitherto have fought only one war with all their strength (and that, a civil war), but who can be induced by their enemies, not by their friends, to devote to the task of making the world tolerable for the United States that tenacity, ingenuity, and power of rational calculation which decided between 1861 and 1865 that there should be a United States which would twice crush the hopes of a nation of military professionals, to whom war is an art and a science, to be lovingly cultivated in peace and practised in war. For Americans, war is almost all of the time a nuisance, and military skill a luxury like Mah-Jongg. But when the issue is brought home to them, war becomes as important, for the necessary period, as business or sport. And it is hard to decide which is likely to be the more ominous for the Axis—an American decision that this war is sport, or that it is business.

Essays

6 Total War

Cyril Falls

Before his retirement, Cyril Falls was Professor of the History of War at Oxford University. His voluminous writings on the subject include The Nature of Modern Warfare, A Short History of the Second World War, *and the brief interpretive essay,* "The Art of War from the Age of Napoleon to the Present Day." *The following essay on "total war" treats the concept in a historical context, a very helpful though never wholly satisfactory endeavor.*

When the phrase "total war" was first used the harnessing of atomic energy had not been carried out and only a minute body of scientists had any conception of how this was to be done. The concept of totality is thus independent of atomic or nuclear warfare. Some of those who first encountered the phrase became intoxicated by its significance, grim though it was, and talked nonsense about it. If we look at the history of war or even examine war in the abstract, we shall find it natural that some wars should be more, or less, limited than others. The causes, the aims of the belligerents, the prospects of outside intervention, the temper and philosophy of the times—these and other factors must influence the manner and means of waging war.

Then, the very fact that a big war has been conducted without restraint or scruple may lead to a reaction. The Thirty Years War was marked by horrible excesses and left a great part of Germany in devastation. This resulted in an effort to canalize war, powerfully influenced by the immortal work of the Dutch jurist Hugo Grotius, who died in 1645, three years before the war dragged its way to an end. He built up a system of jurisprudence to distinguish between just wars and those brought on by ambition and greed for conquest. He took this line because he believed that it was waste of time to try to eliminate war altogether.

From **The Art of War** by Cyril Falls, pp. 144–55. Copyright © 1961 by Oxford University Press. Reprinted by permission of The Clarendon Press, Oxford, England.

In the same spirit he advocated the observance of moral obligations such as respect for neutrality and humanity to women and children. *The Rights of War and Peace*, together with some successors of lesser merit and the memory of rulers and statesmen, played a part in the relative humanity and restraint in the waging of war throughout the remainder of the seventeenth century and the greater part of the next. When these virtues were laid aside, as in the two ravagings of the Palatinate by order of Louis XIV, measures which had been commonplace in the Thirty Years War were found shocking by many.

"Just as limitation can never be absolute, so also totality in war is a relative concept rather than an absolute one." Total war in the absolute would involve fighting without any restrictions, even those of prudence and self-interest. This did not happen. For example, it has often been asserted that the wars sparked off by the Reformation, the "Wars of Religion", approached totality. They were assuredly unrestrained, "unselective" in their aims, and generally barbarous. Yet when Queen Elizabeth intervened in 1585 in the struggle of the Dutch against the Spaniards she did not declare war, any more than did Philip II. She professed a desire to see all the subjects of the King of Spain in the Low Countries living in a state of "due obedience" to him; she engaged from time to time in peace negotiations; and on the Dutch side merchants revictualled the Spaniards by sea.

This is by no means to deny that war has become closer to totality in modern times, since the French Revolution. In earlier chapters an effort has been made to show that the determination of the rulers of revolutionary France to fight a people's war and the response they received initiated the change. Napoleon exploited the virtues of the young armies of the Revolution by his genius. It has also been indicated that railways gave the process a push forward, and that here the prime exploiters were generals of the American Civil War and the elder Moltke. The final impetus was given by the combined progress of science and industry.

The technique of fighting a blockade can justly be considered as part of the art of war. Napoleon showed how clearly he understood the problems of a war not unlimited indeed but approaching in its economic aspect closer to totality than any international conflict of the past. He became the pioneer of the beet-sugar industry because the blockade cut off cane sugar from France. This was only one of his achievements in the stimulation of agriculture, the yield of which increased roughly five-fold during his rule. In eight years the number of silk-looms in France increased threefold. He was the originator of the woollen industry of Roubaix. He set up factories for the machine-printing of fabrics and especially the imitation of Indian cashmeres, which could no longer be imported. It has been said of him that he was to be seen leaning over the customs statements as he did over his reports when on campaign.

The industrial revolution, originating in England, is considered by some to have got into its stride a few years before Napoleon's birth in 1769. In certain respects—for example, the development of iron-smelting by coke—it affected his wars materially, but it did not appear as a decisive factor until the middle of the nineteenth century. How small, or at all events, how uneven, was the psychological impact of the life-and-death struggle with Napoleon is witnessed by the many cases in which this is disregarded in the literature of the period. Sprigs of the nobility and the wealthier squirearchy, whose descendants have in more recent times been the most eager to serve in war, often, like so many of the writers, disregarded the Napoleonic Wars. Fox-hunting was passing through a brilliant phase. George Osbaldeston, the almost legendary hard rider and M.F.H., does not mention Napoleon or Wellington in his memoirs. One passage runs: "We had the most extraordinary sport during my period of office in the Burton country (1810-1813). The gentlemen of the hunt presented me with a large silver waiter having foxes' heads as handles, with a most complimentary inscription on the back, as a token of their appreciation." In 1810 "Squire" Osbaldeston reached the age of twenty-four. Few signs appear of contempt on the part of the country at large or even of officers of their own class for those who lived such lives.

The features of the mid-nineteenth century affecting the form and conduct of war have already been mentioned. They are the power of steam, the more fruitful cultivation of the earth, the increased extent and speed of industrial production, and the closely allied growth of populations. These contributed to a nearer approach to total war, in the sense of involving a far greater proportion of the nation and the national effort. Even now, however, inconsistencies and lacunae are to be found. The American Civil War was unlimited and approached totality in some respects. Both sides put forth tremendous efforts measured in man-power and production. Sherman deliberately destroyed the Confederacy's very means of existence. On the other hand, government controls were of the slightest. Large quantities of boots were held in Virginia at a time when the Confederate armies were nearly barefoot. States' rights were sacred to the Confederacy and Jefferson Davis would not infringe them even in such an emergency. His attitude here is completely opposed to the principle of totality. Governments which adopt this principle are as insistent in their demands on their own citizens as they are ruthless in their conduct of the war against their enemies.

The Franco-Prussian War was in some ways a signpost to totality rather than an example of it. The demands by the opposing States upon their man-power were heavy, but not on the scale of the twentieth century. The French at the time. protested. bitterly against Prussian reprisals for the acts of *francs-tireurs,* but many jurists have since held that the retaliation was not in general contrary to the laws of war. In the siege of Paris the Germans showed restraint. Such bombardments of the city as took place were light and for the most part brief, obviously intended as a warning rather than to cause widespread destruction. The German command has been condemned for forcing prominent Frenchmen to travel on railway engines in order to prevent the wrecking of trains. Even here the greatest English authority on the laws and usages of war, Professor L. Oppenheim, found it difficult to agree with the majority opinion that this practice was indefensible.

How steep has been the descent from the generally accepted standards of the mid-nineteenth century may be measured by two quotations. At the outset of the war of 1848 between Austria and Sardinia, when Milan rose against the garrison, Field-Marshal Radetzky decided to abandon the city. He was supremely confident that he would return victoriously, as in fact he did in the following year; but he took this grave step largely to save Milan from destruction and despite the often inhuman killing of his men in isolated posts. He said himself: "What would Europe have to say, even though we are assailed in our most sacred rights, wounded in our innermost hearts, if we should degrade ourselves to the level of Vandals."

The second is from the book of a senior French officer, General Derrécagaix, writing some twenty years after the Franco-Prussian war, in which he had taken part: "There exists, in a word, a law of war generally regarded as being in force, which forbids the destruction of the enemy because that is an act of barbarism; which condemns vengeance because it is odious; which teaches nations to limit wars to reparation for an injury or the guarantee of a pledge; which forbids the infliction of useless sufferings . . . which condemns burning and devastation. . . . The conqueror ought to be generous; prisoners are brothers in arms whom the lot of conflict has betrayed; they should not be subject to any but good treatment. Goods should never become booty. Pillage is no longer permitted, not even as a reprisal."

He was writing of ideals which he knew were not and would not always be observed, but so is an author who discusses business integrity. He was writing of standards widely accepted. What were the standards of half a century later? In the Second World War fleets of aircraft on both sides set out loaded with bombs for the purpose of devastation and incendiaries for the purpose of burning. And their targets were not as a rule their foes in arms and uniform but the civil populations of cities, including the women and children. Towns were pulverized by bombs because troops lacked the leadership to take them by manoeuvre, sometimes when in fact they were not occupied by hostile troops. The mass slaughter ordered by Hitler, Stalin's deliberate and cold-blooded shooting of a large proportion of the Polish officers in his hands and the most distinguished civilians in all walks of life, were revivals of practices which could not be paralleled for centuries in the annals of warfare between civilized nations.

These last were the savageries of inhumanly savage men. It must not be concluded that all those who permitted and organized the measures of warfare were barbarous by nature. They fought with the weapons which science and industry had put into their hands. Some, even of the most senior air force commanders, had qualms about the policy, notably the Americans, General Henry H. Arnold, Commanding General Army Air Forces, and General Carl Spaatz, Commanding General U.S. Army Air Forces in Europe. "All proposals frankly aimed at breaking the morale of the German people met the consistent opposition of General Spaatz, who repeatedly raised the moral issue involved." How shameful that here American sentiment was humanitarian, and British barbarian! It is beside the point that Spaatz did not protest against "terror" bombing by the British allies of the United States but against being drawn into it himself, and that the Americans had an aircraft suitable for bombing by daylight, whereas the British had not, so that they could only bomb indiscriminately or not at all.

At the moment these words are written the national Red Cross Societies are celebrating the centenary of the Battle of Solferino in 1859 because it was here that the Swiss Henri Dunant, appalled by the break-down of the medical services and the sufferings of the wounded, first conceived the idea of an international organization to canalize war and mitigate its horrors. The celebrations of the International Committee of the Red Cross, which has its seat at Geneva, await the centenary of its actual foundation in 1864. The occasion may be one to justify pride in magnificent work achieved, but it has a melancholy and deeply alarming side. It is the International Red Cross which has from the first worked out schemes to humanize war, to purge it of needless cruelty, to protect civilians and above all women and children, and has presented to Governments detailed and practical schemes, which it has then invited them to sign. The first half-century was heartening; the second has been disappointing. Disregard of their undertakings has been widespread on the part of the most highly civilized states. Unwillingness to undertake fresh obligations has been equally general. When conferences of experts meet to lay the foundations of new conventions, international lawyers, especially those who represent or are citizens of the great powers—men of the highest integrity and the purest philanthropy—intervene to point out that such and such a proposal to protect at least a proportion of those endangered by the abominable weapons is not worth putting forward because it is wholly impracticable. The International Committee can maintain its noble work in relief of suffering as the result of war, in its inspections of the quarters of prisoners of war and concentration camps, where its recommendations are generally carried out. In its greater-scale tasks it is subject to unceasing frustration.

Yet, let it be repeated, governments have seldom acted with conscious brutality, unless when in the hands of savage autocrats such as Hitler and Stalin. They have been borne along upon the social, industrial, and scientific tide. A major war has now come to involve in principle one "waged by means of all the man-power, all the energies, and all the material and moral resources of the state, and directed in 'totality' against the hostile state. It is all-in warfare, nothing being held back by the state which practices it and no objective being avoided, so long as attack upon it may damage the enemy." Where it falls short in practice of this concept the reason has not been doubt of the principle's validity. It has been due to the influence of convenience or to inability to reach the standard, occasionally to the force of public opinion. Since, wholly in theory and in the Second World War nearly in practice, war is directed against nations as such, against their industries which provide the means of war as much as the men in uniform who use these means, it follows that the conception of illegitimate objectives or targets ceases to have any significance. British policy in the Second World War was to break the spirit of the German people by indiscriminate bombing, and the Air Ministry's object was "the elimination of the Reich's fifty largest cities."

The restrictions imposed at home are a natural corollary to this state of affairs. If every hostile activity is to be the object of attack, no home activity can be allowed to go to waste. Finance and agriculture must be organized as thoroughly as industry. Private property must lose its rights. Food consumption must be rationed till it scarcely exceeds the minimum needed for subsistence and enough strength to work for the war effort. These measures are not in themselves shocking, but when in the cause of security laws which have been regarded as among the finest of our heritages are abrogated, when people languish in prison without trial and even without a charge, they become yet another threat to civilization. The bad example is too easily and too often copied in other circumstances when the excuses of danger and fear are absent. The whole system of restrictions has indeed the further disadvantage that it opens the eyes of left-wingers of the autocratic type to opportunities which would not otherwise have become available to them and which they would not otherwise even have perceived. It shows them how to get their hands on banking, industry, trade, communications, transport, the land, in fact upon the State as a whole. They are of course prepared to use a share of the spoils in special subsidies to those most likely to vote for them, for instance, those who rent houses rather than those who have saved up to buy them. This poses the prospect not merely of the Socialist State but, in the long run, of the Marxist-Communist State. A far tougher organization will find its material ready-made and in due time walk in to take possession.

The supreme examples of the methods of total war are to be found, as might be expected, in the Second World War. They are the bombing of London and Berlin, the German attack on England with the flying bomb and rocket bomb (V1 and V2), and the dropping of two atomic bombs on Hiroshima and Nagasaki. They are the supreme examples because the attacks were delivered against non-combatants and as measures of blind destruction. By comparison with the other targets London came off lightly in 1940 and 1941 only because the German Air Force was not adequately designed for strategic bombing. The long-range weapons of 1944 missed their intended effect only because their development had been interrupted by attacks on their experimental station at Peenemünde and on their launching sites, so that they had to be used too early. The lengthy bombardment of Berlin laid practically the whole city in ruins. It was the British night bombing that did most of the damage, and in this case virtually the only objective was Berlin itself. The aim was to get the bombers over the city and then shovel out the bombs as fast as possible. Great pride was expressed in the "block-busters" because a single one of them was supposed to be capable of demolishing a whole block. The atom bombs did far more. Two bombs caused destruction such as the world had never witnessed. Here the aim was to break the will of Government and people without having to fight the Japanese Army. . . .

7   The Garrison State

Harold D. Lasswell

*Harold Lasswell is concerned not with a definition of total war but,
rather, about the impact on modern society of pressures leading to the
institutionalization of armed conflict. In its blunt description of the
emergence of the "specialists on violence" as the most powerful group in
society, aided and abetted by a scientific-technological elite, "The
Garrison State" amounts to a sociological version of George Orwell's
1984. And, although Lasswell wrote this classic essay in 1940, his
"garrison state" shares many characteristics with the more extreme
descriptions of the contemporary "military-industrial complex."*

The purpose of this article is to consider the possibility that we are moving
toward a world of "garrison states"—a world in which the specialists on violence
are the most powerful group in society. From this point of view the trend of our
time is away from the dominance of the specialist on bargaining, who is the
businessman, and toward the supremacy of the soldier. We may distinguish
transitional forms, such as the party propaganda state, where the dominant
figure is the propagandist, and the party bureaucratic state, in which the
organization men of the party make the vital decisions. There are mixed forms in
which predominance is shared by the monopolists of party and market power.

All men are deeply affected by their expectations as well as by their desires.
We time our specific wants and efforts with some regard to what we reasonably
hope to get. Hence, when we act rationally, we consider alternative versions of
the future, making explicit those expectations about the future that are so often
buried in the realm of hunch.

In the practice of social science, as of any skill in society, we are bound to
be affected in some degree by our conceptions of future development. There are
problems of timing in the prosecution of scientific work, timing in regard to
availability of data and considerations of policy. In a world where primitive
societies are melting away it is rational to act promptly to gather data about
primitive forms of social organization. In a world in which the scientist may also
be a democratic citizen, sharing democratic respect for human personality, it is
rational for the scientist to give priority to problems connected with the survival
of democratic society. There is no question here of a scientist deriving his values
from science; values are *acquired* chiefly from personal experience of a given
culture, *derived* from that branch of culture that is philosophy and theology,
implemented by science and practice.

From "The Garrison State" by Harold Lasswell, **The American Journal of Sociology**, XLVI
(January 1941), pp. 455–68. Copyright 1941 by University of Chicago Press. Reprinted by permission of University of Chicago Press.

The picture of the garrison state that is offered here is no dogmatic forecast. Rather it is a picture of the probable. It is not inevitable. It may not even have the same probability as some other descriptions of the future course of development. What, then, is the function of this picture for scientists? It is to stimulate the individual specialist to clarify for himself his expectations about the future, as a guide to the timing of scientific work. Side by side with this "construct" of a garrison state there may be other constructs; the rational person will assign exponents of probability to every alternative picture.

Expectations about the future may rest upon the extrapolation of past trends into the future. We may choose a number of specific items—like population and production curves—and draw them into the future according to some stated rule. This is an "itemistic" procedure. In contrast, we may set up a construct that is frankly imaginative though disciplined by careful consideration of the past. Since trend curves summarize many features of the past, they must be carefully considered in the preparation of every construct. Correlation analysis of trend curves, coupled with the results of experiment, may provide us with partial confirmation of many propositions about social change; these results, too, must be reviewed. In addition to these disciplined battalions of data there is the total exposure of the individual to the immediate and the recorded past, and this total exposure may stimulate productive insight into the structure of the whole manifold of events which includes the future as well as the past. In the interest of correct orientation in the world of events, one does not wisely discard all save codified experience. (The pictures of the future that are set up on more than "item" basis may be termed "total.")

To speak of a garrison state is not to predict something wholly new under the sun. Certainly there is nothing novel to the student of political institutions about the idea that specialists on violence may run the state. On the contrary, some of the most influential discussions of political institutions have named the military state as one of the chief forms of organized society. Comte saw history as a succession (and a progression) that moved, as far as it concerned the state, through military, feudal, and industrial phases. Spencer divided all human societies into the military type, based on force, and the industrial type, based on contract and free consent.

What is important for our purposes is to envisage the possible emergence of the military state under present technical conditions. There are no examples of the military state combined with modern technology. During emergencies the great powers have given enormous scope to military authority, but temporary acquisitions of authority lack the elements of comparative permanence and acceptance that complete the garrison state. Military dictators in states marginal to the creative centers of Western civilization are not integrated with modern technology; they merely use some of its specific elements.

The military men who dominate a modern technical society will be very different from the officers of history and tradition. It is probable that the specialists on violence will include in their training a large degree of expertness in many of the skills that we have traditionally accepted as part of modern civilian management.

The distinctive frame of reference in a fighting society is fighting effectiveness. All social change is translated into battle potential. Now there can be no realistic calculation of fighting effectiveness without knowledge of the technical and psychological characteristics of modern production processes. The function of management in such a society is already known to us; it includes the exercise of skill in supervising technical operations, in administrative organization, in personnel management, in public relations. These skills are needed to translate the complicated operations of modern life into every relevant frame of reference—the frame of fighting effectiveness as well as of pecuniary profit.

This leads to the seeming paradox that, as modern states are militarized, specialists on violence are more preoccupied with the skills and attitudes judged characteristic of nonviolence. We anticipate the merging of skills, starting from the traditional accouterments of the professional soldier, moving toward the manager and promoter of large-scale civilian enterprise.

In the garrison state, at least in its introductory phases, problems of morale are destined to weigh heavily on the mind of management. It is easy to throw sand in the gears of the modern assembly line; hence, there must be a deep and general sense of participation in the total enterprise of the state if collective effort is to be sustained. When we call attention to the importance of the "human factor" in modern production, we sometimes fail to notice that it springs from the multiplicity of special environments that have been created by modern technology. Thousands of technical operations have sprung into existence where a few hundred were found before. To complicate the material environment in this way is to multiply the foci of attention of those who live in our society. Diversified foci of attention breed differences in outlook, preference, and loyalty. The labyrinth of specialized "material" environments generates profound ideological divergencies that cannot be abolished, though they can be mitigated, by the methods now available to leaders in our society. As long as modern technology prevails, society is honeycombed with cells of separate experience, of individuality, of partial freedom. Concerted action under such conditions depends upon skilfully guiding the minds of men; hence the enormous importance of symbolic manipulation in modern society.

The importance of the morale factor is emphasized by the universal fear which it is possible to maintain in large populations through modern instruments of warfare. The growth of aerial warfare in particular has tended to abolish the distinction between civilian and military functions. It is no longer possible to affirm that those who enter the military service take the physical risk while those who remain at home stay safe and contribute to the equipment and the comfort of the courageous heroes at the front. Indeed, in some periods of modern warfare, casualties among civilians may outnumber the casualties of the armed forces. With the socialization of danger as a permanent characteristic of modern violence the nation becomes one unified technical enterprise. Those who direct the violence operations are compelled to consider the entire gamut of problems that arise in living together under modern conditions.

There will be an energetic struggle to incorporate young and old into the destiny and mission of the state. It is probable that one form of this symbolic adjustment will be the abolition of "the unemployed." This stigmatizing symbol will be obsolete in the garrison state. It insults the dignity of millions, for it implies uselessness. This is so, whether the "unemployed" are given a "dole" or put on "relief" projects. Always there is the damaging stigma of superfluity. No doubt the garrison state will be distinguished by the psychological abolition of unemployment—"psychological" because this is chiefly a matter of redefining symbols.

In the garrison state there must be work—and the duty to work—for all. Since all work becomes public work, all who do not accept employment flout military discipline. For those who do not fit within the structure of the state there is but one alternative—to obey or die. Compulsion, therefore, is to be expected as a potent instrument for internal control of the garrison state.

The use of coercion can have an important effect upon many more people than it reaches directly; this is the propaganda component of any "propaganda of the deed." The spectacle of compulsory labor gangs in prisons or concentration camps is a negative means of conserving morale—negative since it arouses fear and guilt. Compulsory labor groups are suitable popular scapegoats in a military state. The duty to obey, to serve the state, to work—these are cardinal virtues in the garrison state. Unceasing emphasis upon duty is certain to arouse opposing tendencies within the personality structure of all who live under a garrison regime. Everyone must struggle to hold in check any tendencies, conscious or unconscious, to defy authority, to violate the code of work, to flout the incessant demand for sacrifice in the collective interest. From the earliest years youth will be trained to subdue—to disavow, to struggle against—any specific opposition to the ruling code of collective exactions.

The conscience imposes feelings of guilt and anxiety upon the individual whenever his impulses are aroused, ever so slightly, to break the code. When the coercive threat that sanctions the code of the military state is internalized in the consciences of youth, the spectacle of labor gangs is profoundly disturbing. A characteristic response is self-righteousness—quick justification of coercive punishment, tacit acceptance of the inference that all who are subject to coercion are guilty of antisocial conduct. To maintain suspended judgment, to absolve others in particular instances, is to give at least partial toleration to countermores tendencies within the self. Hence, the quick substitute responses—the self-righteous attitude, the deflection of attention. Indeed, a characteristic psychic pattern of the military state is the "startle pattern," which is carried over to the internal as well as to the external threat of danger. This startle pattern is overcome and stylized as alert, prompt, commanding adjustment to reality. This is expressed in the authoritative manner that dominates military style—in gesture, intonation, and idiom.

The chief targets of compulsory labor service will be unskilled manual workers, together with counterelite elements who have come under suspicion. The position of the unskilled in our society has been deteriorating, since the machine society has less and less use for unskilled manual labor. The coming of the machine was a skill revolution, a broadening of the role of the skilled and semiskilled components of society. As the value of labor declines in production, it also declines in warfare; hence, it will be treated with less consideration. (When unskilled workers are relied upon as fighters, they must, of course, share the ideological exultation of the community as a whole and receive a steady flow of respect from the social environment.) Still another factor darkens the forecast for the bottom layers of the population in the future garrison state. If recent advances in pharmacology continue, as we may anticipate, physical means of controlling response can replace symbolic methods. This refers to the use of drugs not only for temporary orgies of energy on the part of front-line fighters but in order to deaden the critical function of all who are not held in esteem by the ruling elite.

For the immediate future, however, ruling elites must continue to put their chief reliance upon propaganda as an instrument of morale. But the manipulation of symbols, even in conjunction with coercive instruments of violence, is not sufficient to accomplish all the purposes of a ruling group. We have already spoken of the socialization of danger, and this will bring about some equalitarian adjustments in the distribution of income for the purpose of conserving the will to fight and to produce.

In addition to the adjustment of symbols, goods, and violence, the political elite of the garrison state will find it necessary to make certain adaptations in the fundamental practices of the state. Decisions will be more dictatorial than democratic, and institutional practices long connected with modern democracy will disappear. Instead of elections to office or referendums on issues there will be government by plebiscite. Elections foster the formation and expression of public opinion, while plebiscites encourage only unanimous demonstrations of collective sentiment. Rival political parties will be suppressed, either by the monopolization of legality in one political party (more properly called a political "order") or by the abolition of all political parties. The ruling group will exercise a monopoly of opinion in public, thus abolishing the free communication of fact and interpretation. Legislatures will be done away with, and if a numerous consultative body is permitted at all it will operate as an assembly; that is, it will meet for a very short time each year and will be expected to ratify the decisions of the central leadership after speeches that are chiefly ceremonial in nature. Plebiscites and assemblies thus become part of the ceremonializing process in the military state.

As legislatures and elections go out of use, the practice of petition will play a more prominent role. Lawmaking will be in the hands of the supreme authority and his council; and, as long as the state survives, this agency will exert effective control ("authority" is the term for formal expectations, "control" is the actual distribution of effective power).

This means that instrumental democracy will be in abeyance, although the symbols of mystic "democracy" will doubtless continue. Instrumental democracy is found wherever authority and control are widely dispersed among the members of a state. Mystic "democracy" is not, strictly speaking, democracy at all, because it may be found where authority and control are highly concentrated yet where part of the established practice is to speak in the name of the people as a whole. Thus, any dictatorship may celebrate its "democracy" and speak with contempt of such "mechanical" devices as majority rule at elections or in legislatures.

What part of the social structure would be drawn upon in recruiting the political rulers of the garrison state? As we have seen, the process will not be by general election but by self-perpetuation through co-option. The foremost positions will be open to the officers corps, and the problem is to predict from what part of the social structure the officers will be recruited. Morale considerations justify a broad base of recruitment for ability rather than social standing. Although fighting effectiveness is a relatively impersonal test that favors ability over inherited status, the turnover in ruling families from generation to generation will probably be low. Any recurring crisis, however, will strengthen the tendency to favor ability. It seems clear that recruitment will be much more for bias and obedience than for objectivity and originality. Yet, as we shall presently see, modern machine society has introduced new factors in the military state—factors tending to strengthen objectivity and originality.

In the garrison state all organized social activity will be governmentalized; hence, the role of independent associations will disappear, with the exception of secret societies (specifically, there will be no organized economic, religious, or cultural life outside of the duly constituted agencies of government). Government will be highly centralized, though devolution may be practiced in order to mitigate "bureaucratism." There is so much outspoken resistance to bureaucratism in modern civilization that we may expect this attitude to carry over to the garrison state. Not only will the administrative structure be centralized, but at every level it will tend to integrate authority in a few hands. The leadership principle will be relied upon; responsibility as a rule will be focused upon individual "heads."

We have sketched some of the methods at the disposal of the ruling élites of the garrison state—the management of propaganda, violence, goods, practices. Let us consider the picture from a slightly different standpoint. How will various kinds of influence be distributed in the state? Power will be highly concentrated, as in any dictatorial regime. We have already suggested that there will be a strong tendency toward equalizing the distribution of safety throughout the community (that is, negative safety, the socialization of threat in modern war). In the interest of morale there will be some moderation of huge differences in individual income, flattening the pyramid at the top, bulging it out in the upper-middle and middle zones. In the garrison state the respect pyramid will probably resemble the income pyramid. (Those who are the targets of compulsory labor restrictions will be the principal recipients of negative respect and hence will occupy the bottom levels.) So great is the multiplicity of functions in modern processes of production that a simple scheme of military rank is flagrantly out of harmony with the facts. Even though a small number of ranks are retained in the military state, it will be recognized that the diversity of functions exercised by each rank is so great that the meaning of a specific classification will be obscure. Summarizing, the distribution of safety will be most uniform throughout the community; distribution of power will show the largest inequalities. The patterns of income and respect will fall between these two, showing a pronounced bulge in the upper-middle and middle strata. The lower strata of the community will be composed of those subject to compulsory labor, tending to constitute a permanent pariah caste.

What about the capacity of the garrison state to produce a large volume of material values? The élites of the garrison state, like the élites of recent business states, will confront the problem of holding in check the stupendous productive potentialities of modern science and engineering. We know that the ruling élites of the modern business state have not known how to control productive capacity; they have been unwilling to adopt necessary measures for the purpose of regularizing the tempo of economic development. Hence, modern society has been characterized by periods of orgiastic expansion, succeeded by periods of flagrant underutilization of the instruments of production.

The rulers of the garrison state will be able to regularize the rate of production, since they will be free from many of the conventions that have stood in the way of adopting measures suitable to this purpose in the business state. The business élite has been unwilling to revise institutional practices to the extent necessary to maintain a continually rising flow of investment. The institutional structure of the business state has called for flexible adjustment between governmental and private channels of activity and for strict measures to maintain price flexibility. Wherever the business élite has not supported such necessary arrangements, the business state itself has begun to disintegrate.

Although the rulers of the garrison state will be free to regularize the rate of production, they will most assuredly prevent full utilization of modern productive capacity for nonmilitary consumption purposes. The élite of the garrison state will have a professional interest in multiplying gadgets specialized to acts of violence. The rulers of the garrison state will depend upon war scares as a means of maintaining popular willingness to forego immediate consumption. War scares that fail to culminate in violence eventually lose their value; this is the point at which ruling classes will feel that bloodletting is needed in order to preserve those virtues of sturdy acquiescence in the regime which they so much admire and from which they so greatly benefit. We may be sure that if ever there is a rise in the production of nonmilitary consumption goods, despite the amount of energy directed toward the production of military equipment, the ruling class will feel itself endangered by the growing "frivolousness" of the community.

We need to consider the degree to which the volume of values produced in a garrison state will be affected by the tendency toward rigidity. Many factors in the garrison state justify the expectation that tendencies toward repetitiousness and ceremonialization will be prominent. To some extent this is a function of bureaucracy and dictatorship. But to some extent it springs also from the preoccupation of the military state with danger. Even where military operations are greatly respected, the fighter must steel himself against deep-lying tendencies to retreat from death and mutilation. One of the most rudimentary and potent means of relieving fear is some repetitive operation—some reiteration of the old and well-established. Hence the reliance on drill as a means of disciplining men to endure personal danger without giving in to fear of death. The tendency to repeat, as a means of diminishing timidity, is powerfully reinforced by successful repetition, since the individual is greatly attached to whatever has proved effective in maintaining self-control in previous trials. Even those who deny the fear of death to themselves may reveal the depth of their unconscious fear by their interest in ritual and ceremony. This is one of the subtlest ways by which the individual can keep his mind distracted from the discovery of his own timidity. It does not occur to the ceremonialist that in the spider web of ceremony he has found a moral equivalent of war—an unacknowledged substitute for personal danger.

The tendency to ceremonialize rather than to fight will be particularly prominent among the most influential elements in a garrison state. Those standing at the top of the military pyramid will doubtless occupy high positions in the income pyramid. During times of actual warfare it may be necessary to make concessions in the direction of moderating gross-income differences in the interest of preserving general morale. The prospect of such concessions may be expected to operate as a deterrent factor against war. A countervailing tendency, of course, is the threat to sluggish and well-established members of the upper crust from ambitious members of the lower officers' corps. This threat arises, too, when there are murmurs of disaffection with the established order of things on the part of broader components of the society.

It seems probable that the garrison state of the future will be far less rigid than the military states of antiquity. As long as modern technical society endures, there will be an enormous body of specialists whose focus of attention is entirely given over to the discovery of novel ways of utilizing nature. Above all, these are physical scientists and engineers. They are able to demonstrate by rather impersonal procedures the efficiency of many of their suggestions for the improvement of fighting effectiveness. We therefore anticipate further exploration of the technical potentialities of modern civilization within the general framework of the garrison state.

What are some of the implications of this picture for the research program of scientists who, in their capacity as citizens, desire to defend the dignity of human personality?

It is clear that the friend of democracy views the emergence of the garrison state with repugnance and apprehension. He will do whatever is within his power to defer it. Should the garrison state become unavoidable, however, the friend of democracy will seek to conserve as many values as possible within the general framework of the new society. What democratic values can be preserved, and how?

Our analysis has indicated that several elements in the pattern of the garrison state are compatible with democratic respect for human dignity. Thus, there will be some socialization of respect for all who participate in the garrison society (with the ever present exception of the lowest strata).

Will the human costs of a garrison state be reduced if we civilianize the ruling élite? Just how is it possible to promote the fusion of military and civilian skills? What are some of the devices capable of overcoming bureaucratism? To what extent is it possible to aid or to retard the ceremonializing tendencies of the garrison state?

It is plain that we need more adequate data from the past on each of these problems and that it is possible to plan to collect relevant data in the future. We need, for instance, to be better informed about the trends in the skill pattern of dominant élite groups in different parts of the world. In addition to trend data we need experimental and case data about successful and unsuccessful civilianizing of specialists on violence.

Many interesting questions arise in connection with the present sketch about transition to the garrison state. What is the probable order of appearance—Japan, Germany, Russia, United States of America? What are the probable combinations of bargaining, propaganda, organization, and violence skills in élites? Is it probable that the garrison state will appear with or without violent revolution? Will the garrison state appear first in a small number of huge Continental states (Russia, Germany, Japan [in China], United States) or in a single world-state dominated by one of these powers? With what symbol patterns will the transition to the garrison state be associated? At the present time there are four important ideological patterns.

FOUR WORLD-SYMBOL PATTERNS

In the Name of	*Certain Demands and Expectations are Affirmed*
1. National democracy (Britain, United States)	Universalize a federation of democratic free nations
2. National antiplutocracy (also antiproletarians) (Germany, Russia, Japan, Italy)	Universalize the "axis" of National Socialistic powers
3. World-proletariat (Russia)	Universalize Soviet Union, Communist International
4. True world-proletariat (no state at present)	New élite seizes revolutionary crisis to liquidate "Russian betrayers," all "National Socialisms" and "plutocratic democracies"

The function of any developmental construct, such as the present one about the garrison state, is to clarify to the specialist the possible relevance of his research to impending events that concern the values of which he approves as a citizen. Although they are neither scientific laws nor dogmatic forecasts, developmental constructs aid in the timing of scientific work, stimulating both planned observation of the future and renewed interest in whatever past events are of greatest probable pertinence to the emerging future. Within the general structure of the science of society there is place for many special sciences devoted to the study of all factors that condition the survival of selected values.

This is the sense in which there can be a science of democracy, or a science of political psychiatry, within the framework of social science. If the garrison state is probable, the timing of special research is urgent.

Unit III

The Sort of War It Was

Was the Second World War different from previous wars? Perhaps not in the important ways. Men tried to kill other men. Some succeeded; some did not and were themselves slain. Obviously, the techniques of killing changed, even though death remained the universal constant.

Those who have written about World War II as the first total war do stress certain significant differences. In particular, this conflict stimulated feelings of alienation. One may observe that the act of killing always sets a man apart, but the mechanisms adopted in World War II seemed to intensify in this first post-Freud generation a pervasive sense of alienation. The bombs dropped from 20,000 feet, the silently running torpedoes, the tank shells thudding against the steel carcass of another tank all served to separate the act of killing from the reality of death. Such events also underscored a related phenomenon of the war—its seeming impersonality. The conflict was played out on such a gigantic scale that the individual was dwarfed. Whether he was a foot soldier, a fighter pilot, or a mess cook, he functioned as a small cog in a tremendous machine, the magnitude and purposes of which were beyond his comprehension.

World War II was also characterized by the powerful irony and tragic consequences of anachronism. There was the absurdity of Polish cavalry charging German tanks; of Ethiopian tribesmen with wooden spears dueling Italian machine guns. Fifteenth-century Agincourt had witnessed a similar spectacle when French lancers faced the English longbow, but its incongruity was somehow not as great. Anachronism also dominated the techniques of warfare: the partisan actions in Russia, frogmen clearing invasion beaches, the *kamikaze* attacks. Whether or not these contradictions caused this conflict to be different, they confirmed that World War II shared with all wars the requirement of human sacrifice.

In the last analysis, war is a matter of some universal and many unique effects on the bodies and minds of individual beings, and those who experience the effects usually forget or misconstrue their meaning. With a few brilliant exceptions, only novelists and reporters have succeeded in capturing the flavor and immediacy of combat in the Second World War. Such attempts to impose an order on the chaos of that experience are inevitably distorted portrayals of war's reality; however, they do provide us insights and images otherwise available only to those who can draw upon deeply felt personal experiences.

Documents

1 THE THOUSAND HOUR DAY

W.S. Kuniczak

W.S. Kuniczak's The Thousand Hour Day *is a panoramic novel about the first weeks of Poland's futile struggle against the German and Russian invaders. It is not one of the great novels of the Second World War, but its theme and Kuniczak's exposition of the Polish army's absurdly courageous resistance make it valuable and memorable reading.*

He did not look at the brown coils of barbedwire in front of him, the yellow line of trench. He had the feeling, a complete assurance, that if he looked at them a bullet would strike him in the face.

There were many bullets. They sounded like wind whistling through the shrouds of a sailing ship: one of those tallmasted memories out of the past that sailors were trained on. In all the glittering navies of the world.

I have never seen a real sailing ship, Gzyms thought. Or any kind of ship. Or anything redolent of adventure and distant places. But I can imagine.

This whistling started suddenly when he and all the others came out from under the protecting canopy of trees and crossed the first of the fields, which, grey and billowing, were themselves like a sea trembling in the heat. Somewhere ahead an idiotboy had lit a string of Chinese firecrackers and the earth shook under the drumming of five thousand hooves and he cantered at the regulation pace in the regulation manner, both hands on the reins and saber at right shoulder, back straight, knees tight, with the wind rattling through the lancepennons and whipping the manes of horses. He didn't look ahead towards the wire and the trench and the nearing source of the whistling bullets but only to the right and to the left at the interminable line of men and horses which surged irregularly like a black and silver tide out of the woods. Other waves came behind it, black and silvertipped. It looked as though the woods had moved and

From **The Thousand Hour Day** by W. S. Kuniczak, pp. 208–14, 222–27. Copyright © 1966 by W. S. Kuniczak. Reprinted by permission of the author's agent, Max Gartenberg.

the trees had torn their patient roots out of the earth and were now running out into the fields waving their yellow branches. The fields filled with them from one horizon to the other. Before them was the wire and the trench; many lines of wire and staked-in logs and the black hulls of burned-out armoredcars and tattered flat dolls thrown about the shellholes, and through the gaps in the brown coils of wire came small men bowed under mortars and machineguns who now stopped and began to shout and point at the men and horses boiling out of the woods and across the fields, and who ran and were turned back and put down their machineguns and lay down and pointed rifles at the black mass that rolled towards them and who began to shoot. Smoke moved like a fat, lazy snake above some village in the west.

Gzyms thought about his mother. She knew Napoleonic history. She told him once about the knees of Marshal Murat. They had a way of shaking before every charge. They shook so hard the marshal's feet fell out of his stirrups.—*Let them shake,* the marshal said about his knees. *If they knew what was waiting for them they'd run away and leave me.*

Gzyms looked at his own knees and they too were shaking.

—Let them shake, he said.

We are all nervous. There to the right is Lenski: pale, with a cigarette glued to his lip. The cigarette is dead. There Captain Prus with his torn sleeve flapping like a wing, swaying in the saddle. Up front the colonel with his whitegloved hand hanging down beside him like a sheathed weapon. Ahead of him dust and the smoke and the little men who lay down and knelt and pointed rifles and machineguns. They had machineguns in the gaps in the brown coils of wire. The earth shook and the wire came nearer and Gzyms felt (giggling, feeling foolish) that he was motionless and his mare a statue and that it was the wire and the machineguns and the shooting men who flowed persistently towards him on some mechanical device. And suddenly the whistling shells were gone and then a different sounding shell arrived. (Coming our way, he thought.) Earth fountained up behind him. This was a German shell. He wanted to kick his mare with spurs and send her flying through the field and right, towards the river, to escape the shells, but this was not what the colonel had ordered. The colonel had been quite specific about how he wanted this charge to be made. They—the men and the horses—were to ride at a canter to the first line of wire and then a signal would be given. There was a reason why this charge had to go this way and not another, the colonel had said. He didn't give the reason. But it was probably (Gzyms thought, giggling, watching his feet leap about in the stirrups and his knees shaking) a military reason. He wondered if it was perhaps as Lenski had said: that there was no reason and that the colonel only wished to do it this way because this was the way cavalry used to do it and it was now the last chance he would have of doing it that way. It could be that but he didn't think so. And now the shells came quickly. The field shrank and the wire came near. Earth, logs, sandbags and men flew up like strips of paper and burst in the air. His eyes were full of running water: Small dots and circles moved in them lazily like raindrops running down a pane of glass. Through this wet mist he saw the lines spread out in open order, two long ranks, the colonel ahead with his whitegloved hand going up suddenly like a flagstaff, the flash of sun on lifted trumpets.

My God.

The first three bars of the National Anthem.

Poland Still Lives!

My God.

He could see nothing then. He felt as though this sound had fallen from the sky. It was like fire. It cut into his back. He felt the tears running down his face. Beside him Lenski screamed like a wounded animal: —Form! Form! although everyone was formed. He too began to shout in this highpitched voice of an animal in pain. The lancers shook their weapons and shouted: —Kill! Kill! Hurra-a-a-ah! and the horses, wildeyed like the men and splashing flakes of foam, stood up on their hind legs and beat the air with their hooves.

Was this the colonel's signal? If so it was a devilishly clever one, reaching back to pull the trigger of centuries. It was all there in this music: sabers and lances and trumpets and a thousand battlefields; and the enemy could be anyone: Swedes, Turks, Teutonic Knights, Tartars, anyone.

His face burned. He was burning up. He thought that shortly he would become black and fall apart like a seared timberbeam. He felt his mouth burst like a rotten blister. Heat, fire, blindness.

He shouted orders that no one heard or understood or cared about. Everybody shouted. And the terrible trumpets went on.

When the anthem ended the trumpeters did not lift their brass horns from their lips, did not break off their invocation but picked up the last recognizable note and cracked it and repeated it over and over like the maddened drumming of a fugitive's fist on sanctuary doors: the rasping, monotonous summons of the general charge that was like ice on fevered skin and beat upon the brain and drove spurs into horses' flanks by reflex.

Charge!

He struck his mare with spurs. Felt them sink in.

Ta-ta-ta-ta-ta-ta-ta-taa-a-a-a . . .

Charge!

(Shells explode but you do not hear them.)

Strike! Kill!

(Men vanish under hooves but you do not see them.)

Charge!

Kill!

Jezu! and foul obscenities.

A sound like an avalanche began behind him: hooves and the howl of fourteen hundred men. It drowned the crash of shells so that the leaping feather plumes of earth were robbed of their identity and no longer meant danger, destruction, death or anything. There was only madness: the terribly urgent *now* of it. Earth leaped towards the sky because it wanted to. The good grey earth had had enough of men and rose toward the sky to get away from them.

Shells, shouts, hooves and the tap-tap-tapping of machineguns became one great sound without any meaning.

The horses went insane; the men were already mad.

Earth flew backwards under them. Grey forms fell under the hooves and rolled away like rags pitched from a peddler's cart.

And then the wire.

Like a brown wall smeared with thorns.

Gzyms looked for some way through it and couldn't see one. The hair rose under his cap and he closed his eyes and felt the mare gather herself and leap and soar and land and stagger in recovery and gallop on.

More wires spread before him. This time a triple apron at staggered intervals. The Germans would not have had time to put that up. It was the remnant of some lost position of a lost Polish rearguard. No horse could take that.

He pulled the mare's head to the right, saw a gap in the wire behind him, and thought: There must be more! There must be! and with each word he spurred his bloodysided mare without knowing it. His hands were bloody. Blood had splashed thickly on the mare's neck. He heard the animal's whistling breath.

He wanted to stop and turn back but there were many other hooves behind him and these drove him on. Less than half the squadron had followed him across the wire. Now they galloped down the corridor between the first and second rows of it. Others had dismounted and hacked at stakes and wire with their sabers. He saw men fly out of their saddles as the bullets hit them. He saw mouths open in terror and hands grasping air.

—Left! Left! he shouted and turned his mare that way. The horsemen followed him. Why left and not right or straight ahead or, for that matter, down into the ground or up into the sky? He only knew that he had to go *somewhere* and take the riders with him because to stay in the barbedwire corridor was death, because to move meant life. And then suddenly he saw Lenski in the smoke and felt glad because Lenski would know what to do and where to go, being so professional. He was surprised to see the galloping lieutenant. Lenski had been out on the right when the charge began but now he was in front and riding towards them from the left. His face was as red as a poppyfield and his head was strangely flattened as though his hat had fallen down below his ears and for a moment Gzyms wondered (giggling stupidly) whether the lieutenant had pulled his head down into his collar like a turtle. The thought made him want to laugh terribly hard (because the lieutenant was so *damn* professional about postures and bearing and rules and regulations) and he opened his mouth to shout to the red lieutenant something about flat heads and turtles and, instead, sat with his mouth open, saying nothing. Lieutenant Lenski galloped past him and he saw that the top of the lieutenant's head had been sheared off by the flying sickle of machinegunbullets and now a long red stream trailed behind him like the unwinding coil of a scarlet turban and the lieutenant was shouting something in a terribly high voice and Gzyms didn't understand a word of it. (But he thought: Has he captured any more machineguns? Is he satisfied?) And then new smoke boiled up under the hooves of the lieutenant's horse and man and horse vanished into it and Gzyms could not stop thinking about redfaced turtles but he no longer felt like laughing. His mare flew more than ran through the corridor of wire and it was she not he who found the first green gap in the brown wirewall. The mare took Gzyms into the gap where several hundred men and horses were galloping through. The horses ran into each other and into the wire and kicked each other and bit and screamed and became entangled and tore themselves free and galloped through the smoke into the open field beyond the wire with their red entrails like hobbles on their legs and everywhere soldiers were jumping off their horses to pry the animals loose off the wire and died under their hooves and other soldiers tried to make their way into the open field on foot, abandoning their horses, and riderless horses ran into them and fell on them and crushed them or kicked them into wire, but many more soldiers rode into the gap and through it and more and more of them burst out into the field where the machineguns worked so close to them that they could see the terror in the gunners' eyes. Men fell like puppets off their horses and either hit the ground and did not move or hung suspended in the stirrup by one leg and the horses dragged them off among the strands of wire that reached for them like hungry tentacles and scraped the riders away that way. Sometimes the riders fell directly into wire and sprawled upon it as though tired, sleeping and finally at rest. Plato or somebody had said something about that: how wars were over only for the dead and that the dead were fortunate because of it. Gzyms could no longer hear or think and he wished that he could no longer see.

He wanted this to stop.

The cries of men and the cries of horses and the wildwind whistling of the bullets.

Shells and their orange glow.

Supplications, prayers.

Obscenities: foulness heaped upon desperate foulness.

All of it was a blasphemy.

And it had gone on too long. Surely everybody would agree it was time to call an end to it.

He wanted to ride up to the German gunners and say to them: Look, this is quite enough; we all know—you and I—that it's time to stop; we've had too much of this and so have you, no matter what the trumpets said. And he wanted to shout to the German gunners that he was coming and that they were not to shoot at him because he had something to say to them which was important, which would make it unnecessary for anyone to die. But he forgot the German word for what he wished to say.

If I can only remember the word, he thought.

What is it?

Wait.

Don't shoot.

I'm thinking of the word.

But the only German words which he could remember were the one for mother and the one for God and a blasphemous obscenity.

And then the terrible brown coils and the smoke were behind him, he was in the clear before the machineguns.

Perhaps two dozen men were left of the squadron, but to the right and left of them (where, he thought, there must have been many other gaps in the terrible brown wire) several hundred other men appeared, on foot and on horseback, hurrying towards the Germans. The men and horses were exhausted, he could see that. Their mouths were open as though every animal and man had been suddenly struck down by hideous slackjawed idiocy but their teeth were clenched. Their eyes swam in their heads like the eyes of drunkards.

Gzyms looked for officers. He could see none and thought that they were all dead and did not feel sorrow, and then he saw that no officers were needed: The men formed to charge without command of officers, led by each other in a strange, sleepy slowmotion charge, and he saw (surprised) that he was not a comfortable spectator standing to the side but very much part of the performance, erect in stirrups with his saber high.

The Germans had put up their machineguns in a hurry. It would have been like that everywhere along the line of the attack: a sudden fierce attack and the Germans unready. They had not dug enough emplacements in the fields; the guns were in the open. Around them lay companies of riflemen. The dreamlike, surrealistic charge of desperately tired men on tired horses rolled towards them like the last, faint reaching of a tide that was about to turn.

A hundred meters more.

Eighty meters.

A German officer got to his feet behind the gunners.

The German officer's mouth opened and he raised his arm.

Gzyms pulled back on the reins. The mare ran on.

There was no way to stop the horses anymore. The horses had taken over command from the men and set their own pace and could not be turned and it was then as though the animals had finally decided that they too were involved in the affairs of men and had finally declared their own war on men and had now their own will and their own dark purpose and their own desire to kill and to destroy as though man could no longer tell an animal anything.

Gzyms knew that in a moment all of them would be beaten down by bullets: They were riding headfirst into a wall of iron which would rise up before them when the German officer's arm finally fell and this wall would fall on them and crush them and erase them and he searched his mind for some secret means by which the German's arm could be permanently frozen in the air or by which the interval of time between the German's first and second commands could be compressed so that what was about to happen would come quickly and be quickly over and he, Gzyms, and the rest of them, all the animals and men, would be through it and finished with it and, one way or another, no longer concerned.

He saw the German's hand go down and he heard the sound and saw the smoke that suddenly unfolded between the horsemen and the German gunners, and he bent over the mare's neck as though to hide behind it. Someone tapped him gently enough on the shoulder and someone else gave him an admonitory slap below the knee and someone else laid a hot, restraining hand upon his chest as though to push him back in line with all the others, and he thought: What is this? Wait now, what is this about? Why are you slapping me? I have done nothing.

And then he himself was inside the smoke and saw the dirty, sunburned faces of the Germans looking up at him, and their hands were raised and empty and weaponless and their eyes were wide, and he swung down once and terribly and felt the saber land on something that was neither soft nor hard but a blend of both, and he felt his hand tremble as the saber turned upon bone and then he pulled the saber up and forward in the regulation manner and he was past the Germans.

His mare took him straight to the machineguns. There were, he saw (with a strange new feeling of unconcern, a total lack of interest), seven of them: three watercooled American heavy Brownings from the Skoda Works and four light German guns without tripods. They were set up in a straight line about ten meters apart. He found himself above the center gun. Three men were taking it apart. One had become entangled in the ammunition belts and kept falling down. They tried to get out from under the mare's hooves. The mare trod on the head of the entangled German and the head was flattened. Gzyms tried to lift his saber but it was terribly heavy and he couldn't lift it high enough and he wondered what was the matter with it, whether or not the man whom he had sabered was still on it, invisible on the end of it, and if so why he didn't slide off to make room for another. He let the saber drop towards the biggest German. The German shouted and swung the barrel of the watercooled machinegun and hit the mare between the eyes with it and the animal fell down on her knees with blood coming from her ears in enormous arcs. Gzyms' saber whistled through empty air. He watched it arc prettily in the sunlight . . . turning like a stone . . . round and wet, the way they are when you toss them back into a river on a day out in the country . . . happy day . . . hiking . . . eating on the grass . . . with a thousand small suns leaping off the blade before it hit the ground. And then he himself was in the air and flying and the ground came up quickly to meet him with a hot, red smile, and the ground was not hard but soft and warm and welcoming and comforting and it reached for him and enfolded him and soothed him and he died.

2   Three Russian Women

Quentin Reynolds

Next to Ernie Pyle—who occupies a special place in World War II journalism—Quentin Reynolds was probably the most widely read American correspondent of the war. Reynolds' assignments for Collier's *took him to every corner of the European theater of operations. The sympathetic sketch of three Russian women warriors is from* The Curtain Rises, *a compilation of his dispatches from Russia, North Africa, and the Italian front.*

In fiction, all heroines are slim and beautiful; their eyes are provocative and their hair is as soft as moonlight. It happens that way occasionally in real life, too, but now I speak of a heroine who is neither slim nor beautiful; her eyes are not provocative but, instead, are weary with the pain she has seen and suffered, and her hair is concealed under a shawl. She has no glamorous past and, as for her future, there is little chance of her surviving another year. This, then, is Uliana Alexandrovna Golubkovar, soldier of Russia.

At first glance, Uliana looks like almost any middle-aged peasant woman. She sits hunched over a little, the way women do who have spent too many years bending over the soil, coaxing it to yield wheat and corn and potatoes. Until she tells you, you don't know that she bends forward slightly because that eases the pain of a half-healed wound. Until she tells you that she is only thirty-three, you would indeed think of her as just another middle-aged peasant woman. And you might mistakenly think of her as stupid, until she tells of the time she was left for dead by the Germans, or of an agonizing escape she made, with death often within a few feet of her, or of Germans she and her group of guerrilla fighters had killed.

She was born in the village of Putivl, which is in the soft, lush region of the Ukraine. She had two young sisters, Alexandra and Maria. They were trained as nurses. Uliana herself was a brilliant student and fervent patriot. Her father was postmaster of the village, and he took great pride in the intellectual achievements of young Uliana. So did the rest of the village, for when the old mayor (who had held office for twenty years) died, they elected young Uliana in his place.

In Russia they do not call the head of a community mayor; they call him president of the local soviet; but it means the same thing. She was enrolled as a party member when she was twenty-four, a great honor in the Soviet Union, for there are only two million party members in the whole country. That is one percent of the population. There is a waiting list of more than a million.

As mayor, Uliana settled local disputes over land boundaries, she administered justice, and the village of Putivl was indeed a happy and contented community. And then the German juggernaut rolled through the smooth plains of the Ukraine. Many in the village quite sensibly left, but not Uliana. When the Germans roared into Putivl, Uliana was there, calm and serene, prepared to do her best to make life easier for her fellow villagers.

But the Germans gave her no chance. They took Uliana and some of the other leading citizens, led them to a near-by monastery, lined them up against a wall and shot them.

"There were eight of us," Uliana told me in a peculiarly detached voice, as though she were telling of something which had happened to someone else. "Three of us, two teachers and I, were women. They marched us to an old monastery. They told us to face the wall and to take off our clothes. By now, of course, I knew that we were going to be shot. The Germans usually make people they are going to shoot or hang take off all their clothes first. It saves them a lot of trouble afterward.

"I undressed slowly, and then the shots came. I still had my stockings and underwear on. Nobody cried out when the shots came. Then I felt something hit me in the side and I fell forward. Things became confused. I half remember being carried into the monastery and down a staircase, then I lost consciousness.

"When I came to, it was dark and there was a weight on me. When my mind began to work, I realized that there were bodies on top of me. Upstairs, soldiers were arguing about the clothes. I could hear them and then I heard someone groaning near me. It was one of the men, a doctor, and he was not dead, though the others were. He cried out to the Germans to come and finish him off, but they didn't hear him. I crawled over to him and said that we should try to get out. We were in the cellar of the monastery."

"How did you get out of there?" I asked.

"When the soldiers left," she continued, "I crawled up the stairs very slowly because my side hurt and I was losing a lot of blood. The doctor followed me. It was night now. We crawled to a farmhouse near by. I couldn't stand up to knock at the door. I lay there, trying to cry out and fearing that the Germans would hear me, but they didn't. The people in the farmhouse took us in. The doctor had a bad wound. He died that night.

"The following night they put me in a wagon, piled hay on top of me and sent me to a farmhouse a few miles away. Each night I would be transferred farther away from my village, farther away from the Germans. Then I reached an unoccupied town which had a hospital. The bullet had gone through my side and had injured my lung, and they didn't think I would live. I did, though, and then when I was better I decided to join the partisans. People in our villages always knew where they could be found."

"Were you expert with a gun?" I asked.

She smiled faintly. "I had never held a gun in my hands before, but I soon learned. We were usually behind the German lines. We kept in touch with the people of the occupied villages. Sometimes we raided these villages. There was a great shortage of salt in the Ukraine. I imagine the Germans sent it back to their country. Once we heard that they had a stock of salt in a certain village. We raided the village, took the salt and distributed it among the people of the neighboring villages. We were well armed, but food, of course, was a problem."

"How would you get food?" I asked her.

"They put me in charge of that," she said. "My wound was giving me trouble and I couldn't go on quick marches. I'd take a few men and lie in wait beside a road. When a convoy of German food trucks came along, we would ambush them and run the loaded trucks back to our headquarters. We shifted headquarters every few nights. We slept by day usually, and fought by night."

"What was the partisans' main job?"

She shrugged her shoulders. "Our main job was to blow up railroads and bridges. We blew up a lot of them, hindering the German advance. They decided to send a good force after us. We heard about it. They sent twenty tanks into the valley where we were, but we outflanked them and blew up five of them with hand grenades. Then we moved somewhere else. We were always on the move."

Uliana lived and fought with the partisans for nearly two years. She doesn't know yet what happened to her mother or to her two younger sisters. She would rather not think about that, she said. Why was she in Moscow? Uliana was a little ashamed of it. Her old wound had given her a lot of trouble, so she had been sent to specialists in the capital. But she would be back with the partisans soon, she said grimly, and then, rather surprisingly, she lost her placidity and became vibrant, alive, dynamic.

"Do your American women know the kinds of beasts we are fighting?" Her eyes flashed now and she no longer bent forward. She no longer looked like a middle-aged peasant woman. She was filled with a righteous hatred of the men who had invaded her country.

"Do they know that every time Germans occupy a village they hang or shoot a group of women just as a lesson to the others?" she said. "As a lesson to make others fall into line and obey them. Their motto is, 'Women and children first.' Yes, first hang the women and starve the children. Have American women ever seen the bodies of children who have starved to death? I have—in many villages of the Ukraine." Uliana breathed heavily and put her hand to her side. She got up and bowed, and there was a certain majesty about this stocky Russian who couldn't quite stand up straight. She walked out of the room.

Katia has chestnut hair that tumbles gaily over her forehead, and it is difficult to resist the impulse to run your hand through it. Katia has gray eyes that twinkle when she laughs, and she has even, white teeth and a dimple in her right cheek. She has a slim figure and soft hands, beautifully cared for. She is twenty-four but looks younger.

Katia wears the shining Order of the Red Star and the gold and crimson of it gleam against the dark blue of her uniform. She is a lieutenant and one of the best combat pilots in Russia. She has just returned from the Stalingrad front to receive another decoration. She has been in Moscow ten days and is very bored.

Moscow must seem dull to a pilot who has made 160 operational flights and downed six "certain" German aircraft and received credit for many "probables."

"It will be good to get back," Katia says, her gray eyes gleaming. "Moscow is nice, but it is no place for a fighter pilot to be. Once you've seen the ballet and heard the opera, what else is there to do in Moscow?"

"You might do this," I suggested. "You might tell me the story of how you became a pilot."

Katia was born on a farm near Vyazma in the village of Konoplianka. Her father died when she was very young, and her mother, with five daughters to bring up, had a difficult time. Katia began to work when she was eight. She did housework for a more prosperous family in the village. She had no time to play, no real girlhood, and it is doubtful whether she ever had any dreams. Her dismal future was too obvious. Fortune had destined her to be a household drudge.

Then came Stalin's first great innovation—the collective farm. That meant a great deal to small farmers. It meant a certain amount of security, for one thing.

Katia immediately went to work on a collective farm. Now life was better. She had friends of her own age with whom to talk and play, and she was allowed to attend school for the first time in her life.

Then one day Katia met her destiny. She was walking home from school and, looking up, she saw an airplane. It was the first plane she had ever seen. It circled lazily above her as though it were there for her special benefit. She stared, fascinated.

The pilot glided low, so that she could see the graceful outlines of the plane easily, and then he opened the throttle and roared away, leaving a singing heart below. Katia told herself that one day she, too, would fly an airplane. It was a fantastic ambition for a young girl in an obscure Russian village, but she nursed it, and henceforth everything she did was directed toward that one aim. By now, Katia's older sister, Olga, was working in a Moscow factory—an aircraft factory. Katia headed for the capital.

Her sister laughed when Katia told her of her ambition. Katia had it all planned. She would work in an aircraft factory and her work would be so outstanding that they would immediately send her to a flying school.

"Everyone here is a specialist," Olga told the dismayed Katia. "Everyone has been to a technical school to learn the use of precision instruments. You'll have to go to school before you can get work in an aircraft factory."

Katia went around to technical schools, but found that they had closed for the summer. Then she made the round of factories looking for any kind of job. When you apply for factory work as a pupil in Russia, you must fill out a formal application. Among other questions, you are asked, "What do you want to be?" Invariably Katia wrote down, "Pilot."

One personnel manager grew impatient. "This is a shoe factory," he said. "If you want to be a pilot, it's no place for you."

She went back again to her sister's factory. She pleaded for any kind of job at all. Her persistence was finally rewarded, and Katia was given a job as messenger between departments. Nothing mattered as long as she could hear the roar of engines of planes landing and taking off on the airport which was also part of the factory.

Katia was a good citizen. She became a Pioneer leader—Pioneers are much like our Boy and Girl Scout organizations. She loved children and she worked hard, all of it voluntary unpaid work. In addition, she became a member of the Komsomol (Young Communist League), and she attended night school. But always she kept sight of her main ambition.

At the factory airport, they taught young pilots to fly. Katia never stopped badgering the officials in charge to give her a chance and finally, again perhaps impressed by her persistence or maybe just tired out by it, they reluctantly allowed her to enroll in the school. She didn't mind the tedious months of ground instruction. Soon she would actually fly in a plane.

Then the day when she began her dual instruction finally arrived. She proved an apt pupil, and one spring afternoon when her instructor climbed out of the plane, he waved her back and said casually, "Take it up yourself. See what you can do."

"That was the greatest moment of my life," Katia says, her gray eyes shining. "I took it, and it obeyed me. It was wonderful to be high above Moscow in a plane that did everything you told it to do. I landed, and it was all right, but the instructor said, 'That landing was probably an accident. Take it up again.' And, thank goodness, my second landing was all right, too."

From then on, Katia did nothing but fly. She resented the hours of darkness when she couldn't fly and she became a good pilot, so good that within six months she was acting as an instructor. About this time, aviation clubs were springing up all over Russia. She was given a post as head instructor at one of these clubs. She turned out more than one hundred pilots, some of whom became her colleagues in her squadron at Stalingrad.

"Then one morning," Katia says, "I heard Molotov tell us on the radio that the Germans had invaded us and that we were in a state of war. I said to myself, 'Be calm. Be calm.' But it was hard to be calm. I knew now that I wanted to be a fighter pilot. How? I didn't know. But I would become one."

And, despite every difficulty, she did become a fighter pilot. She found the speedy Yak, the best of all Russian fighters, not much more difficult to fly than the sport planes she had been accustomed to. Gunnery was a little more difficult, but she soon mastered the ground targets, and finally the targets towed in the air by other planes. She was given her wings. Stalingrad was taking a bad beating in those days, and fighter pilots were urgently needed there to stop the German bombers. Katia, wearing her new dark-blue uniform and her new wings, was sent to the Stalingrad squadron.

"Men laughed at first," she said. "They thought it a joke, but not a very good joke. We usually fly in pairs, with each pilot looking after his partner. None of the men wanted to fly with me."

But discipline is discipline, and one of them had to accept her as a flying mate. They took off on a reconnaissance flight, and when they returned an hour later, her partner smiled and cried out, "Khorosho," which meant, "Okay." She had been accepted and henceforth she was one of them.

She got her taste of battle very soon. Alone, she came out of a cloud and was startled to see a full squadron of German bombers just below her. They were heading for Stalingrad. She really had no right to risk herself and her plane against twelve bombers, but if she didn't, these Germans might get to Stalingrad and drop those eggs. She dived, got a German in her sights and pressed the little red button. Smoke poured from the German plane in a lazy trail, and she zoomed above the squadron and into a friendly cloud. She thought she'd try it again. Apparently their fighter escort was very high. She banked and returned to attack.

This time she hit the leader, probably hit his gas tank, for the plane blew up in an orange ball of fire. She saw that the remaining German planes were dropping their bombs. They always did this when they anticipated an attack by a force of fighters. She saw bombs burst harmlessly in white flowers of smoke on the countryside below and then she thought it high time to be getting home.

She had her miraculous escapes as all pilots do. There was the time when she was attacked by two Messerschmitt 109Fs, an awfully good German fighter. She got one of them nicely, and then she and the remaining Messerschmitt, with the sky to themselves, fought for twenty-five minutes—a long time for a dogfight. Each tried to maneuver into good positions. Each cleverly averted and countered every offensive trick.

Finally Katia got him in her sights. She pressed the button—and nothing happened. She was out of ammunition. Well, she would try to make him think she still had ammunition. She circled and climbed and dived, and then he managed to get behind her, and she had a horrible moment when she realized that he was in a beautiful position. She dived. He followed, but the expected fusillade didn't come. Then she realized that he, too, had run out of ammunition.

"It was very silly," Katia says gravely. "There we were flying close to each other and neither of us could do anything about it."

Katia laughed. She had to go, really she did. She had an appointment—at the Kremlin. Rather shyly she confessed that. Yes, she was going to the Kremlin to be decorated again. She was to receive the second Order of the Red Star, and then she would be off to the front again.

Our third Russian woman isn't really a woman at all. She says she is nineteen. She looks fifteen. She seems far too small to carry the long name of Ekaterina Stepanovna Novikova about with her, so it seems quite natural to call her by her diminutive of Katiusha, which really means Kathie. Katiusha always wanted to be a parachutist. She did make one jump. It was from the roof of her parents' farmhouse in the Yaroslavl region, and her parachute was her mother's pet possession—a silk umbrella. The jump was not exactly a success. The umbrella caught on a shutter, and young Katiusha (she was eleven then) landed in very soft mud which injured nothing but her clothes and her feelings.

As a youngster, she never liked dolls, but she did like dogs. Katiusha was the freshest tomboy in the neighborhood and at a very early age she flatly declared her intention of becoming a member of the Red Army. "You're too short," they mocked, and that was true enough. At twelve, she was only a tiny thing with very short legs. She heard of some pills which would make her grow and somehow she managed to get a boxful of them. The instructions said to take one every day. Katiusha took ten at once, which sent her straight to the hospital.

Her parents moved to Moscow to find work in the factories, and Katiusha went to school. There were shooting clubs then in Russia, and Katiusha joined one. At least she would learn to shoot a rifle. She did learn to shoot a rifle, and when she was sixteen she learned to shoot a machine gun. Like any enthusiast, she wanted to spread her gospel, and one day the school authorities were horrified to hear shots in the schoolyard. They hurried out to find Katiusha teaching her young schoolmates how to handle a machine gun.

When war came, sixteen-year-old Katiusha tried hard to enlist. "We have enough men to shoot guns," they told her, "but we need people on the labor front."

She heard the magic word "front," and that was enough. She immediately enlisted in a labor battalion.

"I thought we were going right to the front," Katiusha wails now, "but it was quite different."

She was sent just outside of Moscow with thousands of others who were building trenches and gun sites. It was hard work even for sturdy little Katiusha who had been brought up on a farm. There was an anti-aircraft battery in the vicinity and she and others were given strict orders not to go near the battery. Anyone who broke the rule would be brought up before the commandant. As soon as she heard that, Katiusha's short legs carried her as quickly as possible to the forbidden zone. She was immediately hauled before the angry commandant.

"Why did you go into that section?" he asked.

"It was the only way I could think of to meet you, Tovarisch Commandant," Katiusha said humbly "I am a machine gunner. I want to go to the front."

"How old are you?" he asked, finding it hard to be stern.

"Nineteen," she lied gravely, and when he asked for her passport (all citizens carry passports for identification purposes) she handed him instead her certificates which told of her proficiency with a rifle and machine gun.

"We have plenty of machine gunners," the commandant told her, "but we do need nurses. Will you join us as a nurse?"

To get to the front, Katiusha would have joined anything. Luckily, she had studied nursing at school. A group of infantrymen were just leaving for the front. Katiusha went with them. Her baptism of fire came quickly. They had advanced only a few miles when they were dive-bombed and then strafed by low-flying German planes.

"I just stood there and shook my fist at the planes and yelled at them," Katiusha says. "How I wished I had a gun! All I had were bandages. I did what I could, but it was the first time I had ever seen blood, and it was pretty awful."

Closer to the front, disaster struck again. A group of German parachutists landed behind her detachment and cut them off. They had landed tanks, too, and for six days Katiusha's group held out. There was no question now of what she was to do. She crept out to where a machine gunner had been wounded. His hands still clenched the handles of the gun, but he was dead. Katiusha disengaged his fingers and took the gun in her own hands. Henceforth, she would never be anything but a machine gunner. This was at Belyi in the Smolensk region where fighting was exceptionally heavy.

"I knew the region well," Katiusha says, smiling, and when Katiusha smiles, she shows small white teeth and wide blue eyes. Katiusha has three big freckles on her stubby nose and these make her look even younger than she is.

She was often sent on reconnaissance because she knew the section so well. On one of these long forays she found a cool swimming hole. She used to visit it often, to bathe. One day she found a soldier preparing for a swim. She cried out, *"Zdorovya, tovarisch,"* or "Hello, pal," but his answer was in guttural German, and he went for his gun.

"I had dropped my gun," Katiusha says, frowning as though reproaching herself for her carelessness, "so I reached into my boot and pulled out my knife. I threw myself at him, and just before he got his gun, I stabbed him. He died immediately," Katiusha added grimly.

"Was he the first German you ever killed?" I asked the child.

"Oh, no," Katiusha said. "I had kept track. He was the sixty-seventh one I had killed."

At the front, it was kill or be killed, and killing became commonplace for this youngster. Twice she was wounded, and then a third time she was sent to a hospital with a shell splinter in her head. They found out that she was only seventeen. They told her sternly to go back to Moscow; they wanted no children here at the front.

She started for Moscow but made a detour to wind up with a guerrilla detachment near Sychevka. She spent five months with the guerrillas. During that time she killed, she says almost apologetically, only twelve Germans. Then she was sent to officers' school. The training was ridiculously easy after her practical experience and, within three months, she was made a lieutenant.

Since then, she has been at the front constantly. She received the Order of the Red Star and has another decoration coming up. She has seen the hardest fighting of the war and took part in the defense of Kharkov. The fighting was bitter on the western front when the Russians advanced.

Not long ago Katiusha and her group were given orders to capture a village. They entered it and had to capture house after house. Katiusha, with grenades in her belt, with a revolver at her side and with a Tommy gun in her hands, crashed into one house. She swept the room with her gun, killing two out of three Germans. The third, an officer, held up his hands.

"I walked close to him to get his gun," Katiusha says, "and then he noticed that I was a woman. He was enraged and he hit me on the side of my head. I went sprawling. Well, I was pretty mad, too, so I emptied a whole drum of bullets into him before he could raise his gun. That is seventy bullets. Have you seen *Lady Hamilton?*"

At the moment, the film *Lady Hamilton* was the most popular picture in Russia. Katiusha had just seen it. She would really rather talk of how beautiful

Vivien Leigh looked and how handsome Laurence Olivier was, than she would of the Germans she had killed. That was the commonplace part of everyday existence.

"I have seen *Lady Hamilton* three times," she said, and she looked like any schoolgirl now (except for her wound stripes and her decorations and her uniform). "And now I'm going to see it again. Then tomorrow"—she smiled happily—"I'm going back to the front."

These are three women of Russia I thought you might like to meet.

Moscow, June, 1943

3   The Epic of Stalingrad from Both Sides

The two selections that follow present contrasting views of the Nazi surrender at Stalingrad, a turning point of the war. The Soviet description is from The Epic Story of Stalingrad; *the German piece was published many years later in* Stalingrad, *a gripping narrative of the disaster from the German point of view. Both authors attempted to treat the end of this battle in human terms; thus, despite their ideological differences, the two accounts are, to a surprising extent, complementary.*

The Inglorious Finale of the Nazi Adventure*

by Roman Karmen

We flew to Stalingrad in a "U2" plane. The machine hedgehopped over fields and shell-holes where the greatest battle in the history of war had raged so short a time ago. In the summer the reek of petrol and blood had mingled on these broad plains with the pungent scent of the artemisia of the steppes. On the boundless white steppe where the earth so recently boiled with raging metal, we flitted past thousands of vehicles, guns, tanks, hundreds of planes standing in orderly rows on the aerodromes. Long trains loaded with arms and supplies were to be seen on the railway tracks. As we landed and transferred from the plane to a motor-car this wealth of booty became even more evident. At every corner, in every village, on railway stations and roads we came upon German equipment taken by our forces.

---

*"The Inglorious Finale of the Nazi Adventure" by Roman Karmen. From **The Epic Story of Stalingrad** by Soviet Army Correspondents (London: Hutchinson Publishing Group Ltd.) pp. 240–43. Reprinted by permission of Hutchinson Publishing Group Ltd.

We left Voroponovo and Sadovaya stations behind and entered the city from which the thunder of artillery and the unceasing chatter of machine-gun fire echoed in the frosty air.

The city was nearly cleared of the enemy. Only two nests remained where Germans were still offering futile resistance. Step by step, quarter by quarter, our troops were mopping up in Stalingrad, smoking the Germans out of the houses by artillery fire or digging them out at the point of the bayonet, and after each such drive hundreds and more hundreds of enemy soldiers would give themselves up.

The German prisoners were glad that in spite of the intentions of their commanders they were still alive. They were glad and they showed it. The liberated streets of the city were literally crowded with groups of German prisoners. They walked up to the Red Armymen and asked for food. They stepped over mounds of German bodies to join the great columns of prisoners who were being shepherded by special escort units.

A characteristic trifle: a field kitchen came up to the positions of one of the forward units with hot food. The Red Armymen began to eat. The Germans in their trenches got a whiff of cookhouse smell and scrambled out in a hurry. Within a few minutes, dozens of them surrendered here after shooting their officers who opposed their action.

The German officers had done their best to convince their men that surrender meant certain death, because the Russians killed all prisoners. The soldiers of the German armies surrounded in Stalingrad and now surrendering in their thousands, will have an opportunity of convincing themselves how grossly they have been deceived. Some prisoners begged our commanders to let them return and bring along their comrades. Such prisoners, who were allowed to go back, crawled through some crack in a wall, and in half an hour they returned beaming, and dragging behind them a tail of anything from thirty to fifty fellow-soldiers.

When a certain German infantry division surrendered, its officers stood in an isolated group apart from their soldiers. One of them, a tall *Ober-leutnant*, who managed even under the conditions existing in a surrounded army to preserve some remnants of aristocratic grooming, approached our major, saluted and asked his permission to ask a question.

"Herr Major," he said in broken Russian, "in the camp for prisoners of war will we be given blankets?"

The major clenched his fists. It cost him an effort to control himself.

"Yes, I think so," he said and turned away. The German saluted again and returned to his place.

Some days before this, that Red Army major and his unit had seized a German camp for Soviet prisoners of war. He had had to put his signature to a document describing the monstrous treatment, the inhuman torments to which our soldiers had been subjected in this camp. "Death Camp" was the name our men had given to this ghastly place. Here, in a large space hedged in with barbed wire, our prisoners had lived in the open, in burrows which they themselves had scooped out in the ground. Those of them who were found alive by our liberating troops looked hardly human. They were skeletons covered with skin. They were so feeble they could not even speak, much less move. Living men lay among those of their comrades who had perished as a result of such treatment. Our men captured a document which bears eloquent witness to the attitude of the Germans toward their prisoners of war. This document is the diary of the chief of the "sanitary services" of the camp. Daily entries show the number of men who perished from starvation, disease, ill-treatment or who had been simply shot. The first entries record a daily 20, 18, 22, 19 deaths; then the figures go up to 60, 58, 72 per day and finally to the terrible total of 120, 90, 118 deaths per day.

When they had recovered a bit, the surviving inmates of this camp described the conditions in it. All guards carried sticks. They beat the prisoners at the slightest provocation—for getting out of line in a queue at the distribution of the muddy water called "soup," for a loud word, for a slow movement. The beatings were merciless, bone-breaking. More often prisoners were just shot.

This was why it cost the major such an effort to control himself when he replied to the insolent German officer.

The city was reeling with the shock of artillery fire from guns of every calibre. A violent battle was developing in one quarter. Our troops had taken complete possession of two parks and the great square. Mopping-up operations were in progress in those streets in which small groups of Germans were offering a sporadic resistance.

In the liberated parts of the city the inhabitants immediately began to put in an appearance. I saw women digging in the ruins of their homes. I could hardly believe my eyes when in one of the streets piled with German dead I saw a child—a little girl about seven years old. She was helping her mother drag along their belongings on a little sled. The workers of the Stalingrad factories who in the darkest days took up arms as volunteers to defend their native city, will begin the reconstruction of their work-places in a few days' time.

While fighting is still continuing in the city, railway lines, junctions and stations are being repaired at a rapid rate. Soon, very soon, the military men will say farewell to Stalingrad. They are wanted on other fronts.

I saw a stirring sight: a group of air force men who had come to the end of their job here, were taking leave of the city. . . . They took off from their aerodromes on the outskirts, dozens of planes flying over the city towards the west. The last wave of dive-bombers formed a five-pointed star in the sky. The machines flew over the centre of the city, filling the air with the roar of their mighty engines.

The fighting in the streets was not ended even now. Street by street, quarter by quarter, our Stalingrad was cleared by the Red Army of the last Germans. . . .

In a sector occupied by troops under the command of General Tolbukhin, a group of German officers decided to surrender. In a uniform sparkling with the gold of decorations, a Hitlerite colonel walked slowly along the ruined street, stepping over the dead bodies of other Germans. After him came a few lieutenant-colonels, majors, captains, lieutenants and behind them a long column of soldiers, a straggling procession five hundred yards long, limping on frozen feet.

When one German colonel was told where the front line was at present, he opened his eyes wide. In their encirclement they had no idea of the situation at the front. Proof of this is that a small German detachment, pretending to be prisoners of war "escorted" by their own comrades dressed in Red Army uniforms, tried to leave the city in order to get through to their main forces at—Kalach!

Columns of our men go warily, in single file, to where they hear volleys of rifle fire or the chatter of tommy-guns, where the last nests of resistance of the surrounded German troops are being mopped up. "Get it over quickly" is the feeling which grows stronger in our men and commanders as the time goes by. Get it over with! Free the city!

The end is near. The last nests of stubborn resistance are weakening, the guns are breaking up the defences. Here and there the firing dies down; a pole with a dirty towel on it is poked through a hole in the wall and a crowd of Germans dribble out in the wake of the flag of surrender. Beyond the city the columns of prisoners stretch out for miles and miles; there are tens of thousands of them.

Our troops continue to draw the noose ever tighter round the encircled German forces. Soviet planes incessantly bomb the enemy still holding out in the centre of the city. This bombardment is even beginning to be dangerous. So small have the German islands of resistance become that the bombs may easily hit our own men.

The Fascists have taken up strong positions in a tall, many-storied building. They have even got a gun in there. From behind a corner we could observe the course of the battle. Two of our tanks drove up quite close to the house and opened fire on the spot from where the German tommy-gunners were firing. The gunners brought the gun to bear and, taking careful aim, began to batter at the loopholes. Now the barrel of a tommy-gun gleamed in one of them. Unhurriedly, the gun-layer began to direct his gun on to this loophole, while the Red Army men in cover behind the ruins egged him on: "Come on, mate! Let him have it!" The gun fired and the loophole was immediately transformed into a mass of fire and dense smoke. Done for. But almost instantly little flashes dart out from the next floor—the Germans have climbed up there. Firing shell after shell, as if he were hammering in a nail, our gunner chased the Germans higher and higher up. Already one tiny human figure could be seen on the roof. A shell bit a slice out of the edge of the roof and everything was wreathed in smoke. Our men jumped out from behind their cover and rushed the house. The gunner switched his fire to the next house. It was getting dark and tracers screamed through the air like fiery needles.

On January 29th one could already drive a car along many streets of central Stalingrad. Sometimes one had to get out and struggle through the ruins of houses where one was safe from the bursts of tommy-gun fire. As one walks along the streets and squares of this great and beautiful city destroyed by Hitler, which will now have to be entirely rebuilt, one feels one would like to bare one's head silently in front of these noble ruins, whose every stone, every fragment of it, is stained with the blood of our warriors and bears witness to the glory of the Soviet people. The accurate German strategists took everything into account. But in their variegated military terminology they forgot one word and its meaning: they forgot the word "Russia," and they met their death among the ruins of the city which has become the symbol of the stubborn strength of our country.

We will build you up again, you great city of Stalingrad! Inspired architects, painters and sculptors will create buildings of marble and granite and lay out green squares and parks. Our factories will be rebuilt. But mankind will never forget these ruins, nor the Soviet heroes who fought to the last throb of their hearts on staircases, behind smoking heaps of stones, in cellars and back alleys and held their city.

On the morning of January 30th, 1943, all forces advancing from every direction towards the centre of Stalingrad joined hands completely at last. The German troops were finally routed. Only small groups and single tommy-gun snipers were still shooting from among the ruins. Patrols were scouring the city to mop up the German cutthroats. Lieutenant-General Sanne, commanding the 100th Light Infantry Division, was surrounded and captured. The German soldiers who had surrendered were piling up their rifles, tommy-guns and machine-guns in heaps in the streets when suddenly several German transport planes appeared flying at a great height over the city. They dropped parachutes with loads of food. Our men undid the parcels and greatly enjoyed the sausage destined for Field-Marshal von Paulus.

Our patrols combed the city, and in little clashes finished the mopping-up of the last nests of German resistance. Machine-gun and rifle fire went on throughout the night, but by morning the firing died down. . . .

To-day, February 1st, firing in the central part of the city ceased completely. But at 9 A.M. the thunder of dozens of guns was heard from the direction of the northern outskirts. There the surrounded Germans are still resisting, but their hours are numbered.

Another day or so and this front-line city will suddenly find itself far to the rear. A staff officer, in his dug-out, wearied by many sleepless nights, raises his head from his maps, throws down his red pencil and says with a smile:

"Yes, we're rear-liners now! We must finish things up here and then we shall have to run after the front. And run pretty far and fast if we want to catch up . . . !"

* * *

The Mass Grave at District Command Centre*

by Heinz Schröter

"Care will be taken to ensure that all wounded arriving at Stalingrad are assembled at District Command Centre. Supply Sector Three will be responsible for food and supplies."

This order was issued by the Sixth Army on the 15th of January. All the divisions had been sent a copy and they, in turn, had passed it on to the field hospitals and dressing stations.

". . . assembled at District Command Centre."

Since the 15th of January thousands of wounded soldiers had converged on Stalingrad. The large building with its two wings seemed to exert a magnetic attraction.

The wounded stumbled along, great columns of men from Orlovka and Voroponovo, and from the west as well. Blood and the corpses of those who fell out marked their route. They were often marching for three days, and in many cases it took them two weeks. They were all young, yet their faces were those of old men. They stumbled through the hours of anguish, trying to keep to their feet, fighting against death. They were carried or pulled, they hobbled on sticks and boards. "To Stalingrad Centre," they muttered. "To the District Command."

They imagined a proper hospital, with a roof and a place where they could lie down, hot tea, and dressings for their suppurating wounds. District Command represented for them the island of salvation. It meant help and bandages and clean water and rest. In groups and columns they struggled towards their goal. Those coming from the west never saw the stone pillars that graced the front of the "City Centre" nor the inscription: *The Proletariat of the red Tsaritsyn to the freedom fighters who fell in 1919 in the struggle against Wrangel's hangmen.* While those coming from the south stared with unseeing eyes past the notice beside the Tsaritsa which said: *Keep out. Curiosity endangers your life and the lives of your comrades.*

Onwards, ever onwards, was their sole thought. Day and night the great crowds of wounded men shuffled along towards the apparent security which the large building represented in their eyes.

They reached Stalingrad's "City Centre" and the District Command.

The building of their dreams was filled to overflowing, and had been for many weeks past. It was filled with wounded and sick, shirkers and scroungers.

In the cellars were battle groups of the 29th and 3rd Motorised Infantry Divisions and what was left of the 376th Infantry Division, and the firing went on to right and left of them.

There were no beds and no bandages, no tea and no help. Sixteen doctors fought a hopeless fight, stretcher bearers and medical orderlies worked till they dropped, but the maelstrom of chaos was too much for them.

Newcomers were constantly arriving. They crawled over the heaps of men lying in the halls and corridors, and pushed down into the cellars or up the staircases. And there they stayed. Without a bed, or a word of encouragement, without any help or even the hope of help. They asked for water and food, but neither was given them; they called for a priest, a doctor, an orderly, for morphia, bandages and writing paper, for their friends, mother, wife or child, and some asked for a revolver.

Sometimes they were handed a revolver, and then their place was free for another to occupy.

"They have nowhere to lay their heads and their souls too are without shelter," said the padre of the 44th Infantry Division.

As the battle drew closer, District Command Centre came under fire from the enemy artillery. The building was soon well alight.

The fire started in the west wing and the flames then spread to the attics of the main building.

Those who could move, and who were near the exits, were able to escape, but others blocked the corridors and stairways. Men scrambled over two layers of prostrate bodies. Panic broke out, and some flung themselves over the banisters and out of windows. The main entrance to the building collapsed when the upper floor fell in, thus blocking the way out. Men crowded back up the stairs in an attempt to reach the other part of the building through the upper corridors, but the dead and the dying were in the way, progress was impossible, and then they met another mass of panic-stricken soldiers who were struggling to reach the main entrance, unaware that it had already collapsed.

This desperate attempt to escape from the burning building lasted for three hours. Over three thousand men died there, trampled on, suffocated and burned to death, while others had been killed when they jumped from the windows or were buried under the ruins. Their cries drowned the crackle of the flames and the whine of the shells, and long re-echoed amongst the ruins.

Every house was by now a ruin or a heap of rubble, but most of the cellars were still in good condition. The walls of the houses had fallen across them, thus providing additional security. During the last days of the struggle these cellars acquired a tragic and horrible notoriety.

. . . Any man who entered one of them abandoned all hope of ever coming out alive. This was equally true of the tractor factory cellars, or the G.P.U. prison, the theatre vaults, the cellar of the Red Militia's house, of the library or of the leather exchange. The cellars of the District Command and of the Timoschenko bunker were no better than the vaults under the museum and the power station.

These places of refuge from bombs and mortar fire became collecting points for the dressing stations and field hospitals. They were hells in which men died, singly and *en masse*.

In the cellar under Simonovich's warehouse eight hundred men lay pressed against the walls and all over the damp and dirty floor. Their bodies littered the stairs and blocked the passages. All men were equal here: rank and class had been shed as the dead leaves fall from the November trees. In the Simonovich cellars they had reached the end of life's journey, and if there were any distinctions to be drawn between them it was only in the severity of their wounds or in the number of the days that they still had to live. There was also one other difference, namely the way in which each man met his death.

A man lay on the steps dying of diphtheria, and beside him lay three others who had been dead for days, but no one had moved them because it was dark and they had not been noticed. Behind them a sergeant, whose tongue hung from his mouth like a piece of red hot iron, and whose feet had rotted off up to the ankles, screamed with thirst and pain.

On the wall in the middle of the cellar a foul-smelling wick burned in an old tin. It stank of paraffin, but also of fetid blood and gangrenous flesh and suppurating pus, and over all was the sickly smell of decaying bodies and iodine and sweat and excrement and filth.

The air was well nigh unbreathable, lungs and throat were parched, and eyes streamed tears.

The skin fell in strips from their bodies. They shook with tetanus, they screamed like animals and their bodies were covered with sores. Here a man choked to death, unable to get his breath, while another shivered with fever, calling for his wife and cursing the war or praising God. Spotted fever, typhus, pneumonia, gangrene, all claimed their victims. A lance-corporal was dying in one corner, his stomach and legs fearfully swollen; he neither spoke nor moved, nor asked for help, but just lay there with open eyes and folded hands. Across the passage and up the stairs a young man of twenty kicked and screamed, foaming at the mouth, his eyes rolling wildly, until death came and stilled his pain and stopped his convulsions.

They were given no food and a man who still had any kept it well hidden, for in the darkness a slice of bread was worth more than a man's life. This can only be understood by those who have themselves endured starvation and have known the value that a crumb of bread then has.

The lice were the worst. They bit through the men's skin, crawled into open wounds, and prevented the sleep so desperately needed. In their thousands they swarmed over the men's bodies and tattered underwear; only when death came, or high fever, did they depart, like rats leaving a sinking ship. A disgusting grey, swarming crowd would then move across to the next man and settle on him.

And there was no one there to help them. Whenever possible, the dead were taken out into the courtyard or stacked in bomb craters like logs. For a brief time there had been a doctor in the Simonovich cellar, but he had only taken refuge there during an air raid. His "own" cellar was elsewhere, and men were calling for him just as insistently there as they were here. Even he could only give the most superficial help. The mass of suffering was far too great.

Any man still capable of thinking could work out for himself when his end was due. And he would know that no purpose was served by screaming or complaining.

For to whom could he complain?

Many died, and it was often hours or even days before the next man noticed that they had gone. No one came to take away the dead, who were pushed and rolled from one man to the next, across the room and down the passage. Like logs or sacks, to a hole in the west wall and then out into the crater where the 500-pound bomb had exploded. Through the hole they were tossed, and into the crater. There were already a hundred bodies in it, many of them still warm; those were the men too weak to cry out.

Crowds of wounded waited outside the Simonovich cellar and when there was room slowly made their way down into it. Nobody was surprised that although no one ever came up out of the cellar, there was always room for more to go in. The dead were not counted nor their identity discs removed, though frequently their pockets were searched for bread. The cause of death was of no interest. All that mattered was to die quickly and make room for the others, waiting outside in the icy wind.

Men died not only in the Simonovich cellar but in every cellar. A wave of misery and pain enveloped their weary, broken bodies. They were no longer afraid, there was no terror amongst them nor panic, nor any signs of the demoralisation which had set in amongst the Army staffs above ground. Down in the cellars their fingers were no longer closed about the triggers of their guns, nor did they sit sobbing in dug-outs, like some of those who were fighting to the last round.

"... whatever sacrifice may be demanded of us as individuals is irrelevant. ..." So Hitler had said.

4   1943: Spring and Summer—
The Battle of the Mud

Joseph Stilwell

In his introduction to the chapter from which the following excerpt was taken, Theodore H. White, editor of The Stilwell Papers, *wrote: "Soldiering is a profession which, at every level, swings wildly from the ecstacy of adventure to the bottomless depths of boredom."*

From **The Stilwell Papers** by Joseph W. Stilwell, edited by Theodore H. White, pp. 190–91, 194–96, 198–200, 202–6. Copyright 1948 by Winifred A. Stilwell. Reprinted by permission of William & Morrow Company, Inc.

Lieutenant General Joseph Stilwell, one of the most colorful figures of the war, was commander of all American forces in China. He dealt on a daily basis with Generalissimo Chiang K'ai-shek, with the military leaders of the Allied coalition, and with President Roosevelt himself. However, "Vinegar Joe's" diary entries reveal that he was fighting the same war, though with different weapons, as the lowliest GI, and that red tape, cowardice, and incompetence were to be found at every level.

January 18 Conference. T.V. Soong and Ch'en Ch'eng. Latter seems reasonable. Definitely will be in command. Spoke nicely of U.S. help. Agrees on direct action and no red tape. If Ch'en proves amenable, we can now accomplish something—if the goddam desk-sitters will mind their own business and keep their noses out of ours.

January 19 Conference. Gave Ch'en Ch'eng the program and proposed courses [for the Yoke force training center]. G-mo has indicated general agreement.

Office. P.m. nap. 7:30 to Russian embassy for movies. Excellent. *A Day of War*. June 13, '42. Taken by 160 cameramen. Also views of Stalingrad—recent. The Russians are O.K. Victor Hu there.

What a fight the Russians have made. The nation has obviously found itself. Twenty years of work and struggle. Results: tough physique; unity of purpose; pride in their accomplishments; determination to win. Stalin's decision—*three days* after the war started—to move half of Moscow's heavy industry to the east. (June 25) Leningrad actually exporting munitions to other fronts. Rugged young soldiers. Tough women. Every last man, woman, and child in the war effort.

Compare it with the Chinese cesspool. A gang of thugs with the one idea of perpetuating themselves and their machine. Money, influence, and position the only considerations of the leaders. Intrigue, double-crossing, lying reports. Hands out for anything they can get; their only idea to let someone else do the fighting; false propaganda on their "heroic struggle"; indifference of "leaders" to their men. Cowardice rampant, squeeze paramount, smuggling above duty, colossal ignorance and stupidity of staff, total inability to control factions and cliques, continued oppression of masses. The only factor that saves them is the dumb compliance of the *lao pai hsing* [the common people]. The "intellectuals" and the rich send their precious brats to the [United] States, and the farmer boys go out and get killed—without care, training, or leadership. And we are maneuvered into the position of having to support this rotten regime and glorify its figurehead, the all-wise great patriot and soldier—Peanut. My God.

January 20 & 21 Conference. Ch'en Ch'eng and T.V. (Soong).

Ch'en Ch'eng of course has to protect himself. He gives up his cushy province and zone and takes a job [the Yoke force] he must succeed at. If he fails, his enemies will romp all over him; he'll be through. Ho Ying-ch'in will block and undermine him if he's not extremely careful. He must be sure of his ground, sure that Peanut will support him, and he must line up everybody he can on his side. He's going slow, necessarily. Of course, I have to go over the whole damn story once more, and sell him the idea. He doesn't know about Ramgarh, he doesn't know me, he doesn't know what we can do for him. Even if he understands, he doesn't know he can depend on us. Instead of stepping into a fine command, he's walking into a trap that can be sprung on him unless he sees to it that he has his enemies tied up. Ho Ying-ch'in realizes that if Ch'en succeeds, he'll be the big name, and Ho will slide down into the discard. So Ho will accept the failure of the effort with great equanimity and will perhaps actively try to sabotage it. A fine kettle of fish. And Ch'en knows I'm responsible for pushing him into it. He might very well hate me for it. . . .

Letter to Mrs. Stilwell Ole Pappy has been over the barrel and in the wringer for a solid week but this morning I begin to see light. I am frayed all around the edges and if this has to be fought out all over again, I'll be fit subject for a sanitarium.

The other day as I reached the house, Dorn was at the gate all dressed up, with the staff lined up inside. They lined me up and Joe pinned a medal on me, and then we all went inside and drank whisky. All but me, I still don't like it. I don't know who was behind this business, but I have strong suspicions. The whole thing was bunk, pumped up out of a very minor incident, and entirely undeserved. On that account it is embarrassing, but luckily time moves on and such things are soon forgotten.

We are pinched for personnel and everybody is doing double duty. Do you know that this theater of war is the size of the U.S.? Chungking is at Washington, and Karachi is at San Francisco. A trip from here to Delhi is like one from New York to Denver. And we have to hop over the Japs on the way. And the communications aren't developed quite as well as in the U.S.

January 26 Dinner with Chiang, apparently in my honor, to congratulate me on being decorated. Very simple food and little ritual or ceremony, but oh! the atmosphere. In the presence of the Most High no one dares to make a remark or venture an opinion. The hushed silence continues till a Pearl of Wisdom is dropped, or some brash foreigner asks if the melons came from Hami. You can see from the rigid postures and strained expressions that the sweat is running down the boys' backs. If addressed at all, the recipient of the honor answers briefly in a low respectful tone. No argument, no questions: just poker face and icy dignity. The merry throng was entertained by a movie that we sent over and which nobody understood. There was a lot of kissing and swapping of wives and at this point it was my turn to sweat. What crude barbarians we must still appear to them. There was a short training film on motors, introduced by a shot of a review of the 7th Division. I made some face by announcing it as my outfit. I think I am making progress. If all goes well now, something will have been done that the wise guys said was impossible.

Lights out. Regular thing to save coal. Back to candles, and I've got to save my eyes.

January 27 F.D.R. at Casablanca.

January 29 Arnold and Somervell will be in Delhi tomorrow instead of next week. "Can I make it?" Christ, no. Can't they read a map? "Important conference with Wavell and Dill." If they don't come to Chungking, the Peanut will be furious.

January 30 The Battle of the Mud still continues. These people are hard to help, I have to keep thinking that there are 399,900,000 of them worth helping or I wouldn't be able to stick it out with the other 100,000. Even in the Gang there are bright spots and understanding exceptions who encourage me to stick it out and come back for more. This trip may give me a chance to get my blood pressure down. Having a conference with Chiang at 5:00. I hope he had a good lunch. The destinies of nations sometimes depend on small factors. What a laugh it is to see the continual adulation and glorifying of small potatoes whose reputation grows in *spite* of what they do rather than because of it.

    Date with G-mo at 5:00. He was sour as a pickle. Never one word of gratitude to the U.S. Just what he can get out of us.

February 1 Up at 5:00. Shoved off [for India from Kunming] in C-47 at 7:00. Got up but 100-mile wind held us and we turned back. Changed to C-87 and left at 10:00. Up to 23,000 and made it. Arrived Delhi at 10:30. Waiting dinner for us. Arnold and Somervell here. *No other planes over the Hump today.*

[*Undated* Résumé by General Stilwell of Arnold-Somervell-Dill visit]
    Conferences in New Delhi. Back and forth on plans. Tentative decision. Then Arnold and Dill came up [to Chungking]. Peanut retired to Berchtesgaden Huang Shan, so we went over. Arnold and Dill had their eyes opened. Arnold said, "You ought to have a laurel wreath." After arranging for 137 transports and a heavy bomber group [for Chinese] Arnold thought he had done pretty well. Peanut said he was much disappointed in conference. (*Now* he wants 500 planes, 10,000 tons [a month], and Chennault independent. Last June, 500, 5,000 tons, and three U.S. divisions.) Arnold said, "I'll be God-damned if I take any such message back to the President." He was well fed up.

    At last conference, I pinned Peanut on whether or not he would attack next fall, in case conditions limited naval support. He got mad as hell and said, "Didn't I say I would?" He sent word by T.V. that I had embarrassed him publicly. He can go to hell; I have him on that point. Arnold and Dill got a faint idea of conditions here and it made them sick. . . .

March 4, Chungking ———in. He confirms *all* my most pessimistic opinions. Peanut is really no dictator. He issues an order. Everybody bows and says "sure." But nobody does anything. He knows all about the smuggling and the rottenness, but he hasn't the power to cure it. Ho Ying-ch'in proposed Liu Ch'ih [garrison commander of Chungking garrison] instead of Ch'en Ch'eng for Yoke [command] and the Peanut bawled him out. "What! Would you make a joke out of a serious situation? Would you play politics in such a crisis?" Ho knows all about the rotten conditions, too, but he can't do anything. Lung Yün [governor of Yünnan] is not so bad; he just wants to be let alone in Yünnan. His Sixtieth Army can't be moved—they would refuse to obey the order. Opium traffic in Yünnan still enormous. Guarded by soldiers. Big stocks of hoarded gas, cloth, and other commodities. Gang of rascals around Lung Yün. They are loyal because of the money hookup and he trusts them rather than the Central Government which wants to get his graft away from him. The Yünnan people are suspicious not only of us, but of outside Chinese as well. What saved China was not the fighting by the Army, but the size of the country and lack of communications. We can get our way in Yünnan, but only by going slow. The Chinese Red Cross is a racket. Stealing and sale of medicines is rampant. The Army gets nothing. Malnutrition and sickness is ruining the army; the higher-ups steal the soldiers' food. A pretty picture.

March 6 Chinese military spokesman: "Tali—March 6. After being subjected to furious Chinese counterattacks resulting in heavy casualties, the Jap troops on the west bank of the Nu River [upper reaches of the Salween] have started a general retreat. Many strategic points have been recovered by the Chinese." Utterly false. Jap patrols withdrawing after a reconnaissance. Typical of most Chinese reports.

March 12-18 Took Ch'en Ch'eng to Kunming. Lung Yün did not meet him. Several conferences with Ch'en Ch'eng, who is doing exactly what he agreed to in Chungking. Training is U.S. pigeon; discipline and administration is Chinese. Tu Yü-ming is handling all arrangements for school for Ch'en Ch'eng and in spite of my fears, is doing it as agreed. For the first time since arriving, I feel we are getting real co-operation. Ch'en Ch'eng has decision and appreciates what we are trying to do.

All arrangements made to begin schools on April 1. First infantry class will be Fifth Army, because of difficulty of getting students from outlying units.

Failures by China [Chinese promises] :
Consolidation of divisions [promised] by January 31. Not started.
All units [of 30-division Y force] move [to Yünnan] by January 31. Only two armies started.
No funds allotted for roads.
No action on use of land [for training ranges].
Lung Yün [governor of Yünnan] refused to obey any order from War Department.
All divisions under strength.
No action on Sixtieth Army.

March 10 Midsummer Night's Dream Statement by [Chinese] military spokesman at Chungking:

Jap strength (1937 to date)	6,576,000
Enemy killed	642,647
Enemy wounded	1,286,982
Enemy captured	21,314

March 16 The Japs put out Chinese casualties for 1942 as follows:

Killed	642,657
Wounded	1,287,682
Captured	21,314

Pretty even fight!

March 21, Letter to Mrs. Stilwell I did not write on March 19 because I wanted to let that terrible date ooze by. Now it's over and I can look forward to being seventy. Actually, I am no more creaky than I was last week and I can still go up the 65 steps at the office faster than most. Slowing down but not stopped yet. This is the First Day of Beautiful Spring. Dorn, Bergin and I took a walk.

Lyric to Spring

I welcomed the Spring in romantic Chungking,
I walked in her beautiful bowers.
In the light of the moon, in the sunshine at noon,
I savored the fragrance of flowers.

(Not to speak of the slush, or the muck and the mush
That covers the streets and alleys.
Or the reek of the swill, as it seeps down the hill,—
Or the odor of pig in the valleys.)

The sunset and dawn, and the dew on the lawn,
And the blossoms in colors so rare.
The jasmine in bloom, the magnolia's perfume,
The magic of Spring's in the air.

(The garbage is rich, as it rots in the ditch,
And the honey-carts scatter pollution,
The effluvium rank, from the crap in the tank,
Is the stink of its scummy solution.)

Aromatic Chungking, where I welcomed the Spring,
In a mixture of beauty and stenches,
Of flowers and birds, with a sprinkling of turds,
And of bow-legged Szechuan wenches.

Take me back to the Coast, to the place I love most,
Get me out of this odorous sewer.
I'm in————to my neck, but I'm quitting, by heck!
And I'll nevermore shovel manure. . . .

[April] Famous letter from Roosevelt to George Marshall. [Referring to Chiang K'ai-shek]—"[he] came up the hard way to accomplish in a few years what it took *us* 200 years to attain. . . . One cannot speak sternly or exact commitments from a man like that, as if he were a *tribal chieftain."*

Then orders came for Chennault to have 1,500 out of 4,000 tons [total monthly delivery of Hump airline in China] for his war. Then he gets a separate Air Service Command. Then he is to control the ATC by orders of Arnold, speaking for the President, and giving it to me verbally through Glenn [Chennault's chief of staff]!

Wavell has a grievance. 18,000 of "his" trucks are in U.S. ports, and the goddam Americans won't ship them to him. Furthermore, if he doesn't get 180,000 tons a month, he just can't jump off [for a fall Burma offensive]. He only got 60,000 tons in March, and it's a bloody crime. He's gone to London to squawk. "Can't" is his best word. Everything is so goddam "difficult" that it's practically impossible. This is ominous. If he can contemplate further delay now, we're sunk. . . .

Then the famous call to Washington. Peanut radioed Roosevelt that he and Chennault had been cooking up a plan that Chennault must come and tell him about. George [Marshall] tipped me off. I suggested that he call me, Bissell, and Chennault in, [he] saying he was going to anyway. Roosevelt crossed Bissell off, and George told me to bring one of Bissell's staff. Then I taxed Chennault with the matter, and he knew nothing about it. No new plan and no visit to Washington. So Peanut is just talking about Chennault's "6-months-to-drive-the-Japs-out-of-China" plan. I arranged for priority air travel, but luckily did not alert Win [Mrs. Stilwell]. Will see Peanut on Monday (4/19) and the thing may calm down. Must be in Washington by end of month, as George Marshall leaves soon after.

[This undated paper is General Stillwell's brief summary of the May, 1943, Washington conference in which he participated.]

Washington Continual concessions have confirmed Chiang K'ai-shek in the opinion that all he needs to do is yell and we'll cave in. As we are doing. F.D.R. had decided on an air effort in China before we reached Washington. This suited the British, who want no part of a fight for Burma. Why should they fight to build up China, if we can be euchered into bearing the brunt of the war against Japan? They'll get Burma back at the peace table anyway.

Nobody was interested in the humdrum work of building a ground force but me. Chennault promised to drive the Japs right out of China in six months, so why not give him the stuff to do it? It was the short cut to victory.

My point was that China was on the verge of collapse economically. That we could not afford to wait another year. That Yünnan was indispensable and that a force had to be built up to hold it. That if the Japs took Yünnan, the recapture of Burma would be meaningless. That any increased air offensive that stung the Japs enough would bring a strong reaction that would wreck everything and put China out of the war. Witness the Chekiang campaign, brought on by the Jap belief that Tokyo was bombed from bases there. That the first essential step was to get a ground force capable of seizing and holding airbases, and opening communications to China from the outside world. Overruled. Churchill's idea was, so he said, that China *must* be helped, and the only way to do it within the next few months was by air.

At the same time they decided on Saucy they made it practically impossible for me to prepare the Y force, and then ordered it used in an offensive. But British reluctance caused the wording of the directive to be so loose that it would be up to the commander as to what he could do. He could go the limit or he could quit at any time. With Wavell in command, failure was inevitable; he had nothing to offer at any meeting except protestations that the thing was impossible, hopeless, impractical. Churchill even spoke of it as silly. The Limeys all wanted to wait another year. After the Akyab fiasco, the four Jap divisions in Burma have them scared to death.

The inevitable conclusion was that Churchill has Roosevelt in his pocket. That they are looking for an easy way, a short cut for England, and no attention must be diverted from the Continent at any cost. The Limeys are not interested in the war in the Pacific, and with the President hypnotized they are sitting pretty.

Roosevelt wouldn't let me speak my piece. I interrupted twice, but Churchill kept pulling away from the subject, and it was impossible.

So everything was thrown to the air offensive. F.D.R. pulled 7,000 tons [monthly over the Hump] out of the air when told that 10,000 was impossible, and ordered that tonnage for July. First 4,750 [tons] for air [Fourteenth Air Force], then 2,250 for ground. They will do the Japs some damage but at the same time will so weaken the ground effort that it may fail. Then what the hell use is it to knock down a few Jap planes.

Farewell lunch. Mr. Churchill: "Mr. President, I cannot but believe that an all-wise Providence has draped these great events, at this critical period of the world's history, about your personality and your high office." And Frank lapped it up. . . .

5   Shoot Out That Goddamn Light

Jack Belden

An amphibious landing was perhaps the riskiest tactical operation of the entire war because it was the most complicated and delicately timed. To secure success thousands of details had to synchronize, and the imponderables—the weather, enemy intelligence, mechanical breakdowns, and human error—made perfect planning impossible. Belden, a reporter whose brilliant coverage of the China theater had received international acclaim, was present when the first waves of LCVPs headed for shore to launch the invasion of Sicily.

"Go to your debarkation stations."

The voice on the loud-speaker rang with a harsh metallic note through the wardroom.

The men sat up and blinked their eyes, and for a moment all of them stared at each other with expressions that seemed to say: "This is it." Then a few of them broke out in foolish grins and rose slowly from their chairs . . .

It was pitch-dark in the passageways. In the inky blackness men stumbled against each other, but no one uttered a word. In silence we made our way toward the bulkhead door through which a little light from the boat deck outside shone. As we passed through the door, a hand reached out and squeezed each one of us briefly on the arm. "Good luck," said a voice. It was the chaplain.

The moon was still shining dimly on the deck, but though we could now see, we clung close to each other for fear of becoming separated. From every passageway men, shuffling in dreary, silent attitudes, were coming out to swell the tide of those going in on the assault waves. They made a depressing sight—a composite of dead and dull faces and drab bodies loaded down with military gear. As we turned the corner of a bulkhead, the man ahead of me halted hesitantly before a boat which was swinging violently back and forth, first toward the deck and then away from it. Several voices behind us shouted and tried to allay any feelings of doubt we had. As we hesitated, they shouted cheerfully: "Get in. What are you waiting for?"

These words, spoken to show us that we were at the right boat, did not produce the action desired. The man who was leading our group paused on hearing those words, raised his hands in a helpless gesture and called back to the others: "I can't get in." As he said this, the men back of us yelled as if they were going to throw a fit. The leading soldier, however, remained adamant and made no move to get in the boat.

From my vantage point, it was evident that he was quite right in refusing to do so. The boat was rocking to and fro on its davits, coming close against the ship's side at one moment and swinging far away at the next. The only way to enter the boat was to slide down a short knotted line and drop in. But to attempt to drop in that swinging boat would be suicidal. One slight slip would mean a plunge down into the water, which was slapping now with a loud and menacing sound against the ship's side below us. So both the soldier and I remained standing where we were, looking at the dark void between the swinging boat and the ship, making no attempt to get in.

The crowd behind us, growing impatient, again yelled imperatively at us. Goaded by the angry voices, the soldier by me said: "Goddamit, there's no one here. Where the hell's the navy?" At these words, the men behind us transferred their disapproval from us to the whole American Navy.

"Dammit! Get some sailors!" one officer yelled.

As yet the delay had not been serious, but in our overwrought state of mind it assumed exaggerated proportions, increasing our nervousness to a state of shaking, angry doubt.

"God!" said an officer who had come up beside us, "if we can't get our boats launched from the ship, what's it going to be like in the water when they start shooting at us?"

The soldier by my side laughed bitterly. "Snafu! That's us. Always snafued."

At last two or three sailors arrived, the boat was secured firmly, the soldiers slid one by one down the knotted ropes, and the boat descended past the ship's side into the choppy water.

As we drew away from the ship, our moment's irritability dropped away from us as quickly as it had come. There was an immediate sense of gladness at getting started and a heightened awareness. When we got away from the shelter of the fleet, this feeling, however, soon gave way to another. We became sick.

The rocking of the small landing craft was totally unlike anything we had experienced on the ship. It pitched, rolled, swayed, bucked, jerked from side to side, spanked up and down, undulated, careened and insanely danced on the throbbing, pulsing, hissing sea. The sea itself flew at us, threw the bow in the air, then, as it came down, swashed over us in great roaring bucketfuls of water.

The ensign standing on the high stern of the boat ordered the sailor by the bow to close the half-open ramp. As he moved to do so, the helmsman in the stern yelled: "I can't see. . . ."

He did not finish his sentence. At that moment there was a loud hissing sound, then a dull squashing crash, and a wave of water cascaded through the ramp, throwing down those who were standing on the deck and overrunning the boat with water.

"Bail with your helmets!" called the ensign in a voice of extreme irritation.

Kneeling now in the puddle which sloshed up and down the length of the boat, the men scooped up the water with their helmets, staggered uncertainly to their feet, threw their load overboard and then went down on their knees again to repeat the process.

Meanwhile, the ensign kept the boat zigzagging over the water searching in the sea for the boats of our assault wave. From time to time he would shout out to another boat: "Are you the second wave?" When he would receive a negative answer, he would curse loudly, turn the boat in another direction and begin searching again.

For a long time we coursed back and forth over the water, picking up one boat here and another there. Then we went into a circle, going round and round in the shadow of our fleet till, certain that every boat was present, we broke out of the circle formation and headed in a line toward a blue light, which, shining to seaward, was bobbing up and down some distance ahead of us.

The uneven motion of the boat was now almost unbearable. Hemmed in between the high steel bulkheads of the boat, the men crouched like beasts, shivering from the cold spray, silent, but uneasy with imminent sickness. One by one they vomited, holding their heads away from their loosely clasped rifles, and moaned softly. One man clambered up the side of the boat and crawled out on the narrow ledge running around the top and clung there like a monkey, with one hand clasping the boat and the other fumbling at his pants. The boat was rocking heavily; the man was swaying with its motion, and it seemed momentarily as if he would fall into the sea or a wave would wash him overboard. The ensign in a sharp voice commanded him to get back inside the boat.

"I have to move my bowels, Sir," the man said in a tone of distressed pain.

Someone tittered.

"Jesus! What's so funny about that?" said a soldier, and he got up and grasped the man, who was now half-hanging over the side by his shoulders. "Here, Joe," he said, "hold on to me."

From that time on, our dash toward the unseen shore became a nightmare of sickness, pain and fear. The boat had gathered speed now and we were beginning to bound from one wave crest to the next with a distinct shock. There were no thwarts, no seats of any kind in the boat; only the deck itself to sit on and the steep, high hull of the boat to lean against. The motion of the boat threw us all against one another. My hand in bracing my rolling body had accidentally come to rest on the shoulder of a young boy. I looked down at him and saw that he was holding his head in both of his hands and quietly vomiting. "It's the motion that gets you," I said.

"The what?" the boy said.

"The motion. It's different from on the ship. You'll get used to it. You'll be all right."

"Oh, sure. The motion. You ain't kiddin'. I'll be all right." He bent his head down, a sudden spasm contracting his shoulders, and he spewed from the mouth. "Oh, sure, I'll be all right."

I stood up and took a quick look over the boat's side. Astern our great fleet fled, diminishing, sinking beneath the waves. The boat had begun to pitch and shudder now, swooping forward and down, jolting almost stationary for a moment, then lifting and swooping again; a shot of spray smashed aboard over the bows like a thrown bucket of water, and I knelt down again.

The boat pounded on. It rolled us against iron pipes, smashed us against coils of wire and jammed us on top of one another, compounding us with metal, water and vomit. There was nothing we could do but wait, herded helplessly between the high, blank walls of the boat, huddled together like blind men not knowing where we were going or what was around, behind or ahead of us, only looking at one another with anxious eyes. That not being able to tell what was ahead of us, to catch even one slight glimpse of the universe outside our tossing, rocking world, was almost unbearable, leaving us, as it did, prey to all manner of nighttime fancies. The unnatural and unwholesome motion of the boat, churning my stomach into an uproar, the bare and opaque walls of the hull, shutting out everything but the vault of the sky overhead, evoked in my mind a picture of the world outside that was fantastic and terrifying. Instead of feeling myself part of a group of American soldiers going ashore on a carefully planned invasion, I saw myself and the men as strange phantoms flung out across the maw of the sea, into the blackness of eternity, fast revolving away from any kind of world we ever knew. I felt as if we had been caught up in some mysterious rocket, and that we were being borne onward in this bouncing projectile of machinery toward a nether-world goal as incapable of taking command over our own destinies as a squirrel in a cage.

In a moment of hollow doubt I stood up, edging my eyes over the gunwale and looking out into the comparative world of light around us. The sea was sparkling with tossed spray. Ahead, and on either side of us, boats were dodging and twisting through the choppy waves, and from their sterns, waving from side to side with the motion of the boats, showers of gleaming water streamed out. behind like the plumes of birds. What was causing the water to gleam was a wide streak of light. It sprang like the tail of a stationary comet from a ball of incandescent yellow that was shining on the edge of the blackness off to our left.

Suddenly, the light swung across the water, fastened on our boat and illuminated us like actors on a darkened stage. In the glare, I saw the green, pale faces of the soldiers and their bodies huddling close against the hull. Then the light shot past and over us.

"Why don't they shoot out that goddam searchlight?" growled a voice from the depths of the cavernous boat. "Jesus! We'll be drowned without knowing what hit us!"

"Steady there!" said the voice of Captain Paul Carney. "Take it easy."

Again I craned my neck upward, just getting the top of my helmet above the hull and looking out with fascinated eyes. The light had now swung onto a small group of boats which were thrashing wildly from side to side trying to escape off into the darkness. From somewhere ahead faint red flashes began to flicker like fireflies. Then red balls, describing a high arc like a tennis lob, arched over our heads and fell down toward the illuminated boats which could not seem to shake off the hunting glare of the searchlight. At this I drew in my breath and involuntarily I shouted: "They're shooting at the boats." Below me, from the soldiers crouching with their heads toward the bottom of the boat, floated up an echo: "Shooting at the boats—Jesus!"

Abruptly, our boat slowed down. Above me, and slightly to the right, hung a blue light, seemingly suspended in the air. Dimly I discerned the outlines of a naval patrol vessel. Out of the darkness above mysteriously came a metallic voice: "Straight ahead! Go straight ahead. You'll see a small light on your right. Land there. Look out for mines. Good luck."

It was all very eerie—rocking there on the sea and hearing a voice calling out of the black above us. But I had no time to think of this. Our engine gave a sudden full-throated roar as the ensign cut off the underwater exhaust. The boat leapt forward. The other boats behind us raced around to either side of us, and we sped forward like a charging football line. "Hurry!" I thought. "God! If we can only make it!" The sea cascaded through the ramp and a broadside of water catapulted down on us. The boat shuddered, bucked, then plunged onward in a confident show of power.

All my senses were now alerted to the straining point. A flush of thrill and excitement shot through me like flame. It was wonderful. It was exhilarating.

Smash! Pound! Roar! Rush!—toward the goal. Here we come! Wheee! My mouth was open and I giggled with insane laughter.

The sailor by the bow tapped me on the shoulder. I peered around. The boy was pointing. Ahead—directly ahead—two strings of dotted red lights were crossing each other. They came out from right and left, like two necklaces of strung red and black beads, and crossed each other in the air some distance before us.

"Machine guns!" the sailor shouted. "Theirs." The little fireflies of light were growing very close now. "Going right through them!" the sailor shouted. He made a gesture with his hand across his throat. "Right through them."

Snap! I heard a sharp cracking sound. Snap! Snap! Snap! Jittering, I ducked down below the side of the boat. Then I half slid, half fell to the deck, huddling low with the rest of the soldiers. I was on fire inside, but outside I was cold. I could feel all my flesh jerking. It was not from excitement. No longer did I feel any thrill. The boat was pitching and rocking like a roller coaster. I knelt now and was sick. Gasping for breath I wiped the strings of sputum from my lips, drawing my sleeve across my chin. Dimly I saw the boy beside me on all fours with his mouth wide open and his head bent down. I tried to pull myself together and sidled over and held his head. My gesture was almost automatic. I told myself I had to be of some use. But I no longer cared about anything. The boat seemed to be spinning like a merry-go-round. Dazed, I wished that a shell would come along and end all this horror, wetness and misery. If we could only get out of this insanely rocketing prison. If the boat would only stop for just a moment.

Soon I was almost beyond feeling. All I knew was that we were enclosed in an infernal machine, shuddering through the darkness, toward the edge of the world, toward nowhere. I did not feel the boat slow down. I neither heard nor saw men get to their feet. At first, all I felt was a violent shudder. Then I heard the engine break out into a terrible throbbing roar. At last, there was a jerk and a bump and the boat came to a halt.

"Open ramp!" shouted the ensign at the stern.

Glancing fearfully toward the bow of the boat, I saw it swinging down, like a huge jaw opening. Halfway down it stopped, stuck. We could see nothing. Only a half-open hole.

The soldiers stared at the hole as if fascinated. Grappling at the side of the boat, they pulled themselves to their feet, and peered uncertainly out into the darkness through the ramp. For a brief moment they stared at each other, then bent their heads down, shuffling their feet. No one moved.

The ramp jerked down farther until it was level with the water. Still nothing could be seen. Still no one moved.

"Get off!" Major Grant's voice was imperious.

No one moved.

"Jump off!" he hollered again. "You want to get killed here? Get on that beach!"

With these words he leapt out into the darkness. Another man with a coil of wire followed. The others hesitated as if waiting to see what happened to those who had jumped.

I felt I would go crazy if I stayed in the boat any longer. I advanced to the ramp. "Here it comes," I thought and jumped.

The water struck me like a shock. I kept going down. "It's over my head," I thought. My feet sank down and touched bottom. My chin was just at the water. I started to push forward. A sharp crackle burst the air near by. There was a whine and whizz overhead. Then a metallic, plunking sound as if something was striking the boat.

The water was growing shallower. I bent my knees, keeping only my helmet-covered head above the water. I felt as if I were wearing a shield. Finding I wasn't hit, I realized the machine-gun fire was so far surprisingly light. "Hell!" I said to myself, "this is not as bad as the Mareth Line."

It was dark. The fires that had been visible from the ship could not be seen here. Ahead of me I made out a sandy beach, rising in a slight slope. Figures were crawling on hands and knees up the slope. Every few moments they halted and lay flat on their stomachs. By now the water was really shallow. I straightened up and dashed for the beach. Bullets snapped overhead. I threw myself flat on the sand. At last, I was on dry land.

6   These Nips Are Nuts

Technical Sergeant Herman Kogan

Shaped by fear and preconceptions, the combat infantryman's opinions of the enemy were scarcely objective. A belief that the enemy was demented or fanaticized by crazy ideas served to ease the soldier's anxiety about his own conduct and encouraged the process of detachment from the business of killing other human beings. The following piece, excerpted from an anthology of combat reports by U.S. Marine Corps correspondents, is probably a typical example of the operation of this stereotyping defense mechanism. The description of Japanese tactics is basically accurate, but the American soldier's response to those tactics was conditioned by his attitudes about the Japanese as contrasted with the German enemy.

Wherever they have fought in this war, the Japs have shown an amazing aptitude for the queer and fantastic. They have staged solemn funeral processions in the midst of hot battles. They have blown themselves to bits with hand grenades, have stabbed themselves with daggers, sabers, bayonets, and even with scythes. They have plunged forward in stupidly blind banzai charges, and they have danced wildly atop ridges while exposed to American fire.

Some of these acts are part of their ancient philosophy that it is glorious to die for the emperor. Some are designed to terrorize and demoralize the foe, so that he will respond with a burst of rifle or machine-gun fire and thus reveal his position. And some are so freakish that they defy explanation. Whatever the motivation, these strange things have been etched sharply on the minds of the men who have witnessed them in every campaign of the Pacific war and who have been chilled, angered, puzzled—and even amused—by them.

In the third week of the battle for Saipan, Marines had fought their way to within sight of Makunsha village. Then the Japanese began one of the most furious—and futile—counterattacks of the campaign. One of the few who witnessed this banzai of banzais was Marine Lieutenant Colonel Lewis B. Rock, of Dayton, Ohio. From his vantage point high on a mountain, he saw thousands of Japs headed for the American defensive positions. At their head were half a dozen soldiers bearing a huge, blood-red naval flag.

"It was like a throwback to medieval battle scenes, gripping and dramatic," said Colonel Rock. But what followed in the wake of these front-line soldiers was even more startling.

From **Semper Fidelis: The U.S. Marines in World War II**, edited by Robert B. Asprey, pp. 220–23. Copyright © 1967 by Robert Asprey. Reprinted by permission of the publisher, Grosset & Dunlap, Inc.

"It was an unbelievable spectacle. Following these troops were the enemy's wounded. There were men with bandaged heads, men without arms, men on crutches, the great majority of them unarmed. They were tagging along, sometimes a mile or so behind the fighting troops, to participate in this last banzai charge, to have the privilege of dying for the emperor."

Two days later, the ground between Tanapag and Makunsha was covered with the bodies of these Japs who had made the vain assault. And on the Saipan coast line lay the huge red naval battle flag, now a prized Marine trophy.

On a smaller scale, but no less ferocious or crackbrained, was the exploit of a Japanese officer on Guam who led nine men in a suicidal attack on a forward CP in the Tumon Bay area. In the light of a full moon, they leaped from the jungle, shrieking and stomping wildly. The enemy soldiers were cut down instantly by grenade and rifle fire. But the officer, clutching a wound with one hand and waving his saber with the other, lurched on. He staggered into a medical aid station and wounded four corpsmen before rifle and pistol fire finally ended his foolish foray.

Such saber rushes are common in front-line fighting in the Pacific. A Jap troop leader, either to impress his own men or to frighten the enemy, has often leaped out of a foxhole and rushed singlehanded against his adversaries.

The Marines who fought on Guam will not soon forget the "Dancing Officer" or the "Trumpet Player." The first appeared one day on the crest of a hill about 1,400 yards from the American lines.

"There he was," related Corporal Donald S. Griffin, of San Jose, California, "jumping up and down, cutting this way and that. Maybe he was exhorting his men, but it's my guess he was going through some sort of ritualistic dance. Or maybe he was trying to impress us with his bravery by doing a dance while exposed to the enemy."

The Trumpet Player was a Jap who pulled a similar stunt on Guam, except that he stood on the hill and blew on a long horn, similar to the kind blown at New Year's Eve parties.

Several other Japs also showed our men some fancy didos on Guam. During the heavy fighting on the Agat front, they suddenly ran out of an emplacement. All were shirtless. First they paraded solemnly in a single file in front of the Marine line. Then they moved forward again. They executed this step several times before they were shot down. And there was another Jap on Guam with more nerve than sense. Just before the opening of a banzai attack, this Nip jumped to the crest of a ridge above the Marines.

"One, two, three, you can't catch me!" he shouted.

Two dozen 30-caliber bullets promptly proved him wrong.

This eccentric could easily have been first cousin to the Jap on Eniwetok who took a shot at Private First Class Richard Kyhill, of Brooklyn, and missed. So irate was he at his poor marksmanship that he threw his rifle away and waved his hands in the air.

"He started hollering and screaming," said Kyhill. "He was really sore. And then he started swearing. Bad language always annoys me. So I shot him in the head."

Sometimes these weird things the Japs do verge on the near-heroic, although, in a military sense, they constitute useless expenditure of life. On Guam, several waves of Japanese infantry charged a squad of huge 34-ton medium tanks. One of the infantrymen drove his bayonet into the periscope of a tank driven by Sergeant Joe Rzesutek, of Oxford, Connecticut, before he was mowed down. Another jammed a grenade down the barrel of a 75-millimeter cannon and held his hand over the cannon barrel so the grenade would not drop out. The explosion blew his hand off.

There are other incidents Marines will always remember with a puzzled brow. There was the group of Japs who stormed a hill on Cape Gloucester, shouting, "Gimme back my hill; gimme back my hill!"

There was the attack by a band of Japs on one of the Marshall Islands in which each wore an oversized gas mask and uttered hideous cries. The "crazy howls" were first heard on Guadalcanal. They came at night—shrieks and bloodcurdling yells from the darkness of the jungles. They were intended by the Japs to frighten the Marines into a state of complete inability to fight. The battle cries of the Japs have become familiar to thousands of Marines, too. "Banzai!" and "Marines, you die!" and "Marines, we kill you!" and "More blood for the Emperor!" were common enough, but on Cape Gloucester one unit of Japs tried a new one. As they stormed a Marine strong point in a hopeless attack, they yelled, "To hell with Babe Ruth! To hell with Babe Ruth!" This cry, however, was no more profitable for the Japs than the others. Marines wiped them out.

7   Kamikazes: An Eyewitness Account

Phelps Adams

The lengths to which fanaticism was carried during the Second World War were exemplified by the phenomenon of kamikaze, *the Japanese suicide attacks on United States warships during the last months of the war. "Berserkers," warriors willing to trade their lives for guaranteed admission to Paradise, are part of the West's cultural heritage; however, the decision for self-destruction was usually thought of in the West as an individual act, undertaken without premeditation and normally to save other lives. The cold-blooded planning behind the* kamikaze *attacks repelled Americans and confirmed the widespread belief that "Japs"*

"Kamikazes: An Eyewitness Account of Attack on Admiral Mitscher's Flagship by Japanese Suicide Pilots off Okinawa" by Phelps Adams. From **Masterpieces of War Reporting: The Great Moments of World War II**, edited by Louis Snyder, pp. 487–94. Copyright © 1962 by Julian Messner, Inc. Reprinted by permission of Simon and Schuster, Inc.

*were alien, subhuman creatures. Not even the most fanatical Nazi would
throw away his life as did the Japanese.*

It is absolutely out of the question for you to return alive. Your mission
involves certain death. Your bodies will be dead but not your spirits. The
death of a single one of you will be the birth of a million others. . . . Do not
be in a hurry to die. If you cannot find your target turn back. Next time you
may find a better opportunity. Choose a death that brings maximum results.

Aboard a Fast Carrier in the Forward Pacific Area, May 11
(Special—Delayed)—Two Japanese suicide planes carrying 1,100 pounds of
bombs plunged into the flight deck of Vice Admiral Marc A. Mitscher's own
flagship early today, killing several hundred officers and men and transforming
one of our biggest flat-tops into a floating torch, with flames soaring nearly
1,000 feet into the sky.

For eight seemingly interminable hours that followed the ship and her crew
fought as tense and terrifying a battle for survival as had ever been witnessed in
the Pacific, but when dusk closed in, the U.S.S. *Bunker Hill*—horribly crippled
and still filmed by wisps of smoke and steam from her smoldering embers—was
plowing along under her own power on the distant horizon, safe. Tomorrow she
will spend another eight terrible hours burying at sea the men who died to save
her.

From the deck of a neighboring carrier a few hundred yards distant I
watched the *Bunker Hill* burn. It is hard to believe that men could survive those
flames or that metal could withstand such heat.

One minute our task force was cruising in lazy circles about 60 miles off
Okinawa without a care in the world and apparently without a thought of an
enemy plane. The next the *Bunker Hill* was a pillar of flame. It was as quick as
that—like summer lightning.

The oriental equivalent of Lady Luck was certainly riding with Japan's
suicide corps today. Fleecy-white, low-hanging clouds studded a bright sky to
conceal the intruders from lookouts manning all the stations on the ships of
Task Force 58. Not until the Japs began their final plunge from the cover of
these clouds did the *kamikazes* become visible.

And it was sheer luck, of course, that they happened to strike on the
particular day and at the exact hour when their target was most vulnerable.
Since there was no sign of the enemy and because the *Bunker Hill* and her men
were weary after 58 consecutive days in the battle zone off Iwo Jima, Tokyo,
the Inland Sea and Okinawa, her crew was not at general quarters when she was
hit.

For the first time in a week, our own ship had secured from general
quarters an hour or two before. Some of the water-tight doors that imprisoned
men in small, stifling compartments were thrown open. The ventilators were
unsealed and turned on, and those men not standing the regular watch were

permitted to relax from the deadly sixteen-hour vigil they had put in at battle stations every day since we had entered the danger area.

So it was on the *Bunker Hill*. Exhausted men not on watch were catching a catnap. Aft, on the flight deck, 34 planes were waiting to take off. Their tanks were filled to the last drop with highly volatile aviation gasoline. Their guns were loaded to the last possible round of ammunition.

Young pilots, mentally reviewing the briefing they had just received, were sitting in the cockpits warming up the motors. On the hangar deck below, more planes—also crammed with gasoline and ammunition—were all set to be spotted on the flight deck, and in the pilots' ready rooms, other young aviators were kidding around, waiting their turn aloft.

Just appearing over the horizon were the planes returning from an early mission. They jockeyed into the landing circle and waited until the *Bunker Hill* could launch her readied craft and clear the deck for landing.

Then it was that a man aboard our ship caught the first glimpse of three enemy planes and cried a warning. But before general quarters could be sounded on this ship, and before half a dozen shots could be fired by the *Bunker Hill*, the first *kamikaze* had dropped his 550-pound bomb on the ship and plunged his plane squarely into her 34 waiting planes in a shower of burning gasoline.

The delayed-action bomb pierced the flight deck at a sharp angle, passed through the side of the hull and exploded in mid-air before striking the water. The plane, a single-engined Jap fighter, knocked the parked aircraft about like ten-pins, sent a huge column of flame and smoke belching upward, and then skidded crazily over the side.

Some of the pilots were blown overboard by the explosion. Many managed to scramble to safety. But before a move could be made to fight the flames, another *kamikaze* came whining out of the clouds, straight into the deadly anti-aircraft guns of the ship. This plane was a Jap dive bomber, a Judy.

A five-inch shell that should have blown him out of the sky set him afire and riddled his plane with metal. But still he came. Passing over the stern of the ship he dropped his bomb right in the middle of the blazing planes. Then he flipped over and torched through the flight deck at the base of the "island."

The superstructure, which contains many of the delicate nerve centers from which the vessel is commanded and controlled, was enveloped in flames and smoke which were caught in turn by the maws of the ventilating system and sucked down into the inner compartments of the ship. Scores of men were suffocated in these below-deck chambers.

Minutes later a third Jap suicider zoomed down to finish the job. Ignoring the flames and the smoke that swept around them, the men in the *Bunker Hill's* gun galleries stuck to their posts, pumping ammunition into their weapons and filling the sky with a curtain of lead. It was a neighboring destroyer, however, which finally scored a direct hit on the Jap and sent him splashing harmlessly into the sea.

That was the end of the attack and beginning of the fight for survival. The entire rear end of the ship by this time was burning with uncontrollable fury. It looked much like the newsreel shots of a blazing oil well only worse, for this fire was feeding on highly refined gasoline and live ammunition. Smoke rose in a huge column from the stern of the ship, shot through with angry tongues of flame.

Blinding white flashes appeared continuously as ready ammunition in the burning planes or in the gun galleries was touched off. Every few minutes the whole column of smoke would be swallowed in a great burst of flame as another belly tank exploded or as the blaze reached another pool of gasoline flowing from the broken aviation fuel lines on the hangar deck below.

For more than an hour there was no visible abatement in the fury of the flames. They would seem to die down slightly as hundreds of thousands of gallons of water and chemicals were poured on them only to burst forth more hungrily than ever as some new explosion occurred within the stricken ship.

The carrier itself was listing and as each new stream of water was poured into her, the angle increased more dangerously. Crippled as she was she plowed ahead at top speed, and the wind that swept her decks blew the flames and smoke astern over the fantail, prevented the blaze from spreading forward on the flight deck and through the island structure. Trapped on the fantail itself, men faced the flames and fought grimly on; with only the ocean behind them, and no way of knowing how much of the ship remained on the other side of that fiery wall.

Then, somehow, other men managed to break out the huge openings in the side of the hangar deck, and I saw the interior of the ship. That, I think, was the most horrible sight of all. The hangar deck was a raging blast furnace. Even from where I stood the glow of molten metal was unmistakable.

By this time the explosions had ceased and a cruiser and three destroyers were able to venture alongside with hoses fixed in their rigging. Like fire boats in harbor they pumped great streams of water into the ship, and the smoke at last began to take on that grayish tinge which showed that somewhere a flame was dying.

Up on the bridge, meanwhile, Capt. George A. Seitz, the skipper, was concerned about the list his ship had developed. He resolved to take a gambling chance. Throwing the *Bunker Hill* into a 70-degree turn, he heeled her cautiously over onto the opposite beam so that the tons of water which had accumulated on one side were suddenly swept across the decks and overboard on the other. This wall of water carried the heart of the hangar deck fire with it.

That was the turning point in this battle. After nearly three hours of almost hopeless fighting, she had brought her fires under control, and though it was many more hours before they were completely extinguished, the battle was won and the ship had been saved.

A goodly thick book could not record all the acts of heroism that were performed aboard that valiant ship today.

There was the executive officer, Commander H.J. Dyson, who was standing within 50 feet of the second bomb when it exploded and who was badly injured, yet refused medical aid and continued to fight the blaze until it was safely under control.

There was the squad of Marines who braved the white heat of the hangar deck to throw every bomb and rocket out of a near-by storage room.

But the most fruitful work of all, perhaps, was performed by the pilots of the almost fuelless planes that had been circling overhead for a landing when the ship was struck. In the hours that followed, nearly 300 men went overboard, and the fact that 269 of these were picked up by other ships in the fleet was due, in no small measure, to the work of these sharp-eyed airmen.

Although our own flight deck had been cleared for their use and they had been instructed to land on it, these pilots kept combing every inch of the surface of the sea, tearing packets of dye marker from their own life jackets and dropping them to guide destroyers and other rescue vessels to the little clusters of men they saw clinging to bits of wreckage below them.

Calculating their fuel supply to a hair's breadth, some of them came aboard us with such a close margin that a single wave-off would have sent them and their planes into the sea before they could make another swing about the landing circle and return.

In all, I am told, 170 men will be recommended for awards as a result of this day's work.

Late today, Admiral Mitscher and 60 or more members of his staff came aboard us to make this carrier his new flagship. He was unhurt—not even singed by the flames that swept the *Bunker Hill*—but he had lost three officers and six men of his own staff and a number of close friends in the ship's company. It was the first time in his long years of service that he had personally undergone such an experience.

As he was hauled aboard in a breeches buoy across the churning water that separated us from the speedy destroyer that had brought him alongside, he looked tired and old and plain, downright mad. His deeply lined face was more than weather-beaten—it looked like a badly eroded hill. But his eyes flashed fire and vengeance.

He was a man who had a score to settle with the Japs and who would waste no time going about it. He had plans that the Japs will not like, not at all.

But the enemy is already on the losing end of the *Bunker Hill* boxscore. Since she arrived in the Pacific in the Fall of 1943, the *Bunker Hill* had participated in every major strike. She was initiated at Rabaul, took part in the invasions of the Gilberts and the Marshalls, pounding at Kwajalein and Eniwetok. With Task Force 58 she had struck twice at Tokyo and also at Truk, the China coast, the Ryukyus, Formosa, the Bonins, Iwo Jima and Okinawa.

During this time the pilots of her air groups have sunk or damaged nearly a million tons of Jap shipping. They have shot 475 enemy planes out of the air, 169 of them during the last two months. In two days here off Okinawa, they splashed 67 Nipponese aircraft and the ship herself has brought down 14 more by anti-aircraft fire.

On a raid last March at Kure Harbor, when the Japanese fleet was hiding out in the Inland Sea, *Bunker Hill* planes scored direct bomb hits on three carriers and one heavy cruiser, and then sent nine torpedoes flashing into the side of the enemy's beautiful new battleship, *Yamoto*, sinking her.

In the Jap column stands the fact that at the cost of three pilots and three planes today the enemy killed a probable total of 392 of our men, wounded 264 others, destroyed about 70 planes and wrecked a fine and famous ship. The flight deck of that ship tonight looks like the crater of a volcano. One of the great 50-ton elevators has been melted almost in half. Gun galleries have been destroyed and the pilots' ready rooms demolished. Virtually the entire island structure with its catwalks . . . is a twisted mass of steel, and below decks tonight hospital corpsmen are preparing 352 bodies for burial at sea, starting at noon tomorrow.

But the ship has not been sunk. Had it been, it would have taken years to build another. As it is the *Bunker Hill* will steam back to Bremerton Navy Yard under her own power and there will be repaired. While she remains there, one American carrier with a hundred or so planes and a crew of 3,000 men will be out of action. But within a few weeks she will be back again, sinking more ships, downing more planes, and bombing out more Japanese airfields.

Perhaps her next task will be to cover the invasion of Tokyo itself.

Essays

8 The Significance of the
Soviet Partisan Experience

John A. Armstrong

> *Partisan activities during the Second World War have recently been receiving careful attention by military professionals and thus by historians. Such doctrines as the "war of national liberation," such painful experiences as Vietnam, have stimulated the reassessment of partisan operations in World War II. Indeed, one nation, the People's Republic of China, has taken basic strategic assumptions from the Chinese Communist experience with guerrilla warfare during the 1930's and 40's. The "lessons" from this aspect of World War II are, however, diverse and contradictory. Were guerrilla movements effective substitutes for conventional military forces? Did partisans anywhere tip the scales of the military balance? In France, in Northern Italy, in the Philippines and Burma, partisans were fighting armies of occupation; of necessity they replaced conventional forces. But their importance in these regions, though large, was not decisive. On other fronts—perhaps in the Balkans, China, and the Soviet Union—as John A. Armstrong states in his essay, partisan activities may have played a decisive role.*

Viewed from the perspective of the 1960's, partisan activities in the USSR during World War II appear as part of a series of guerrilla movements which have constituted a most significant aspect of twentieth-century warfare. There are indeed important resemblances between Soviet partisan activity and other contemporary guerrilla operations. In several respects, however, the Soviet experience is highly unusual, though not entirely unique. One way to approach an understanding of this experience is to analyze the peculiar objectives of the

From **Soviet Partisans in World War II,** edited by J. A. Armstrong (Madison: the University of Wisconsin Press; © 1963 by the Regents of the University of Wisconsin), pp. 3–7. Reprinted by permission of the University of Wisconsin Press.

antagonists which shaped the conflict in the German-occupied territory of the Soviet Union.

The Soviet Objective

Historically, guerrilla forces have been the weapon of the side which is militarily weaker. When they first arise, guerrillas are a substitute for an adequate conventional force, though they may become the auxiliaries of an offensive army if the military balance shifts in the course of the war. From a strategical standpoint, the Soviet partisans clearly played these traditional roles. When the Soviet regime began developing partisan forces, its conventional armed forces were apparently greatly inferior in strength, though not in over-all size, to those which Nazi Germany could employ on the eastern front. At least until December 1941 the very existence of the Soviet system was in doubt; the margin by which the Red Army succeeded in stopping the German advance was an extremely narrow one. Under these circumstances, even a very small increment of help from irregular forces could have been decisive; consequently, it seems clear the prime immediate objective in developing the partisan forces was military. No human costs, in individual or social terms, were regarded as too high, so long as the partisan activity contributed to the overriding goal of preserving the Soviet system. In this respect, there was little distinction between the sacrifices exacted from Soviet citizens affected by partisan activity and the sacrifices exacted from those involved in other aspects of the war effort, as exemplified by the starving population of besieged Leningrad, the millions dispatched to industrial relocation sites with wholly inadequate living conditions, or the Red Army soldiers. The principle that no opportunity to impede the enemy should be renounced because of "humanitarian" considerations was emphatically stated by the Soviet regime from the moment it became involved in the war and has been reiterated consistently since then. Even major allies such as the United States were criticized for weakness in surrendering positions to avoid loss of life. This accusation of pusillanimity has been a constant theme in Soviet attacks on the non-Communist European resistance movements which sought to preserve their forces by avoiding action until the general military balance became more favorable.

As the threat to the existence of the Soviet system gradually diminished, political objectives for the partisan forces became more significant; indeed (as will be discussed in Sect. III below) one may infer that they became dominant. But the position of the Soviet regime in this regard was peculiar. Ordinarily, a government which employs guerrilla forces to help it *regain* its territory is interested in maintaining the social system of the country *and* restoring the authority of the government. Certainly the Soviet regime was interested in restoring Soviet government in the occupied territories. Moreover, the objective was clearly the restoration of the embracing Communist totalitarian system, of which the government was only a subsystem. But, before 1941, Communist totalitarianism was a goal rather than the status quo even within the USSR. The Communist prescription calls not only for the imposition of a new set of institutions upon a pre-existing society, but for a complete reshaping of society and even of individual psychology.

It is true that in those parts of the USSR which had been under Soviet control since the end of the Civil War the process of reshaping society had by 1941 made considerable headway. Especially after the agricultural collectivization and forced industrialization of the 1930's, much of the old social fabric had been disrupted. From the formal standpoint Soviet society had been reconstituted on a new basis. However, one-fourth of the population in the territory occupied by the Germans had lived under Soviet rule for such a short time (since 1939 or 1940) that the process of reconstructing society had hardly begun. In those areas, therefore, the existing social structure was fundamentally objectionable to the regime. Even in the "old" Soviet areas many traits of the pre-Soviet society survived. The bulk of the population (particularly, as will appear later, in areas where partisan activity was feasible) consisted of peasants. Although formally grouped in collective farms (which were officially regarded as only a step in the direction of "socialization"), the peasants retained many of their traditional communal and familial ties. Under normal circumstances the regime hesitated to disrupt these ties violently. The political and economic costs to the peacetime Soviet system of the resistance which such disruption might provoke would be high. Moreover, the traditional ties served certain short-run purposes of the regime, such as maintenance of a high rural birth rate and suppression of juvenile delinquency. These considerations, however, ceased to have much if any force once the population passed under the enemy control. On the other hand, if the objectionable social features dissolved in general chaos, the ultimate construction of Communist society in the postwar era might even be facilitated.

There is no direct evidence that the Soviet leaders pursued the calculation presented above, nor is it likely that any will be forthcoming. It is quite possible, indeed, that no one in authority ever consciously reasoned along these lines. However, it is evident, at least, that the Soviet leaders had far less reason to be concerned with preserving the traditional substructure of society than would normally be the case with a regime seeking to restore its authority. The Soviet regime's position in this respect was, of course, entirely consistent with its insistence on all-out attack against the enemy, regardless of human cost:

> I knew, of course, that the Hitlerites might send a punitive expedition to the village, accuse its citizens of contacts with the partisans and cruelly avenge themselves on the peaceful population. But I also knew that the population, which was driven to repair the enemy's roads, whether voluntarily or involuntarily, delayed the hour of victory by some time. But who can determine what a minute of military activity costs?

One is forced to conclude, therefore, that, while on the surface the Soviet partisan movement appears to resemble that of a guerrilla force seeking to restore the authority of an invaded state, in many respects it was really closer to the guerrilla movements in countries where Communists are trying to build a new system on the wreckage of the traditional administrative and social structure. As Franz Borkenau has pointed out, Communist partisans in Europe during World War II had an incalculable advantage over the non-Communist resistance movements, for the former, having a vested interest in social disruption, were prepared to face drastic reprisals, while the latter were constantly restrained in their tactics both by moral considerations and by the desire to avoid extreme civilian losses. The paradox of the Soviet situation lies in the fact that a guerrilla movement enjoying the support of the established government of the country could be used for ruthless, unlimited action.

The German Objective

In its way, the German position in regard to the partisans was just as unusual as the Soviet. Most contemporary antiguerrilla forces have been seeking to re-establish legitimate authority. Their task is usually enormously more difficult than the guerrillas' because the latter have only to smash an intricate and delicate web of economic installations and social relations while the defenders must not only defeat the guerrillas but do so in such a way as to preserve the system which is under attack. Failure to realize this basic difference between objectives, or lack of the patience and resources required to complete the more difficult defensive task, have been major causes for failure in antiguerrilla operations. Occasionally commentators on the Germans' antipartisan activities attribute the same shortcomings to them. In fact, however, the German objectives were so basically different from those of "defensive" antiguerrillas that the comparison has little meaning.

The overriding German objective at all times was to knock the Soviet Union out of the war. This objective was, of course, essentially Adolf Hitler's personal goal, for he realized that only complete victory would preserve his own position. Once Hitler had taken the foolhardy step of attacking the USSR, his only real prospect of eventual victory over the "Grand Coalition" of his enemies lay in eliminating Soviet military strength before Great Britain and the United States could bring the full weight of their resources to bear on Germany. At most, Hitler had only one or two years in which to achieve this goal. All longer-range considerations in Eastern Europe were subordinated to the military defeat of the Soviet Union. Though his premises are abhorrent, and his specific measures were often absurd by any standard, there was logic in the way in which Hitler tenaciously pursued this objective.

Hitler's overriding objective of destroying Soviet military power within a very short time meant that the German command regarded the partisans as crucially important only insofar as they impeded the German war effort. Whatever success the partisans might achieve in controlling territory or influencing the population was insignificant, as long as it did not reduce German capacity to strike at the basic Soviet military position. The vast stretches of occupied Europe between Germany itself and the German armies at the front were important only as a necessary avenue of communication and a source of materials (including slave labor) for pursuing the war. As a result, the German authorities did not feel that they were faced with many of the problems which usually confront an antiguerrilla force. Secure control of territory, allegiance of the population, maintenance of institutional patterns or the traditional social system did not per se interest the German authorities. Of course, the Nazi regime intended to dominate and exploit the occupied areas of Eastern Europe for centuries. Nazi ideology, however, regarded the inhabitants of the area (or at least the Slavic majority) as inferiors who were to be exploited ruthlessly and slowly reduced in numbers if not exterminated. If the course of military operations produced chaos which reduced the numbers and social viability of the Slavs, so much the better.

Consequently, no considerations of the welfare of the people in the area of partisan activity were in principle to act as impediments to ruthless conduct of antiguerrilla warfare. The Nazi leadership itself sometimes recognized the desirability of securing the cooperation of the local population for the sake of the war effort. The limits which Hitler placed on this cooperation, however, suggest the limits to the "rationality" of Hitler's conduct of the war. Until the war was almost certainly lost, he refused to allow former Soviet citizens (with minor exceptions) to bear arms even to fight the Soviet regime. To be sure, it seems very likely that even an early and massive attempt to enlist military manpower in the occupied territories would not have been decisive, for the crucial battles were lost by the Germans long before (given shortages of matériel and other factors) the Slavic anti-Communist armies could have become really effective forces.

The Resultant of the German and Soviet Objectives

The combination of Soviet and German objectives produced a situation in which measures of almost unparalleled ruthlessness became the norm of guerrilla and antiguerrilla warfare alike. Nazi doctrine glorified the use of violence and looked with distrust upon anyone who exhibited inclinations toward showing mercy. For the German antiguerrillas, ruthlessness became not only a practical norm, but a rule. While some antiguerrilla leaders, particularly among the middle and lower army officer corps, did try to exercise moderation, for reasons both of expediency and of humanity, among others sadistic tendencies toward wanton brutality and destructiveness led to excesses even beyond those encouraged by the official policy. Apart from individual instances of sadism, Soviet partisan activity was guided not by *desire* to inflict suffering, but by *disregard* of suffering, which was viewed as "necessary" for war purposes. Frequently the practical distinction between the two types of motivations was not very evident, however. . . .

9   The *Kamikaze* Controversy

Rikihei Inoguchi

In The Chrysanthemum and the Sword, *a perceptive study of the historical developments that determined Japanese thought, Ruth Benedict explained the "Kamikaze spirit" as "an illustration of the power of mind over matter". The concluding chapters of* The Divine Wind: Japan's Kamikaze Force *in World War II offer partial confirmation of this view. Its authors recognize that one motive of the Special Attack Force was a conscious effort to duplicate the exploits of the* Samurai, *those semimythical heroes whose fantastic achievements against impossible odds were also examples of mind over matter. The selection that follows discusses the postwar Japanese response to the* kamikaze *tactics and reproduces several letters from young fliers who participated. One must then deal with the basic point at issue: Did the* kamikaze *phenomenon represent the existence of diametrical differences between Japanese and Western outlooks, or was it merely a desperate tactical maneuver that might have been ordered by any military establishment in similar circumstances?*

Japanese Attitudes

The annals of war yield many instances of the use of death-scorning tactics. The motives and incentives have been as varied and varying as the techniques, but defiance of death has been the common ground. The history of Japan is full of examples, since the Japanese have been taught that a duty must always be performed, even at the risk of life. Why, then, did the kamikaze special attacks arouse such a storm of controversy in Japan?

What was there about these suicide actions to distinguish them from all historical precedents? The use of airplanes was a modern touch, of course, but this was only a matter of form. The fundamental difference was the protracted period—October 1944 to August 1945—during which these organized suicide attacks continued. In this respect they were without parallel in history. Suicidal military efforts of the past had always been sudden, swift, and drama-packed; from concept to conclusion in these previous instances there was not time enough for the "victim" to dwell on his prospects. Crisis, volunteer for death, death—that idea had been acceptable to the individual and lauded by his countrymen. But the idea of systematically planned suicide attacks carried out over a period of months, while acceptable to the individuals most concerned,

From **The Divine Wind: Japan's Kamikaze Force in World War II** by Roger Pineau et al. (Annapolis: U.S. Naval Institute, 1958), pp. 188–94, 196–208. Reprinted by permission of Roger Pineau.

seems to have been too much for the Japanese public. Thus the system and its leaders came in for severe criticism from the home front.

It is not strange that the *Ohka* attack method was ridiculed by the enemy, who referred to the weapon as the *"Baka"* bomb. This weapon had been invented and developed for months before it was finally called into use, out of sheer desperation, and its successes were few. No wonder it drew the scorn of the Americans, when we ourselves were skeptical about its chances of success. Our enemies, on the other hand, appear to have had real respect for kamikaze attacks, probably because these scored such telling blows.

When the war was over, some Japanese vehemently denounced the kamikazes without having given any thought or study to them. These outbursts could generally be traced and attributed to a general animosity of the civilian public toward the Army and Navy, and citing them would add nothing here.

There are, however, many responsible and informed people who, after due consideration and reflection, have expressed views on the kamikaze attacks. One of these is Admiral Kantaro Suzuki, a senior naval officer and the country's Premier at the time of Japan's surrender. In the Sino-Japanese War he had personally led a group of torpedo boats in a daring assault which truly exemplified the Japanese Navy's tradition of death-scorning tactics. In his book, *The Phases of Terminating the War*, he said:

> The spirit and the deeds of kamikaze pilots naturally arouse profound admiration. But, considered from the standpoint of strategy, these tactics are a product of defeat.
>
> An able commander would never resort to such extreme measures. The daring attempt to blockade Port Arthur during the Russo-Japanese War was not approved until it was shown that there was a fair chance of rescuing the participants. Their only aim was to sink boats at the entrance to the harbor, but the commanding officer refused his permission for the operation until he was assured that rescue boats would be provided. That is the way of a good commander.
>
> In the midget submarine attack on Pearl Harbor at the outbreak of war we have another example. Admiral Yamamoto would not authorize that part of the operation until it was shown that there was at least some chance of retrieving the small two-man submarines.
>
> Kamikaze attacks, on the other hand, were carried out with no possible hope of return. It is clear evidence of our fear of inevitable defeat that no other chance of turning the tide of war was visualized. The aerial operations which were begun in the Philippines left no possibility of survival. As the able pilots were expended, less experienced pilots had to be used, and finally men who had practically no training were being sent on kamikaze missions.

What Admiral Suzuki said is true. And yet it is not the way we would have liked things to be. We would have preferred to follow the precepts of what a good commanding officer should do, but the extraordinary circumstances of the war rendered conventional tactics valueless.

It is interesting to observe the parallels and the differences in comments from a non-military point of view as expressed by Dr. Daisetsu Suzuki (unrelated to Admiral Kantaro Suzuki), a noted authority and proponent of the Zen Sect of the Buddhist religion. Writing in the March 1946 issue of the *Sekai* magazine, he said:

> The recent war must be considered from many angles. Certain characteristics peculiar to the Japanese deserve our special consideration. One manifestation of these peculiarities is the special attack corps. . . .
> The Japanese Army was imbued with certain German ideologies, including the thought that war is destruction. The war potential of the enemy, whatever it be, must be destroyed. . . . War is the collision of two physical forces. The opposing force must be destroyed as quickly as possible. Soldiers, therefore, should not be thought of as human beings, but merely as a means of destruction. In this concept there in no distinction between the opposing forces.
> The kamikaze was born of such thinking! Shrink from nothing that may serve to destroy the war potential of the enemy. There were uttered such specious phrases as "the highest cause of our country," but thoughtful visions of the utterers never went beyond the physical realities of war. They were totally blind to the spiritual side of things.
> These war professionals strove endlessly to preserve from special attacks the members of their own group who were best trained to fight. They first threw into the maw of battle the non-members of their clique—the civilian non-professionals fresh from colleges and universities.
> It is most regrettable that Japanese military men have consistently been so irreligious in their outlook. Army and Navy men reiterate endlessly such Shinto ideas as "the Divine Glory of His Majesty," "the Divine Nation," "the Holy War," "the Imperial Host," and similar phrases. But they neglect or ignore such truly universal ideas as love, humanity, and mercy.
> Shinto is replete with gods of war, but there are no gods or goddesses of love. These war gods, as a consequence of Japan's insularity, are totally lacking in universality. They do not give life; they only take it.
> Deeming destruction the only way of war, the goal was to kill the enemy by any means at all. And the eternal thought was, "The essence of life is to die like a true samurai." Kamikaze attacks, the product of these two feudalistic concepts, provided a maximum of efficiency from man and material. And professional militarists cunningly took advantage of the situation.

Thus does Dr. Suzuki pass judgment on the "professional militarists" who organized and directed kamikaze attacks, pronouncing it a mental defect on our part. He then launches his attack against the people of Japan generally, saying that the spirit behind the kamikaze tactics is attributable to their lack of scientific spirit.

They attempted to overcome this deficiency by means of spiritual and physical strength applied through kamikaze tactics. The unscientific mentality of the Japanese military man was common to the rest of the country as well.

This compensatory tactic was bound to be suicidal. Far from being a matter of pride, it must remain a blemish on the people of Japan.

Dr. Suzuki's argument has some validity but, as he admits elsewhere in his writing that he was not familiar with kamikaze tactics in detail, it also involves some misunderstanding. He is obviously swayed as to some points by prejudice and dogmatism. Nevertheless, his views are presented here as being characteristic of certain of the thinking groups in Japan.

Another writer who expressed his opinion of kamikaze attacks and their proponents was Mr. Kazuo Watanabe, an assistant professor at Tokyo University, who wrote an article "Vacillating Youth" which appeared in the 9 September 1946 issue of *Nippon Dokusho Shimbun*. There he said:

Among the young men of my acquaintance, several were enrolled in the Kamikaze Corps. These men had been students, and in talking with them I found no evidence that their souls were unstable.

When they were dispatched to the battle front with a flourish of brass bands, or when in uniform they were roughly treated as belonging to the intelligentsia, they merely said to themselves, "Wait and see!" Or, when they were forced to volunteer for kamikaze attacks and were going through the training which they knew was preparing them to take the place of their professional comrades in arms, they consoled themselves with the inward words, "Wait and see!" Their conduct and bearing were founded on this stoic attitude. I have great respect for this spirit, and admire the men who were able to achieve it.

These young men could not express their resentment in positive acts against the environment which we, the older generation, had created. But they instinctively protected what they believed to be right. If today's survivors of the kamikaze effort are embarrassed by the thought that the course they followed was wrong, this is an *ex post facto* consideration. At the time, everyone concerned was guided more by instinct than by reason. There really was very little chance for reflection.

Mr. Watanabe's use of the word "instinct" is interesting in that it denotes a rather skeptical or negative attitude. Although contrary to the traditional or militaristic way of thinking, his idea must still be considered because it represents another school of kamikaze critics.

I cannot help wondering, in considering these remarks, what grounds Dr. Suzuki and Professor Watanabe have for asserting that the students-turned-soldiers were offered merely as victims to preserve the professional soldiers. If there is substance to this allegation I am unaware of it.

The editorial column of the newspaper *Yomiuri* carried an article in its issue of 1 June 1946 by its president, Mr. Tsunego Baba:

I am inclined to think that the spiritual strength of the Japanese people shows itself only in fits of passion. In the long run the Japanese people taper off and become slack. A case in point is the kamikaze attack. We must build a more tenacious race which will not have to resort to mere momentary heroism. . . .

This attitude may be construed as sympathetic to kamikaze participants, but I cannot accept his assertion that Japanese become slack in the long run. Kamikaze attacks are certainly no example of this. Those pilots had to live facing death over a long period of time, day in and day out, never knowing when it would come. And yet their spirit and determination never wavered.

In his book *Reflections upon Our National Character*, Mr. Masanori Oshima, an avowed atheist, wrote:

When confronted with a national crisis there is an urgency for immediate action. It is at such times that merits and demerits are most markedly apparent. There is no opportunity for delay or pause in which the true character may be concealed. It is then that true character is manifested; the loyalty and patriotism of the people, the real virtues of our nation, are revealed. These virtues are epitomized in the conspicuous valor of our kamikaze pilots.

It is often said that the Japanese excel in loyalty and courage. To the Japanese, death is shorn of terror. Their brave conduct on the field of battle serves as evidence of this attitude. It is a point of strength. But it is also a point of weakness, for the Japanese are prone to make light of their lives and to be too ready to die. Courage is all too often a matter of impulse rather than a matter of mature deliberation.

On the other hand, Occidentals place high value on the life of the individual. They do not die so readily, and, therefore, they cannot comprehend the psychology of kamikaze pilots. It is not a question of bravery, since Occidentals display great bravery in conquering nature, hunting wild beasts, and in exploration. But when they embark upon a hazardous undertaking it is done with the utmost of individual enterprise and intellect. That approach should serve as a good lesson for us.

There have been innumerable Japanese critics of the kamikaze attacks. Most of them, however, seem to have been made by uninformed people who stood merely as spectators of the great crisis which their nation faced. The reader must understand that the criticisms chosen for inclusion here represent the more knowledgeable Japanese observers of the kamikaze phenomenon.

* * *

Last Letters Home

What, then, were the thoughts and feelings of the suicide pilots themselves as they volunteered, waited their turn, and went out on their missions?

Mr. Ichiro Ohmi made a nationwide pilgrimage for four and a half years after the war to visit the homes of kamikaze pilots. The families showed him mementoes and letters of their loved ones. He has kindly provided the authors of the book with copies of these letters, some of which express more clearly than could any other words the thoughts and feelings of the pilots about to die.

In general, what little the enlisted pilots wrote was of a simple, straightforward nature. Academy graduates also wrote very little—perhaps because they were thoroughly indoctrinated in the way of the warrior and thus accepted their fate matter-of-factly. It was the reserve officers from civilian colleges and universities, who had had only a hasty military training before receiving their assignments, who wrote the most. A few typical letters serve to convey the spirit of kamikaze pilots.

The following was written by Ensign Susumu Kaijitsu of the Genzan (Wonsan) Air Group in Korea. Kaijitsu was born in 1923 at Omura City, Nagasaki Prefecture of northern Kyushu. He had graduated from Nagoya Technical College just before entering the naval aviation school.

Dear Father, Mother, brothers Hiroshi and Takeshi, and sister Eiko:

I trust that this spring finds you all in fine health. I have never felt better and am now standing by, ready for action.

The other day I flew over our home and bade a last farewell to our neighbors and to you. Thanks to Mr. Yamakawa I had a chance recently to have a last drink with father, and there now remains nothing but to await our call to duty.

My daily activities are quite ordinary. My greatest concern is not about death, but rather of how I can be sure of sinking an enemy carrier. Ensigns Miyazaki, Tanaka, and Kirmura, who will sortie as my wingmen, are calm and composed. Their behavior gives no indication that they are momentarily awaiting orders for their final crash-dive sortie. We spend our time in writing letters, playing cards, and reading.

I am confident that my comrades will lead our divine Japan to victory.

Words cannot express my gratitude to the loving parents who reared and tended me to manhood that I might in some small manner reciprocate the grace which His Imperial Majesty has bestowed upon us.

Please watch for the results of my meager effort. If they prove good, think kindly of me and consider it my good fortune to have done something that may be praiseworthy. Most important of all, do not weep for me. Though my body departs, I will return home in spirit and remain with you forever. My thoughts and best regards are with you, our friends, and neighbors. In concluding this letter, I pray for the well-being of my dear family.

The following letter is by Flying Petty Officer First Class Isao Matsuo of the 701st Air Group. It was written just before he sortied for a kamikaze attack. His home was in Nagasaki Prefecture.

28 October 1944

Dear Parents:

Please congratulate me. I have been given a splendid opportunity to die. This is my last day. The destiny of our homeland hinges on the decisive battle in the seas to the south where I shall fall like a blossom from a radiant cherry tree.

I shall be a shield for His Majesty and die cleanly along with my squadron leader and other friends. I wish that I could be born seven times, each time to smite the enemy.

How I appreciate this chance to die like a man! I am grateful from the depths of my heart to the parents who have reared me with their constant prayers and tender love. And I am grateful as well to my squadron leader and superior officers who have looked after me as if I were their own son and given me such careful training.

Thank you, my parents, for the 23 years during which you have cared for me and inspired me. I hope that my present deed will in some small way repay what you have done for me. Think well of me and know that your Isao died for our country. This is my last wish, and there is nothing else that I desire.

I shall return in spirit and look forward to your visit at the Yasukuni Shrine. Please take good care of yourselves.

How glorious is the Special Attack Corps' Giretsu Unit whose *Suisei* bombers will attack the enemy. Our goal is to dive against the aircraft carriers of the enemy. Movie cameramen have been here to take our pictures. It is possible that you may see us in newsreels at the theater.

We are 16 warriors manning the bombers. May our death be as sudden and clean as the shattering of crystal.

Written at Manila on the eve of our sortie.

Isao

Soaring into the sky of the southern seas, it is our glorious mission to die as the shields of His Majesty. Cherry blossoms glisten as they open and fall.

The following letter was written by Ensign Ichizo Hayashi, born in 1922, in Fukuoka Prefecture of northern Kyushu. He had been reared in the Christian faith. Upon graduation from Imperial University at Kyoto he joined the Genzan (Wonsan) Air Group, from which he was assigned to the Special Attack Corps.

Dearest Mother:

I trust that you are in good health.

I am a member of the *Shichisei* Unit of the Special Attack Corps. Half of our unit flew to Okinawa today to dive against enemy ships. The rest of us will sortie in two or three days. It may be that our attack will be made on 8 April, the birthday of Buddha.

We are relaxing in an officers' billet located in a former school building near the Kanoya air base. Because there is no electricity we have built a roaring log fire and I am writing these words by its light.

Morale is high as we hear of the glorious successes achieved by our comrades who have gone before. In the evening I stroll through clover fields, recalling days of the past.

On our arrival here from the northern part of Korea we were surprised to find that cherry blossoms were falling. The warmth of this southern climate is soothing and comforting.

Please do not grieve for me, mother. It will be glorious to die in action. I am grateful to be able to die in a battle to determine the destiny of our country.

As we flew into Kyushu from Korea the route did not pass over our home, but as our planes approached the homeland I sang familiar songs and bade farewell to you. There remains nothing in particular that I wish to do or say, since Umeno will convey my last desires to you. This writing is only to tell you of the things that occur to me here.

Please dispose of my things as you wish after my death.

My correspondence has been neglected recently so I will appreciate it if you remember me to relatives and friends. I regret having to ask this of you, but there is now so little time for me to write.

Many of our boys are taking off today on their one-way mission against the enemy. I wish that you could be here in person to see the wonderful spirit and morale at this base.

Please burn all my personal papers, including my diaries. You may read them, of course, mother, if you wish, but they should not be read by other people. So please be sure to burn them after you have looked at them.

On our last sortie we will wear regular flight uniforms and a headband bearing the rising sun. Snow-white mufflers give a certain dash to our appearance.

I will also carry the rising sun flag which you gave to me. You will remember that it bears the poem,"*Even though a thousand men fall to my right and ten thousand fall to my left....*" I will keep your picture in my bosom on the sortie, mother, and also the photo of Makio-san.

I am going to score a direct hit on an enemy ship without fail. When war results are announced you may be sure that one of the successes was scored by me. I am determined to keep calm and do a perfect job to the last, knowing that you will be watching over me and praying for my success. There will be no clouds of doubt or fear when I make the final plunge.

On our last sortie we will be given a package of bean curd and rice. It is reassuring to depart with such good luncheon fare. I think I'll also take along the charm and the dried bonito from Mr. Tateishi. The bonito will help me to rise from the ocean, mother, and swim back to you.

At our next meeting we shall have many things to talk about which are difficult to discuss in writing. But then we have lived together so congenially that many things may now be left unsaid. "I am living in a dream which will transport me from the earth tomorrow."

Yet with these thoughts I have the feeling that those who went on their missions yesterday are still alive. They could appear again at any moment.

In my case please accept my passing for once and for all. As it is said, "Let the dead past bury its dead." It is most important that families live for the living.

There was a movie shown recently in which I thought I saw Hakata. It gave me a great desire to see Hakata again just once before going on this last mission.

Mother, I do not want you to grieve over my death. I do not mind if you weep. Go ahead and weep. But please realize that my death is for the best, and do not feel bitter about it.

I have had a happy life, for many people have been good to me. I have often wondered why. It is a real solace to think that I may have some merits which make me worthy of these kindnesses. It would be difficult to die with the thought that one had not been anything in life.

From all reports it is clear that we have blunted the actions of the enemy. Victory will be with us. Our sortie will deliver a *coup de grace* to the enemy. I am very happy.

We live in the spirit of Jesus Christ, and· we die in that spirit. This thought stays with me. It is gratifying to live in this world, but living has a spirit of futility about it now. It is time to die. I do not seek reasons for dying. My only search is for an enemy target against which to dive.

You have been a wonderful mother to me. I only fear that I have not been worthy of the affection you have lavished on me. The circumstances of my life make me happy and proud. I seek to maintain the reason for this pride and joy until the last moment. If I were to be deprived of present surroundings and opportunities my life would be worth nothing. Standing alone, I was good for little. I am grateful, therefore, for the opportunity to serve as a man. If these thoughts sound peculiar, it is probably because I am getting sleepy. But for my drowsiness there are many other things I should like to say.

There is nothing more for me to say, however, by way of farewell.

I will precede you now, mother, in the approach to Heaven. Please pray for my admittance. I should regret being barred from the Heaven to which you will surely be admitted.

Pray for me, mother.

Farewell,
Ichizo

Ensign Heiichi Okabe was born in 1923. His home was Fukuoka Prefecture of northern Kyushu. Before enlisting he was graduated from Taihoku Imperial University. His first duty was in the Wonsan Air Group, and he was transferred thence to *Shichisei* Unit No. 2 of the Special Attack Corps. He kept a diary which was sent to his family after his final sortie. The following is an excerpt from one of his last entries in that diary:

22 February 1945

I am actually a member at last of the Kamikaze Special Attack Corps.

My life will be rounded out in the next thirty days. My chance will come! Death and I are waiting. The training and practice have been rigorous, but it is worthwhile if we can die beautifully and for a cause.

I shall die watching the pathetic struggle of our nation. My life will gallop in the next few weeks as my youth and life draw to a close. . . .

. . . The sortie has been scheduled for the next ten days.

I am a human being and hope to be neither saint nor scoundrel, hero nor fool—just a human being. As one who has spent his life in wistful longing and searching, I die resignedly in the hope that my life will serve as a "human document."

The world in which I lived was too full of discord. As a community of rational human beings it should be better composed. Lacking a single great conductor, everyone lets loose with his own sound, creating dissonance where there should be melody and harmony.

We shall serve the nation gladly in its present painful struggle. We shall plunge into enemy ships cherishing the conviction that Japan has been and will be a place where only lovely homes, brave women, and beautiful friendships are allowed to exist.

What is the duty today? It is to fight.

What is the duty tomorrow? It is to win.

What is the daily duty? It is to die.

We die in battle without complaint. I wonder if others, like scientists, who pursue the war effort on their own fronts, would die as we do without complaint. Only then will the unity of Japan be such that she can have any prospect of winning the war.

If, by some strange chance, Japan should suddenly win this war it would be a fatal misfortune for the future of the nation. It will be better for our nation and people if they are tempered through real ordeals which will serve to strengthen.

10 Combat Attitudes and Behavior

Samuel A. Stouffer et al.

*In late 1943 the United States War Department's Information Division
Research Branch initiated an investigation of the attitudes of American
soldiers before and after they engaged in combat. A team of social
psychologists interviewed selected units during training and again after
they had undergone extended periods in combat in the European or
Pacific theaters. The conclusions derived from this study were published
after the war in four volumes* (The American Soldier: Adjustment
During Army Life; Combat and Its Aftermath; Experiments on Mass
Communication; and Measurement and Prediction). *The second volume,
which treats the responses of American soldiers to combat conditions,
has been rightly termed a body of knowledge unique in the annals of
war.*

Attitudes of Individuals in Training as Related to Performance in Combat

In the fall and winter of 1943 it was possible to ascertain attitudes of a sample
of a newly activated division, then in training at Camp Adair, Oregon, and to
identify the questionnaires by comparing background information like induction
date, age, and state of birth with information on the Form 20 personnel cards.
The questionnaires were filled out anonymously and faith was kept with the
men, since by agreement with the commanding general the identifying
information was known only to the Research Branch and never revealed to the
local command.

One of the purposes of obtaining these individual identifications was
eventually to compare the attitudes of individuals with their performance in
combat. The division transferred more than half of its infantrymen as overseas
replacements early in 1944, thus reducing greatly the number who could be
followed up in their original units. However, the questionnaire responses of
those transferred and those remaining were almost identical on all items, so that
those remaining proved to be representative of the division with respect to
attitudes.

The 274th Infantry Regiment, to which were assigned the greater part of
the men for whom precombat data were available, arrived in France in December
1944, as part of a task force along with two other regiments. Until the artillery
and the rest of the divisional troops arrived, they were attached to other

From **The American Soldier: Combat and Its Aftermath,** vol. IV of **Studies in Social Psychology in World War II,** edited by Samuel A. Stouffer et al., Social Science Research Council, pp. 30–36, 69–88, 95–100. Copyright 1949 by Princeton University Press. Reprinted by permission of Princeton University Press.

divisions to plug the lines, here and there, wherever needed. Then, in February, they operated as part of the 70th Division. Their battle history includes heavy fighting at Philippsbourg, France, and in cracking the Siegfried Line outside of Saarbrucken. In their main actions they suffered quite severe casualties. The 275th and 276th Infantry Regiments and the 270th Engineer Battalion had much the same history. The four field artillery battalions, however, did not come into the line until mid February and had had only a little over a month of combat and few casualties when the entire division was withdrawn from combat on March 25, 1945.

Shortly after VE Day, a team of psychologists from the Research Branch, ETO, was sent to the 70th Division to obtain data on the combat performance of as many as possible of the individuals who had participated in the attitude surveys in Oregon. The division command was fully cooperative. A carefully planned interviewing procedure was employed, and out of the interviewing were obtained reliable evaluations of the combat performance of individuals. The conditions were perhaps optimal for obtaining the kind of evaluation sought. Most of the men had been in the line for about three months—long enough to provide a thorough test under fire, yet short enough so that there were still some men left to tell about it. And memories were still fresh. These conditions, and the manner in which the ratings were obtained, are critical factors in assessing the validity of the combat performance data. The rating interviews were conducted by specially trained interviewers, and in almost all cases the raters were the officers or noncoms who had worked most closely in combat with the man being rated.

At least two independent ratings were obtained on each man relative to *other men in the same outfits*, and men were regarded as "above average" or "below average" in the analysis only if the judgments of the raters showed substantial agreement as to the way in which a man had performed relative to the performance of other men in comparable jobs in the same outfit. . . . Usable combat ratings were obtained for 393 men for whom personnel and questionnaire data also were available. These men fell into three categories, as follows:

Above average in combat performance	33%
Average or indeterminate in combat performance	39
Below average in combat performance	28
	100%

Because it was particularly desired to control the influence of education, AGCT score, age, and marital condition on performance, and to evaluate the relationship between attitudes and combat ratings with these background factors held constant, the sample was reduced to 279 cases in the process of matching the three performance groups on these background factors.

Attitudes Relating to Combat as Correlated with Combat Performance

In the initial attitude surveys in Oregon, four questions were asked which had a direct reference to combat. These were:

If you were sent into actual fighting after finishing one year of training, how do you think you would do?
Do you ever worry about whether you will be injured in combat before the war is over?
How do you think you would feel about killing a Japanese soldier?
How do you think you would feel about killing a German soldier?

[The results of the initial surveys are shown in Chart I on the following pages.] . . .

* * *

General Characteristics of Ground Combat

The Combat Situation in Europe and the Pacific

There were important differences between the European and Pacific campaigns which the reader should keep in mind in evaluating the discussions and data to follow. Some of these differences may appropriately be summarized here.

In Italy and on the mainland of Europe after the landings in Normandy, the main bodies of combat troops were almost continually committed to action up to the closing weeks before the capitulation of Germany. Although men were given short rest periods, there were divisions in which a majority of the troops were in the line for months on end. Furthermore, the Germans made extensive and effective use of artillery. Partly for this reason, casualties were very heavy during many of the periods in which the front was relatively stable. Long periods of such heavy losses occurred, for example, in Normandy, in the Hurtgen Forest, in the fortified areas centering on the Siegfried Line, and at Anzio and Cassino. On the other hand, the troops were fighting in urbanized countries among people with a culture broadly similar to their own. Therefore, when they were out of the line, there were relatively favorable opportunities for familiar types of relaxation among relatively friendly populations. The troops were also favored by climatic conditions which, although at many times difficult, were not enervating and were reasonably similar to those encountered in their past experience. Furthermore, even with the winter menaces of trench foot and respiratory illness, they did not have to contend with such a persistent physical hazard as malaria proved to be in the Pacific.

In the Pacific, for the first two years of the war, battle casualties were relatively light. Only small bodies of troops were committed to action, and these only intermittently. The strategy of island-hopping typically meant that combat

CHART I

Attitudes While in Training as Related to
Combat-Performance Ratings Over a Year Later

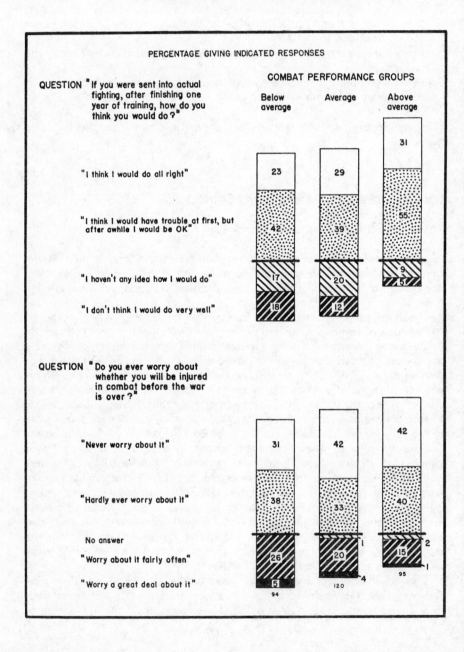

PERCENTAGE GIVING INDICATED RESPONSES

QUESTION "If you were sent into actual fighting, after finishing one year of training, how do you think you would do?"

COMBAT PERFORMANCE GROUPS

Below average   Average   Above average

"I think I would do all right"

"I think I would have trouble at first, but after awhile I would be OK"

"I haven't any idea how I would do"

"I don't think I would do very well"

QUESTION "Do you ever worry about whether you will be injured in combat before the war is over?"

"Never worry about it"

"Hardly ever worry about it"

No answer

"Worry about it fairly often"

"Worry a great deal about it"

CHART I (Continued)

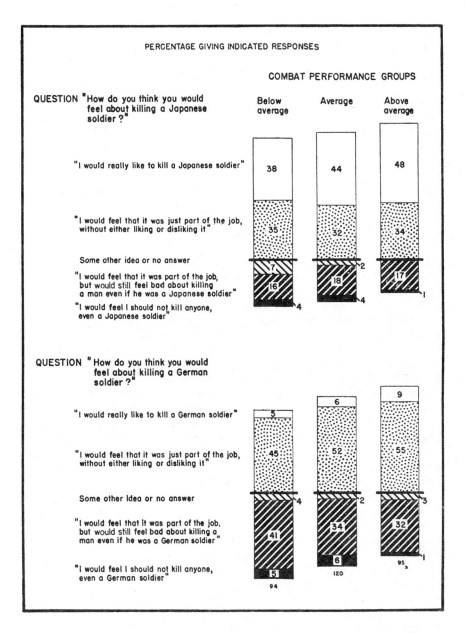

The numbers at the bottom of the bars are the numbers of cases on which the percentages are based.

troops experienced short periods of intense fighting followed by long intervals out of combat. The sporadic character of any given organization's fighting was in sharp contrast to the situation in Europe. Japanese resistance was determined, and the fighting was often incredibly grueling, but the actual incidence of battle casualties suffered by the average division was considerably less than in the war against Germany. It must be remembered that the Pacific campaigns in which the Japanese made much use of artillery and heavy weapons generally came very late in the war. The heavy casualties in such actions as those on Saipan, Iwo Jima, and Okinawa were certainly not typical of what had happened in the preceding three years. Thus, with respect to *duration of continuous combat* and *incidence of battle casualties*, the Pacific fighting during the greater part of the war may be said to have been less severe than the combat in Europe.

In nearly every other respect, however, the men in the Pacific faced conditions which severely tested morale and combat efficiency. Infiltration warfare rather than a well-defined front was the rule. As compared with the forces in Europe, a high proportion of the combat troops had spent a long time overseas. Opportunities for relaxation when out of combat were typically poor. Many soldiers had the experience of going through a campaign only to camp for long months under trying physical circumstances on an isolated island. The incidence of malaria and other diseases was high, especially in the earlier phases of the war. For example, among two divisions surveyed by the Research Branch in the South Pacific in March and April 1944, 66 per cent of the enlisted Infantry veterans in one division, which had been overseas for more than two years, said they had been hospitalized or sent to a rest camp for malaria, as did 41 per cent in the other division, which had been overseas for a year and a half.

. . . As Chart II shows, both officers and enlisted infantrymen in divisions which fought in the Mediterranean were more likely than their compatriots in the Pacific to say that combat became more frightening the more they saw of it. The officer samples in the two theaters are comparable, having been obtained at the same time in 1944. Although the officers in both theaters were markedly less likely than the enlisted men to admit fear in battle, there is a striking difference between the responses of officers in the two theaters. The enlisted sample from the Mediterranean theater was surveyed a year later, and includes troops who saw more prolonged combat than any others in the war. Probably the average of combat troops who fought in France and Germany would not have differed so greatly in their responses from the men who fought in the Pacific. But the difference does illustrate a real contrast between the two major campaigns of the war. . . .

In Chart III a comparison is presented of the responses of officers in two divisions which saw heavy jungle fighting against the Japanese in the Solomons with the responses of officers in two divisions which played a large part in the North African and Sicilian campaigns. . . .

As would be expected from the previous discussion, the officers in the Pacific considerably more frequently cited "Lack of endurance due to poor physical condition" than did the officers in Europe (41 per cent as against 26 per cent).

CHART II

Fear of Battle in Mediterranean and Pacific Campaigns

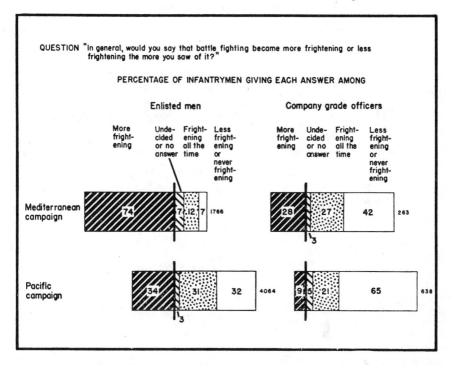

QUESTION "In general, would you say that battle fighting became more frightening or less frightening the more you saw of it?"

PERCENTAGE OF INFANTRYMEN GIVING EACH ANSWER AMONG

There were only two items which were significantly more frequently cited in Europe than in the Pacific as having a bad effect on battle performance. One was "Inadequate communications with other companies and with higher headquarters" (34 per cent in the Pacific and 47 per cent in Europe), a factor related perhaps to the more rapid mobility of the North African and Sicilian campaigns. The other was "Lack of conviction about what we are fighting for"—a phenomenon obviously difficult for officers to observe, and one which was seldom cited in either area as having a bad effect on battle performance. However, the fact that only 8 per cent cited this in the Pacific, as compared with 22 per cent in Europe, reflects a statistically significant difference and one which may very likely be attributable to the attitude toward the enemy in the Pacific as compared with the attitude toward the enemy in Europe. . . .

Combat as a Situation of Stress

The one all-pervading quality of combat which most obviously marks it off as the object of special interest is that it was a *situation of stress*. It combined in one not-too-neat package a large number of major factors which men everywhere

CHART III

Testimony of Company Officers as to Factors
in Battle Performance—Pacific and Europe

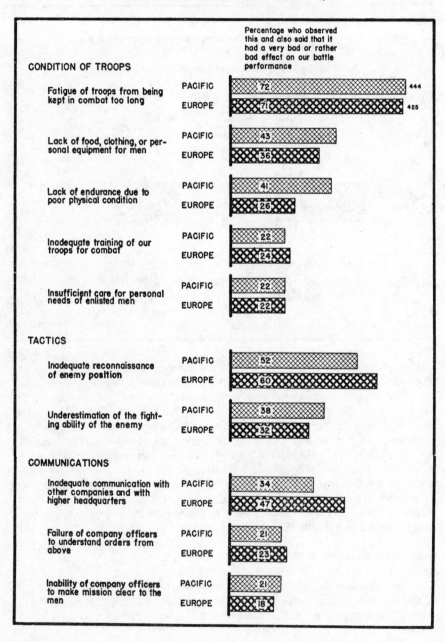

Percentage who observed this and also said that it had a very bad or rather bad effect on our battle performance

CONDITION OF TROOPS

Fatigue of troops from being kept in combat too long
- PACIFIC: 72 — 444
- EUROPE: 71 — 425

Lack of food, clothing, or personal equipment for men
- PACIFIC: 43
- EUROPE: 36

Lack of endurance due to poor physical condition
- PACIFIC: 41
- EUROPE: 26

Inadequate training of our troops for combat
- PACIFIC: 22
- EUROPE: 24

Insufficient care for personal needs of enlisted men
- PACIFIC: 22
- EUROPE: 22

TACTICS

Inadequate reconnaissance of enemy position
- PACIFIC: 52
- EUROPE: 60

Underestimation of the fighting ability of the enemy
- PACIFIC: 38
- EUROPE: 32

COMMUNICATIONS

Inadequate communication with other companies and with higher headquarters
- PACIFIC: 34
- EUROPE: 47

Failure of company officers to understand orders from above
- PACIFIC: 21
- EUROPE: 23

Inability of company officers to make mission clear to the men
- PACIFIC: 21
- EUROPE: 18

CHART III (Continued)

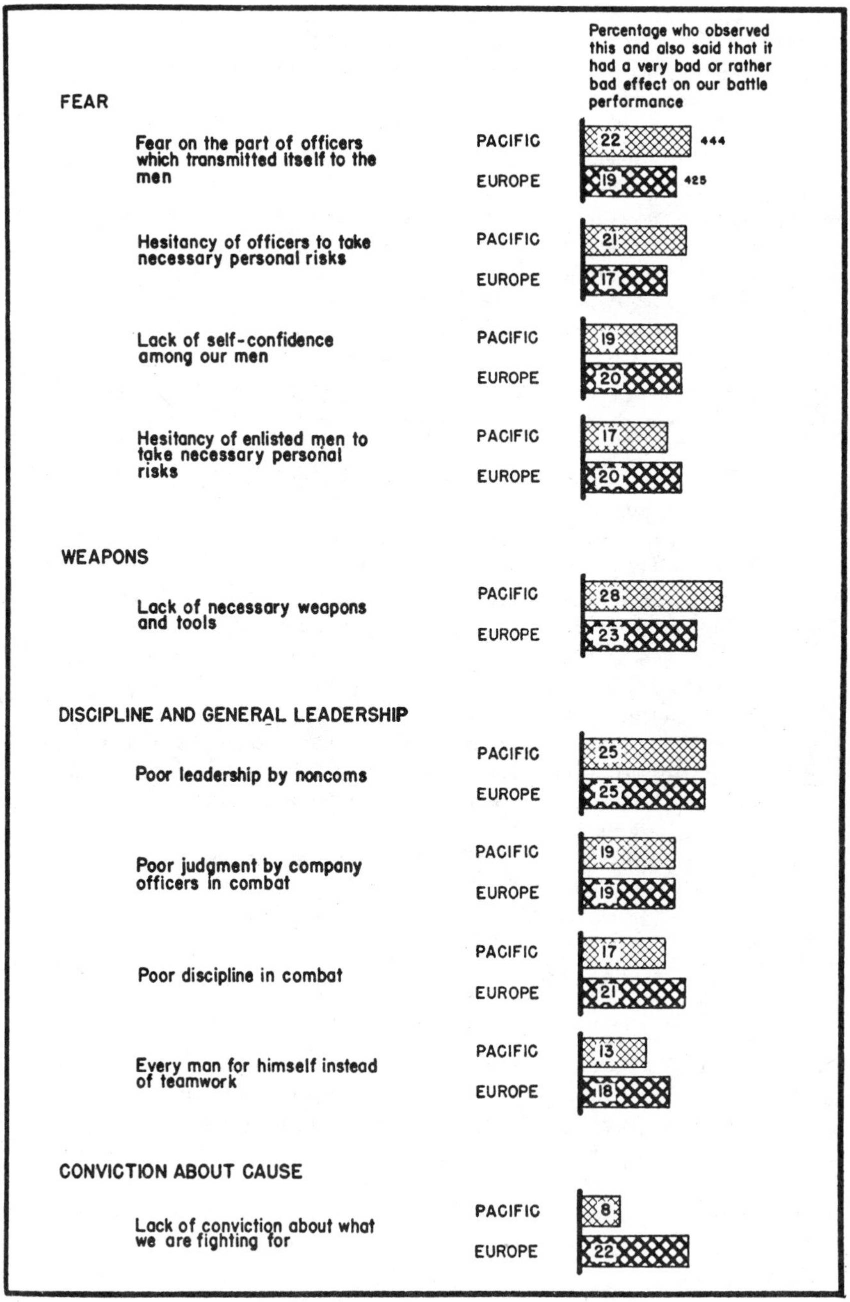

Percentage who observed this and also said that it had a very bad or rather bad effect on our battle performance

FEAR

Fear on the part of officers which transmitted itself to the men

PACIFIC 22 444

EUROPE 19 425

Hesitancy of officers to take necessary personal risks

PACIFIC 21

EUROPE 17

Lack of self-confidence among our men

PACIFIC 19

EUROPE 20

Hesitancy of enlisted men to take necessary personal risks

PACIFIC 17

EUROPE 20

WEAPONS

Lack of necessary weapons and tools

PACIFIC 28

EUROPE 23

DISCIPLINE AND GENERAL LEADERSHIP

Poor leadership by noncoms

PACIFIC 25

EUROPE 25

Poor judgment by company officers in combat

PACIFIC 19

EUROPE 19

Poor discipline in combat

PACIFIC 17

EUROPE 21

Every man for himself instead of teamwork

PACIFIC 13

EUROPE 18

CONVICTION ABOUT CAUSE

Lack of conviction about what we are fighting for

PACIFIC 8

EUROPE 22

tend to regard as things to be avoided: "Adjustment to combat . . . means not only adjustment to killing, but also adjustment to danger, to frustration, to uncertainty, to noise and confusion and particularly to the wavering faith in the efficiency or success of one's comrades and command."

The main types of stress in combat are reasonably clear. Not necessarily in order of their importance, they are:

1. Threats to life and limb and health.
2. Physical discomfort—from lack of shelter, excessive heat or cold, excessive moisture or dryness, inadequacy of food or water or clothing; from insects and disease; from filth; from injuries or wounds; from long-continued fatigue and lack of sleep.
3. Deprivation of sexual and concomitant social satisfaction.
4. Isolation from accustomed sources of affectional assurance.
5. Loss of comrades, and sight and sound of wounded and dying men.
6. Restriction of personal movement—ranging from the restrictions of military law to the immobility of the soldier pinned down under enemy fire.
7. Continual uncertainty and lack of adequate cognitive orientation.
8. Conflicts of values
   a. between the requirements of duty and the individual's impulses toward safety and comfort
   b. between military duty and obligations to family and dependents at home, to whose well-being the soldier's survival is important
   c. between informal group codes, as of loyalty to comrades, and the formal requirements of the military situation which may sometimes not permit mutual aid
   d. between previously accepted moral codes and combat imperatives.
9. Being treated as a means rather than an end in oneself; seemingly arbitrary and impersonal demands of coercive authority; sense of not counting as an individual.
10. Lack of "privacy"; the incessant demands and petty irritations of close living within the group.
11. Long periods of enforced boredom, mingled with anxiety, between actions.
12. Lack of terminal *individual* goals; poverty and uncertainty of individual rewards.

All of these broad categories of stress were found in combat situations. Not all of them were always operative for a given group or individual; some combat soldiers never experienced some of them *as stress* at all. Depending upon circumstances, also, the intensity of any particular sort of stress varied greatly. Each type of stress deserves preliminary comment. Although much that will be said is obvious, an explicit consideration has the advantage of giving at the outset a fairly full picture of what the combat men had to withstand.

Fear of death or injury is potentially present among persons generally. Combat as the prime occasion of deliberate risks to life and limb imposed severe stress, involving the deepest anxieties and the most primitive threats to personal integrity. . . .

Whereas any newspaper reader or movie-goer has a definite, sometimes exaggerated, notion of the dangers of combat, the degree of stress imposed by sheer physical discomfort is perhaps less widely appreciated. Many a soldier will remember the mud and the K-rations after the memory of danger has grown dim. Rarely, furthermore, was the combat soldier subject merely to one kind of physical discomfort; his ills came in flocks. It is thus not merely that he was cold and wet, but that he was also deadly tired, dirty, and without prospect of shelter. Or, it is not only that his stomach staged a minor revolt against still another can of pork loaf, but that he was simultaneously lying in a filthy foxhole under steaming heat and incessantly irritated by swarms of malaria-bearing mosquitoes. The effects of long-continued, multiple physical discomforts of this sort were intensely distressing; and if no relief was in prospect for an indeterminable future, they could come to seem well nigh insupportable. It is believed that most ground troops who saw front-line duty in this war will agree with this general appraisal.

Two illustrations to bring home the omnipresence of this kind of combat stress may be drawn from a survey made in Italy shortly before the end of the campaign in that theater. Although the front had been quiet for several months of holding action at the time the survey was made—and conditions were therefore probably as favorable as ever exist in combat—nearly one third of the men said that they averaged 4 hours or less of sleep out of each 24 hours the last time they were in the line, while only 13 per cent said they averaged 7 or more hours of sleep a day (Table 1).

TABLE 1

Average Amount of Sleep Reported by Infantrymen During a Quiet Period

Question: "When you were last on active duty, how many hours of sleep did you average each 24 hours?"

	Percentage of infantrymen giving each answer
Less than 2 hours	3
2 to 4 hours	28
5 to 6 hours	54
7 or more hours	13
No answer	2
Total	100

Over half the men said they did not get as much to eat as they needed. Those who said they did not, gave the reason for the most part that they did not like the food available, or that they couldn't get the food. (Table 2.) Again it should be remembered that conditions in the months prior to administration of the questionnaire had been exceptionally favorable. Hot food at the front at this time was by no means unheard of.

TABLE 2

Eating Frustrations Reported by Combat Infantrymen
During a Quiet Period

Questions: "When you were last on active combat duty, did you get as much to eat as you needed?"

"If you did not get as much to eat as you needed, what was the reason?"

	Percentage of infantrymen giving each answer
We couldn't get food	22
I didn't like the kind of food we had	30
I didn't feel like eating	10
Some other reason	*
I got as much as I needed	36
No answer	2
Total	100

*Less than 0.5 per cent.

Opportunities for regularized sex relations are a necessary part of the institutions of every large social system. The average young man in our culture does not make a virtue out of sexual deprivation. Furthermore, there are few psychiatric generalizations which are more widely documented than that sexual relations typically involve much more than physical gratification as such. They are bound up with needs for security, for feeling oneself a valued person, for reassurance that one is considered worth affection. The ostensibly sexual is often the bearer of many personal needs which have little to do with physical gratification as usually viewed. For men in combat there was a particular significance in all this. Under great anxiety and insecurity, men tended to lose many of their usual long-term perspectives. At the same time, their need for emotional reassurance was especially great; faced with the immediate possibility of personal annihilation amid the vast impersonal destruction of war, hedonistic drives and socially derived needs combined to make sexual deprivation a major stress. A closely allied fact is the strain imposed upon most normal individuals by having to live under conditions of great difficulty without the taken-for-granted affectional support which is typically supplied by one's family, close friends, and local community.

Grief, rage, and horror are emotions which occurred among masses of men in every day of battle. Because the combat soldier was trained to anticipate and meet the shocks which occasion those emotions, he was better able to bear them than his civilian counterparts. Still, the recurring evidences of death, destruction, and mutilation imposed a sapping emotional drain upon the typical American soldier. And because men in combat were closely bound together by mutual dependence and affectional ties they were correspondingly shaken by the loss of comrades. Grief was added to fear, fatigue, and discouragement.

The extent to which the front-line infantryman was exposed to the sight of death and suffering during a combat career may be underlined by data from the survey of combat infantrymen in Italy, only 10 per cent of whom had seen less than 3 months of combat and 54 per cent of whom had seen 6 months of combat or more. Of these men, 87 per cent said they had seen a close friend killed or wounded in action, while 83 per cent said they had seen "a man's nerves crack up" at the front. Data from a division which saw combat in the South Pacific indicate that, as might be expected, the effect of these stresses was cumulative. The men were asked how often they had various physical reactions to the dangers of battle when they were under fire. On the assumption that men who were successfully resisting the effects of combat stress should show relatively fewer of these physical symptoms when under fire, one would expect men who have been exposed to more severe stresses to admit to a greater number of symptoms. As Chart IV indicates, such is indeed the case. Men who said that their companies had suffered heavy casualties, that they had seen one of their best friends killed in action, and that they had witnessed enemy atrocities, reported many more fear symptoms than those who had not been subjected to any of these stresses; groups intermediate in amount of stress were also intermediate in respect to fear symptoms. The reservation must be made that, to the extent that more fearful men were more likely to overestimate casualties and more likely to interpret a given enemy action as an atrocity, the relationship may be spuriously high. . . .

War is a special province of chance, and the gods of luck rise to full stature on the field of battle. Uncertainty and confusion are inseparable from combat: "Every action . . . only produces a counteraction on the enemy's part, and the thousands of interlocking actions throw up millions of little frictions, accidents and chances, from which there emanates an all-embracing fog of uncertainty . . . the unknown is the first-born son of combat and uncertainty is its other self."

In combat, the individual soldier was rarely sure of what had just happened, what was going on at the moment, or what was likely to occur next. He was subject to continual distraction by violent stimuli, and lived always under the tension of expecting the unexpected. This kind of unceasing confusion—the lack of firm constance to which behavior could be oriented—exposed the individual to insidious anxieties. All people need some stability in their environment; it has been repeatedly shown that personality integration and the development of

CHART IV

Degree of Reported Bodily Expression of Fear in Battle, in Relation to Various Sources of Stress, in Combination

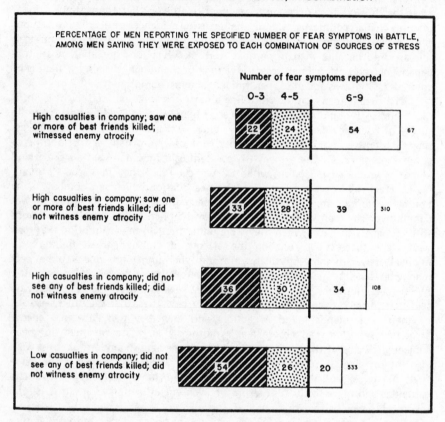

PERCENTAGE OF MEN REPORTING THE SPECIFIED NUMBER OF FEAR SYMPTOMS IN BATTLE, AMONG MEN SAYING THEY WERE EXPOSED TO EACH COMBINATION OF SOURCES OF STRESS

Number of fear symptoms reported

0-3   4-5   6-9

High casualties in company; saw one or more of best friends killed; witnessed enemy atrocity — 22 | 24 | 54 | 67

High casualties in company; saw one or more of best friends killed; did not witness enemy atrocity — 33 | 28 | 39 | 310

High casualties in company; did not see any of best friends killed; did not witness enemy atrocity — 36 | 30 | 34 | 108

Low casualties in company; did not see any of best friends killed; did not witness enemy atrocity — 54 | 26 | 20 | 533

regularized patterns of behavior are strongly conditioned upon the existence of stable referents for activity. One of the prime functions of any sort of social organization is to provide the individual with a dependable set of expectations. Unless one knows, at least within broad limits, what behavior to expect from others, the very concept of adjustment becomes meaningless. So it is that the uncertainties and confusions of combat were themselves identifiable sources of stress. The frictions of battle, the mistiness of knowledge that goes under the name of "the fog of war," could be minimized by good provisions for transportation and communication, and by good discipline and administrative organization; but uncertainty always remained. Enemy movements would not always be known; supplies would sometimes fail to arrive when and where most needed; reinforcements would be delayed; radios would refuse to work and telephone lines would be broken. The necessities of secrecy, among other things, would sometimes prevent the mass of soldiers from knowing the "big picture." Men would become lost from their units, enemy surprise attacks would be launched, units would be cut off from other units. The fact of never knowing what to expect was thus a sharply distinguishing mark of the situation of men in combat.

In some respects a group in conflict with another group represents a maximum of value integration: all are united in a common task with a definite and agreed-upon goal. Yet in other respects the combat situation was permeated with conflicts of values and obligations. Most clearly evident was the struggle between the individual's impulses toward personal safety and comfort and the social compulsions which drove him into danger and discomfort: "Sometimes a guy would say, 'How do I keep going?' You have to fight with yourself. You didn't want to be a quitter. You know you're all right." In the case of the combat soldier, this internal fight was one of the factors which sometimes lay at the root of neuropsychiatric breakdowns involving gross disorganization of behavior. . . .

Finally, combat required a sharp break with many moral prescriptions of peacetime society. As easy as it seems to be for men to kill when their immediate group sanctions it, and as ambivalent as normal people often are about killing, it is still true that to kill other human beings requires of most men from our culture an effort to overcome an initial moral repugnance. Under the requirements of the situation, men in combat were careful to hide this feeling, and it was not a subject of much discussion among soldiers. Killing is the business of a combat soldier, and if he is to function at all he must accept its necessity. Yet the acceptance of killing did not prevent men from feeling the ambivalence revealed by such comments as that of a veteran rifleman who said, "I'll tell you a man sure feels funny inside the first time he squeezes down on a Kraut."

Not so often recognized as a fundamental source of strain was the sheer impersonality of combat. Over all else hung the thought that "we are expendable" and a sense of the enormous impersonal forces upon which one's personal fate might depend. In the nature of the case, the combat soldier was to a large extent used as a means rather than an end. He was an instrument of war. It is usual for people in our culture to feel an aversion to being treated as numbers, to react negatively to being impersonally used. Although it could be increased or decreased, the feeling that "nobody gives a damn about us" was always ready to spring to the surface among the men who repeatedly were sent into situations resulting in high casualties. The stress was worsened by any seemingly capricious, arbitrary, and impersonal acts of higher authority. Acts interpreted by the men in these terms were not necessarily so regarded by the command, nor would they necessarily be so viewed by an impartial outside observer. But men's beliefs could represent the orders of higher command as further assaults on their already vulnerable sense of counting for something as individuals; and it must be remembered that commanders were themselves under stress and did not always see a necessity for keeping the men informed, for minimizing nonfunctional demands upon them, or for doing other things to bolster men's sense of personal worth. . . .

Combat as actually experienced consisted of periods of intense activity and excitement punctuating the periods of routine and boredom. When men were not actually in the line of battle or even when they were in the line during quiet periods, the often spent long periods of enforced idleness in which the intense boredom of having no goals for activity was intermingled with the anticipatory anxiety of waiting for further combat. Monotony and boredom may appear to have been trivial compared with the shocks of the attack, but they did take a psychological toll of more than negligible importance.

Finally, for American ground troops there was the particular burden of the apparent endlessness of combat—the lack of any terminal individual goal short of the end of the war. Under our system of replacing personnel losses by individuals rather than by units and of keeping divisions in action for extended periods, men easily concluded that there would be no end to the strain until they "broke" or were hit. In the words of an Infantry scout who was wounded at Salerno after fighting through the Sicilian campaign: "Men in our division gave up all hope of being relieved. They thought the Army intended to keep them in action until everybody was killed . . . that they would simply replace casualties. . . . All the men have hope of getting back, but most of the hope is that you'll get hit someplace that won't kill you. That's all they talk about." Or, later in the same interview: "You give up. You feel that you'll never get back anyway. You just try to postpone it as long as possible."

Infantrymen who had seen very extensive action were asked, near the end of the Italian campaign, "While you were in combat, did you have the feeling that it was just a matter of time until you would get hit?"

	The percentage of infantrymen giving each answer was:
I almost always felt that way	26
I usually felt that way	13
I sometimes felt that way	23
I felt that way once in a while	21
I practically never felt that way	15
No answer	2
Total	100 . . .

General Social Characteristics of the Combat Situation Which Resist Stress

From what has now been said one might well wonder how soldiers ever managed to fight at all, if so many destructive and disorganizing forces were at work upon them. This wonder is justified and it is an indication of the strength of opposing factors that soldiers did fight—fight well, for long periods, and often without gross personality disorganization. Evidently the combat situation included factors other than those of stress which warrant attention. In this section, some of these important social features of the combat situation will be indicated. . . .

Features Which Are Part of the Definition of the Combat Situation

From the mere fact that combat always consists in one group fighting an enemy, there follow certain features which make for social cohesion. In the first place, combat involves *a major threat from outside to the group as a whole*. Alone, the threat does not automatically result in group solidarity. In conjunction, however, with other factors to be discussed later which keep the group in the situation, it results in a dramatic increase in mutually supportive action among members of the group. In the face of great external danger common to the entire group, there is strong pressure to resolve or repress internal antagonisms and discordant behavior patterns.

Also inherent in the combat situation is the existence of a *socially approved outlet for aggressions* which are ordinarily tabooed within our society. Many an intragroup quarrel has been checked by the curt advice from fellow soldiers: "Save that for the Germans." The enemy is a suitable target for many of the hostilities arising from the individual's personal history and his experience within the group.

A third characteristic of organized combat without which there would be no combat is that the activities of the men are *directed toward definite and tangible goals*. Regardless of the extent to which the individual soldier accepts it as his own, there is always an unambiguous goal inherent in the situation: to overcome the enemy. Any unit is almost always under orders to take or hold a specific objective, and each man in action has a definite set of duties to perform. The men have weapons which, ideally, they know how to use. Their task, although difficult, is in a sense simple and straightforward. But over and above the fact that the task is set by orders—a characteristic, after all, of most other military situations—is the immediacy and manifest importance of the combat goal. Whether the particular task was to capture an enemy observation post, or to hold a position, or even to engage in an action the strategic usefulness of which was not at all apparent, it directly involved overcoming or resisting the enemy, and this goal was a primary feature of the structure of the situation. The goals set for the combat soldier were much less indirect than those of a soldier in the chain of supply.

There are, of course, many other concrete personal and group goals in combat, which may support or conflict with this goal in different degrees. Also, men may vary in the extent to which they accept the goal of combat as important; that it is there to make simple sense of their behavior, however, raises it to a position of peculiar potency. It is in part this immediacy of the goal which lends meaning to the phrase, "the battle is the pay-off."

Institutional Features Which Are Primarily Brought to the Combat Situation

Both informal and formal institutional factors entered into the control of behavior in combat. While certain aspects of the informal controls grew out of attitudes common to our culture or were developed during the training period, the strong intragroup ties which lent so much potency to the informal controls in combat arose for the most part within the combat situation. . . . No understanding of combat behavior would . . . be possible if the obvious fact were ignored that the fighting is done by armies, which bring with them to the field a complex social organization and a set of prescribed ways of doing, interpreting, and evaluating things. . . . The special relevance in combat of certain of these institutional characteristics will be considered [here].

The rigid and complexly hierarchical Army organization, with its accompanying set of formal rules, was the Army's main answer to the stress and confusion of battle. The soldier was not an individual atom in the tide of warfare; he was an integral part of a vast system of discipline and coordination. The chain of command was implemented by stringent sanctions for failures to conform. Men faced combat in tightly organized formal groups, and were held in those groups by the ultimate sanctions their society wielded, including the power, almost never used, of punishment by death. Thus, the individual in combat was simultaneously guided, supported, and coerced by a framework of organization.

A prime characteristic of the Army is the extent to which it relies on these impersonal controls. Army organization is devised to work even when personal ties cannot be depended on—as in the last analysis they cannot be when any individual may have to be replaced as a combat casualty. So great is the need for coordinated behavior in the battle situation, and so obdurate are the difficulties in the way of securing it, that the Army tries to aim for a margin of safety in establishing an organizational structure with supporting habits and sentiments to ensure prompt and exact carrying out of orders. This is the rationale for much that was resented by the men in their precombat training. Whether or not close-order drill and garrison discipline actually do aid in knitting together this automatically functioning organization and, if they do, whether or not they are more efficient than alternative types of training are moot questions which it is not possible to settle here. There can be little doubt, however, of the crucial importance of the mechanical, quasi-automatic aspects of Army operation in combat which such training is intended to promote. "You get a habit of taking orders when you're in training so that when they tell you to do something, you do so without hardly thinking," a wounded veteran of the Sicilian and early Italian campaign put it. During the confusion of combat, in which any course is problematical and dangerous and individual judgment must operate under a tremendous handicap, the fact that one knew to whom to look for direction and orders, that such orders were forthcoming, and that the range of possible behavior was closely limited by established rule, was one of the most important single determinants of behavior.

Social Features Which Arise Primarily Within the Combat Situation

Within the framework of formal organization on the one hand and of the inherent features of organized combat on the other, characteristic informal social features developed which, it will be seen in the following [section], supported a potent system of informal controls.

The combat situation was one of mutual dependence. A man's life depended literally and immediately upon the actions of others; he in turn was responsible in his own actions for the safety of others. This vital interdependence was closer and more crucial in combat than in the average run of human affairs. Any individual's action which had conceivable bearing on the safety of others in the group became a matter of proper concern for the group as a whole. Mutual dependence, however, was more than a matter of mere survival. Isolated as he was from contact with the rest of the world, the combat man was thrown back on his outfit to meet the various affectional needs for response, recognition, approval, and in general for appreciation as a significant person rather than a means—needs which he would normally satisfy in his relations with his family and with friends of his own choosing. Most aspects of combat as a stress situation served only to make these needs the more urgent. The group was thus in a favored position to enforce its standards on the individual.

Some illustrations of the close affectional ties which develop in combat may be drawn from an interview with an Infantry private first class who fought through seven months of the North African campaign before being returned to the United States as a casualty:

The men in my squad were my special friends. My best friend was the sergeant of the squad. We bunked together, slept together, fought together, told each other where our money was pinned in our shirts. We write to each other now. Expect to get together when the war is over. . . . If one man gets a letter from home over there, the whole company reads it. Whatever belongs to me belongs to the whole outfit.

An armored Infantry veteran says, "Practically all of the boys in your company are your friends. One of the things a fellow learns in the Army is to make friends with anybody, and hold that friendship."

The isolation of the front-line unit was such as to make the combat man feel completely set apart. Even in the midst of his fellows, each man had the inner loneliness that comes from having to face death at each moment. This psychological isolation was mitigated by the presence, example, and support of other soldiers in the unit. But the unit itself lived and died apart from that other great world of the rear—and that meant, for the rifleman, everyone out of range of small arms and mortars. The "taken-for-grantedness" of personal survival vanished in the realization that death might come at any time and that often it was more likely to come than not. In a thousand ways, great and small, the soldier coming into the line had defined for him a world that felt itself to be and was, in fact, removed physically and psychologically from all that lay behind it.

Behind the front the great military machine inexorably continued to send forward supplies and men—and the orders that sent men into attack. But the rifleman's world shrank to the tremendous immediacies of staying alive and destroying the enemy.

In this setting developed the feeling of fraternity of combat soldiers. Those who had shot at the enemy and had themselves been fired upon in that thin forward zone, had a consciousness of shared experience under great emotional stress which they felt others could never understand. This consciousness became clear mostly after action, when in the rear or in reminiscence. But even during battle, soldiers at the front felt strongly their mutual dependence, their common loneliness, their separate destiny apart from all who were not at the front. The significant experience they had shared was a further bond between individual and group. . . .

* * *

Combat Motivations Among Ground Troops

. . . Notice has already been taken of certain general aspects of the situation which made it possible for the combat soldier to sustain the extraordinary stresses to which he was subjected. In the present section this problem will be given closer attention.

It must be noted that this is a very different question from "why men fight," or why the population at large may want a war or acquiesce in it. As a man changes from civilian to front-line soldier, the factors conditioning his behavior change and so do the motives to which he refers to account for his actions. It is also a more restricted problem than "why soldiers fight." A career army, a guerrilla army, or an army fighting in its own homeland may be expected to fight for a quite different cluster of "reasons" than the American combat man in the recent war.

Furthermore, it is necessary to be specific as to the meaning of "why." It would be possible to raise the question "why" in such a form as to require a complete knowledge of the individual life histories of every person in our culture. On the other hand, it would be possible to pose the problem solely in terms of institutional factors without reference to individual motives. The meaning of "why" depends on the frame of reference in terms of which the analysis is carried out.

In the following account, the central concern will be the more important ways in which social and situational factors impinge on the behavior of the ground soldier to keep him in combat. The focus will be on the individual, but no systematic attempt will be made to trace out the intricacies of combat motivation in intrapersonal terms. Indeed, the nature of the data available virtually imposes such a limitation, since without extensive psychiatric interviewing any attempt at a thorough account of intrapersonal factors would be merely speculative. The analysis therefore in general will not be concerned with personal traits, needs, or drives at the level of aggressiveness, wish for recognition, or need for affection. It will, on the other hand, touch upon such factors as hatred of the enemy, the prestige of the combat man, and the loyalty to one's buddies—factors at a level of abstraction fairly close to the immediate combat situation. . . .

The major interest in the present discussion is, then, to analyze the typical and general determinants of behavior in the immediate combat situation. A tired, cold, muddy rifleman goes forward with the bitter dryness of fear in his mouth into the mortar bursts and machine-gun fire of a determined enemy. A tremendous psychological mobilization is necessary to make an individual do this, not just once but many times. In combat surely, if anywhere, we should be able to observe behavioral determinants of great significance, since we already know that most soldiers did fight in the face of all the cumulative stresses tending to drive them out of combat. . . .

As an overview of this investigation of combat motivation, an analysis of the unguided statements of combat men and officers on the subject is instructive. Chart 2 presents a summary classification of the responses of enlisted infantrymen in a veteran division which saw action in two Mediterranean campaigns and of company grade officers in divisions in both European and Pacific theaters to questions in regard to the incentives which kept the men fighting. A more detailed presentation of the same data may be found in Tables 3 and 4. Both the question asked of the enlisted men and that asked of the officers invited answers of a somewhat more restricted scope than that of this chapter. The enlisted men were asked what was most important to them in making them *want* to keep going and do as well as they could, while the officers were asked what *incentives* kept their men fighting. One would not expect these questions to elicit reference to the several factors which appear to have been important in giving the men support without, however, providing a spur to further fighting, for instance prayer or fatalism. Neither would one expect the men's answers to make much of coercive institutional authority, since only indirectly can it be said to have been an incentive or to have made the men want to keep going. In other respects, the men's answers touch in one way or another on most of the principal sources of motivation with which we will be concerned.

Most frequently mentioned by the enlisted men was the prosaic goal of ending the task—getting the war over with to get home again, or hope of more immediate relief at the end of a particular mission. Presumably "thoughts of home and loved ones" had somewhat similar import, as something to look forward to when the job was over. Various aspects of solidarity with the group were mentioned second in frequency: sticking together, loyalty to comrades, pride in outfit, etc. The importance of the strong group ties that developed in combat will be the subject of considerable later discussion. A sense of duty and self-respect was mentioned by a number of the men. Rather than considering this as a separate motivational category, it will be treated as evidence of the internalization of both institutional and informal group requirements.

All of the incentives listed thus far (excepting "thoughts of home and loved ones," if this is considered separately from "ending the task") were also mentioned by substantial numbers of officers. The most striking discrepancy

CHART V

Combat Incentives Named by Officer and Enlisted Veterans

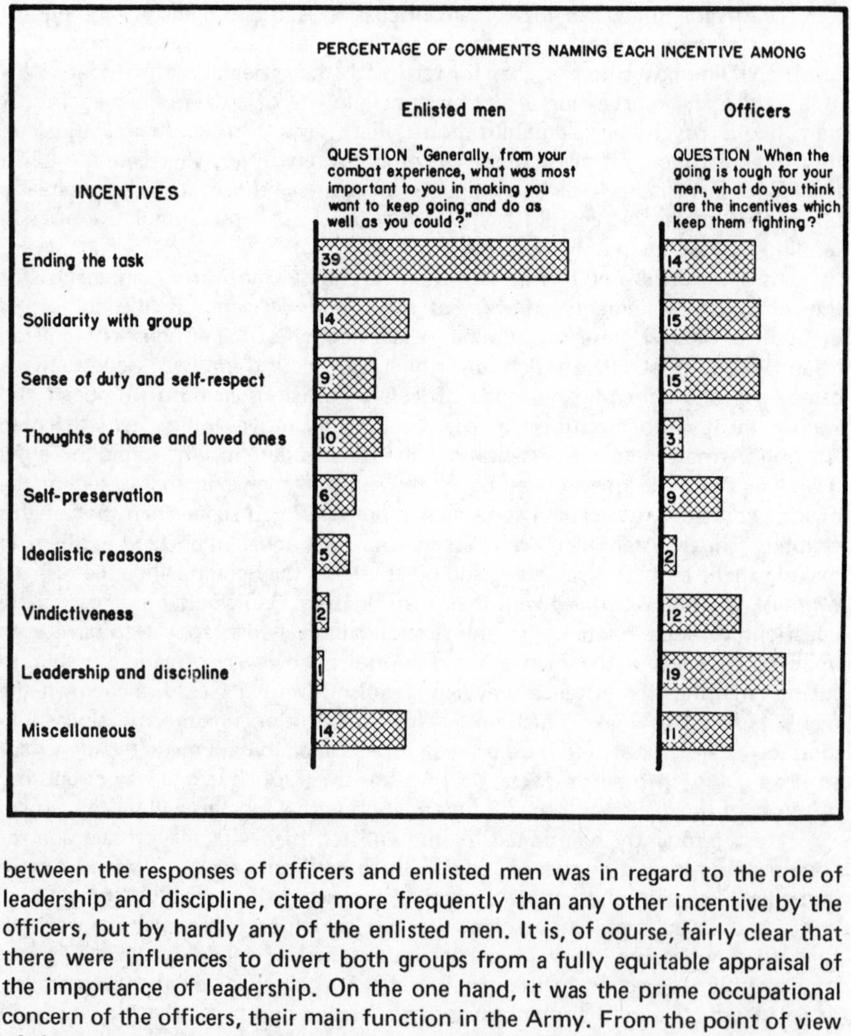

PERCENTAGE OF COMMENTS NAMING EACH INCENTIVE AMONG

INCENTIVES	Enlisted men QUESTION "Generally, from your combat experience, what was most important to you in making you want to keep going and do as well as you could?"	Officers QUESTION "When the going is tough for your men, what do you think are the incentives which keep them fighting?"
Ending the task	39	14
Solidarity with group	14	15
Sense of duty and self-respect	9	15
Thoughts of home and loved ones	10	3
Self-preservation	6	9
Idealistic reasons	5	2
Vindictiveness	2	12
Leadership and discipline	1	19
Miscellaneous	14	11

between the responses of officers and enlisted men was in regard to the role of leadership and discipline, cited more frequently than any other incentive by the officers, but by hardly any of the enlisted men. It is, of course, fairly clear that there were influences to divert both groups from a fully equitable appraisal of the importance of leadership. On the one hand, it was the prime occupational concern of the officers, their main function in the Army. From the point of view of the enlisted men, on the other hand, one would not expect mention here of the coercive aspects of leadership and discipline for reasons already stated, while one may suppose that the feelings many of them had toward officers as a group may have kept them from talking more about such of the other aspects of leadership as they had experienced.

Officers and enlisted men alike attached little importance to idealistic motives—patriotism and concern about war aims. Their evaluation appears to be

TABLE 3

Combat Incentives Named by Enlisted Infantrymen

Question: "Generally, in your combat experience, what was most important to you in making you want to keep going and do as well as you could?"

	Percentage of comments naming each incentive	
Ending the task	39	
Thoughts of getting the war over		*34*
Thoughts of getting relief or a rest		*5*
Solidarity with group	14	
Cannot let the other fellows or the outfit down; sticking together; "buddies depending on me"; "my friends around me"		
Sense of duty and self-respect	9	
Personal pride, self-respect		*7*
"Doing my part, my duty"		*2*
Thoughts of home and loved ones	10	
Self-preservation; "kill or be killed"	6	
A job to be done; "somebody has to do the fighting"	5	
Idealistic reasons	5	
Making a better world; crushing aggressor; "belief in what I'm fighting for"		*3*
Patriotism, protecting our people and their freedom		*2*
Vindictiveness	2	
Anger, revenge, "fighting spirit"		
Lack of any alternative action	2	
"There was nothing else to do"; "easier to keep going"		
Leadership and discipline	1	
Indifference	1	
"Too tired or mad to care"; "don't give a damn any more"		
Miscellaneous	6	
Total	100	
Number of comments	*568*	

in fundamental accord with other sources of evidence, though attributable in part to a socially prescribed avoidance of idealistic references that will be noted later. An intermediate proportion of both officers and enlisted men mentioned self-preservation as a motive; that combat was, as they put it, a matter of kill or be killed. In regard to vindictiveness—anger, revenge, etc.—the fact that the chart shows it to have been cited by more officers than enlisted men may be somewhat misleading. Reference to Table 4 will reveal that . . . officers in

TABLE 4

Combat Incentives Named by Company Officers

Question: "When the going is tough for your men, what do you think are the incentives which keep them fighting?"

	Percentage of Comments Naming Each Incentive		
	Division A	Division B	Division C*
Ending the task	15	11	15
Thought of getting the war over	*9*	*9*	*12*
Thoughts of getting relief or a rest	*6*	*2*	*8*
Solidarity with group	17	17	11
Pride in outfit and esprit de corps; loyalty to comrades; opinions of other men; seeing others doing their job			
Sense of duty and self-respect	14	16	14
Personal pride, self-respect	*12*	*12*	*9*
Sense of duty	*2*	*4*	*5*
Thoughts of home and loved ones	3	3	2
Self-preservation; "kill or be killed"	10	9	9
A job to be done; "somebody has to do the fighting"	4	5	†
Idealistic reasons	2	1	2
Ideals, patriotism, "what we're fighting for"			
Vindictiveness	9	8	18
Anger, revenge, "fighting spirit"			
Lack of any alternative action	5	3	†
"nothing else for them to do"; "easier to keep going"			
Leadership and discipline	18	19	20
Indifference; "don't give a damn"	1	1	†
Miscellaneous	2	7	9
Total	100	100	100
Number of comments	*304*	*256*	*556*

*Divisions A and B fought in North Africa and Sicily; Division C fought in the Central Pacific.

†These categories were not used in the analysis, and such comments were classed as miscellaneous.

combat against the Japanese were more likely than officers in Europe to say that vindictiveness was an important incentive. Since the present questions were not asked of enlisted men in the Pacific, the difference may be ascribable principally to the lack of comparability of the samples in this respect. . . .

The broad picture given by the men's free comments is one which we will have little need to modify or correct, aside from including factors other than positive incentives. It is one of a matter-of-fact adjustment to combat, with a minimum of idealism or heroics, in which the elements which come closest to the conventional stereotype of soldier heroism enter through the close solidarity of the immediate combat group. . . .

Unit IV

Dimensions of Grand Strategy

To the private soldier of any army the grandiose schemes of generals and politicians, which move him and his comrades around the world like pawns in a gigantic chess game, often seem of no relevance to his day-to-day struggle for survival. There was in World War II an updated version of an ancient epigram that conveyed the soldier's dislike of armchair strategy: "The mimeograph machine is mightier than the machine gun." Nonetheless, the elaborate planning so much caricatured during the Second World War was essential, probably more so in this war because of its greater complexity and scope.

Strategy may be defined as "the overall planning and conduct of large-scale combat operations." Grand strategy is strategy combined with concern for the political, economic, and psychological factors that establish limits on global strategic planning. *Barbarossa, Torch, Overlord*, and the other glamorously named major operations of the war were the product of agreed decisions at the highest level—decisions on the assignment of matériel produced, on the relative priorities to be accorded the various theaters of war. Although it is often said that the Second World War was preeminently a war of production and resources, there was never enough production and never enough manpower to do everything, everywhere, at the same time. Therefore grand strategy.

A partial listing of strategic issues in World War II might include Hitler's decision to attack the Soviet Union, the "Europe-first" strategy adopted by the Western Allies, Japan's fateful southward advance, and the Anglo-American move into the Mediterranean. The most controversial issue of grand strategy was, of course, the opening of a "Second Front" in Europe. In wrestling with this dilemma, Allied leaders had to face just about every difficulty imaginable: the coordination of fierce political pressures from the members of a shaky wartime coalition; the resolution of serious personal and philosophical differences between British and American leaders; and, most challenging of all, the incredible task of mounting and putting ashore the largest amphibious force in history. These problems and the solutions found in opening up the Second Front form an outstanding case study of the dominant strategic aspects of World War II.

Documents

1 Minutes on Grand Strategy

Winston S. Churchill

The three memoranda printed below form what was the first full description of a "British" strategy for winning the war in Europe. The strategic concepts underlying these notes were presented at the Washington Conference between Churchill, President Roosevelt, and their military advisers in December, 1941. The proposed plan encountered strong opposition from American representatives, and a bitter struggle ensued—a struggle of tremendous significance for the course of the war and the postwar world. While admiring Churchill's comprehensive grasp of strategy, the Americans objected that his plan was unnecessarily cautious and overly complex, that it underestimated Allied offensive capacity and exaggerated the enemy's ability to counteract a direct assault on the continent of Europe.

The Atlantic Front

1. Hitler's failure and losses in Russia are the prime facts in the war at this time. We cannot tell how great the disaster to the German Army and Nazi régime will be. This régime has hitherto lived upon easily and cheaply won successes. Instead of what was imagined to be a swift and easy victory, it has now to face the shock of a winter of slaughter and expenditure of fuel and equipment on the largest scale.

Neither Great Britain nor the United States have any part to play in this event, except to make sure that we send, without fail and punctually, the supplies we have promised. In this way alone shall we hold our influence over Stalin and be able to weave the mighty Russian effort into the general texture of the war.

From **Grand Strategy, World War II,** I (London: Her Majesty's Stationery Office, 1964), pp. 325–36. Reprinted by permission of the Controller of Her Britannic Majesty's Stationery Office.

2. In a lesser degree the impending victory of General Auchinleck in Cyrenaica is an injury to the German power. We may expect the total destruction of the enemy force in Libya to be apparent before the end of the year. This not only inflicts a heavy blow on the Germans and Italians, but it frees our force in the Nile Valley from the major threat of invasion from the west under which they have long dwelt. Naturally, General Auchinleck will press on as fast as possible with the operation called 'Acrobat', which should give him possession of Tripoli, and so bring his armoured vanguard to the French frontier at Tunis. He may be able to supply a forecast before we separate at Washington.

3. The German losses and defeat in Russia and their extirpation from Libya may of course impel them to a supreme effort in the spring to break the ring that is closing on them by a southeastward thrust either to the Caucasus or to Anatolia, or both. However, we should not assume that necessarily they will have the war energy for this task. The Russian Armies, recuperated by the winter, will lie heavy upon them from Leningrad to the Crimea. They may easily be forced to evacuate the Crimea. There is no reason at this time to suppose that the Russian Navy will not command the Black Sea. Nor should it be assumed that the present life-strength of Germany is such as to make an attack upon Turkey and a march through Anatolia a business to be undertaken in present circumstances by the Nazi régime. The Turks have 50 divisions; their fighting quality and the physical obstacles of their country are well known. Although Turkey has played for safety throughout, the Russian command of the Black Sea and British successes in the Levant and along the North African shore, together with the proved weakness of the Italian Fleet, would justify every effort on our part to bring Turkey into line, and are certainly sufficient to encourage her to resist a German inroad. While it would be imprudent to regard the danger of a German south-west thrust against the Persia-Iraq-Syrian front as removed, it certainly seems much less likely than heretofore.

4. We ought therefore to try hard to win over French North Africa, and now is the moment to use every inducement and form of pressure at our disposal upon the Government of Vichy and French authorities in North Africa. The German setback in Russia, the British successes in Libya, the moral and military collapse of Italy, above all the declarations of war exchanged between Germany and the United States, must strongly affect the mind of France and the French Empire. Now is the time to offer to Vichy and to French North Africa a blessing or a cursing. A blessing will consist in a promise by the United States and Great Britain to re-establish France as a Great Power with her territories undiminished. It should carry with it an offer of active aid by British and United States expeditionary forces, both from the Atlantic seaboard of Morocco and at convenient landing-points in Algeria and Tunis, as well as from General Auchinleck's forces advancing from the east. Ample supplies for the French and the loyal Moors should be made available. Vichy should be asked to send their fleet from Toulon to Oran and Bizerta and to bring France into the war again as a principal.

This would mean that Germany would take over the whole of France and rule it as occupied territory. It does not seem that the conditions in the occupied and the hitherto unoccupied zones are widely different. Whatever happens, European France will inevitably be subjected to a complete blockade. There is of course always the chance that the Germans, tied up in Russia, may not care to take over unoccupied France, even though French North Africa is at war with them.

5. If we can obtain even the connivance of Vichy to French North Africa coming over to our side we must be ready to send considerable forces as soon as possible. Apart from anything which General Auchinleck can bring in from the east should he be successful in Tripolitania, we hold ready in Britain (Operation 'Gymnast') about 55,000 men, comprising two divisions and an armoured unit, together with the shipping. These forces could enter French North Africa by invitation on the twenty-third day after the order to embark them was given. Leading elements and air forces from Malta could reach Bizerta at very short notice. It is desired that the United States should at the same time promise to bring in, via Casablanca and other African Atlantic ports, not less than 150,000 men during the next six months. It is essential that some American elements, say 25,000 men, should go at the earliest moment after French agreement, either Vichy or North African, had been obtained.

6. It is also asked that the United States will send the equivalent of three divisions and one armoured division into Northern Ireland. These divisions could, if necessary, complete their training in Northern Ireland. The presence of American forces there would become known to the enemy, and they could be led to magnify their actual members. The presence of United States troops in the British Isles would be a powerful additional deterrent against an attempt at invasion by Germany. It would enable us to nourish the campaign in North Africa by two more divisions and one complete armoured division. If forces of this order could be added to the French Army already in North Africa, with proper air-support, the Germans would have to make a very difficult and costly campaign across uncommanded waters to subdue North Africa. The North-West African theatre is one most favourable for Anglo-American operations, our approaches being direct and convenient across the Atlantic, while the enemy's passage of the Mediterranean would be severely obstructed, as is happening in the Libyan enterprise.

7. It may be mentioned here that we greatly desire American bomber squadrons to come into action from the British Isles against Germany. Our own bomber programme has fallen short of our hopes. It is formidable and is increasing, but its full development has been delayed. It must be remembered that we place great hopes of affecting German production and German morale by ever more severe and more accurate bombing of their cities and harbours, and that this, combined with their Russian defeats, may produce important effects on the will to fight of the German people, with consequential internal reactions upon the German government. The arrival in the United Kingdom of, say, twenty American bomber squadrons would emphasize and accelerate this process, and would be the most direct and effective reply to the declaration of war by Germany upon the United States. Arrangements will be made in Great

Britain to increase this process and develop the Anglo-American bombing of Germany without any top limit from now on until the end of the war.

8. We must however reckon with a refusal by Vichy to act as we desire, and on the contrary they may rouse French North Africa to active resistance. They may help German troops to enter North Africa; the Germans may force their way or be granted passage through Spain; the French fleet at Toulon may pass under German control, and France and the French Empire may be made by Vichy to collaborate actively with Germany against us, although it is not likely that this would go through effectively. The overwhelming majority of the French are ranged with Great Britain, and now still more with the United States. It is by no means certain that Admiral Darlan can deliver the Toulon fleet over intact to Germany. It is most improbable that French soldiers and sailors would fight effectively against the United States and Great Britain. Nevertheless, we must not exclude the possibility of a half-hearted association of the defeatist elements in France and North Africa with Germany. In this case our task in North Africa will become much harder.

A campaign must be fought in 1942 to gain possession of, or conquer, the whole of the North African shore, including the Atlantic ports of Morocco. Dakar and other French West African ports must be captured before the end of the year. Whereas however entry into French North Africa is urgent to prevent German penetration, a period of eight or nine months' preparation may well be afforded for the mastering of Dakar and the West African establishments. Plans should be set on foot forthwith. If sufficient time and preparations are allowed and the proper apparatus provided, these latter operations present no insuperable difficulty.

9. Our relations with General de Gaulle and the Free French movement will require to be reviewed. Hitherto the United States have entered into no undertakings similar to those comprised in my correspondence with him. Through no particular fault of his own his movement has created new antagonisms in French minds. Any action which the United States may now feel able to take in regard to him should have the effect, *inter alia*, of redefining our obligations to him and France so as to make these obligations more closely dependent upon the eventual effort by him and the French nation to rehabilitate themselves. If Vichy were to act as we desire about French North Africa, the United States and Great Britain must labour to bring about a reconciliation between the Free French (de Gaullists) and those other Frenchmen who will have taken up arms once more against Germany. If, on the other hand, Vichy persists in collaboration with Germany and we have to fight our way into French North and West Africa, then the de Gaullists' movement must be aided and used to the full.

10. We cannot tell what will happen in Spain. It seems probable that the Spaniards will not give the Germans a free passage through Spain to attack Gibraltar and invade North Africa. There may be infiltration, but the formal demand for the passage of any army would be resisted. If so the winter would be the worst time for the Germans to attempt to force their way through Spain. Moreover, Hitler, with nearly all Europe to hold down by armed force in the

face of defeat and semi-starvation, may well be chary of taking over unoccupied France and involving himself in bitter guerrilla warfare with the morose, fierce, hungry people of the Iberian peninsula. Everything possible must be done by Britain and the United States to strengthen their will to resist. The present policy of limited supplies should be pursued.

The value of Gibraltar harbour and base to us is so great that no attempts should be made upon the Atlantic islands until either the peninsula is invaded or the Spaniards give passage to the Germans.

11. To sum up, the war in the West in 1942 comprises, as its main offensive effort, the occupation and control by Great Britain and the United States of the whole of the North and West African possessions of France, and the further control by Britain of the whole North African shore from Tunis to Egypt, thus giving, if the naval situation allows, free passage through the Mediterranean to the Levant and the Suez Canal. These great objectives can only be achieved if British and American naval and air superiority in the Atlantic is maintained, if supply-lines continue uninterrupted, and if the British Isles are effectively safeguarded against invasion.

Notes on the Pacific

1. The Japanese have naval superiority, which enables them to transport troops to almost any desired point, possess themselves of it and establish it for an air-naval fuelling base. The Allies will not have for some time the power to fight a general fleet engagement. Their power of convoying troops depends upon the size of the seas, which reduces the chance of interception. We can arrive by surprise from out of the wide seas at some place which we hold. Even without superior sea-power we may descend by surprise here and there. But we could not carry on a sustained operation across the seas. We must expect, therefore, to be deprived one by one of our possessions and strong points in the Pacific, and that the enemy will establish himself fairly easily in one after the other, mopping up the local garrisons.

2. In this interim period our duty is one of stubborn resistance at each point attacked, and to slip supplies and reinforcements through as opportunity offers, taking all necessary risks. If our forces resist stubbornly and we reinforce them as much as possible, the enemy will be forced to make ever larger overseas commitments far from home; his shipping resources will be strained and his communications will provide vulnerable targets upon which all available naval and air forces, United States, British and Dutch—especially submarines—should concentrate their effort. It is of the utmost importance that the enemy should not acquire large gains cheaply; that he should be compelled to nourish all his conquests and kept extended, and kept burning up his resources.

3. The resources of Japan are a wasting factor. The country has been long overstrained by its wasteful war in China. They were at maximum strength on the day of the Pearl Harbor attack. If it is true, as Stalin asserts, that they have, in addition to their own Air Force, 1,500 German aeroplanes (and he would have opportunities of knowing how they got there), they have now no means of

replacing wastage other than by their small home production of 300/500 per month. Our policy should be to make them maintain the largest possible number of troops in their conquests overseas and to keep them as busy as possible so as to enforce well-filled lines of communications and a high rate of aircraft consumption. If we idle and leave them at ease they will be able to extend their conquests cheaply and easily, work with a minimum of overseas forces, make the largest gains and the smallest commitments, and thus inflict upon us an enormous amount of damage. It is therefore right and necessary to fight them at every point where we have a fair chance, so as to keep them burning and extended.

4. But we must steadily aim at regaining superiority at sea at the earliest moment. This can be gained in two ways; first, by the strengthening of our capital ships. The two new Japanese battleships built free from Treaty limitations must be considered a formidable factor, influencing the whole Pacific theatre. It is understood that two new American battleships will be fit for action by May. Of course, all undertakings in war must be subject to the action of the enemy, accidents and misfortune, but if our battleship strength should not be further reduced, nor any new unforeseen stress arise, we should hope to place the *Nelson* and the *Rodney* at the side of these two new American battleships, making four 16-inch gun modern vessels of major strength. Behind such a squadron the older reconstructed battleships of the United States should be available in numbers sufficient to enable a fleet action, under favourable circumstances, to be contemplated at any time after the month of May. The recovery of our naval superiority in the Pacific, even if not brought to a trial of strength, would reassure the whole western seaboard of the American continent and thus prevent a needless dissipation on a gigantic defensive effort of forces which have offensive parts to play. We must therefore set before ourselves, as a main strategic object, the forming of a definitely superior battle fleet in the Pacific and we must aim at May as the date when this will be achieved.

5. Not only then, but in the interval, the warfare of aircraft-carriers should be developed to the greatest possible extent. We are ourselves forming a squadron of three aircraft-carriers, suitably attended, to act in the waters between South Africa, India and Australia. The United States have already seven regular carriers compared to Japan's ten, but those of the United States are larger. To this force of regular warship carriers we must add a very large development of improvised carriers, both large and small. In this way alone can we increase our sea-power rapidly. Even if the carriers can only fly a dozen machines, they may play their part in combination with other carriers. We ought to develop a floating air establishment sufficient to enable us to acquire and maintain for considerable periods local air superiority over shore-based aircraft and sufficient to cover the landing of troops in order to attack the enemy's new conquests. Unless or until this local air superiority is definitely acquired even a somewhat superior fleet on our side would fight at a serious disadvantage. We cannot get more battleships than those now in sight for the year 1942, but we can and must get more aircraft-carriers. It takes five years to build a battleship, but it is possible to improvise a carrier in six months. Here then is a field for

invention and ingenuity similar to that which called forth the extraordinary fleets and flotillas which fought on the Mississippi in the Civil War. It must be accepted that the priority given to sea-borne aircraft of a suitable type will involve a retardation in the full-scale bombing offensive against Germany which we have contemplated as a major method of waging war. This, however, is a matter of time and of degree. We cannot in 1942 hope to reach the levels of bomb discharge in Germany which we had prescribed for that year, but we shall surpass them in 1943. Our joint programme may be late, but it will come along. And meanwhile the German cities and other targets will not disappear. While every effort must be made to speed up the rate of bomb discharges upon Germany until the great scales prescribed for 1943 and 1944 are reached, nevertheless we may be forced by other needs to face a retardation in our schedules. The more important will it be therefore that in this interval a force, be it only symbolic, of United States bombing squadrons should operate from the British Isles against the German cities and seaports.

6. Once the Allies have regained battle-fleet superiority in the Pacific and have created a sea-borne air-power sufficient to secure local supremacy for certain periods, it will be possible either to attack the Japanese in their overseas conquests by military expeditions or to attack them in their homeland. It may well be the latter will be found the better. We must imagine the Japanese Air Force as being steadily and rapidly reduced and having no adequate power of replenishment. The approach to the shores of Japan near enough for our sea-borne air-power to ravage their cities should be freed from its present prohibitive cost and danger. Nothing will more rapidly relieve the Japanese attacks in the East Indian theatre. Under the protection of the superior battle fleet and the sea-borne air-power aforesaid, it should be possible to acquire or regain various island bases, enabling a definite approach to be made to the homeland of Japan. The burning of Japanese cities by incendiary bombs will bring home in a most effective way to the people of Japan the dangers of the course to which they have committed themselves, and nothing is more likely to cramp the reinforcing of their overseas adventures.

7. The establishment of air bases in China or Russia from which attacks can be made upon the Japanese cities is in everyone's mind. It is most desirable that Russia should enter the war against Japan, thus enabling her own and Allied aircraft to bomb all the main cities in Japan from a convenient distance. This would also make available a force of about seventy Russian submarines to harass the Japanese lines of communication with their overseas commitments, especially at the point of departure from Japan. However, this is not a point upon which we can press the Russians unduly at the present time. They have withstood and are withstanding the giant assault of the German Army. They have achieved undreamed of success. If their resistance to the German Armies were to break down, or even if their pressure upon them were relaxed, all the problems of the Caucasus, Syria, Palestine and Persia would resume the menacing shape they have only lately lost, entailing immense diversions of force upon Great Britain, and offering no satisfactory assurance of success. The influence of the German losses and defeats against Russia upon the German people must be very depressing, and if this is prolonged it may provoke stresses

within the German régime of the utmost hopeful consequence. M. Stalin has indicated that perhaps in the spring he may be able to act against Japan. If he does not feel able or willing to do so now, it would be a mistake to press him unduly. Russia has more than rowed her weight in the boat, and she alone must judge when to take on more burdens. The question of whether air bases in Russia could be acquired without entailing war between Japan and Russia is worth while studying. It would certainly not be in Japan's interest, any more than that of Russia, to open up this new front of war. It might mean that an attitude of non-belligerency might be adopted by Russia at a period before she would be willing to come into the war. Such an attitude of non-belligerency might permit aircraft, based on China, to refuel in Siberia before and after bombing Japan.

8. The danger of the Japanese using their numerous cruisers to raid all shipping between Australia and the Middle East, and even to assail our convoys round the Cape, will require to be met by the provision of battleship escort. We propose to use the four 'R' Class battleships for this purpose if we need to. It is to be hoped that United States will also be ready to help in convoying work against cruiser attacks in the Pacific.

9. Lastly, there is the question of whether we should ask the United States to base her battle fleet on Singapore, or perhaps make such a movement conditional on our adding our two battleships from the Atlantic. I am in much doubt about this. When we see what happened to the *Prince of Wales* and the *Repulse* in these narrow waters, soon to be infested with aircraft based at many points, we cannot feel that they would offer an inviting prospect to the United States. It would be represented as a purely British conception. One is not sure of the work they could do when they got there, and whether they would not suffer unduly heavy losses. It would redouble the anxieties and waste of force upon the defences of the Pacific seaboard of America. It would put out of the way all chances of a sea-borne offensive against the homelands of Japan. It is inconceivable that the United States' authorities would agree to it at any time which can at present be foreseen.

10. We cannot tell what will happen in the Philippines, and whether or for how long United States troops will be able to defend themselves. The defence or recapture of the Philippines cannot be judged upon theoretical principles. Wars of the present scale are largely wars of attrition and a wise choice of a particular battlefield is not necessarily the only criterion. The Philippines will undoubtedly appear to the United States as an American battleground which they are in honour bound to fight for. The Japanese will have to expend war-power and aircraft in this conflict, and even if it does not proceed in the best chosen theatre the process of exhaustion and wearing down of the weaker country by the stronger is of very great advantage and relief to us in the Pacific sphere.

11. For these reasons it would not be wise to press the Americans to move their main fleet to Singapore.

12. Nor need we fear that this war in the Pacific will, after the first shock is over, absorb an unduly large proportion of United States' forces. The numbers of troops that we should wish them to use in Europe in 1942 will not be so large

as to be prevented by their Pacific operations, limited as these must be. What will harm us is for a vast United States Army of 10 millions to be created which, for at least two years while it was training, would absorb all the available supplies and stand idle defending the American continent. The best way of preventing the creation of such a situation and obtaining the proper use of the large forces and ample supplies of munitions which will presently be forthcoming, is to enable the Americans to regain their naval power in the Pacific and not to discourage them from the precise secondary overseas operations which they may perhaps contemplate.

The Campaign of 1943

1. If the operations outlined in Parts I and II should prosper during 1942 the situation in 1943 might be as follows:
   (a) The United States and Great Britain would have recovered effective naval superiority in the Pacific, and all Japanese overseas commitments would be endangered both from the assailing of their communications and from British and American expeditions sent to recover places lost.
   (b) The British Isles would remain intact and more strongly prepared against invasion than they were before.
   (c) The whole West and North African shores from Dakar to the Suez Canal and the Levant to the Turkish frontier would be in Anglo-American hands.

Turkey, though not necessarily at war, would be definitely incorporated in the American-British-Russian front. Russian positions would be strongly established, and the supplies of British and American material as promised would have in part compensated for the loss of Russian munition-making capacity. It might be that a footing would already have been established in Sicily and Italy, with reactions inside Italy which might be highly favourable.

2. But all this would fall short of bringing the war to an end. The war cannot be ended by driving Japan back to her own bounds and defeating her overseas forces. The war can only be ended through the defeat in Europe of the German armies, or through internal convulsions in Germany produced by the unfavourable course of the war, economic privations, and the Allied bombing offensive. As the strength of the United States, Great Britain and Russia develops and begins to be realized by the Germans an internal collapse is always possible, but we must not count on this. Our plans must proceed upon the assumption that the resistance of the German Army and Air Force will continue at its present level and that their U-boat warfare will be conducted by increasingly numerous flotillas.

3. We have therefore to prepare for the liberation of the captive countries of Western and Southern Europe by the landing at suitable points, successively or simultaneously, of British and American armies strong enough to enable the conquered populations to revolt. By themselves they will never be able to revolt, owing to the ruthless counter-measures that will be employed, but if adequate and suitably equipped forces were landed in several of the following countries,

namely, Norway, Denmark, Holland, Belgium, the French Channel coasts and the French Atlantic coasts, as well as in Italy and possibly the Balkans, the German garrisons would prove insufficient to cope both with the strength of the liberating forces and the fury of the revolting peoples. It is impossible for the Germans, while we retain the sea-power necessary to choose the place or places of attack, to have sufficient troops in each of these countries for effective resistance. In particular they cannot move their armour about laterally from north to south or west to east; either they must divide it between the various conquered countries—in which case it will become hopelessly dispersed—or they must hold it back in a central position in Germany, in which case it will not arrive until large and important lodgements have been made by us from overseas.

4. We must face here the usual clash between short-term and long-term projects. War is a constant struggle and must be waged from day to day. It is only with some difficulty and within limits that provision can be made for the future. Experience shows that forecasts are usually falsified and preparations always in arrear. Nevertheless, there must be a design and theme for bringing the war to a victorious end in a reasonable period. All the more is this necessary when under modern conditions no large-scale offensive operation can be launched without the preparation of elaborate technical apparatus.

5. We should therefore face now the problems not only of driving Japan back to her homelands and regaining undisputed mastery in the Pacific, but also of liberating conquered Europe by the landing during the summer of 1943 of United States and British armies on their shores. Plans should be prepared for the landing in all of the countries mentioned above. The actual choice of which three or four to pick should be deferred as long as possible, so as to profit by the turn of events and make sure of secrecy.

6. In principle, the landings should be made by armoured and mechanised forces capable of disembarking not at ports but on beaches, either by landing-craft or from ocean-going ships specifically adapted. The potential front of attack is thus made so wide that the German forces holding down these different countries cannot be strong enough at all points. An amphibious outfit must be prepared to enable these large-scale disembarkations to be made swiftly and surely. The vanguards of the various British and American expeditions should be marshalled by the spring of 1943 in Iceland, the British Isles and, if possible, in French Morocco and Egypt. The main body would come direct across the Ocean.

7. It need not be assumed that great numbers of men are required. If the incursion of the armoured formations is successful, the uprising of the local population, for whom weapons must be brought, will supply the corpus of the liberating offensive. Forty armoured divisions at 15,000 men apiece or their equivalent in tank brigades, of which Great Britain would try to produce nearly half, would amount to 600,000 men. Behind the armour another million men of all arms would suffice to wrest enormous territories from Hitler's domination. But these campaigns, once started, will require nourishing on a lavish scale. Our industries and training establishments should by the end of 1942 be running on a sufficient scale.

8. Apart from the command of the sea, without which nothing is possible, the essential of all these operations is superior air-power, and for landing purposes a large development of carrier-borne aircraft will be necessary. This however is needed anyhow for the war in 1942. In order to wear down the enemy and hamper his counter-preparations, the bombing offensive of Germany from England and of Italy from Malta, and if possible from Tripoli and Tunis, must reach the highest possible scale of intensity. Considering that the British first-line air strength is already slightly superior to that of Germany, that the Russian Air Force has already established a superiority on a large part of the Russian front and may be considered to be three-fifths the first-line strength of Germany, and that the United States resources and future development are additional, there is no reason why a decisive mastery of the air should not be established even before the summer of 1943, and meanwhile heavy and continuous punishment be inflicted upon Germany. Having regard to the fact that the bombing offensive is necessarily a matter of degree and that the targets cannot be moved away, it would be right to assign priority to the fighter and torpedo-carrying aircraft required for the numerous carriers and improvised carriers which are available or must be brought into existence.

9. If we set these tasks before us now, being careful that they do not trench too much upon current necessities, we might hope, even if no German collapse occurs beforehand, to win the war at the end of 1943 or 1944. There might be advantage in declaring now our intention of sending armies of liberation to Europe in 1943. This would give hope to the subjugated peoples and prevent any truck between them and the German invaders. The setting and keeping in movement along our courses of the minds of so many scores of millions of men is in itself a potent atmospheric influence.

2   The American Bid for a Second Front

Sir Arthur Bryant

The debates within the Allied coalition over grand strategy were determined as much by the force of personality as by the superiority of one point of view over another. Churchill and F.D.R. both were prone to intervene in the discussions over strategy, and often their interventions were for political or personal reasons. The military professionals learned

From **The Turn of the Tide** by Arthur Bryant, pp. 36–39. Copyright © 1957 by Arthur Bryant. Used by permission of Doubleday & Company, Inc. and William Collins Sons & Co., Ltd.

to live with the meddling by their civilian superiors, but, as the following excerpt suggests, they were never entirely happy about this state of affairs. After gaining access to the diaries and papers of Field Marshal Sir Alan Brooke, Churchill's principal military adviser, Sir Arthur Bryant wrote The Turn of the Tide, *a fascinating study of the conflicts between contrasting strategies and personalities at the highest level.*

It was not . . . the Battle of the Atlantic, but the invasion of France which, in the spring of 1942, was growing in the Prime Minister's mind like a canker. When the Americans came into the war after Pearl Harbour they began to plan for the day when the Allied armies would land again upon the French shore. It was General Marshall's conviction that only in that way could the war be won. Mr. Churchill was as sure that only by the premature invasion of France could the war be lost. To postpone that evil day, all his arts, all his eloquence, all his great experience were spent.

Why did Winston so much dread this particular operation? He feared the casualties. It was the carnage on the first day of the Battle of the Somme which led the P.M. to invent a monster tank of his own. He told me this before we left London for Washington.

"The War Office," Winston began, "is always said to be preparing for the last war. I certainly entered this war with a mentality born in the last war. I had a waterproof suit made so that I might keep dry in the communication trenches. I wanted to be prepared for those visits to the front line which," the P.M. added with a mischievous smirk, "I felt my position as First Lord of the Admiralty entitled me to make. What I had learned in the last war was deeply rooted in my mind—the terrible losses in an assault on a prepared position. But I still believed that the Siegfried Line facing us could be broken with the increased fire power of this war without those losses."

"This was the way I planned to do it. In the last war the tanks went overland. In this way they would have to plough through the surface of the ground. In the next war," Winston added with a grin, "they will be underground. So I evolved a plan in which a tank of great length," and here the P.M.'s eyes dilated, "weighing sixty or seventy-five tons, ploughed a way six feet deep by six feet wide, giving the troops cover to attack through this communication trench. There were to have been eighty or ninety of these tanks," Winston added reflectively, "but it all came to nothing."

The whole episode was pure Winston. On the one hand, the never-failing fertility of ideas and the astonishing capacity to impose them on others:

"It passed the Cabinet," he said. "It was demonstrated to Gamelin and Georges. All were impressed."

On the other hand, the unscientific approach to a problem. The P.M. admitted that he had not followed the development of tanks between the two wars. He did not know that the tank he invented was already obsolete. De Gaulle's conception of tank warfare, outlined in his book, *La France et son*

Armée, published in 1938, and adopted by the German's in the invasion of France, was quite new to Churchill in 1940.

Winston's service with a battalion in France in the First World War had not weaned him from the great game of playing at soldiers. But it must be his kind of war. He shrank back from the bloody immobility of Continental warfare. His imagination was staggered by the thought of what might happen if things went wrong in an invasion of France or Belgium.

President Roosevelt was impressed at that time by the P.M.'s knowledge of military matters; his dread of a frontal attack·on the French coast appeared reasonable. Roosevelt was a humane man, and the P.M.'s picture of the probable fate of the cross-Channel operation appalled him. However, he had complete confidence in his Chief of Staff, and Marshall was convinced that there was only one way to shorten the war—to invade France. Full of that conviction, he set out to educate the President.

Early in April, Roosevelt, with the zeal of a convert, sent Hopkins and Marshall to London to say that his heart and mind were in this plan for landing on the French coast.

Brooke and Marshall, who now met, had a good deal in common. They both came of virile stock. Brooke's ancestors, the "Fighting Brookes," had taken part as soldiers in the settlement of Ulster in the reign of Queen Elizabeth, while a forebear of Marshall's, an Irish Captain of Horse, fought for Charles I against Cromwell.

However, the acquisitive instinct, common enough among full-blooded men, had no part in their lives. Their one ambition was to lead armies in the field, but they would not lift a finger to bring this about. They were both selfless men with a fine contempt for the pressures of the mob.

Brooke, who had a feeling for character, decided in Washington that Marshall was "a great gentleman and a great administrator," while Marshall, in his own slow and rather cautious manner, came to much the same conclusion about Brooke. When, however, the two men first met in London, neither impressed the other.

To Brooke it was inexplicable that Marshall would cross the Atlantic to advocate the early invasion of France without first priming himself by a prolonged study of all the relevant factors. And yet when he asked Marshall on the eighth day of the Conference, "Do we go west, south or east after landing?" he found that the American had not begun to think of it. As for Marshall, he decided that Brooke "lacked Dill's brains". . . .

Marshall was a man of strong convictions; he did not find it easy to give way. It appeared inevitable that there would be a prolonged tussle between these two obstinate men, whereas, in fact, the mission from Washington seemed to get almost at once what they wanted, and it was decided that a force of forty-eight divisions should take part in the invasion of France.

I was puzzled at the time by the manner in which the P.M. agreed with Marshall, almost, as it were, without a fight. It was not like him. I made this note in my diary:

"The P.M. is an experienced and tenacious campaigner, and he may have decided that the time has not yet come to take the field as an out-and-out opponent of a Second Front in France. Anyway, 1943 seems a long way off, and a good deal may happen in the meanwhile."

From what the P.M. said to me then, I know that he was still fearful that the President might be driven by public clamour to concentrate on the war with Japan. It was not a time for argument. Winston put it like this: "I had to work by influence and diplomacy in order to secure agreed and harmonious action with our cherished ally."

Whatever may be the truth, we know that the Americans left London in great heart; they were satisfied that there was complete agreement, and that the question of a Second Front had been settled once and for all. However, if the P.M. had yielded too quickly, he soon made amends. In the first days of June he sent a cable to the President impressing on him that we must never let *Torch* (the invasion of North Africa) pass from our minds, while Mountbatten was sent to Washington to explain that certain difficulties had arisen in the planning of an invasion of France.

The P.M. did not doubt that he could convince the President of the folly of such an invasion at the present time, if only he could talk with him. He determined to make such an opportunity without more delay.

3   Official Allied Correspondence

The conference of Roosevelt and Churchill at Casablanca ended any hopes for an Anglo-American invasion of the continent in 1943. Pleading lack of preparation and the desirability of expanded operations in the Mediterranean, the British on this occasion prevailed. Those who took part in the Casablanca discussions convinced themselves that the postponement of the Second Front operation (which had been promised the Soviet Union and their own peoples for 1943) was necessary. It was another matter to convince their Russian ally that the decision was not some devious plot to have Germany and the U.S.S.R. fight each other to exhaustion. The exchanges between the Western leaders and Premier Stalin revealed that this effort was something less than a total success. The Second Front issue led to intense Russian bitterness and fuelled the smoldering hostility among the members of the Allied coalition.

From President Roosevelt and Prime Minister Churchill
to Premier Stalin*

We have been in conference with our military advisers and have decided on the operations which are to be undertaken by the American and British forces in the first nine months of 1943. We wish to inform you of our intentions at once. We believe that these operations, together with your powerful offensive, may well bring Germany to her knees in 1943. Every effort must be made to accomplish this purpose . . .

2. We are in no doubt that our correct strategy is to concentrate on the defeat of Germany with a view to achieving an early and decisive victory in the European theater. At the same time we must maintain sufficient pressure on Japan to retain the initiative in the Pacific and the Far East and sustain China and prevent the Japanese from extending their aggression to other theaters such as your Maritime Provinces.

3. Our main desire has been to divert strong German land and air forces from the Russian front and to send Russia the maximum flow of supplies. We shall spare no exertion to send you material assistance in any case by every available route.

4. Our immediate intention is to clear the Axis out of North Africa and set up naval and air installations to open:

(1) an effective passage through the Mediterranean for military traffic, and
(2) an intensive bombardment of important Axis targets in Southern Europe.

5. We have made the decision to launch large-scale amphibious operations in the Mediterranean at the earliest possible moment. The preparation for these operations is now under way and will involve a considerable concentration of forces, including landing craft and shipping, in Egypt and the North Africa ports. In addition we shall concentrate within the United Kingdom a strong American land and air force. These, combined with the British forces in the United Kingdom, will prepare themselves to re-enter the continent of Europe as soon as practicable. These concentrations will certainly be known to our enemies but they will not know where or when or on what scale we propose striking. They will, therefore, be compelled to divert both land and air forces to all the shores of France, the Low Countries, Corsica, Sardinia, Sicily and the Levant, and Italy, Yugoslavia, Greece, Crete and the Dodecanese.

6. In Europe we shall increase the Allied bomber offensive from the United Kingdom against Germany at a rapid rate and by midsummer it should be double its present strength. Our experiences to date have shown that day bombing attacks result in the destruction of, and damage to, large numbers of German fighter aircraft. We believe that an increased tempo and weight of daylight and night attacks will lead to greatly increased material and moral damage in Germany and rapidly deplete German fighter strength. As you are aware, we are

*From Ministry of Foreign Affairs of the U.S.S.R., **Correspondence between the Chairman of the Council of Ministers of the U.S.S.R. and the Presidents of the U.S.A. and the Prime Ministers of Great Britain during the Great Patriotic War, 1941–1945,** II (Moscow: Foreign Languages Publishing House, 1957), pp. 51–52.

already containing more than half the German Air Force in Western Europe and the Mediterranean. We have no doubt that our intensified and diversified bombing offensive, together with the other operations which we are undertaking, will compel further withdrawals of German air and other forces from the Russian front.

7. In the Pacific it is our intention to eject the Japanese from Rabaul within the next few months and thereafter to exploit the success in the general direction of Japan. We also intend to increase the scale of our operations in Burma in order to reopen this channel of supply to China. We intend to increase our Air Forces in China at once. We shall not, however, allow our offensives against Japan to jeopardize our capacity to take advantage of every opportunity that may present itself for the decisive defeat of Germany in 1943.

8. Our ruling purpose is to bring to bear upon Germany and Italy the maximum forces by land, sea and air which can be physically applied.

Received January 27, 1943

* * *

Personal and Secret Message from Premier J.V. Stalin to the Prime Minister, Mr. W. Churchill*

Your message of June 19 received.

I fully realise the difficulty of organising an Anglo-American invasion of Western Europe, in particular, of transferring troops across the Channel. The difficulty could also be discerned in your communications.

From your messages of last year and this I gained the conviction that you and the President were fully aware of the difficulties of organising such an operation and were preparing the invasion accordingly, with due regard to the difficulties and the necessary exertion of forces and means. Even last year you told me that a large-scale invasion of Europe by Anglo-American troops would be effected in 1943. In the Aide-Mémoire handed to V.M. Molotov on June 10, 1942, you wrote:

"Finally, and most important of all, we are concentrating our maximum effort on the organisation and preparation of a large-scale invasion of the Continent of Europe by British and American forces in 1943. We are setting no limit to the scope and objectives of this campaign, which will be carried out in the first instance by over a million men, British and American, with air forces of appropriate strength."

Early this year you twice informed me, on your own behalf and on behalf of the President, of decisions concerning an Anglo-American invasion of Western Europe intended to "divert strong German land and air forces from the Russian

*From Ministry of Foreign Affairs of the U.S.S.R., Correspondence between the Chairman of the Council of Ministers of the U.S.S.R. and the Presidents of the U.S.A. and the Prime Ministers of Great Britain during the Great Patriotic War, 1941-1945, II (Moscow: Foreign Languages Publishing House, 1957), pp. 74-76.

front." You had set yourself the task of bringing Germany to her knees as early as 1943, and named September as the latest date for the invasion.

In your message of January 26 you wrote:

> "We have been in conference with our military advisers and have decided on the operations which are to be undertaken by the American and British forces in the first nine months of 1943. We wish to inform you of our intentions at once. We believe that these operations together with your powerful offensive, may well bring Germany to her knees in 1943."

In your next message, which I received on February 12, you wrote, specifying the date of the invasion of Western Europe, decided on by you and the President:

> "We are also pushing preparations to the limit of our resources for a cross-Channel operation in August, in which British and United States units would participate. Here again, shipping and assault-landing craft will be the limiting factors. If the operation is delayed by the weather or other reasons, it will be prepared with stronger forces for September."

Last February, when you wrote to me about those plans and the date for invading Western Europe, the difficulties of that operation were greater than they are now. Since then the Germans have suffered more than one defeat: they were pushed back by our troops in the South, where they suffered appreciable loss; they were beaten in North Africa and expelled by the Anglo-American troops; in submarine warfare, too, the Germans found themselves in a bigger predicament than ever, while Anglo-American superiority increased substantially; it is also known that the Americans and British have won air superiority in Europe and that their navies and mercantile marines have grown in power.

It follows that the conditions for opening a second front in Western Europe during 1943, far from deteriorating, have, indeed, greatly improved.

That being so, the Soviet Government could not have imagined that the British and U.S. Governments would revise the decision to invade Western Europe, which they had adopted early this year. In fact, the Soviet Government was fully entitled to expect that the Anglo-American decision would be carried out, that appropriate preparations were under way and that the second front in Western Europe would at last be opened in 1943.

That is why, when you now write that "it would be no help to Russia if we threw away a hundred thousand men in a disastrous cross-Channel attack," all I can do is remind you of the following:

First, your own Aide-Mémoire of June 1942 in which you declared that preparations were under way for an invasion, not by a hundred thousand, but by an Anglo-American force exceeding one million men at the very start of the operation.

Second, your February message, which mentioned extensive measures preparatory to the invasion of Western Europe in August or September 1943, which, apparently, envisaged an operation, not by a hundred thousand men, but by an adequate force.

So when you now declare: "I cannot see how a great British defeat and slaughter would aid the Soviet armies," is it not clear that a statement of this kind in relation to the Soviet Union is utterly groundless and directly contradicts your previous and responsible decisions, listed above, about extensive and vigorous measures by the British and Americans to organise the invasion this year, measures on which the complete success of the operation should hinge.

I shall not enlarge on the fact that this responsible decision, revoking your previous decisions on the invasion of Western Europe, was reached by you and the President without Soviet participation and without inviting its representatives to the Washington conference, although you cannot but be aware that the Soviet Union's role in the war against Germany and its interest in the problems of the second front are great enough.

There is no need to say that the Soviet Government cannot become reconciled to this disregard of vital Soviet interests in the war against the common enemy.

You say that you "quite understand" my disappointment. I must tell you that the point here is not just the disappointment of the Soviet Government, but the preservation of its confidence in its Allies, a confidence which is being subjected to severe stress. One should not forget that it is a question of saving millions of lives in the occupied areas of Western Europe and Russia and of reducing the enormous sacrifices of the Soviet armies, compared with which the sacrifices of the Anglo-American armies are insignificant.

June 24, 1943

4   The Tehran Conference

In November, 1943, Churchill, Roosevelt, and Stalin conferred together for the first time. Their meeting at Tehran, the high point of wartime diplomacy, resulted in agreements on critical issues related to the conduct of the war. Policies that were to dominate international affairs after the war—creation of the United Nations, political arrangements in Eastern Europe, the treatment of Germany—germinated at Tehran. This was foremost, however, a conference on grand strategy, and its central

From **Foreign Relations of the United States: The Conferences at Cairo and Tehran, 1943** (Washington, D. C.: U. S. Government Printing Office, 1961), pp. 540–55.

focus was on the Second Front: when, where, and how much relief, if any, it would offer the Soviet Union.

Secondary Plenary Meeting
November 29, 1943, 4 P.M., Soviet Embassy

Combined Chiefs of Staff Minutes

The President said he had no formal agenda for today's meeting. He thought it would be a good idea if Marshal Stalin, the Prime Minister, and possibly Marshal Voroshiloff, would give the meeting their ideas.

Marshal Stalin asked whether the military committee had completed its work.

General Brooke gave an outline of the proceedings of the conference this morning. . . .

General Marshall stated that he had little to add to the statement of General Brooke but that the problems concerning the United States are not those of troops nor equipment but rather problems of ships, landing craft and airfields in sufficient proximity to the scene of immediate operations under consideration. Furthermore he said, in speaking of landing craft, he was speaking particularly of a special type which carries about 40 tanks or motor vehicles. He said he desired to make clear, as far as the United States forces for *Overlord* are concerned, that the build-up has proceeded according to schedule. Especially should it be noted that the supplies and equipment have now been assembled to the extent of one million tons in the United Kingdom, in advance of the arrival of the troops anticipated. All supplies and equipment have been set up according to schedule. The variable or questionable factor is the subject of landing craft. He said there was a schedule of landing craft construction which had been accelerated both in the United Kingdom and the United States. The purpose of this acceleration is involved with two considerations, (a) the matter of the initial assault for *Overlord*, and (b) operations in the Mediterranean, which could be done if additional landing craft could be made available. In brief, the *Overlord* build-up is going ahead according to schedule as regards ground troops, air forces and equipment. Discussions and problems regarding *Overlord* were related almost entirely to the employment and movement of available landing craft. Transfer of certain United States and British divisions from the Mediterranean to the United Kingdom for the *Overlord* build-up had virtually been completed at the present time.

Marshal Voroshiloff said that the information given by General Brooke and General Marshall corresponded to the talks which had been held this morning on the questions concerning *Overlord*—specifically, technical questions. Continuing, Marshal Voroshiloff said as far as the matters discussed by General Brooke concerning [concerned?] Italy, Yugoslavia, Turkey and Southern France, it was hoped that these matters would be the subject of the next meeting of the *ad hoc* committee. The committee also had under discussion the date of *Overlord* and the details of that operation, with the thought that they would be able to discuss these matters further at the next meeting.

Marshal Stalin asked who will be the commander in this Operation *Overlord*. (The President and Prime Minister interpolated this was not yet decided.) Marshal Stalin continued, "Then nothing will come out of these operations." He further inquired as to who carries the moral and technical responsibility for this operation. He was informed by the President and Prime Minister that the British General Morgan, who is Chief of Staff to the Supreme Allied Commander (Designate), is charged with the plans and preparations which have been and are continually being made and carried out by a Combined U.S.-British Staff.

In reply to a question from Marshal Stalin as to who has the executive responsibility for *Overlord* preparations, The President replied that we have already decided the names of all the commanders except that of the Supreme Commander.

Marshal Stalin said that it could happen that General Morgan might say that all matters were ready; however, when the Supreme Commander reports, he, the Supreme Commander, might not think that everything necessary had been accomplished by the Chief of Staff. He felt that there must be one person in charge.

The Prime Minister informed Marshal Stalin that General Morgan had been charged with the preparation and carrying out of plans in the preliminary stages for *Overlord*. His Majesty's Government had expressed willingness to have Operation *Overlord* undertaken under the command of a United States commander. The United States will be concerned with the greatest part of the build-up, and this United States commander will have command in the field.

Mr. Churchill added that in the Mediterranean the British have large naval and air forces which are under direct British command under the Allied Commander in Chief. A decision had not yet been reached between the President and Prime Minister regarding the specific matter of high command. Decisions here at this conference will have a bearing on the choice. Therefore the President can name the Supreme Allied Commander for *Overlord* if he desires to accept the British offers to serve under a United States commander. The Prime Minister further suggested that Marshal Stalin be given an answer in confidence between the three Chiefs of State regarding who the Supreme Allied Commander would be.

Marshal Stalin said he desired it to be understood that he did not presume to take part in the selection of a commander for *Overlord* but merely wanted to know who this officer would be and felt strongly that he should be appointed as soon as possible and be given the responsibility for preparations for *Overlord* as well as the executive command of the operation.

The Prime Minister agreed it was essential that a commander be appointed for the *Overlord* operation without delay and indicated that such an appointment would be made within a fortnight. He hoped that it might be accomplished during his current meeting with the President.

The Prime Minister then went on to say that he was concerned with the number and complexity of problems which presented themselves before the conference. He said that the meeting was unique in that the thoughts of more than 140,000,000 people were centered upon it. He felt that the principals should not separate until agreements on political, moral, and military problems had been reached. He said that he wished to present a few points which would require study by a subcommittee. Both he and the British Staff had given long study to the Mediterranean position, in which area Great Britain has a large army. He was anxious that the British Mediterranean army should fight throughout 1944 and not be quiescent. From that point of view he asked the Soviets to survey the field and examine the different alternatives put before them and submit their recommendations.

The Prime Minister said that the first point which required study was what assistance could be given to the *Overlord* operation by the large force which will be in the Mediterranean. He asked in particular what the possibilities of this force might be and what should be the scale of an operation that might be launched from Northern Italy into Southern France. He did not feel that such an operation had been studied in sufficient detail but he welcomed the opportunity to give it close examination. He thought it might be well for the U.S. and U.K. staffs to consider this matter together in the light of their special knowledge concerning resources available. He pointed out that Marshal Stalin had stressed the value of pincer operations. He said that for such operations timing is of great importance. A weak attack several months in advance might result in it[s] being defeated and permit the enemy to turn his whole strength to meet the main attack.

The Prime Minister said he wanted landing craft to carry at least two divisions. With such an amphibious force it would be possible to do operations seriatim, that is, first, up the leg of Italy by amphibious turning movements, thus offering the possibility of cutting off the enemy's withdrawal and capturing the entire German force now in Central Italy; second, to take Rhodes in conjunction with Turkey's entry into the war; and, third, to use the entire force for operations six months hence against the southern coast of France in order to assist *Overlord*. He said that none of these operations would be excluded but that the timing would require careful study. This force of two divisions cannot be supplied in the Mediterranean without either setting back the date of *Overlord* for six or eight weeks or without drawing back from the Indian Ocean landing craft which were now intended to be used against the Japanese. He said that this is one of the dilemmas which the Anglo-American staffs are balancing in their minds. In reaching their conclusions they would be greatly assisted by the views of Marshal Stalin and his officers. He welcomed these views because of his admiration for the military record of the Red Army. He therefore suggested that the military staffs continue to study these subjects. . . .

The Prime Minister concluded by saying he felt that the whole Mediterranean situation should be carefully examined to see what could be done to take weight off the Soviet front.

Marshal Stalin said, . . .if we are here in order to discuss military questions, among all the military questions for discussion we, the U.S.S.R., find *Overlord* the most important and decisive. Marshal Stalin said he would like to call the attention of those present to the importance of not creating diversions from the most important operation in order to carry out secondary operations. He suggested that the *ad hoc* committee, which was created yesterday, should be given a definite task as to what they were to discuss. He said if a committee is created in the U.S.S.R., we always give that committee a specific directive or instructions. . . . He said it was, of course, true that the U.S.S.R. needed help and that is why the representatives of the Soviet are here at this conference. He said the Soviets expect help from those who are willing to fulfill Operation *Overlord*. The question now was what shall be the directive to the *ad hoc* committee? What shall be the instructions that should be given to the committee under the guidance of General Brooke? First of all, this directive must be specific with regard to the fact that *Overlord* should not be postponed and must be carried out by the limiting date. Secondly, the directive to the committee should state that Operation *Overlord* must be reinforced by a landing in the South of France a month or two before undertaking the *Overlord* assault. If not possible two or three months earlier, then the landing in the South of France should be at the same time. If a landing can not be effected in the South of France at the same time as *Overlord*, possibly this operation could be mounted a little later than *Overlord*.

Marshal Stalin thought this operation in the South of France would be an auxiliary or supporting operation and would help and be considerably effective in contributing toward *Overlord*. On the other hand, operations . . . in the Mediterranean would be diversions. Operations in the South of France would influence and contribute directly to *Overlord*. He said that the directive to the *ad hoc* committee must also state that the appointment of the Supreme Commander for *Overlord* should be made forthwith. The decision regarding the *Overlord* commander should be made here in Tehran. If it can not be done here, it should be done within a week at the latest. The Soviets believe that until such a commander has been appointed, no success from *Overlord* can be expected in the matter of organization for this operation. He added that it is the task of the British and the United States representatives to agree on the commander for *Overlord*. The U.S.S.R. does not enter into the matter of this selection but the Soviets definitely want to know who he will be. The above are the points of the directive which should be given to the *ad hoc* committee, and the work of this committee should be completed immediately.

Marshal Stalin asked the conference to seriously consider the points which he had just outlined. He added that he felt if the three points he had made were carried out, they would result in the successful and rapid accomplishment of *Overlord*.

The President said . . . that if we are all agreed on *Overlord*, the next question would be regarding the timing of *Overlord*. Therefore, if we come down to a matter of questions, the point is either to carry out *Overlord* at the appointed time or to agree to the postponement of that operation to some time in June or July. There are only one or two other operations in the Mediterranean which might use landing craft and air forces from some other theater. The President said there are two dangers in creating a delay in *Overlord*. One of them is that the use of two or three divisions in the Eastern Mediterranean would cause a delay to *Overlord* and would necessitate the sending of certain landing craft for those operations which in turn could not be withdrawn from the Eastern Mediterranean in time to return for the *Overlord* date. He said it was believed that once we are committed to specific operations in the Eastern Mediterranean, we would have to make it a supreme operation and we probably could not then pull out of it.

Marshal Stalin observed that maybe it would be necessary to utilize some of the means for *Overlord* in order to carry out operations in the Eastern Mediterranean. . . .

The President said we should . . . work out plans to contain the German Divisions [in the area]. This should be done on such a scale as not to divert means from doing *Overlord* at the agreed time.

Marshal Stalin observed, regarding the President's statement, "You are right"—"You are right."

The President said we again come back to the problem of the timing for *Overlord*. It was believed that it would be good for *Overlord* to take place about 1 May, or certainly not later than 15 May or 20 May, if possible.

The Prime Minister said that he could not agree to that.

Marshal Stalin said he observed at yesterday's conference that nothing will come out of these proposed diversions. In his opinion *Overlord* should be done in May. He added that there would be suitable weather in May.

The Prime Minister said he did not believe that the attitudes of those present on this matter were very far apart. He said he (the Prime Minister) was going to do everything in the power of His Majesty's Government to begin *Overlord* at the earliest possible moment. However, he did not think that the many great possibilities in the Mediterranean should be ruthlessly cast aside as valueless merely on the question of a month's delay in *Overlord*.

Marshal Stalin said all the Mediterranean operations are diversions, aside from that into Southern France, and that he had no interest in any other operations other than those into Southern France. He accepted the importance of these other operations but definitely considered that they are diversions.

The Prime Minister continued that in the British view their large armies in the Mediterranean should not be idle for some six months but should be, together with the United States Allies, working toward the defeat of Germany in Italy, and at the same time be active elsewhere. He said for the British to be inert for nearly six months would be a wrong use of forces, and in his opinion would lay the British open to reproach from the Soviets for having the Soviets bear nearly all the burden of land fighting.

Marshal Stalin said that he did not wish the British to think that the Soviets wished them to do nothing.

The Prime Minister said if all the landing craft were taken away from the Mediterranean they will not affect the battle. Marshal Stalin must remember that at Moscow it was stated under what conditions *Overlord* could be mounted and that under those conditions alone could it be launched. Operation *Overlord* was predicated on the assumption that not more than 12 German mobile divisions would be located behind the coastal troops, and furthermore, that not more than 15 reinforcement divisions could enter the fray within 60 days. He said that that was the basis on which he (Mr. Churchill) had stated the British would do *Overlord*. On those conditions, the Allies will have to utilize as many divisions in the Balkans and so forth as are necessary to contain German troops. If Turkey comes into the war, this will be particularly necessary. The German divisions now in Italy have largely come from France. Consequently, if there should be a slackening off in Italy, it would mean that the German divisions would withdraw and appear in the South of France to meet us there. On the other hand, if we do the Eastern Mediterranean, we will contain more German divisions and will create conditions indispensable to the success of *Overlord*.

Marshal Stalin inquired, "What if there are 13 divisions, not 12?"

The Prime Minister replied, "Naturally.". . .

The Prime Minister added that he agreed with General Marshall in his statement that the chief problem is one of transportation across the water and that that matter is largely a question of landing craft. He said that the British were prepared to go into the matter in great detail, and a very small number of landing craft could make the subsidiary operations feasible. If these landing craft cannot be kept in the Mediterranean because of *Overlord* or cannot possibly be found from some other arrangement [area?] such as the Indian Ocean, then this matter should be resolved by the technical committee. A landing in Southern France will require a great number of landing craft. He begged that this important point should be carefully weighed.

The Prime Minister said in conclusion that he accepted the proposal that a directive should be drawn up for this technical committee. He further suggested that the Soviet Government draw up terms of reference, that the United States draw up terms of reference, that Great Britain draw up terms of reference and then he felt sure that all three nations would not be far apart.

The President inquired how long will the conference be in session until the staff comes to a conclusion on these matters.

The Prime Minister in this connection said he can give his own opinion on behalf of the British Government tonight. . . .

The President suggested that if the three Chiefs of State were in agreement, the committee need not have any written directive because they have been confronted with every suggestion made at this afternoon's meeting. He said if the Chiefs of State could agree on the proceedings of the afternoon conference as a directive, then the staff would definitely have only one directive.

Marshal Stalin said he considered that the *ad hoc* committee was unnecessary. It could not raise any new questions for the military conference. He believed that all that was necessary to be solved was the selection of the commander for *Overlord*, the date for *Overlord* and the matter of supporting operations to be undertaken in Southern France in connection with *Overlord*. . . .

The President then read a proposed directive for the *Ad Hoc* Committee of the Chiefs of Staff:

"1. The Committee of the Chiefs of Staff will assume that *Overlord* is the dominating operation.
"2. The Committee recommends that subsidiary operation(s) be included in the Mediterranean, taking into consideration that any delay should not affect *Overlord*."

Marshal Stalin observed that there was no mention regarding the date of *Overlord* in the proposed directive. He said for the U.S.S.R. it is important to know the date *Overlord* will be mounted in order that the Soviets could prepare the blow on their side. He said he insisted on knowing the date.

The President remarked that the date for *Overlord* had been fixed at Quebec and that only some much more important matter could possibly affect that date, that is to say, this was the President's view.

The Prime Minister said he would like to have an opportunity to reply to the President's remarks. He said there was no decisive difference in principle. . . . It was not clear to him what the President's plans were, however. He said he was in favor of the continuance of the *ad hoc* committee if that could be done. . . . He considered that the timing of the supreme Operation *Overlord* as regards any subsidiary operations would be most necessary as a condition for the success of *Overlord*. Furthermore, he believed that the *ad hoc* staff committee should recommend what subsidiary operations should be carried out. The Prime Minister believed that we should take more time in drawing up a proper directive to the *ad hoc* committee.

The President said he found that his staff places emphasis on *Overlord*. While on the other hand the Prime Minister and his staff also emphasize *Overlord*, nevertheless the United States does not feel that *Overlord* should be put off.

The President questioned whether it would not be possible for the *ad hoc* committee to go ahead with their deliberations without any further directive and to produce an answer by tomorrow morning.

Marshal Stalin questioned, "What can such a committee do?" He said, "We Chiefs of State have more power and more authority than a committee. General Brooke cannot force our opinions and there are many questions which can be decided only by us." He said he would like to ask if the British are thinking seriously of *Overlord* only in order to satisfy the U.S.S.R.

The Prime Minister replied that if the conditions specified at Moscow regarding *Overlord* should exist, he firmly believed it would be England's duty to hurl every ounce of strength she had across the Channel at the Germans. . . .

* * *

Tripartite Dinner Meeting
November 29, 1943, 8:30 P.M., Soviet Embassy

Bohlen Minutes

The most notable feature of the dinner was the attitude of Marshal Stalin toward the Prime Minister. Marshal Stalin lost no opportunity to get in a dig at Mr. Churchill. Almost every remark that he addressed to the Prime Minister contained some sharp edge, although the Marshal's manner was entirely friendly. He apparently desired to put and keep the Prime Minister on the defensive. At one occasion he told the Prime Minister that just because Russians are simple people, it was a mistake to believe that they were blind and could not see what was before their eyes.

In the discussion in regard to future treatment of Germans, Marshal Stalin strongly implied on several occasions that Mr. Churchill nursed a secret affection for Germany and desired to see a soft peace.

Marshal Stalin was obviously teasing the Prime Minister for the latter's attitude at the afternoon session of the Conference, he was also making known in a friendly fashion his displeasure at the British attitude on the question of *Overlord*.

Following Mr. Hopkins' toast to the Red Army, Marshal Stalin spoke with great frankness in regard to the past and present capacity of the Red Army. He said that in the winter war against Finland, the Soviet Army had shown itself to be very poorly organized and had done very badly; that as a result of the Finnish War, the entire Soviet Army had been re-organized; but even so, when the Germans attacked in 1941, it could not be said that the Red Army was a first class fighting force. That during the war with Germany, the Red Army had become steadily better from [the] point of view of operations, tactics, etc., and now he felt that it was genuinely a good army. He added that the general opinion in regard to the Red Army had been wrong, because it was not believed that the Soviet Army could reorganize and improve itself during time of war.

In regard to the future treatment of Germany, Marshal Stalin developed the thesis that he had previously expressed, namely, that really effective measures to control Germany must be evolved, otherwise Germany would rise again within 15 or 20 years to plunge the world into another war. He said that two conditions must be met:

(1) At least 50,000 and perhaps 100,000 of the German Commanding Staff must be physically liquidated.
(2) The victorious Allies must retain possession of the important strategic points in the world so that if Germany moved a muscle she could be rapidly stopped.

Marshal Stalin added that similar strong points now in the hands of Japan should remain in the hands of the Allies.

The President jokingly said that he would put the figure of the German Commanding Staff which should be executed at 49,000 or more.

The Prime Minister took strong exception to what he termed the cold blooded execution of soldiers who had fought for their country. He said that war criminals must pay for their crimes and individuals who had committed barbarous acts, and in accordance with the Moscow Document, which he himself had written, they must stand trial at the places where the crimes were committed. He objected vigorously, however, to executions for political purposes.

Marshal Stalin, during this part of the conversation, continuously referred to Mr. Churchill's secret liking for the Germans.

With reference to the occupation of bases and strong points in the vicinity of Germany and Japan, The President said those bases must be held under trusteeship.

Marshal Stalin agreed with the President.

The Prime Minister stated that as far as Britain was concerned, they do not desire to acquire any new territory or bases, but intended to hold on to what they had. He said that nothing would be taken away from England without a war. He mentioned specifically, Singapore and Hong Kong. He said a portion of the British Empire might eventually be released but that this would be done entirely by Great Britain herself, in accordance with her own moral precepts. He said that Great Britain, if asked to do so, might occupy certain bases under trusteeship, provided others would help pay the cost of such occupation.

Marshal Stalin replied that England had fought well in the war and he, personally, favored an increase in the British Empire, particularly the area around Gibraltar. He also suggested that Great Britain and the United States install more suitable government[s] in Spain and Portugal, since he was convinced that Franco was no friend of Great Britain or the United States. In reply to the Prime Minister's inquiry as to what territorial interests the Soviet Union had, Marshal Stalin replied, "there is no need to speak at the present time about any Soviet desires, but when the time comes, we will speak."

Although the discussion between Marshal Stalin and the Prime Minister remained friendly, the arguments were lively and Stalin did not let up on the Prime Minister throughout the entire evening.

Essays

The essays that conclude the present unit present two shades of the broad spectrum of controversy over and interpretation of Allied efforts to open a Second Front in Europe. Although the diversity of viewpoints in this great strategic debate is much greater than these two arguments might suggest, they do offer contrasting perspectives of the important issues. The two authors' thoughtful and carefully reasoned analyses, based primarily on the same sources, ask similar questions but reach quite different conclusions.

5   The Consequences of Winston Churchill's War Doctrine, 1943-1945

Trumbull Higgins

A specialist in modern European history, Trumbull Higgins has earned wide acclaim for his studies of World War II strategy. Winston Churchill and the Second Front, *from which the following material was excerpted, was published in 1957 and was immediately hailed as "a masterly presentation" and "a work of great scholarship." Most interesting is Higgins' treatment of Winston Churchill's strategic views, an evaluation founded on provocative theories about modern strategy and the nature of decision-making in wartime.*

"To say the truth, I do not believe we had in the last war, and, according to all appearance, we shall not have in the present one either; plans of a sufficiently large scale to force France to keep within her proper limits. Small measures produce only small results."——Horatio Nelson

"Has there ever been such a thing as absolute war since nations ceased to exterminate or enslave the defeated? Nineteenth Century Europe has passed beyond the Mongol stage."——Captain Liddell Hart

From **Winston Churchill and the Second Front,** 1940–1943 by Trumbull Higgins, pp. 183–214. Copyright © 1956 by Oxford University Press, Inc. Reprinted by permission.

*"The uncontrollable momentum of war, the inadequacy of unity and leadership among Allies, the tides of natural passion, nearly always force improvident action upon Governments or Commanders. Allowance must be made for the limits of their knowledge and power . . . But do not let us obscure the truth. Do not found conclusions upon error. Do not proclaim its melancholy consequences as the perfect model of the art of war or as the triumphant consummation of a great design."——*Winston Churchill

*"There is no greater fatuity than a political judgment dressed in a military uniform."——*David Lloyd George

By the time of the Casablanca Conference in January 1943, the form of war advocated so indirectly, yet so effectively, by the British Prime Minister had reached its apogee. The production priority of landing craft on the U.S. Navy's Shipbuilding Precedence List was dropped from second to twelfth place, or lower than in the dark days of March 1942, and in Great Britain field artillery shell production was drastically cut back. Neither of these essential prerequisites of large-scale land warfare would be restored to their 1942 levels until early 1944.

The U.S. Army was to send only seven divisions abroad in the ten months following the North African landings, compared with double that number in 1942. The General Staff of the Army was forced to suspend, if not to abandon completely, its long-held concept of an immense force designed to operate as a single unit and solely against the army of the principal enemy. Consequently, as had also occurred to the British Army, the total United States troop list was again reduced, on this occasion from one hundred and fourteen to one hundred divisions. Recognizing the implications for land warfare of the British narrowing-ring approach to the European Axis, General Marshall had found it necessary to insist upon this reduction in divisional strength against the unanimous advice of his staff.

The results of the failure of the U.S. Army to achieve a durable agreement on a dominant theater in western Europe were now becoming more apparent. On January 14, at the first meeting at Casablanca of the Chiefs of Staff, in opposing "interminable operations" in the Mediterranean, General Marshall joined Admiral King in the advocacy of further reinforcements for the South and Southwest Pacific as well as new assaults against Burma and the Marshall Islands. Marshall was again reviving the old issue of the American Pacific threat despite his full awareness that only a few weeks before the President had complained that the United States was much more heavily engaged in the Southwest Pacific than he had expected. The U.S. Army Chief of Staff was also conscious of the current desire of the President to give the operations in North Africa precedence over all other projects until adequate preparations had been made against any Axis assault in Spanish Morocco or in Tunisia.

The British Chiefs of Staff opposed their American colleagues on this Pacific proposal; instead at last they frankly urged an all-out effort in the Mediterranean. To thwart the emphasis of Marshall and King upon the Pacific, the British now discovered the necessity for a plan that would bring victory "quickly and decisively" in the European theater. As the Prime Minister would put it, the danger which faced his Grand Alliance was no longer defeat, but stalemate.

Unfortunately, notwithstanding that, in Mr. Churchill's phrase, Admiral King had been "paid off" once already in 1942, by May 1943 the American preoccupation with the war against Japan had risen to such a crescendo that it required a careful answer by Mr. Churchill before a Joint Session of the United States Congress. Moreover, the United States Chiefs of Staff were not willing to sacrifice a full-fledged effort in their own popular Pacific theater for the sake of a limited campaign of expediency in the Mediterranean. War might be all hell and no glory, according to the prophetic General William Sherman, but by Calvinist definition there could be no mere purgatory of limited war in General Marshall's still absolute war doctrine.

Thus, with both United States military doctrine and popular opinion against him, there can be little doubt as to why the Americans had so unfavorable a reaction to Mr. Churchill's now triumphant conception of war. The Combined Chiefs were unable to answer General Eisenhower's request for his next objective, an impasse which Eisenhower terminated by remarking: "Oh you just want to go on fighting, do you, well we can find plenty of places to do that."

Only a month previously the Prime Minister himself had conceded in a communication to President Roosevelt that "at present we have no plan for 1943 which is on the scale or up to the level of events." More privately, Mr. Churchill would grumble to his own Chiefs concerning the inadequacy of the Western Allies "playing about" with six German divisions while the Russians were facing one hundred and eighty-five. For himself the Prime Minister favored an ample program which included not merely the conquest of Tunisia and Sicily and the recapture of Burma; he also still desired a preliminary invasion of France, a weakening phrase which presumably reflected his exposure to the overwhelming fact of Torch.

So long as they had the decisive support of the President the British would win in the essentials, and this they did at Casablanca. It was decided to push ahead, officially at least, only to Sicily in the Mediterranean. This new commitment was facilitated by the now obvious impossibility of conquering Tunisia in time to permit even a theoretical revival of Roundup in 1943. Nevertheless, the United States Chiefs of Staff had extracted their price and would continue to do so. Of the sixteen American Army and Marine divisions arriving at United States Ports of Embarkation in 1942, two-thirds had been sent to the Pacific by the beginning of 1943. So late as January 1944 there were 40 per cent more of what Mr. Churchill has considered American divisions "in fighting contact" with the enemy in the Pacific than in the Mediterranean.

What, indeed, one might ask, had become of the concept of Germany first? By Casablanca the Allies were perilously close to the most deadly error of the Axis, that of fighting private and separate wars against their preferred and widely separated enemies. Between the late spring of 1940 and the surrender of Italy in

September 1943, the bulk of Great Britain's fighting strength on land was engaged chiefly against Italians. Until the summer of 1944 the majority of American divisions actually in combat were waging war against Japan. The Soviets, of course, had been given no choice regarding the area of their basic conflict. The Western Allies alone could shift their weight in order to work with the U.S.S.R. against the strongest Axis partner; the United States alone, as would become ever more apparent throughout 1943, had the will to do so.

From early 1941, when advance elements of Hitler's Afrika Korps began landing in Libya, until the final overture of the cross-Channel invasion in June 1944, the entire strength of the British Empire and Commonwealth intermittently fought between two and eight divisions of the principal Axis power, Germany. On the other hand, during all but the first six months of this same period the Russians contained an average of about one hundred and eighty German divisions in more or less continuous action. Moreover, in the policy advocated by the British, the United States was also compelled to limit its effort against Germany during 1943 and the first five months of 1944 to an average of four or five divisions in actual combat most of the time. As Mr. Churchill himself had explained, this contrasts most impressively with the original intention of the U.S. Army General Staff to wage a continuous and continental warfare against the Reich, a war designed to begin in the spring of 1943 with a commensurate force of some forty-eight British and American divisions.

Under the inspiration of this essentially British colonial type of war, it took an average of twelve divisions of the Western Allies some two and one-half years to push about the same number of Axis divisions back from northwest Egypt to northeast Italy, a distance of some two thousand miles over terrain chiefly distinguished by its poverty of good communications and its frequency of highly defensible positions. At the end of several bitterly contested campaigns the greatest natural barrier in Europe, the Alps, still lay between the Anglo-American armies and the Reich.

Under the leadership of the U.S. Army, following the Anglo-American landings in France on June 6, 1944, an Allied land force averaging fifty to sixty divisions attacked German armies of nominally the same number of divisional units, but in fact a great deal weaker in all respects. Within eleven months the Allied troops had advanced a distance of some five hundred and fifty miles over a terrain notable chiefly for its comparative flatness, for a superb transportation network, and for the heart of Axis war industry. At the termination of this type of campaign, undertaken in conjunction with the Red Army, there existed neither a German Army nor a German war economy.

As the German General Staff had warned Hitler in 1938, in no year between 1941 and 1944 did the German Army have the resources either in manpower or equipment to fight continental warfare on two fronts for any length of time. The long-planned German Army attempt upon Hitler's life in July 1944 merely recognized as much in an overdue, but finally concrete form. Conducting war according to Mr. Churchill's mode any longer than absolutely necessary played right into the hands of German policy; the Reich always could spare small forces to dally with the Allies in the Mediterranean. Mr. Broderick's charge so early as 1901 that Churchill suffered from a "hereditary desire to run Imperialism on the cheap" may well be recalled. In addition, the terrible dependence of the Western Allies upon Soviet military successes implicit in this form of war in the long run involved the grave danger of as great a political dependence.

From the evidence available today, it seems likely that the most important motive in policy for a Mediterranean denouement in 1942 lay in Mr. Churchill's desire to retain for at least another year the low British casualty rate established at the opening of the Second World War. So late as the period September 1943 through May 1944, land conflict in Europe resulted in only 14,300 deaths to soldiers from the British Empire during these nine ineffectual months. To be sure, this conflict was at last necessarily fought against the German Army, but only within the narrow confines of the Italian peninsula. On the other hand, the decisive eleven-month campaign across the Channel so much dreaded by the Prime Minister and his whole generation of Britons, in fact, cost the British Isles no more than about 30,000 dead. Unlike the Italian campaign, the cross-Channel thrust would not drag on thereafter with further casualties and negligible rewards.

Above all, Mr. Churchill significantly has not pointed out that even with the American version of war policy superimposed upon his own, by the end of the Second World War the United Kingdom would suffer a total of no more than 264,000 military deaths, of which approximately one-quarter were in the Royal Air Force. By contrast, in the First World War the United Kingdom had sustained 744,000 deaths in the shorter period of four and one-quarter years. Furthermore, in the First War almost all of these deaths were incurred in land warfare in France, while at that time the Salonika front afforded the safest, if also the most futile theater of war for the British Army.

This immense drop in war losses was more than simply desirable in Great Britain for, as Wing Commander J.C. Slessor had put it in 1937 in his influential Gold Medal Essay: "In war we could not afford again to be the mainstay of an alliance at sea, in the air, and in the economic sphere, while at the same time maintaining huge armies in the field. Moreover—and the sooner we face the fact the better—*the country will not stand it again*. It will take a very just cause, cleverly stated, to get the British people to go to war again at all; for that just cause they will fight with air forces, they will spend their money and energies; but they will not again tolerate casualties in the scale of those suffered by the National Armies in the Great War."

Hitler was no further off in this basic postulate of his, that Britain did not have the determination to fight an all-out land war against Germany, than he had been in his belief that the Soviets would collapse in 1941 or that the Americans would have to fight a war principally directed against Japan. But in each case these relatively narrow misses proved decisive.

A closely related aspect of the current triumph of the war of attrition advocated by Winston Churchill may be found in the frank dependence of the Casablanca Conference upon air power as the principal weapon of the West for the defeat of Germany. Certainly the increasingly discrete impersonality of life in the more civilized Western states, in a military and, perhaps, moral sense, led directly to the theories of Douhet in the air and of Liddell Hart on land. Facing the practical consequences of personal and infantry combat was now too distasteful to societies which in other realms had already successfully evaded so many of the traditional agonies of the human condition. In the famous air directive issued at the Conference which accurately foreshadowed the war of the future, breaking of the German will-to-fight was openly admitted to be a major objective of the bombing offensive, although it was subordinated somewhat by references to military, industrial, and economic targets.

Perhaps the chief rational, if not necessarily the principal intended, object of this renewed stress upon area bombing would be for the sake of appeasing the popular clamor for action while at the same time diverting attention from the all-too-visible possibility of conducting major land warfare across the Channel. To be sure, the Air Force Chiefs, if not Mr. Churchill, believed that they could win the war by their action alone. At the very least, however, should the Allied public, if not the Axis populations, become fully enough convinced of the value of strategic bombing, an invasion of France even in 1944 might be deflected.

It is only fair to emphasize that the faith in the effectiveness of bombing so frequently manifested by the Allied leaders at this time stemmed in part from mistaken intelligence analyses. Far from recognizing that German munitions production was increasing more than three times between 1942 and 1944, Allied Intelligence circles held as a fixed article of belief that Germany had passed her production maximum in the previous year. It was only too easy to jump to the conclusion that the totalitarian German state must have achieved her full production by the start of the war she had initiated in 1939. Nevertheless, as Max Werner could still write so late as 1943, "the algebraic sum total of a land defensive and an air offensive will not be offensive, but defensive action."

By March 1944, when Britain was at last irrevocably committed to the cross-Channel invasion, Sir James Grigg, the British Secretary of State for War, estimated that there were as many workers employed on the R.A.F. heavy bomber program alone as upon the whole British Army program for the large-scale land campaign then imminent. At this late date the United Kingdom was still devoting 40 to 50 per cent of her war production to her air forces. Under these circumstances it can be understood why authorities such as General Fuller, Allen Dulles, and Admiral Gallery believe that because of its cost in raw materials and manpower this air policy up to the spring of 1944 did not shorten the war but instead prolonged it. There is certainly no mystery why Mr. Churchill's Britain, of her own accord, would never have been able and ready to cross the Channel and wage major land battles in France.

While, in effect, postulating the defeat of Germany without large-scale land warfare on the part of the Western Allies at Casablanca in January 1943, at the same time, quite inconsistently, Mr. Churchill also accepted President Roosevelt's policy of unconditional surrender. The policy of the President was, of course, a political reflection of the American Army's philosophy of absolute war rather than of the Prime Minister's own more limited form of warfare. As that apostle of Winston Churchill's strategy, Captain Liddell Hart, has pointed out in an uncharacteristic exposition of Clausewitz, a strategy of a limited aim is usually a result of a war policy of a limited aim. Subsequently the Prime Minister was uncomfortable over the consequences of unconditional surrender; decidedly less than the President was Mr. Churchill a pacifist in war-paint, inclined "to overact the unfamiliar part" he was at last able to play.

Not merely was Mr. Churchill incorrect with regard to his *de facto* reliance before 1944 upon area bombing as the West's principal contribution to defeating Germany, he was also fundamentally mistaken in treating Africa as one of Hitler's major objectives before the defeat of the U.S.S.R. After the survival of Russia in the battle of Moscow, and notwithstanding the simultaneous American entry into the war, it may be concluded that Churchill quite consciously used the continuing fear of a German threat to Africa—a threat which he had done so much to evoke—as the method by which he was able to initiate an Anglo-American offensive against Italy instead of Germany. Unlike those of the Nazi Fuehrer, the intentions of Winston Churchill were never essentially defensive on the periphery and, in particular, not in the Mediterranean.

On the other hand, like Adolph Hitler in the summer of 1940, the British Prime Minister staved off the continuing possibility of a campaign across the Channel from 1941 until 1944, choosing instead to suffer comparable losses elsewhere in campaigns which could never lead to the defeat of the Reich. As the Duke of Marlborough had emphasized to his cautious, overburdened, and weary Dutch ally, in the long run the pursuit of victory without slaughter is likely to eventuate in slaughter without victory. But, Mr. Churchill has written, Marlborough was not attracted "by small warfare or limited objects." His purpose was to annihilate the French Army in a great battle.

Like Hitler with respect to Great Britain, Winston Churchill's significant if subconscious fear of an absolute decision in a general war made him prefer no more than a *guerre d'usure* against his German enemy. Each man displayed an excessive anxiety concerning operations within the chosen realm of the other, e.g. on land and sea respectively. But only through the admittedly difficult and unattractive Channel route could either obtain a final decision as opposed to simply another triumph.

The parallels between the attitudes of Hitler and Churchill toward war and strategy go deeper than the problem of a cross-Channel invasion and beyond the tedious ambivalence of Anglo-German relations in the last century. If, for example, as romantics each man tended to overestimate the newer technological factors in war, more surprisingly they also seemed to have underemphasized such traditional military influences as the terrain of the supposed soft underbelly of the Axis of the climate and immensity of Russia. Yet neither ignored geography; indeed both generally pursued geographical objectives to the exclusion of any real concentration upon the destruction of the chief forces of their enemies.

Actually their successes resulted from their keen insight in politics rather than from their military proclivities—fortunately for Mr. Churchill's reputation his opportunity for political judgment came late in a victorious war won, as in 1918, by others; a war which, however had gradually excluded Hitler from any further chance to exercise his remarkable talents for political blackmail.

It is hardly surprising that with personalities so opposed to the authority of others, and imbued with such similar conclusions concerning the fatuity and parochialism of the military in the First World War, the Prime Minister and the Fuehrer should have desired to make their respective General Staffs vehicles for the expression of their own strategic views. To be sure, unlike Hitler, Mr. Churchill would hardly reproach his generals for their "obsolete concepts of the chivalrous conduct of war." It is also questionable whether anyone but a parvenu with his back to the wall would express himself so bluntly as did Hitler in 1945 when he told Guderian: "It is intolerable to me that a group of intellectuals should presume to press their views upon their superiors. But such is the General Staff system and that system I intend to smash." Unquestionably there could be no easy reconciliation between the improvisation and opportunism inherent in the strategy of these forceful advocates and the emphasis upon long-range and determinist planning embodied in such a revolutionary development as the General Staff system.

The similarities between the great British nationalist and the rulers of Japan are equally illuminating. Like the Japanese government, Winston Churchill saw in the opening of the decisive struggle of the Second World War between Germany and Russia a better opportunity to seize territory from a still weak opponent in the south than to open a second front against his more powerful enemy in the north. Like the Japanese on their Manchurian frontier in 1938-39, Winston Churchill made a pretense at a correct coalition strategy at Dieppe in 1942; in each instance the timing was premature and in the case of Dieppe any real punch was lacking as well. In August 1942, in Mr. Churchill's concept of land warfare, Dieppe was not planned to lead anywhere, as the great air raid on Cologne in May 1942 was planned to accomplish so much—with Allied public opinion. As a wit had said of the elder Pitt's raid on Rochefort in 1757:

> *We went, we saw, were seen, like Valiant Men*
> *Sailed up the Bay and then—sailed back again.*

It is interesting to recall why Britain's Prime Minister at the beginning of the First World War, Herbert Asquith, had begun to lose faith in Winston Churchill's judgment even before the Dardanelles. According to Lord Beaverbrook, Asquith's disillusionment had resulted from a series of hit-and-run raids launched by Churchill along the Flemish coast with the intention of encouraging the Belgians and alarming the Germans "by making a great parade of force without fighting any general action." In September 1943 a still purer theatrical enterprise—a part of which was appropriately named "Harlequin"—was staged by British forces in the Channel in an unsuccessful simulation of a second front assault. Wisely, with the high cost of Dieppe in mind, on this occasion the British Army did not disembark in France at all.

Certainly in the art of staging martial drama the nautical impresario of the Dunkirk Circus, as the actions of 1914 were known, had few peers. But it can be seen why that realistic organizer of mass British Armies, Lord Kitchener, had then become so weary of what he called Churchill's "wild-cat schemes" that he threatened to resign the War Office to his irrepressible rival, although the latter already held the Admiralty. Churchill had long grated on the feelings of so rigid a planner as Kitchener, and the latter may be forgiven for doubting whether what Churchill advocated was magnificent, let alone whether or not it constituted war. After all, few Puritans had approved of theater, even in times of peace.

In the Second World War the policy of Mr. Churchill in many fundamentals also resembled that of the more conservative elements among the military masters of Japan, who according to Herbert Rosinski did not realize that they had "no *choice*; that their cautious, 'independent' and 'limited' strategy was radically unsound in a world-wide conflict and that the only slender chance of salvation depended precisely on such a seemingly reckless, 'unlimited' global strategy. The fatal effect of their plan for a 'limited war' also prevented them from acting with full concentrated energy in any direction." Unlike the Japanese military conservatives, however, Mr. Churchill was saved from the full force of a war of attrition on the part of Hitler's Reich by the unexpected recovery of the Soviet Union. Of course the Prime Minister had already received his share of bad luck in the First World War.

Lastly, this British statesman so often considered a soldier of fortune was admittedly an opportunist, quite willing to engage in a great conflict without any clear-cut and responsible plans or methods for obtaining a final military decision; essentially the military doctrines of Winston Churchill, like those of the Axis, made sense only in terms of a mediated peace. Although in 1918 Mr. Churchill may have favored such a peace or, as was his aristocratic custom, a magnanimous victory, in the Second World War he would engage in no negotiations of any sort with the Third Reich.

On the other hand, Hitler at least did seek such a peace in 1940 with Great Britain and possibly in 1943 with the U.S.S.R.; this latter an effort eagerly fostered by his Japanese ally. Likewise, Tokyo's whole policy in undertaking war with America was dependent upon the theory that eventually the Americans would weary of fighting and accept a Japanese *fait accompli* in the Far East. The Axis rulers did not direct societies which, after fighting no more than limited wars, still demanded the absolute victories of Puritanism.

The question may be posed as to what extent any British belief that Hitler would win in Russia would enhance their desire to advance in the Mediterranean while this theater was not dominated by Germany. Of course, it is perfectly possible that, like the Japanese, the British Government formulated its policy after June 22, 1941, on the hypothesis that, sooner or later, the Soviet Union would be defeated by Germany. If so, like Tokyo, Mr. Churchill held to the strategic consequences of his probable beliefs regarding the course of the Barbarossa campaign in 1941 with remarkable tenacity thereafter. In 1942 the Japanese would not even help their German ally through India, let alone in the Russian Far-Eastern provinces, although with the wrong timing, as usual, and for their own purposes, they attempted to invade India from Burma in 1944. Similarly in 1942, Mr. Churchill refused to stick to a more or less settled engagement to attack Germany rather than Italy; even at the end of 1943 he was willing to reaccept a major attack upon Germany perhaps only because of *force majeure* applied by his more powerful Allies.

Most surprisingly, in the course of an eloquent tribute to Mr. Churchill, Sir James Grigg has illuminated one of the Prime Minister's most salient characteristics, his seeming inability to grow with the war. Although starting from a lower level of military experience than the Prime Minister, neither of the leaders of the other two chief Allied states reflected this particular weakness to the same degree; as deliberate social innovators, their development in military affairs was both obvious and profound. As statesmen, using nationalism rather than being used by it, Roosevelt and Stalin would in time come to dominate the course of the Second World War perhaps as much through their aggressive military attitudes as through the immense potentials of their respective nations. On the other hand the Axis leaders, men of the extreme Right, far from growing with their war, shrank almost to nothingness as it developed. With the dubious exception of Mussolini, they had little of that extraordinary understanding of the world outside their national states which so enlightened a moderate Conservative such as Otto von Bismarck.

If, unlike the Axis leaders, Mr. Churchill's peculiar qualities of magnanimity, imagination, courage, and humor led him to the utmost magnificence in defeat, as a man of the moderate Right he would also diminish in size as victory approached without reference to his policies. To be sure, his great design of imposing a war strategy based on the stringent British necessities of 1940-41 upon the Grand Alliance of 1942-43 can be explained on the grounds that his countrymen had not sufficiently abandoned the pacifism of the earlier 1930's to be able to conduct an effective coalition war on the land against the German Army. At the same time an important explanation for the desire for a limited war manifest in the dominant circles of the British Government after Pearl Harbor must be sought in its predominantly conservative cast.

In contrast to the First World War, the Second World War was essentially a struggle favored by the political Left among the Allied coalition; it seems improbable that a British Government of the Left would have sought to resist the early creation of a second front to relieve Russia with either the persistence or the passion manifested by Mr. Churchill for three full years. Moreover a British Labour Government, in spite of occasional yearnings toward its traditional pacifism, would hardly have opposed the desire of the United States General Staff for a war conducted according to a long-range plan with the ideological enthusiasm of this great Conservative advocate of strategic opportunism.

Indeed, in discussing an era more to his taste, Mr. Churchill has written of the early eighteenth century that, like his own mentor in strategy, Admiral Fisher, the British Tories had "obstinately championed the policy that if we were drawn into a war we should go as little to the Continent, send as few troops, fight as near to the coast as possible, and endeavor to secure territory and traffic across the oceans." As Mr. Churchill's Liberal Imperialist colleagues had done in the First World War, so the eighteenth-century Whigs dwelt upon "the theory familiar to us as the doctrine of 'the decisive theatre' and sought, with the largest army that could be maintained, to bring the war to an end by a thrust at the heart of France, the supreme military antagonist, arguing that thereafter all the rest would be added unto them. It should be noticed that the Tories favored the popular idea that the Navy should be stronger and the Army stinted . . . Marlborough's march to Blenheim was there . . . the greatest violation of Tory principles which could be conceived."

Winston Churchill, then, as a Conservative, looked to the past in preference to the future, although it has been pointed out that it was his knowledge of history which helped distinguish him from the more common run of Conservatives. As occurred with the U.S. Army in the Second World War, Churchill had won the distrust of many Britons of an earlier generation for his notably plangent and impulsive romanticism—a romanticism obliquely recognized in the once popular appellation of poor judgment.

As a romantic Winston Churchill could see the cinema *Lady Hamilton* for the fifth time with deep emotion. As a romantic Winston Churchill was the man who in 1914 wished to abandon the Admiralty for the "glittering commands" of the Army, then in his opinion in the hands of "dug-out trash" or of "mediocrities who have led a sheltered life, mouldering in military routine." Churchill had gone on to tell Herbert Asquith that a political career was nothing to him in comparison with military glory. He also was the man who told Henry Stimson in the Second World War that any blow to President Roosevelt's basic war policy, such as that which would result from the abandonment of a cross-Channel attack in 1944, could be cured by victories elsewhere. As a romantic he was the man who would consider the alternatives between attacking southern Italy or the island of Sardinia as the difference between a "glorious campaign and a mere convenience." As a romantic he always felt it would be "very foolish to discard the reasons of the heart for those of the head." Like Admiral Fisher he wanted to enjoy both.

In fact, Mr. Churchill's dislike of the drab impersonality of contemporary warfare went hand in hand with his distaste for democratic or mass warfare as a whole. Certainly the grimly predetermined warfare of the political Left, so explicitly proletarian and Puritan, as in the Bolshevik Reformation, or even the bourgeois New Models inspired by Gustavus Adolphus and his successors, would distress Mr. Churchill regardless of what the ablest practitioners of such warfare—Cromwell, Marlborough, and Napoleon—actually achieved in the field.

Unfortunately for Mr. Churchill, as the great connoisseur of chivalric postures, Edmund Burke, had long ago conceded: "It is a dreadful truth, but is a truth that cannot be concealed: in ability, in dexterity, in the distinctness of their views, the Jacobins are our superiors. They saw the thing right from the beginning. . . . The British and the Austrians, [on the other hand] refused to take any steps which might strike at the heart of affairs. . . . They always kept on the circumference; and the wider and remoter the circle was, the more eagerly they chose it as their sphere of action in this centrifugal war. The plan they pursued, in its nature, demanded great length of time." Or as Mr. Churchill's *bête noire* in Calvinist warfare, Oliver Cromwell, put it, "without a more speedy, vigorous and effectual prosecution of the War—casting off all lingering proceedings like [those of] soldiers of fortune . . . we shall make the kingdom weary of us, and hate the name of a Parliament." Probably, as his earlier career had demonstrated, Mr. Churchill did not recognize that overdisciplining the means of war is a necessary compensation for the disorder inherent in its ends.

The rather complex nature of Winston Churchill's deliberate rejection of Clausewitz and his disciples in World War II did not grow out of the traumatic experiences of the First World War alone, although of that war Mr. Churchill has readily admitted that his general principles ran counter to the dominant military views.

Between 1919 and 1939 the bitter legacy of Passchendaele and the Somme had enthroned Captain Liddell Hart as the prophet of a more traditional form of warfare for Britain, a form of warfare which the modern military theorist, Delbrück, has termed the *"Ermattungsstrategie,"* or strategy of exhaustion. Recognized by Clausewitz only shortly before his death, this strategy is in many fundamentals diametrically opposed to that strategy of annihilation at any cost more generally associated with this famous theorist.

Embodying, as Winston Churchill did, a rather Anglican repudiation of any Calvinist tendency toward clear-cut or absolute solutions, the strategy of exhaustion would encounter a most sympathetic pupil in this conserver of so many of the older and finer values of Occidental society. Such a form of warfare was condoned in Clausewitz either when the political ends or conflicts of the war were small or when the military means were inadequate to bring about an absolute victory. The political tensions between the Anglo-Americans and the Third Reich were unquestionably beyond compromise in the Second World War; more germane, after Pearl Harbor the military means of the Western Allies were not inadequate to accomplish a war of annihilation should they really set out to do so.

Nevertheless, from the start of the conflict in 1939, the future Prime Minister had thrown all his influence on behalf of that type of warfare so persuasively presented by Hart, Fuller, and others in post-1918 Britain; a defensive warfare of limited liability on land, of blockade, of economic conflict, and of a small but elite army concentrated in Britain and the Middle East instead of in France. He was naturally supported by the Royal Air Force and Navy; more important, the C.I.G.S. after 1941, Sir Alan Brooke, and many Army generals of Churchill's generation agreed with their Prime Minister wholeheartedly. One long-standing critic of Mr. Churchill, Victor Germains, summed up the demoralizing influence of the period before 1939 when he wrote: "For more than a decade the British public was trained to put faith in every conceivable means of winning wars save by fighting battles and beating the enemy."

Mr. Churchill believed at the beginning of his career that wars of the people might be more terrible than those of the kings, but as Captain H.M. Curteis felt compelled to point out after Munich: "It may not be entirely coincidence that the last two major wars—the Napoleonic and the German—in which Great Britain has fought, have not been decided by 'traditional' or 'amphibious' strategy . . . The chances that our strategical problems in any future European war would more nearly resemble 1914-1918 than those of the XVIIIth Century appear too strong to ignore; and traditional strategy applied in circumstances no longer traditional is likely to prove inadequate and perhaps disastrous."

In order to preserve and, if possible, to exalt such a traditional type of war, Mr. Churchill had only to resort to his conclusion from 1915 that the least-guarded strategic points should be selected for attack, rather than the more guarded. Unfortunately, the least-guarded points, in the Second World War at any rate, were almost invariably the least important points. Combat undertaken for its own sake rather than for a decision violated another principle of Clausewitz, that of not losing time. In the Prussian theorist's well-known interpretation, everything that does not happen is to the credit of the defense. The defender "reaps where he had not sowed."

Another closely related example of Mr. Churchill's strategic principles for land warfare derived from the First World War merits a more extended analysis, for it lies even closer to the heart of his strategic thesis in the Second World War. "In any hostile combination," wrote the future Prime Minister, "once it is certain that the strongest cannot be directly defeated itself, but cannot stand without the weakest, it is the weakest that should be attacked." Leaving aside the infinitely debatable issue of whether or not Germany could have been attacked directly through France in 1943, it would in any event seem clear that the defeat of the weakest hostile power does not necessarily bring about either the certain or probable defeat of the strongest. Furthermore, the dissipation of military resources against such a secondary enemy as Italy militated against the decisive conflict with the major hostile power. Nevertheless, to Mr. Churchill, his Eastern policy in the First World War was vindicated in the end since "the collapse of Bulgaria . . . was the signal for the general catastrophe of the Central Powers."

The belief that the surrender of Bulgaria in 1918 had enforced that of Germany is indeed remarkable, and certainly a belief at variance with many of Churchill's civilian colleagues, not to mention the military, in the First War. For example, Lord Grey, who had played such a decisive role at the Foreign Office, decided that the principal mistakes in British strategy between 1914 and 1918 could be summed up in the phrase *"side-shows."* Grey concluded that Britain had not sufficiently concentrated on the one cardinal point: "It was the German Army which had to be beaten and this could be done only on the Western Front. For to attempt it anywhere else was to give the Germans the advantage of interior and safe lines of communication as compared with our own." In fact, on occasion Mr. Churchill himself appears to have recognized full well both the necessity for raising large British armies in 1914 and their absolute essentiality as a means of achieving victory in 1918.

Whatever may be said of the merits of the Dardanelles, without the immense potential of the American Expeditionary Force in the First World War, without that terrible main *and* decisive theater sustained by ravaged armies of Sir Douglas Haig in France, there would have been no "black day" for Erich

Ludendorff and no capitulation of the Second Reich. Hitler's propaganda notwithstanding, in 1918 Germany faced an overwhelming and inescapable land assault in the next year aimed directly at her fatherland, an assault which she had no reasonable assurance of resisting. Unlike Hitler, the rulers of the Kaiserreich were men as relatively reasonable as the peace terms of their enemies.

An additional basis in strategic theory on which Winston Churchill disagreed with Clausewitz and, for that matter, with his own General Frederick Morgan, is in his apparent opinion that an attack on exterior lines is preferable to one on interior lines. In *The World Crisis* Mr. Churchill asserted: "If the fronts of centres of armies cannot be broken their flanks should be turned. If these flanks rest on seas the manoeuvers to turn them must be amphibious and dependent on sea power." Clausewitz, however, has written that in strategy, he who finds himself "in the midst of his enemies is better off than his opponent who tries to envelop him, particularly if the forces on each side are equal, and, of course, still more so if there is an inferiority on the enveloping side. . . . The strategic enveloping movement is therefore never advisable unless we are (physically and morally) so superior, that we shall be strong at the decisive point, and yet can, at the same time, dispense with the detached corps." No better commentary upon Mr. Churchill's North African operation and its consequences can be found.

One authority has interpreted Clausewitz as being particularly interested in the problems arising from coalition warfare. To him the basic problem confronting the strategist is "one of discerning the 'center of gravity' against which the military push must be directed. . . . In wars of coalition, the 'center' lies in the army of the strongest of the allies or in the community of interest between the allies." Here lies Winston Churchill's best military base in Clausewitz; nonetheless, we notice a choice is posed by Clausewitz even in this instance.

From 1939 the destruction of the community of interest between Germany and Italy was continuously planned by the future Prime Minister, but far from seriously damaging the Reich by the destruction of this uneasy Axis rapport, the Anglo-Americans found themselves entangled in a situation in which the possibility of returning to their original coalition plan of attacking the army of their strongest enemy tended more and more to put a strain upon their own alliance. Yet, as the United States War Department had anticipated, having bet wrongly on the alliance between the Axis powers as the enemy's true center of gravity, the British and Americans would still have to face that inescapable German Army again. Fundamentally, the bet was misplaced because the power of Germany so enormously outweighed that of Italy that it made little difference one way or another what happened to the Latin partner. With Allies of more equal strength such as Britain and France in 1940, the destruction of the alliance might well have yielded decisive fruit.

The efforts of Mr. Churchill and his supporters after the Second World War to refute the impressive evidence of his own earlier attitude in order to maintain that he always favored the Allied assault-in-force of 1944 across the Channel has taken two principal forms. The first, in general adduced for the public, can be termed the timing or *coup de grâce* argument. The second, more frequently employed by and against the professional military critic, has been dressed up into a philosophy of expediency or of opportunism.

The first argument has been well presented by Mr. Churchill's wartime personal chief of staff, General Sir Hastings Ismay. In 1948, accurately anticipating the Prime Minister's own dialectic in a review of Eisenhower's *Crusade in Europe*, he wrote: "Mr. Churchill and his military advisors always recognized that ultimately the death blow to Germany must be delivered across the Channel; but they were determined that it should not be delivered prematurely. There was no difference as to the principle, but only as to the timing."

With respect to the thesis that the wartime Prime Minister always favored the principle of a major cross-Channel invasion, wishing to delay it only until it was a reasonably safe bet, the true character of this cross-Channel operation emerges in Ismay's expressions, "ultimately" and "death blow." Not for small reason had his old friend Jacky Fisher terminated his historic controversy with Mr. Churchill in 1915 on the following note: "You are bent on forcing the Dardanelles and nothing will turn you from it—*nothing*. I know you so well!"

So late as 1943, in no fundamental had Winston Churchill abandoned his belief of 1941 in a cross-Channel assault undertaken solely in the event that German morale showed signs of a serious weakening. As before, his concept of a safe and sound cross-Channel venture constituted a technique to exploit a German collapse rather than a method of evoking it.

For example, in early May 1943, Admiral Leahy heard that the British Chiefs of Staff would not agree to an invasion, such as was envisaged in the American Roundup plan, until Germany had collapsed under pressure from Russia and from the Allied air attack. In the same month General Eisenhower, who had been told by Mr. Churchill himself in January of this year that the British did not plan "to scuttle Roundup," understood Sir Alan Brooke to say that he would be glad to reconsider the cross-Channel project to the point of eliminating it entirely.

Returning to the inverted logic which served them so well in 1942, and with the cordial approval of Mr. Churchill, in late 1943 the British Chiefs of Staff officially declared that without continued major operations in the Mediterranean, Overlord would be impossible in 1944. Justifying the profound doubts of both their Russian and American Allies concerning their sincerity on this fundamental issue, the British Chiefs then suggested that Overlord might involve no more than a limited number of divisions against weak opposition (that is, actually, their own Rankin plans) and that no cross-Channel operation on "a fixed date" should be regarded "as the pivot of our whole strategy on which all else turns." In short, regardless of the hegemony implicit in its name, Overlord would merely remain no more than one peer among many.

In this period the Prime Minister left Eisenhower uncertain regarding his own views, but, as the American general has indicated suspiciously, in the spring of 1943 Churchill did want to pour into Italy the maximum number of Allied forces available in the Mediterranean instead of saving at least a part of these forces for the cross-Channel invasion in 1944. Rather less guardedly, Mr. Churchill told Eisenhower that he would prefer to wait until after the war and then write "impressions, so that, if necessary, he could correct or bury his mistakes." Perhaps, like d'Alembert, Mr. Churchill believed a man of letters should be very careful of what he writes, fairly careful of what he does, and relatively careless of what he says—in private.

Again in October 1943, in protesting the movement of landing craft from the Mediterranean for Overlord, Mr. Churchill had told President Roosevelt that the latter operation was possible "only if certain hypothetical conditions are fulfilled which may very likely not be fulfilled." When the Prime Minister made his customary affirmation to the principle of Overlord, he emphasized to the President that he did not wish his agreement with the United States on this score to be interpreted "rigidly and without review in the swiftly-changing situations of war." Mr. Churchill had a hearty dislike of the "lawyer's" covenants with which his distrustful Allies attempted to bind him irrevocably to Overlord.

Another strong advocate of an all-out cross-Channel attack, Henry Stimson, has likewise expressed grave doubts concerning the real determination of the Prime Minister for such an operation. In preparing the President for the Quadrant Conference in August 1943, Mr. Stimson wrote:

> First: We cannot now rationally hope to be able to cross the Channel and come to grips with our German enemy under a British commander. His Prime Minister and his Chief of the Imperial [General] Staff are frankly at variance with such a proposal. . . . Though they have rendered lip service to the operation their hearts are not in it. . . .
>
> Second: The difference between us is a vital difference of faith. . . . The British theory (which cropped out again and again in unguarded sentences of the British leaders . . .) is that Germany can be beaten by a series of attritions in northern Italy, in the eastern Mediterranean, in Greece, in the Balkans, in Rumania and the other satellite countries. . . .
>
> To me in the light of the postwar problems we shall face, that attitude . . . seems terribly dangerous. We are pledged quite as clearly as Great Britain to the opening of a real second front. None of these methods of pinprick warfare can be counted on by us to fool Stalin into the belief that we have kept that pledge.

Over the years the British have had plenty of experience in opportunist raids such as those dispatched by both Pitts to warm the coasts of France and the Netherlands in preference to a serious and effective war in Germany. So fine a British soldier as Sir John Moore had then, perforce, employed that "disastrous term 'a littoral warfare' " and Charles James Fox had aptly compared these operations to "breaking windows with guineas." A British general who certainly should know has written of the Second World War that if the Allies had continued such "non-profit making" raids—as Mr. Churchill advocated against

Norway and the Dodecanese in 1943—the chances for the success of their invasion of France in 1944 would have been "gravely jeopardized."

If President Roosevelt was also an opportunist in military affairs, as his reaction to Stimson's pressure had made clear, Winston Churchill alone was prepared by training and temperament to elevate opportunism into a philosophy of war. To the Prime Minister, "the American mind runs naturally to broad, sweeping logical conclusions on the largest scale," but the British mind does not work quite this way. "We do not think," Mr. Churchill maintains, "that logic and clear-cut principles are necessarily the sole keys to what ought to be done in swiftly changing and indefinable situations. In war particularly we assign a larger importance to opportunism and improvisation, seeking rather to live and conquer in accordance with the unfolding event than to aspire to dominate it often by fundamental decisions. There is room for much argument about both views. The difference is one of emphasis, but is deep-seated." Or in the phrase of another slightly chastened romantic:

> *When precept and the pedantry*
> *of dull mechanic battle do enslave.*

One Briton who fortunately did not think in such Arminian terms as Winston Churchill was General Frederick Morgan, in 1943 the chief of the tremendous and long-range planning project for the Overlord invasion of France in 1944. In his disarmingly restrained and modest reminiscences General Morgan has written that in the beginning of 1943 there was much talk in Britain of the need for flexibility in her strategy, and it seemed to him at this time that the British authorities had "no real plan for the day when they would have to stop being flexible." Of course, Morgan had been one of that something more than a minority of Englishmen in the First World War, a "confirmed" Westerner. In World War II he again reflected a marked preference for a Puritan straight line from London to Berlin, namely that across the Channel. Whether or not these opinions represented the true Briton's outlook, as General Morgan avers, or whether the typical inhabitant of the British Isles thought so flexibly as Mr. Churchill has judged, would seem to be a matter of individual interpretation.

The Calvinist crusader who was to carry out General Morgan's predetermined cross-Channel plan in the field, Dwight Eisenhower, has recorded that in 1943 he also had to cope with the theory that "opportunity should be exploited as it arises, and . . . if things went well in the 'soft underbelly' we should not pause merely because we had made up our minds to conduct the cross-Channel operation." Like Morgan, Eisenhower concluded sharply: "The doctrine of opportunism, so often applicable in tactics, is a dangerous one to pursue in strategy. Significant changes in the field of strategy have repercussions all the way back to the factory and the training center."

In reluctantly facing the formal demise of Roundup at the Casablanca Conference General Marshall had likewise considered Mr. Churchill's strategy as one of opportunity or expediency. Yet in so reacting to the Prime Minister's concept of war Marshall had gone further and had questioned the sincerity of the term so freely accepted by Winston Churchill himself. He had asked pointedly whether the British Chiefs of Staff considered that an attack now against Sicily was a means to an end or an end in itself.

In short, by this date General Marshall was coming to recognize the purpose behind the British strategy, a strategy so opportunely called opportunist. Actually, as the U.S. Army Chief may have now perceived, Mr. Churchill almost certainly knew perfectly well where he was going and had known it years in advance—his old Influx and Whipcord war plans of 1941-42 for the invasion of Sicily are cases in point. At Casablanca Mr. Churchill and his military chiefs must have been aware that they could get the U.S. Army to accept a further Mediterranean push chiefly because the American Army would hope that this also would be the last such effort. In other words, Marshall had accepted Sicily as the next Allied objective, partly because the island's geographic position made it a fine place to close down all subsequent operations in the Mediterranean in order to give priority to a revivified cross-Channel assault.

When the logical denouement of the Sicilian campaign necessarily unfolded in the southern or wrong end of the Italian peninsula, General Marshall—like Kitchener with the Dardanelles—did not wish "a vacuum" created in Italy into which the resources of the cross-Channel operation would be again dissipated in 1943 as they had been the previous year.

Had the British suggested at Casablanca that in their conception the seizure of Sicily was designed to lead on to Italy the American Army would instead have preferred Sardinia as the logical Mediterranean objective to follow the conquest of Tunisia. From Sardinia, and its natural corollary, Corsica, it would have been infinitely simpler to have cut off the bulk of Italy by landings in Liguria or Tuscany without fighting all the way up the crenelated boot of the peninsula. Alternatively, and of far greater potential importance, as actually took place in 1944, the still unfortified and under-garrisoned coast of southern France might have been assaulted in 1943 from this Sardinian-Corsican *point d'appui*.

But although such British amphibious planners as Morgan and Mountbatten had preferred Sardinia to Sicily as the militarily sensible way of approaching even Italy, they had been overruled by the Prime Minister and his Chiefs of Staff on the grounds that the political effect of Sicily's surrender was a more important consideration. In fact, Mountbatten, who finally seemed to string along with the American desire for Sicily, appeared embarrassed when the Americans learned of his switch from a Sardinian approach to the nominal dead-end in Sicily and cautioned them to say nothing to his superiors concerning his own advocacy of the Sardinian route. The trouble with Sardinia may have been that too obviously it did lead somewhere, and Mr. Churchill's careful and patient policy of winning American acquiescence in what is too often represented as a strategy of opportunism or expediency could not tolerate such an honest and logical anticipation of the future. One may decide that although the Prime Minister's strategy might be termed opportunist in the larger sense that he followed the easier rather than the harder path in waging war, it can scarcely be considered completely improvised, as it was disclosed to his Allies, step by step.

The parallel between the pattern of the unduly cautious or self-defeating approach set at Casablanca and that of Torch is striking, and it was a pattern which would continue onto the Italian mainland in a manner which General Fuller eventually described as "daft." In each case, in order to evade a direct American refusal to countenance the prospect of an indefinite advance in the Mediterranean in the direction of southeastern Europe, the British sacrificed their initially logical plans for the execution of their strategy, e.g. the landings at Bône and Philippeville or in Sardinia. For the policy of concealment of Mr. Churchill and the obstinacy of the U.S. Army with respect to this so-called eccentric approach many Allied soldiers would die unnecessarily and much time and matériel would be expended in the mountains of southern and central Italy. While two of Mr. Churchill's true objectives in his war policy, namely a political as well as a military victory and one at a low cost in casualties to Great Britain, were in no sense morally reprehensible objectives from the point of view of the United Kingdom alone, the necessity of concealing these objectives from his more powerful Allies would have most unhappy consequences for Britain in the long run as in the short.

It may well be felt that the role and responsibility of Winston Churchill for British war policy and strategy after he became Prime Minister in 1940 has been overstressed. There are, however, very substantial grounds for emphasizing it. A variety of Americans have taken note of the unquestioned dominance of Mr. Churchill in the Second World War over a tremendous variety of British military issues, great and small.

General Arnold, for one, observed at the first general Allied Conference following Pearl Harbor, the Arcadia Conference, that the British Chiefs of Staff seemed to be reluctant to commit themselves to any new war plans until they could check them over with their Prime Minister. General Eisenhower, who was in a better position to know, expressed himself more forcefully. He considered the Prime Minister a "virtual member" of the British Chiefs of Staff. He could not remember any major discussion with the British Chiefs in which Churchill did not participate. According to Eisenhower, Mr. Churchill even joined his Chiefs of Staff in tactical instructions. Indeed, in 1915 the resignations of Fisher and Churchill had been precipitated, at least nominally, over this very issue. Harry Hopkins might well write the President in his first report on Winston Churchill: "Your 'former Naval person' is not only the Prime Minister, he is the directing force behind the strategy and the conduct of the war in all of its essentials."

Churchill himself has made no bones about the Erastian nature of his conception of the duties of the British Chiefs of Staff. As he wrote of the First World War: "A series of absurd conventions became established in the public mind. First and most monstrous was that generals and admirals were more competent to deal with the broad issues of war than abler men in other spheres of life." In 1943 Mr. Churchill reiterated this theme: "Modern war is total, and it is necessary for its conduct that the technical and professional authorities should be sustained and if necessary directed by the Heads of Government, who have the knowledge which enables them to comprehend not only the military but the political and economic forces at work, and who have the power to focus them all upon the goal." Of the Second World War Winston Churchill could wind up contentedly that, for his Britain, at least, there had been "no division, as in the previous war, between politicians and soldiers, between the 'Frocks' and the 'Brass Hats'—odious terms which darkened counsel."

It is, of course, difficult to say how much such unwonted felicity had resulted from Mr. Churchill's having learned from previous unhappy experience not to overrule his Chiefs on strictly military issues when they stood firm and united against him and how much this agreement was evoked by his selection of military chiefs in fundamental accord with himself. In any event it is clear that Winston Churchill had not the slightest intention of finding himself, like his political colleague and rival in the First World War, David Lloyd George, in the position of being unable to impose his will on the military. Like Churchill, and most of their generation, including Adolf Hitler, Lloyd George had come to believe that British statesmen had shown undue caution in exerting their authority over their subordinates in uniform. Another dedicated man of crisis, the witty and cynical Georges Clemenceau, had already immortalized this overwhelming lesson of 1914-18 in the aphorism that war was too important a matter to leave to the generals.

Far more than Lloyd George with his hard-won conception of the proper relationship between the Prime Minister and his Chiefs of Staff, Winston Churchill was prepared in World War II to resume his continuous conflict with the expert—in this war with the American expert. Such more or less independent Britons as Beaverbrook, Morgan, and occasionally, Mountbatten, the Prime Minister could ignore without especial difficulty. Furthermore, by 1942, Mr. Churchill could cut a very fine figure as a military expert himself. His fervent supporter, Air Marshal Sir Arthur Harris, had never known Churchill without an answer for any question of pure strategy.

As his biographers have often recognized, Winston Churchill had been trained primarily for war, at the Admiralty, at the Ministry of Munitions, and at the War Office, and almost all his writings involved military issues. The Prime Minister was an acknowledged expert on espionage and had played a significant role in founding the Royal Air Force. Moreover, in some measure he was responsible for the conversion of the Royal Navy from coal to oil before the First World War. In addition to his pioneer work with tanks in the First World War and with landing craft in the Second, Mr. Churchill had worked closely with the Air Defence Research Committee in connection with the development of radar for the R.A.F. and for the Admiralty.

In his exaltation of the civilian head of government over the military chiefs, Mr. Churchill was in close accord with orthodox military doctrine. Clausewitz—normally so repugnant to the Prime Minister as the formulator of the revolutionary military practices of Napoleon—has written: "The subordination of the political point of view to the military would be contrary to common sense, for policy has declared the war; it is the intelligent faculty, War only the instrument, and not the reverse. The subordination of the military point of view to the political is, therefore, the only thing which is possible."

It may be contended that it was precisely because in this instance the British Prime Minister was in such essential accord with the classic theory that he proved ultimately correct in his continuing dispute with the United States War Department in 1944-45. In the desperate argument over the Anvil plan for a French and American landing in southern France in August 1944, a landing proposed in part to drain Allied divisions out of Mr. Churchill's beloved Mediterranean, the now probably dominant anxiety of the Prime Minister over the post-war position of the West in Eastern Europe may well have deserved priority over the logistic needs of the American Army for the port of Marseille. Certainly, having been sucked into Italy in 1943 by her surrender, the U.S. Army was more determined than ever not to allow the eager Hungarians to have a similar effect, and in 1944 President Roosevelt backed up his Army leaders.

Mr. Churchill was on still stronger ground in the spring of 1945 when he urged the Anglo-American seizure of Berlin and his Chiefs urged that of Prague. Fortunately for the Soviet Union, even at this point amid the collapsing ruins of the Third Reich, and notwithstanding lip service to the contrary theory, General Eisenhower continued to operate on the assumption that military plans should be devised with "the single aim of speeding victory." Ignoring the point of any war, General Marshall backed up Eisenhower's crusade in Europe. He cabled: "I would be loath to hazard American lives for purely political purposes." It may be that to Puritans, facing the evil of war is only to be condoned by fighting for purely moral purposes, although the U.S. Army's Prussian model had reflected a similar military egocentricity after the intoxicating victories of the elder Moltke. But however much he might wish to limit Great Britain's casualties, Winston Churchill was an old hand at accepting the struggle for political power endemic in war.

To a very considerable extent this gross U.S. Army violation of the doctrines of Clausewitz must have resulted from its now confirmed and fundamental distrust of the sincerity of the military policies of Mr. Churchill, a distrust which at the Trident and Quadrant conferences Stimson and Marshall had finally succeeded in conveying to President Roosevelt. After the middle of 1943 the President could no longer be induced to believe that his British colleague was driving deeper and deeper into the Mediterranean for the sake of a cross-Channel invasion. When this American disillusionment was accentuated by the apparent alienation of the Russians at this time, it is not surprising that in Mr. Churchill's careful language: "There was emerging a strong current of opinion in American governmental circles, which seemed to wish to win Russian confidence even at the expense of co-ordinating the Anglo-American war effort."

The ultimate effect of this distrust appeared at the Teheran Conference in November-December 1943, when after the United States joined up with the Russians to push through the cross-Channel invasion, this policy of Russo-American military collaboration tended to continue in the even more delicate realm of politics, a realm in which Mr. Churchill was a true master, a master solidly based on Clausewitz. But by 1944-45 the British Prime Minister had misled the Americans too often on the military end to expect to be respected and heeded on the political. Conversely, General Marshall, who had made no public speeches concerning his many "difficult scenes" with President Roosevelt in 1942, had so won the latter's confidence by 1944-45 that there was no debate "whatsoever" between them in this era in which political considerations should have dominated the scene.

Stalin, who followed Clausewitz in the military sphere properly enough until the realization of a true second front in the West had sealed the fate of Germany, abruptly suspended his own drive upon Berlin in August 1944, and concentrated upon conquering the Balkans himself, notwithstanding the fact that he had discouraged Mr. Churchill from doing the same thing the year before. Although subsequent to the war he formally repudiated some of the military theses of the great military theorist, Stalin understood and followed Clausewitz in both his political and military senses; the Soviet ruler first and necessarily had concentrated everything upon defeating the strongest force of the chief Axis power, the German Army, and only afterward started to cash in his political chips. Mr. Churchill made the serious mistake of attempting to reverse this logical order of action under the cloak of a policy of supposed opportunism.

It is a striking fact that the two states which emerged from the Second World War with the most power, the United States and the U.S.S.R., were also the two states with the most effective coalition strategies in this war. Of course, this was no accident. Only these two states had the resources to support the self-confidence and courage which led to a long-range strategy of concentration. After 1943, when the full effects of the growing mobilization of their enormous resources began to be felt, both of these states could look primarily outward to the problem of defeating the enemy rather than essentially inward to the questions of domestic opinion, tradition, or morale.

By the autumn of 1943 the U.S.S.R. had largely overcome her grave problem of internal dissidence and was prepared to commit herself to aid the United States against Japan following the defeat of Germany; by the autumn of 1943 the United States had the strength to impose long-planned and truly offensive strategies of concentration directly against the seats of Axis power in both the Central Pacific and in the Western European theaters on top of those opportunist and defensive strategies, based on conditions of comparative impotence, which for political reasons had been accepted in 1942 in the South Pacific and in the Mediterranean.

As a result, regardless of their motives, both states would eventually face and successfully encompass their fundamental problems in two-front strategies, first with Germany and then with Japan. In subordinating a war not yet won to personal inclinations or to considerations of domestic policy, Great Britain under Winston Churchill's otherwise inspiring leadership never could achieve this. That in 1944-45 the Americans either forgot that war is not more than an instrument of foreign policy, or followed a foreign policy based upon false assumptions, illustrates again what Mr. Churchill himself once wrote with such prophetic irony: "those who can win a war well can rarely make a good peace and those who could make a good peace would never have won the war."

6   American and British Strategy: How Much Did They Differ?

Kent Roberts Greenfield

Before his death in 1970, Kent Greenfield enjoyed a brilliant career as a military historian and editor. He served from 1946 to 1958 as Chief Historian of the Department of the Army and was responsible for the formative stages of that massive historical work, The United States Army in World War II. *Drawing on fifteen years of familiarity with his subject, Greenfield published in 1963* American Strategy in World War II: A Reconsideration, *a discussion of the major elements in United States strategy. Although he should not be considered an apologist for an official view of wartime decisions, Greenfield does understate the seriousness of Anglo-American differences and claims that what happened happened for the best.*

It is generally agreed that the Anglo-American coalition in World War II was the closest and most effective partnership in war that two great powers have ever achieved. Their strategy evolved in an unbroken series of agreements as to what it was necessary or desirable to do next in order to gain a maximum of military advantage from the situations that successively confronted them. But these agreements were attended by controversy. This revolved around the cross-Channel attack of the Allies. Flaring up first within six months after the United States entered the war it continued until the invasion of France was well on its way to success in August 1944. The controversy generated a heat that at times seemed to endanger the Anglo-American alliance, and it has continued to generate heat in the histories and memoirs of the war.

Dr. Richard M. Leighton has recently recalled attention to this controversy in studies based on his research in the logistics and strategy for the United States Army's history of World War II. He has concluded that the suppositions that animated it, particularly those of the Americans, were unfounded, and that the British were on firmer ground in suspecting the motives and intentions of the Americans than the Americans were in suspecting those of the British. In short, he has challenged the version of the controversy that has become all but a stereotype in American thought about Allied strategy in the war.

According to this version the heated debates between the Americans and the British that preceded their decisions arose from opposing conceptions of strategy. The Americans believed in concentration of power at the earliest possible moment at a decisive point, and the delivery of a blow to the solar plexus. The British believed that the correct strategy was to work vigorously but more cautiously from a ring which sea-power and Russia's resistance enabled the Allies to close around Axis-dominated Europe; keep the Russians supplied and fighting; blast and burn the German and Italian cities with bombs; stir up and arm resistance in the occupied countries; jab through the ring whenever an opportunity presented itself, while ever tightening it, until the enemy was so strangled and bled that the final offensive need be only a coup de grace.

American writers on the subject have consistently represented *Overlord*—the great cross-Channel drive launched in June, 1944—as a triumph of American over British views. They have maintained that the British, though they repeatedly accepted a decisive power-drive in principle, did everything they could to evade or postpone its execution; that Mr. Churchill having induced Mr. Roosevelt to put the bulk of our forces into the Mediterranean in November, 1942, the British became intent on keeping them there indefinitely; and that only by dint of persistent argument and pressure the Americans, with decisive support from Stalin at Tehran, finally succeeded in getting Allied strategy back on the right track. The result, after some further displays of reluctance, was British support for a cross-Channel drive to the heart of Germany, and a spectacular success. This is commonly represented, in American writings, as a triumph of the American conception of correct strategy imposed on the unwilling British.

Dr. Leighton sharply challenges the view that the British tried to evade a cross-Channel invasion in 1944, and gave their support to it only under pressure from the Americans. He finds no evidence for such evasiveness except in the suspicions of the Americans. His conclusion is that the successive agreements that defined the course of Anglo-American strategy were governed by practical considerations, of which, in 1942-43, the most pressing was the availability of critical military resources. To these practical exigencies both Allies had to trim their concepts, interests, and desires. In the end the course they pursued conformed more closely to the British concept of sound strategy than to that for which, after March, 1942, the Americans persistently contended.

Basic Principles and a Proposed Speed-up

Dr. Leighton reminds us that as soon as Pearl Harbor brought the United States into the war the two Allies agreed, in principle, on the strategy by which they would be guided. They reached this agreement at the so-called Arcadia conference, which, immediately after Pearl Harbor, brought Mr. Churchill and Mr. Roosevelt, and the British and American Chiefs of Staff together in Washington. The strategy agreed on was as follows:

1. Beat Germany first, meanwhile containing the Japanese.
2. Wear down the strength of the enemy by closing around Axis-held territory a ring to be tightened as fast as the resources of the Allies permitted.

3. The means to be used: naval blockade; all-out aid to the Russians; strategic bombing; intensive cultivation of resistance in Nazi-occupied countries; limited offensives with mobile forces at points where locally superior Allied forces, particularly forces strong in armor, could be brought to bear with telling effect—all directed toward a final knockout punch.

No plan for a drive to the heart of German power then seemed possible to envisage and none was developed.

But only three months later the Americans proposed such a plan which, if adopted, would be a radical departure from the Arcadia agreement. They proposed that the Allies proceed at once to the blow that would knock Germany out of the war. Dubbed *Bolero-Roundup*, it called for concentration in the United Kingdom of all the then available resources of the Allies (*Bolero*). This was to begin at once and be given first claim on all new resources as they became available, with a view to launching a massive power-drive across the English Channel in the spring of 1943 (*Roundup*). Forty-eight divisions would be used—over 1,000,000 Americans in thirty divisions, the rest British. The Americans would also supply a powerful air force to be combined with British air in support of the operation. The assault would go in on a six-division front, between Le Havre and Boulogne, with 77,000 men, 18,000 vehicles, and 2,250 tanks.

To this master plan the Americans attached a rider, known as *Sledgehammer*. This was to prepare an assault force to be launched across the Channel in September, 1942. By then only three and a half American divisions could be made available in England, and only enough landing craft to put the combat elements of two divisions ashore in the assault. *Sledgehammer* was to be undertaken in only one of two contingencies: (1) if the Russians were on the verge of collapse, in order to create a diversion that might keep them from capitulating; or (2) in the unlikely event that the Germans were crumbling and a small-scale invasion might suffice to finish them off.

The *Bolero-Roundup* plan originated in the War Plans Division of the War Department General Staff, to which it offered the solution for a problem that seemed all but desperate. The United States, thrown on the defensive at Pearl Harbor, unready for war in spite of its preliminary mobilization, saw its unfinished structure of forces and materiel now being dismantled and dribbled away in small packets to meet demands for reinforcement from all over the world. Nobody could see an end to this dissipation. On December 15, General Marshall had brought young Colonel Eisenhower into his War Plans Division and in February made him its Chief. In January Eisenhower wrote in his notes to himself: "The struggle to secure the adoption by all concerned of a common concept of strategy is wearing me down. Everybody is too much engaged with small things of his own. We've got to go to Europe and fight—and we've got to quit wasting resources all over the world."

Into this chaos General Eisenhower's Division projected its plan for a cross-Channel drive through France into Germany, in 1943. It was so beautifully logical, so completely an expression of the principles of war and it also answered so perfectly the need of the Americans to stop the scatteration of their strength and get it mobilized to end the war in Europe at the earliest possible date, that the War Department, including the ambitious young American air force, fell in love with it, and the Navy accepted it. F.D.R. approved it and in April sent General Marshall and Harry Hopkins to London to sell it to the British.

To the relief and jubilation of the Americans the British accepted it. Eisenhower now wrote in his notes: ". . . at long last . . . we are all committed to one concept of fighting! [Now] . . . we won't be just thrashing around in the dark." The Americans at once put *Bolero*—the build-up in the United Kingdom—into effect. But the British soon began to express anxiety about *Sledgehammer*, and finally concluded that that would be a rash and unfeasible undertaking. *Sledgehammer* was a subordinate feature of the American concept and the Americans could not press hard for it since the British would have to provide most of the force necessary for its execution. But the Americans refused to abandon it. When in June the American and British Chiefs came to a deadlock over *Sledgehammer*, the American Joint Chiefs went to Mr. Roosevelt and proposed that the United States suspend its support of the whole *Bolero-Roundup* plan and go all out against Japan in the Pacific. The President firmly said, "no": that would be a little like threatening to "take up your dishes and go home," and in July he sent Harry Hopkins, General Marshall, and Admiral King to London under firm orders to agree with the British on some plan that would bring American ground forces into action in Europe before the end of the year.

The result was *Torch* and the invasion of North Africa in November 1942.

Encirclement Pursued: the Mediterranean and Pacific Offensives

The American military chiefs were bitterly disappointed by the decision for *Torch*. Eisenhower said on the day of the decision that he thought it "could well go down as the 'blackest day in history'." It threw the Americans' carefully arrayed plans into confusion. They saw all their disposable strength, including the troops, equipment, aircraft, and assault shipping that had already been built up in the United Kingdom under *Bolero*, being sucked into the Mediterranean. Concluding that *Torch* would make *Roundup* in 1943 an impossibility, the Army chiefs were again left with no master plan to govern the mobilization of their military and productive resources. To the American military chiefs *Torch* meant that Allied strategy had been diverted from the highroad to victory into a dead-end theater from which no decisive blow at Germany could ever be delivered.

When Churchill, Roosevelt, and the Combined Chiefs of Staff met at Casablanca in January to decide what they could do in 1943, both sides readily agreed that their three primary tasks for the year were to quell the U-boat menace, get all possible aid to Russia, and concentrate their air power on the bombing of Germany. The sore point was what to do in the Mediterranean. The declared objectives of *Torch* had been to occupy North Africa and reopen the line of communication through the Mediterranean to the Middle and Far East.

But Mr. Churchill and Mr. Roosevelt were now talking cheerfully about using the forces victorious in Africa for an invasion of Sicily, not only to complete the security of this line, but as a step toward knocking Italy out of the war. This, said Mr. Churchill, with unfortunate rhetorical exuberance, would be "to strike into the underbelly of the Axis."

The Americans, having no alternative to offer, accepted the invasion of Sicily. It clearly made military sense to keep the only Anglo-American forces that were in contact with the Germans fully employed in wearing them down as long as any object of strategic importance was within reach. But in the vista that now seemed to be opening, the American military staff and chiefs anxiously foresaw a progressive commitment to the Mediterranean of ground strength and amphibious lift which would make it possible for the British to argue successfully against a cross-Channel attack even in 1944. For at Casablanca their conviction hardened that the British would hold out for a peripheral strategy—what one irritated American officer called "periphery pecking." Secretary Stimson later called it "pinprick warfare." The suspicion had already taken root that when the British argued for a "flexible" strategy, as against an overriding commitment to *Roundup* in 1944, they were also intent on securing their imperial interests in the Mediterranean.

Suspicion had become conviction in the stern, unbending mind of the American Navy's Chief, Admiral Ernest J. King. He had backed the *Bolero-Roundup* plan vigorously only in order to get the war in Europe out of the way quickly. He now, in the spring of 1943, easily won from his American colleagues authorization to "extend" as well as "maintain" "unremitting pressure on the Japanese." This was a departure from the basic agreement of the Allies on the conduct of the war. It seemed to the British that the Americans were saying to them: "if you insist on committing our strength in Europe to indecisive employment in a theater in which your interests are paramount, we will insist on reserving a larger share of our growing resources for the theater in which our interest is paramount."

The American Army staff went home from Casablanca convinced that they had been outwitted and outmaneuvered by the British. General Wedemeyer, General Marshall's chief adviser at that conference, wrote: ". . . we lost our shirts . . . we came, we listened, and we were conquered." They determined never to let it happen again. Beginning with the next conference with the British in May (the Trident Conference) they went to these "summit" meetings with the British—Quadrant at Quebec in August and the Cairo-Tehran conferences in November and December—armed to anticipate and counter every imaginable argument of the British and backed by ranks of experts whose brief cases bulged with studies and statistics; and they devoted themselves to getting Mr. Roosevelt to throw his weight in their favor. They concentrated their growing argumentative skill and resourcefulness on getting from the British an inescapable commitment to a cross-Channel invasion in force in the spring of 1944.

A 1944 Cross-Channel Attack Desirable: Is It Feasible?

At each of the conferences the British readily agreed to accept a cross-Channel drive in the spring of 1944 as a major Allied objective. But they refused to commit themselves to a conclusively dated decision until conditions could be foreseen that would give the operation a reasonable chance of success at that date; and they argued earnestly that the only correct strategy was to remain flexible, that is, free to adopt alternative moves until the last possible moment. To the Americans such flexibility seemed irreconcilable with the complex business of organizing, assembling, and mounting a huge expeditionary force and providing in time the equipment to meet its multifarious specialized needs. And the conditions which the British attached to ratification of their consent deepened the suspicion of the Americans that the British meant to evade or postpone indefinitely a direct blow at Germany through France, and were wedded to a peripheral strategy and an inconclusive opportunism. Anxious over what they believed—with some justice—to be Mr. Churchill's proclivity, they even feared that the British would try to involve them in an invasion of the Balkans. To their great relief Stalin, at Tehran, threw his weight on their side, and insisted on giving *Overlord* (as it was now called), and a complementary invasion of southern France (*Anvil*), first claim on all the resources of the Allies. The British offered no objection to this. Eisenhower was chosen to be Supreme Commander. The point of no return had been passed.

Even so, and even after *Overlord* was launched, the Americans, still suspicious of the uses the British wished to make of American forces in the Mediterranean, pressed hard for the invasion of southern France, which was repeatedly postponed until it finally went ashore on August 15. By then the Americans had beaten down the last claim of the British on the American divisions required for a strong push into northern Italy. Indeed, it was in this hassle that the Anglo-American conflict of interest over the Mediterranean entered its most acrimonious phase, and the Americans for the first time rode rough-shod over the unanimous military judgment of Mr. Churchill and his military chiefs, leaving them feeling, as Mr. Churchill wished Washington to know, "that we have been ill-treated and are furious."

Dr. Leighton, in the study mentioned above, argues plausibly that if in 1943 the British were reluctant to sacrifice all other projects in Europe to a cross-Channel attack in 1944, they had as much ground for suspecting the Americans' real intentions as the Americans had for suspecting theirs. This becomes clearer if one looks more closely at the question of nuts and bolts, or, to speak more grandly, at the logistics of strategy. For the *sine qua non* of a strong assault on the coast of France for which the Americans were contending was enough assault landing craft, which only the Americans were in a position to supply.

At the Trident Conference in May the question of assault shipping—above all of tank-landing ships (LST's)—came into focus as the critical factor in planning for a 1944 cross-Channel assault. The American Joint Chiefs brought to the conference a plan for a massive cross-Channel blow in the spring of 1944 on much the same scale as their plan for *Roundup* in 1943. The British experts immediately challenged and demolished the Americans' assumption that enough landing craft of the needed types would be available to carry out the heavy assault that they proposed. It had to be recognized that without more assault landing craft, particularly without more LST's, the best that the Allies could hope to achieve in the spring of 1944 was an initial assault by only three divisions, backed by two afloat, against the armed and defended coast of France. It was assumed, and was reasonable to assume, that not as large an assault force would be needed in 1944 as in 1943, since it now looked as if the combined bomber offensive would have knocked the *Luftwaffe* out of the air over France by May, 1944. But a five-division assault against "Fortress Europe" would have less initial punch and be smaller by almost half than the eight-division assault that the Allies were about to launch against the lightly defended coast of Sicily in July, 1943. Facing up to the facts, the Combined Chiefs agreed to plan for a cross-Channel assault of this modest weight, plus two airborne divisions. In all twenty-nine divisions, including those to be assembled in the United Kingdom ready to be fed into the lodgment area, were to form the Allied invading force.

Obviously, to have any chance of success an assault on this scale would have to be attended by very favorable conditions. One was Allied supremacy in the air. Another was that only a limited number of German divisions should be in France to oppose the invasion. This being so, the British urged their contention that to keep German divisions away from France the Allies should press the Germans harder in the Mediterranean where they then had them on the run. The Americans continued to argue that this violated the principle of concentration at the decisive point. They at least obtained a joint declaration that all future operations in the Mediterranean should be planned to prepare the way for the cross-Channel invasion.

A Dilemma: How Find Enough Assault Craft?

It had become sharply clear at Trident that the critical item limiting the prospect of a cross-Channel attack in 1944 was tank-landing-ships (the LST). This put the Americans in an awkward bind. The LST was a British invention, but in 1943 only the Americans were equipped to produce LST's or other large landing craft in anything like the necessary quantity and, unlike small landing craft, LST's could be built only in shipyards capable of producing large vessels for the Navy. Furthermore the American chiefs had agreed that the building of LST's was an American responsibility. But they had fully committed the qualified shipyards to the production of other types of ships. The first charge on Navy shipyard capacity had been the construction of escort carriers and destroyer escorts to quell the submarine menace. This was agreed to be right and proper when the Combined Chiefs at Casablanca in January had made anti-submarine warfare the first charge on all the resources of the Allies. The peak of this load on the shipyards had passed in March. But crowding it for priority was the stupendous task of constructing a new, modernized United States fleet to replace the one shattered at Pearl Harbor, and equip the Navy to drive the Japanese out of the Pacific. And when the turn of the LST's came, Admiral King would certainly claim the bulk of them to carry out the operations in the Pacific which he and Admiral Nimitz were now planning, under the authorization that he had obtained at Trident, to expand the Navy's offensives against the Japanese.

The British were well aware of all this. And it put them in a position to think (and to say): "If we are to have a power-drive across the Channel in 1944, on whose prior claim to our joint strength you are so insistent, only you Americans can provide the means indispensable to its success."

Meanwhile, the Combined Chiefs had taken a practical step which was more important than anyone could then foresee. This was to create a small headquarters under General Sir Frederick Morgan, who was designated *Cossac*—that is, Chief of Staff to the [future] Supreme Allied Commander. At Trident, giving General Morgan the strength of assault there agreed on as predictable, they instructed him to work out, within its limits, a plan of attack for a cross-Channel invasion on May 1, 1944 and estimate the conditions necessary for its success. He would then submit it for judgment as to whether the Allies could safely adopt it.

To this complex, laborious, and baffling task General Morgan and his staff applied themselves with remarkable breadth of vision and integrity of purpose. From the first, General Morgan instructed his staff not to think or act as planners but as the embryo of the future Supreme Headquarters. He had his plan ready to submit when the Allies met again at Quebec in August. There the Allied chiefs—Mr. Roosevelt, Mr. Churchill, and the Combined Chiefs—adopted it, and they now authorized General Morgan, subject to their approval, to issue the necessary orders for the assemblage of forces and the preparatory operations that his plan required.

Overlord (as it was now called) had passed from planning to preparations keyed to an accepted plan. But nobody was happy about its prospects. Its execution remained highly conditional. And the conditions turned, and continued to turn, on the limited strength allotted to it at Trident, a five-division seaborne assault, supported by two airborne divisions. The Allies had committed themselves to its execution as their main objective in Europe. But by putting a ceiling on the size and strength of the force to be used they had got themselves into the position of giving their chief operation for 1944 a strictly limited claim on their resources, while their other enterprises became the residuary legatees of American production, which was now beginning to pour out munitions and supplies in an abundance beyond expectation.

The British, and the United States Army staff, were dissatisfied with the modest scale of invasion adopted. Mr. Churchill asked for a twenty-five percent increase in its strength. But no action was taken. It did not make sense to build up a more massive attacking force without a reasonable hope of having in hand enough assault craft to lift it. Assault shipping, above all the LST, remained the crux of the problem, and the key to its solution was in the hands of the Americans, and specifically, barring intervention by the President, in the hands of Admiral King.

A month after Quebec the Navy ordered the construction of landing craft. In October the American shipyards began to launch LST's at the rate of about twenty a month. But Admiral King laid claim to all but three months of this output as necessary for the great amphibious drive through the Central Pacific which the Combined Chiefs had authorized him to launch, and Mr. Roosevelt made no visible move to deny his claim. Only the November, December, and January output of LST's was allocated to *Overlord*. General Morgan soon pointed out that the new LST's promised, plus the LST's to be transferred from the Mediterranean, would still not be enough even for the minimal *Overlord* required by his plan. On November 5, Admiral King offered a bonus of twenty-one LST's from his allocation—hardly "a princely gift," Dr. Leighton remarks, since it was to be made up from production that exceeded his original calculations of his requirements and since not all of the additional craft he offered could arrive in time for a May 1 *Overlord*. That operation—now less than six months away—was still left with a big deficit of assault ships. If *Overlord* was to be executed, it was clear that the deficit would have to be made up either at the expense of the Pacific in which the American interest was paramount, or of the Mediterranean in which the British interest was paramount. Such was the situation on the eve of the "showdown" Cairo-Tehran conferences in November and December, 1943. The British had served notice that they would demand a review of the relation between the Mediterranean and *Overlord*. The Americans, therefore, went to the conference tense and anxious about the positions that the British would take, and feeling that only a firm stand by Roosevelt and Stalin could save *Overlord*.

The proposals of the British proved to be anything but unreasonable, and after meeting with Stalin at Tehran, the Allies came back to Cairo committed to an agreement that a May, 1944 *Overlord* was to have first claim on the resources and military efforts of the Allies, world-wide. This was what the Americans had been contending for since Trident. But to the British it might well seem a concession, since for the first time it put into reserve for that operation the assault shipping in the Pacific, which Admiral King, firm in his skepticism about British intentions had guarded as sacrosanct and not even to be discussed with the British.

Still to come was a hassle over means with which to carry out operations in the Mediterranean during the winter and spring that the Cairo-Tehran agreements recognized as desirable. As soon as Eisenhower and Montgomery got into their *Overlord* saddles in January, they demanded that the assault on Normandy be greatly strengthened—which created a big new demand for landing craft. How meet this and at the same time find enough to put three divisions ashore in an invasion of southern France (Operation *Anvil*), which the Americans insisted on mounting simultaneously with *Overlord*? In Italy the amphibious end run to Anzio in January failed dismally. "I had hoped," said Mr. Churchill, "that we were hurling a wild cat onto the shore but all we got was a stranded whale." The Anzio beachhead had now to be defended and reinforced. Finding enough LST's and other landing craft to meet all these requirements tested to the limit the ingenuity and tempers of both the English and the

Americans. But by "veering and hauling," trimming and recalculating, and by the postponement of *Anvil*, the assault shipping for a much expanded *Overlord* was found, and the biggest amphibious force in history, which had been given the objective of driving to the heart of Germany, was lifted across the Channel on June 6. No one doubts that the British put everything they had into the final strain and effort that made this possible.

British Contributions and Reasons for Caution

Looking back one can now see that from the first the British had taken an impressive number of practical measures that paved the way to success for the invasion of France. If they refused *Sledgehammer*, they did not flinch from undertaking alone the bloody cross-Channel raid on Dieppe as early as August, 1942. It was a failure. But the British diligently wrung from the experience lessons that were valuable in making *Overlord* successful. It was the British who invented and first engineered the instrument of war, the LST, that made a cross-Channel assault in force a feasible military operation. It was Mr. Churchill who dreamed up, and the bold ingenuity of his engineers that constructed, the indispensable offshore harbors by which the Allied expeditionary force was supplied over the beaches throughout the summer and fall of 1944. General Morgan (*Cossac*) was a British officer, completely loyal to the concept of a cross-Channel invasion. He had an able American deputy and an Anglo-American staff. But from first to last *Cossac* got more vigorous co-operation and support from the British than from us. It was *Cossac* that brought planning down out of the clouds into the realm of problem-solving, and this, in my opinion, had more effect than any other one thing in bringing to pass a firm agreement to see *Overlord* through. British urgings in 1942 took us into the Mediterranean where in the spring of 1943 the Anglo-Americans bled the Axis in Africa. The Allies then invaded Sicily, thereby shaking down Mussolini's regime and bringing about the surrender of Badoglio's Italy. Thereupon, staging a major campaign on the mainland, they pinned down and wore out the divisions Hitler threw into Italy after Badoglio's surrender, and by arming and supplying Tito's guerillas kept wastefully occupied the German divisions with which he garrisoned the Balkans. These measures were taken in compliance with British arguments. In these arguments the British may have been—and probably were—animated by their own political interests, but the arguments made military sense. From Quadrant on it was Mr. Churchill and his military chiefs, and not the Americans, who urged the need for a stronger cross-Channel assault, and certainly they pulled their full weight in the provision of ocean shipping and other measures to insure a build-up for the invasion that would make it decisive. As early as May, 1943, they had activated an army group and an army headquarters that went to work on detailed plans for the assault, in contrast with the Americans, who made no similar provision until October. In short, it can be plausibly argued that it was the British (and Mr. Roosevelt) who are to be credited with the realistic approach to *Overlord* that insured its success.

The effective co-operation of the British and Americans in World War II was an unprecedented achievement in the history of nation-states. But the fact of mutual suspicion remains, standing out more starkly against the lack of any evidence, except the suspicion of the Americans, that the British were ever unfaithful to their repeated pledge to support a full-bodied cross-Channel attack—always with the proviso that the situation as the due date approached must be such as to offer a reasonable prospect of success—a proviso that certainly made common sense.

It cannot be denied that the British approached *Roundup* and *Overlord* more cautiously than the Americans, and this is not surprising in view of past experience and their situation in 1943.

In 1942 they were suffering from fresh and terrible wounds that made them more feelingly aware of German might than we could be. The insistence of the American military chiefs on *Sledgehammer*, in the spring of 1942, had undoubtedly confirmed their impression that the Americans were as reckless as they were inexperienced in military affairs. A year later General Marshall admitted that *Sledgehammer* might have been suicidal. The British, although they acquired a genuine admiration for Marshall and Eisenhower, could not overlook the fact that neither of them had ever commanded even a regiment in battle. They were naturally convinced of the superiority of their own military wisdom based on experience and were disposed to regard the Americans as bright but annoyingly persistent children. Nor could they dismiss the grim memories of their experience in World War I. Then, when for once they had committed a huge ground force on the continent, they had seen a whole generation of young Englishmen destroyed. Churchill's mind was haunted by the thought of the Channel running "red with the blood of British and American youth" and the beaches "choked with their bodies." When the Americans pointed to the overpowering resources they could put behind a cross-Channel drive, the British remembered the similar promises we had made in World War I and then had failed to make good, except in manpower. This time we more than made good. We delivered, by 1944, an overwhelming abundance of materiel, on time, at the decisive points. But in 1943 what the British had before them was the fact that the Americans were offering to put in the Channel by 1 May 1944 only enough LST's for an attack that would be anything but overwhelming.

As the hour for *Overlord* drew near, the British had a very grave reason for caution as they counted what it would cost them in basic strength as a world power. They were facing the fact that in the fall of 1943 their economy and military manpower were mobilized to the limit of endurance. They had far more to lose than the Americans. *Overlord* on a big scale would be their last shot. Even if it succeeded, they would be unable to replace the losses it would inflict. The strength of their nation would decline not only relatively to that of the United States, but absolutely, leaving Great Britain a second or third-rate power in world affairs. Failure of the invasion would mean, if not ruin, a prolongation of the war all but certainly beyond their power to sustain. These prospects they weighed with deliberation in the fall of 1943 and accepted with characteristic realism and courage as they made their final commitment to *Overlord*.

Was American Strategy Excessively Rigid?

The British, on their part, did less than justice to the Americans in blaming them for rigidity in their military thinking. "The President," exclaims Mr. Churchill in his memoirs, "was oppressed by the prejudices of his military advisers," and lets us know in a well-known outburst of impatience how oppressed he himself felt by the "American clear-cut, logical, large-scale, mass-production style of thought." The English seem not fully to have grasped either the capabilities or the limiting conditions of the American system of industrial production. When the American military chiefs insisted on adoption of a plan with a target date long in advance of a large operation, it was because they could not see how otherwise in a huge mass-production economy such as ours, they could ready for a great offensive, forces armed with intricate mechanized equipment whose production had to be scheduled back through the whole war economy, and whose delivery and supply on the far shore required the preparation and assembly of a fleet of ships of all kinds; not to mention the task of keeping all these requirements co-ordinated with the demands of the other theaters of a world-wide war. Given our highly subdivided system of mass-producing the complex and varied implements of modern warfare, it can be argued that the American military chiefs, far from being rigid theorists, were guided by practical sense in insisting on steadfast adherence to large and definitely scheduled objectives. As Gordon Harrison has observed, when Mr. Churchill characterizes our undeviating adherence to a cross-Channel attack on a given date in the spring of 1944, as typical of American mass-production thinking, this amounts to accusing the Americans of having a mass-production economy. The corollary of the British concept was elasticity, the seizure of opportunities as they arose, the shifting of forces from one point to another, to take advantage of the enemy's weakness. The experience of *Torch* should have been enough to show that this was no easy matter once a large force was committed and its massive structure of overseas bases and communications established. This was a fact that Mr. Churchill's restless imagination seems never to have grasped.

Finally, it must be said in justice to the Americans that when Mr. Roosevelt gave the English so much anxiety by loosening the tether on Admiral King and General MacArthur in the Pacific, he was favoring the evolution of a strategy more appropriate to a global two-front war than rigid adherence to the Germany-first strategy.

The Resolution of Differences

In their debates about the cross-Channel attack and Mediterranean operations the British and Americans both argued tenaciously for their points of view and their vigorous, and sometimes heated, debates left a mark on their strategy. But they always ended with a compromise agreement on what to do next. Two forces, I believe, kept them together. One was the determination of Mr. Roosevelt and Mr. Churchill that everything else must be secondary to the solidarity of the Anglo-American alliance. The other was common sense, or preferably perhaps, a capacity to deal sensibly with concrete issues as they arose, on which both the Americans and the English pride themselves as a quality in their common tradition of jurisprudence and management of affairs. Thanks to their determination to stick together and to move only by steps on which they could agree, the strategy they actually pursued reflected the concepts of both. Step by step throughout 1943, they moved nearer to concentration on the massive blow that the Americans desired, but this step-by-step advance permitted much of the elasticity and follow-up of immediate opportunities in which the British believed. In the plan that was executed each side got in fair measure what it had contended for. The ring around the area controlled by the enemy had been tightened until it was becoming a noose. His cities had been blasted and burned, his air force knocked out of the sky over France. The resistance in Jugoslavia and France had been armed and organized. "His armies had been dispersed, pinned down and bled by concentric Russian and Allied offensives until he could no longer form an effective reserve for counterattack. To this extent the strategy urged by the British had prevailed, with tremendous effect." If the Americans had had their way and *Roundup* had been launched in 1943, it would have been a one-shot affair which, if it had miscarried, could have been disastrous. At best it would not improbably have led to the slaughters that the British dreaded. On the other hand when *Overlord* came, "it was the power-play for which the Americans had always contended, and the Allies put behind it the force and weight needed to drive it to the heart of Germany."

Looking back now, it is interesting to observe that the strategy in Europe which the Americans followed, step by step, as events unfolded, and which they found it wise to follow, was much closer to that which the British proposed at the Arcadia Conference in December, 1941, and which the Americans had then accepted, than it was to the deviation from that strategy which the Americans proposed in the spring of 1942, and for which for more than a year they vociferously contended.

Unit V

Death from the Skies

In the First World War aerial combat had been considered a beautiful albeit deadly game, one whose intricate rules and elaborate chivalry recalled the Middle Ages. Death in the sky compared with death in the trenches had seemed somehow less horrible; it was ennobling, even glorious. World War II destroyed the nobility of air warfare and thus was a brutal shock to a generation weaned on the exploits of Eddy Rickenbacker and the "Red Baron," Manfred von Richtofen. Air war turned out to be no less final nor any less terrible than other varieties of combat. This was partly because the Second World War, a "people's war," took the war in the air away from a gentlemanly elite, expanding it and bringing into the "club" such "undesirables" as peacetime plumbers and automobile mechanics.

For the most part, however, attitudes toward air warfare changed because a changed role was demanded of it. Death *in* the sky became death *from* the skies. The Second World War developed to a fine art the ingenious practice of loading explosive devices aboard airplanes, transporting them to distant places (such as troop concentrations, railway marshalling yards, and large cities), and then dropping them with fair precision on these targets. There was, notably, no parallel development of a code of conduct to control this novel technique of warfare. Nor, despite intense prewar speculation about the potential effects of air attacks, did there develop well-defined views on the morality of bombing. Most people condemned indiscriminate bombing of civilian populations, but no one suggested how the killing of civilians by air bombardment could be avoided in practice. Consequently, the "legitimacy" of strategic bombing as it was practiced during World War II was one of the most awkward and confusing moral issues that arose from the war.

Although the moral question has not yet been answered, the policy was justified at the time on several grounds. Distasteful means often must be adopted to accomplish good ends. (Bombing was only another though admittedly devastating technique of war, and, if its use would hasten the war's end, it should be used.) The Allies claimed that the Germans had been first to bomb nonmilitary targets; Germany naturally asserted the opposite. Each side thus excused its actions by pointing the finger of guilt elsewhere.

Meanwhile, a related debate within the Allied camp was raging over area or saturation bombing versus precision bombing. The British decided that maximum effectiveness—and minimum aircraft losses—would be realized by night attacks and pulverization of selected areas in which Axis war plants were known to be located. The United States Air Force rejected saturation bombing as inherently inefficient and morally repugnant. American leaders asserted that "precision bombing," daytime attacks on precisely identified targets, guaranteed larger returns per bomb and avoided unnecessary killing of civilians. The argument continued unabated and unresolved throughout the war.

While the public in both Axis and Allied countries acquiesced in the necessity of strategic bombing and was not much concerned about the enemy civilian deaths that resulted, the use of the atomic bomb at Hiroshima and Nagasaki was a different matter. After an initial period of shocked acceptance, there was an outpouring of guilt and moral condemnation. But why? Was the destruction of 100,000 people by one bomb dropped from one plane so objectionable—more so than the killing of 100,000 people by 1,000 bombs dropped from 100 planes? This kind of moral arithmetic is errant nonsense. The moral issue is not how many died by how many bombs, not whether the explosion that killed them was caused by atomic energy or TNT, not even whether the atomic bomb produced new and unique effects (for example, radiation damage). Defenseless people died and other people suffered horribly in *both* atomic and conventional bombing. The actual moral issue—if ever morality can be discussed in the context of war—was the decision to drop bombs on civilians in the first place. Leaving aside the matter of the use of the atomic bomb at Nagasaki, which may have been unnecessary and thus reprehensible, the point at issue is that Hiroshima was an instance of saturation bombing. If Hiroshima is morally indefensible then so were Coventry, Hamburg, Dresden, Tokyo, and the East End of London—all the victims of saturation bombing.

Documents

1 Bombing Policy

Historically international law has been slow to adjust to changing conditions, especially to those of warfare. Its inability to deal with the novel situation resulting from large-scale use of the submarine in World War I is but one example of the inflexibility and impotence of international law. A strenuous effort was made between the wars to establish rules dealing with another military innovation of the First World War, the bombardment airplane. But no agreement had been reached when the Second World War began. The following material from Grand Strategy, *part of the official British history of the war, traces the early development of policy on air bombardment.*

Allied Policy, September 1939–May 1940

The Anglo-French Declaration of 2 September 1939, of which the text is given below, was issued in answer to President Roosevelt's appeal of the previous day to every belligerent Government "publicly to affirm its determination that its armed forces shall in no event and under no circumstances undertake bombardment from the air of civilian populations or unfortified cities, upon the understanding that the same rules of warfare will be scrupulously observed by all their opponents."

Speaking in the House of Commons on 21 June 1938 Mr. Chamberlain, the Prime Minister, after prefacing that there was in fact at present "no international code of law with respect to aerial warfare which is the subject of general agreement," had stated that none the less there were three rules or principles of international law which were as applicable to warfare from the air as to war at sea or on land. First, it was against international law to bomb civilians as such and to make deliberate attacks upon civilian populations. Secondly, targets aimed at from the air must be legitimate military objectives and must be capable of identification. Thirdly, reasonable care must be taken in attacking such military objectives not to bomb a civilian population in the neighbourhood.

From **Grand Strategy, World War II,** II (London: Her Majesty's Stationery Office, 1957), pp. 567–70. Reprinted by permission of the Controller of Her Britannic Majesty's Stationery Office.

These principles, which had been unanimously approved by the Assembly of the League of Nations, were quoted in Air Ministry Instructions of 22 August 1939.

Hitler replied to President Roosevelt in the same sense as the Allies, stating that the German Air Force had received the command to confine itself to military objectives.

During the Polish campaign the British War Cabinet considered on several occasions whether in view of the activities of the German Air Force they should change their own policy. The question was decided in the negative on grounds of expediency, but the Chiefs of Staff reported also on the question of fact. Up to September 12 it did not appear to them, on the available evidence, that the Germans had adopted a policy of disregarding the accepted principles; but soon afterwards reliable evidence was received of the indiscriminate bombing of open towns, and the bombing of Warsaw on September 24 and 25 was by no means confined to military objectives. On October 16, after a meeting of the Cabinet on the 14th, the Chief of the Air Staff informed Air Marshal Barratt, Head of No. 1 Air Mission in France, as follows: "Owing to German action in Poland we are no longer bound by restrictions under the instructions . . . of 22 August, nor by our acceptance of Roosevelt's appeal. Our action is now governed entirely by expediency, i.e., what it suits us to do having regard to (a) the need to conserve our resources, (b) probable enemy retaliatory action, and (c) our need still to take into account to some extent influential neutral opinion." In fact our policy remained unchanged until 15 May 1940.

Anglo-French Declaration on the Conduct of Warfare
"The Governments of the United Kingdom and France solemnly and publicly affirm their intention, should a war be forced upon them, to conduct hostilities with a firm desire to spare the civilian population and to preserve in every way possible those monuments of human achievement which are treasured in all civilised countries.

"In this spirit they have welcomed with deep satisfaction President Roosevelt's appeal on the subject of bombing from the air. Fully sympathising with the humanitarian sentiments by which that appeal was inspired they have replied to it in similar terms.

"They had indeed some time ago sent explicit instructions to the commanders of their armed forces prohibiting the bombardment, whether from the air or the sea, or by artillery on land, of any except strictly military objectives in the narrowest sense of the word.

"Bombardment by artillery on land will exclude objectives which have no strictly defined military importance, in particular large urban areas situated outside the battle zone. They will furthermore make every effort to avoid the destruction of localities or buildings which are of value to civilisation.

"As regards the use of naval forces, including submarines, the two Governments will abide strictly by the rules laid down in the Submarine Protocol of 1936, which have been accepted by nearly all civilised nations.

Further, they will only employ their aircraft against merchant shipping at sea in conformity with the recognised rules applicable to the exercise of belligerent rights by warships.

"Finally the two Allied Governments re-affirm their intention to abide by the terms of the Geneva Protocol of 1925, prohibiting the use in war of asphyxiating or poisonous or other gases or of bacteriological methods of warfare. An enquiry will be addressed to the German Government as to whether they are prepared to give an assurance to the same effect.

"It will of course be understood that in the event of the enemy not observing any of the restrictions which the Governments of the United Kingdom and France have imposed on the operations of their armed forces these Governments reserve the right to take all such action as they may consider appropriate."

The German Bombing of Rotterdam

The bombing of Rotterdam on 14 May 1940 presents a problem of some complexity. There are two aspects to be considered. Firstly, the legitimate tactical use of air bombardment in support of the ground operations. Secondly, the more questionable use of air power to hasten the surrender of the town.

On the first point, the German attitude, as revealed by contemporary Army documents, was that Rotterdam could no longer be regarded as an "open city" as areas of the town had been fortified and troops were defending them against the Germans, who were, in fact, being hard pressed to hold their positions. The G.O.C. XXXIX Corps (General Schmidt) accordingly prepared an assault to be launched on 14 May, preceded by a bombing attack from 13.30 to 14.00 hours, for which one Stuka Geschwader (about 100 aircraft) of Fliegerkorps Putzier was allotted. Göring and Kesselring (who was commanding Luftflotte 2 at the time), in their post-war statements, have claimed that the actual attack was carried out solely as a tactical operation, but an examination of all the available evidence clearly shows that there were other considerations.

This leads us to the second point—the significance of the raid in relation to the surrender of the city. To appreciate this fully, it will be useful to give some account of the actual events.

On the evening of 13 May, Eighteenth Army sent the following order to General Schmidt: "Resistance in Rotterdam will be broken with every means; if necessary destruction of the town will be threatened and carried out." At 10.30 the following morning, therefore, the Dutch authorities received an ultimatum which threatened the "complete destruction" of the city unless resistance ceased forthwith. The Dutch were given two hours in which to reply. At 12.10, although there was still no official answer from the Dutch, General Schmidt learnt that surrender was likely and he immediately took steps to postpone the bombing, scheduled for 13.30. The War Diary of XXXIX Corps records that "Fliegerkorps Putzier received at 12.10 hours, through 7th Parachute Division, the following order: 'bombing attack Rotterdam postponed owing to surrender negotiations'."

The Dutch reply was received at about 12.30 but it merely asked for the signature and rank of the officer sending the ultimatum—which had, by some chance, been omitted. The Germans interpreted this, probably correctly, as an attempt to play for time. Accordingly, Schmidt drew up the terms of surrender, which demanded that all negotiations must be completed in time for the German occupation to take place before dark. A new time-limit of 3 hours (up to 16.30) was fixed, but no threats were made. This communication was handed over to the Dutch representative, who left the meeting-place at 13.20. A few minutes later, a formation of bombers was seen approaching and General Schmidt gave the order to fire red flares as a signal to the aircraft to refrain from bombing. Nevertheless, at 13.30 the bombing started, causing large fires and considerable damage. Two hours later, Rotterdam formally surrendered and the German troops took possession of the city. The capitulation of the whole Dutch Army followed the next morning (15 May). It is clear, from the above evidence, that General Schmidt did his best to call off the air attack. Why, then, was it carried out when surrender negotiations were in progress? In his memoirs, Kesselring declares that he had no knowledge of these negotiations but this is hard to believe, particularly as Göring admitted at Nuremberg that there was radio communication between Rotterdam and Luftflotte 2 via his (Göring's) headquarters. It seems reasonable to assume, therefore, that the message from General Schmidt to the Air Corps, postponing the attack, must have been known to Kesselring and probably also to Göring. There is, unfortunately, no record of what was said during the telephone conversation between Göring and Kesselring which, according to the latter, went on throughout the morning on the question of the air attack. However, it is unlikely that Göring would ignore the psychological effect of the attack and, with Warsaw in mind, he must have realised that a display of air power would probably hasten the Dutch surrender. He may, therefore, have decided to over-ride the Schmidt request on the grounds that the surrender was not yet an accomplished fact. When the bomber force arrived over Rotterdam, about one-half saw the red flares and did not drop their bombs on the city. The other half either did not see the flares or failed to appreciate their significance, and bombed according to plan.

To sum up, it can fairly be said that, even if the attack was not completely indiscriminate, it was quite unnecessary, and cannot be excused, as Göring and Kesselring have suggested, on the grounds of inadequate means of communication between ground and air. We have clear evidence that the Germans were prepared to be ruthless and had threatened the destruction of the city if it did not surrender. Although complete evidence is lacking, it would appear probable that Göring decided to hasten the surrender by intimidating the defenders with a display of air power, not unmindful of the probable repercussions on the Dutch Army as a whole. In fact, as the German air attaché, Wenninger, told Kesselring, in consequence of the attack, the whole of the Dutch Army capitulated.

It is not, perhaps, without significance that, after the bombing, General Schmidt expressed his regret to the Dutch Commander in Rotterdam that the attack had been carried out.

2 The Present War Situation as It Relates to Air

Lord Trenchard

It was logical that Great Britain would embrace some form of the doctrine of strategic bombing—the British possessed neither the resources nor, it must be said, the necessary zeal for a "slugging match" on the ground with Nazi Germany. The circumstances in which the British found themselves after the fall of France made strategic bombing, in combination with economic blockade and subversion, seem the best method for bringing about Germany's defeat. The following memorandum by the Marshal of the Royal Force was written May 19, 1940. Soon after, Prime Minister Churchill told his staff that "all concentration should be given to the Air Force as the war would be won by bombing." Unable to launch an invasion of the Continent, unwilling even to face the prospect, many Englishmen saw air power as an ideal—indeed the only—solution.

When we have surveyed the whole area of the struggle and the factors involved, what is the outstanding fact? It is the ingrained morale of the British nation which is nowhere more strongly manifest than in its ability to stand up to losses and its power to bear the whole strain of war and its casualties.

History has proved that we have always been able to stand our Casualties better than other Nations.
Strategically it must be sound to hammer the weak points of the enemy. When we talk of weak points we mean the spheres in which we are relatively stronger than he is. Where are those points to be found? Certainly not in land fighting.
The German army, with its eight to ten million trained and disciplined fighting men, well equipped and containing countless mechanised units, is a far more powerful weapon than we have to-day, or can have. At sea, though we have an infinite naval superiority, there is no point at which we can strike decisively with our navy, and the German submarine is a very powerful weapon.

It must be realised that to-day the Sea is a Source of Weakness to us as well as a Source of Strength.

From **The Strategic Air Offensive Against Germany** by Charles Webster and Noble Frankland, IV (London: Her Majesty's Stationery Office, 1961), pp. 194–97. Reprinted by permission of the Controller of Her Britannic Majesty's Stationery Office.

Germany has been able to turn the weapon of the blockade against us, and it is we, owing to our sea approaches, who are being increasingly blockaded, while Germany, owing to her land frontiers, is enabled to draw on the resources of the whole of Europe and the vast areas of Russia beyond. We cannot therefore find that weak point which we should attack either on the sea or by the blockade.

Germany, and Germany alone, is the Enemy that we have got to beat.

It may be argued that Italy is the weak point, but this would be false, as nothing that we can do to Italy will win the war for us.

Where then is Germany's weak point? It is to be found in precisely the sphere in which I began this paper by stating that we had a great strength. All the evidence of the last war and of this shows that the German nation is peculiarly susceptible to air bombing. While the A.R.P. services are probably organised with typical German efficiency, their total disregard to the well-being of the population leads to a dislocation of ordinary life which has its inevitable reaction on civilian morale. The ordinary people are neither allowed, nor offer, to play their part in rescue or restoration work; virtually imprisoned in their shelters or within the bombed area, they remain passive and easy prey to hysteria and panic without anything to mitigate the inevitable confusion and chaos. There is no joking in the German shelters as in ours, nor the bond which unites the public with A.R.P. and Military services here of all working together in a common cause to defeat the attacks of the enemy.

This, then, is their weak point compared with ourselves, and it is at this weak point that we should strike and strike again.

When we examine the technical factors governing our Air Force, and its use, we find striking confirmation that this policy is correct.

Taking all in all the percentage of Bombs which hit the Military Target at which they are aimed is not more than one per cent.

This means that, if you are bombing a target at sea, then 99 per cent. of your bombs are wasted, but not only 99 per cent. of the bombs are wasted, but 99 per cent., too, of the pilots and of the training which went to produce them, and of all the machines and the labour and plant and raw material which went to their construction, and, further back, 99 per cent. of all the ships which have transported the raw materials and of the finance which purchased these raw materials are all equally wasted. So, too, if the bombs are dropped in Norway, Holland, Belgium or France, 99 per cent. do Germany no harm, but do kill our old allies, or damage their property or frighten them or dislocate their lives. It is more than wasted. If, however, our bombs are dropped in Germany, then 99 per cent. which miss the military target all help to kill, damage, frighten or interfere with Germans in Germany and the whole 100 per cent. of the bomber organisation is doing useful work, and not merely 1 per cent. of it.

So technical factors also point to the wisdom of striking at what in fact is Germany's weak point. We should therefore exploit to the uttermost this vulnerable spot in the German nation and we should bomb persistently military targets in every town in Germany and never let up on them.

The Germans have an advantage over us in that their geographical situation enables them to utilise every single type of bomber to drop bombs on England if they want to, and they do. While obviously their long-range bombers can attack any part of the British Isles, their short-range bombers, their reconnaissance machines, their fighters and even obsolete models all can hit Portsmouth, Southampton and Dover, whereas only our fairly long-range bombers can reach even the nearest target in Germany. Again, owing to the shortness of summer nights we can only bomb them for a relatively short time, whereas they can bomb England almost all the hours of darkness.

Our long-range bombers constitute only a comparatively small part of our total Air Force.

In the face, therefore, of these handicaps it is vital that none of our *long-range bombers* should be diverted from the single task of bombing military targets in Germany. By Germany, I do not mean only Western Germany, I mean Munich, Berlin, Stuttgart, and if possible in time even Vienna, where I understand Headquarters of the Army and other departments have been moved to from Germany. There is at present a far too large percentage of our bomber force which cannot be used to attack the military objectives in Central or Southern Germany either in winter or summer—a percentage which must be continually reduced. Meanwhile this percentage can be used, and only it should be used, for hitting at the oil in Rotterdam, the shipping on the coasts, the invasion ports, the empty barges, the ships in Brest and the other opportunities that exist for weakening the enemy outside Germany.

There should be established the same sort of clear priority for the use of bomber aeroplanes based on strategical reasons as exists in the economic sphere and is maintained by the Cabinet.

Absolute priority should be given to the long-range bombers for this work and this prior claim on the use of the long-range bombers must be backed up by a sufficient priority being accorded for the supply and training of pilots, air and ground staff, as also for the planes and the necessary materials of this branch of the Air Service. The training of these bomber crews must be given priority over the training of the crews for Coastal Command aircraft, Army Co-operation Squadrons, the Fleet Air Arm, Photography and Fighters, and this priority must be maintained despite the pressure on the Air Force by various departments, which I know must be great, with the Army wanting invasion ports bombed, the Navy wanting submarine bases and ships bombed, and the Ministry of Economic Warfare wanting the oil in Rotterdam and elsewhere bombed, a demand which becomes all the more acute owing to the small size of the bomber force, due not merely to the lack of belief in the efficacy of hitting with the bomber, but to its appalling neglect in the years before the war and at the beginning of the war.

What do I mean by persistent bombing? I mean that on every single night, and most days, some bombing of military targets in Germany must take place, even if sometimes only one machine can be sent. When all the conditions are favourable a great force can go to destroy some military objective of first-class importance. At other times perhaps military objectives in twenty towns should be selected for an attack by ten machines each. On another night perhaps one machine should be sent to towns in Germany with over 5,000 inhabitants to attack some military objective in that town. The plan must be flexible, but must result in unremitting nightly and daily bombing of military targets in Germany, sometimes here, sometimes there, sometimes with a large concentrated force and at others with widely dispersed small forces or single machines. Day bombing must necessarily be less than night bombing as it can only be done in bad weather and in very fast machines, but more day bombing must be done. The object of this night and day bombing of military targets in Germany is to make the civil population realise what war means, and make them realise that if there is a military objective in their town it is going to be bombed.

Hitherto, we have not done this. There have been months or weeks without a machine going into Germany. Not a single day or night should pass without a visit from our machines.

Such a policy may necessarily involve fairly heavy casualties, but the counting of our losses has nothing to do with the soundness of the plan once you accept the view that the nation can stand their casualties. The pilots in the last war stood it, and the pilots of this war are even better, and, I feel, would welcome a policy of this description. It will need the very best and most up-to-date type of long-range bombers from America and this country, and it will also mean that great reserves are essential. It is quite possible to lose as many as 70 per cent. of your machines in a month, though these will not be all completely written off, as some can be repaired to fly again after crashes and accidents in England. Reserves will be needed of 400 to 500 per cent., not the mere 100 per cent. mentioned by the late Minister of Aircraft Production, a statement at which every airman must have said to himself: 'What—only 100 per cent. reserves!'

In the last war casualties of pilots were sometimes 30 per cent. per month or more, but now, owing to the universal use of parachutes, the percentage of those killed and wounded will be greatly reduced.

I am convinced that when this policy has been adopted, and then only if it has been pursued unrelentingly and persistently, will it be possible, when the morale of the German nation has begun to crumble, to utilise with success in victory over the German military forces the necessarily smaller British Army which is slowly but surely being equipped 100 per cent. with the necessary mechanical instruments of modern warfare, such as tanks, guns, munitions and aircraft.

It is because it is the only effective way in which we can hit at our enemy—Germany—now, and it is the only way that we can make effective for victory our eventually assembled forces of weapons and men that I so stongly advocate the dropping on military targets in Germany of every possible bomb where a 100 per cent. of every load dropped will have its value.

Provided nothing is allowed to interfere with the fullest possible production of bomber aircraft, I do not underestimate the importance of reinforcing strongly, with machines, tanks, munitions and men, Africa, Iraq and

Singapore—the three areas vital to the Empire—and of constructing the largest possible fleet of fast surface craft to keep open the American artery which is so essential during the eighteen months or two years while the policy I urge is exploited persistently and unflinchingly.

3   The Bombing of Cologne

Robert Bunnelle

The first really large-scale Allied bombing effort was the British night raid on Cologne on May 30, 1942. Some 1,250 heavy bombers were mustered for this attack. The target was an important industrial center in the Rhineland, heavily defended by antiaircraft units and several squadrons of fighter interceptors. British Bomber Command claimed the raid was an overwhelming success. Although the RAF lost forty-four bombers, approximately 300 acres in the center of the city, including numerous munitions factories, were destroyed. When the planes returned home, Associated Press reporter Robert Bunnelle was on hand to get the story.

The grass grew neatly to the edge of England's flare-lighted runways with peaceful lushness of a country club lawn. But there peace ended, for it was 8:08 P.M.—and take-off time for the greatest raid in all aerial warfare.

In the soft dusk of England's spring, dozens of heavily loaded bombers squatted at the top of the line. Their propellers beat an impatient rattle awaiting the green light from the control tower. And the same thing was happening at hundreds of hidden bomber bases over England. Already the sky was filled with roar of planes from the other fields, all getting ready for the 1,250-bomber party at Cologne—the world's first four-figure air raid.

The best way to describe the unprecedented battle perhaps will be to describe what happened aboard one of those planes. It was a feat that was being duplicated by all the others.

The captain of a four-motored Stirling in one group of waiting ships suddenly heard an anxious voice on the intercommunicating telephone.

"Bombing of Cologne" by Robert Bunelle. Associated Press article, May 30, 1942. Reprinted by permission of The Associated Press.

"Captain," the voice said, "if we have to wait much longer, we'd better switch off. Engine three's getting hot."

But before the captain could reply, the green light flashed from the control tower. The big plane began to move. The raid was on.

The crew in the Stirling looked to the left. In the flickering light of flare-path number two, they saw the others taking off—plane after plane like streetcars leaving a terminal. The Stirling moved faster. As it began to lift, a voice on the interplane phone sang: "We're off to see the Wizard, the wonderful Wizard of Oz." The field dropped swiftly away and the Stirling circled to set its course. The crew suddenly felt a mighty bump—but it was only the slipstream from another Stirling that roared near by.

Before the planes reached the coast they were climbing through clouds. A dejected voice on the Stirling's phone complained: "Just our luck to find ten-tenths cloud (thick clouds) at Cologne." But the clouds began to break and soon dykes and towns in Holland loomed in the moonlight. The moon was to the starboard and straight ahead was a rose-colored glow in the sky.

"It's probably something to do with the German-Dutch frontier searchlight belt," somebody said. But just then the captain broke in on the plane's phone to warn the Stirling's three gunners: "We're in the danger zone now. Keep your eyes skinned for any aircraft of the enemy."

The front gunner spoke up quickly.

"Light ahead to port," he reported.

All eyes turned to the front, just in time to see a sudden shower of incendiaries, apparently jettisoned by a bomber under attack by a Nazi night fighter. Soon they saw the burning wreckage of a plane on the ground. Disaster had struck in the soft moonlight. By this time the Stirling was in the searchlight belt and in the blue streaks piercing the sky the crew saw other planes—some traveling their way and others headed back for England. The going was rougher now because the captain was dodging and weaving the ship to avoid lights and flak that sailed up from the ground like white mushrooms.

The front gunner broke the tenseness. "Keep weaving, captain," he shouted on the plane's phone. "The flak is getting so thick you could walk on it."

"There's a plane on our tail," cut in the rear gunner, then, half disappointedly, he added: "Hell, it's only one of ours."

The rose-colored glow was still ahead and the captain came on the phone again.

"How much longer before we're there, navigator?"

"About ten minutes," replied the navigator.

"Well, we don't need you any more. That light's Cologne. The fellows have built up quite a fire."

By this time the sky became so full of flak, tracers, shell bursts, and spotlight streaks that it was like the fireworks at the county fair. The Germans were throwing everything they had at the attackers. From the bomb aimer's hatch, Cologne glowed like a big cigarette end in a blackout. Then the plane was directly over the fires and the captain ordered: "Bomb doors open!"

"Bomb doors open," came the reply.

The captain spoke again. He said: "Hell, wait a minute. No use wasting stuff on burning buildings. Let's look for a black spot."

Block after block of the town was blazing under the craft, smoke drifting past the flame-outlined wings. In the blaze could be seen what appeared to be white-hot skeletons of steel framework.

There were Wellingtons, Halifaxes, Manchesters, more Stirlings—in fact, about everything but helicopters—flying above, below, and on either side of the Stirling. All were silhouetted against the towering flames of Cologne. And all were dropping their loads on Cologne. While the town blazed like a furnace, the blasts of high explosive bombs continued to hurl the walls of buildings across the flames. From time to time, in the outer dark spaces, showers of incendiaries poured down in platinum-colored flashes that turned slowly red.

One tiny dark spot showed on the Rhine river's flowing west bank.

"That might be Elektra Stahldraht Fabrik (a steel wire plant)," said the captain. "Let's try it."

There followed an anxious moment of leveling off and moving right and left to get on the target. Then the bomb aimer pressed the button and the plane gave a lift from the release of the heavy bomb cargo. A piece of flak tore through the ship six inches above the pilot's head and for a few minutes everybody was busy with the guns, rudders, and cameras as the Stirling wove its way out of a blazing curtain of anti-aircraft fire. The ship slipped through the flak and the rear gunner shouted: "We got it! I saw the white flash of debris flying, then red and yellow flames shooting up."

There were shouts of elation on the ship's phone. The job had been done. The Stirling's bombs had found their mark. The Stirling skirted the city, setting a homeward course. The burning area had increased tremendously in the eight minutes over the target. New fires were springing up everywhere. About ninety miles from Cologne, the captain turned in a complete circle to take another look. From this distance, the three major fires had merged into one immense volcano of flame.

The Stirling dodged and spiraled on to England, trying to confuse Nazi night fighters and ground observers.

"Can't anybody see our coast yet?" the captain asked.

"Not yet," the phone said. Then—with obvious relief—came: "Yes, there it is and you can still see Cologne."

"Well," said the captain, "throw the navigator overboard. We won't need him any more tonight!"

It was a breeze from there on to the home station. The Stirling radioed in and the flare-path control informed the pilot he was fourth in and gave him the height at which to circle for a landing. As he rounded the field awaiting his turn to land, a Wellington fluttering from the opposite direction, nipped past one wing.

"What's wrong with that idiot!" growled the navigator. But he quickly added: "Sorry, looks like he had a rough trip."

It turned out later that the Wellington was short-cutting home with a badly wounded crew.

Three planes ahead of the Stirling were shepherded in quickly without incident—one every three minutes with timetable precision—and within a few moments after the Stirling touched ground she was in the hands of a ground crew hurrying to heal her battle wounds.

The bus that took the cheerful crew to quarters for interrogation by intelligence officers also carried others just back from Cologne. One lanky pilot with sun-reddened face and white eyebrows said with a laugh:

"Well, that was the only time I enjoyed being over Cologne—and this is my fifth trip. God, what a pretty fire!"

"Damned good show," another agreed.

Interrogation finished, the crews went off to eat bacon and eggs—a special treat.

4　An Estimate of the Effects of an Anglo-American Bomber Offensive Against Germany

Charles Portal

Inside the headquarters of the American and British air forces it was considered heretical to question the effectiveness of the bomber offensive. Doubts about the military significance of strategic bombing were widely expressed by the public and by spokesmen for ground forces. The doubters were fond of using Germany's experience with Great Britain to ask why Allied air attacks against Germany should be any more decisive. Infuriated by their critics, defenders of the heavy bomber were often guilty of overstating their case. The November 3, 1942, memorandum by the Chief of the Air Staff is an example of this sort of response.

At the 137th Meeting of the Committee, held on the 5th October, I was invited to circulate a Note setting out the facts and arguments which support the Air Staff view that a heavy bomber force rising to a peak of between 4,000 and

From **The Strategic Air Offensive Against Germany** by Charles Webster and Noble Frankland, IV (London: Her Majesty's Stationery Office, 1961), pp. 258–64. Reprinted by permission of the Controller of Her Britannic Majesty's Stationery Office.

6,000 heavy bombers in 1944 could shatter the industrial and economic structure of Germany to a point where an Anglo-American force of reasonable strength could enter the Continent from the West.

2. The only difficulty in complying with this request is that of dealing with this very wide subject in a Paper of reasonable length. I have accordingly been obliged to restrict this note to an outline of the salient points. Some of the factors involved are treated more fully in Appendices.

3. As the starting point for an appreciation of this kind it is necessary to decide upon a reasonable estimate of the results likely to be achieved by a given weight of bombs. From photographs and intelligence reports we have a very good idea of the damage being inflicted on Germany by the current operations of the Bomber Command. Nevertheless, this information is far from complete and would not serve as a satisfactory basis for the study.

4. The only comprehensive analysis of the results of bombing is that derived from the German bombing raids on this country during the twelve months ended the 30th June, 1941. Estimates derived from the results of these attacks are accordingly employed to forecast the effect of the very much heavier scale of bombing contemplated under the plan in question.

5. During the twelve months ended the 30th June, 1941, the Luftwaffe dropped 55,000 tons of bombs on this country, of which 36,000 tons were directed at industrial areas. These attacks caused 41,000 deaths and serious injury to 45,000 persons. Nearly 350,000 houses were rendered uninhabitable for the duration of the war and one million people were displaced from their homes. In addition there were some 2½ million "incidents" of housing damage, many of which caused the temporary displacement of the occupants and all of which required repairs. Beyond these results, the destruction caused to factories, power plants, shipping and harbour facilities and public utilities had a direct reaction on the war effort, but is not susceptible of exact numerical assessment.

6. Judging by contemporary standards, the German attacks were an inferior example of bombing technique. The attacks were not well planned; the Luftwaffe was only partly prepared for night operations; the effort was widespread over the country and the methods of reaching and marking targets were, on the whole, unreliable. Above all, the small raids of those days effected only a fraction of the damage per ton of bombs achieved with the large-scale concentrated attacks of to-day employing the latest incendiary technique.

7. It follows that the estimates of damage made later in this paper and based on the achievements of the German Air Force over this period are likely to be far short of reality.

8. It is worth turning aside from the main argument for a moment to deal with the not uncommon suggestion that the German attacks against this country proved that large-scale bombing is not a decisive weapon.

9. The first comment which must be made on this suggestion is that the large-scale raids were brought to an end, not because Germany believed they were paying an unsatisfactory dividend, but because it was necessary for the Luftwaffe to move East for the invasion of Russia.

10. Nevertheless, it is a fact that the German raids of 1940/41 produced no major interruption of the British war effort. The reasons for this lie partly in the small scale of the German attacks and partly in the degree of resilience which characterised the British war economy at that stage.

11. The scale of the German attacks was far below that necessary to produce a decisive effect. The total tonnage of bombs dropped by the Luftwaffe throughout the year amounted to less than two-thirds of the peak monthly scale of attack contemplated in this paper.

12. Again, the German attacks came at a time when the British war effort was running far below its potential maximum. With certain important exceptions, alternative manufacturing capacity was available or could be adapted to replace damaged factories. Nearly a million building trade operatives were available for repair work and could be supplemented by military personnel. Our own efforts were backed up by access to the resources of the United States of America located far beyond the reach of enemy bombing and undisturbed by the effects of war. Our resources in man-power were free from any vast operational commitment of the character imposed on Germany by the Russian campaign. From the moral standpoint, the attack came at a time when the British people were comparatively fresh, well-fed and well-clothed. They were braced by the ordeal of Dunkirk and sustained by the triumph of the Battle of Britain. They had been warned to expect heavy air raids and they were convinced that the attack was a temporary hardship to which an answer would soon be found and which would undoubtedly be repaid with interest.

13. Thus the British industries and the British people possessed a degree of resilience and recuperative power adequate to sustain a greater shock than was in fact inflicted.

14. For all these reasons the German attacks fell short of their aim. Nevertheless, their importance must not be underestimated. Nearly 18 months have passed since the last major air attack on this country, and it is easy to forget how gravely the German bombing offensive was regarded by responsible authorities at the time. Many who were in close touch with the events would support the view, that, had even this small scale of attack been more concentrated and persistent, the effect on our war effort and on civilian morale might have assumed a most serious character.

15. For the purpose of this paper I have assumed that the Anglo-American Bomber Force based in the United Kingdom would expand to a first-line strength of 5,000 by June 1944 rising to a peak of 6,000 by the end of the year.

16. During the period of development of this force the scale of attack would amount to 25,000 tons a month by June 1943, to 50,000 tons per month by December 1943, to 65,000 tons a month by June 1944, and to a peak of 90,000 tons a month by December 1944. Under such a plan 1¼ million tons of bombs would be dropped on Germany during 1943 and 1944.

17. A simple calculation based on the results of the German bombing raids referred to in paragraph 5 would suggest that apart from the direct destruction of industries and public utilities, an attack on this scale would lead to the destruction of eight million German houses. But regard must be paid to the fact

that the proportion of undamaged houses would be a steadily decreasing quantity. Allowing for this, the estimate of houses rendered permanently uninhabitable falls to six million. In addition there would be some sixty million "incidents" of bomb damage to houses. Civilian casualties are estimated at about 900,000 killed and about 1,000,000 seriously injured. These estimates make no allowance for the fact that the number of persons per house would tend to increase as the destruction of dwellings progressed. Altogether the calculations suggest that some 25 million Germans would be rendered homeless and many additional millions would have to be temporarily evacuated elsewhere.

18. It is now necessary to consider the effect of destruction of this order on the German war machine.

19. Assuming that the attacks were concentrated on urban areas, the scale of devastation described in paragraph 17 would be adequate to render homeless three-quarters of the inhabitants of all German towns with a population of over 50,000. Superimposed upon the destruction of dwellings there would be a proportionate destruction of industrial plant, sources of power, means of transportation and public utilities.

20. It is possible to paint an even clearer picture of the degree of destruction involved by describing it in terms of attacks of a specified intensity.

21. On the night of the 30th/31st May, 1942, a major attack was carried out on Cologne. In the space of 90 minutes, 770 tons of bombs fell in the city. As a result, nearly one-third of the inner zone of the town was completely destroyed and the areas of total devastation aggregated nearly a square mile. 20,000 houses were completely destroyed and many others damaged. 200,000 persons had to be evacuated. 250 factories were destroyed or suffered varying degrees of damage.

22. Taking this attack as a unit of measurement the probable results of the attacks can be described in rather more definite terms, as follows: During 1943 and 1944 every industrial town in Germany with a population exceeding 50,000 could receive *in proportion to its size*, ten attacks of "Cologne" intensity.

23. In practice, the attacks would be more concentrated. Assuming, for example, they were directed against such a selection of towns as those listed . . . each of these towns would receive, *in proportion to its size,* some 17 attacks of "Cologne" intensity during the period.

24. The towns listed in Appendix I comprise between one-quarter and one-third of the total urban population of Germany and it is safe to conclude that they contain more than one-third of total German industry. The method of selection employed ensures that they are the most important third of the German economy.

25. It is not, I think, unreasonable to suppose that under a policy of concentrated attack the contribution to the German war effort of these 58 towns would be eliminated and that they would become instead a serious liability to the German war machine.

26. Germany is in no condition to withstand an onslaught of this character. Her strength has passed its peak and is diminishing. The heavy drain of the Russian war, the campaign in Libya, the existing air offensive and the

blockade are all contributing to a progressive attrition. Damaged resources, plant and stock of materials cannot now be adequately replaced; structural damage can no longer be adequately repaired; replenishments obtainable from the stocks of occupied countries are a waning asset. The output of German labour is falling through war weariness, food difficulties and other domestic problems, while that of foreign labour—whether in Germany or in the occupied territories—falls with Germany's diminishing prospects.

27. It should not be supposed, moreover, that the effect of destroying one-third of German industry as contemplated in paragraphs 23-25 would be limited to a corresponding drop in the German war potential. In practice the effect would be very much greater. A certain minimum proportion of the industrial effort of any country must always be devoted to maintaining a minimum standard of subsistence throughout the country as a whole. In Germany it is believed that this minimum has already been reached. It follows that any large-scale damage inflicted on industry as a whole cannot be absorbed evenly but must be borne to an ever-increasing degree by that part of industry which is maintaining the armed forces. The only alternative is to face a collapse of the Home Front.

28. This point can be illustrated numerically. It is believed that the urban working population of Germany is divided as two-thirds in industries engaged in maintaining the national economy and one-third in the munitions industries. It is also believed that the former proportion is now at its minimum. In these circumstances any general loss to German industry as a whole must be borne almost exclusively by the munitions element. . . .

29. The proportions quoted above may not be entirely accurate. But that the loss of one-third of German industry would be attended by a far greater proportionate loss to her war potential as a whole can scarcely be disputed.

30. In considering the estimates included in the foregoing paragraphs it is instructive to note the results achieved in certain recent heavy-scale attacks on Germany. Details of the damage inflicted during attacks on Cologne, Dusseldorf and Karlsruhe are accordingly included . . . [elsewhere].

31. I have purposely said nothing about the moral factor as this is a subject on which opinions differ widely. It is, in fact, difficult to estimate the moral consequences of a scale of bombardment which would far transcend anything within human experience. But I have no doubt whatever that against a background of growing casualties, increasing privations and dying hopes it would be profound indeed.

32. The foregoing discussion is based entirely on the assumption that the results of our future bombing will be proportionate to those attained by Germany during the attacks of 1940/41. This has the merit of providing a cautious estimate. It is, however, very far from corresponding to our reasonable expectations. The technique of bombing is improving rapidly. Better training, the Pathfinder Force, incendiary technique, better bombs and radio aids have all to play their part. The ability to concentrate a large-scale attack into the shortest possible time has already proved itself as a means both of reducing casualties and of increasing the damage caused per ton of bombs. There is every chance that

together these various factors will make possible a substantial improvement over the results achieved by Germany against this country.

33. There is also the possibility that the United States will prove successful in their daylight technique, in which case a high proportion of the total effort contemplated in this paper will take the form of precision bombing by daylight.

34. The higher standards of efficiency we hope to attain from these improvements in air tactics and technique are dealt with in greater detail . . . [elsewhere]. If these expectations are realised the forecast decline of German war potential will, of course, be greatly accelerated.

35. The development of our offensive would certainly result in a desperate expansion of the air defences of Germany. I have carefully considered this possibility and I am convinced that the German defences would be incapable of dealing effectively with attacks on the scale proposed. . . .

36. In fact, I think there is a distinct possibility that the implementation of the plan would result in a progressive deterioration of the air defence system of Germany. The rapid development of the offensive would force upon the German defences a scale of effort and a scale of wastage far greater than anything they have yet encountered. The pressure would be applied at a time of acute and increasing industrial difficulties. To the extent that they failed to meet the threat, the difficulties would intensify. Thus the task might grow increasingly beyond their ability to control.

37. I believe that the operations of an Anglo-American force of the size contemplated in this paper might well create a situation of this kind which would lead to the whole of Germany being laid open to deliberate bombing by day and night.

Meanwhile, the ever-increasing demands made upon a waning aircraft industry for the support of the Home Front could not but inflict a most serious handicap on Axis operations by land, sea and air in all other theatres.

38. For the reasons described above, I am convinced that an Anglo-American bomber force based in the United Kingdom and building up to a peak of 4,000-6,000 heavy bombers by 1944 would be capable of reducing the German war potential well below the level at which an Anglo-American invasion of the Continent would become practicable. Indeed, I see every reason to hope that this result would be achieved well before the combined force had built up to peak strength.

Summary

(i) The paper assumes that an Anglo-American Heavy Bomber Force would be based in the United Kingdom and built up to a first-line strength of 4,000 to 6,000 by 1944.

(ii) Such a force could deliver a monthly scale of attack amounting to 50,000 tons of bombs by the end of 1943, and to a peak of 90,000 tons by December 1944.

(iii) Under this plan 1¼ million tons of bombs would be dropped on Germany between January 1943 and December 1944.

(iv) Assuming that the results attained per ton of bombs equal those realised during the German attacks of 1940-41, the results would include:

(a) the destruction of 6 million German dwellings, with a proportionate destruction of industrial buildings, sources of power, means of transportation and public utilities;

(b) 25 million Germans rendered homeless;

(c) an additional 60 million "incidents" of bomb damage to houses;

(d) civilian casualties estimated at about 900,000 killed and 1,000,000 seriously injured.

(v) If the attacks were spread over the main urban areas the result would be to render homeless three-quarters of the inhabitants of all German towns with a population of over 50,000.

(vi) Expressed in other terms, this scale of attack would enable every industrial town in Germany with a population exceeding 50,000 to receive, in proportion to its size, ten attacks of "Cologne" intensity.

(vii) If the attacks were concentrated on the 58 towns specified . . . each would receive, in proportion to its size, some 17 attacks of "Cologne" intensity.

(viii) A concentrated attack of this character would destroy at least one-third of the total German industry.

(ix) A substantial proportion of the total industry of Germany is necessary to maintain minimum standard of subsistence among the German people. As the German economic structure is now stretched to the limit this proportion cannot be further reduced. Consequently, the loss of one-third of German industry would involve either the sacrifice of almost the entire war potential of Germany in an effort to maintain the internal economy of the country, or else the collapse of the latter.

(x) It is hoped that our bombing efficiency will prove to be substantially better than that achieved in the German attacks of 1940-41. In that case the process of attrition will be much accelerated.

(xi) It is considered that the German defences will be incapable of stopping these attacks.

(xii) It is certain that the diversion of more and more of a waning aircraft production to the defence of Germany will heavily handicap all German operations by land, sea and air in other theatres.

(xiii) It is concluded that an Anglo-American bomber force of the size proposed could reduce the German economic and military strength to a point well below that at which an Anglo-American invasion of the Continent would become possible. This result might well be achieved before the combined force had built up to peak strength.

5 Report on the Raids on Hamburg

Police President of Hamburg

The most terrible result of saturation bombing was the "firestorm," a raging inferno of superheated air that destroyed everything and everyone within its reach. Firestorms occurred after the great air raids on Dresden, Tokyo, and, of course, Hiroshima; but the first and in some ways most devastating firestorm developed after the Allied bombing of the north German city of Hamburg during the night of July 27, 1943. Following is a description of the July and August raids on Hamburg, published as an appendix to the British work, The Strategic Air Offensive Against Germany, 1939-1945.

This short account of the course of the raids cannot . . . give any idea of the destruction and terror. Description of the course of the raids and their effects pales before the occurrences in Hamburg during those ten days. The impression made by a gutted area is colourless compared with the actual fire, the howling of the firestorm, the cries and groans of the dying and the constant crash of bombs. It seems important to record this. Because the calamity is as much perceived in the process of destruction as in the accomplished fact. Just as a great part of all Air Protection measures are in vain or incomplete in moments of danger, without the requisite human strength behind them, so experience of these Air Protection measures can only be discussed if account is taken of the extraordinarily heavy strain, both physical and mental, to which human beings are exposed during raids. If the efficacy of an Air Protection measure depends on a man and if he, by reason of *force majeure*, is powerless, this must receive consideration and attempts must be made to find a solution when a final decision is to be taken on the measure. The conduct of persons, whether good or bad, sound or misguided, can only be judged with a precise knowledge of the circumstances.

The cause of the enormous extent of the heavy damage and particularly of the high death rate in comparison with former raids is the appearance of firestorms. In consequence of these a situation arose in the second large scale raid during the night of July 27th/28th which must be regarded in every respect as new and unpredictable.

As a result of H.E. bombs and land mines, roofs were laid bare in large numbers, windows and doors blown in and smashed and the Self Protection Service was driven into the cellars. The incendiary bombs of all kinds then dropped in great concentration found ample food amongst the destruction

From **The Strategic Air Offensive Against Germany** by Charles Webster and Noble Frankland, IV (London: Her Majesty's Stationery Office. 1961), pp. 310–15. Reprinted by permission of the Controller of Her Britannic Majesty's Stationery Office.

already caused. More H.E. bombs and land mines drove the Self Protection personnel, who, despite the complete failure of the municipal water supply, had hurried out to fight the fires, back again into the shelters. This constantly alternating dropping of H.E. bombs, land mines and incendiary bombs made possible an almost unimpeded spread of fires. It should be observed that as a result of these tactics by the enemy and of the dropping of countless liquid incendiary bombs, fires occurred not only in attics and upper floors, but often at the bottom of buildings. The immediate fanning out thus made possible an immense number of individual fires caused within barely half an hour huge area fires. And these produced firestorms.

An appreciation of the force of these firestorms, transcending all human experience and imagination, can only be obtained by sober observation of the physicometeorological phenomenon. Only in this way can an appreciation be formed of the powerlessness of all personnel through the lack of water and of the special experiences of the so far unique major incidents in Hamburg. For it would be absurd and impossible to try and draw conclusions generally applicable to Air Protection from the major incidents in Hamburg, unless the special circumstances arising out of the many firestorms are taken into consideration.

The firestorm and its phenomena are clear and well known conceptions in the history of city fires. The explanation of the physical occurrence is simple. As a result of the confluence of a number of fires, the air above is heated to such an extent that in consequence of its reduced specific gravity a violent up draught occurs which causes great suction of the surrounding air radiating from the centre of the fire. Through this firestorm, and especially the tremendous suction, movements of air are produced of greater force than normal winds. With firestorms just as in meteorology, movements of air result from the compensation of differences in temperature. Whereas these amount in meteorology as a rule to from 20° to 30° Celsius, in firestorms, it is a question of differences in temperature of 600°, 800° or even 1000° Celsius. This circumstance explains the colossal force of firestorms, which cannot be compared to normal meteorological phenomena. Another result of this great force is that weather conditions, even the strongest wind, have no effect or influence on the development of the firestorm. This power of the firestorm to overcome ruling weather conditions together with the centripetal suction effect on surrounding masses of fresh air is also the reason that as a rule firestorms do not tend to spread sideways. These fires therefore only spread as a result of flying sparks or radiating heat. It should be remembered that the danger from radiating heat is not to be underestimated in view of the extraordinarily high temperature developed.

In this attempt, by considering the physicometeorological phenomena, to explain the origin, effect and the spread, which was to some extent apparent, of the firestorms in Hamburg, certain impulses must be taken into account which result from special circumstances. No special evidence is needed to show that conditions ruling locally may have great influence on the development of firestorms. Urban building conditions in the affected area may assist or delay the formation of firestorms, as may the nature, extent and size of the original individual fires. In Hamburg the firestorms originated in densely built up and thickly populated areas, where, therefore, by reason of the type of building and the densely massed houses affected, conditions were favourable for the development of firestorms. In the affected areas in Hamburg there were mostly large blocks of flats in narrow streets with numerous houses behind them, with terraces (inner courtyards), etc. These courtyards became in a very short time cauldrons of fire which were literally man-traps. The narrow streets became fire-locks through which the tall flames were driven.

In these areas, owing to the concentration of the enemy raid and the great number of bombs dropped an immense number of fires were caused. And it should be noted especially that these were not exclusively attic fires but that, as a result of phosphorus and liquid incendiary bombs, at many points large blocks of flats were set on fire in a moment from the ground floor upwards. The fires spread with incredible speed, because, owing to the concentration of the H.E. bombs and land mines, roofs were torn off, walls blown in, windows and doors torn from their frames or smashed and the flames were, therefore, fed unhindered. The intermediate stage of incipient fires, when in former raids fire-fighting was possible and had been carried out with success by the Self Protection Service in Hamburg, did not therefore occur. At many points area fires developed in this way in a very short time. In every one of these area fire zones, a firestorm developed for the reasons of physical laws given above. The suction of the firestorm in the larger of these area fire zones had the effect of attracting the already over-heated air in smaller area fire zones. The most powerful firestorm centres therefore attracted the fire from the smaller area fire zones. One effect of this phenomenon was that the fire in the smaller area fire zones was fanned as by a bellows as the central suction of the biggest and fiercest fires caused increased and accelerated attraction of the surrounding masses of fresh air. In this way all the area fires became united in one vast area fire.

In order to appreciate the force of this huge firestorm caused by the blending of great numbers of smaller firestorms, it should be recalled that, for example, in the raid on the night of the 27th/28th July the area affected was 5½ Km. long by 4 Km. wide, an area therefore of 22 square Km.

It should further be remembered, in considering the situation described, that on account of the type of building in the city not only was there every opportunity for such firestorms to develop rapidly but that the particular way in which the firestorm was developed was due to it. The particular structural conditions, the existence of the terraces (inner courtyards) and narrow streets naturally had the effect that the masses of air attracted could not be drawn to the centre in a geometrically precise centripetal direction. The masses of air had to find their way through locks formed by the streets, terraces, open windows and doors, etc. The bellows—like effect of the draught on the fires on the outskirts, therefore, gave a concentric direction, though individually eddying to and fro, to the extremely overheated masses of air through the whole district affected. The extraordinary force of the currents of air is the obvious explanation of the fact that not only sparks but whole beams and parts of cornices, etc. aflame and of enormous size, were involved, leading of course to a spread of the fire in the districts they traversed.

Thus in a very short time there developed a hurricane of fire probably never known before, against which all human resistance seemed vain and was in point of fact, despite all efforts, useless.

Even this attempt to portray the situation in Hamburg will have given some idea of the extraordinary difficulties with which all personnel were faced. Small as were the opportunities of personnel for fire-fighting, they were further impeded by the complete absence of any water supply.

The struggle by all personnel against the fire as an overpowering enemy increased in the course of the raids. It reached its climax in the last heavy raid during the night of August 2nd/3rd, in which the detonation of exploding bombs, the peals of thunder and the crackling of the flames and ceaseless downpour of the rain formed a veritable inferno.

The rapidity with which the fires and firestorms developed, made every plan and every prospect of defence by the inhabitants purposeless. Houses, which in previous raids might have been preserved by the courageous efforts of Self Protection and other personnel, now fell victims to the flames. Before the necessity of flight could be realized, often every path to safety was cut off.

After the alarm, Self Protection personnel in their shelters, fireguards of the Extended Self Protection and Works Air Protection Services in the places assigned to them, awaited the beginning and development of the raid. H.E. bombs and land mines in waves shook the houses to their foundations. Only very shortly after the first H.E. bombs had fallen an enormous number of fires caused by a great concentration of incendiary bombs—mixed with H.E. bombs—sprang up. People who now attempted to leave their shelters to see what the situation was or to fight the fires were met by a sea of flame. Everything round them was on fire. There was no water and with the huge number and size of the fires all attempts to extinguish them were hopeless from the start.

Many members of the Self Protection Service on their patrols or when courageously fighting the fires, were either buried by H.E. bombs or cut off by the rapid spread of the fires. The same fate overtook many fireguards in Extended Self Protection or Works Air Protection establishments while bravely doing their duty. One eyewitness report says: "None knew where to begin firefighting." The constant dropping of H.E. bombs and land mines kept driving people back into the shelters. The heat, which was becoming unbearable, showed plainly that there was no longer any question of putting out fires but only of saving their lives. Escape from the sea of flame seemed already impossible. Women, especially, hesitated to risk flight from the apparently safe shelter through the flames into the unknown. The continual falling of H.E. and incendiary bombs increased their fears. So people waited in the shelters until the heat and the obvious danger compelled some immediate action, unless action was forced upon them by rescue measures from outside. In many cases they were no longer able to act by themselves. They were already unconscious or dead from carbon monoxide poisoning. The house had collapsed or all the exits had been blocked. The fire had become a hurricane which made it impossible in most cases to reach the open. The firestorm raging over many square kilometres had cut off innumerable people without hope of rescue. Only those got away who had risked an early escape or happened to be so near the edge of the sea of fire that it was possible to rescue them. Only where the distance to water or to open spaces of sufficient size, was short, was flight now possible, for to cover long distances in the redhot streets of leaping flames was impossible.

Many of these refugees even then lost their lives through the heat. They fell, suffocated, burnt or ran deeper into the fire. Relatives lost one another. One was able to save himself, the others disappeared. Many wrapped themselves in wet blankets or soaked their clothes and thus reached safety. In a short time clothes and blankets became hot and dry. Any one going any distance through this hell found that his clothes were in flames or the blanket caught fire and was blown away in the storm.

Numbers jumped into the canals and waterways and remained swimming or standing up to their necks in water for hours until the heat should die down. Even these suffered burns on their heads. They were obliged to wet their faces constantly or they perished in the heat. The firestorm swept over the water with its heat and its showers of sparks so that even thick wooden posts and bollards burned down to the level of the water. Some of these unfortunate people were drowned. Many jumped out of windows into the water or the street and lost their lives.

The number of deaths is still not finally settled. This is not due to faulty methods of investigation but solely to unimaginable immensity of the destruction and the limited amount of staff available. The fact that even now up to 100 bodies are found and recovered on some days, will give some idea of the situation. The destruction was so immense that of many people literally nothing remains. From a soft stratum of ash in a large air raid shelter the number of persons who lost their lives could only be estimated by doctors at 250 to 300. Exact information will only be available when everyone at that time resident in Hamburg if still alive, has reported himself.

The scenes of terror which took place in the firestorm area are indescribable. Children were torn away from their parents' hands by the force of the hurricane and whirled into the fire. People who thought they had escaped fell down, overcome by the devouring force of the heat and died in an instant. Refugees had to make their way over the dead and dying. The sick and the infirm had to be left behind by rescuers as they themselves were in danger of burning.

This sad fate, which befell Hamburg, exceeded in effect and extent any catastrophic fire—with the exception of Tokyo—of the past. It is distinguished in the first place by the fact that never before in a city of a million inhabitants everyone, prepared and equipped for fire-fighting, supported by great experience and great success in fire-fighting in many earlier raids, was waiting at the signal of the sirens for duty and the necessity of fighting the fire. In earlier cases it developed as a rule gradually during many hours or days from a small incipient fire. Here a population ready and prepared for the alarm were literally overwhelmed by the fire which reached its height in under an hour.

Even taking the conditions of those days into consideration, the fire in Hamburg in 1842, bears only a faint likeness to the fire in Hamburg in 1943. The catastrophes of Chicago and San Francisco, the fire in the Paris Opera house, all these events, of which the scenes of fantastic and gruesome terror have been described by contemporaries, pale beside the extent and the uniqueness of the Hamburg fire of 1943. Its horror is revealed in the howling and raging of the firestorms, the hellish noise of exploding bombs and the death cries of martyred human beings as well as in the big silence after the raids. Speech is impotent to portray the measure of horror, which shook the people for ten days and nights and the traces of which were written indelibly on the face of the city and its inhabitants.

And each of these nights convulsed by flames was followed by a day which displayed the horror in the dim and unreal light of a sky hidden in smoke. Summer heat intensified by the glow of the firestorms to an unbearable degree; dust from the torn earth and the ruins and debris of damaged areas which penetrated everywhere; showers of soot and ashes; more heat and dust; above all a pestilential stench of decaying corpses and smouldering fires weighed continually on the exhausted men.

And these days were followed by more nights of more horror, yet more smoke and soot, heat and dust and more death and destruction. Men had not time to rest or salvage property according to any plan or to search for their families. The enemy attacked with ceaseless raids until the work of destruction was complete. His hate had its triumph in the firestorms which destroyed mercilessly men and material alike.

The Utopian picture of a city rapidly decaying, without gas, water, light and traffic connections, with stony deserts which had once been flourishing residential districts had become reality.

The streets were covered with hundreds of corpses. Mothers with their children, youths, old men, burnt, charred, untouched and clothed, naked with a waxen pallor like dummies in a shop window, they lay in every posture, quiet and peaceful or cramped, the death-struggle shown in the expression on their faces. The shelters showed the same picture, even more horrible in its effect, as it showed in many cases the final distracted struggle against a merciless fate. Although in some places shelterers sat quietly, peacefully and untouched as if sleeping in their chairs, killed without realization or pain by carbon monoxide poisoning, in other shelters the position of remains of bones and skulls showed how the occupants had fought to escape from their buried prison.

No flight of imagination will ever succeed in measuring and describing the gruesome scenes of horror in the many buried air raid shelters. Posterity can only bow its head in honour of the fate of these innocents, sacrificed by the murderous lust of a sadistic enemy.

The conduct of the population, which at no time and nowhere showed panic or even signs of panic, as well as their work, was worthy of the magnitude of this disaster. It was in conformity with the Hanseatic spirit and character, that during the raids, friendly assistance and obligation found expression and after the raids an irresistible will to rebuild.

6   The Effects of the Allied Bombing of Germany

Following the defeat of Germany, both Great Britain and the United States dispatched investigatory teams to various German production centers to evaluate the effects of Allied bombing. The "United States Strategic Bombing Survey" concluded that the air offensive had seriously, perhaps decisively, weakened Germany's industrial capacity and thus its military strength. The survey also claimed that the evidence demonstrated the superiority of precision over saturation bombing. The USSBS report was given great public exposure, and, despite later criticism of its data and conclusions, it has been the basis of continued faith in the efficacy of air power. The British investigation was less sanguine about the value of precision bombing and, to an even lesser degree, about the bombing offensive itself. An important source of information on the effects of Allied bombing was Reich Minister Albert Speer. His interview with the British, which is reproduced below, is one of many Speer gave British and American officers after his capture. Notably, Speer gave major credit to the American precision attacks.

Q. At what stage of the war did strategic bombing begin to cause the German High Command and Government real concern, and why?

A. The first heavy attack on Hamburg in August 1943 made an extraordinary impression. We were of the opinion that a rapid repetition of this type of attack upon another six German towns would inevitably cripple the will to sustain armaments manufacture and war production. It was I who first verbally reported to the Fuehrer at that time that a continuation of these attacks might bring about a rapid end to the war. At first, however, the raids were not repeated with the same weight and in the meantime it became possible for the civilian population to adapt themselves to these air attacks both from the point of view of morale and the experience gained, whilst at the same time the armaments industry was able to gather useful experience.

The raids on the ball-bearings industry at Schweinfurt in July 1943 evoked a renewed crisis, the full import of which was likewise made known to the Fuehrer in all its gravity. Here again the delay in development of repetitions of the attack gave us the necessary time to take defensive precautions.

The raids on the aircraft industry and tank engine factories early in 1944 caused a serious renewal of anxiety and doubt, although as it became evident in this case also that our industry was more elastic than had at first been assumed, our anxieties in this connection lessened.

From **The Strategic Air Offensive Against Germany,** IV (London: Her Majesty's Stationery Office, 1961), pp. 378–85, 392–95. Reprinted by permission of the Controller of Her Britannic Majesty's Stationery Office.

In May and June 1944 the concentrated day and night attacks on the Ruhr transport and communications system first began to cause most serious anxieties about future developments, since supplies to industry in the rest of the Reich of the numerous products of the Ruhr, ranging from coal to single items, were bottled up in the Ruhr owing to transport difficulties and could no longer be conveyed to the intended recipients. That these effects did not immediately manifest themselves was due only to the fact that industry throughout the Reich was in possession of considerable stocks of goods, and that in the case of coal it was possible to make a priority delivery for armaments and war production in the summer months at the expense of household deliveries and of the provision of stocks for the winter. A memorandum was delivered by me to the Fuehrer in June 1944 on the subject of the Ruhr and its problems.

The planned assaults on the chemical industry which began on 12th May 1944 caused the first serious shortages of indispensable basic products and therefore the greatest anxiety for the future conduct of the war. Information on this subject is to be found in the numerous memoranda addressed to the Fuehrer in June 1944, in which the further prosecution of the technical side of the war (*eines technischen Krieges*) is repeatedly shown to be impossible. I had the impression that these attacks were to mark the beginning of the *long expected* and long feared series of *planned attacks upon industrial economy* and moreover upon a sphere which owing to its complicated structure was particularly difficult to restore and impossible to decentralise. In actual fact, this type of attack was the *most decisive in hastening* the end of the war.

The attacks on transport and communications *only* produced serious consequences as their intensity was increased. The communications system *proved itself however extremely resistant*, so that in spite of the attacks an emergency transport system for the needs of armament and war production could be maintained until the late autumn of 1944. In this connection, from autumn 1944 onwards the *Reichsbahn* on my instigation continuously submitted written reports to the Fuehrer regarding the serious anxieties which future developments must inevitably produce.

Q. What measures were taken to deal with the threat, and how effective did they prove? Did the German High Command consider they could stop strategic bombing by these measures?

A. . . . I was not of the opinion that the effects of planned air operations against industrial targets could be avoided. . . . The opponent in the air is able to choose his objectives and *in so doing he can plan to concentrate on any vital target such a weight of attack as hitherto has never been possible in the whole history of war. There was consequently no means of defence.*

In spite of all this, however, the Allied air attacks remained without decisive success until early 1944. This failure, which is reflected in the armaments output figures for 1943 and 1944, is to be attributed principally to the tenacious efforts of the German workers and factory managers and also to the haphazard and too scattered form of attack of the enemy *who until the attacks on the synthetic oil plants based his raids on no clearly recognisable economic planning. . . .*

Q. Did the effects of strategic bombing at any time cause any of the three branches of the German High Command to modify, postpone or abandon planned operations?

A. I am not aware that any material alteration had to be made in the timing of a planned operation, or that any operation was abandoned on account of air attack. The reason for this was not that the air raids had not caused material damage before such an operation began, but rather that our supreme command refused to see and to admit the consequences of such attacks.

As an example of this I can quote the beginning of the Ardennes offensive. The attack was ordered to begin although the units had only one or two fuel supply units; the entire supplies of bridge-building equipment still lay in the rear areas, whilst the rest of the supply organisation for the units was insufficient for the distant goal in view. *Feldmarschall* Model and *Oberstgruppenfuehrer* Dietrich called attention to this state of affairs but the time table for the attack was persisted in. *Without any doubt the lack of supplies was due to the transport difficulties caused by air attack.*

Q. Which forms of attack at various periods of the war were most effective in weakening the German war effort?

A. Only the mass attacks by day, because these were based upon economic considerations and inflicted heavy damage on precise targets.

Some "Oboe" night attacks with Mosquitoes upon the Goldenberg power station and the August Thyssen Huette were disturbing on account of the precision with which they were carried out. The last night attack upon the Krupp works, which was carried out by a large number of four-engined bombers, caused surprise on account of the accuracy of the bomb pattern. We assumed that. this attack was the first large-scale operation based on "Oboe" or some other new navigational system.

The last series of night attacks on Poelitz, Bruex and Leuna were more effective in their results than the day attacks by reason of the fact that the superheavy bombs caused shattering damage to these plants. On the other hand, the previous night attacks on towns had no decisive effect upon armaments output.

Q. What was the relative importance of: (a) Attack on cities? (b) Attack on specific types of production? (c) Attack on communications? (d) Use of heavy bombers for the bombardment of front line positions? (e) Attack of naval installations and shipping including the effects of mining? (f) Attack of airfields and air parks?

A. From the point of view of armaments the relative importance of the various forms of attack was as follows:

(a) Attacks on key points in the basic industries or supplies.

(b) Attacks on transport and communications, but the effect of these was long delayed on account of the density of the transport network.

(c) Attacks on front line positions, also because of the psychological effect upon the troops.

(d) Attacks on final stages of manufacture in industry.

(e) Attacks on towns.

(f) Attacks on naval installations, shipping activity and airfields.

Q. Which of the above forms of attack were most difficult to counteract and for what reasons?

A. The attacks on the chemical industry were the most difficult to deal with, since chemical works form an extraordinarily complex organism. Before activity can be recommenced at a chemical factory, the entire plant must be restored in at least one phase of manufacture in order that the chemical process, which forms a self-contained unit, can pass through all its stages.

On the other hand, in the final stages of all other industrial manufacturing processes work can be recommenced shortly after an attack with the remaining undamaged machine tools, and in this way the factory concerned can take up production again in successive stages.

The highly rationalised automobile industry was also extraordinarily difficult to restore owing to the multi-storey buildings in use in the trade, the destruction of which brought to a standstill whole sections of the continuous belt production system. These breakdowns could not be offset by emergency improvisations as in the case of other industries. In any event these attacks had exceptionally serious effects.

Q. Which, at various periods of the war, caused most concern; British or American heavy bomber attacks, day or night attacks; and why?

A. The American attacks, which followed a definite system of assault on industrial targets, *were by far the most dangerous. It was in fact these attacks which caused the breakdown of the German armaments industry*. The night attacks did not succeed in breaking the will to work of the civilian population. Two mistakes were made in this connection:

(1) The weight of the attack was *gradually stepped up* and consequently it was possible to improve defensive measures and the civilian population was able to accustom itself' to the raids. In every case in which the R.A.F. *suddenly* increased the weight of its attacks, as for example the first attack on Cologne and Hamburg and the attacks on Dresden, the effect not only upon the population of the town attacked but upon the whole of the rest of the Reich was terrifying, even if only temporarily so.

(2) The powers of resistance of the German people were underestimated and no account was taken of the fatalistic frame of mind which a civil population finally acquires after numerous air raids. Other peoples, as perhaps the Italians, would have certainly collapsed under a similar series of night attacks and would have been unable to undertake further war production.

Q. To what extent did the diversion of forces and equipment to counter the strategic bomber offensive detract from the fighting power of the *Wehrmacht*?

A. The continuous bomber offensive kept a considerable amount of the German armament production inside Germany, thus withholding it from the Front.

Some 30% of the total output of guns in 1944 consisted of Flak guns, while some 20% of that year's output of the heavier calibres of ammunition (from 7 cm. upwards) consisted of A.A. shells.

Between 50% and 55% of the armaments production capacity of the electro-technical industry was engaged on the manufacture of radar and signals equipment for defence against bomber attacks.

33% of the optical industry was engaged on the production of aiming devices for A.A. guns and for other anti-aircraft equipment.

The fighting power of the *Wehrmacht* was considerably weakened by reason of the above, since the production of valuable Flak guns would have supplied us with excellent anti-tank weapons and the use of Flak ammunition at the Front, in addition to other types would have provided a very substantial increase in stocks. Both were used only to a small extent in the final battles.

I cannot say to what extent the fighting capacity of the *Luftwaffe* was weakened by the use of fighters and night-fighters in Germany itself. One may assume, however, that the small number of fighters retained for Reich defence would have done little to improve the position if they had been used at the Front instead.

The shortage of signals equipment, such as W/T pack-sets, artillery ranging equipment, (sound-ranging devices) and, in fact, the whole supply situation of every type of signals equipment in the Army was particularly serious. This shortage, which made the task of command extraordinarily difficult, was caused by the employment of the electrical industry on priority defence measures against the bombing offensive.

In addition, for the same reason, the radar equipment industry was unable to keep up with the requirements of the Army and Navy, either from the point of view of development or production.

The position was made even more grave by the fact that 50% of the valves produced for G.A.F. purposes were diverted for home defence.

Q. Do you believe strategic bombing alone could have brought about the surrender of Germany? What scale and form of attack would have been required to achieve this?

A. The answer to the first part of the question is *yes. The attacks on the chemical industry would have sufficed, without the impact of purely military events, to render Germany defenceless.* Further targets of the same kind were to be found in the ball bearings industry and in power stations.

Q. What effect did the bombing of the Homeland have upon the morale of the three fighting forces?

A. The morale of the fighting troops at the Front was considerably influenced by the bombing of the Homeland. In this connection the attacks on the towns undoubtedly had some effect. The stories recounted by soldiers returning from leave in a town which had been destroyed made a big impression on the front line troops. Such stories became very numerous after soldiers were granted the right to home leave following the total destruction of their dwelling. Owing to the poor channels of communication, the troops were very disturbed regarding the fate of their relatives whenever they learned from the *Wehrmacht* communiqué that their home town had been bombed.

Q. What effect did strategic bombing have upon the willingness and ability of the civilian population to sustain the war effort? Was German morale more affected by the destruction of cities or by knowledge of the damage caused to essential industries?

A. We drew distinction between morale and conduct. *The morale following attacks upon towns was bad, the conduct of the civil population on the other hand was admirable.* In the armament and war production industries the conduct of the workers could be measured in terms of output which right up to the end of the war did not diminish despite all the raids, as production figures prove. Moreover, the will to rebuild the factories remained unimpaired right up to the end. Neither of these results could be achieved by means of compulsion but only by virtue of the voluntary response of the German workers. . . .

Q. (a) To what extent did the attack of cities cause direct damage to plant and equipment of vital war factories?

(b) How far was the production of vital war factories affected by damage to essential services (power, gas, water, transport etc.)?

(c) How far was war production in bombed cities affected by the effects of area attack on the productivity of labour? To what extent did conditions change in this respect as the war proceeded?

(d) To what extent did the loss of records affect the efficiency of production and public administration?

(e) To what extent and when did the attack of cities cause the dispersal of industry, and what was the nett effect of this dispersal on the overall level of production?

(f) How far did general administration and accommodation difficulties caused by the attack of cities affect the German war effort as a whole? What would have been the position if both bomber forces had thrown their effort continuously into the attack of cities?

(g) What was the effect of Mosquito raids on Berlin and other cities? How could these have been made more effective?

(h) What diversion of manpower and resources was necessary to meet the threat and results of area attack, including A.R.P. and essential repair work, and how far did this affect the resources available for war products and the armed forces?

A. (a) It often occurred naturally that attacks on cities caused damage to plants and equipment of vital war industries, but this was mostly of a temporary nature, as it was due to the failure of electricity and gas supplies.

The best gauge of the effects of night attacks upon production was provided by the demands on power supplies following the attacks; these frequently dropped to between 30% and 40% although after a week they usually rose again rapidly to their original level. Such graphs showing the demand for current were prepared in respect of all major night attacks and are to be found in the records of the *Reichslastverteiler*. They give the *best overall impression* of the effects of the various night attacks upon production.

(b) A particularly difficult situation was caused by the failure of transport facilities in all areas where employees had to cover large distances on the way to work. Thus in the case of the attacks on Berlin, on every occasion individual groups of factories remained idle for several days, although their buildings were intact.

Heavy damage was caused by the destruction of the gas grid in the Ruhr, which resulted in a serious and continuous reduction in the processing of products. In this connection the graphs kept by the *"Ruhrgas"* organisation (Director Wunsch), showing the rise and fall in gas supplies, present an exact picture of the situation.

As a result of the breaching of the Mohne Dam, the Ruhr valley was flooded and the fresh-water pumping station in the Ruhr was put out of action by mud and silt; despite this, however, adequate supplies of water were restored after a lapse of a week. The simultaneous destruction of the other Ruhr valley dams would have resulted in a considerable drop in output in the Ruhr.

Works lying idle owing to shortages of electric power could always be restored to activity within a comparatively short space of time.

(c) Up to the end of the war the productivity of labour remained as high as ever.

(d) On the contrary, the loss of records led to a temporary loosening of the ties of bureaucracy. We very often received the message "Administrative building burnt out, production continues at full pressure." I do not know how far the loss of records affected the difficulties of local administrative authorities.

(e) The dispersal of important industries from west and north-west Germany to central and eastern Germany was carried out in 1942 and 1943. From 1944 onwards vital key industries were transferred to caves and other underground installations.

These dispersals did not at first affect production as it was possible to execute them within a short space of time. Production was hindered by dispersal and decentralisation only after transport and communications facilities had been shattered.

(f) The accommodation available for the workers was of course entirely insufficient but this state of affairs was willingly borne right up to the end of the war. Even if all the raids had been concentrated upon the towns and cities this would still not have had any decisive effect if the old system of attacks with long intervals between each, had been continued. The effects would, however, have been more important *if the raids had been based on a different system*. After the first raid it was generally the case that the water mains were heavily damaged and that consequently the water pressure in the town was considerably reduced. A renewal of these attacks on the next two or three nights *would have had a considerably greater effect, since damage caused by the night raids was in the main due to fire*.

A pre-requisite for attaining such results is that the town attacked should be reduced by a succession of raids separated only by short intervals. If intervals of considerable length elapsed between the attacks which raised the first fires, the danger of new conflagrations was considerably reduced by the restoration of the water mains and the creation of natural fire-breaks. Day attacks made in addition to night raids would only have had some effect if in the main they, like the night raids, had taken the form of incendiary attacks.

Such a system of attack was employed on Dresden and, despite all previous raids throughout the Reich during the three preceding years, it caused a considerable shock effect. Nevertheless, the industrial life of Dresden recovered with comparative rapidity.

Consequently it can be said in conclusion *that a bomb load is more effective if it is dropped upon economic targets than if it is expended upon towns and cities.*

(g) The Mosquito attacks on Berlin and other towns with the exception of the "Oboe" attacks had no considerable effect. They were felt as purely nuisance raids and it would have been more effective if they had been continued over a longer period of time, because their most disturbing aspect was the loss of sleep which they caused. Moreover, the regular time-table of the attacks enabled people to make their own arrangements to correspond. *Irregular attacks, spread as widely as possible would have been more effective.*

(h) I do not know the detailed figures of personnel engaged in A.R.P. and in bomb damage repair organisations, but in the year 1943-1944 the figure may be reckoned at some 1,000,000-1,500,000. Needless to say, this was one reason why industry was unable to make good its shortages of manpower. It is not, however, to be assumed that a materially greater output of armaments would have been attained even had the necessary manpower been available, since the bottlenecks in materials (raw steel, etc.) would still have persisted.

There is no doubt that, in the absence of air raids, it would have been possible to withdraw several hundred thousand more soldiers from the armaments industry at the end of 1943. A large proportion of German skilled labour was required at the factories for bomb damage clearance, where their specialised knowledge and keenness to restore the plants made their presence indispensable after air attacks. If no air raids had taken place, we should have been able to increase the proportion of foreign and unskilled labour.

Furthermore, during 1944 Army training units were increasingly employed on bomb damage clearance work, leading to a reduction in the standard of training and to a lengthening of training schedules.

Q. In attacks on German cities what was the relative effect of H.E. and I.B. respectively on:

(1) The production of industries associated with the city.

(2) Absenteeism among workers in those industries.

(3) The morale of the population?

A. (1) In so far as concentrated area attacks are concerned, the effect of incendiary bombs was greater than that of high-explosive bombs owing to the wide area affected. The effect of high-explosive bombs was merely to render the incendiaries more effective. On the other hand, the effects caused by the heaviest type of mines were fearful.

The difference between the effects of high-explosive and incendiary bomb attacks was to be seen in Berlin. Here the American Air Force carried out several attacks on the centre of the city, exclusively with H.E., but considering the number of aircraft engaged, these did not have the effect of a comparable night attack.

The damage caused to industrial plants by concentrated high-explosive attacks was of varying character. The best and most effective attacks were the last raids by the R.A.F. on Poelitz and Bruex, which, *thanks to the mixed bomb loads had excellent results*.

(2) Fire was also much more effective in destroying workers' dwellings than high explosive, which often left a part of a house still habitable. Consequently the worker was kept from his place of employment for a longer period by conflagrations than by high-explosive attacks.

(3) Fires made the greatest impression on the general morale of the population which after events in Hamburg and elsewhere was extremely afraid of the outbreak of large area conflagrations.

7   The Flaming X

Martin Caidin

In March, 1945, the capital city of the Japanese Empire was largely destroyed in a massive raid by B-29 heavy bombers. It is ironic that the United States Air Force adopted in its attacks on Japan the very tactics it had previously scorned in Europe. Martin Caidin's Torch to the Enemy *provides a masterful account of the fire attack on Tokyo, in which more people were killed than at either Hiroshima or Nagasaki.*

The Pathfinders rushed in first, well ahead of the first massed wave of the bomber stream, their striking time coordinated down to the last second. Over an area of Tokyo with 103,000 persons to the square mile, one of the most congested spots of the world, the lead B-29's raced in at less than five thousand feet. Engines wide open, diving slightly to bring their speed to well over 300 miles per hour, they sped over Tokyo with almost total surprise.

The 100-pound, M47A2 napalm bombs worked with devastating success. It was what the crews called a good bombing night. The skies were clear with scattered clouds; initially the visibility was better than ten miles, and the cloud cover never reached more than three-tenths.

Into the designated target area of ten square miles poured the clusters of pathfinder bombs. At a hundred feet over the city the 500-pounders split open, shredding the napalm bombs outward. These scattered, and the napalm blazed immediately upon contact, feeding hungrily upon the flimsy walls and rooftops where they struck.

The first two airplanes streaked across the city, nearly two hundred bombs showering downward along their high-speed runs. First one B-29 laid a blazing swath along its target path; immediately after, the second plane dashed in, crossing the line of falling bombs.

The napalm is an insidious, sticky incendiary, and it sows fire on contact, sets aflame its objectives in less than a second. The first Japanese searchlights were stabbing the sky as the pathfinders fled.

Behind them they left a wide, perfect flaming X, directly in the heart of the target area. That blazing X was all that was needed.

The message flashed back to XXI Bomber Command Headquarters—*"Bombing the target visually. Large fires observed. Flak moderate. Fighter opposition nil."*

The first bombs fell at exactly fifteen minutes after midnight. There was a brisk wind blowing in Tokyo, and in seconds the situation was disastrous. The flame grasped at the wood-bamboo-plaster construction, and leaped with explosive fury from wall to wall, from roof to roof. Within thirty minutes—by a quarter of one—as the fire chief of Tokyo was to report later, the situation "was completely out of control; we were absolutely helpless."

Following the first two pathfinders came ten more of the giant B-29's. They dumped their bombs into the area marked by the blazing X carved out in the heart of the Tokyo slums. Behind them came an armada that was to pour fiery hell into Tokyo for three hours of continuous attack.

Millions of the deadly incendiary bombs rained from the sky into Tokyo. In the city, fear mounted to stark terror. The pilots of the early planes reported that Tokyo was illuminated like a forest of brightly lighted Christmas trees. The flames were still separate, but beginning to spread. They were thousands and thousands of tiny flickering candles. But they grew, and they merged.

In the beginning, the crews commented with interest on the scene. The last planes brought men into something entirely different. It was the maw of hell; like flying over a super-blast furnace that shrieked and roared with its insane fires.

Several miles outside of the attacked area stood the house of a member of the Swedish legation. Fascinated and horrified, he watched the entire scene develop right before his eyes. Later, when it was all over and the shock of the fantastic sight had subdued, he said: "It seems to me when I think of it now that the B-29's started to come in like a fan, coming in from two sides, very low. The fan seemed to come to a point right over my house. The bombers were beautiful. Their colors changed like chameleons. They were greenish as they passed through the searchlights, and red as they flew over the glare of the fire. At first the anti-aircraft fire was rather strong but seemed badly aimed. Later, as the fires grew worse, it died away. I saw one plane being shot down, falling in several pieces. An intense fire broke out where it fell. Another developed a huge golden, glowing bowl underneath it—I expected one of the incendiaries had exploded inside—and limped off over the horizon.

"The flames were very colorful. The white buildings of brick and stone were burning, and they gave off a very deep color. The wooden houses gave off a light yellow flame, and a huge billow of smoke hung over the edge of the bay."

The Japanese who stared in fright and terror at the wind-whipped flames bearing down upon them saw no beauty nor any pattern developing from the screaming fires. The wind shifted and roared, and quickly shot to hurricane force, bearing down upon tens of thousands of people with the speed of an express train.

But before we move deeply into Tokyo, into the heart of the single most devastating fire the human race has ever known, let us return to the waves of bombers in their loose stream, as they approach the city in which the great, flaming X has been burned. It is a scene that few men have ever witnessed; and those who saw it from the sky, the executioners, have stated that they hope that never again will they, or other men, ever be forced to look straight into the very heart of hell.

The first sight of Japan is a faint, barely seen pink glow on the distant horizon. It is at first no more than a flickering touch of luminescence; you would not know that a city is burning. The visibility is ten miles; seen from a greater distance, the glow is fuzzy and indistinct, more of a blur than truly a light.

But the great bombers rush at nearly three hundred miles per hour toward the capital of Japan, and the miles flee quickly. The glow increases in size, becomes brighter. Now the mountains of Japan are distinct against the sky; the ridges are black and silhouetted, but familiar to the veteran crews. In the nose of the bombers, over the greenish glow of the instrument panels, the pilots and co-pilots, the bombardiers and the navigators, the flight engineers—they all stare out. They have been over Japan before, they have sown explosive and incendiary bombs.

But they have never seen the heart of a city being gouged out of existence by flame.

Tokyo rushes closer, and soon the light is reflected on the glass of the bomber noses, it shines off the leading edges of the wings, glints off the propellers. Then the haziness of the light has vanished, and the men see clearly the intense white spears of the larger fires, spawn of the original napalm, whipped to insane frenzy by the M-69 missiles. Magnesium burns in air; it blazes with an intolerable white light, and in those areas where the greater flames have not yet reached, there can be seen the intense pinpoints of light. Here the B-29's have unleashed thousands of bombs that are just starting to burn.

Each Superfortress rushed in with twenty-four 500-pound bombs, and each of these 500-pounders released a cluster of the magnesium incendiaries. In the pathfinders the intervalometers were set to release the napalm bombs at 100-foot intervals; the main stream of raiders had theirs set for fifty feet. It was very precise, very carefully planned. On this basis the attacked area was receiving a minimum density of twenty-five tons—8,333 magnesium bombs—per square mile!

The stream of bombers attacked an area of rectangular shape, roughly four by three miles. But so rapidly did the flames spread, that the bombardiers were able to follow their orders to fan out and hit those areas as yet unbombed. Thus fires were created over a much greater area than had been anticipated. It is terrible to contemplate the effect of fire in areas with a population density of 103,000 persons per square mile; the Japanese realized immediately, however, that the casualties would be beyond belief when a long stream of B-29's concentrated on the Asakusa Ward—where there were nearly 140,000 people to the square mile, and a building density exceeding 50 percent!

The bombers rush in, the crews stare, many of them unable to speak of the holocaust raging below. There are clouds in the sky, but even at some distance from Tokyo, the clouds passing beneath the airplanes do not block out the light that expands and swells with every passing second.

Nor is there only light; there is heat. The fire is a thing alive now. It dances and writhes on the ground, back of the waters of Tokyo Bay; it swells monstrously as the men stare with mixed horror and fascination.

When they look up at the higher layer of clouds there is still light. The sky changes. The angry red that boils and seethes on the ground vanishes at these heights; it is an unbelievably beautiful pink, a soft illumination that suffuses the bottoms of the higher clouds, that turns the heavens into a vast amphitheater of light that at any other time *would* be beautiful.

There is light in the skies over Tokyo from sources other than the flames. The Japanese are defending their city. They have been caught unawares and they are stunned by the catastrophe unfolding before them; they see the flames advancing toward their gun positions, but until the flames wash over the guns, or the heat sets their clothes afire, the gunners remain at their positions, blasting away. They have little radar, and what they do have is almost useless. Searchlights stab the sky, but they are not needed. The great bombers are clearly outlined by the dancing flames; they form a long river in the skies, unreal shapes rushing overhead, their thunder nearly drowned out by the crashing of the flames.

Seen from a distance at night, flak is unreal. If it were not deadly, it would be lovely. Tiny sparks appear in the sky as if by magic; they wink into being, and subside almost immediately, soundless, shapeless. These are the heavy shells exploding. Sometimes, out of the angry, flaming carnage on the ground, brighter sparks appear, red and yellow; these ascend slowly into the heavens in long red streaks. They are rockets, new defenses for Tokyo, blazing shells that trace strange arcs upward from the tortured earth.

There are also curving, twisting necklaces of glowing lights; tracer shells from the smaller guns. The Japanese are firing frantically, hysterically, pumping shells and bullets into the air as fast as their overheated guns will allow. In the midst of all this blazing reception, a different white appears; a soft and diffused glow of white that sends streamers out in all directions—smoking tendrils. These are the arms and the fingers of phosphorous shells hurled into the air by Japanese defenses.

Sometimes the shells strike, and a great, flaming fireball plummets from the heavens to mark the death of a bomber and the men within. But even this success has its own curse, for every Superfortress brought down is a bomb weighing sixty tons, filled with metal and magnesium and oil and thousands of gallons of high-octane fuel. Each bomber that crashes—though they are few—is certain to wipe out not one, but several huge blocks, and to kill hundreds of hapless Japanese who have time only to look up and see the meteoric mass plunging down upon them before the world blots out in a stabbing knife of red.

The study of Tokyo during the approach is brief, for the bombers close in rapidly to the IP (Initial Point), where they will turn and then rush for their bombing strikes. As they approach the IP there comes the first change in power; pilots shove the four throttles all the way forward and the engines answer back with a richer, huskier roar. At the same moment the pilots cry *"Props!"* to the men at their right; the co-pilots push forward on the propeller controls, the blades turn and go into flatter pitch, and the propellers throw off their knife-edged, keening, metallic sound. The bombers gain in power and in speed.

The B-29's climb above their assigned bombing altitudes. The pilots have been briefed to maintain a certain speed during the bomb run, but this is impossible with the heavy load of bombs and the still-heavy load of fuel aboard. So the Superfortresses come into their positions for the IP with every ounce of power in their great engines; the speed gain is slight, but not the power, and the thrashing propellers drag the bombers to greater heights.

The navigator chants into the interphone, counting down the seconds to the IP, where the pilot will turn for the run over the blazing target. "Four—three—two—one—start your turn now. . . ."

Now the IP is behind the airplane, and the B-29 is committed to the test of fire. The pilot pushes forward on the control column and there comes another change in sound, meaningful to the experienced. The nose goes down, the labored rhythm of the engines eases as the propellers spin faster. The giant airplane is moving downhill now, and she runs before her power, weight, and gravity and drops out of the sky in the long, slanting race. Then there is all the speed that the pilot needs, and the control column inches back.

A new sound comes; subdued, but meaningful to the men aboard the airplanes. It is a change in the sound of wind. The bombardier coordinates with his pilot, and a switch has been closed. Four doors are open now, exposing the hellish cargo carried in the two great bays.

With a peal of thunder the bombers rush toward downtown Tokyo. What had first been a distant glow, is now a shifting, writhing mass on the earth. Tokyo does not exist; at least not the heart of the city. The earth itself has been torn away by a great blade of burning steel. There is left a jagged tear, a massive, gaping fissure in the earth itself. It pulses with fire like a live creature. Separated from the people below by several thousand feet of superheated air, the bomber crews see the streets only as avenues and rivers of fire. People burn, their skin peeled suddenly like grapes thrown into a furnace, but all of this is hidden from the air.

Even at this instant a living wall of flame sweeps through Tokyo. Not a pillar of fire, or a great mass of flame, but literally a tidal wave of flame that advanced over the earth, devouring everything combustible in its path. It leaves behind it embers and lesser fires, total death and ashes and the remnants of terror in the form of bodies charred and pulverized by heat that cannot be believed.

From the air this wall of fire is not sharp and defined, but yet it is visible. The men in the bombers look down and do not believe what they see. The base of the wave is streaked with white; the intense, impossible white that comes from an arc lamp, or the heart of a pressure-fed, white-hot blast furnace. The city is an ocean, a great churning mass burning and writhing in its own cremation.

But there is no end to it. The radarmen in the B-29's stare into their scopes and shout to the bombardiers, "Drop 'em! Drop your bombs! The scope is blank—drop 'em now!"

And another seven tons of hell spill into the city, cascading earthward to feed the creature below that is consuming Tokyo with its ravenous, unquenchable thirst of fire.

What began in Tokyo at fifteen minutes past midnight was an incipient firestorm. This was the same kind of towering flame that had consumed the heart of the German city of Hamburg and other great urban centers in the Reich. All the conditions were ripe in Tokyo for the greatest blaze ever known: building density and the inflammability of the target area promised a firestorm reaching to fifteen or twenty thousand feet above the earth.

The concentration of bombs per square mile—and in a period of only a few hours—exceeded in severity the attack on Hamburg by the Royal Air Force. But there was no firestorm—and all because of a wind.

Assuming combustibility and building density, a fire-storm requires the creation of tens of thousands of individual fires within a limited area and in a short period of time. In merging, these fires create immediately a cyclonic effect, as do all large fires.

In the absence of a prevailing ground wind, the fires rapidly merge into great central blazes, all drawing in air from the perimeter of their flames. The suction of these flames overcomes natural prevailing weather; the several great fires join into a single blaze that is known as the firestorm. In Hamburg this fire reached fantastic proportions, producing heat on the periphery of the fire of 1,472 degrees Fahrenheit and winds of hurricane force. Everything within the firestorm was utterly consumed; if it could burn, it burned. If it could not burn, it often melted. Any living creature trapped within the periphery of the firestorm was doomed.

Within ten to twenty minutes after the original flaming X was carved into the heart of downtown Tokyo, conditions were even more favorable for a firestorm than they had been in Hamburg in July of 1943, with the one exception of an existing surface wind at the moment the fires began to leap upward.

At this period in the attack, nature itself decided the outcome of the flames. Without that wind, an enormous pillar of fire would have leaped into existence. Because of the wind, the potential firestorm was transformed at once into an even deadlier force—*the sweep conflagration*.

Just as Hamburg in July of 1943 became the first city in history ever to know the firestorm, so Tokyo in March of 1945 became the world's first city ever to suffer the sweep conflagration. A technical term, sweep conflagration means something quite different from "a large fire blazing out of control." What leaped into being in Tokyo was literally a tidal wave of flame.

As the fires ignited by the initial attack flashed through the inflammable Japanese homes, they shot almost instantly high above the buildings. The spread of fire was beyond belief; it was like a great forest fire blazing in dry timber. Under these conditions fire does not simply spread, it *explodes* as it moves along. It gathers itself into great blazing spheres and like a living creature leaps from building to building, shoots across hundreds of feet, and smothers its objective in a great searing flash that in an instant transforms an entire block, or group of blocks, into an inferno.

Whipped by 28 mile-per-hour surface winds, the fires spread rapidly to leeward. But as they did so, they merged with new fires already started, pools of flame and heat and suction from the tens of thousands of magnesium bombs blazing fiercely, unchecked, ignored by the Japanese who fled for their lives.

The tidal wave began to gather its strength.

A pillar of flame appeared, grew to a solid wall of fire leaping high above the blazing rooftops. Then it bowed to the increasing force of the wind, and began to bend.

It bent more and more toward the ground, like the curving lip of a great breaker about to smash itself against a rocky shore. Only the breaker is alive, an enormous, thundering comber of flame. The higher the wind, the more the pillar leans over.

The more it leans over, the closer the flaming gases and searing radiated heat come to the combustible materials on the ground. And, the closer the pillar—extending rapidly on each side—comes to the ground, the richer the content of the oxygen it burns. Correspondingly, its temperature is higher. In Tokyo on this night, it exceeded the fantastic level of 1,800 degrees Fahrenheit!

The chief characteristic of this sweep conflagration, to approach it in a clinical sense, is the presence of a massed fire front, an extended wall of fire that moves to leeward, preceded by a mass of preheated vapors so hot that it can bring unconciousness and even death to the victims caught in its path.

This is what was happening below the B-29's as they came in over Tokyo, at altitudes extending from 4,200 feet to 9,000 feet.

Below them, everywhere, incredible agony stalked the blazing streets. People were dying, roasting alive, by the thousands. But it could not be seen or felt from the air. There were the slashing flames and the fantastic mixtures of color—white and orange and crimson—the great masses of superheated, flaming gases that shot ahead of the fire wall like the jet from a gigantic furnace. There were great boiling clouds of smoke that thundered upward from the flaming carnage, smoke that momentarily obscured from view the fire, but could never hide the deep, angry, glowing, fearful red. It was as though the men looked down upon the surface of a planet still in its throes of creation, still lashed and whipped by vast and terrible volcanic fury.

There was fear in Tokyo below the airplanes, and also hate. Many a Japanese gunner died at his post, screaming hate and pumping shells futilely into the air, until a blast of superheated air exploded his clothes and hair and body into flames.

Until the guns were overrun by heat or flame, Tokyo showed its defiance. Tracers and shells and rockets spat into the air. The guns fired until the barrels turned white hot and began to melt. No less than forty-two of the great raiders were hit; these flew home to show their scars to the men on Saipan or Guam, or perhaps Iwo or Tinian.

Nine of the great bombers fell into the city of Tokyo, to contribute by their very death to the savage flames. Another five, crippled but flyable, managed to stagger away from Tokyo, to reach out to the south to the ocean, finally to ditch on the water. All five crews were saved.

The men in the bombers had never known anything like what was happening to them. The skies over Tokyo became a sea of absolute violence, a vast devil's cauldron boiling and raging. Tremendous blows smashed at the wings and the bodies of the Superfortresses. Waves of heat danced and shimmered visibly.

The thermals that soared upward from Tokyo were too much to believe. Sixty-ton bombers were flung about like matchsticks; B-29's at five thousand feet were thrust upward in a few seconds to eight or nine thousand feet. More than likely these thermal forces were as important as the anti-aircraft fire in downing several of the bombers. If a pilot attempted to hold his bombing altitude against the violent vertical columns of superheated air, he would exceed the structural limitations of his plane. It was as if he had shoved the control column all the way forward and dived the airplane at great speed until the wings collapsed.

The thermals spread out four miles laterally from the center of the fire. Japanese fighter pilots in the air over Tokyo reported they were unable to control their light airplanes, that they were flung helplessly around the sky and could not swing into pursuit curves to attack the racing B-29's.

"Gusts from the inferno were so powerful," wrote one sergeant, "that the men were rattled around inside the ships like dice in a cup. Floor boards were uprooted. All loose equipment was hurled about like shrapnel. More than one man was hurt that night because of those violent thermals."

B-29's at six thousand feet were caught by the shattering force of the superheated air, and flipped upside down, onto their backs. Often the planes fell several thousand feet before the shaken pilots could recover.

One bomber was caught in a particularly severe rising column of superheated air. Without warning the heavy airplane shot skyward, the pilot helpless at the controls. Within several seconds the airplane was flung from seven thousand to more than twelve thousand feet; the nose flashed upward, went straight up, and in those few seconds the B-29 was inverted at nearly two and a half miles above the city. By some miracle, the Superfortress completed its maneuver with the crew and all loose gear against the ceiling, fell down and back in a screaming loop, and streaked earthward. With both the pilot and copilot straining with all their might the airplane came out of its wild plunge only two hundred feet over Tokyo Bay. Wings bent sharply upward from the terrible strain, the B-29 leveled out at nearly 450 miles per hour and went howling out of range of the shore guns before the astonished Japanese could react.

The men in the early waves reported that, from a mile and a half above, the city looked like a vast bed of red-hot and burned-out embers. Those who flew over Tokyo in the final waves said they could almost hear the city screaming in its agony. The streets were barely visible in the midst of the sea of flames. Along the fire front the fire was a blinding white. Where the great tidal wave had passed whole city blocks glowed a dark red.

In many parts of the city even the dark lines of streets had vanished, spattered with strange flickering lights. These were burning trees and telephone poles, the fires getting the contents of a fireproof building, the scorched shell of a truck or a trolley car. Buildings had collapsed into the streets, gas lines flamed. Tokyo had become a slag heap, a garish wasteland of still-burning wreckage.

But above all else, there was one thing which brought home vividly what was happening down there in one of the world's greatest cities.

Because of the low altitudes of the mission, the B-29's remained unpressurized. The men did not need to wear their oxygen masks.

Inside the airplanes the fumes swept in from the city. A mist began to fill the cabins; a strange mist, blood-red in color.

The men could not bear what that mist brought with it.

Choking, spluttering, coughing—many of them vomiting forcefully—they grabbed their masks, slapped the rubber to their faces, drank in gratefully of the clean oxygen.

They could take everything else. But not the overpowering, sweet-sick stench of the burning flesh that permeated the skies two miles over the tortured city.

Essays

8   The Legacy of Dresden

Edward Jablonski

The final selection in this unit is the epilogue to Flying Fortress, *Edward Jablonski's biography of the B-17 heavy bomber in World War II. Jablonski's essay serves as a counterweight to critical accounts (such as Rolf Hochhuth's devastating play,* Soldiers) *of the policy of saturation bombing. This historian, biographer, and lifelong aviation enthusiast is entirely convinced that the Allied Air attacks were militarily and morally justified. Jablonski argues that, after all, the Germans began it all by bombing undefended cities. And, he concludes, even if Allied bombing were "uncivilized"—which he stoutly denies—it was not remotely comparable to the incivilities the Nazis perpetrated at Dachau and Auschwitz.*

When Göring boasted before the onset of the Second World War that his *Luftwaffe* would make it impossible for an enemy aircraft to fly over the Reich (he referred specifically to the industrial Ruhr), there were few among his admirers who would have attempted to contradict the pink, beaming, arrogant, and cherubic German *Reichsmarschall*.

Less than a month later his *Luftwaffe* demonstrated what it could do in coordination with the German troops and Panzer divisions. The Germans introduced the concept of lightning warfare—the blitzkrieg—to the world. With ruthless and characteristic disregard for anything but its own ends, the apparently indomitable German war machine raced across Poland, crushing everything in its path.

The *Luftwaffe* was employed mainly as a tactical adjunct to the ground forces, its screaming Stukas terrorizing the refugees choking the roads in an attempt to flee the battle zones. But there were actually no clearly defined battle zones in the style of good old-fashioned war; as the Stukas strafed the columns, clearing a path for the advancing Wehrmacht, they left behind them a terror of confusion and death. The Germans had also introduced the concept of modern total war in which all, soldiers and civilians, were grist for the mills of Mars.

The Polish Air Force, weak and equipped with obsolete aircraft, was no match for the Messerschmitts which were faster and more heavily armed than anything the Poles could muster. In about two days of war the Polish Air Force no longer existed, wiped out on the ground.

Within twenty-seven days after crossing the Polish border in an undeclared war (after, of course, providing for an "incident"), the Germans were in possession of Warsaw. With the Russians moving in from the east and the Germans from the west, the Poles had no chance.

Göring's *Luftwaffe* had proved itself, particularly in its devastating ground support with the frightful Stukas (these were equipped with noise-making devices which added to the terror), and in contending with inferior and outnumbered Polish and French aircraft. Obviously the preening Göring knew whereof he boasted. That his 1500 or so long-range bombers were primarily intended for tactical support of land army operations or, because of a deficiency in armament, might prove easy victims to heavily armed fighters seemed unimportant in the heady run of victories.

The only opponent, actually, confronting Germany was Britain. Both adversaries approached the employment of strategic bombardment warily and tentatively, confining their attacks mostly to strictly military targets or the dropping of leaflets upon enemy cities.

And then occurred the first bombing of a city of little military importance. During the afternoon of May 10, 1940, three bombers appeared over the German city of Freiburg, attacked and left behind fifty-seven dead, thirteen of them children.

"This kind of aerial terrorism is the product of sick minds of the plutocratic world-destroyers," Dr. Goebbels would say three years later. "A long chain of human suffering in all German cities blitzed by the Allies has borne witness against them and their cruel and cowardly leaders—from the murder of German children in Freiburg on May 10, 1940, right up to the present day."

Herr Goebbels did not reveal of course that he knew then, and in 1940, that the planes that bombed Freiburg were Heinkel 111s which had been dispatched to bomb a fighter airfield in France, got lost in the clouds, and bombed one of their own cities. Nor did Goebbels refer to the bombing of Rotterdam, which occurred four days after the bombing of Freiburg, a systematic, methodical, and one would be tempted to say Germanically thorough, destruction of a portion of an open city.

"Rotterdam," General Henri Winkelman, the Dutch commander announced, "bombed this afternoon, suffered the fate of total war . . . We have ceased to struggle."

The German bombers, ironically, dropped their bombs on the center of Rotterdam at the same time that surrender negotiations were under way. Although propaganda at the time exaggerated the casualties (30,000), the sixty or so attacking He-111s literally saturated the city with bombs killing about 980 and rendering 78,000 homeless. Although the attack could not be termed strategic, for it had been brought to bear as ground support, the distinction to the people of Rotterdam was unimportant. The British initiated, thereafter, the strategic assault upon the Ruhr on May 15-16.

Even more importantly, the Germans emphasized the concept of total war: people against people, not army against army. The tragedy is that, like the Freiburg bombing, the wiping out of Rotterdam was probably an error. The attacking planes continued on to Rotterdam although they had been called back when it became known that surrender negotiations had begun.

It has been said that war is an art; it is not. War is a succession of more or less controlled calamity—and even what control exists (which is never revealed on large-scale maps with their impressive lines and arrows) is frightfully dependent upon whim, chance, luck, and any number of unpredictable variables.

Germany had launched the Second World War and it had won impressive victories by using quite new methods of warfare. When its juggernaut leaped over the supposedly impregnable Maginot line, Germany proved, even more than the military realized, that the concept of the static "front line" was truly passé. So was the innocent civilian, many of whom lay strewn along the roads of Poland, in the center of Rotterdam and—ironically—Freiburg.

The gloves were off. On the night of August 24-25, 1940, bombs fell on the city of London for the first time since the First World War. On the night of August 25-26 the RAF dropped bombs upon Berlin. Thus was begun the reprisal raids, a deadly stick-on-the-shoulder retaliatory game in which each power took turns in attacking the cities of the other.

The RAF carried the war into the Ruhr Valley and the Germans, recalling the boast of Göring began to ask bitterly, "Where is Hermann Meier?" The air raid sirens, which wailed with unrelenting regularity, were called "Meier's Hunting Horns." Total war was turned upon its practitioners.

Since the war the Germans, somewhat encouraged and backed by some British writers, have adopted a curious pose in reference to the subject of the strategic air war. In a curiously dishonest book, *The Bombing of Germany* (Holt, Rinehart and Winston, 1963), the German writer Hans Rumpf marshals a battery of cold, precise statistics which are used to suggest that the real victim of the Second World War was Germany. The most chilling aspect of the book, however, is its tacit acceptance of war itself, just so long as it is "civilized" and, no doubt, fought on German terms. Although the American Air Forces are blackened here and there in the book, it is the RAF which is painted as the most cruel villain. Because, early in the war, the RAF learned that it was unable (like the Germans during the Battle of Britain and the London Blitz) to take the terrible losses which were inevitable during day bombing raids and had concentrated on nighttime bombing, the concept of "area" bombing was adopted.

This meant that when a military target was to be hit at night, the only possible means of actually hitting it (and frequently it was missed altogether) was by saturating the area in which the target lay. The result was that dwellings around the target area were also struck, civilians killed and wounded and their homes destroyed. This was regarded as perfectly proper for London, Birmingham, Portsmouth, and Coventry but unlawful and cruel when applied to Essen, Kassel, Stuttgart, Berlin, and Hamburg. In short, the concept of half a war.

In *The Bombing of Germany*, Herr Rumpf employs such phrases as a "lawful act of war," the "ideals of humanitarianism in war" and the "acknowledged laws of humanity in war," as if such exist and as if these were practiced by the Germans and not by the Allies. War, then, is acceptable if played according to rules.

Rules imply legality, but strategic bombardment was not a legal form of war. True, the bulk of the American bombs fell upon military targets but as the war reached the climax before the bloody *finale*, even the Americans helped the British destroy the lovely little German cities.

The facts assembled by Herr Rumpf are carefully chosen, just as other facts (especially those pertaining to German atrocities) are ignored.

Without a doubt the Germans suffered and terribly, the innocent along with the guilty. But in the glorious days of the Third Reich who did not belong to the Master Race and who did not worship at the altar of Hitler and who did not condone the acts of war, as long as things were going well?

Even the "good" German generals who were, after all, exponents of the fine classic approach to war, did not attempt to depose Hitler because he had committed crimes against all human reason but because he was giving the German military caste a bad name. As a war leader, the mad little World War I corporal was to prove himself the Allies' "own dearest enemy."

The German cities and their inhabitants paid for all this. So long as the war remained in Poland, France, Holland, and Britain it was a nice war. But when "Meier's Hunting Horns" began to blow and their cities were destroyed, their homes burned, their children killed, it was not a very glorious war after all.

That terrible personal tragedies on an enormous scale resulted from strategic bombardment cannot be denied, but it does seem that the popular position since the war is an attempt, as followed the First World War, to misplace the guilt. Had Hitler and his cheering, triumphant Germans never invaded Poland in 1939 then it is very likely that Dresden would not have been all but obliterated in 1945.

Impressive numbers are appalling, but so is each individual tragedy. Piling on of detail after detail of how terribly many innocent German women and children were killed is also awesome, but death by freezing in a supposed medical study is no less terrible than being fused with the street paving by fire.

Strategic bombardment has been called a failure because it did not always eradicate the military installations or factories it was supposed to bomb. Nor did it break civilian morale as many believed it would. These so-called "terror raids" were not the main objective of the RAF area bombings but merely a hoped for side effect. The Battle of Britain had amply proved that the human spirit is capable of withstanding impossible punishment; there was no reason to believe that the Berliner was less brave than the Londoner.

Of all German cities, Berlin was struck most often and most heavily—no less than 363 attacks—during which 45,517 tons of bombs were dropped. Berlin was, as has been said, both a military as well as political target, the heart of Hitler's Germany. It was a costly target to hit and the Allies suffered great losses over Berlin, with its ring of flak guns and fighters. After the *Luftwaffe*—which is rapidly becoming the scapegoat responsible for Germany's losing the war—was neutralized, it could not defend the German capital as well as it would have liked. But when the fighters rose to attack the bomber formations they fought gallantly and desperately. The "Big B" was never a popular target for the bomber crews. But when the war came to a close, it had been reduced to rubble as had many other historic cities.

If examples of medieval architecture, such as that at Dresden, were destroyed, so were the exponents of primordial political ethics and social concepts. Tragically, the innocent suffered and the innocent did not number among them merely the classic examples of women, children, and the aged. The great masses of soldiers were equally innocent. The Germans had permitted themselves to be deluded and led by madmen into committing massive brutalities that still jars the imagination and belief. One day they found themselves in a burning asylum. Hitler had built a fortress around Europe and, in the phrase of Franklin D. Roosevelt, "forgot to put a roof on it."

Great architectural treasures were devastated (as they also had been in London and Coventry) and examples of art, too, were destroyed in the frightful fire storms. But one wonders how much of that art had been looted from conquered countries.

In total war there really are no innocent civilians, for the means are produced by them. Civilians supply the weapons, the ammunition and even the beautifully efficient German ovens. Thus a good German businessman appealed to the SS in Belgrade for business, saying in reference to "equipment . . . for the burning of bodies" that he was "submitting plans for our perfected cremation ovens which operate with coal and which have hitherto given full satisfaction." The firm, C.H. Kori, went so far as to "guarantee the effectiveness of the cremation ovens as well as their durability, the use of the best materials and our faultless workmanship."

Nothing was too good for the 5,000,000 enemies of the German Reich.

Although knowledge of the death camps was denied by Germans after the war, such an open bid for business would tend to obviate that. Undoubtedly large numbers of Germans were unaware of extermination camps, but they were unaware of a lot of aspects of the Thousand Year Reich. All they knew was that the weak, ineffectual British and Americans were flying over with their Lancasters and Flying Fortresses and teaching them how to war.

They would look up, and then around them asking, "Where's Hermann Meier?" Where was the *Luftwaffe*? Where was the fuel, the oil and the steel? The now damned strategic bombardment program had wiped them out. While it was not a complete success, it was not a failure and without question contributed to the fall of Germany. This was accomplished at great cost to the young men—none of them brutal killers, nor, for that matter were their leaders—who flew in the heavy bombers.

Young American lives (and British too) were lost in great air battles. It was a fearful kind of barter, the hope being that each life might be traded for a moment or an hour nearer the war's end. There was no means of knowing, at the time, whether or not this would prove true. We now know that the casualty toll for the 8th and 15th Air Forces up to May 8, 1945, was 24,288 killed, 18,804 wounded, 31,436 taken prisoner, and 18,699 missing. A great number of the missing have never been heard from and may be presumed dead. The loss rate of bomber crews, if analyzed statistically, was second only to the infantry.

Had the price paid achieved the hoped for results? A year after the war's end Senator Elbert D. Thomas of Utah published an article in a popular magazine in which he stated that "One of the outstanding hoaxes of military history was the myth of 'precision bombing.' There was no such thing." He then proceeded to prove his point with an amazing compendium of misinformation and a surprising ignorance of the mission of the air forces.

Those who had suffered the weight of this mission, professional airmen and others who should have known, had other views. *Generaleutnant* Adolf Galland, who had commanded the fighter forces for a time, said, "In my opinion, it was the Allied bombing of our oil industries that had the greatest effect on German war potential . . . [Also] disorganization of German communications in the West by strategic bombing caused withdrawal to the German frontiers. In the last two months of the war, the crippling of the German transport system brought about the final collapse."

Alfred Krupp, head of the German armament empire, stated that "Allied air attacks left only 40 per cent of the Krupp works able to operate . . . These plants of mine, and German industry as a whole, were more hampered by lack of speedy and adequate transportation facilities since the beginning of 1943 than by anything else."

General Feldmarschall Hugo Sperrle said, "Allied bombing was the dominant factor in the success of the [Normandy] invasion. I believe the initial landing could have been made without assistance from the air forces, but the breakthrough that followed would have been impossible without the massive scale of bombing, particularly of German communications far in the rear. Allied air power was the chief factor in Germany's defeat."

The broken and deposed Hermann Göring had this to say: "Allied precision bombing had a greater effect on the defeat of Germany than area bombing, because destroyed cities can be evacuated but destroyed industry was difficult to replace.

"Allied selection of targets was good, particularly in regard to oil. As soon as we started to repair an oil installation, you always bombed it again before we could produce one ton.

"We didn't concentrate on the four-engine Focke-Wulf planes as heavy bombers because we were developing the He-177 and the Me-264, which was designed to go to America and return . . ."

Thus the defeated proclaimed immediately after the fall of the Third Reich. Since then, however, out of the ashes have risen such apologists as Hans Rumpf who revealed a decided lack of remorse and little more than passing recognition of the fact that Hitler, backed by Germans grown arrogant and rapacious by easy victories, had plunged the world into total war.

All that seems to remain of historical fact is that the Germans suffered heavily at the hands of the Allies and, ultimately, through betrayals, or because of Hitler (just like "the last time" of the Kaiser's war) lost. Few of these apologists speculate on what kind of a world it might have been had the Germans won—or to what military extremes they might have gone had they been able.

Much is made of Germany's inability to strike back at the Allies in kind—that is, with heavy retaliatory strategic bombing. This was not Nazi humanitarianism but rather simple ineffectuality. The German Air Force had not been designed for strategic bombardment and when Hitler awakened to its possibilities, it was too late: the RAF and the U.S. Air Force had canceled it out for him. However, had Germany been able to launch its "New York Bomber" (the Me-264, wistfully mentioned by Göring), armed with an atomic bomb (on which the Germans were working) there can be no doubting that New York would have suffered heavily during the Second World War.

As it was, the V-1s and V-2s were pointed in the general direction of England with no real knowledge of where they would actually come to earth. England itself—and her people, the old, women, and children—was the target; military definitions no longer held.

The basic error in the thinking of so many who now decry the "work" of the strategic bombardment forces is that, as stated by military analyst Liddel Hart, it was "the most uncivilized method of warfare the world has known since the Mongol devastations."

What, indeed, is civilized about any aspect of war? It is not the means, but war itself which is the major tragic illusion. Still, there are those who are willing to accept it so long as it can be played according to the rules of the nineteenth century.

This is their theme, just at it is the theme of the tract by Rumpf, one of whose chapters is entitled "At Least There Was No Gas War." There was—at Dachau, at Buchenwald, at Mauthausen and Auschwitz.

Unit VI

Of War Crimes and Operational Necessity

The punishment of soldiers by their own governments for having committed criminal acts during wartime was not unique to World War II. Precedents for such action can be found throughout the history of war, and a contemporary parallel exists in the My Lai trials. As yet, however, the decision of the victorious nations in the Second World War to prosecute various officials of the defeated powers for "war crimes" is unique. The problems of what constitutes war crimes and how and by whom such acts may be punished were placed on a wholly new basis in this war. "International military tribunals" were set up to try Germans and Japanese charged with having committed war crimes. The punishment of such persons via judicial procedures was itself revolutionary, for international law had not previously recognized individuals as being subject to its jurisdiction. These courts were further empowered to deal with three broad categories of war crimes: criminal acts related to battlefield conduct, waging aggressive war, and crimes against humanity. Prosecution of persons for the latter two crimes was a startling departure since they had neither been defined nor identified as criminal offenses before the war began. It is therefore understandable that the Nuremberg and Tokyo trials stimulated tremendous controversy.

Basic to the issues in this unit is the question whether "war" and "crime" are not mutually exclusive, whether ethical standards have any meaning in time of war. Many have argued that war itself is the negation of morality. Indeed, moral relativists oppose the concept of war crimes on the basis that participants in modern war are required to use any means necessary to achieve victory. It would seem that the practice of total war—the killing of as many of the enemy as expeditiously as possible—has rendered a complete mockery of the "laws of war" and, thus, of war crimes. Even in the Second World War, however, certain rules governing the conduct of warfare were recognized as having practical value and were therefore espoused, if not always followed, by the belligerents. For example, there existed elaborate regulations on the treatment of the wounded, prisoners of war, and dead on land and at sea; on the protection of medical personnel; on the responsibilities toward civilian internees; and on the rights and duties arising from occupation of enemy territory. Failure to observe rules accepted as articles of the law of war justified criminal prosecution of the guilty parties. It may be said as a general principle that, only if war is viewed as the total collapse of ethical values (mob violence) or, alternatively, as a holy crusade, may it be claimed that *all* efforts to control wartime conduct are meaningless.

As has been noted, regulation of new weapons was achieved rarely—or too late—through international law. Chemical and biological warfare had been outlawed by the Geneva Protocol of 1925. But there was no similarly effective outlawry or control of the bomber airplane and the submarine—for a very simple reason. World War I experience had shown that gas warfare was difficult to control, dangerous to user and victim alike, and not really effective. Bombers and submarines displayed no such disadvantages. Properly used, they might prove war-winning weapons; thus no nation was willing to abandon them. It should be remembered that the chief bulwarks of international law are expediency and concern for precedent.

Even where law did exist, there was no guarantee that it would be applied justly. In the absence of absolute moral standards, the plea of "operational necessity" carries considerable logical appeal. Who is to decide when a particular act is an atrocity or a legitimate measure of self-protection? The Japanese pilot who machine-gunned parachuting American fliers could argue that if he did not kill them they might shoot him down the next day. The German U-boat commander could contend that personnel from the ship he had just torpedoed, if not silenced, might call down on him the fury of an antisubmarine task force. Operational necessity was used as a defense for conduct that would be considered brutal and reprehensible by peacetime standards. An additional complication was the familiar assertion by defendants in war-crimes trials that they "were just following orders," that they should not be made to bear personal responsibility for action carried out at the behest of higher authority.

The prosecution of enemy persons for the crimes of "waging aggressive war" and "crimes against humanity" confounded these already confusing issues.

The Bataan Death March, the Malmedy massacre, the annihilation of Lidice were but particularly terrible episodes in a clear pattern of Axis brutality toward Allied soldiers and civilians. And, of course, the Nazis' cold-blooded slaughter of Europe's Jews occupied a unique plane of cruelty. It was certain that acts of savagery so incredible and perverse as to defy comprehension had been committed. But on what grounds and by what authority could those who had started this war and had killed millions of innocent people be brought to justice?

The fateful decision of the Allies to use the mechanisms of international law must be counted as less than totally successful. The idea of crimes against humanity defined as genocide was rejected by the Nuremberg Tribunal. Axis leaders were convicted of the "crime" of waging aggressive war; but it is doubtful whether this decision, which raised many more questions than it answered, will ever serve as a legal precedent.

We should not be surprised that the war-crimes trials of World War II have left an ambiguous legacy. Despite their judicial trappings, they were the products of political expediency and naked force, and thus the conclusions they reached are in some measure suspect. If the Axis had won the Second World War, would Allied leaders have been tried for war crimes? Would Churchill, Stalin, and Roosevelt have been accused of fomenting a war of aggression? Might not a major indictment have been the Anglo-American policy of saturation bombing? By what authority *does* one side declare that the other is guilty of war crimes? Were the war-crimes trials after World War II examples of "victor's justice," or were they legitimate and necessary acts by nations representing the conscience of mankind?

Documents

1 The Bataan Death March

International Military Tribunal for the Far East

Brutal treatment of prisoners of war occurred with dismaying frequency during World War II. Both sides were guilty of atrocities, but probably the most infamous episode of this sort was Japanese cruelty toward American and Filipino POW's during the "Bataan Death March." In April, 1942, some 76,000 defenders of the fortress of Corregidor surrendered to the Japanese army. During a subsequent march up the Bataan Peninsula to prison camps outside Manila, these men were deprived of adequate medical treatment and sanitary facilities, given little food and water, and subjected to vicious physical abuse. Many were slain. It has been estimated that between 8,000 and 12,000 of the marchers died from disease, starvation, beatings, or execution. The official Japanese viewpoint, reflecting their belief that surrender was cowardly, was the most blatant form of the "operational-necessity" argument: "To show Allied prisoners mercy is to prolong the war."

We present as our next witness, Donald F. Ingle, to testify as to mistreatment, torture, and improper conditions at the Prisoners of War Camps at Nicholes Field and Pasay.

Donald F. Ingle, called as a witness on behalf of the prosecution, being first duly sworn, testified as follows:

Direct Examination by Mr. Lopez:

Q Please give us your full name, age, position and address.

A My name is Donald Ingle, age is 27 and my permanent address is Laurel, Illinois.

Q Were you with the United States Army that surrendered at Bataan in April of 1942?

From **International Military Tribunal for the Far East: Proceedings**, VII (Washington, D.C.: U.S. Government Printing Office). Microfilm edition.

A Yes.

Q At the time of surrender what was the state of your health?

A Well, in the first part of April of 1942 I had contracted malaria and it was suspected that I had pneumonia, so I was sent to the rear to Field Hospital No. 1. About 30 minutes after my arrival there Japanese planes appeared overhead and bombed the hospital on 3 consecutive runs.

Q Were you wounded?

A I was wounded, well, minorly, in the right shoulder.

The President: Did the hospital have Red Cross signs of any kind?

The Witness: Yes, the hospital was plainly marked.

Q What part of the building was marked?

A There were several wards and on the top of each of the buildings was a large red cross.

Q At the time of the actual surrender where were you, please?

A I was at—Just after the bombing a medical officer came by and asked if I was seriously wounded. I told him, "no," and he ordered me to leave the area. So, I wandered up the road about a kilometer to USAFFE Headquarters bivouac area at Kilometer Post 165.

Q Were you in bed when the first Japanese soldier approached and placed you under arrest?

A I was lying on a stretcher under a tree. It was the only type of bed available. I was—

Q Where were you lying in this stretcher?

A In the USAFFE bivouac area.

Q I said, "why?"

A I did have bronchial pneumonia and malaria. My temperature was 105.6.

Q What did the Japanese soldier do to you?

A The first one that approached prodded me in the back with a bayonet, ordered me to stand up. Well, I complied with as much alacrity as possible and in the next few minutes he took from me my watch, ring and everything in my billfold with the exception of a couple of pictures which I managed to convince him were those of my mother.

Q Did he see that you were plainly sick?

A I would say it was comparatively obvious.

Q Despite the fact that you were sick were you forced to join the Death March?

A Yes.

Q How long did it take you to make it?

A 9 days.

Q During the march did you have food and water provided for you by the Japanese?

A For the first five days not a drop of food or water or rest was given by any of the Japanese.

Q Where did you get your water?

A Well, there were many that didn't get any, many that died that tried to get water. All that was available was from an occasional artesian well along the side of the road or possibly a caribou well. That water in the ponds and in the ditches was so polluted that it was highly dangerous to drink and that which came from the artesian wells was of such small amount that when the great numbers of men tried to get it, well, the troops would simply raise their weapons and fire into the group and when the smoke and dust cleared away it was proven that pure water could cause your death as well as polluted water.

Q During the first five days how were you able to manage to get some food, if at all?

A The Filipino civilians tried on many occasions to give food to the men that were marching. However, they done so at the risk of their lives and a lot of the civilians did lose their lives trying. Other than that, only an occasional sugar cane patch offered food and even that was at the risk of your life.

Q How were you treated during the march by the Japanese guards?

A Well, even the lack of food could have been stood and I suppose that going without water could have been taken, but a person must have rest. But the continued marching and sitting for hours in the hot sun, undergoing search after search by members of the Japanese Army, continual harrassing; members, friends, buddies right close being taken out of column and shot or bayonetted for no reason, was a continual strain.

Q Do you recall a Captain by the name of—a Chaplain by the name of Captain Day?

A Yes, he is an Episcopalian Chaplain, I believe.

Q Was he with you during the march, please?

A There were thousands of men in the march but we ordinarily were segregated into groups of one hundred, for the convenience of the guards, I would assume, and Chaplain Day was in the same group of one hundred that I was in.

Q Will you kindly tell us what happened to the Chaplain, Captain Day, during the march?

A Well, Chaplain Day had taken a drink from a stream or pond beside the road and had contracted dysentery. As a result it was necessary for him to answer Nature's call several times every day every few minutes. His usual procedure was to step out of line quickly, relieve himself and back into the column. It was only a matter of a few seconds. On one occasion he followed the same procedure and a Japanese guard nearby spotted him and immediately charged up. Well, before the Chaplain could regain his place in ranks the Japanese charged and wounded him with his bayonet.

Q After the Chaplain was wounded did you aid him, Mr. Ingle?

A I was one of several that helped to aid him. I personally helped carry him until the next rest period and throughout the following days we took turns, two men at a time helping the Chaplain on the march.

Q Could the Japanese guards see with their own eyes that here is a Chaplain wounded?

A Rank or branch of service meant nothing. As I just stated, we were in groups of one hundred and I recall one day very vividly there were sixteen

Americans out of the group of one hundred men that I was in—sixteen of those men were taken from the ranks and bayonetted, killed, and left by the roadside in one day.

Q What I was trying to say to you, Mr. Ingle, was this: Notwithstanding the fact that Captain Day was wounded, he was made to continue to march and he was given no medical treatment; was that it?

A Not only wasn't he given any medical treatment but if we had not been able to assist him or hadn't assisted him, then he, too, would have been left by the roadside because they would not tolerate anyone not being able to walk.

Q How many cases of killings and bayonettings or shootings did you actually see during the march?

A That I couldn't say accurately. I would say that when a thing becomes so commonplace you lose track of the importance of it so after the first few hundred I didn't try to keep track.

Q Those who were killed during the march, were they buried?

A They were usually rolled to the roadside. I have seen on occasions some of them buried, but mostly they were left lying where they were killed.

Q On the sixth day of your march how was it that you were able to get some food?

A We were informed through an interpreter that if we would turn in our watches, rings, and whatever valuables we had that we would be given food. By that time there was very few men that had those same valuables; however, those that did have were more than glad to give them up on the prospect of being fed and they did so. Well, we received the food that was promised all right. It was about, I would say, a teacupful of boiled rice, nothing more, nothing less, just boiled rice.

Q Were you given some salt to make it quite palatable?

A No salt.

Q On the 9th day what happened to you and your group?

A Well, I felt pretty relieved on the 9th day because we were informed we wouldn't walk anymore. We were going to ride. However, the relief was relatively short-lived. We found that we were to be crowded into the real small Filipino railroad cars, 100 men to the car.

Q Could you give us a rough idea of how crowded you were in one small car with 100 persons in [it]?

A With that many men in the car there were a number of men that never touched the floor from the beginning of the trip to the end. There were several men that fainted from lack of air in the back part of the car, and those men couldn't be tended; they couldn't be given any treatment because of the close quarters. There was five guards in the car, and they kept the space directly in front of the doors, and whenever the train stopped at each stop along the way the Filipino civilians tried to give us food and water, but the guards would run them away. . . .

Cross-Examination by Mr. Logan:

Q If the Tribunal please. Did you hold a commission—Mr. Ingle, is it?

A No.

Q I understand when you were taken prisoner your temperature was 105.6, and you said that the Japanese soldier obviously knew you were sick. How did he know that?

A Because I was lying on a stretcher in the heat of the day covered with about five blankets and a shelter-half.

Q Were you in the hospital?

A No.

Q Have you ever testified in any cases before?

A No.

Q With respect to any atrocities?

A No.

Q Do you know anything about who was in command of this Bataan death march?

A I didn't know the man personally, but it was General Homma from newspapers and, well, rumor—that would be discounted I suppose, but the talk was General Homma. He was everything, General Homma, he was in all the Philippine newspapers at that time.

Q Was that the General Homma who was executed?

A Yes.

Q But you don't know what rank the officer had who was in charge of the march itself, do you?

A How could I?

Q I do not know, Mr. Witness, I was not there. I thought you might know.

A I was a prisoner of people whom I had never seen except in markets in the United States. I didn't at that time know anything about the ranks in their military organizations.

Q You sound rather bitter about this, Mr. Ingle. Are you?

A Well, there are several thousand buddies that aren't here today that would be here if it weren't for that. Use your own judgment.

Mr. Logan: No further questions, your Honor. . . .

Cross-Examination by Mr. Shimanouchi:

Q Was it during the night or was it during the day that bombs fell on the field hospital at Bataan?

A It was during the day.

Q About what time?

A About 10 o'clock in the morning.

Q Was it fair or cloudy?

A It was very clear.

Q You said that bombs fell soon after you arrived at the field hospital. At the time were you inside the hospital or outside?

A I was outside.

Q Did you immediately go somewhere else?

A About, I would say, forty-five minutes later.

Q How were you transported?

A I walked.

Q How did you know that the roof of this hospital had the insignia of the Red Cross?

A Parts of the roofs were visible from the ground. They were very low buildings.

Q Were there any military installations near this hospital?

A I don't know.

Q Were there any important traffic junctions such as railway bridges or railway stations?

A No.

Q Was not the American military school which you attended a military installation? Was not USAFFE which you attended right after being discharged from the hospital a military installation? You said that after the hospital was bombed you went, you were sent to an American military school. Was that not a military installation?

A I said nothing about a school.

Q How far did you walk?

A The Number 1 hospital was about 167 and a half, I believe, kilometer post. USAFFE headquarters was at 165.

Q You walked that distance, didn't you?

A Yes.

Q Was the Japanese who woke you when you were lying under the branches of a tree an officer or an enlisted man?

A At that time I didn't know how to differentiate ranks in the Japanese military.

Q Did he have a rifle or a saber?

A He had a rifle.

Q Did this soldier speak English?

A He said "hello."

Q Did he speak any other words?

A No.

Q Then were you able to get across to him what kind of sickness you were suffering from?

A I didn't try to tell him I was sick.

Q You said that during the death march Chaplain Day was wounded by a bayonet. How seriously was he wounded?

A I am not a physician but the wound was of such depth and of serious enough extent that it took the aid of myself and friends to assist him that he might continue the march.

Q How did you—in what manner did you help him to walk?

The President: There is no need to answer that question which is utterly foolish.

Q How many days did you help him?

A That happened on the third or fourth day. We assisted him from then on until the ninth day, which was the termination of our hike.

Q Did your sickness become worse during this march?

A I seemed to have sweated out a portion of the malaria and temporarily I felt somewhat better.

Q What route did this death march take?

A I am not too familiar with the routes in the Philippines but I know that we passed up through the Pampanga Province and boarded the train at San Fernando, Pampanga.

Q Was this a mountain path or a wide road?

A A portion of it was through the jungle. The rest of it was through rice fields.

Q Was there not the possibility then that when the captives broke ranks to drink water that they would escape and it would be difficult for them to be found?

A In the area of the mountains where the roads were there were no artesian wells, and through the rice paddies and the belt where the sugar cane fields were in existence there was no vegetation close enough to the road to offer any possible cover for escaping soldiers.

Q Did freight carts and water carrying carts pass on that road?

A I don't recall.

Q Did the Japanese Army have some means of distributing water?

A There was quite heavy traffic on the road and even the water that was available in the village was, well, off limits to the marching men.

Q What was the situation of the American Army in Bataan in regard to food before the surrender?

A I wasn't with the quartermaster. I am not familiar with that.

Q The commander of the American troops in the Bataan area said that before the surrender provisions were one-fourth of the usual rations. Is that so?

The President: You are attempting to give evidence now. You know he isn't aware of the position. As he told you, he wasn't with the quartermaster.

Mr. Shimanouchi: I am just asking him whether the food rationed out to him was less or not.

A We were on a fighter's rations, two meals per day.

Q Did the Japanese troops march with the captives also?

A They changed guards about three times per day.

Q When they rested what kind of place did they rest in?

A Invariably in the open in a rice paddy.

Q Did the Japanese soldiers rest there also?

A Yes.

Q Where did the Japanese troops drink water?

A Whenever they felt like it.

Q Did they drink from streams?

A On many occasions they took canteens from the marching men if they had water in them. If they didn't have water in them they would throw the canteen to the roadside.

The President: Answer the question, witness. Did the Japanese soldiers drink from streams on the way?

The Witness: No.

Q You have testified that one hundred men were packed in one freight car. Is it not true that the railroads were damaged by the war and that there wasn't enough carriages to transport the men?

A I am not familiar with the railroad situation due to war damages.

The President: How broad and how long were the cars in feet?

The Witness: I would estimate about forty feet.

The President: How broad?

The Witness: Not more than eight feet. . . .

Cross-Examination by Mr. Levin:

Q What was the entire distance of your hike, as you call it?

A I started at 165 kilometer post and ended at San Fernando.

The President: How far was it? Just say. Have you ever worked it out?

Mr. Levin: The President asked you have you ever worked it out?

The President: How many miles or kilometers?

The Witness: It is about 100 kilometers. . . .

2 The Moscow Declaration on German Atrocities

On November 1, 1943, Roosevelt, Churchill, and Stalin signed a declaration that publicly stated the Allies' determination to punish those responsible for "atrocities, massacres, and executions" in the territories occupied by the Axis powers. Though this statement referred only to German acts, because the USSR was not at war with Japan, the policy proclaimed here was to be general in its application.

The United Kingdom, the United States and the Soviet Union have received from many quarters evidence of atrocities, massacres and cold-blooded mass executions which are being perpetrated by the Hitlerite forces in the many countries they have overrun and from which they are now being steadily expelled. The brutalities of Hitlerite domination are no new thing and all the

From **Foreign Relations of the United States, 1943,** I (Washington, D.C.: U.S. Government Printing Office, 1963), pp. 556–57.

peoples or territories in their grip have suffered from the worst form of government by terror. What is new is that many of these territories are now being redeemed by the advancing armies of the liberating Powers and that in their desperation, the recoiling Hitlerite Huns are redoubling their ruthless cruelties. This is now evidenced with particular clearness by monstrous crimes of the Hitlerites on the territory of the Soviet Union which is being liberated from the Hitlerites, and on French and Italian territory.

Accordingly, the aforesaid three allied Powers, speaking in the interests of the thirty-two [*thirty-three*] United Nations, hereby solemnly declare and give full warning of their declaration as follows:

At the time of the granting of any armistice to any government which may be set up in Germany, those German officers and men and members of the Nazi party who have been responsible for, or have taken a consenting part in the above atrocities, massacres and executions, will be sent back to the countries in which their abominable deeds were done in order that they may be judged and punished according to the laws of these liberated countries and of the free governments which will be created therein. Lists will be compiled in all possible detail from all these countries having regard especially to the invaded parts of the Soviet Union, to Poland and Czechoslovakia, to Yugoslavia and Greece, including Crete and other islands, to Norway, Denmark, the Netherlands, Belgium, Luxemburg, France and Italy.

Thus, the Germans who take part in wholesale shootings of Italian officers or in the execution of French, Dutch, Belgian or Norwegian hostages or of Cretan peasants, or who have shared in the slaughters inflicted on the people of Poland or in territories of the Soviet Union which are now being swept clear of the enemy, will know that they will be brought back to the scene of their crimes and judged on the spot by the peoples whom they have outraged. Let those who have hitherto not imbrued their hands with innocent blood beware lest they join the ranks of the guilty, for most assuredly the three allied Powers will pursue them to the uttermost ends of the earth and will deliver them to their accusers in order that justice may be done.

The above declaration is without prejudice to the case of the major criminals, whose offences have no particular geographical localisation and who will be punished by the joint decision of the Governments of the Allies.

(Signed):

Roosevelt
Churchill
Stalin

3   Chief U.S. Prosecutor's Opening Statement at Nuremburg

Robert H. Jackson

The convocation of the International Military Tribunal at Nuremberg, Germany, was a pivotal event in international jurisprudence. While punishment of losers by victors was certainly not new or even unusual, the Nuremberg Trials draped the mantle of international law over an activity hitherto regarded as mere "victor's justice." This was a bold and dangerous experiment, as Justice Robert Jackson himself warned at the onset of the trials.

May it please your honors, the privilege of opening the first trial in history for crimes against the peace of the world imposes a grave responsibility. The wrongs which we seek to condemn and punish have been so calculated, so malignant and so devastating, that civilization cannot tolerate their being ignored because it cannot survive their being repeated. That four great nations, flushed with victory and stung with injury, stay the hand of vengeance and voluntarily submit their captive enemies to the judgment of the law is one of the most significant tributes that Power ever has paid to Reason.

This Tribunal, while it is novel and experimental, is not the product of abstract speculations nor is it created to vindicate legalistic theories. This inquest represents the practical effort of four of the most mighty of nations, with the support of fifteen more, to utilize International Law to meet the greatest menace of our times—aggressive war. The common sense of mankind demands that law shall not stop with the punishment of petty crimes by little people. It must also reach men who possess themselves of great power and make deliberate and concerted use of it to set in motion evils which leave no home in the world untouched. It is a cause of this magnitude that the United Nations will lay before Your Honors.

In the prisoners' dock sit twenty-odd broken men. Reproached by the humiliation of those they have led almost as bitterly as by the desolation of those they have attacked, their personal capacity for evil is forever past. It is hard now to perceive in these miserable men as captives the power by which as Nazi leaders they once dominated much of the world and terrified most of it. Merely as individuals, their fate is of little consequence to the world.

What makes this inquest significant is that these prisoners represent sinister influences that will lurk in the world long after their bodies have returned to

From **Trial of the Major Criminals before the International Military Tribunal, Nuremberg** (Nuremberg: 1947–1949), pp. 1–12.

dust. They are living symbols of racial hatreds, of terrorism and violence, and of the arrogance and cruelty of power. They are symbols of fierce nationalisms and of militarism, of intrigue and war-making which have embroiled Europe generation after generation, crushing its manhood, destroying its homes, and impoverishing its life. They have so identified themselves with the philosophies they conceived and with the forces they directed that any tenderness to them is a victory and an encouragement to all the evils which are attached to their names. Civilization can afford no compromise with the social forces which would gain renewed strength if we deal ambiguously or indecisively with the men in whom those forces now precariously survive.

What these men stand for we will patiently and temperately disclose. We will give you undeniable proofs of incredible events. The catalogue of crimes will omit nothing that could be conceived by a pathological pride, cruelty, and lust for power. These men created in Germany, under the *"Führerprinzip,"* a National Socialist despotism equaled only by the dynasties of the ancient East. They took from the German people all those dignities and freedoms that we hold natural and inalienable rights in every human being. The people were compensated by inflaming and gratifying hatreds toward those who were marked as "scapegoats." Against their opponents, including Jews, Catholics, and free labor, the Nazis directed such a campaign of arrogance, brutality, and annihilation as the world has not witnessed since the pre-Christian ages. They excited the German ambition to be a "master race," which of course implies serfdom for others. They led their people on a mad gamble for domination. They diverted social energies and resources to the creation of what they thought to be an invincible war machine. They overran their neighbors. To sustain the "master race" in its war-making, they enslaved millions of human beings and brought them into Germany, where these hapless creatures now wander as "displaced persons." At length bestiality and bad faith reached such excess that they aroused the sleeping strength of imperiled Civilization. Its united efforts have ground the German war machine to fragments. But the struggle has left Europe a liberated yet prostrate land where a demoralized society struggles to survive. These are the fruits of the sinister forces that sit with these defendants in the prisoners' dock.

In justice to the nations and the men associated in this prosecution, I must remind you of certain difficulties which may leave their mark on this case. Never before in legal history has an effort been made to bring within the scope of a single litigation the developments of a decade, covering a whole Continent, and involving a score of nations, countless individuals, and innumerable events. Despite the magnitude of the task, the world has demanded immediate action. This demand has had to be met, though perhaps at the cost of finished craftsmanship. In my country, established courts, following familiar procedures, applying well-thumbed precedents, and dealing with the legal consequences of local and limited events seldom commence a trial within a year of the event in litigation. Yet less than eight months ago today the courtroom in which you sit was an enemy fortress in the hands of German SS troops. Less than eight months ago nearly all our witnesses and documents were in enemy hands. The law had not been codified, no procedures had been established, no Tribunal was in existence, no usable courthouse stood here, none of the hundreds of tons of official German documents had been examined, no prosecuting staff had been assembled, nearly all the present defendants were at large, and the four prosecuting powers had not yet joined in common cause to try them. I should be the last to deny that the case may well suffer from incomplete researches and quite likely will not be the example of professional work which any of the prosecuting nations would normally wish to sponsor. It is, however, a completely adequate case to the judgment we shall ask you to render, and its full development we shall be obliged to leave to historians.

Before I discuss particulars of evidence, some general considerations which may affect the credit of this trial in the eyes of the world should be candidly faced. There is a dramatic disparity between the circumstances of the accusers and of the accused that might discredit our work if we should falter, in even minor matters, in being fair and temperate.

Unfortunately, the nature of these crimes is such that both prosecution and judgment must be by victor nations over vanquished foes. The world-wide scope of the aggressions carried out by these men has left but few real neutrals. Either the victors must judge the vanquished or we must leave the defeated to judge themselves. After the first World War, we learned the futility of the latter course. The former high station of these defendants, the notoriety of their acts, and the adaptability of their conduct to provoke retaliation make it hard to distinguish between the demand for a just and measured retribution, and the unthinking cry for vengeance which arises from the anguish of war. It is our task, so far as humanly possible, to draw the line between the two. We must never forget that the record on which we judge these defendants today is the record on which history will judge us tomorrow. To pass these defendants a poisoned chalice is to put it to our own lips as well. We must summon such detachment and intellectual integrity to our task that this trial will commend itself to posterity as fulfilling humanity's aspirations to do justice.

At the very outset, let us dispose of the contention that to put these men to trial is to do them an injustice entitling them to some special consideration. These defendants may be hard pressed but they are not ill-used. Let us see what alternative they would have to being tried.

More than a majority of these prisoners surrendered to or were tracked down by forces of the United States. Could they expect us to make American custody a shelter for our enemies against the just wrath of our Allies? Did we spend American lives to capture them only to save them from punishment? Under the principles of the Moscow Declaration, those suspected war criminals who are not to be tried internationally must be turned over to individual governments for trial at the scene of their outrages. Many less responsible and less culpable American-held prisoners have been and will be turned over to other United Nations for local trial. If these defendants should succeed, for any reason, in escaping the condemnation of this Tribunal, or if they obstruct or abort this trial, those who are American-held prisoners will be delivered up to our continental Allies. For these defendants, however, we have set up an

International Tribunal and have undertaken the burden of participating in a complicated effort to give them fair and dispassionate hearings. That is the best-known protection to any man with a defense worthy of being heard.

If these men are the first war leaders of a defeated nation to be prosecuted in the name of the law, they are also the first to be given a chance to plead for their lives in the name of the law. Realistically, the Charter of this Tribunal, which gives them a hearing, is also the source of their only hope. It may be that these men of troubled conscience, whose only wish is that the world forget them, do not regard a trial as a favor. But they do have a fair opportunity to defend themselves—a favor which these men, when in power, rarely extended to their fellow countrymen. Despite the fact that public opinion already condemns their acts, we agree that here they must be given a presumption of innocence, and we accept the burden of proving criminal acts and the responsibility of these defendants for their commission.

When I say that we do not ask for convictions unless we prove crime, I do not mean mere technical or incidental transgression of international conventions. We charge guilt on planned and intended conduct that involves moral as well as legal wrong. And we do not mean conduct that is a natural and human, even if illegal, cutting of corners, such as many of us might well have committed had we been in the defendants' positions. It is not because they yielded to the normal frailties of human beings that we accuse them. It is their abnormal and inhuman conduct which brings them to this bar.

We will not ask you to convict these men on the testimony of their foes. There is no count of the Indictment that cannot be proved by books and records. The Germans were always meticulous record keepers, and these defendants had their share of the Teutonic passion for thoroughness in putting things on paper. Nor were they without vanity. They arranged frequently to be photographed in action. We will show you their own films. You will see their own conduct and hear their own voices as these defendants re-enact for you, from the screen, some of the events in the course of the conspiracy.

We would also make clear that we have no purpose to incriminate the whole German people. We know that the Nazi Party was not put in power by a majority of the German vote. We know it came to power by an evil alliance between the most extreme of the Nazi revolutionists, the most unrestrained of the German reactionaries, and the most aggressive of the German militarists. If the German populace had willingly accepted the Nazi program, no Stormtroopers would have been needed in the early days of the Party and there would have been no need for concentration camps or the Gestapo, both of which institutions were inaugurated as soon as the Nazis gained control of the German state. Only after these lawless innovations proved successful at home were they taken abroad. . . .

A failure of these Nazis to heed, or to understand the force and meaning of this evolution in the legal thought of the world is not a defense or a mitigation. If anything, it aggravates their offense and makes it the more mandatory that the law they have flouted be vindicated by juridical application to their lawless conduct. Indeed, by their own law—had they heeded any law—these principles were binding on these defendants. Article 4 of the Weimar Constitution provided that "the generally accepted rules of International Law are to be considered as binding integral parts of the law of the German Reich." Can there be any doubt that the outlawry of aggressive war was one of the "generally accepted rules of International Law" in 1939?

Any resort to war—to any kind of a war—is a resort to means that are inherently criminal. War inevitably is a course of killings, assaults, deprivations of liberty, and destruction of property. An honestly defensive war is, of course, legal and saves those lawfully conducting it from criminality. But inherently criminal acts cannot be defended by showing that those who committed them were engaged in a war, when war itself is illegal. The very minimum legal consequence of the treaties making aggressive wars illegal is to strip those who incite or wage them of every defense the law ever gave, and to leave war-makers subject to judgment by the usually accepted principles of the law of crimes.

But if it be thought that the Charter, whose declarations concededly bind us all, does contain new law I still do not shrink from demanding its strict application by this Tribunal. The rule of law in the world, flouted by the lawlessness incited by these defendants, had to be restored at the cost to my country of over a million casualties, not to mention those of other nations. I cannot subscribe to the perverted reasoning that society may advance and strengthen the rule of law by the expenditure of morally innocent lives but that progress in the law may never be made at the price of morally guilty lives.

It is true, of course, that we have no judicial precedent for the Charter. But International Law is more than a scholarly collection of abstract and immutable principles. It is an outgrowth of treaties and agreements between nations and of accepted customs. Yet every custom has its origin in some single act, and every agreement has to be initiated by the action of some state. Unless we are prepared to abandon every principle of growth for International Law, we cannot deny that our own day has the right to institute customs and to conclude agreements that will themselves become sources of a newer and strengthened International Law. International Law is not capable of development by the normal processes of legislation for there is no continuing international legislative authority. Innovations and revisions in International Law are brought about by the action of governments designed to meet a change in circumstances. It grows, as did the Common Law, through decisions reached from time to time in adapting settled principles to new situations. The fact is that when the law evolves by the case method, as did the Common Law and as International Law must do if it is to advance at all, it advances at the expense of those who wrongly guessed the law and learned too late their error. The law, so far as International Law can be decreed, had been clearly pronounced when these acts took place. Hence, I am not disturbed by the lack of judicial precedent for the inquiry we propose to conduct.

The events I have earlier recited clearly fall within the standards of crimes, set out in the Charter, whose perpetrators this Tribunal is convened to judge and punish fittingly. The standards for war crimes and crimes against humanity are too familiar to need comment. There are, however, certain novel problems in applying other precepts of the Charter which I should call to your attention. . . .

The American dream of a peace and plenty economy, as well as the hopes of other nations, can never be fulfilled if those nations are involved in a war every generation so vast and devastating as to crush the generation that fights and burden the generation that follows. But experience has shown that wars are no longer local. All modern wars become world wars eventually. And none of the big nations at least can stay out. If we cannot stay out of wars, our only hope is to prevent wars.

I am too well aware of the weaknesses of juridical action alone to contend that in itself your decision under this Charter can prevent future wars. Judicial action always comes after the event. Wars are started only on the theory and in the confidence that they can be won. Personal punishment, to be suffered only in the event the war is lost, will probably not be a sufficient deterrent to prevent a war where the war-makers feel the chances of defeat to be negligible.

But the ultimate step in avoiding periodic wars, which are inevitable in a system of international lawlessness, is to make statesmen responsible to law. And let me make clear that while this law is first applied against German aggressors, the law includes, and if it is to serve a useful purpose it must condemn, aggression by any other nations, including those which sit here now in judgment. We are able to do away with domestic tyranny and violence and aggression by those in power against the rights of their own people only when we make all men answerable to the law. This trial represents mankind's desperate effort to apply the discipline of the law to statesmen who have used their powers of state to attack the foundations of the world's peace and to commit aggressions against the rights of their neighbors.

The usefulness of this effort to do justice is not to be measured by considering the law or your judgment in isolation. This trial is part of the great effort to make the peace more secure. One step in this direction is the United Nations organization, which may take joint political action to prevent war if possible, and joint military action to insure that any nation which starts a war will lose it. This Charter and this trial, implementing the Kellogg-Briand Pact, constitute another step in the same direction—juridical action of a kind to ensure that those who start a war will pay for it personally.

While the defendants and the prosecutors stand before you as individuals, it is not the triumph of either group alone that is committed to your judgment. Above all personalities there are anonymous and impersonal forces whose conflict makes up much of human history. It is yours to throw the strength of the law back of either the one or the other of these forces for at least another generation. What are the real forces that are contending before you?

No charity can disguise the fact that the forces which these defendants represent, the forces that would advantage and delight in their acquittal, are the darkest and most sinister forces in society—dictatorship and oppression, malevolence and passion, militarism and lawlessness. By their fruits we best know them. Their acts have bathed the world in blood and set civilization back a century. They have subjected their European neighbors to every outrage and torture, every spoliation and deprivation that insolence, cruelty, and greed could inflict. They have brought the German people to the lowest pitch of wretchedness, from which they can entertain no hope of early deliverance. They have stirred hatreds and incited domestic violence on every continent. These are the things that stand in the dock shoulder to shoulder with these prisoners.

The real complaining party at your bar is Civilization. In all our countries it is still a struggling and imperfect thing. It does not plead that the United States, or any other country, has been blameless of the conditions which made the German people easy victims to the blandishments and intimidations of the Nazi conspirators.

But it points to the dreadful sequence of aggressions and crimes I have recited, it points to the weariness of flesh, the exhaustion of resources, and the destruction of all that was beautiful or useful in so much of the world, and to greater potentialities for destruction in the days to come. It is not necessary among the ruins of this ancient and beautiful city, with untold members of its civilian inhabitants still buried in its rubble, to argue the proposition that to start or wage an aggressive war has the moral qualities of the worst of crimes. The refuge of the defendants can be only their hope that International Law will lag so far behind the moral sense of mankind that conduct which is crime in the moral sense must be regarded as innocent in law.

Civilization asks whether law is so laggard as to be utterly helpless to deal with crimes of this magnitude by criminals of this order of importance. It does not expect that you can make war impossible. It does expect that your juridical action will put the forces of International Law, its precepts, its prohibitions and, most of all, its sanctions, on the side of peace, so that men and women of good will in all countries may have "leave to live by no man's leave, underneath the law."

4   Dissent to the Verdict of the International Military Tribunal for the Far East

Rabhabinad Pal

The International Military Tribunal for the Far East, created to deal with Japanese war crimes, reflected greater diversity of opinion on its jurisdiction and prerogatives than was present at Nuremberg. For example, Justice Rabhabinad Pal of India denounced the Tokyo judgment as "sham employment of legal process for the satisfaction of a thirst for revenge." Pal implied that, according to standards adopted by the IMTFE, use of the atomic bomb was a criminal act as terrible as anything the Germans and Japanese had perpetrated. His objections were ignored.

. . . The so-called trial held according to the definition of crime now given by the victors obliterates the centuries of civilization which stretch between us and the summary slaying of the defeated in a war. A trial with law thus prescribed will only be a sham employment of legal process for the satisfaction of a thirst for revenge. It does not correspond to any idea of justice. Such a trial may justly create the feeling that the setting up of a tribunal like the present is much more a political than a legal affair, an essentially political objective having thus been cloaked by a juridical appearance. Formalized vengeance can bring only an ephemeral satisfaction, with every probability of ultimate regret; but vindication of law through genuine legal process alone may contribute substantially to the "re-establishment of order and decency in international relations.". . .

The Allied Powers have nowhere given the slightest indication of their intention to assume any power which does not belong to them in law. It is therefore pertinent to inquire what is the extent of the lawful authority of a victor over the vanquished in international relations. I am sure no one in this twentieth century would contend that even now this power is unlimited in respect of the person and the property of the defeated. Apart from the right of reprisal, the victor would no doubt have the right of punishing persons who had violated the laws of war. But to say that the victor can define a crime at his will and then punish for that crime would be to revert back to those days when he was allowed to devastate the occupied country with fire and sword, appropriate all public and private property therein, and kill the inhabitants or take them away into captivity. . . .

From **International Military Tribunal, Far East: Dissenting Judgment** (Calcutta: 1953), pp. 3–12.

Under international law, as it now stands, a victor nation or a union of victor nations would have the authority to establish a tribunal for the trial of war criminals, but no authority to legislate and promulgate a new law of war crimes. When such a nation or group of nations proceeds to promulgate a Charter for the purpose of the trial of war criminals, it does so only under the authority of international law and not in exercise of any sovereign authority. I believe, even in relation to the defeated nationals or to the occupied territory, a victor nation is not a sovereign authority. . . .

Whatever view of the legality or otherwise of a war may be taken, victory does not invest the victor with unlimited and undefined power now. International laws of war define and regulate the rights and duties of the victor over the individuals of the vanquished nationality. In my judgment, therefore, it is beyond the competence of any victor nation to go beyond the rules of international law as they exist, give new definitions of crimes and then punish the prisoners for having committed offense according to this new definition. This is really not a norm in abhorrence of the retroactivity of law: It is something more substantial. To allow any nation to do that will be to allow usurpation of power which international law denies that nation.

Keeping all this in view my reading of the Charter is that it does not purport to define war crimes; it simply enacts what matters will come up for trial before the Tribunal, leaving it to the Tribunal to decide, with reference to the international law, what offense, if any, has been committed by the persons placed on trial. . . .

I believe the Tribunal, established by the Charter, is not set up in a field unoccupied by any law. If there is such a thing as international law, the field where the Tribunal is being established is already occupied by that law and that law will operate at least until its operation is validly ousted by any authority. Even the Charter itself derives its authority from this international law. In my opinion it cannot override the authority of this law and the Tribunal is quite competent, under the authority of this international law, to question the validity or otherwise of the provisions of the Charter. At any rate unless and until the Charter expressly or by necessary implication overrides the application of international law, that law shall continue to apply and a Tribunal validly established by a Charter under the authority of such international law will be quite competent to investigate the question whether any provision of the Charter is or is not ultra vires. The trial itself will involve this question. Its specific remittance for investigation by the Charter will not be required. . . .

It is not the prosecution case that "war," irrespective of its character, became a crime in international law. Their case is that a war possessing the alleged character was made illegal and criminal in international law and that consequently persons provoking such criminal war by such acts of planning, etc., committed a crime under international law.

Two principal questions therefore arise here for our decision, namely:
1. Whether the wars of the alleged character became criminal in international law.

2. Assuming wars of the alleged character to be criminal in international
law, whether the individuals functioning as alleged here would incur any
criminal responsibility in international law. . . .

The atom bomb during the Second World War, it is said, has destroyed
selfish nationalism and the last defense of isolationism more completely than it
razed an enemy city. It is believed that it has ended one age and begun
another—the new and unpredictable age of soul.

Such blasts as leveled Hiroshima and Nagasaki on August 6 and 9, 1945,
never occurred on earth before—nor in the sun or stars, which burn from
sources that release their energy much more slowly than does Uranium. [So
said John J. O'Neill, the Science Editor, New York Herald Tribune.] In a
fraction of a second the atomic bomb that dropped on Hiroshima altered our
traditional economic, political, and military values. It caused a revolution in
the technique of war that forces immediate reconsideration of our entire
national defense problem.

Perhaps these blasts have brought home to mankind "that every human
being has a stake in the conduct not only of national affairs but also of world
affairs." Perhaps these explosives have awakened within us the sense of unity of
mankind,—the feeling that:

We are a unity of humanity, linked to all our fellow human beings,
irrespective of race, creed or color, by bonds which have been fused
unbreakably in the diabolical heat of those explosions.

All this might have been the result of these blasts. But certainly these
feelings were non-existent at the time when the bombs were dropped. I, for
myself, do not perceive any such feeling of broad humanity in the justifying
words of those who were responsible for their use. As a matter of fact, I do not
perceive much difference between what the German Emperor is alleged to have
announced during the First World War in justification of the atrocious methods
directed by him in the conduct of that war and what is being proclaimed after
the Second World War in justification of these inhuman blasts.

I am not sure if the atom bombs have really succeeded in blowing away all
the pre-war humbugs; we may be just dreaming. It is yet to be seen how far we
have been alive to the fact that the world's present problems are not merely the
more complex reproductions of those which have plagued us since 1914; that
the new problems are not merely old national problems with world implications,
but are real world problems and problems of humanity.

There is no doubt that the international society, if any, has been taken ill.
Perhaps the situation is that the nations of the international group are living in
an age of transition to a planned society.

But that is a matter for the future and perhaps is only a dream.

The dream of all students of world politics is to reduce the complex
interplay of forces to a few elementary constants and variables by the use of
which all the past is made plain and even the future stands revealed in lucid
simplicity. Let us hope it is capable of realization in actual life. I must, however,
leave this future to itself with the remark that this future prospect will not in the
least be affected even if the existing law be not strained so as to fix any criminal

responsibility for state acts on the individual authors thereof in order to make the criminality of states more effective. The future may certainly rely on adequate future provisions in this respect made by the organizers of such future.

During and after the present war, many eminent authors have come forward with contributions containing illuminating views on the subject of "War Criminals—Their Prosecution and Punishment." None of these books and none of the prosecutions professed to be prompted by any desire for retaliation. Most of these contributors claim to have undertaken the task because "miscarriage of justice" after World War I shocked them very much, particularly because such failure was ascribable to the instrumentality of jurists who deserved the epithets of being "stiff-necked conceptualists," "strict constructionists," and men "afflicted with an ideological rigor mortis." These Jurists, it is said, by giving the appearance of legality and logic to arguments based on some unrealistic, outworn and basically irrelevant technicality, caused the greatest confusion in the minds of ordinary laymen with regard to the problems of war criminals. These, it is claimed, were the chief present-day obstacles to the just solution of the problem and these authors have done their best to remove such obstacles and to supply "not a mere textbook on some remote technically intricate phrase of a branch of law," but "a weapon with which to enforce respect for the tenets of international law with its underlying principles of international justice."

Some of these authors have correctly said that law is not merely a conglomeration of human wisdom in the form of rules to be applied wherever and whenever such rules, like pieces in a jigsaw puzzle, may fit in. "Law is instead a dynamic human force regulating behaviour between man and man and making the existence and continuity of human society possible."

Its chief characteristic is that it stems from man's reasonableness and from his innate sense of justice. "Stability and consistency are essential attributes of rules of law, no doubt," says such an author:

Precedent is the *sine qua non* of an orderly legal system. But one must be certain that the precedent has undoubted relevancy and complete applicability to the new situation or to the given set of facts. And if applicable precedent is not available, a new precedent must be formed, for at all times law must seek to found itself on common sense and must strive for human justice.

With all respect to these learned authors, there is a very big assumption in all these observations when made in connection with international law. In our quest for international law are we dealing with an entity like national societies completely brought under the rule of law? Or, are we dealing with an inchoate society in a stage of its formation? It is a society where only that rule has come to occupy the position of law which has been unanimously agreed upon by the parties concerned. Any new precedent made will not be the law safeguarding the peace-loving law-abiding members of the Family of Nations, but will only be a precedent for the future victor against the future vanquished. Any misapplication of a doubtful legal doctrine here will threaten the very formation of the much coveted Society of Nations, will shake the very foundation of any future international society.

Law is a dynamic human force only when it is the law of an organized society; when it is to be the sum of the conditions of social co-existence with regard to the activity of the community and of the individual. Law stems from a man's reasonableness and from his innate sense of justice. But what is that law? And is international law of that character? . . . .

In my judgment no category of war became a crime in international life up to the date of commencement of the world war under our consideration. Any distinction between just and unjust war remained only in the theory of the international legal philosophers. The Pact of Paris did not affect the character of war and failed to introduce any criminal responsibility in respect of any category of war in international life. No war became an illegal thing in the eye of international law as a result of this Pact. War itself, as before, remained outside the province of law, its conduct only having been brought under legal regulations. No customary law developed so as to make any war a crime. International community itself was not based on a footing which would justify the introduction of the conception of criminality in international life. . . .

The question of introduction of the conception of crime in international life requires to be examined from the viewpoint of the social utility of punishment. At one time and another different theories justifying punishment have been accepted for the purpose of national systems. These theories may be described as (1) Reformatory, (2) Deterrent, (3) Retributive and (4) Preventive. "Punishment has been credited with reforming the criminal into a law-abiding person, deterring others from committing the crime for which previous individuals were punished, making certain that retribution would be fair and judicious, rather than in the nature of private revenge, and enhancing the solidarity of the group by the collective expression of its disapproval of the law-breaker." Contemporary criminologists give short shrift to these arguments. I would however proceed on the footing that punishment can produce one or the other of the desired results.

So long as the international organization continues at the stage where the trial and punishment for any crime remains available only against the vanquished in a lost war, the introduction of criminal responsibility cannot produce the deterrent and the preventive effects.

The risk of criminal responsibility incurred in planning an aggressive war does not in the least become graver than that involved in the possible defeat in the war planned.

I do not think any one would seriously think of reformation in this respect through the introduction of such a conception of criminal responsibility in international life. Moral attitudes and norms of conduct are acquired in too subtle a manner for punishment to be a reliable incentive even where such conduct relates to one's own individual interest. Even a slight knowledge of the processes of personality-development should warn us against the old doctrine of original sin in a new guise. If this is so, even when a person acts for his own individual purposes, it is needless to say that when the conduct in question relates, at least in the opinion of the individual concerned, to his national cause, the punishment meted out, or criminal responsibility imposed by the victor nation, can produce very little effect. Fear of being punished by the future possible victor for violating a rule which that victor may be pleased then to formulate would hardly elicit any appreciation of the values behind that norm.

In any event, this theory of reformation, in international life, need not take the criminal responsibility beyond the State concerned. The theory proceeds on this footing. If a person does a wrong to another, he does it from an exaggeration of his own personality, and this aggressiveness must be restrained and the person made to realize that his desires do not rule the world, but that the interests of the community are determinative. Hence, punishment is designed to be the influence brought to bear on the person in order to bring to his consciousness the conditionality of his existence, and to keep it within its limits. This is done by the infliction of such suffering as would cure the delinquent of his individualistic excess. For this purpose, an offending State itself can be effectively punished. Indeed the punishment can be effective only if the delinquent State as such is punished.

In my opinion it is inappropriate to introduce criminal responsibility of the agents of a state in international life for the purpose of retribution. Retribution, in the proper sense of the term, means the bringing home to the criminal the legitimate consequences of his conduct, legitimate from the ethical standpoint. This would involve the determination of the degree of his moral responsibility, a task that is an impossibility for any legal Tribunal even in national life. Conditions of knowledge, of training, of opportunities for moral development, of social environment generally and of motive fall to be searched out even in justifying criminal responsibility on this ground in national life. In international life many other factors would fall to be considered before one can justify criminal responsibility on this retributive theory.

The only justification that remains for the introduction of such a conception in international life is revenge, a justification which all those who are demanding this trial are disclaiming. . . .

After giving my anxious and careful consideration to the reasons given by the prosecution as also to the opinions of the various authorities I have arrived at the conclusion:

1. That no category of war became criminal or illegal in international life;
2. That the individuals comprising the government and functioning as agents of that government incur no criminal responsibility in international law for the acts alleged;
3. That the international community has not as yet reached a stage which would make it expedient to include judicial process for condemning and punishing either states or individuals.

I have not said anything about the alleged object of the Japanese plan or conspiracy. I believe no one will seriously contend that domination of one nation by another became a crime in international life. Apart from the question of legality or otherwise of the means designed to achieve this object it must be held that the object itself was not yet illegal or criminal in international life. In any other view, the entire international community would be a community of criminal races. At least many of the powerful nations are living this sort of life and if these acts are criminal then the entire international community is living that criminal life, some actually committing the crime and others becoming accessories after the fact in these crimes. No nation has as yet treated such acts as crimes and all the powerful nations continue close relations with the nations that had committed such acts. . . .

We need not stop here to consider whether a static conception of peace is at all justifiable in international relations. I am not sure if it is possible to create "peace" once for all, and if there can be status quo which is to be eternal. At any rate in the present state of international relations such a static idea of peace is absolutely untenable. Certainly, dominated nations of the present day status quo cannot be made to submit to eternal domination only in the name of peace. International law must be prepared to face the problem of bringing within juridical limits the politico-historical evolution of mankind which up to now has been accomplished chiefly through war. War and other methods of self-help by force can be effectively excluded only when this problem is solved, and it is only then that we can think of introducing criminal responsibility for efforts at adjustment by means other than peaceful. Before the introduction of criminal responsibility for such efforts the international law must succeed in establishing rules for effecting peaceful changes. Until then there can hardly be any justification for any direct and indirect attempt at maintaining, in the name of humanity and justice, the very status quo which might have been organized and hitherto maintained only by force by pure opportunist "Have and Holders," and which, we know, we cannot undertake to vindicate. The part of humanity which has been lucky enough to enjoy political freedom can now well afford to have the deterministic ascetic outlook of life, and may think of peace in terms of political status quo. But every part of humanity has not been equally lucky and a considerable part is still haunted by the wishful thinking about escape from political dominations. To them the present age is faced with not only the menace of totalitarianism but also the actual plague of imperialism. They have not as yet been in a position to entertain a simple belief in a valiant god struggling to establish a real democratic order in the Universe. They know how the present state of things came into being. A swordsman may genuinely be eager to return the weapon to its scabbard at the earliest possible moment after using it successfully for his gain, if he can keep his spoil without having to use it any more. But, perhaps one thing which you cannot do with weapons like bayonets and swords is that you cannot sit on them. . . .

It may be suggested, as has very often been done in course of this trial, that simply because there might be robbers untried and unpunished it would not follow that robbing is no crime and a robber placed under trial for robbery would gain nothing by showing that there are other robbers in the world who are going unpunished. This is certainly sound logic when we know for certain that robbery is a crime. When, however, we are still to determine whether or not a particular act in a particular community is or is not criminal, I believe it is a pertinent enquiry how the act in question stands in relation to the other members of the community and how the community looks upon the act when done by such other members.

Before we can decide which meaning should be attached to the words "aggressor," "aggression" and "aggressive," we must decide which of the views as to a certain category of war having become criminal is being accepted by us. It is needless to say that we are now proceeding on the assumption that a certain category of war is a crime under the international law. . . .

There is yet another difficult matter that must enter into our consideration in this connection. We must not overlook the system of Power Politics prevailing in international life. It will be a pertinent question whether or not self-defense or self-protection would include maintenance of a nation's position in the system. The accused in the present case claim such defensive character also for their action in the Pacific. . . .

I would only like to observe once again that the so-called Western interests in the Eastern Hemisphere were mostly founded on the past success of these western people in "transmuting violence into commercial profit." The inequity, of course, was of their fathers who had had recourse to the sword for this purpose. But perhaps it is right to say that "the man of violence cannot both genuinely repent of his violence and permanently profit by it.". . .

The Kaiser Wilhelm II was credited with a letter to the Austrian Kaiser Franz Joseph in the early days of that war, wherein he stated as follows:

"My soul is torn, but everything must be put to fire and sword; men, women and children and old men must be slaughtered and not a tree or house be left standing. With these methods of terrorism, which are alone capable of affecting a people as degenerate as the French, the war will be over in two months, whereas if I admit considerations of humanity it will be prolonged for years. In spite of my repugnance I have therefore been obliged to choose the former system."

This showed his ruthless policy, and this policy of indiscriminate murder to shorten the war was considered to be a crime.

In the Pacific war under our consideration, if there was anything approaching what is indicated in the above letter of the German Emperor, it is the decision coming from the allied powers to use the atom bomb. Future generations will judge this dire decision. History will say whether any outburst of popular sentiment against usage of such a new weapon is irrational and only sentimental and whether it has become legitimate by such indiscriminate slaughter to win the victory by breaking the will of the whole nation to continue to fight. We need not stop here to consider whether or not "the atom bomb comes to force a more fundamental searching of the nature of warfare and of the legitimate means for the pursuit of military objectives." It would be sufficient for my present purpose to say that if any indiscriminate destruction of civilian life and property is still illegitimate in warfare, then, in the Pacific war, this decision to use the atom bomb is the only near approach to the directives of the German Emperor during the First World War and of the Nazi leaders during the Second World War. Nothing like this could be traced to the credit of the present accused. . . .

Essays

5 Killing Center Operations

Raul Hilberg

No brief summary could convey the enormity of the crimes Nazi Germany perpetrated against the Jews. A real awareness of the Reich's terrorism and atrocities could perhaps be gained only by personally observing Anne Frank's garret in Amsterdam and the charnelhouses at Dachau and Buchenwald. Because most of us do not have such an opportunity, a selection from The Destruction of the European Jews *by Raul Hilberg is included here. In cold, unemotional prose it provides a detailed account of the German planning and implementation of the "Final Solution," the systematic extermination of some three million human beings.*

The most secret operations of the destruction process were carried out in six camps located in Poland in an area stretching from the incorporated areas to the Bug. These camps were the collecting points for thousands of transports converging from all directions with Jewish deportees. In three years the incoming traffic reached a total of close to three million Jews. As the transports turned back empty, their passengers disappeared inside.

The killing centers worked quickly and efficiently: a man would step off a train in the morning, and in the evening his corpse was burned and his clothes packed away for shipment to Germany. Such an operation was the product of a great deal of planning, for the death camp was an intricate mechanism in which a whole army of specialists played their parts. Viewed superficially, this smoothly functioning apparatus is deceptively simple, but upon closer examination the operations of the killing center resemble in several respects the complex mass-production methods of a modern plant. It will therefore be necessary to explore, step by step, what made possible the final result.

From **The Destruction of the European Jews** by Raul Hilberg, pp. 555, 561–85, 618, 624–28. Copyright © 1961, 1967 by Quadrangle Books, Inc. Used by permission of the publisher, Franklin Watts, Inc.

The most striking fact about the killing center operations is that, unlike the earlier phases of the destruction process, they were unprecedented. Never before in history had people been killed on an "assembly line" basis. The killing center, as we shall observe it, has no prototype, no administrative ancestor. This is explained by the fact that it was a composite institution which consisted of two parts, the camp proper and the killing installations in the camp. Each of these two parts has its own administrative history. Neither was entirely novel. As separate establishments, both the concentration camp and the gas chamber had been in existence for some time. The great innovation was effected when the two devices were fused. . . .

To keep up with the influx of victims, the camp network had to be extended. In 1939 there were 6 relatively small camps. In 1944 Pohl sent Himmler a map which showed 20 full-fledged concentration camps (*Konzentrationslager*—KL) and 165 satellite labor camps grouped in clusters around the big KL's. (Again the camps of the Higher SS and Police Leaders were not included.) . . . Pohl's empire was huts characterized by a three-fold growth: the jurisdictional expansion, the increase in the number of camp slaves, and the extension of the camp network.

The six killing centers appeared in 1941-42, at a time of the greatest multiplication and expansion of concentration camp facilities. This is a fact of great importance, for it insured that the construction and operation of the killing centers could proceed smoothly and unobtrusively. Let us now trace the history of these special camps.

The death camps operated with gas. There were three types of gassing installations, for the administrative evolution of the gas method had proceeded in three different channels. One development took place in the Technical *Referat* of the RSHA. This office produced the gas van. We have already observed the use of the van in two places, Russia and Serbia. In both of these territories the vans were auxiliary devices used for the killing of women and children only, but there was to be one more application. In 1941, *Gauleiter* Greiser of the Wartheland obtained Himmler's permission to kill 100,000 Jews in his *Gau*. Three vans were thereupon brought into the woods of Chelmno, the area was closed off, and the first killing center came into being.

The construction of another type of gassing apparatus was pursued in the Führer Chancellery, Hitler's personal office. After the outbreak of war, Hitler signed an order (predated September 1, 1939) empowering the chief of the Führer Chancellery, *Reichsleiter* Bouhler, and his own personal physician, Dr. Brandt, "to widen the authority of individual doctors with a view to enabling them, after the most critical examination in the realm of human knowledge, to administer to incurably sick persons a mercy death." Actually this order was intended for and applied to incurably insane persons only. The administrative implementation of the plan, which became known as the "euthanasia program," was in the hands of Bouhler's Führer Chancellery. The man who was actually in charge of the operation was a subordinate of Bouhler, *Reichsamtsleiter* Brack. The *Reichsamtsleiter* obtained the services of one *Kriminalkommissar* Wirth, chief of the Criminal Police office in Stuttgart and an expert in tracking down criminals, for the technical side of the project. Wirth constructed carbon monoxide gas chambers, a device which overwhelmed its victims without their apprehension and which caused them no pain.

In the summer of 1941 "the final solution of the Jewish question" was officially inaugurated. Himmler consulted with the Chief Physician of the SS, *Reichsarzt SS und Polizei Gruppenführer* Dr. Grawitz, upon the best way to undertake the mass-killing operation. Grawitz advised the use of gas chambers.

At this point the SS and the Führer Chancellery got together. In October, 1941, three officials in Berlin—Brack, Eichmann, and *Amtsgerichtsrat* Wetzel of the East Ministry—were considering the introduction of gassing apparatus in the *Ostland*. Brack offered to send his chemical expert, Dr. Kallmeyer, to Riga for an inspection of sites. Wetzel was in complete agreement. "As affairs now stand," wrote Wetzel, "there are no objections to doing away with those Jews who are not able to work, with the Brack remedy.". . .

. . . Before long, four killing centers were established in the *Generalgouvernement*: Belzec, Sobibor, and Treblinka on the Bug river, and Lublin (Maydanek) near the city of that name. . . .

. . . The first question which should logically be asked is: How did it happen that a killing center had any inmates at all? Why should anybody have been left alive? Jews were left alive mainly for three reasons: temporary congestion of the killing installations (gas chambers and crematoriums), camp construction and maintenance, and labor for industrial purposes. Persons remaining in barracks because of temporary overcrowding in the gas chambers or the ovens were no administrative problem at all. They were not registered; they were not given numbers. In most cases they were not given clothes or food. Administratively speaking, they were already written off, already dead. Camp maintenance did not require many inmates; in the pure killing centers and in those which had little industrial activity (Kulmhof, Belzec, Sobibor, and Treblinka) there were relatively few work parties. Only two camps had a large inmate population: the WVHA camps, Auschwitz and Lublin. These, then, were the only camps which posed a maintenance problem: the provision of shelter, food, and medical care for the prisoners.

Maintenance planning was characterized by a lack of concern for life itself. It is significant that "accounting for the life of an inmate" (even a German inmate) was defined as a complete and accurate report of his death (name, birth date, nationality, etc.). When a Jew died, no special report had to be made; a death list sufficed. Whether an individual Jew lived or died did not matter at all.

There had to be a sufficient number of inmates to take care of work requirements, and if the supply was too big, the SS weeded out the Jewish inmate population by sending the excess number to the gas chamber. The inmate count was therefore subject to great fluctuation. Depending on the arrival of new transports or a selection of victims to be put to death, the camp population could be doubled or halved within a matter of weeks or even days.

Obviously, expenditures of money for the upkeep of inmates were extremely low. Living quarters were about as primitive as could be imagined.

Lublin, for example, in the fall of 1942 had five blocks with a total of twenty-two barracks. The barracks were partially unfinished. Some had no windows. Others had cardboard roofs. None had water. Provisional latrines (fill-in type) spread odors throughout the habitat. During an Auschwitz construction conference on June 16, 1944 (Pohl, Maurer, Höss, Bischoff, Bär, and Wirths participating, among others), the "completion" (*Ausbau*) of barracks in Camp II was still a subject of discussion. In this connection, it was pointed out that the installation of washing and toilet facilities was necessary only in every third or fourth barrack.

The overcrowding in the barracks was a constant plague for the inmates; there was simply no limit to the number of people who could be put into a hut. Inmates slept without blankets or pillows on so-called *Pritschen*, wooden planks joined together. On October 4, 1944, the administrative division of Auschwitz II wrote to the central administration for 230 new *Pritschen*. Instead of having been used by five inmates, as regulations prescribed, each of the *Pritschen* had held up to fifteen inmates. Because of this weight the upper layer of the *Pritschen* had broken apart, and all the inmates had fallen on top of the people lying on the middle layer. The second layer had thereupon collapsed, and everybody had crashed through the lowest layer. The result was a twisted mass of bodies and splinters.

In the matter of clothes the situation was even worse. Jews arriving in camps were deprived of all their belongings, including their clothes. Up to the beginning of 1943, prisoners' clothing was issued to all inmates. Estimates of requirements were sent by *Amtsgruppe D* to *Amt B*-II, which had to bargain with the civilian sector (Speer and Economy Ministry) for allocation. As shortages increased, the supply of prisoners' clothing was choked off. On February 26, 1943, it was therefore ordered that inmates were to get ordinary clothes (properly marked), with remaining supplies of the striped variety to be given only to work parties moving about outside the camp compounds. Since any clothes which could be dignified by the word were generally picked out for distribution to needy Germans—a complicated confiscation process to be described later—the Jewish inmates usually received only rags. Such things as toilet articles, handkerchiefs, and paper (including toilet paper) were not issued at all. During 1944, conditions were such that many thousands of people had to go around without any clothes whatsoever.

The third plague was the lack of food. The administrative basis for food allocation in the camps was the ration system worked out by the Food and Agriculture Ministry, complete with discriminatory rations for Jews. Each camp administration obtained the supplies from the food depots of the *Waffen-SS* (*Standartenführer* Tschentscher) and in the open market. What happened to the food after it got into the camp was the administration's own business. The basic diet of Jewish inmates was watery turnip soup drunk from pots; it was supplemented by an evening meal of sawdust bread with some margarine, "smelly marmalade," or "putrid sausage." Between the two meals inmates attempted to lap a few drops of polluted water from a faucet in a wash barrack.

The living conditions in the killing centers produced sickness and epidemics—dysentery, typhus, and skin diseases of all kinds. Sanitation measures were almost nil. The Auschwitz grounds were not suitable for canalization; hence fill-in latrines were the only facilities available. Water was not purified. Soap and articles for cleansing were very scarce. Rats ran loose in the barracks. Only occasionally was a block fumigated with Zyklon. Hospitals were barracks, and inmate doctors worked with few medicines and few instruments. When the sickrooms became overcrowded, the SS doctor made an inspection and dispatched the worst cases to the gas chamber.

The prisoners tried to survive, and they worked out a few compensatory mechanisms. Food was stolen and traded in the black market. Inmate doctors worked frantically and tirelessly, but the tide of death was too great. Up to the end of 1942, Lublin had received 26,258 *registered* Jewish inmates. A total of 4568 had been released; 14,348 had died. Auschwitz had obtained 5849 *registered* Jewish inmates up to the same date; 4436 had died. In July, 1943, Auschwitz was short of inmates for its industrial requirements, and a commission was sent to Lublin to take some prisoners from there. Out of 3800 people set aside for Auschwitz a preliminary check revealed only 30 per cent fit for work. The Auschwitz commission was so indignant that the Lublin administration scraped up everyone whom it could call fit for work "with a good conscience"; after a second examination a Lublin doctor, *Untersturmführer* Dr. Rindfleisch, admitted that Lublin inmates could not really be classified as employable. Fifteen hundred inmates were finally chosen. When they arrived, five women were already dead, forty-nine were dying, and most others had skin erruptions or were suffering from "exhaustion" (*Körperschwäche*). Whatever other talents the camp officials may have had, keeping prisoners alive was not one of them—even if on rare occasions that became necessary.

For the SS, a far more serious task than maintaining inmates was the problem of keeping them under control. To have an iron grip on the inmate population, the camp administration expended a great deal of money and effort. The three elements of inmate control were guards, contraptions, and internal controls. We shall examine these measures in reverse order, for the most important means by which inmates were held in check were internal controls.

The Germans proceeded from the fundamental assumption that an individual prisoner would not resist. He would obey an order even if it were against his interests. When confronted with a choice between action and inertia, he would be paralyzed; he would reason that nothing is ever certain, not even death in Auschwitz. The primary danger of resistance was consequently not the reasoning power of the individual—for he was helpless in spite of it and because of it—but the establishment of an organization which would pit against the concentration camp a compulsive mechanism of its own. Internal controls sought to prevent the formation of any such resistance movement. Camp commanders were ordered to watch developments in their camps at all times, lest one day they be surprised by "major unpleasant events." The commanders were to keep track of things by making use of inmate spies, and inmate resistance was frustrated further by the institution of an inmate bureaucracy and inmate privileges.

The distribution of power and privilege among the inmates was determined in the first instance by the racial hierarchy. Even in a concentration camp a German was still a German; a Pole was a Pole; a Jew, a Jew. This stratification could not be broken by the inmates; the racial hierarchy was as rigid as any bureaucratic hierarchy had ever been. No combining, no delegation of power, no mutiny, was possible here. . . .

Not only were German prisoners in the most important positions of the inmate bureaucracy; they also enjoyed the most extensive privileges within the framework of concentration camp life, such as the right to receive packages, supplementary food rations, less overcrowding in barracks, and bed linen in camp hospitals. Far less privileged and much worse off were Poles, Czechs, and other Slavs. On the bottom were the Jews. Between the Jewish and the German inmates there was an unbridgeable gulf: the Germans were entitled to live—they had at least a minimum of privileges to make a fight for life; the Jews were doomed. It is characteristic that the Jews in Auschwitz were hoping that an air raid might destroy the killing installations, while the Germans were consoled by the thought "that the Allied airmen knew and avoided the camp.". . .

Another internal control measure was marking. In the concentration camp, too, the Jewish inmate had to wear the six-pointed Star of David. In addition, his registration number was tattooed on his arm. Still another precaution was taken in the form of daily roll calls which sometimes lasted hours. The roll calls kept track of all prisoners and prevented hiding within the camp. The prisoners were not dismissed until everyone was accounted for, dead or alive. As a last means the Germans also resorted to reprisal, usually a public hanging. They thus sought to frustrate the formation of an internal resistance movement by a system of spies, inmate bureaucracies, inmate privileges, marking, roll calls, and reprisals. However, preventive measures did not stop with these devices.

In February, 1943, Himmler became worried that air raids on the concentration camps might occasion mass breaks. To prevent any such occurrence he ordered that each camp be divided into blocks, 4000 inmates per block, each block to be fenced in with barbed wire. Every camp was to be surrounded by a high wall, and barbed wire was to be strung on *both* sides of the wall. The interior passageway between wire and wall was to be patrolled by dogs; the outer passageway was to be mined, just in case a bomb tore a hole in the wall. In the vicinity of the camp, dogs trained to tear a man apart (*zerreissen*) were to roam at night. All these elaborate contraptions were set up pursuant to Himmler's wishes. Searchlights were mounted on poles of the wire fence, and the interior wire was electrically charged. Inmates who tired of life had only to lean on this wire to end their misery.

The third element of inmate control was the guard force. In spite of all internal measures and the construction of contraptions, there had to be an armed body of men to deal with the eventuality of "major unpleasant events." However, these camps, in which more than 3,000,000 people were killed, were—all other devices notwithstanding—rather thinly guarded. All in all, about

6000-7000 men may have manned the killing centers at any one time; about 10,000-12,000 if rotation is taken into account. Auschwitz had about 3000 guards; Lublin had a battalion; Treblinka may have had about 700 men, including Ukrainians; Kulmhof was run by a *Sonderkommando* of 150 to 180 men. Little is known about the guard forces of Belzec and Sobibor, except that they numbered in the hundreds and that, again, they were mostly Ukrainian. In the WVHA camps the guards were equipped with small arms, including machine guns mounted on observation towers. . . .

We turn now to the second part of the organic killing center operations—the death of three million Jews.

The success of the killing operations depended, in the first instance, upon the maintenance of secrecy. Unlike any other administrative task confronting the bureaucracy, secrecy was a continuous problem. Precautionary measures had to be taken before the victims arrived, while they went through the processing, and after they were dead. At no point could any disclosure be permitted; at no time could the camp management afford to be caught off guard. The killers had to conceal their work from every outsider; they had to mislead and fool the victims; and they had to erase all traces of the operation. . . .

The Jewish crowds which surged into the gas chambers were incapable of striking back. In two thousand years they had deliberately unlearned the art of revolt. They were helpless. It is true that in a moment of extreme despair long-forgotten and long-repressed powers of combat may be recalled, to be applied in a last-minute struggle for survival. But such extreme despair depends upon very precise knowledge, and the Jewish knowledge of the danger that faced them was not that precise. Undoubtedly, many incoming Jews had a premonition that they had arrived in a killing center. Reports, rumors, and logical deductions had accomplished that. But the victims did not know the details of the killing operation, the when and the how. They did not know what to expect from step to step.

Resistance, in short, depends upon two factors: the disposition and readiness to think in terms of opposition, and the knowledge of the danger of compliance. The less disposition a people has to resist, the greater must be its precise knowledge of the threat with which it is confronted. The Jews needed all the details. They had few, if any. The Germans exploited Jewish submissiveness and Jewish ignorance to the utmost. The killing operation was a masterful combination of physical layout and psychological technique. The camp officials covered every step, from the train platform to the gas chamber, with precise orders, and in that way the Germans took maximum advantage of the long-conditioned Jewish reaction pattern. In addition, they supplied misleading explanations. These deceptive measures calmed the Jews sufficiently so that they obeyed once more—and for the last time.

The procedure following arrival varied from camp to camp. At Kulmhof the deportees were brought to a large mill in the nearby village of Zawadki; they were then taken in small groups by truck to the waiting vans, where their clothes were collected and where they were gassed.

In Belzec the process started at the platform. Instructions were given by loudspeaker to undress. The SS-man told the Jews that they would be marched into an inhalation chamber. "Breathe deeply," he said, "it strengthens the lungs." This crude deception did its work. Even when doubts were raised in the minds of the victims, their nakedness benumbed any thought of resistance. The collection of clothes thus had the effect of facilitating the killing operation. From the platform the naked columns were marched a considerable distance to the gas chambers. Near the entrance, guards received the Jews with whips to facilitate the last step. Without counting, they drove men and women into the death chamber, crushing them like sardines in the enclosed space.

What the outside-undressing method meant in the winter is told by a survivor of Treblinka. At temperatures of 20 to 30 degrees below zero, mothers were forced to take off their children's clothes. The "bath" hoax did not work; Höss tells us that at Treblinka the victims almost always knew that they were about to die. Some of them suffered nervous shock, crying and laughing alternately. Irritated guards made use of their whips. Babies who interfered with the shaving of their mother's hair were grabbed by the legs and smashed against the wall. Upon occasion the guard handed the bloody mess to the mother.

In Auschwitz the process was more elaborate. On the platform camp doctors (i.e., König, Mengele, Thilo, Klein) were waiting to choose employable Jews for the industrial machine. The separation of those fit for work—which we shall call positive selection—was haphazard in nature; the victims were paraded in front of the doctor, who made spot decisions by pointing with the thumb. "Right" was Auschwitz (work); "left" was Birkenau.

Those who were sent right augmented the Jewish inmate population and were detailed to forced labor and, occasionally, to medical experiments. For those who had to go left the first step was the loss of their luggage. Next the men and women were separated. Then the condemned Jews were led from the platform to the Birkenau area, still unaware of what was going on. Sometimes they passed the outdoor inmate symphony orchestra, conducted by the Jewish violinist Alma Rose—an Auschwitz specialty. Most of the Birkenau arrivals saw great flames belching from the chimneys and smelled the strange, sickening odor of the "bakery" (crematoriums). In the halls in front of the gas chamber, which had signs reading *Wasch- und Disinfektionsraum* ("Wash- and Disinfection room"), clothes and valuables were collected. Receipts were given for the clothes. Women had their hair cut off. Then, under the eyes of guards and Jewish work parties, the deportees were crowded into the gas chambers. Many believed that they were going to take a shower, but those who hesitated were driven in with rods and whips.

Once there was a major incident in front of an Auschwitz gas chamber. A transport which had come in from Belsen revolted. The incident occurred when two thirds of the arrivals had already been shoved into the gas chamber. The remainder of the transport, still in the dressing room, had become suspicious. When three or four SS men entered to hasten the undressing, fighting broke out. The light cables were torn down, the SS men were overpowered, one of them was stabbed, and all of them were deprived of their weapons. As the room was plunged into complete darkness, wild shooting started between the guard at the exit door and the prisoners inside. When Höss arrived at the scene, he ordered the doors to be shut. A half-hour passed. Then, accompanied by a guard, Höss stepped into the dressing room, carrying a flashlight and pushing the prisoners into one corner. From there they were taken out singly into another room and shot.

In Auschwitz selections were carried out not only on the platform, in order to pick out deportees who would be able to work, but also within the camp, to eliminate inmates too sick or too weak to work any longer. We have called the first procedure a positive selection; let us call the second a negative one. The principal agents of both were the camp doctors. Jewish inmates were constantly living in dread of the negative selections.

The usual occasion for the choosing of victims was the roll call, where everybody was present; another place was the hospital; and sometimes selections were carried out block by block. The victims tried every subterfuge to escape. They tried to hide. Occasionally they tried to argue. A nineteen-year-old girl asked the Auschwitz women's camp commander, Hössler, to excuse her. He replied: "You have lived long enough. Come, my child, come." Driven with whips between cordons of *Kapos* and guards, the naked people who had been picked out were loaded on trucks and driven to the gas chamber or to a condemned block. Before Christmas, 1944, 2000 Jewish women were packed into Block 25, which had room for 500. They were kept there for ten days. Soup cauldrons were pushed through a gap in the door by the fire guard. At the end of ten days 700 were dead. The rest were gassed.

The gassing was a short process in Auschwitz. As soon as the victims were trapped in the *Badeanstalt* or *Leichenkeller*, they recognized in a flash the whole pattern of the destruction process. The imitation shower facilities did not work. Ouside, a central switch was thrown to turn off the lights. A Red Cross car drove up with the Zyklon, and a masked SS-man lifted the glass shutter over the lattice, emptying one can after another into the gas chamber. *Untersturmführer* Grabner, political chief of the camp, stood ready with stop watch in hand. As the first pellets sublimated on the floor of the chamber, the law of the jungle took over. To escape from the rapidly rising gas, the stronger knocked down the weaker, stepping on the prostrate victims in order to prolong their life by reaching the gas-free layers of air. The agony lasted for about two minutes; then the shrieking subsided, the dying men slumping over. Within four minutes everybody in the gas chamber was dead. The gas was now allowed to escape, and after about a half-hour the doors were opened. The bodies were found in tower-like heaps, some in sitting or half-sitting position under the doors. The corpses were pink in color, with green spots. Some had foam on their lips; others bled through the nose.

In the carbon monoxide camps the agony was prolonged. . . . With no room to move—for these chambers were very small—the victims had to stand for an hour, two hours, or even three hours. One of the visitors in Belzec, Professor Pfannenstiehl, wanted to know what was going on inside. He put his ear to the wall and listened. After a while he remarked, "Just like in a synagogue." Not only was the gassing operation longer in the carbon monoxide chambers; apparently it also left a bigger mess. When the gas chamber doors were opened, "the bodies were thrown out blue, wet with sweat and urine, the legs covered with excrement and menstrual blood."

The disposal of the bodies—a very nasty job—was left to Jewish work parties known as *Sonderkommandos.* Membership in these work parties was brief, indeed, since the *Sonderkommandos* were periodically gassed. The first task of the body disposal squads was to haul out the corpses from the gas chambers; for this task they were sometimes equipped with special hook-tipped poles. Then the *Kommandos* had to examine the corpses, lest some jewelry be hidden in them, and extract gold teeth from the mouths. Only then could the corpses be destroyed. . . .

6   The Scientists: Their Views 20 Years Later

William L. Laurence

Twenty years after the first atomic bombs were dropped, The New York Times *published a retrospective collection of essays and articles about the decision. William Laurence, a former science editor of* The Times *who had flown with the mission to Nagasaki, interviewed some of the scientists who had participated in the development of the bomb. The scientists' statements provide an excellent study of the "operational-necessity" argument. Most replied, "The weapon was there; ergo, it should have been used."*

"Why did you help make the bomb?"

"Knowing what you do now, would you do the same again?"

Repeatedly, the scientists and the military and civilian leaders who participated in the decision to build and use the atomic bomb are asked such questions. A number of the leading protagonists have died during the past two decades. The dead, all of whom agreed that the bomb be used without prior

From "Would You Make the Bomb Again?" by William L. Laurence. **New York Times Magazine,** August 1, 1950, pp. 114–25. Copyright © 1965 by The New York Times Co. Reprinted by permission.

warning or demonstration, include Enrico Fermi, Ernest O. Laurence and Arthur H. Compton, among the scientists; Sir Winston Churchill, Henry L. Stimson, General George C. Marshall, Admiral Ernest King and General Henry H. Arnold, among the civilian and military leaders. Very few who played equal roles in arriving at the great decision are left. Hence the twentieth anniversary of the fateful date on which the decision was carried out over Hiroshima suggested itself as a propitious time for asking leading representatives among these survivors whether, in contemplating the past in the light of more recent knowledge, they would do it again. The men and their replies:

Dr. J. Robert Oppenheimer

[Director, Institute for Advanced Study, Princeton, N.J. Headed the Los Alamos team—the greatest scientific team ever assembled—which designed, developed and fabricated the atomic bomb. Later opposed the development of the hydrogen bomb.]

Q.: *After what has happened during these past twenty years, would you, under conditions as they were in 1942, accept once again the invitation to work on the development of the atomic bomb?*

A.: Yes.

Q.: *Even after Hiroshima?*

A.: Yes.

Q.: *Do you think it was necessary to drop the two atomic bombs over Japan when Japan was already on her knees?*

A.: From what I know today, I do not believe that we could have known with any degree of certainty that the atomic bomb was necessary to end the war. But that was not the view of those who had studied the situation at the time and who were thinking of an invasion of Japan. Probably they were wrong. Japan had already approached Moscow to sound out the United States about terms of peace. Probably a settlement could have been reached by political means. But the men who made the decision—and I am thinking particularly of Secretary [of War Henry L.] Stimson and President Truman—were sure that the choice was either invasion or the bomb. Maybe they were wrong, but I am not sure that Japan was ready to surrender.

Dr. Oppenheimer added:

I never regretted, and do not regret now, having done my part of the job. I have a deep, continuing, haunting sense of the damage done to European culture by the two world wars. The existence of the bomb has reduced the chance of World War III and has given us valid hope.

I believe it was an error that Truman did not ask Stalin to carry on further talks with Japan, and also that the warning to Japan was completely inadequate.

But I also think that it was a damn good thing that the bomb was developed, that it was recognized as something important and new, and that it would have an effect on the course of history. In that world, in that war, it was the only thing to do. I only regret that it was not done two years earlier. It would have saved a million or more lives.

Dr. Edward Teller

[Lawrence Radiation Laboratories of the University of California at Berkeley. A member of the Los Alamos team. Known as "the father of the hydrogen bomb."]

To develop the bomb was right. To drop it was wrong. We could have used the bomb to end the war without bloodshed by exploding it high over Tokyo at night without prior warning. If it had been exploded at an altitude of 20,000 feet, instead of the low altitude of 2,000 feet (as was the case at Hiroshima and Nagasaki), there would have been a minimum loss of life, if any, and hardly any damage to property, but there would have been tremendous sound and light effects. We could then have said to the Japanese leaders: "This was an atomic bomb. One of them can destroy a city. Surrender or be destroyed!"

I believe they would have surrendered just as they did following the destruction of the two cities. If that had happened it would have been a tremendous moral as well as military victory. We could have said to the world: "See what science can do? It has ended the war without shedding a drop of blood!" On the other hand, if they had failed to surrender they would have given us good reason for using the bomb as we did, though we might have waited a longer interval before we dropped the second bomb.

Like most of the other scientists, Dr. Teller worked on the bomb because he believed we were in a race against the Nazi scientists. But, he said:

Even when it was found out that there was no race, I still wanted to continue working on the bomb as an instrument to end the war, but without unnecessary bloodshed.

Dr. Teller added:

I was positive then, and I am positive now, that we made a mistake dropping the bomb without a previous bloodless demonstration. But I am quite willing to work on such a project again because I believe that in a democratic government such mistakes are the exception rather than the rule.

To abstain from progress is a medieval idea. I am in favor of any advance in knowledge or any development of the greater power of man. I believe in such advances because I feel that on the whole they will be used in the right way by democratic nations.

Does a scientist have a choice? In an emergency, it is obvious that everyone's choice is more restricted. The pressures are greatly increased. Everyone's responsibility is greater. However, an emergency does not eliminate any individual's responsibility, choice or conscience.

Dr. Eugene P. Wigner

[Princeton University. One of the group, led by Enrico Fermi, who lighted the first atomic pile under a squash court at the University of Chicago on December 2, 1942. The only winner of the world's three major honors in physics—the Fermi Award of the U.S. Atomic Energy Commission, the Atoms for Peace Award and the Nobel Prize.]

On the basis of admittedly scant information at the time the use of the nuclear weapon against Japan was contemplated, I came to the conclusion that

Japan would surrender without its use, and that such use was unnecessary. For this reason I signed the so-called Franck petition [the report of a group of scientists headed by James Franck, Nobel Prize-winner in physics, opposing the use of the bomb].

Subsequently, particularly as a result of my reading Herbert Feis's book *Japan Subdued*, serious doubts concerning this question have been raised in my mind. I am now inclined to believe that the use of the nuclear bomb to terminate the war was a more humane way and led to less suffering and loss of life than any other way that was contemplated.

There was no difference in my attitude concerning the possible use of a nuclear weapon against Germany, on the one hand, and against Japan, on the other. In both cases my attitude would have been governed at that time by the view of whether peace could be obtained without the use of a nuclear weapon.

I signed the Franck petition because I believed at the time that it would be possible to terminate the war without the use of the nuclear weapon. Today I would try to avoid responsibility for using it or not using it. I would leave it to other people to decide, on the grounds that it was not my job.

As for my participation in making the bomb, there was no choice. The original discovery that made it possible was made in Germany, and we had believed that the German scientists were ahead of us in the development of a nuclear weapon. I shudder to think what would have happened if Germany had been first to acquire the weapon.

I had volunteered for the Army as a soldier, but was refused. I knew I had to leave the ivory tower and go out into the world, because what was at stake in the war was just too much.

Believing as I did that the use of the weapon was unnecessary, I was very unhappy about it, and I would have been equally unhappy had I believed that it was necessary to use it. But I had no sense of guilt, since I did not make the decision.

The scientist in a democracy has the right to refuse to do anything distasteful to him. But as long as scientists in totalitarian countries have no such choice, it would not be right to exercise such legal rights for, if one did, there soon would not be any democracy. The scientist, like any other civilian, should not act in such a way as to make democracy impossible.

Dr. Emilio Segre
[University of California at Berkeley. One of Fermi's original associates at the University of Rome. Winner of the Nobel Prize in Physics.]

Q.: *If you knew then what you know now, would you have worked on the bomb?*

A.: Under the circumstances prevailing at the time, yes. We had Hitler around. We knew the Nazis would make the bomb and were working on it. We would have been crazy not to make the bomb under the circumstances. We could not be sure atomic bombs would not start dropping on us. If that had happened, Hitler would have won the war.

Q.: *Did you approve the use of the bomb?*

A.: The President had hardly any alternative. On the basis of the information available—the probability that the war would go on for a long time—I thought, and still think, the decision was the only one possible. But I am glad I was not the President.

Dr. Luis W. Alvarez
[University of California at Berkeley. Played a major role on the Los Alamos team and served as a key member of the group that assembled the two nuclear weapons on Tinian. Flew aboard the B-29 *Enola Gay* on its atomic-bomb run over Hiroshima.]
Q.: *Did you approve the use of the bomb in 1945?*
A.: Of course. We had been in the war a long time. It seemed certain to continue for a long time, with enormous loss of life on both sides. We had the means to end the war quickly, with a great saving of human life. I believed it was the only sensible thing to do, and I still do.
Q.: *Would you do it over again? Would you still work on the bomb?*
A.: Of course. The weapon was possible. So far as we knew, we were in a race with the Germans. We had to beat them to it, or risk losing the war.
Q.: *Would you have done it, knowing subsequent history?*
A.: Yes. I am proud to have had a part in a program that by most modern estimates saved a million lives, both Japanese and American, that would otherwise have been lost in the projected invasion. This pride is reinforced by the knowledge that the world has not had a major war in the past 20 years, and that most responsible people feel the risk of a World War III has diminished steadily with time in these same years. I am confident that both of these admirable situations are directly traceable to the existence of nuclear weapons.

Lieutenant General Leslie R. Groves U.S.A. Ret.
[As head of the Manhattan Project, in less than two and a half years built the $2 billion industrial empire which produced the atomic bomb on schedule.]
There was never any question as to the use of the bomb, if it was successfully developed, on the part of anyone who was in a top position on the project and who knew what was going on. One group that objected to the use of the bomb did not object until after V-E Day. That group was mostly centered around people who were bitterly anti-Germany and who did not appear to feel the same way toward Japan.

John J. McCloy
[Attorney and civic leader. Former U.S. Military Governor and High Commissioner for Germany. As Assistant Secretary of War under Stimson, participated in the wartime inner councils.]
Q.: *We made the A-bomb because we believed we were in a race with the Nazis. Would we have made it if we had known, as we know now, that the Nazis were actually very far from making the A-bomb?*
A.: Yes, we would have done it because of the mere fact that atomic

energy was in the air. I don't believe you could have checked it. We couldn't afford to take a chance that somebody wouldn't come along and do it.

We were in a race with ideas. At that stage, under the pressure of war, we would have gone ahead anyway. Here there was something to end the war, to bring about peace, to prevent war in the future.

Q.: *Knowing what you know today, would you approve dropping the bomb as we did?*

A.: I tried to tell Stimson to advise the Japanese that we had the bomb. I am absolutely convinced that had we said they could keep the Emperor, together with the threat of the atomic bomb, they would have accepted and we would never have had to drop the bomb.

However, if they had refused our offer, then there is no question that we should have used the bomb.

The final decision was that there was no alternative; that neither air bombardment nor blockade would end the war. It was either invasion or the bomb. It was decided not to mention the bomb because it was still not known whether it would work (it was before Alamogordo) and because there was at that time an inhibition against talking about it.

Under the circumstances we had to go ahead with it, because an invasion would have cost terrible casualties. However, I wish we had given them better notice about the Emperor and the bomb. Then our position before the world would have been better.

As to my own position, it was to bring the war to an end sooner than it would otherwise be ended, and thus to save American lives. We were losing about 250 men a day in the Pacific. The estimated American casualties for landing on Japanese shores were anywhere between 250,000 and 1,000,000, while the Japanese casualties were conservatively estimated to run as high as 10 million. We were therefore faced with a very serious question: Should we go on with the war and face the American soldiers who were subjected to unnecessary danger and the families of all those who were killed after we could have stopped the war?

The reason that we did not have a demonstration of the bomb was, first, that it would have completely wiped out the element of surprise, which in my opinion was extremely important. As it turned out, that was one of the reasons why Japan surrendered so quickly. They weren't prepared for it. It was a bolt out of heaven. There has never been a surprise to equal it since the Trojan horse.

Also, if we had had a demonstration or warning, and if neither had any effect—and I don't believe they would have—then the Japanese would have made every effort to see that the plane that carried the bomb was brought down, and it would have increased the hazards of the men who were carrying the bomb manyfold.

Above all else was the very strong feeling on the part of President Truman, which was the same feeling that the rest of us who knew about it had, that it was criminal and morally wrong for us to have means to bring this war to a proper conclusion and then not use the means.

It is true we didn't need the bomb to win, but we needed it to save American lives.

Remember this, that when the bomb was used, before it was used and at the time it was used, we had no basic concept of the damage that it would do. We thought it would do a great deal, but we didn't know at that time whether the explosion might not be a little too high or a little too low. We didn't know whether the fusing would work. The bomb used over Hiroshima had never been tested. A lot of features had been tested, but only of the gun-part—it was a gun-type bomb in which a projectile of uranium 285 was fired into a uranium 235 target. We had no real knowledge that the thing would work. The fact that the bomb had exploded at Alamogordo—the implosion type, the kind used over Nagasaki—was no indication that the Hiroshima type would go off.

Also, the one tested in New Mexico was put up on a tower. It had none of the mechanisms that were necessary to set it off at the proper height. The actual proximity fusing for control of the height at which it would be exploded was tested in the United States about 48 hours before it was actually used over Nagasaki. It was tested over the Tinian area 24 hours ahead of time. And nobody could tell just what was going to happen, and particularly we couldn't tell how severe the explosion would be and how many people would be injured.

The decisions recommending the use of the bomb, made by the interim committee formed by President Truman, were reached after thorough exploration of every possible angle; Could you have a demonstration? What would that mean? How and where would you have a demonstration? What would be its effects? We had not at that time seen the explosion at Alamogordo, but I can just say that if I had been a Japanese observer and had seen the bomb go off at Alamogordo, I would not have advised surrender. It's one thing to see something go off, causing no damage at all but creating a great ball of fire and obviously of tremendous power, but it's another thing to say: "Well, now, they set this off on a tower; maybe it weighs 50 tons. How do we know they can deliver it? That they can get all the mechanisms perfected to deliver it?" And I am sure that anyone who was a sound thinker would have said: "No, that doesn't convince us. In the first place, would they have another?" For example, the German scientists believed that it would be impossible for us to make an atomic bomb, and that if we did we could make only one. The Germans thought of an atomic bomb as something that would have to contain as much as 20 tons of uranium 235, a practically impossible quantity.

7   The Enthronement of Naked Force

Fred J. Cook

*Fred Cook is an American journalist who has written extensively on
political and social issues. His essay is relevant because it deals, not with
the question of war crimes per se, but with the decision to drop the
atomic bomb. That decision, Cook argues, rendered obsolete "in one
blinding flash" all considerations of morality in time of war. It is
interesting to contrast his assessment of the atomic scientists with the
viewpoints expressed in the preceding selection.*

The atomic bomb that fell on Hiroshima exploded with only slightly less impact
among America's civilian institutions. Yet only a small minority at the time
appreciated its implications. The public at large, the Military and the statesmen
united in a mood of patriotic awe and pride at the immensity of our
achievement, and few persons, in high place or low, had the vision to recognize
its true significance. Plainly, however, such super-destructive power rendered all
the old criteria of power obsolete; clearly, the ruthless employment of that
power to obliterate 80,000 men, women and children in one blinding flash
meant that all considerations of morality, all moral restraint, had now become
archaic concepts; and this combination—the possession of the limitlessly lethal
weapon, the demise of morality—signified that naked force had been enthroned
over the world as never before. This stark fact carried with it inevitable
corollaries. The final enthronement of force spelled inevitably the beginning of
the world's most awesome arms race in which each nation would seek to possess
that force; and it virtually insured the complete dominance of the Military since
only the Military would be supposed to know all the answers in the realm of
force.

All of this was implicit in the development and use of the atomic bomb.
America had made the bomb, and it could not escape the decisions that the
possession of the bomb entailed. We had it. No one else did. Having it, what
should we do with it? Should we share our knowledge or seek some international
custodian of the "secret" we had discovered by prodigious wartime effort and
the expenditure of some $2 billion? Or should we husband it, should we keep it
all to ourselves? These were the fateful questions, and on the answers to them
depended in large degree the climate of the postwar world and the direction that
world would take. The answers lay in the realm of science, which alone could
gauge the validity of our secret and estimate the degree of our true choice; and

because these answers, like the questions, involved entire new worlds of techniques and knowledge, it could not be expected that they would be widely and clearly understood. Inevitably, the issue of the bomb, the most momentous issue of our time, would be debated and settled in the inner councils of government; and, inevitably, under these circumstances, with knowledge largely confined to the high-circle inner club, it was foreordained that the Military, which already dominated this club, would define the argument in its own terms and dictate the decision. For this was clearly the Military's province, was it not? Who else could possibly know with their certainty?

The simplicity of this logic, viewed in the perspective of the years, now seems to have been the great delusion of our times. For anyone studying the record is forced to the conclusion that the Military, preoccupied with their own narrow professional interests, simply did not know best. Trained always to seek out the more powerful weapon, drilled to the point of instinct to protect such weapons by the tightest of secrecy, the military mentality was precisely the worst possible type of mentality with which to meet the special challenges of the new and infinitely complicated age of nuclear science. Great vision would be needed to recognize and deal with the unimaginable host of problems that we had willed ourselves in the birth of our horrible brain child. But the military mind, by its very nature, would fall prey to the obsession that it possessed a great and final "secret" when in reality it had no secret at all, or at best only one of fleeting duration. This first delusion of the military mind would lead directly to a second. Convinced we alone held the "secret" of this supreme power, we would soon envision ourselves as the guardian of the world, the policeman of its security and its peace—a decision that ignored the elemental fact that other nations almost certainly would not desire a guardian and one of them, Russia, would not trust or countenance our policing. Along such paths were we to be driven into the ever-mounting tensions of the Cold War that sane men know can hardly be expected to continue and remain forever cold.

The tragedy is that we need not have walked so often to so many precarious brinks. There were men who saw the issues clear and whole. But these men were not of the Military. They were civilian scientists whose only claim was that they had created the atomic monster. They knew its terrible power. They knew that the scientific knowledge on which it was based was world-wide, not the exclusive province of any single country. They could glimpse the still more horrifying potentials that lay in the nuclear future now that the door was open, and they clearly saw that an arms race to achieve these higher horrors would escalate into the most desperate competition the world had ever seen. The views of the scientists were reflected in the eloquent voice of one far-visioned statesman in the top-level councils of government, Secretary of War Henry L. Stimson. The scientists raised their voices in protest. Stimson tried to bring to the issue the power of prophetic vision and common sense and high ideals. But the scientists and Stimson lost. Inevitably, because the Military was against them. This is the story of that defeat—a defeat that led directly to all our future points of no return.

Both the moral and strategic dilemmas of the coming atomic age had been foreseen by the more perceptive men, and they were to be argued to their preordained wrong turnings. If World War I had undermined the fibre of western man and led to the depravity of Hitler, World War II had marked the virtual death of western morality. The fascist dictators began it, and democracy, giving only lip service to the principles of Christianity, had aped the ways of the dictators. Hitler had ordered the mass-bombing extermination of Rotterdam; the Allies replied, as soon as they had the power, with the indiscriminate bombing of German cities. War, a barbarity that for generations had been waged under strict rules of conduct for the protection of the homes and the civilization of a nation, now lost the justification of this purpose, for mass slaughter became one of its primary objectives. No longer were women and children to be protected by the armies; they were to be one of the prime targets of armies everywhere under the Fascist-Nazi theory that such sub-human horrors would break the national will to resist. No longer was there even the pretext that high-flying bombers were seeking out military targets. In night bombing raids such as the one in which the R.A.F. destroyed Hamburg by blast and fire storm, total destruction of an entire population became the goal. As Lewis Mumford has written, the "democratic governments sanctioned the dehumanized techniques of fascism. This was Nazidom's firmest victory and democracy's more servile surrender."

Once the surrender had been made, there is considerable evidence that the war lords of the Allies came to relish the slaughter. The dedicated fanatics of air power had to prove, at whatever cost, the validity of their thesis that bombing alone could bring a great nation to its knees, and so the raids over Germany were mounted in ever greater fury against centers of civilian population in which the military targets were minimal. In the closing days of the war in Europe, with the Nazi system obviously doomed, crushing area attacks were launched against the cities of Augsburg, Bochum, Leipzig, Hagen, Dortmund, Oberhausen, Schweinfurt and Bremen. These cities, as the U.S. Strategic Bombing Survey later acknowledged, contributed only minute percentages to over-all German production. In all of them, there were just three big war plants, the steel works at Dortmund and the aircraft plants at Bremen and Leipzig. Each was a specific target that could have been bombed separately, but in each case the city, not the installation, became the objective.

"On what basis was the death of these eight cities decided upon?" Professor Fleming has asked with reason. "We have elaborate precautions to prevent the execution of one innocent individual. He must be clearly guilty, beyond peradventure of doubt, but when we are engaged in mass destruction the death of cities will be decided by a few military men, doubtless estimable men, who write down the names of the doomed cities on a piece of paper.

"Does a board of generals gravely decide that ten more cities must die? Or does a single man condemn ten cities to death by putting their names on a list of the doomed?"

This was war, World War II style. Armies no longer fought armies alone; they sought the death and destruction of an entire population. Yet we had not become, in the early stages at least, so callous as not to recognize that this changed concept *did* pose a moral issue. This, naturally, we recognize no longer. We calmly discuss obliterating people by the millions as if such a deed were nothing more than an exercise in semantics. The inhumanity implicit in our calm acceptance of the concept marks in itself the illimitable horizon of the barbarous once it has become the acknowledged norm. Under the pressures of war, without as yet the active presence of the A-bomb, the moral issue could hardly have been expected to be perceived in the terms of the ultimate crisis it has become; but it is at least significant that its implications were foreseen in higher military circles and were for a time quite seriously debated.

"As late as the spring of 1942," Lewis Mumford has written, "as I know by personal observation, a memorandum was circulated among military advisers in Washington propounding this dilemma: If by fighting the war against Japan by orthodox methods it might require five or ten years to conquer the enemy, while with incendiary air attacks on Japanese cities Japan's resistance might be broken in a year or two, would it be morally justifiable to use the second means? Now it is hard to say which is more astonishing, that the morality of total extermination was then seriously debated in military circles or that today its morality is taken for granted, as outside debate, even among a large part of the clergy.

"More than any other event that has taken place in modern times this sudden radical change-over from war to collective extermination reversed the whole course of human history."

By 1945 the vital decision had been made, the generals calmly chalked off the cities that were to die, and only the most wild-eyed idealists had any qualms about the inhuman process. We devised napalm bombs and built 1,000-bomber air fleets to fry the Japanese in their homeland. One fire raid on Tokyo incinerated an estimated 125,000 persons; another, nearly 100,000. So a precedent was established. When mass slaughter on such horrifying scale once was accepted as a fact of war, why be squeamish about whether the deed was to be done with napalm bombs in long, flaming, agonizing hours, or by the demoniac energy of the atom in a few blinding minutes? The mind of man had already been conditioned to accept, even to welcome and cheer, the most fiendish slaughter that the mind of man was capable of devising.

Only men of exceptional vision could see that the moral issue was not quite that simple, that with the advent of the atom it had escalated in its ultimate cost so that what was now involved, or was about to become involved, was not the death of people by the hundreds of thousands, not the destruction of single cities, but the death of people by the millions, of entire nations, perhaps the destruction of the whole world. Only the scientists who had worked to perfect the atomic bomb could realize its horrible potential power. Only they could know with some degree of certainty the details of the new epoch of destructiveness that their brainchild was about to create. To the credit of the scientists, they read the future and tried to warn the men of government of its hideous dimensions.

In early 1945, with work on the A-bomb nearing fruition, scientists engaged on the super-secret project began to write and circulate among themselves memoranda discussing the potentials and the implications of the force they were about to unleash. These various memoranda finally crystallized in a document that was to become known as the Franck Report, named after Professor James Franck who headed a "Committee on Social and Political Implications." The Franck Report was forwarded to the Secretary of War on June 11, 1945, and it was to become one of the most discussed documents of the atomic age.

One feature of the Franck Report ever since has claimed major attention—its recommendation that we first use the bomb, not in anger and inhumanity, but in a test demonstration on a barren or desert island with representatives from all nations present to witness for themselves the incredible power of the new weapon. This suggestion, which was rejected, was the single most controversial feature of the Franck Report, and it has tended to obscure the fact that the report brought into sharp perspective all of the thronging issues posed by the mere existence of the bomb and made a series of major deductions whose validity was to be corroborated by future events.

Most important, the report tried to dispel the belief that was to become a fetish of our time—that we possessed the scientific secret of the ages and that we could retain it for our own exclusive use. The Franck Report warned that, in Russia, the basic facts about nuclear power were well understood in 1940 and that the experience of Russian scientists was "entirely sufficient to enable them to retrace our steps in a few years." In other words, here at the very start was raised a clear warning flag against what was to become the most fateful delusion of our times: We were to persist in believing we had a great secret whereas, in reality, *we had no secret*.

Because we had not, the Franck Committee warned that a nuclear arms race was inevitable. We could not prevent such a race by cornering raw materials or keeping our advance steps secret. The materials were too broadly dispersed over the surface of the earth, the basic scientific knowledge was too widely held, and it was inevitable that, within a relatively short span of years, other nations would possess our weapon—and be able to menace us with it.

When this happened, we would become vulnerable as we had never been before. Indeed, we would be more vulnerable than some other nations. Looking far into the future and analyzing the possibilities, the Franck Report concluded that only two nations, Russia and China, as a result of their vast land areas and dispersed resources, would be able in time to come to survive an atomic attack.

For all of these reasons, the atomic scientists called for restraint and pleaded for a demonstration of the weapon rather than its abrupt, unheralded use in war. "The highest political leadership of this country," the scientists wrote, should consider "what the effects would be if the bomb were used first without warning as a military weapon."

The scientists, displaying a statesmanship that unfortunately was to be lacking in the statesmen, then accurately forecast the future in this perceptive paragraph:

"Russia, and even allied countries which bear less mistrust of our ways and intentions, as well as neutral countries may be deeply shocked by this step. It may be very difficult to persuade the world that a nation which was capable of secretly preparing and suddenly releasing a new weapon, as indiscriminate as the rocket bomb and a thousand times more destructive, is to be trusted in its proclaimed desire of having such weapons abolished by international agreement."

The saving of American lives in the war with Japan might well be outweighed by "a wave of horror and revulsion sweeping over the rest of the world and perhaps even dividing public opinion at home. . . . If the United States were to be the first to release this new weapon of indiscriminate destruction upon mankind, she would sacrifice public support throughout the world, precipitate the race for armaments, and prejudice the possibility of reaching an international agreement on the future control of such weapons."

Such was the remarkably perceptive forecast of the future written by the atomic scientists well in advance of Hiroshima. In its essential details, it was to prove almost uncannily accurate, and certainly the major evils that it foresaw—a desperate nuclear arms race and the impossibility of reaching agreements for international control—have become the crucial realities of our times. . . .

Unit VII

The Nature of Wartime Diplomacy

Carl von Clausewitz' famous pronouncement—that "war is a continuation of diplomacy by other means"—has often been misinterpreted as meaning that the art of diplomacy is consigned to limbo for the duration of a war. This idea has caused great harm, especially when, as during the Second World War, national leaders accept and act on such a mistaken conception of diplomacy's function. Diplomatic activities continued throughout the Second World War because the need for negotiation and resolution of international differences continued. With a few significant exceptions, these activities took place among members of the Allied coalition.

Discussions among Great Britain, the United States, the Soviet Union, and to a lesser extent China dealt with (and often confused) various political, military, and diplomatic concerns. In very many, perhaps most, cases the diplomatic element proved to be of most significance. But the intimate interrelationships among the three major types of considerations form one important aspect of wartime diplomacy. These relationships can be seen most clearly in the efforts of Allied leaders to resolve the pressing issues of a "Second Front" in Europe, of aid to keep China in the war, and of postwar policy toward the Axis powers.

Equally important for understanding the nature of wartime diplomacy are the peculiar pressures that derive from the temporary cooperation of nations with divergent expectations and interests. One may speculate that the "summit conferences," which typified World War II diplomacy, intensified those pressures in this war. The atmosphere of these meetings, arising from poor preparation and inaccurate assumptions about the aims of one's allies, was hardly conducive to realistic, farsighted decisions. It may be, as certain of the documents and essays in this unit suggest, that by bringing into close proximity such gigantic egos as Churchill, Roosevelt, and Stalin the wartime summit conference did a great disservice. One should also note, however, that much recent scholarship has stressed underlying causes—such as hysterical anticommunism, American or British or Russian imperial ambitions, economic motives—rather than the "trivia" of personal diplomacy, to explain the course of international relations during World War II.

Documents

1   The German-Soviet Non-Aggression Pact

The German-Soviet Non-Aggression Pact signed in August, 1939, was a pivotal event in the progress of Europe toward general war. Whatever else may be claimed about it, this "foothill" conference did establish stylistic precedents for much of World War II diplomacy. Having been assigned plenipotentiary status by their governments, German Foreign Minister Von Ribbentrop and Commissar for Foreign Affairs Molotov met in secret, drank an impressive number of toasts, and decided the fate of peoples who were neither represented nor consulted while their futures were being sealed. A cynic might say this represents an apt summary of all conference diplomacy in the Second World War.

PUBLIC TEXT

The Government of the German Reich and the Government of the Union of Soviet Socialist Republics, desirous of strengthening the cause of peace between Germany and the U.S.S.R., and proceeding from the fundamental provisions of the Neutrality Agreement concluded in April, 1926, between Germany and the U.S.S.R., have reached the following agreement:

Article I. Both High Contracting Parties obligate themselves to desist from any act of violence, any aggressive action, and any attack on each other, either individually or jointly with other powers.

Article II. Should one of the High Contracting Parties become the object of belligerent action by a third power, the other High Contracting Party shall in no manner lend its support to this third power.

Article III. The Governments of the two High Contracting Parties shall in the future maintain continual contact with one another for the purpose of consultation in order to exchange information on problems affecting their common interests.

From **Documents on German Foreign Policy, 1918–1945,** Series D, VII, (Washington, D.C.: U.S. Government Printing Office, 1966), pp. 245–47.

Article IV. Neither of the two High Contracting Parties shall participate in any grouping of powers whatsoever that is directly or indirectly aimed at the other party.

Article V. Should disputes of conflicts arise between the High Contracting Parties over problems of one kind or another, both parties shall settle these disputes or conflicts exclusively through friendly exchange of opinion or, if necessary, through the establishment of arbitration commissions.

Article VI. The present treaty is concluded for a period of ten years. . . .

Article VII. The present treaty shall be ratified within the shortest possible time. . . . The agreement shall enter into force as soon as it is signed.

Moscow, August 23, 1939

For the Government of the German Reich: V. RIBBENTROP
With full power of the Government of the U.S.S.R.:   V. MOLOTOV

SECRET PROTOCOL

On the occasion of the signature of the Nonaggression Pact between the German Reich and the Union of Soviet Socialist Republics the undersigned plenipotentiaries of each of the two parties discussed in strictly confidential conversations the question of the boundary of their respective spheres of influence in Eastern Europe. These conversations led to the following conclusions:

1. In the event of a territorial and political rearrangement in the areas belonging to the Baltic States (Finland, Estonia, Latvia, Lithuania), the northern boundary of Lithuania shall represent the boundary of the spheres of influence of Germany and the U.S.S.R. In this connection the interest of Lithuania in the Vilna area is recognized by each party.

2. In the event of a territorial and political rearrangement of the areas belonging to the Polish state the spheres of influence of Germany and the U.S.S.R. shall be bounded approximately by the line of the rivers Narew, Vistula, and San.

The question of whether the interests of both parties make desirable the maintenance of an independent Polish state and how such a state should be bounded can only be definitely determined in the course of further political developments.

In any event both Governments will resolve this question by means of a friendly agreement.

3. With regard to Southeastern Europe attention is called by the Soviet side to its interest in Bessarabia. The German side declares its complete political disinterestedness in these areas.

4. This protocol shall be treated by both parties as strictly secret.

Moscow, August 23, 1939

For the Government of the German Reich: V. RIBBENTROP
Plenipotentiary of the Government of the U.S.S.R.:   V. MOLOTOV

2 Imperial Conference

The summer of 1941 was a critical period for Japan. Dissatisfaction with the progress of military operations in China and growing fear of encirclement by the Western powers led Japanese leaders to fateful decisions. In this atmosphere the German invasion of the Soviet Union had tremendous effect. It forced the dominant government faction, already committed to expansion, to choose the direction of advance. On July 2, 1941, Japanese civil and military leaders met in the presence of Emperor Hirohito and reached an agreement on a course of action. As the following document reveals, that course ultimately took Japan into war with the United States.

Agenda: "Outline of National Policies in View of the Changing Situation."

Policy

1. Our Empire is determined to follow a policy that will result in the establishment of the Greater East Asia Co-prosperity Sphere and will thereby contribute to world peace, no matter what changes may occur in the world situation.

2. Our Empire will continue its efforts to effect a settlement of the China Incident, and will seek to establish a solid basis for the security and preservation of the nation. This will involve taking steps to advance south, and depending on changes in the situation, will involve a settlement of the Northern Question as well.

3. Our Empire is determined to remove all obstacles in order to achieve the above-mentioned objectives.

Summary

1. Pressure applied from the southern regions will be increased in order to force the capitulation of the Chiang regime. At the appropriate time, depending on future developments, the rights of a belligerent will be exercised against the Chungking regime, and hostile Foreign Settlements will be taken over.

2. In order to guarantee the security and preservation of the nation, our Empire will continue all necessary diplomatic negotiations with reference to the southern regions, and will also take such other measures as may be necessary.

In order to achieve the above objectives, preparations for war with Great Britain and the United States will be made. First of all, on the basis of "Outline of Policies Toward French Indochina and Thailand" and "Acceleration of the Policy Concerning the South," various measures relating to French Indochina and Thailand will be taken, with the purpose of strengthening our advance into

From **Japan's Decision for War: Records of the 1941 Policy Conferences,** edited and translated by Nobutaka Ike, pp. 78–90. Copyright © 1967 by the Board of Trustees of the Leland Stanford Junior University. Reprinted by permission of the publishers, Stanford University Press.

the southern regions. In carrying out the plans outlined above, our Empire will not be deterred by the possibility of being involved in a war with Great Britain and the United States.

3. Our attitude with reference to the German-Soviet war will be based on the spirit of the Tripartite Pact. However, we will not enter the conflict for the time being. We will secretly strengthen our military preparedness vis-à-vis the Soviet Union, and we will deal with this matter independently. In the meantime, we will conduct diplomatic negotiations with great care. If the German-Soviet war should develop to the advantage of our Empire, we will, by resorting to armed force, settle the Northern Question and assure the security of the northern borders.

4. In carrying out the various policies mentioned above [in Section 3], and especially in deciding on the use of armed force, we will make certain that there will be no great obstacles to the maintenance of our basic posture with respect to war with Great Britain and the United States.

5. In accordance with established policy, we will strive to the utmost, by diplomatic and other means, to prevent the entry of the United States into the European war. But if the United States should enter the war, our Empire will act in accordance with the Tripartite Pact. However, we will decide independently as to the time and method of resorting to force.

6. We will immediately turn our attention to putting the nation on a war footing. In particular, the defense of the homeland will be strengthened.

7. Concrete plans covering this program will be drawn up separately.

Statement by Prime Minister Konoye:

I would like to explain the main points of today's agenda.

I believe that it is most urgent for our Empire to decide quickly what policies it should adopt in view of the present world situation—especially the outbreak of war between Germany and the Soviet Union and its subsequent development, the trends in the United States, the developments in the European war situation, and the settlement of the China Incident. Accordingly, the Government and the Army and Navy sections of Imperial Headquarters have deliberated at length; and as a result, the "Outline of National Policies in View of the Changing Situation," which is on the agenda today, was drawn up.

First of all, I will discuss the Policy Section. As has been repeatedly made clear in Imperial Rescripts, the basis of our national policy is to establish the Greater East Asia Co-prosperity Sphere, and thereby to contribute to the achievement of world peace. I believe, furthermore, that this national policy should not be altered in the least by changes and developments in the world situation.

It goes without saying that in order to establish the Greater East Asia Co-prosperity Sphere, it will be necessary to expedite the settlement of the China Incident, which is still pending. Moreover, I also believe that to lay the basis for the security and preservation of the nation we must proceed south, on the one hand; and, on the other, to get rid of our difficulties in the North we must settle the Northern Problem at an appropriate time, taking advantage of the world situation and especially of developments in the German-Soviet war. This [the Northern Problem] is of utmost importance, not only for the defense of our Empire but also for stability in all of Asia.

It is to be expected that in trying to achieve these objectives our Empire will encounter interference and obstruction from various quarters. But since our Empire absolutely must achieve these objectives, we are making clear our firm determination to remove all obstacles.

Next I will speak about the full-scale strengthening of our domestic wartime structure. In order to carry out the policies mentioned in the Summary it is vital that we quickly strengthen our domestic wartime structure as much as possible, and especially vital that we do our utmost to strengthen the defense of our homeland. The Government expects to remove all obstacles resolutely and put this policy into effect immediately.

The Army Chief of Staff and the Navy Chief of Staff will speak on matters pertaining to the disposition of the armed forces and to [military and naval] operations, while the Foreign Minister will speak on diplomatic matters.

With this I conclude my remarks.

Statement by Army Chief of Staff Sugiyama:
Let me explain the principal items.

On the settlement of the China Incident: Under present circumstances, I believe that in order to hasten the settlement of the Incident it will be absolutely necessary for our Empire to increase its direct pressure on the Chungking regime, and at the same time move southward and sever the links between the Chungking regime and the British and American powers, which support it from behind and strengthen its will to resist. The movement of our troops into southern French Indochina at this time is based on these considerations.

Moreover, I believe that in order to expedite the surrender of the Chunking regime it would be effective and appropriate for us to exercise the rights of a belligerent and take over the hostile Foreign Settlements in China at the appropriate time, which will be determined by an overall analysis of possible developments: for instance, the declaration of war against Germany by the United States, the imposition of an embargo against Japan by the United States, Great Britain, and the Netherlands, and the acquisition of a foothold in southern French Indochina by our Empire.

On the solution of the Northern Question: It goes without saying that we should act in accordance with the spirit of the Tripartite Pact with reference to the German-Soviet war; but it seems appropriate for us not to participate in that war for the time being, since we are presently acting to settle the China Incident, and since our relations with Great Britain and the United States are in a delicate state. Nevertheless, if the development of the German-Soviet war should turn out to be favorable to our Empire, I believe that we will have to decide on using force to settle the Northern Problem and assure the security of our northern borders. Therefore, it is vitally important for us to make in secret the necessary preparations for military operations, and to be in a position to act independently.

I further believe that in carrying out various measures for the solution of the Northern Problem, especially in using force, it is vital that we maintain, whatever the obstacles, our basic position of always being prepared for war with Great Britain and the United States, since the attitude of these countries toward Japan cannot be viewed with optimism.

Statement by Navy Chief of Staff Nagano:

Let me explain the principal items.

On the solution of the Southern Question: I believe that under present circumstances our Empire, in order to secure our defenses in the South and attain a position of self-sufficiency within the Greater East Asia Co-prosperity Sphere, must take immediate steps to push steadily southward by coordinating political and military action with reference to key areas in the South, in accordance with developments in the situation.

However, Great Britain, the United States, and the Netherlands are currently stepping up their pressure against Japan. If they obstinately continue to obstruct us, and if our Empire finds itself unable to cope with this, we may, it must be anticipated, finally have to go to war with Great Britain and the United States. So we must get ready, resolved that we will not be deterred by that possibility. As the first step, it will be necessary for us to carry out our policy with respect to French Indochina and Thailand in accordance with "Outline of Policies Toward French Indochina and Thailand" and "Acceleration of Policy Concerning the South," and thereby increase our ability to move southward.

On the attitude of our Empire regarding American participation in the war: It goes without saying that if the United States should enter the war in Europe, our Empire will act in accordance with the Tripartite Pact. This action should not be limited to fulfilling our obligations to assist Germany and Italy. I believe that we should also endeavor to carry out our policy to establish the Greater East Asia Co-prosperity Sphere, even if this ultimately involves the use of force.

However, it cannot be predicted when and under what circumstances the United States may enter the war in Europe. Therefore, I believe it will be necessary for us to decide independently when and in what manner we should use armed force against Great Britain and the United States, taking into consideration the situation at the time.

Statement by Foreign Minister Matsuoka:

Let me discuss matters relating to diplomacy.

It has been established, and remains unchanged, that our basic national policy consists of establishing the Greater East Asia Co-prosperity Sphere with the view of achieving permanent world peace. We have conducted our diplomacy in keeping with this national policy, taking into consideration such matters as the China Problem, relations with the United States, developments in the European situation, and the Southern Problem. However, a new situation has arisen with the outbreak of war between Germany and the Soviet Union. Hence

I believe that it is vitally important in conducting our diplomacy to reaffirm our position regarding current national policy.

As the Army and Navy Chiefs of Staff have just stated, it is necessary in conducting our diplomacy to decide beforehand what circumstances will call for the use of force. Nevertheless, it is obvious that even though we may ultimately be compelled to resort to force, we must do our utmost until then to achieve our aims through diplomatic means. For example, in settling the China Incident we will, on the one hand, do our utmost to strengthen the National Government in Nanking; and on the other hand, we will endeavor, by various diplomatic measures directed at the Chunking regime on both domestic and foreign fronts, to force Chungking to capitulate, get her to merge with or form a coalition with the National Government, or persuade her to enter into peace negotiations. These measures will help us to carry out our policies toward French Indochina and Thailand and to satisfy our demands in the South in accordance with the "Outline of Policies toward French Indochina and Thailand" and "Acceleration of the Policy Concerning the South." Moreover, it goes without saying that our diplomatic policies in connection with the war between Germany and the Soviet Union should be based on the goals and spirit of the Tripartite Pact. However, it will be necessary for us to give full consideration in our diplomacy to the overall picture, embracing the entire area of Greater East Asia.

I further believe that it is important for us to be prepared to conduct our foreign policy vis-à-vis the Soviet Union in such a way that it conforms to the realities as seen by the Supreme Command and others. Furthermore, in our relations with the United States we must maintain a very cautious diplomatic attitude in order to prevent America from entering the European war, and to prevent her from clashing with our country.

Since it is difficult in our time to predict what will happen in international relations, we cannot exclude the possibility of totally unexpected developments in the international situation. Under the present circumstances, there is no alternative but to adhere firmly to the policy set forth in the Summary and to conduct our diplomacy with great care and caution. Even from the point of view of diplomacy, I believe that our Empire is confronted with a literally unprecedented danger; our people must see this clearly and deal with it in a truly determined and united manner.

Proceedings

Konoye: With your permission we will proceed with the meeting.

President of the Privy Council Hara: I have no questions or objections regarding the Policy portion of today's agenda as explained by the Prime Minister. I am going to raise some questions regarding the Summary.

First, in taking over hostile Foreign Settlements will we resort to force if necessary? Won't this raise problems with Great Britain and the United States? We have to be concerned with this matter, since we are going to adopt a strong policy toward French Indochina at the same time. I would like to know when and how the takeover will be made. Things would be different if it were to be done after we had begun a war with Great Britain and the United States. Otherwise, shouldn't we rely on peaceful diplomatic means? What is meant by "at the appropriate time"? I would like to know the relationship between the takeover of the Foreign Settlements and the war against Great Britain and the United States.

Matsuoka: The words "depending on future developments" cover the entire sentence to the end. This problem is very important, and should be treated carefully. We hope to control the Foreign Settlements as a possible step in the settlement of the China Incident. Although we will have to resort to force if necessary, we will certainly try diplomatic means first. We want to avoid, if possible, the takeover of the Foreign Settlements by Japanese forces. We would rather have the National Government in Nanking take them over. We will consider a takeover by Japanese troops only as a temporary measure when no other solution is available. I believe the takeover of the Foreign Settlements will provoke Great Britain and the United States more than our action in French Indochina.

War Minister Tojo: We shall proceed carefully, as the Foreign Minister states. As you know, the Foreign Settlements stand in the way of settling the Incident. Foreign Settlements are found in Tientsin, Shanghai, and other places, and they all stand in the way. The Imperial Army has suffered heavily because of the need to stay out of the Foreign Settlements. During the four years of the China Incident the situation has changed, but I think that both diplomatic negotiations and military operations are needed to solve the problem. However, the matter should be handled carefully. I would especially call your attention to the fact that the Foreign Settlements constitute a serious obstacle to the settlement of the Incident.

Sugiyama: The Foreign Settlements in China obstruct our military operations, and we have suffered great losses during these four years. In order to settle the Incident quickly, we must act decisively and take over the Foreign Settlements in such cases, as I explained earlier. We might well deal with this problem when the United States has entered the war, or when Great Britain, the United States, and the Netherlands have imposed an embargo, or when the dispatch of our troops to southern Indochina, which is scheduled to be carried out soon, has been accomplished without greatly provoking Great Britain and the United States.

Hara: I asked the question because I wondered whether the words "will not be deterred by the possibility of being involved in a war with Great Britain and the United States" in Section 2 meant that we are prepared to go to war with Great Britain and the United States when we deal with the Foreign Settlements mentioned in Section 1. I think that we should deal with this problem after we have considered the possibility of a war against Great Britain and the United States, as the Army Chief of Staff has explained.

Another question: does the phrase "all necessary diplomatic negotiations" in Section 2 of the Summary refer to negotiations with the Netherlands East Indies?

Matsuoka: It refers chiefly to French Indochina. It may also apply to Thailand and the Netherlands East Indies.

Hara: Since you state that French Indochina is included, I would like to ask about "Acceleration of the Policy Concerning the South." Section 3 [of that document] says that we might resort to force. I believe that this matter should be considered in connection with the settlement of the Incident. Is our policy [in Indochina] to be carried out chiefly by diplomatic means or by military action?

Matsuoka: The chances are that diplomatic measures will not be successful.

We have asked Germany for her good offices, but we have received no answer yet. The reply is expected by about tomorrow. Germany seems to think that she would not be successful if she approached the Vichy regime. We have told Germany that we would not ask for her good offices if she were not certain of success in approaching the Vichy regime; but we have yet to receive her reply. We hope for Germany's good offices; otherwise it does not seem likely that diplomatic negotiations will succeed.

Therefore, we must tackle this problem determined to resort to military action. However, we will try until the last minute to solve it by diplomatic means. These may or may not prove to be successful. However, we managed to deal successfully with northern French Indochina last year, although the chances were only one in ten that diplomacy would be successful. This time I do not think that the situation is as favorable as it was last year, so I do not know whether or not we will succeed. We will try our best, since the Supreme Command prefers to avoid military action.

Hara: I agree that it will be difficult if we rely only on diplomatic negotiations. But military action is a serious matter. I regard a war against Great Britain and the United States, which is mentioned in Section 2 of the Summary, as a very serious matter.

The Foreign Minister has referred to Hakko Ichiu and he has frequently advocated the Imperial Way in diplomacy. I do not think that the scheduled movement of our military forces into French Indochina is consistent with the circumstances: we assured Indochina last year that we would respect her territorial integrity, and we are just about to ratify the treaty between Japan and France. What does the Foreign Minister think about this? The situation would be different if Great Britain and the United States had used armed force against Indochina. Otherwise, isn't sending our troops inconsistent with the Imperial Way in diplomacy? The Foreign Minister says that he wishes to avoid military action. I think it is all right to persuade Indochina with armed force in the background; but I do not think it wise for Japan to resort to direct and unilateral military action and be called an aggressor. I offer my opinion to all of you, and will conclude this question.

Next, I believe all of you would agree that the war between Germany and the Soviet Union really represents the chance of a lifetime for Japan. Since the Soviet Union is promoting Communism all over the world, we will have to attack her sooner or later. Since we are now engaged in the China Incident, I feel that we cannot attack the Soviet Union as easily as we would wish. Nevertheless, I believe that we should attack the Soviet Union when it seems opportune to do so. Our Empire wants to avoid going to war with Great Britain and the United States while we are engaged in a war with the Soviet Union. The people are eager for a war against her. I want to see the Soviet Union attacked on this occasion. I ask you to try to give Germany whatever advantage we can in accordance with the spirit of the Tripartite Pact. Has Germany sent us any messages asking us to attack the Soviet Union?

Matsuoka: I have carefully listened to your advice and opinion. The Imperial ratification of the agreement between Japan and French Indochina, which is now being acted on, is an important matter, and we must proceed with caution so that we will not be discredited. I will see to it that we will not appear to be engaging in an act of betrayal in the eyes of the world. As for cooperation with Germany in the German-Soviet war, Ribbentrop asked for our cooperation on the 26th, and he cabled us again on the 28th. At the time we were considering "Acceleration of Policy Concerning the South"; we were expecting a war between Germany and the Soviet Union. Consequently we do not want to give Germany the impression at this point that we are shirking our responsibility.

Hara: Has the Soviet Union indicated her wishes?

Matsuoka: Four days after the outbreak of war between Germany and the Soviet Union, the Soviets asked us to clarify our attitude toward the Neutrality Pact between Japan and the Soviet Union. We replied that the war had nothing to do with the Tripartite Pact, and since then the Soviet Union has lodged no protest. She also asked what attitude Japan would take toward the present war, and we replied that we had not yet reached a decision.

A few more comments on this matter: Even if our Empire does not take part in the war between Germany and the Soviet Union, it will not be an act of betrayal according to the letter of the Tripartite Pact. In view of the spirit that led to the alliance, however, I think it would be proper for us to take part in the war.

Hara: Some people say that it would be improper for Japan to attack the Soviet Union in view of the Neutrality Pact; but the Soviet Union is notorious for her habitual acts of betrayal. If we were to attack the Soviet Union, no one would regard it as treachery. I am eagerly waiting for the opportunity to attack the Soviet Union.

I want to avoid war with the United States. I do not think that the United States would take any action if we were to attack the Soviet Union.

I have one more question. It is said that in carrying out our policy toward French Indochina, we are prepared to go to war, if necessary, with Great Britain and the United States. But the impending establishment of bases in Indochina is said to be preparation for a war with Great Britain and the United States. Haven't we already prepared for a war with them? I think that such a war will occur if we take action against Indochina. What is your opinion on this matter?

Matsuoka: It is difficult to answer your question. The trouble is that the officers in the front lines are aggressive, convinced that we will use force. A war against Great Britain and the United States is unlikely to occur if we proceed with great caution. Of course, I have sanctioned the aggressive behavior of the officers, trusting in the wisdom of the Supreme Command.

Because of the war between Germany and the Soviet Union, Germany's invasion of Great Britain will be postponed. Great Britain and the United States, therefore, might think that Germany will not attempt an invasion of the British Isles; but I think it is probable that Germany will do so while she is still engaged in war with the Soviet Union. Even Ribbentrop did not know that war between Germany and the Soviet Union was imminent. It is Hitler alone who will decide whether or not to carry out an invasion of Great Britain during the German-Soviet war. If Germany invades Great Britain, the United States might be too astounded to take part in the war; or, on the other hand, she might take positive action against Japan from the north. I can envisage the latter possibility in view of the American national character, so it is very difficult to make a judgment.

Hara: What I want made clear is whether the United States would go to war if Japan took action against Indochina.

Matsuoka: I cannot exclude the possibility.

Sugiyama: Our occupation of Indochina will certainly provoke Great Britain and the United States. After our successful mediation of the dispute in Indochina earlier this year, our influence has become quite strong there and in Thailand. At present, however, the intrigues of Great Britain and the United States in Thailand and Indochina have increased steadily, and we cannot tell what will happen in the future. At this juncture, Japan must resolutely carry out the policy she now has in mind: this policy is absolutely necessary in order to stamp out the intrigues of Great Britain and the United States.

Future developments in the German-Soviet war will have a considerable effect on the United States. If the Soviet Union is defeated quickly, the Stalin regime is likely to collapse, and the United States will probably not enter the war. If something goes wrong with German calculations, the war will be prolonged, and the probability of American entry into the war will be increased. Since the war situation is favorable to Germany, I do not believe that the United States will go to war if Japan moves into French Indochina. Of course, we wish to do this peacefully. We also wish to take action in Thailand; but that might have serious consequences, since Thailand is near Malaya. This time we will go only as far as Indochina. We will be careful in sending our troops into Indochina, since this will greatly influence our future policy with regard to the South.

Hara: I understand. I agree with you fully. I think that the Government and the Supreme Command are in agreement on this point: that is, we will try our best to avoid a clash with Great Britain and the United States. I believe that Japan should avoid taking belligerent action against the United States, at least on this occasion. Also, I would ask the Government and the Supreme Command to attack the Soviet Union as soon as possible. The Soviet Union must be destroyed, so I hope that you will make preparations to hasten the commencement of hostilities. I cannot help but hope that this policy will be put into effect as soon as it is decided.

For the reasons I have already given, I am in complete agreement with the proposal put before us today.

Tojo: I am of the same opinion as Mr. Hara, President of the Privy Council. However, our Empire is now engaged in the China Incident, and I hope that the President of the Privy Council understands this.

Foreign Minister Matsuoka just now expressed his opinion on the matter of the young officers. As a person responsible for supervising soldiers and military personnel, I wish to say a few words on the remarks made by the Foreign Minister in the presence of the Emperor.

Foreign Minister Matsuoka implied that some members of the Army in the front lines are intemperate; but I wish to say that the Army acts on orders issued by the Emperor. What the Foreign Minister implied has never happened. We took severe [disciplinary] measures when we sent troops to French Indochina. Coordination between military and diplomatic action is very difficult. I will try to avoid problems in this respect by cooperating with the Supreme Command.

Sugiyama: I completely agree with the War Minister. We will exercise strict supervision to prevent misconduct, so set your mind at ease. I will take this opportunity to describe the situation with respect to the Kwantung Army. Of the Soviet Union's thirty divisions, four divisions have already been sent to the West; but the Soviet Union still maintains an absolutely overpowering force, ready for strategic deployment. The Kwantung Army, on the other hand, is in the condition I have already described. I want to reinforce the Kwantung Army, so that it can defend itself, can provide backing for diplomatic negotiations, can be prepared for offense, and can take the offensive when the opportunity comes. I think that the outcome of the war between Germany and the Soviet Union will become clear in fifty or sixty days. Until then we will have to mark time in the settlement of the China Incident and in the negotiations with Great Britain and the United States. This is why the phrase "will not enter the conflict for the time being" was inserted in the proposal.

Sugiyama: [Remarks after the conference.] Throughout the conference no one on the Navy side expressed an opinion. Nagano, Navy Chief of Staff, was once going to take the floor when there were questions on southern French Indochina, but he stopped when some other person stood up to speak.

The questions put by President of the Privy Council Hara were relevant and pointed. The Emperor seemed to be extremely satisfied. [The Imperial assent was given at one-thirty, immediately after lunch.] The answers by the Government and the Supreme Command were fluent and well done.

After the conference, the President of the Privy Council came to see me, and courteously explained that he had inquired about the phrase "without intervening" because he had not understood it, and that he had no intention of asking about military preparedness in Manchuria. He assured me that he had meant no offense.

3 The Casablanca Press Conference

Franklin Delano Roosevelt

*President Roosevelt's announcement of the "unconditional surrender"
doctrine at a press conference following his meeting with Prime Minister
Churchill at Casablanca is well established in the "mythology" of
wartime diplomacy. That F.D.R. chose this occasion to make public this
important policy is indisputable, for it is documented in the transcript of
the press briefing. Why he chose this method is usually explained by
pointing to one of Roosevelt's personality quirks—his penchant for
throwing out startling ideas as casually as he brandished his ivory
cigarette holder. Of course, extended discussions had preceded the
President's carefully staged announcement, and it can be said that the
statement merely expressed prevailing attitudes about treatment of the
Axis. It was already a "no-quarter" war. Was, therefore, a public
announcement necessary? Did this statement serve other purposes?
Whether answers to these questions are ever found, Roosevelt's
post-Casablanca press conference will stand as a typical example of his
diplomatic style.*

CASABLANCA, January 24, 1943

The President: This meeting goes back to the successful landing operations last
November, which as you all know were initiated as far back as a year ago, and
put into definite shape shortly after the Prime Minister's visit to Washington in
June.

After the operations of last November, it became perfectly clear with the
successes, that the time had come for another review of the situation, and a
planning for the next steps, especially steps to be taken in 1943. That is why we
came here, and our respective staff came with us, to discuss the practical steps to
be taken by the United Nations for prosecution of the war. We have been here
about a week.

I might add, too, that we began talking about this after the first of
December, and at that time we invited Mr. (Josef) Stalin to join us at a
convenient meeting place. Mr. Stalin very greatly desired to come, but he was
precluded from leaving Russia because he was conducting the new Russian
offensive against the Germans along the whole line. We must remember that he is
Commander in Chief, and that he is responsible for the very wonderful detailed
plan which has been brought to such a successful conclusion since the beginning
of the offensive.

From "Casablanca Press Conference," from **FRUS: Conferences at Washington, 1941–1942,
and Casablanca, 1943** (Washington, D.C.: U.S. Government Printing Office, 1968), pp. 726–31.

In spite of the fact that Mr. Stalin was unable to come, the results of the staff meeting have been communicated to him, so that we will continue to keep in very close touch with each other.

I think it can be said that the studies during the past week or ten days are unprecedented in history. Both the Prime Minister and I think back to the days of the first World War when conferences between the French and British and ourselves very rarely lasted more than a few hours or a couple of days. The Chiefs of Staffs have been in intimate touch; they have lived in the same hotel. Each man has become a definite personal friend of his opposite number on the other side.

Furthermore, these conferences have discussed, I think for the first time in history, the whole global picture. It isn't just one front, just one ocean, or one continent—it is literally the whole world; and that is why the Prime Minister and I feel that the conference is unique in the fact that it has this global aspect.

The Combined Staffs, in these conferences and studies during the past week or ten days, have proceeded on the principle of pooling all of the resources of the United Nations. And I think the second point is that they have re-affirmed the determination to maintain the initiative against the Axis Powers in every part of the world.

These plans covering the initiative and maintenance of the initiative during 1943 cover certain things, such as united operations conducted in different areas of the world. Secondly, the sending of all possible material aid to the Russian offensive, with the double object of cutting down the manpower of Germany and her satellites, and continuing the very great attrition of German munitions and materials of all kinds which are being destroyed every day in such large quantities by the Russian armies.

And, at the same time, the Staffs have agreed on giving all possible aid to the heroic struggle of China—remembering that China is in her sixth year of the war—with the objective, not only in China but in the whole of the Pacific area, of ending any Japanese attempt in the future to dominate the Far East.

Another point. I think we have all had it in our hearts and heads before, but I don't think that it has ever been put down on paper by the Prime Minister and myself, and that is the determination that peace can come to the world only by the total elimination of German and Japanese war power.

Some of you Britishers know the old story—we had a General called U.S. Grant. His name was Ulysses Simpson Grant, but in my, and the Prime Minister's, early days he was called "Unconditional Surrender" Grant. The elimination of German, Japanese and Italian war power means the unconditional surrender by Germany, Italy, and Japan. That means a reasonable assurance of future world peace. It does not mean the destruction of the population of Germany, Italy, or Japan, but it does mean the destruction of the philosophies in those countries which are based on conquest and the subjugation of other people.

While we have not had a meeting of all of the United Nations, I think that there is no question—in fact we both have great confidence that the same purposes and objectives are in the minds of all of the other United Nations—Russia, China, and all the others.

And so the actual meeting—the main work of the Committee—has been ended, except for a certain amount of resultant paper work—has come to a successful conclusion. I call it a meeting of the minds in regard to all military operations, and, thereafter, that the war is going to proceed against the Axis Powers according to schedule, with every indication that 1943 is going to be an even better year for the United Nations than 1942.

You will want to know about the presence of General (Henri Honoré) Giraud, and General (Charles) de Gaulle. I think that all that should be said at this time is that the Prime Minister and I felt that here we were in French North Africa and it would be an opportune time for those two gentlemen to meet together—one Frenchman with another Frenchman. They have been in conference now for a couple of days, and we have emphasized one common purpose, and that is the liberation of France. They are at work on that. They are in accord on that, and we hope very much that as a result of getting to know each other better under these modern, new conditions, we will have French armies, and French navies, and French airmen who will take part with us in the ultimate liberation of France itself.

I haven't got anything else that relates to the United Staffs conference, but—it is purely personal—but I might as well give it to you as background. I have had the opportunity, during these days, of visiting a very large number of American troops—went up the line the other day and saw combat teams and the bulk of several divisions. I talked with the officers, and with the men. I lunched with them in the field, and it was a darn good lunch. We had to move the band, because it was a very windy day, from leeward to windward, so we could hear the music.

From these reviews we went over to a fort—I don't know whether you can use the name or not—that is up to (Brigadier) General (Robert A.) McClure. Actually, it was at the mouth of Port Lyautey where the very heavy fighting occurred and where a large number of Americans and Frenchmen were killed. Their bodies, most of them, lie in a joint cemetery—French and American. I placed a wreath where the American graves are, and another wreath where the French graves are.

I saw the equipment of these troops that are ready to go into action at any time; and I wish the people back home could see it, because those troops are equipped with the most modern weapons that we can turn out. They are adequately equipped in every way. And I found them not only in excellent health and high spirits, but also a very great efficiency on the part of officers and men, all the way from top to bottom. I am sure they are eager to fight again, and I think they will.

I'd like to say just a word about the bravery and the fine spirit of the French whom we fought—many of whom were killed. They fought with very heavy losses, as you know, but the moment the peace came and fighting stopped, the French Army and Navy, and the French and Moroccan civil population have given to us Americans wholehearted assistance in carrying out the common objective that brings us to these parts—to improve the conditions of living in these parts, which you know better than I do have been seriously hurt by the fact that during the last two years so much of the output, especially the food output of French North Africa, has been sent to the support of the German Army. That time is ended, and we are going to do all we can for the population of these parts, to keep them going until they can bring in their own harvests during this coming summer.

Also, I had one very delightful party. I gave a dinner party for the Sultan of Morocco (Sidi Mohammed) and his son. We got on extremely well. He is greatly interested in the welfare of his people, and he and the Moroccan population are giving to us the same kind of support that the French population is.

So I just want to repeat that on this trip I saw with my own eyes the actual conditions of our men who are in this part of North Africa. I think their families back home will be glad to know that we are doing all we can, not only in full support of them, but in keeping up the splendid morale with which they are working at the present time. I want to say to their families, through you people, that I am mighty proud of them.

This is not like a Press Conference in Washington. We have 200 to 250 that crowd into one rather small room, and it is almost impossible there to meet everyone personally. You are an elite group, and because it is not too big a group, the Prime Minister and I want to meet all of you.

One thing, before we stop talking—on the release date of this thing—sometimes I also am under orders. I have got to let General McClure decide the release date. There are certain reasons why it can't be for a few days, but as I understand it, one of your problems is the bottle-neck at Gibraltar. I think you have enough background to write your stories and put them on the cables, and General McClure will decide what the actual release date will be. I told him that it should be just as soon as he possibly could.

4   The Tehran Conference

As was pointed out in Unit IV, the conference at Tehran was the high-water mark of wartime diplomacy. It is of particular interest because it brought together for the first time all three leaders of the Allied coalition. During the various meetings at Tehran, Churchill, Roosevelt, and Stalin ranged over almost every problem related to the war and postwar issues. Their dinner meetings were especially revealing, for at these occasions the personal tensions between the three leaders were often dragged into the open.

Tripartite Dinner Meeting, November 28, 1943, Soviet Embassy

Bohlen Minutes

During the first part of the dinner the conversation between the President and Marshal Stalin was general in character and dealt for the most part with a suitable place for the next meeting. Fairbanks seemed to be considered by both the most suitable spot.

Marshal Stalin then raised the question of the future of France. He described in considerable length the reasons why, in his opinion, France deserved no considerate treatment from the Allies and, above all, had no right to retain her former empire. He said that the entire French ruling class was rotten to the core and had delivered over France to the Germans and that, in fact, France was now actively helping our enemies. He therefore felt that it would be not only unjust but dangerous to leave in French hands any important strategic points after the war.

The President replied that he in part agreed with Marshal Stalin. That was why this afternoon he had said to Marshal Stalin that it was necessary to eliminate in the future government of France anybody over forty years old and particularly anybody who had formed part of the French Government. He mentioned specifically the question of New Caledonia and Dakar, the first of which he said represented a threat to Australia and New Zealand and, therefore, should be placed under the trusteeship of the United Nations. In regard to Dakar, the President said he was speaking for twenty-one American nations when he said that Dakar in unsure hands was a direct threat to the Americas.

Mr. Churchill at this point intervened to say that Great Britain did not desire and did not expect to acquire any additional territory out of this war, but since the 4 great victorious nations—the United States, the Soviet Union, Great Britain and China—will be responsible for the future peace of the world, it was

From **Foreign Relations of the United States: The Conferences at Cairo and Tehran, 1943** (Washington, D.C.: U.S. Government Printing Office, 1961), pp. 509–12.

obviously necessary that certain strategic points throughout the world should be under the [*their?*] control.

Marshal Stalin again repeated and emphasized his view that France could not be trusted with any strategic possessions outside her own border in the post-war period. He described the ideology of the Vichy Ambassador to Moscow, Bergery, which he felt was characteristic of the majority of French politicians. This ideology definitely preferred an agreement with France's former enemy, Germany, than with her former allies, Great Britain and the United States.

The conversation then turned to the question of the treatment to be accorded Nazi Germany.

The President said that, in his opinion, it was very important not to leave in the German mind the concept of the Reich and that the very word should be stricken from the language.

Marshal Stalin replied that it was not enough to eliminate the word, but the very Reich itself must be rendered impotent ever again to plunge the world into war. He said that unless the victorious Allies retained in their hands the strategic positions necessary to prevent any recrudescence of German militarism, they would have failed in their duty.

In the detailed discussion between the President, Marshal Stalin and Churchill that followed Marshal Stalin took the lead, constantly emphasizing that the measures for the control of Germany and her disarmament were insufficient to prevent the rebirth of German militarism and appeared to favor even stronger measures. He, however, did not specify what he actually had in mind except that he appeared to favor the dismemberment of Germany.

Marshal Stalin particularly mentioned that Poland should extend to the Oder and stated definitely that the Russians would help the Poles to obtain a frontier on the Oder.

The President then said he would be interested in the question of assuring the approaches to the Baltic Sea and had in mind some form of trusteeship with perhaps an international state in the vicinity of the Kiel Canal to insure free navigation in both directions through the approaches. Due to some error of the Soviet translator Marshal Stalin apparently thought that the President was referring to the question of the Baltic States. On the basis of this understanding, he replied categorically that the Baltic States had by an expression of the will of the people voted to join the Soviet Union and that this question was not therefore one for discussion. Following the clearing up of the misapprehension, he, however, expressed himself favorably in regard to the question of insuring free navigation to and from the Baltic Sea.

The President, returning to the question of certain outlying possessions, said he was interested in the possibility of a sovereignty fashioned in a collective body such as the United Nations; a concept which had never been developed in past history.

After dinner when the President had retired, the conversation continued between Marshal Stalin and Mr. Churchill. The subject was still the treatment to be accorded to Germany, and even more than during dinner Marshal Stalin appeared to favor the strongest possible measures against Germany.

Mr. Churchill said that he advocated that Germany be permitted no aviation of any character—neither military or civilian—and in addition that the German general staff system should be completely abolished. He proposed a number of other measures of control such as constant supervision over such industries as might be left to Germany and territorial dismemberment of the Reich.

Marshal Stalin to all of these considerations expressed doubt as to whether they would be effective. He said that any furniture factories could be transformed into airplane factories and any watch factories could make fuses for shells. He said, in his opinion, the Germans were very able and talented people and could easily revive within fifteen or twenty years and again become a threat to the world. He said that he had personally questioned German prisoners in the Soviet Union as to why they had burst into Russian homes, killed Russian women, etc., and that the only reply he had received was they had been ordered to do so.

Mr. Churchill said that he could not look more than fifty years ahead and that he felt that upon the three nations represented here at Teheran rested the grave responsibility of future measures of assuring in some manner or other that Germany would not again rise to plague the world during the [*that?*] period. He said that he felt it was largely the fault of the German leaders and that, while during war time no distinction could be made between the leaders and the people particularly in regard to Germany, nevertheless, with a generation of self-sacrificing, toil and education, something might be done with the German people.

Marshal Stalin expressed dissent with this and did not appear satisfied as to the efficacy of any of the measures proposed by Mr. Churchill.

Mr. Churchill then inquired whether it would be possible this evening to discuss the question of Poland. He said that Great Britain had gone to war with Germany because of the latter's invasion of Poland in 1939 and that the British Government was committed to the reestablishment of a strong and independent Poland but not to any specific Polish frontiers. He added that if Marshal Stalin felt any desire to discuss the question of Poland, that he was prepared to do so and he was sure that the President was similarly disposed.

Marshal Stalin said that he had not yet felt the necessity nor the desirability of discussing the Polish question (After an exchange of remarks on this subject from which it developed that the Marshal had in mind that nothing that the Prime Minister had said on the subject of Poland up to the present stimulated him to discuss the question, the conversation returned to the substance of the Polish question).

Mr. Churchill said that he personally had no attachment to any specific frontier between Poland and the Soviet Union; that he felt that the consideration of Soviet security on their western frontiers was a governing factor. He repeated, however, that the British Government considered themselves committed to the reestablishment of an independent and strong Poland which he felt a necessary instrument in the European orchestra.

Mr. Eden then inquired if he had understood the Marshal correctly at dinner when the latter said that the Soviet Union favored the Polish western frontier on the Oder.

Marshal Stalin replied emphatically that he did favor such a frontier for Poland and repeated that the Russians were prepared to help the Poles achieve it.

Mr. Churchill then remarked that it would be very valuable if here in Teheran the representatives of the three governments could work out some agreed understanding on the question of the Polish frontiers which could then be taken up with the Polish Government in London. He said that, as far as he was concerned, he would like to see Poland moved westward in the same manner as soldiers at drill execute the drill "left close" and illustrated his point with three matches representing the Soviet Union, Poland and Germany.

Marshal Stalin agreed that it would be a good idea to reach an understanding on this question but said it was necessary to look into the matter further.

The conversation broke up on this note.

5   The Yalta Agreements

In February, 1945, with Germany toppling into defeat and Japan reeling under heavy blows, the "Big Three"—Churchill, Roosevelt, and Stalin—met at Yalta in the Russian Crimea to discuss basic questions relating to the war and the postwar world. The agreements reached at the Yalta Conference have been subjected to violent criticism; many Americans came to believe that President Roosevelt "sold out" United States interests on such issues as the United Nations, the occupation of Germany, and territorial arrangements in the Far East. But in fact, for the most part Yalta merely confirmed decisions that had been made earlier.

The Crimea Conference of the Heads of the Governments of the United States of America, the United Kingdom, and the Union of Soviet Socialist Republics which took place from February 4th to 11th came to the following conclusions.

From **Foreign Relations of the United States: The Conferences at Malta and Yalta, 1945** (Washington, D.C.: U.S. Government Printing Office, 1955), pp. 969–74.

WORLD ORGANISATION

It was decided:

(1) that a United Nations Conference on the proposed world organisation should be summoned for Wednesday, 25th April, 1945, and should be held in the United States of America.

(2) the Nations to be invited to this Conference should be:

(a) the United Nations as they existed on the 8th February, 1945 and

(b) such of the Associated Nations as have declared war on the common enemy by 1st March, 1945. (For this purpose by the term "Associated Nation" was meant the eight Associated Nations and Turkey). When the Conference on World Organization is held, the delegates of the United Kingdom and United States of America will support a proposal to admit to original membership two Soviet Socialist Republics, i.e. the Ukraine and White Russia.

(3) that the United States Government on behalf of the Three Powers should consult the Government of China and the French Provisional Government in regard to the decisions taken at the present Conference concerning the proposed World Organisation.

(4) that the text of the invitation to be issued to all the nations which would take part in the United Nations Conference should be as follows:

Invitation

"The Government of the United States of America, on behalf of itself and of the Governments of the United Kingdom, the Union of Soviet Socialist Republics, and the Republic of China and of the Provisional Government of the French Republic, invite the Government of _____ to send representatives to a Conference of the United Nations to be held on 25th April, 1945, or soon thereafter, at San Francisco in the United States of America to prepare a Charter for a General International Organisation for the maintenance of international peace and security.

"The above named governments suggest that the Conference consider as affording a basis for such a Charter the Proposals for the Establishment of a General International Organisation, which were made public last October as a result of the Dumbarton Oaks Conference, and which have now been supplemented by the following provisions for Section C of Chapter VI:

C.   Voting

1.   Each member of the Security Council should have one vote.

2.   Decisions of the Security Council on procedural matters should be made by an affirmative vote of seven members.

3.   Decisions of the Security Council on all other matters should be made by an affirmative vote of seven members including the concurring votes of the permanent members; provided that, in decisions under Chapter VIII, Section A and under the second sentence of paragraph 1 of Chapter VIII, Section C, a party to a dispute should abstain from voting.

"Further information as to arrangements will be transmitted subsequently.

"In the event that the Government of _____ desires in advance of the Conference to present views or comments concerning the proposals, the

Government of the United States of America will be pleased to transmit such views and comments to the other participating Governments."

Territorial Trusteeship

It was agreed that the five Nations which will have permanent seats on the Security Council should consult each other prior to the United Nations Conference on the question of territorial trusteeship.

The acceptance of this recommendation is subject to its being made clear that territorial trusteeship will only apply to (a) existing mandates of the League of Nations; (b) territories detached from the enemy as a result of the present war; (c) any other territory which might voluntarily be placed under trusteeship; and (d) no discussion of actual territories is contemplated at the forthcoming United Nations Conference or in the preliminary consultations, and it will be a matter for subsequent agreement which territories within the above categories will be placed under trusteeship.

DECLARATION ON LIBERATED EUROPE

The following declaration has been approved:

"The Premier of the Union of Soviet Socialist Republics, the Prime Minister of the United Kingdom and the President of the United States of America have consulted with each other in the common interests of the peoples of their countries and those of liberated Europe. They jointly declare their mutual agreement to concert during the temporary period of instability in liberated Europe the policies of their three governments in assisting the peoples liberated from the domination of Nazi Germany and the peoples of the former Axis satellite states of Europe to solve by democratic means their pressing political and economic problems.

"The establishment of order in Europe and the re-building of national economic life must be achieved by processes which will enable the liberated peoples to destroy the last vestiges of Nazism and Fascism and to create democratic institutions of their own choice. This is a principle of the Atlantic Charter—the right of all peoples to choose the form of government under which they will live—the restoration of sovereign rights and self-government to those peoples who have been forcibly deprived of them by the aggressor nations.

"To foster the conditions in which the liberated peoples may exercise these rights, the three governments will jointly assist the people in any European liberated state or former Axis satellite state in Europe where in their judgment conditions require (a) to establish conditions of internal peace; (b) to carry out emergency measures for the relief of distressed peoples; (c) to form interim governmental authorities broadly representative of all democratic elements in the population and pledged to the earliest possible establishment through free elections of governments responsive to the will of the people; and (d) to facilitate where necessary the holding of such elections.

"The three governments will consult the other United Nations and provisional authorities or other governments in Europe when matters of direct interest to them are under consideration.

"When, in the opinion of the three governments, conditions in any European liberated state or any former Axis satellite state in Europe make such action necessary, they will immediately consult together on the measures necessary to discharge the joint responsibilities set forth in this declaration.

"By this declaration we reaffirm our faith in the principles of the Atlantic Charter, our pledge in the Declaration by the United Nations, and our determination to build in co-operation with other peace-loving nations world order under law, dedicated to peace, security, freedom and general well-being of all mankind.

"In issuing this declaration, the Three Powers express the hope that the Provisional Government of the French Republic may be associated with them in the procedure suggested."

DISMEMBERMENT OF GERMANY

It was agreed that Article 12 (a) of the Surrender Terms for Germany should be amended to read as follows:

"The United Kingdom, the United States of America and the Union of Soviet Socialist Republics shall possess supreme authority with respect to Germany. In the exercise of such authority they will take such steps, including the complete disarmament, demilitarisation and the dismemberment of Germany as they deem requisite for future peace and security."

The study of the procedure for the dismemberment of Germany was referred to a Committee, consisting of Mr. Eden (Chairman), Mr. Winant and Mr. Gousev. This body would consider the desirability of associating with it a French representative. . . .

REPARATION

The following protocol has been approved:

1. Germany must pay in kind for the losses caused by her to the Allied nations in the course of the war. Reparations are to be received in the first instance by those countries which have borne the main burden of the war, have suffered the heaviest losses and have organised victory over the enemy.

2. Reparation in kind is to be exacted from Germany in three following forms:

a) Removals within 2 years from the surrender of Germany or the cessation of organised resistance from the national wealth of Germany located on the territory of Germany herself as well as outside her territory (equipment, machine-tools, ships, rolling stock, German investments abroad, shares of industrial, transport and other enterprises in Germany, etc.), these removals to be carried out chiefly for purpose of destroying the war potential of Germany.

b) Annual deliveries of goods from current production for a period to be fixed.

c) Use of German labour.

3) For the working out on the above principles of a detailed plan for exaction of reparation from Germany an Allied Reparation Commission will be set up in Moscow. It will consist of three representatives—one from the Union of

Soviet Socialist Republics, one from the United Kingdom and one from the United States of America.

4. With regard to the fixing of the total sum of the reparation as well as the distribution of it among the countries which suffered from the German aggression the Soviet and American delegations agreed as follows:

"The Moscow Reparation Commission should take in its initial studies as a basis for discussion the suggestion of the Soviet Government that the total sum of the reparation in accordance with the points (a) and (b) of the paragraph 2 should be 20 billion dollars and that 50% of it should go to the Union of Soviet Socialist Republics."

The British delegation was of the opinion that pending consideration of the reparation question by the Moscow Reparation Commission no figures of reparation should be mentioned.

The above Soviet-American proposal has been passed to the Moscow Reparation Commission as one of the proposals to be considered by the Commission.

MAJOR WAR CRIMINALS

The Conference agreed that the question of the major war criminals should be the subject of enquiry by the three Foreign Secretaries for report in due course after the close of the Conference.

POLAND

The following Declaration on Poland was agreed by the Conference:

"A new situation has been created in Poland as a result of her complete liberation by the Red Army. This calls for the establishment of a Polish Provisional Government which can be more broadly based than was possible before the recent liberation of the Western part of Poland. The Provisional Government which is now functioning in Poland should therefore be reorganised on a broader democratic basis with the inclusion of democratic leaders from Poland itself and from Poles abroad. This new Government should then be called the Polish Provisional Government of National Unity.

"M. Molotov, Mr. Harriman and Sir A. Clark Kerr are authorised as a commission to consult in the first instance in Moscow with members of the present Provisional Government and with other Polish democratic leaders from within Poland and from abroad, with a view to the reorganisation of the present Government along the above lines. This Polish Provisional Government of National Unity shall be pledged to the holding of free and unfettered elections as soon as possible on the basis of universal suffrage and secret ballot. In these elections all democratic and anti-Nazi parties shall have the right to take part and to put forward candidates. . . .

MEETINGS OF THE THREE FOREIGN SECRETARIES

The Conference agreed that permanent machinery should be set up for consultation between the three Foreign Secretaries; they should meet as often as necessary, probably about every three or four months.

These meetings will be held in rotation in the three capitals, the first meeting being held in London.

* * *

The leaders of the three Great Powers—the Soviet Union, the United States of America and Great Britain—have agreed that in two or three months after Germany has surrendered and the war in Europe has terminated the Soviet Union shall enter into the war against Japan on the side of the Allies on condition that:

1. The *status quo* in Outer-Mongolia (The Mongolian People's Republic) shall be preserved;

2. The former rights of Russia violated by the treacherous attack of Japan in 1904 shall be restored, viz:

(a) the southern part of Sakhalin as well as all the islands adjacent to it shall be returned to the Soviet Union,

(b) the commercial port of Dairen shall be internationalized, the preeminent interests of the Soviet Union in this port being safeguarded and the lease of Port Arthur as a naval base of the USSR restored,

(c) the Chinese-Eastern Railroad and the South-Manchurian Railroad which provides an outlet to Dairen shall be jointly operated by the establishment of a joint Soviet-Chinese Company it being understood that the preeminent interests of the Soviet Union shall be safeguarded and that China shall retain full sovereignty in Manchuria;

3. The Kuril islands shall be handed over to the Soviet Union.

It is understood, that the agreement concerning Outer-Mongolia and the ports and railroads referred to above will require concurrence of Generalissimo Chiang Kai-Shek. The President will take measures in order to obtain this concurrence on advice from Marshal Stalin.

The Heads of the three Great Powers have agreed that these claims of the Soviet Union shall be unquestionably fulfilled after Japan has been defeated.

For its part the Soviet Union expresses its readiness to conclude with the National Government of China a pact of friendship and alliance between the USSR and China in order to render assistance to China with its armed forces for the purpose of liberating China from the Japanese yoke.

6   Personal and Top Secret for
Marshal Stalin from President Roosevelt

The precarious consensus established at Yalta threatened to collapse even before final victory in Europe was achieved. President Roosevelt strove valiantly to preserve a spirit of trust and cooperation within the Allied coalition, even at the risk of appearing to appease the Soviet Union. However, Russian actions in Eastern Europe, particularly in Poland, mocked his efforts for reasonable compromise. On April 1, 1945, just ten days before his death, F.D.R. sent Stalin a message that may have marked a basic change in American policy. Many students of the period believe that this message proves President Roosevelt had given up any hope of working with the Russians.

I cannot conceal from you the concern with which I view the developments of events of mutual interest since our fruitful meeting at Yalta. The decisions we reached there were good ones and have for the most part been welcomed with enthusiasm by the peoples of the world who saw in our ability to find a common basis of understanding the best pledge for a secure and peaceful world after this war. Precisely because of the hopes and expectations that these decisions raised, their fulfillment is being followed with the closest attention. We have no right to let them be disappointed. So far there has been a discouraging lack of progress made in the carrying out, which the world expects, of the political decisions which we reached at the conference particularly those relating to the Polish question. I am frankly puzzled as to why this should be and must tell you that I do not fully understand in many respects the apparent indifferent attitude of your Government. Having understood each other so well at Yalta I am convinced that the three of us can and will clear away any obstacles which have developed since then. I intend, therefore, in this message to lay before you with complete frankness the problem as I see it.

Although I have in mind primarily the difficulties which the Polish negotiations have encountered, I must make a brief mention of our agreement embodied in the Declaration on Liberated Europe. I frankly cannot understand why the recent developments in Roumania should be regarded as not falling within the terms of that Agreement. I hope you will find time personally to examine the correspondence between our Governments on this subject.

However, the part of our agreements at Yalta which has aroused the greatest popular interest and is the most urgent relates to the Polish question. You are aware of course that the Commission which we set up has made no progress. I feel this is due to the interpretation which your Government is

From Ministry of Foreign Affairs of the U.S.S.R, **Correspondence between the Chairman of the Council of Ministers of the U.S.S.R. and the Presidents of the U.S.A. and the Prime Ministers of Great Britain during the Great Patriotic War, 1941–1945**, II (Moscow: Foreign Languages Publishing House, 1957), pp. 201–4.

placing upon the Crimea decisions. In order that there shall be no misunderstanding I set forth below my interpretations of the points of the Agreement which are pertinent to the difficulties encountered by the Commission in Moscow.

In the discussions that have taken place so far your Government appears to take the position that the new Polish Provisional Government of National Unity which we agreed should be formed should be little more than a continuation of the present Warsaw Government. I cannot reconcile this either with our agreement or our discussions. While it is true that the Lublin Government is to be reorganized and its members play a prominent role, it is to be done in such a fashion as to bring into being a new government. This point is clearly brought out in several places in the text of the Agreement. I must make it quite plain to you that any such solution which would result in a thinly disguised continuance of the present Warsaw régime would be unacceptable and would cause the people of the United States to regard the Yalta agreement as having failed.

It is equally apparent that for the same reason the Warsaw Government cannot under the Agreement claim the right to select or reject what Poles are to be brought to Moscow by the Commission for consultation. Can we not agree that it is up to the Commission to select the Polish leaders to come to Moscow to consult in the first instance and invitations be sent out accordingly. If this could be done I see no great objection to having the Lublin group come first in order that they may be fully acquainted with the agreed interpretation of the Yalta decisions on this point. It is of course understood that if the Lublin group come first no arrangements would be made independently with them before the arrival of the other Polish leaders called for consultation. In order to facilitate the agreement the Commission might first of all select a small but representative group of Polish leaders who could suggest other names for the consideration of the Commission. We have not and would not bar or veto any candidate for consultation which Mr. Molotov might propose, being confident that he would not suggest any Poles who would be inimical to the intent of the Crimea decision. I feel that it is not too much to ask that my Ambassador be accorded the same confidence and that any candidate for consultation presented by any one of the Commission be accepted by the others in good faith. It is obvious to me that if the right of the Commission to select these Poles is limited or shared with the Warsaw Government the very foundation on which our agreement rests would be destroyed.

While the foregoing are the immediate obstacles which in my opinion have prevented our Commission from making any progress in this vital matter, there are two other suggestions which were not in the agreement but nevertheless have a very important bearing on the result we all seek. Neither of these suggestions has been as yet accepted by your Government. I refer to:

(1) That there should be the maximum of political tranquility in Poland and that dissident groups should cease any measures and counter-measures against each other. That we should respectively use our influence to that end seems to me eminently reasonable.

(2) It would also seem entirely natural in view of the responsibilities placed

upon them by the Agreement that representatives of the American and British members of the Commission should be permitted to visit Poland. As you will recall Mr. Molotov himself suggested this at an early meeting of the Commission and only subsequently withdrew it.

I wish I could convey to you how important it is for the successful development of our program of international collaboration that this Polish question be settled fairly and speedily. If this is not done all of the difficulties and dangers to Allied unity which we had so much in mind in reaching our decisions at the Crimea will face us in an even more acute form. You are, I am sure, aware that the genuine popular support in the United States is required to carry out any government policy, foreign or domestic. The American people make up their own mind and no government action can change it. I mention this fact because the last sentence of your message about Mr. Molotov's attendance at San Francisco made me wonder whether you give full weight to this factor.

Received April 1, 1945

Essays

7   The Atlantic Conference

Theodore A. Wilson

The first of the World War II summit conferences on the Allied side was the dramatic sea meeting of President Roosevelt and Prime Minister Churchill. The meeting off Argentia, Newfoundland, coming as it did before formal American entry into the war, was in many ways the most novel of the wartime meetings. It determined the style and much of the agenda for subsequent conferences. But the most important result of the "first summit" was the Atlantic Charter, a statement of high principle that was to become the basic expression of Allied war and peace aims. In his essay, Wilson contends that the Atlantic Charter was primarily an outgrowth of Roosevelt's desire to achieve a propaganda coup. While the statement did reflect strong convictions—particularly the American vision of an open international economic system as the basis for lasting peace—its transformation from press release into something approaching divine writ was supremely ironic.

That the Atlantic Charter proved the longest-lived result of their meeting at Argentia amazed Roosevelt and Churchill. Its chief rationale was propaganda; yet the joint declaration on war and peace aims turned up like a copper penny throughout the war—alternately embarrassing and pleasing its designers.

Planning for some such statement had been going on for a long time in England and especially in the United States. Statements about war aims and the structures of peace were congenial to Roosevelt and his advisers on foreign policy—as such pronouncements have been to most Americans over the years. On many matters F.D.R. bypassed his Department of State; in regard to postwar planning he gave the inhabitants of "foggy bottom" great if not sole responsibility, and he listened to their recommendations.

Long before America became involved in the war Roosevelt felt that "if

From **The First Summit** by Theodore A. Wilson (Boston: Houghton Mifflin, 1969), pp. 173–202. Copyright © 1969 by Theodore A. Wilson. Reprinted by permission of the author.

could come out of the Second World War, it would be the opportunity afforded the Americans and the British to bring order out of the resulting chaos and, in particular, to disarm all those powers who in his belief had been the primary cause of so many of the wars of the preceding century." These words, put in his mouth by Sumner Welles, do not have the compelling ring of Wilson's "make the world safe for democracy"; but the purpose was the same.

Roosevelt's views on international affairs might justifiably be termed unsophisticated; and on some problems he had no views at all. However, he held to his opinions with tenacity. He was not and did not claim to be an original thinker, but he possessed in abundance the gift of using men and ideas to his own advantage and of giving clear expression to the vague ideas of others. . . .

Attachment to "internationalism" was one of Roosevelt's convictions, but there was confusion as to the best means of achieving the goal. According to Louis Wehle, the President believed that "war must still be the touchstone of policy in foreign affairs. At thirty Roosevelt was a worshiping Wilsonian. Into middle age he espoused a world order under a union of nations; but unlike Wilson, the evangelist, while pursuing peace, he never neglected military preparedness." There was to be much Wilsonian idealism in the Atlantic Charter, as there was much of Wilson in the moral outlook of Roosevelt; but he came to advocate what he believed were "realistic" methods of achieving world order. Such reasoning was the basis for his scoffing in 1928 at the Kellogg-Briand Pact, and for his attempt in the 1930's to substitute national power for platitudes. One finds it ironic that this point of view culminated in the Atlantic Charter.

Oddly existing with this "realistic approach" were principles from his Wilsonian heritage. F.D.R. said to Adolf A. Berle, Jr. in June, 1941: "Don't forget that the elimination of costly armaments is still the keystone—for the security of all the little nations and for economic solvency. Don't forget what I discovered—that over ninety percent of all national deficits from 1921 to 1939 were caused by payments for past, present, and future wars;" and in 1942 he told Mackenzie King that the "main emphasis" in the peace settlement should be on "the complete disarmament of Germany, the constant and thorough inspection of their industry, coupled with an international police force, particularly an aviation bombardment force." Indeed, forcible disarmament of all nations must be contemplated.

Sumner Welles, not one to criticize the President, had to admit F.D.R.'s attitude toward small powers was "unduly impatient."

He maintained stubbornly that they should be satisfied if the English-speaking powers were able to assure them security from aggression, and in return should be willing to spend their national revenues upon education and upon raising living standards rather than upon armaments for which they would have no further need. He brushed aside all references to national pride, or to the age-old international hatreds of Eastern Europe. He dismissed as of little account the argument that no responsible government of a small country could be compelled to liquidate the military establishment upon which it believed the safety of the nation depended, unless the self-appointed policemen were prepared to occupy that country by force. He occasionally spoke of his project for an Anglo-American policing of the world as being "realistic." He could enumerate in considerable detail the various advantages that the peoples of the smaller countries would derive from such a policy of realism.

Although for domestic economic reasons, early in his first administration, he had "torpedoed" the London Economic Conference, Roosevelt soon demonstrated his attachment to liberal trade policy. He succeeded in having enacted into law the reciprocal trade ideas of his Secretary of State, Cordell Hull. From that time he was an advocate—in theory, and sometimes in practice—of free, equal trade for all nations, but his advocacy varied with circumstances.

Then perhaps the most important of Roosevelt's principles as the United States moved closer to war was another Wilsonian ideal—conveyed by the jaw-breaking phrase "no predetermination." The President was joined by other top-ranking American leaders in the desire that there be no "advance agreements" regarding frontiers or related questions. Belief that territorial agreements and "other political bargains" should await a universal peace conference merged nicely with F.D.R.'s desire to preserve flexibility in foreign affairs; it was, however, "a part of the entire fabric of wartime diplomacy," as Raymond Dawson correctly points out.

The President did not suffer from lack of advice about the proper course for the United States. Naturally, suggestions increased in volume and in urgency as American involvement became a stronger possibility. For example, on October 29, 1940, the famous English novelist, H.G. Wells, proffered a statement of war aims. Disturbed about his government's failure to offer more than "vague and unconvincing promises," he turned to Roosevelt. "There is something better to be done for which there exists a number of precedents . . . from *Magna Carta* onward and that is to make a clear restatement in modern terms in view of modern conditions of the natural *Rights of Man*." Hadley Cantril, a member of the Princeton Institute of Public Opinion Research, had been providing the White House with résumés of the Institute's surveys. On March 20, 1941, he wrote: "When listening to the President's speech the other night I was then, as I have been so frequently, somewhat disappointed that he did not spell out . . . the personal effects of a Nazi victory or the whole Nazi ideology. Wouldn't it be sensible if sometime he could elaborate with profuse illustrations what he means by the four freedoms? . . . I am convinced that the great majority of people in this country have no idea how their own self-interest would be involved in any radical departure from the democratic way of life." . . .

An elaborate commentary on postwar policy issued from a meeting of high administration officials in early May, 1941. The memorandum recording the gist of this discussion not only rationalizes the role of the United States in the postwar world but also calls for a conference between the President and Prime Minister Churchill. The views therein, if not formally those of Roosevelt, represent the thinking of the inner circle.

Certainly the introductory sentence of the memorandum conformed to F.D.R.'s view of the postwar situation: "The years ahead are divisible into three periods, the period of war, the period of postwar transition, the period of the new world order." Only the last two were discussed by the group. As a first principle they agreed that the United States "should and would take much more responsibility in the coming peace than in the peace which is now past." Later conversation showed they assumed America would claim a dominant position after the war. The group scrutinized the interwar period "with a view to past error and future promise." One speaker argued that a return to the Versailles Treaty, by men who had learned from its tragic mistakes, might result in a satisfactory peace settlement. Although there was disagreement about his contention, all accepted the necessity of Anglo-American domination. It was suggested that many of the League's failures "could be traced to the failure of the Tripartite Treaty to come into effect; because of the absence of this instrument of order during the transition period, France began a lone search for security which distorted the future of the League." To avoid any such development after the current war close cooperation between the United States and the United Kingdom was essential.

Someone observed that the "avoidance of quarrels"—an obvious reference to the difficulties over trade policy—was crucial. It was true that England's postwar financial position would push her toward currency controls and even more exclusive trading systems, and that "the story of British attitudes on raw materials in the 1920's and particularly in the 1930's . . . warns us of present dangers." America presently held a strong hand, "but it is important to come to agreements while Great Britain is willing to deal." The situation demanded "an immediate opening of conversations leading to the establishment of common institutions." One speaker noted that the democracies were given an opportunity to "grow" a League of Nations rather than to "make" one. A suggested agenda for such discussion included plans for immediate and joint action, and for postwar cooperation throughout the world. The issue of access to raw materials also belonged on the agenda. These questions could not be postponed much longer; and in fact some participants indicated impatience with the current rate at which the "fusion" of American and British interests was taking place. Some believed that immediate union was needed, and that it should be "open-ended" for adherence by nations presently under the Nazi yoke. At least, provision for the merger of America and England was essential.

The group called for a "statement of our alternative to Hitler's new order, a definition of the New Order of the Ages proclaimed on the Great Seal of the United States," which would answer these questions and generate the "dynamic" for the task ahead. One speaker suggested a revision of Wilson's Fourteen Points, a "formulation" which could serve as both peace aim and war instrument. Such a double-barreled statement, he believed, "would have real propaganda value for bringing peace." For the President's benefit the secretary of the meeting wrote, "The need for a vigorous lead was repeated over and over . . . Without outspoken leadership, we are in the position of fighting something with nothing." Obviously, the propaganda effect of a statement of war aims, and the steps presumably to follow, had highest priority.

Proposals of this kind in part duplicated activities already being carried on within high-ceilinged offices in the antiquated State-War-Navy Building next to the White House. Study of postwar problems in the Department of State had begun in December, 1939, with a committee "on problems of peace and reconstruction." Sumner Welles was largely responsible, although the Secretary approved. The committee acquired the title of Advisory Committee on Problems of Foreign Relations. Welles assumed the chairmanship. There were three subcommittees to consider respectively, political problems (including organization of peace), limitation and reduction of armaments, and economic questions. They met without agenda, minutes, or preparatory studies; and they functioned in this form for less than a year.

The group dealing with economic problems continued its studies longer than the other two. Secretary Hull offered enthusiastic support and gave elaborate suggestions. Problems of international trade were, he devoutly believed, the source of all other international difficulties. Breckinridge Long said of the Secretary's obsession with economic policy: "Of course *that* is Hull. That is his . . . *raison d'etre* . . . His trade agreements . . . are the base on which rest his whole foreign activity. Without that base the structure falls." He spelled out his ideas on economic policy in a radio address in May, 1941. "The main principles," he asserted, " are few and simple": 1., extreme nationalism "must not again be permitted to express itself in excessive trade restrictions"; 2., "non-discrimination in international commercial relations must be the rule"; 3., raw materials must be available to all nations; 4., international finance must "lend aid to the essential enterprises and the continuous development of all countries."

Hull's principles seemed an amplification of the goals of the President. Roosevelt's Annual Message of January, 1941, had expressed his definition—for the first time—of the foundation for a secure future, the so-called Four Freedoms (freedom of speech, expression, and worship; freedom from want and from fear). Roosevelt said these aims were "no vision of a distant millenium," but the basis "for a kind of world attainable in our time and generation." He knew such vague words would not move the American people. He must find a way to bring the words into focus, to stamp them in American hearts and identify them with the policy of assisting Great Britain.

Circumstances ensured that some kind of statement on war aims would arise at Argentia. That it would take the form of the Atlantic Charter was not at all certain. As noted, Roosevelt passionately desired to postpone territorial and general political questions until a peace conference. The Department of State had campaigned to commit the United Kingdom to a liberal postwar economic policy: Hull and his helpers wanted the British to abolish "imperial preference." American planners adopted the notion that security was indivisible, and they opted for a general international organization over tight regional groupings. Their attitude on economic policy reflected these beliefs. . . . There had been several efforts to force Britain to an agreement. Then some bright officer in the

Department had proposed that the United States link postwar abolition of closed economic systems with the negotiation concerning Lend-Lease agreements. The Department followed this suggestion with notable sprightliness. . . .

The early summer of 1941 was a trying period for the Churchill government. While the British suffered Nazi attacks, their "friends" bombarded them with memoranda. Churchill steadfastly refused to pronounce on postwar questions, which might divide British opinion. Mackenzie King admitted that his fellow Prime Minister "was so concentrated on the war that he could not see that settling certain broad problems of the peace now would in effect help the actual war effort."

British political parties, of course, had placed on the record general statements about war aims. As early as March, 1940, before Churchill took office, the government had established a committee to study problems in connection with peace, proposing an exchange of ideas with American planners; but Hull squelched the suggestion.

Churchill in January, 1941, was pressed in the House of Commons for clarification of principles for which Great Britain was fighting. The Prime Minister irritably responded: "As I have said, when a good opportunity presents itself, I or other Ministers will certainly be on the look-out to turn that opportunity to the best advantage."

Soon after, the Schuster Committee, reorganized under Clement Attlee, sent to the Department of State, and thence to Roosevelt, a short memo which may be called a semiofficial statement of the Churchill government's war aims. The document called for a New Deal for the English people and all nations. It recommended: 1., "positive lines of action" for outlawry of war; 2., maintenance of security; 3., greater economic equality; 4., production for human welfare; and, 5., social justice. With regard to the third point, it proposed that the United Kingdom offer "international solutions" to colonial problems and access to raw materials, "lowering of trade barriers which are essential if greater economic equality between nations is to be brought about." There was strong emphasis on measures primarily national. Bruce concluded: "If Britain declares her revolutionary intentions in no uncertain voice, her determination will be followed in the Dominions, and we shall have provided the closest bond of cooperation with President Roosevelt, namely an identity of ideas."

The Prime Minister did come to recognize the need for some public statement, and an address at Mansion House, May 29, 1941, by Foreign Secretary Anthony Eden, was intended to pacify the critics. Eden's speech was a repetition of Keynesian views and his description of the postwar economic scene disturbed the State Department. Continental Europe he saw as emerging from the war "starving and bankrupt." Liberated countries and "maybe" others would require resources, and Eden suggested that the United Kingdom contribute. Otherwise, the speech was vague. It endorsed Hull's point about creating international financial institutions; but as Leo Pasvolsky, Special Assistant and Chief, Division of Special Research, commented to the Secretary: "It is too bad that Mr. Eden does not similarly endorse the other four points of your program, especially points 1 and 2, relating to excessive trade barriers and non-discriminatory treatment." Hull's adviser preferred the ideas of the British Labour Party, which viewed the world as a single economic unit, over Eden's "rather cryptic phrases" about social security.

For better or worse, American leaders thought Eden's speech "one of the authoritative indications of British war aims." Until the Atlantic Conference, Churchill's regime took no further action although more statements were issued. The Roosevelt administration knew only that Churchill held sharply different views from their own on aspects of the postwar world. As Pasvolsky lamented in June, the "vagueness" of Churchill's statements and of other British pronouncements "argue strongly for joint exploration of postwar problems by representatives of the two governments and for vigorous effort to work out a more or less precise post-war program." He was not alone in requesting some joint negotiations. Other voices, for a variety of reasons, were calling for a meeting, preferably at the highest level, of American and British leaders.

In spite of all that had been done, creation of the Atlantic Charter proved as complicated as the earlier debate about war aims. From whence came the decision to link the Roosevelt-Churchill meeting with a statement of ideals is not entirely clear. The joint declaration certainly was of American inspiration. Churchill has written that he hardly had set foot on *Augusta's* deck when the President brought up the notion of a declaration "laying down certain broad principles which should guide our policies along the same road." As has been shown, F.D.R. had some such purpose in mind for several months, and expressed his desire for a statement at the luncheon of Saturday. Churchill gracefully acceded. The two leaders and their principal assistants, Welles and Cadogan, carried forward the project.

Preliminary work occurred in meetings between the two Under Secretaries. Churchill and Cadogan had not much time to consult about the President's suggestion before this first meeting. Cadogan was conversant with his superior's views. At the meeting Saturday afternoon Welles revealed he was privy to Roosevelt's position. . . .

Cadogan said the question of secret treaties was one of the "main matters" Churchill desired to discuss with President Roosevelt. He had with him the texts of all agreements into which Britain had entered, and would be "very glad" to go over them. Cadogan gave the "most specific and positive assurance" that his government had made no commitments on frontiers or territorial readjustment—with one exception, an "oral statement" to Yugoslavia before the coup d'état. The British Minister at Belgrade had stated "that at the conclusion of the war the subject of the jurisdiction over Istria was a matter which might well come up for reconsideration." There had been no mention either of Goritza or Trieste. In their alliances with Poland and Czechoslovakia the British had made no decision as to boundaries. Great Britain, in the cases of Norway, the Netherlands, and Belgium, had committed itself only to their "reestablishment" as nations. The French alliance, whatever its present status, was similar.

These confidences "much heartened" Welles. He was not personally sympathetic to the Rooseveltian doctrine of "no predetermination" but, he did oppose political concessions at that time. He gave Cadogan a convincing explanation of the source of the policy. Cadogan would remember, he said, the damage during the First World War "by the sudden revelation of the series of agreements which Great Britain had previously entered into." Rumors that Churchill's regime had made similar secret agreements had created "disquiet and suspicion." Cadogan asserted that Churchill "had it very much in mind" and the two diplomats agreed to consider a statement "at an appropriate moment" on postwar commitments. The matter remained unsettled several weeks after the conference, and in September the Roosevelt administration was still demanding a British disavowal of secret treaties.

The other source of the joint declaration—a satisfactory formula for postwar economic arrangements—formed the final topic of this Saturday conversation. Cadogan said he had received the text of the proposed Lend-Lease Agreement the day before he left London but asked for a copy to refresh his memory. This Welles gave him and also copies of Acheson's memorandum of conversations with Keynes, and Keynes' letter to Acheson the following day.

After allowing Cadogan time to read these documents the Under Secretary said there was no need "to undertake a dissertation upon fundamental economics." Describing the conversations, he stated: "I felt sure from my conversations with Sir Alexander during the past few years that he and I saw eye to eye with regard to the freest possible economic interchange without discriminations, without exchange controls, without economic preference utilized for political purpose, and without all of the manifold economic barriers which had in my judgment been so clearly responsible for the present world collapse." Welles was disturbed that Keynes represented "some segment of British public opinion" which desired after the war to resume "exactly that kind of system which had proved so fatal during the past generation." A healthy world demanded not policies already proven disastrous but identity of purpose and a spirit of self-sacrifice. Welles believed the Lend-Lease Agreement provided such assurances. One of the factors "poisoning" British-American relations in the interwar period had been the British debt, and he assured Cadogan that the formula, as drafted, would prevent any recurrence of that issue. Welles avoided direct reference to Article VII, which called for abolition of all discriminatory trade arrangements.

This lecture placed Cadogan in an awkward position. He said that he could offer only his own opinion with regard to the economic issue. "He himself found the formula exactly what was required." He wished Wells to know—off the record—that he had "bitterly opposed" the Ottawa Agreements and that, in his opinion, they had nearly proved fatal. "He saw no hope for the future unless our two countries agreed, no matter what the obstacles might later prove, to press for the resumption of liberal trade practices and for the abolition of discriminations at the earliest possible moment." The Prime Minister would speak with President Roosevelt about this subject, and Cadogan claimed not to know what Churchill's "considered judgment" might be.

Each man immediately reported this conversation to his chief. One might construct imaginary but logical descriptions of these interviews. Roosevelt would have been delighted and relieved that the British accepted his proposal—even though there would be difficulties. The Prime Minister was less enthusiastic but willing to go along. If his campaign for American entry into the war failed, a pledge of Anglo-American solidarity (into which he could read various meanings) would help.

Both sides now gave attention to the declaration. Churchill may have received warning of the President's intent. Welles, however, in the few hours before leaving Washington, had drafted a statement drawn from his conversations with Roosevelt and Department studies. His draft—which has never come to light—focused probably on the political aims of F.D.R. and on liberal economic policies.

This result of his frantic effort was not used at Argentia, probably because of another of Roosevelt's stratagems. The President feared an American proposal would challenge the British Empire, that it would attack colonialism and trade discrimination. Convinced that discussion on this basis would founder, F.D.R. arranged that the British furnish the working draft. He evidently instructed Hopkins to notify the Prime Minister. The President then rested in knowledge that Churchill would come through with an inspiring if vague manifesto. It would be possible to insert American principles in this proposal.

It was ever British policy to make draft proposals, so Churchill went along. After listing some of the ideas the President could expect in the document on Saturday night, he retired to his cabin and put a draft declaration—which he may already have prepared—into polished form. Churchill has written of this effort: "Considering all the tales of my reactionary, Old-World outlook, and the pain this is said to have caused the President, I am glad it should be on record that the substance and spirit of what came to be called the 'Atlantic Charter' was in its first draft a British production cast in my own words." This "production," given to the Americans Sunday morning, read as follows:

> The President of the United States of America and the Prime Minister, Mr. Churchill, representing His Majesty's Government in the United Kingdom, being met together to resolve and concert the means of providing for the safety of their respective countries in face of Nazi and German aggression and of the dangers to all peoples arising therefrom, deem it right to make known certain principles which they both accept for guidance in the framing of their policy and on which they base their hopes for a better future for the world.
>
> First, their countries seek no aggrandizement, political or other;
>
> Second, they desire to see no territorial changes that do not accord with the freely expressed wishes of the peoples concerned;
>
> Third, they respect the right of all peoples to choose the form of government under which they will live; they are only concerned to defend the rights of freedom of speech and of thought without which such choosing must be illusory;
>
> Fourth, they will strive to bring about a fair and equitable distribution of

essential produce not only within their territorial jurisdiction but between the nations of the world.

Fifth, they seek a peace which will not only cast down forever the Nazi tyranny but by effective international organization will afford to all States and peoples the means of dwelling in security within their own bounds and of traversing the seas and oceans without fear of lawless assault or need of getting burdensome armaments.

. . . The President went over Churchill's creation with his assistant late Sunday afternoon. Neither was happy with the British draft, but it did form a basis for discussion. The first three points, if not clear, answered Roosevelt's desire of no secret territorial or political agreements. Point four, which contained a meaningless promise "to bring about a fair and equitable distribution of essential produce . . . between the nations of the world," brought a cry of outrage from Welles. Roosevelt's reaction is not recorded. He was disturbed by the last clause, since he did not believe—at that time—in international organization. Also, F.D.R. had no wish to throw such a bone to the isolationists at home. He told Welles to redraft the declaration.

Welles' anxiety about British policy was confirmed Sunday night, at the informal dinner of Roosevelt, Churchill, and their personal staffs. He was not invited, but reports of the Prime Minister's statements must have set him working into the night on a redraft. According to Elliott Roosevelt, F.D.R. provoked Churchill into a full defense of the British Empire. This dialogue, even if untrustworthy, deserves full quotation.

"Father started it," his son wrote. "Of course," he remarked with a sly sort of assurance, "of course, after the war, one of the preconditions of any lasting peace will have to be the greatest possible freedom of trade." He paused. The P.M.'s head was lowered; he was watching Father steadily, from under one eyebrow. "No artificial barriers," Father pursued. "As few favored economic agreements as possible . . . Markets open for healthy competition . . ."

Churchill shifted in his armchair. "The British Empire trade agreements," he began heavily, "are—." Father broke in. "Yes. Those Empire trade agreements are a case in point. It's because of them that the people of India and Africa, of all the colonial Near East and Far East, are still as backward as they are."

Churchill's neck reddened and he crouched forward. "Mr. President, England does not propose for a moment to lose its favored position among the British Dominions. The trade that has made England great shall continue, and under conditions prescribed by England's ministers."

"You see," said Father slowly, "it is along in here somewhere that there is likely to be some disagreement between you, Winston, and me. I am firmly of the belief that if we are to arrive at a stable peace it must involve the development of backward peoples. . . . How can this be done? It can't be done, obviously, by eighteenth century methods . . ." The P.M. . . . was beginning to look apoplectic. "You mentioned India," he growled. "Yes. I can't believe that we can fight a war against facist slavery, and at the same time not work to free people all over the world from a backward colonial policy" . . . "There can be no tampering with the Empire's economic agreements." They're artificial . . ." "They're the foundation of our greatness."

"The peace," said Father firmly, "cannot include any continued despotism. The structure of the peace demands and will get equality of peoples. Equality of peoples involves the utmost freedom of competitive trade. Will anyone suggest that Germany's attempt to dominate trade in central Europe was not a major contributing fact to war?"

Elliott brought the exchange to a close on this note. Churchill may have made some such statement. Elsewhere, he accused the President of wanting to destroy the Empire. One doubts, however, if F.D.R. would have waved such a large red flag before the Prime Minister. As already stated, he believed the things Elliott has him say on this occasion; but rarely did he allow them to influence his negotiations.

Welles was not entirely convinced of the President's loyalty to anticolonialism and freedom of trade. The alternative draft which he gave Roosevelt Monday morning was a way of committing the President as well as Churchill. It read,

> The President of the United States of America and the Prime Minister, Mr. Churchill, representing his Majesty's Government in the United Kingdom, being met together to consider and to resolve the steps which their Governments should take in order to provide for the safety of the respective countries in face of the policies of the world-wide domination and of military conquest upon which the Hitlerite Government of Germany and the other dictatorships associated therewith have embarked, deem it right and proper to make known certain principles which they both accept for guidance in the framing of their respective policies and on which they base their hopes for a better future for the world.
>
> First, their countries seek no aggrandizement, territorial or other;
>
> Second, they desire to see no territorial changes that do not accord with the freely expressed wishes of the peoples concerned;
>
> Third, they respect the right of all peoples to choose the form of government under which they will live;
>
> Fourth, they will strive to promote mutually advantageous economic relations between them through the elimination of any discrimination in either the United States of America or in the United Kingdom against the importation of any product originating in the other country; and they will endeavor to further the enjoyment by all peoples of access on equal terms to the markets and to the raw materials which are needed for their economic prosperity;
>
> Fifth, they hope to see established a peace, after the final destruction of

Nazi tyranny, which by effective international organization, will afford to all states and peoples the means of dwelling in security within their own boundaries, and the means of assurance that human beings may live out their lives in freedom from fear. They likewise hope to see established by such a peace safety for all peoples on the high seas and oceans, and the adoption of such measures as will prevent the continuation of expenditures for armaments other than those which are purely defensive.

. . . Roosevelt suggested several further changes—a few important, some minor. Welles later claimed they "considered and discussed" every word; the President wished to ensure that nothing should work out to his embarrassment. F.D.R. eliminated most of Churchill's bellicos preamble. The joint declaration was to affirm an Anglo-American alliance, but only in principle. It must not, he considered, contain references to "immediate issues" such as American participation in the war.

This attitude led to the pruning of the first part of Welles' fourth article. After the shenanigans of Sunday night Roosevelt realized that commitment to free trade between the United States and the British Commonwealth was too powerful a draft for Churchill. The reference to access to markets and raw materials remained. In his own handwriting Roosevelt inserted the words "without discrimination," a condensation of the first clause. To the third article he added a hope for restoration of self-government "to those from whom it has been forcibly removed." Churchill's casual reference to "safety for all peoples in the high seas and oceans" was given the status of a separate article, and the language stiffened to conform with traditional American policy regarding freedom of the seas. The President excised all reference to international organization. In its place went a statement dealing with disarmament of aggressors.

Welles returned to *Tuscaloosa* and prepared another draft. He appreciated Roosevelt's firmness regarding economic policy, but he opposed the position, taken apparently out of cynicism, on international organization. The new draft contained seven articles, since the President had added one and divided the fifth point:

The President . . . and the Prime Minister . . . being met together, deem it right to make known certain common principles in the national policies of their respective countries on which they base their hopes for a better future for the world.

First, their countries seek no aggrandizement, territorial or other;

Second, they desire to see no territorial changes that do not accord with the freely expressed wishes of the peoples concerned;

Third, they respect the right of all peoples to choose the form of government under which they will live; and they wish to see self-government restored to those from whom it has been forcibly removed.

Fourth, they will endeavor to further the enjoyment by all peoples, without discrimination and on equal terms, to the markets and to the raw materials of the world which are needed for their economic prosperity;

Fifth, they hope to see established a peace, after the destruction of the Nazi tyranny, which will afford to all nations the means of dwelling in security within their own boundaries, and which will afford assurance to all peoples that they may live out their lives in freedom from fear and want.

Sixth, they desire such a peace to establish for all safety on the high seas and oceans;

Seventh, they believe that all of the nations of the world, for realistic as well as spiritual reasons, must come to the abandonment of the use of force. Because no future peace can be maintained if land, sea, or air armaments continue to be employed by nations which threaten, or may threaten, aggression outside of their frontiers, they believe that the disarmament of such nations is essential. They will likewise further all other practicable measures which will lighten for peace-loving peoples the crushing burden of armaments.

Welles had exercised considerable freedom in transcribing the President's language but left intact the spirit of the changes.

In this, its third incarnation, the proposed declaration differed markedly from Churchill's original essay. Roosevelt and Welles could not be sure how the Prime Minister would react. The references to disarmament would not be objectionable, for they were satisfactorily vague and idealistic. Absence of any reference to international organization, they knew, would distress the Prime Minister. The redraft of article four was expected to do more than distress him.

The joint declaration came up between the two leaders late Monday morning. F.D.R., Churchill, Hopkins, Cadogan, and Welles met in the Admiral's cabin on *Augusta*. . . . After more pressing diplomatic matters had been dealt with, Churchill asked that the company take up the proposed declaration. F.D.R. at first took this suggestion as meaning arrangements for its announcement. He said he thought the "best solution" was an "identic statement" in London and Washington on Thursday, August 14, announcing that "the Prime Minister and the President had met at sea, accompanied by the various members of their respective staffs; that these officers had discussed the question of aid under the terms of the Lend-Lease Act to nations resisting aggression, and that these military and naval conversations had in no way involved any future commitments between the two Governments, except as authorized under the terms of the Lend-Lease Act; that the Prime Minister and the President had between them discussed certain principles relating to a better future for the world and had agreed upon a joint declaration. In reply, Churchill indicated that he cared not how and when they proclaimed the joint declaration; he was concerned about its contents and how it was received. He said he could not allow the announcement made as the President described it. The President considered this rank heresy.

The Prime Minister objected "very strongly" to the way in which the statement made clear there had been no commitments. Roosevelt replied the point was extremely important "inasmuch as a statement of that character would make it impossible for extreme isolationist leaders in the United States to allege that every kind of secret agreement had been entered into." Churchill was also concerned with public opinion. He feared the effect on the British people; and thought "any categorical statement of that character would prove deeply discouraging to the populations of the occupied countries and would have a very serious effect upon their morale." Might not the announcement, he wondered, "be worded in such a way to make it positive rather than negative, namely, that the members of the staffs of the Prime Minister and of the President had solely discussed questions relative to the furnishing of aid to countries resisting aggression under the terms of the Lend-Lease Act?" Once he grasped the meaning behind the Prime Minister's convoluted phrasing, Roosevelt agreed to have the announcement couched in this manner. If he were interrogated by those nasty isolationists, "he need merely reply" that nothing had been discussed or decided except matters referred to in the declaration. With this agreeable evasion confirmed the company turned to the declaration.

Welles gave the President, Churchill, and Cadogan copies of the rewritten proclamation he had finished just prior to the meeting. Apparently, the Prime Minister began to read it aloud. There was no hesitation as he droned through the first three points. He did suggest insertion in point three of "sovereign rights and" before the words "self-government." This minor change found ready acceptance. On reading the fourth article his voice likely trailed off into silence. The article bore little resemblance to the one he had drafted Saturday evening. "He immediately inquired whether this was meant to apply to the terms of the Ottawa Agreements." Welles replied firmly, "Of course, it did." He launched into a lecture about attempts by the United States "for the better part of nine years" to remove "all of those artificial restrictions and controls . . . which had created such tragic havoc to world economy during the past generation." Welles understood the "immediate difficulties" this caused the Prime Minister; but the phrase "they will endeavor to further" did not require a "formal and immediate contractual obligation" on the part of the United Kingdom. Roosevelt supported his subordinate because of article four's propaganda value. He believed the point of great importance "as a measure of assurance to the German and Italian peoples that after the war they would receive equal economic opportunities."

Churchill demonstrated impressive restraint. He pleaded his lack of authority—introducing his listeners to the constitutional complexities of the British Commonwealth. The government of the United Kingdom was unable to agree to the article without consulting the Dominions. The member nations were unlikely to accede to destruction of the Ottawa Agreements. And Churchill never intended to submit the outrageous fourth article to them. The wily Prime Minister was displaying what he believed a trump card. He could play this constitutional requirement against the President's desire for announcement of the Atlantic Charter immediately after the conference's end.

Churchill claimed to be on the side of the angels in liberalization of trade. The issue, he said, was connected intimately with "his personal life history." He treated the Americans to a brief history of "the days at the outset of the century when Joseph Chamberlain first brought up the proposal for Empire preferences and the predominant part which this issue had played in the political history of Great Britain during the past forty years." He was "heartily in accord" with the principle of free trade. "As was well known," he had always opposed the Ottawa Agreements. Whatever Churchill's theoretical attitude, the dictates of British politics controlled his response. Again he flashed that hole card. "It would be at least a week," he said, "before he could hope to obtain by telegraph the opinion of the Dominions with regard to this question."

At this awkward moment Hopkins stepped in and resumed the role of intermediary. The President's aide was always willing to gloss over disagreements. "It was inconceivable," he stated, "that the issuance of the joint declaration should be held up by a matter of this kind." Hopkins proposed that Welles and Cadogan draft new phrasing "which would take care of these difficulties and prevent the delay of which Mr. Churchill spoke." This offhand rejection of long months of effort infuriated Welles, who thought further revision "would destroy completely" the fourth article. It was not a question of phrasing, he insisted, but vital principle. "If the British and the United States Governments could not agree to do everything within their power to further, after the termination of the present war, a restoration of free and liberal trade policies, they might as well throw in the sponge and realize that one of the greatest factors in creating the present tragic situation . . . was going to be permitted to continue unchecked." Without support by the President and Prime Minister a policy of "constructive sanity" would never see the light, Welles pleaded.

Churchill and Cadogan both admitted the difficulty lay not merely with wording. The Prime Minister then put his cards on the table. "The Dominions would have to be consulted," he sighed. It was even possible the Commonwealth nations would turn down article four and "consequently the proposed joint declaration could only be used some time after news of the meeting . . . had been given out." To "ease the situation" he suggested insertion of a simple qualifying phrase, "with due regard for our present obligations." The maneuver had the predictable effect on F.D.R., who was more concerned with issuing a statement of some kind than with the Department's economic policy. Too softhearted to concede the point in front of Welles, F.D.R. suggested that Churchill "try and draft some phraseology which would make that situation easier." The Prime Minister graciously acceded. It was arranged that Welles call on the English representatives later in the afternoon to go over Churchill's redraft.

With that crisis settled in his favor, the Prime Minister returned to reading the American draft. He expressed "entire accord" with the fifth and sixth articles—little different from his version. He came to point seven, and first raised a minor objection. In the second sentence "aggression" should replace "to use force." The article, which Churchill may have recognized as the President's creation, received enthusiastic approval. But he missed any reference to a revived League of Nations. "He inquired . . . whether the President would not agree to support some kind of 'effective international organization' as suggested . . . in his original draft." Roosevelt's first reaction was negative. He could not agree to those three little words "because of the suspicions and opposition" at home.

F.D.R. touched on his prejudice against revival of a world organization. He could not support any new "Assembly of the League" until after a period of transition. During this stage an international force staffed by the United States and Great Britain would police the world. Churchill possessed considerable sympathy for this view, but his concern was with *British* public opinion. "He did not feel he would be candid if he did not express to the President his feeling that point seven would create a great deal of opposition from the extreme internationalists." Roosevelt would not budge. He came back to his conviction that "the time had come to be realistic and that . . . the main factor in the seventh point was complete realism." Churchill had no choice but to accept the President's decision.

The Prime Minister remarked that he did not intend to leave until at least 5:00 P.M. the next day. He attached so much importance to reaching "a complete meeting of minds" that he was willing to stay an additional twenty-four hours. Welles feared the Prime Minister's cordiality, and attempted to convince F.D.R. to use this extra time to American advantage. He urged him "to see whether Mr. Churchill might not be induced to cut corners and expedite his communications with the Dominions' governments." If pressure of time were removed, the President would stand behind his Department—and Welles. The fourth point as Churchill intended to rewrite it would mean nothing. F.D.R. seemed to agree, or so Welles believed. He knew Churchill was using the President's desire for an immediate declaration to force a disastrous compromise; but there was little he could do. . . .

. . . A meeting of Welles, the P.M., and Cadogan had been arranged for 3:00 P.M. Just a few minutes before the hour a messenger from *Augusta* handed Welles a surprising but not entirely unexpected note. At 2:30 the President had written out his decision on point four. "Dear Sumner: Time being of the essence I think I can stand on my own former formulas—to wit: access to raw materials. This omits entirely the *other* subject which is the only one in conflict: discrimination in trade. The fourth paragraph would then read 'of access to the raw materials of the world,' etc. For *me* that is consistent." Welles thought it was not at all consistent. He was shocked and deeply disappointed by Roosevelt's defection—but there was nothing he could do. A few words from the President destroyed his hopes and those of the Department that Argentia would bind the British to trade liberalization. The Under Secretary blamed Harry Hopkins; probably he was right.

The meeting with Cadogan (the Prime Minister did not attend) was anticlimactic. Welles had no further reason to delay an agreement—on British terms. His English colleague asked him to read a summary of the morning discussion, and Welles passively approved. Cadogan stated that the Prime Minister had dispatched to London a text of the joint declaration, which incorporated certain "modifications" of points four and seven. The revised fourth article read: "They will endeavor, with due respect for their existing obligations, to further the enjoyment by all States, great or small, victor or vanquished, of access on equal terms to the trade and to the raw materials of the world." The article did refer both to commerce and raw materials, and Welles accepted ·this minor concession. Welles explained that "inasmuch as the Prime Minister's draft of point four was far broader and more satisfactory than the minimum which the President had instructed me . . . to accept" nothing would be gained by raising objection.

The Under Secretary bestirred himself to approve the changes in point seven. Perhaps he reasoned that he could salvage something of value. The two diplomats engaged in frank exchange about the President's and Prime Minister's attitudes on international organization. Cadogan said the Prime Minister "felt very strongly—perhaps exaggeratedly—the opposition which would be created on the part of a certain League-of-Nations element to the contents of point seven." He believed this sentiment received undue importance; but it would be tragic "to place sole emphasis upon the transition period after the war." Some reference to an agency to function after the transition stage was essential. Welles was in sympathy, but stressed that, "as recent experience had shown," only the President could decide the matter. While the British draft of point seven was completely satisfactory, he "had no idea what the President's decision might be." It was now Welles' turn to play the role of marionette.

The Under Secretary subsequently took these revisions to his master. F.D.R. accepted the redraft of point four as "better than he had thought Mr. Churchill would be willing to concede." He accepted Churchill's version of the seventh article without question, since it conveyed the idea of a transition period before the creation of any international organization. If Welles had doubted the Prime Minister's cards before, these words removed any question. . . .

* * *

In one sense the aftermath of Argentia comprehended the history of the Second World War. Long after the site of the first conference between Roosevelt and Churchill had been forgotten, when the discussions with Japan and Vichy and Premier Salazar were remembered only by file clerks in the Department of State and Foreign Office archives, the Atlantic Charter was a live issue. Subsequent problems with regard to each of the eight points were great. The history of these conflicting interpretations is outside the scope of this study. It is sufficient to understand how much a part of national desires and anxieties were the "peace aims" contained in the joint declaration. The Charter somehow survived identification with the crisis of 1941, and, in truth, of the period 1941-45. It comprised principles, not policies. There is a direct connection between the eight-point declaration and establishment of the United Nations. Seen as a goal for those nations which fought the Axis, the Charter became the beacon toward which the Allied nations were to strive. As Cordell Hull was to write, "It is a statement of basic principles and fundamental ideas and policies that are universal in their practical application."

The joint declaration attained multilateral sanction by action of the Inter-Allied Meeting in London, September 24, 1941, when representatives of the United Kingdom, Canada, Australia, New Zealand, South Africa, the governments-in-exile of Belgium, Czechoslovakia, Greece, Luxembourg, the Netherlands, Norway, Poland, and Yugoslavia, and representatives of the Free French signed a resolution "adhering to the common principles of policy set forth in the Atlantic Charter and expressing their intention to cooperate in giving them effect." The delegation from the U.S.S.R. expressed qualified agreement. In an address before the conference Ambassador Maisky stated: "Considering that the practical application of these principles will necessarily adapt itself to the circumstances, needs, and historic peculiarities of particular countries, the Soviet Government can state that a consistent application will secure the most energetic support on the part of the Government and peoples of the Soviet Union." The Inter-Allied Meeting's decision preceded approval by the legislative organs of most signatory states, and endorsement by national and international agencies such as the International Labor Organization—and even by the moribund League of Nations. Representatives of twenty-six nations on January 1, 1942, signed the United Nations Declaration. By this act each subscribed to the Atlantic Charter and pledged cooperation in achievement of its principles. The Roosevelt-Churchill statement became the approved vehicle of Allied war aims, the ideal basis for the war and the peace.

In practice the Charter's influence was severely limited. More important were national ambitions and fears, and the changes in them as the fortunes of war fluctuated. One is tempted to claim that the primary relevance of the Charter during the Second World War lay in its usefulness in justifying the policies of one or another parties. The Polish leader Stanislaw Mikolajczyk based his objections to Teheran and Yalta on the Charter. On occasion Churchill was not averse to finding in the joint declaration an excuse for avoiding commitments, "secret or public, direct or implied," which were not in England's immediate interest. Soon after the meeting he claimed that it was never intended that the eight points be applied to the British Empire. The sad history of the Charter is best expressed by the rapid shift of Russia from support to denigration. "I thought that the Atlantic Charter was directed against those people who were trying to establish world dominion. It now looks as if the Charter was directed against the U.S.S.R.," exclaimed Stalin in December, 1941, to Sir Anthony Eden. Ideals, of course, became increasingly burdensome to the Russian leadership as the war progressed.

The Roosevelt-Churchill statement was the embodiment of a real yet informal alliance between the two men and their countries. It was a tentative compromise statement of their credos. As such the Charter possessed whatever force was inherent in the power and determination of Roosevelt and Churchill to influence international affairs. One has to conclude that the exact legal position of the joint declaration is, as President Roosevelt was fond of saying, an "iffy" question.

8　Unconditional Surrender:
A Study in Historical Continuity

Theodore Livingston

The following essay was written originally for a graduate seminar in United States diplomatic history at The University of Kansas. Never before published, the essay has been included here because it combines freshness of approach with mature scholarship and, most important, because it expresses assumptions about the nature of history and the nature of World War II diplomacy that are receiving increasing attention and popularity. There exist numerous other examples of so-called "New Left" history that deal, perhaps more expertly, with the questions of concern to Theodore Livingston. However, his honest commitment to a relevant past and his belief that historical events reflect, not discontinuity, but a consistent and continuing process (with which view, by the way, the editor emphatically disagrees) should be of special interest to members of the first postwar generation.

Between January 14 and 24, 1943, Roosevelt, Churchill, and their chiefs of staff conferred at the Anfa Hotel, some five miles from Casablanca in Morocco, North Africa. Out of this conference came the rough outlines of Allied military strategy that were to prevail in large measure for the duration of the war. But more significantly, this, the most important *military* conference of the war, saw the birth of what was to become, if not the most important, then at least the most controversial *political* policy of the war—that of "unconditional surrender."

The phrase—and the far-reaching policy it implied—were first introduced by Roosevelt at the joint press conference that marked the close of the conference: ". . . Peace can come to this world only by the total elimination of German and Japanese war power. . . . The elimination of German, Japanese, and Italian war power means the *unconditional surrender* by Germany, Italy, and Japan." The controversy began almost at once and has continued unabated into the postwar period. Indeed, a cursory perusal of pertinent materials published between 1945 and 1955 suggests that the controversy actually intensified after the close of the war.

The reasons for this intensification are easily discernible: the scholarly dispute has for the most part addressed itself to the consequences of unconditional surrender—consequences which, more often than not, were

---

From "Unconditional Surrender: A Study in Historical Continuity" by Theodore Livingston. Unpublished seminar thesis, The University of Kansas, 1970. Reprinted by permission of the author.

applied to a broader context than the immediate wartime. That is, the dispute over consequences concerned itself mainly with the way in which the policy affected the postwar world. Hanson Baldwin's comments in 1954 are typical of the critical view: "It meant the creation of a vacuum of power, the complete destruction of two nations . . . which in modern history had been the traditional counterpoise to Soviet Russia. . . . It was the foundation stone of the politico-strategic edifice the United States erected during the war upon the quicksand of unreality. . . . We substituted one enemy for another; and today's enemy, Soviet Russia, is more threatening than the old." This is not to say that the controversy over consequences germane to the immediate wartime was not important. It was. But by the time the question had come under the scrutiny of historians, the postwar world was upon us, and it was only natural that their treatment should reflect their immediate concern.

Unfortunately, the emphasis on consequences has led to an almost universal neglect of the other side of the historical problem posed by unconditional surrender: why was it promulgated? Scholarship has emphasized "what it did" almost to the point of losing sight of "why it was."

What follows is an attempt to view unconditional surrender as a logical outgrowth of its historical context—in order to better understand it as well as its consequences. Answering "why" can cast invaluable light upon "what came of it."

Unconditional surrender has been besieged by a number of popular myths. Prominent among these misconceptions has been the idea that the policy constituted a complete break with the historical context from which it emerged, that it was an "historical anomaly." This myth is supported by considerable evidence. "Originally, this principle had not formed part of the State Department's thinking," maintains Cordell Hull. "We were as much surprised as Mr. Churchill when, for the first time, the President, in the Prime Minister's presence, stated it suddenly to a press conference during the Casablanca Conference in January, 1943. I was told that the Prime Minister was dumbfounded."

In a letter to Robert Sherwood in 1947, Churchill corroborated this account, stating that he had "heard the words 'unconditional surrender' for the first time from the President's lips at the Conference." Sherwood relates that "Roosevelt himself absolved Churchill from all responsibility for the statement. Indeed, he suggested that it was unpremeditated on his own part." Sherwood goes on to quote Roosevelt: "We had so much trouble getting those two generals together [de Gaulle and Giraud] that I thought to myself that this was as difficult as arranging the meeting of Grant and Lee—and then suddenly the press conference was on, and Winston and I had no time to prepare for it, and the thought popped into my mind that they had called Grant, 'Old Unconditional Surrender' and the next thing I knew, I had said it." Louis Snyder supports this "unpremeditated" view of unconditional surrender, referring to it as "an unfortunate slip."

Sherwood later dissents from this view and tells us that "Roosevelt, for some reason, often liked to picture himself as a rather frivolous fellow who did not give sufficient attention to the consequences of chance remarks." He feels that Roosevelt's account was—to put it as delicately as possible—"inaccurate." Sherwood appears convinced, the evidence he cites notwithstanding, that the policy "was very deeply deliberated," that it was "Roosevelt's considered policy." What evidence does Sherwood offer in support of this assertion? He refers rather vaguely to Roosevelt's consistent refusal to retract or alter the policy once it had been announced, an intransigence noted by both Hull and Wallace Carroll, Deputy Director of the Overseas Branch of the Office of War Information during the war. But could not Roosevelt's subsequent attitude be attributed to an ingrained stubbornness and a marked reluctance to admit error? Unless we know why he thought it important, the fact of his intransigence is meaningless. Sherwood's only other evidence is Roosevelt's consultation of notes during his remarks at the press conference—notes which contained the controversial announcement. But although this belies Roosevelt's account, it does not give support to the idea that the policy was "deeply deliberated" and "considered." After all, the notes could have been composed just prior to the announcement itself.

Churchill comes to Sherwood's assistance in a volume that appeared in 1950 in which he repudiates the version recounted in his letter of 1947. He notes in his report to the British War Cabinet on January 20, 1943—four days prior to Roosevelt's announcement—that he had asked his colleagues for their reaction to the idea of including in the conference communiqué a declaration "of the firm intention of the United States and the British Empire to continue the war relentlessly until we have brought about the 'unconditional surrender of Germany and Japan.' " He goes on to say that the War Cabinet had disapproved, not out of distaste for the principle, but because of the omission of Italy. Not wishing to include Italy, Churchill claims he simply dismissed the idea entirely. This state of affairs, coupled with the fact that no mention of the principle appeared in the official communiqué, occasioned the Prime Minister's surprise at Roosevelt's announcement of the policy and explains in large part the letter of 1947.

That Roosevelt's policy was "considered" is further supported in a study by Matloff and Snell, who set the official introduction of the phrase even earlier. The President used it during a meeting with his Joint Chiefs of Staff on January 7, fully two-and-a-half weeks before Casablanca. This evidence, Churchill's later testimony, and other data gathered from the War Department's files appear incontrovertible: the policy of unconditional surrender was indeed *premeditated*; it was "deliberated" and "considered."

However, even though the myth was ostensibly founded on the idea that the Casablanca policy was introduced completely unexpectedly, the myth did not fall with the demise of this idea. It has been demonstrated that the policy was "considered"—but considered and deliberated by whom? Excepting the isolated exchange between Churchill and his War Cabinet, unconditional surrender appears to have been the considered policy of one man—President Roosevelt. And it is self-evident that the product of one man's deliberation does not necessarily reflect the prevailing assessment of the historical situation; his conception of the historical context in which he forms his "policy" might be totally alien to the generally accepted conception.

Therefore, without forfeiting allegiance to the myth, its advocates can concede that unconditional surrender was indeed the product of deliberation, that Roosevelt did have carefully considered reasons for endorsing it. And Hanson Baldwin does just that: "Unconditional surrender was laid down as a *diktat*—a one man decision . . . and was announced publicly and unilaterally at a press conference to the surprise of the nation's chief ally, Great Britain. Historians may agree or disagree as to the validity of the unconditional-surrender policy, but history can describe the manner in which this policy was born in just one way: 'This is a hell of a way to run a railroad.'" Matloff and Snell provide him with impressive corroboration: "The most striking illustration of the want of understanding between the White House and the military staffs was the President's announcement, at the 7 January meeting, of his intention to support the 'unconditional surrender' concept as the basic Allied aim in the war. . . . No study of the meaning of this formula for the conduct of the war was made at the Army staff. . . ."

It appears indisputable that the actual explicit enunciation of unconditional surrender was unilateral and that it was greeted by surprise on all sides. Indeed, Hull's remark that the "principle had not formed part of [our] thinking" seems to have been the almost universal reaction.

But was the surprise valid? Did not the actual promulgation of unconditional surrender occur in a context in which it was already present by implication?

The idea of a "negotiated" or "compromise" peace was apparently alien to basic American thought about the war from the outset. Indeed, as early as November, 1941, Roosevelt refused to use his position as the leader of an eminent neutral to help bring about a negotiated peace between Great Britain and the Axis powers—a course of action strenuously urged upon him by the leaders of the Vichy government in France. In his "fireside chat" on December 9, 1941, Roosevelt gave explicit form to the idea that the aim of the U.S. in prosecuting the war was *total* victory as opposed to a negotiated peace: "Powerful and resourceful gangsters have banded together to make war upon the whole human race. . . . The United States can accept no result save victory, final and complete. . . . The sources of international brutality, wherever they exist, must be absolutely and finally broken. . . . There is no such thing as security for any Nation—or any individual—in a world ruled by the principles of gangsterism." He elaborated on this theme in his annual message to Congress on January 6, 1942:

Our own objectives are clear; the objective of smashing the militarism imposed by war lords upon their enslaved peoples—the objective of liberating the subjugated nations. . . . Many people ask, "When will this war end?" There is only one answer to that. It will end just as soon as we make it end, by our combined efforts, our combined strength, our combined determination to fight through and work through until the end—the end of militarism in Germany and Italy and Japan. . . . We shall not settle for less. . . . No compromise can end . . . [the] conflict. There never has been—there never can be—successful compromise between good and evil. Only total victory can reward the champions of tolerance, and decency, and freedom, and faith.

One may object that this concept of "total victory"—especially as it was informed by Roosevelt with the significance of a moral crusade—was merely a rhetorical construct which the President used to garner widespread support for the war effort. Certain aspects of the concept were undoubtedly intended as propaganda. But, for reasons I will make clear below, it would be a grave mistake to view the concept as completely contrary to the President's real thought about war. Furthermore, even if the idea of total victory was merely the rhetorical smoke screen behind which Roosevelt hid his real aims and purposes, the point is that the concept itself was not new in January, 1943. Whether or not it was seriously entertained by the country's leaders, total victory was an integral part of American thought about the war for over a year prior to the announcement of unconditional surrender—if for no other reason than the continual explicit expression of it in the public speeches of the President.

But total victory was more than empty rhetoric. It was a concept that permeated the whole of official thought about the war. The truth of this proposition is confirmed by the various designs for postwar Germany entertained by America's leaders. At Tehran in November, 1943, Roosevelt proposed that postwar Germany be partitioned into five parts, the apparent reason being to irreversibly weaken the ability of the German state to make war. Stalin concurred. But Churchill dissented, pointing out that there was nothing in the President's plan that would preclude a future reuniting of the parts; rather he wished to see, above all else, an effective and permanent isolation of Prussia—implying that this was the center of German war mania. Roosevelt countered that "all Germans are the same," but he did agree that Prussia, with its officer corps, was the "cement." The substance of these designs is not as important as what they inherently implied—a postwar situation that precluded a negotiated peace, one that could only be brought about by the total defeat of Germany.

The same total victory ideology characterized the thought of Dwight Eisenhower when he was Supreme Allied Commander in the European theater. Harry Butcher, in recounting a conversation between Eisenhower and his chief of staff, General Walter Bedell Smith, notes that Eisenhower advocated extermination or exile of the Prussian officer corps, and Smith warned against mere imprisonment because he feared their lethal ambitions would be unleashed again when the American public, as it almost invariably had in the past, grew "soft-hearted and conciliatory." Thus, *total* victory was also the precondition of the realization of the military's war aims. And this was the same military that appealed to Washington in November of the same year for a modification of unconditional surrender.

Churchill's endorsement of the principle of partition detracts considerably from the credibility accorded his surprise at Casablanca. Evidently he was committed to the idea of total victory. Beyond this, he insisted throughout the war that ". . . justice must be done upon the wicked and the guilty, and within her proper bounds justice must be stern and implacable. No vestige of Nazi . . . power . . . will be left to us when the work is done, and done it certainly will be."

It is clear then that the idea of total victory, given explicit form by Roosevelt's announcement at Casablanca, was characteristic of official thought throughout the war—thought whose scope exceeded Roosevelt's alone to include that of American military leaders and the British Prime Minister. The fact that Churchill couched his war aims in terms of total victory suggests that the concept was Anglo-American rather than solely American. This view is substantiated by the text of the Atlantic Charter, signed by Roosevelt and Churchill on August 12, 1941, several months prior to America's entry into the war. The document called for the "final destruction of Nazi tyranny."

The general commitment to total victory in World War II points to an even more significant repudiation of the myth: the conviction widely held in Anglo-American circles that, historically, the total defeat of Germany was prerequisite to a lasting peace. The evidence cited above suggests the basis of this conviction. The German state was viewed as irrevocably war- and conquest-oriented; as long as there was a German nation as then constituted, world peace and security would be in jeopardy. Beyond this, Prussia was viewed as the center of German militarism. Eisenhower gave frank expression to this attitude when he stated that "this war and the preceding one" were viewed by the German General Staff as "military campaigns in their dogged determination, first to dominated Europe and eventually the world."

The validity of the historical conception latent in this attitude is extraneous to the present thesis. What is important is that this attitude did exist within official circles at the time of the war, and that it manifested itself in the total-victory theme that served as the central fiber in official Anglo-American thought. When viewed in this context, the unconditional-surrender announcement, far from being an historical anomaly, was really anticlimatic. Failure to realize this led to widespread opposition from those implicitly wedded to the concept of total victory—Churchill and elements within the U.S. military stand out in this regard—and gave birth to the myth which has been enshrined by so much subsequent scholarship.

The second, and perhaps the most pervasive, myth associated with unconditional surrender contends that the policy, rather than being a political decision—or at any rate a principle determined by political considerations—represented a sacrifice of the political goals of the war to the military. Further, the policy was a cause as well as a symptom of the American propensity to emphasize military victory to the point of completely neglecting political aims. Baldwin's characterization of unconditional surrender as a "negative peace aim, not a positive one," one that "meant the subordination of political aims to military ones," is a typical expression of the myth's basic tenets. Ann Armstrong reaches a similar conclusion. "The major decisions, at least during the first years of the war, were military," she writes. "Policy trailed in the wake of strategy, and strategy seemed to be aimed solely at the destruction of the enemy. The policy of Unconditional Surrender is both a reflection and a symptom of the nature of the thinking of the Anglo-American policy makers on the conduct of war and the role of policy in war time. The Casablanca Conference . . . was a case in point. . . . Policy . . . was a by-product and an afterthought."

A considerable portion of postwar scholarship has shunned such an extreme adherence to this myth. The interpretation almost universally offered in its stead is that unconditional surrender was a tactical ploy dictated by the exigencies of coalition warfare: the announcement was made to alleviate Soviet suspicions born of repeated failures on the part of Anglo-American forces to open a "second front." William L. Langer gives pointed expression to this view: "Whether sincerely or otherwise, . . . [the Soviets] took the line that refusal to open a second front was an indication of unwillingness to crush Nazi power or permit . . . Russia an unqualified victory. It was this . . . that . . . lay behind the demand for unconditional surrender as formulated by the Casablanca Conference of January 1943 . . . . The primary objective of the President and Mr. Churchill at that conference was to reassure the Bolshevik leaders that there would be no compromise with Hitler and that the Allies would fight on to total victory." In an effort to forge and maintain a workable coalition, Roosevelt promulgated unconditional surrender to establish a "common denominator" that would serve to unify the Allies.

But the view of unconditional surrender as a political tactic does no violence to the conception of it as essentially apolitical. This fact is evident in the conclusions drawn by the proponents of the "modified" myth. Gaddis Smith's pronouncement is typical: "Unconditional surrender was in spirit the antithesis of careful long-range planning. It encouraged the delusion that once the Axis was defeated there would be few obstacles in the way of establishing . . . peace." That is to say, Roosevelt's "common denominator," while it may have been successful in quieting Soviet suspicions and thus facilitating the coalition effort was devoid of real political substance save that of winning the war. Therefore, whether unconditional surrender is viewed as a tactic of coalition warfare or merely as a blanket endorsement of the war as an entirely military venture, the myth of the policy's apolitical nature stands unscathed, making Hanson Baldwin's harsh indictment compatible with both versions: "We fought to win and we forgot that wars have political aims and that complete destruction and unconditional surrender cannot contribute to a more stable peace."

Despite this formidable opposition, I persist in my dissent; this second myth, much as the first, stems from a tendency to view unconditional surrender in too narrow a context. Unconditional surrender was the enunciation of what was primarily a political decision, one of far-reaching import. It was formulated with a specific postwar political objective in mind: the realization of a secure peace based on American politico-economic-military hegemony. It was apolitical only in that it was the antithesis of traditional European political conceptions. In 1943 European statesmen viewed the task of preserving peace as one of maintaining a sometimes delicate balance of power, much as had their forbearers over the course of previous centuries. Unconditional surrender heralded a new concept of peace and security, that of singular hegemony—the supremacy of one nation whose force and pervasiveness would be sufficient to the task of keeping the peace.

The Atlantic Charter provides us with an insight into the nature of this "peace" that was to become the central aim of the U.S. during the war: "First their countries [Great Britain and the United States] seek no aggrandisement, territorial or other. . . . They will endeavor . . . to further the enjoyment by all States . . . to the trade and to the raw materials of the world which are needed for . . . economic prosperity. . . . Since no future peace can be maintained if . . . armaments continue to be employed by nations which threaten . . . aggression outside of their frontiers, they believe, pending the establishment of a wider and permanent system of general security, that the disarmament of such nations is essential." It may be argued—indeed it has been, and quite persuasively so—that the foregoing is really void of any determinate content, that it is essentially Wilsonian idealism without the concomitant specificity. Advocates of this position would further argue that the expression of Anglo-American solidarity, rather than the content, was the real significance of the statement. And I agree—up to a point. Churchill probably viewed the Charter in this fashion; at least his later chagrin in the face of American demands for strict adherence indicates that he did not regard it as a truly definitive statement of policy.

Yet implicit in the Charter statement are the general outlines of the political aims that Roosevelt and his administration pursued in consistent fashion throughout the war. Not only does the unconditional-surrender principle underlie the discussion of the total disarmament of the Axis, but the nature of the peace that unconditional surrender would later be called on to enforce is revealed. The ideas of "no territorial aggrandisement" and "equal economic access" (i.e., the "open-door" policy applied on a global scale) combined to form a vision of American hegemony based on economic expansion, that is, political control facilitated by economic control. That total victory would be followed by an interim in which the Allies—presumably America—would "supervise" the peace "pending the establishment of a wider and permanent system of general security" is further indication of the plan for American hegemony. The validity of this interpretation is supported by the subsequent position adopted by Roosevelt and the role played by unconditional surrender in facilitating that position.

But the actual Charter proclamation was even more than the implication that the postwar world would be a community of nations united and pacified by the politico-economic dominance of the United States. There was another dimension to the statement's design. It was aimed against a peace founded on the traditional balance of power. It was specifically aimed against a Soviet hegemony in Eastern Europe constructed on the precepts of that tradition. Unconditional surrender, while implying a specific postwar world, was in its immediate impact directed against the main threat to that world—the Soviet Union.

When the United States entered the war as an active belligerent in December, 1941, it was immediately greeted by a challenge to its peace—the territorial demands of the Soviet Union. These demands centered around the Soviet desire for Anglo-American recognition of her 1941 frontiers. The value attached to such recognition was hinted at in a series of exchanges between Churchill and Stalin following Germany's invasion of the Soviet Union in June, 1941. In a dispatch dated July 18, 1941, Stalin told Churchill that "the German forces would have been far more advantageously placed if the Soviet troops had had to counter the blow, not along the line Kishinev-Lvov-Brest-Bialystok-Kaunas and Vyborg, but along the line Odessa-Kamenets-Podolsk-Minsk and the vicinity of Leningrad." Churchill's reply of July 21 acknowledged the tactical advantages afforded the Soviets by their 1941 frontiers: "I fully realize the military advantage you have gained by forcing the enemy to deploy and engage on forward Western fronts, thus exhausting some of the force of his initial effort." Clearly Stalin wished to emphasize the security gained from the expansion of Soviet borders between 1939 and 1941, security based on a traditional view of European politics. Churchill's agreement, also based upon this traditional view, was soon to involve him in an unpleasant confrontation with the United States and its peace.

The occasion for the actual Soviet demand for recognition of its 1941 frontiers was provided by the December 16-22, 1941, Moscow trip of Anthony Eden, Britain's Foreign Secretary, to engage in talks with Stalin about a general coalition agreement. In the course of these talks Stalin quite pointedly pressed Eden to commit his government to an agreement on the western boundaries of Russia. Stalin went so far as to make the signing of an agreement contingent upon British acquiescence on this point. Eden, although "personally impressed with the reasonableness of the Russian demand," was unable to so commit his government prior to American approval because of the nature of the Anglo-American alliance.

British response apparently arose from a twofold concern: their belief that the Russian demand was reasonable (which seems plausible in light of British commitment to conventional concepts of security), and their conviction that the success of the coalition effort depended on a concession. The U.S. chargé in the Soviet Union reported that British Ambassador to the Soviet Union Cripps felt "that an understanding should be reached with the Soviets by Great Britain, with the acquiescence of the United States, with respect to frontiers.... He feared that if it [the impasse in reaching a coalition agreement because of Eden's inability to commit his government to Stalin's territorial demands on his own cognizance] was not disposed of, full cooperation could not be achieved."

The United States proved intransigent. Hull and Roosevelt adhered to a strict interpretation of the Atlantic Charter which "clearly" precluded, in its antiaggrandizement clause, any agreement of the sort pending between Britain and Russia. The American leaders continually dwelt on the point that both Britain and Russia had agreed to the "spirit and content" of the Charter (the latter in September, 1941, as a prelude to a definitive coalition agreement). Hull felt that "the test of our good faith with regard to the Soviet Union should not be our willingness to agree to the recognition of extended Soviet frontiers at this time, but rather the degree of determination which we show . . . to carry out our promises to aid the Soviet Government with equipment and supplies."

In a message to Roosevelt dated March 7, 1941, Churchill tried to overcome American resistance founded on the conviction that the nature of the pending Anglo-Soviet accords violated the Atlantic Charter: "The increasing gravity of the war has led me to feel that the principles of the Atlantic Charter ought not to be construed so as to deny Russia the frontiers she occupied when Germany attacked her. This was the basis on which Russia acceded to the charter."

But more was at stake than the "letter" of the Charter; the peace implicit therein—the American peace—was endangered. In a memorandum dated February 20, 1942, Sumner Welles, Under Secretary of State, reported that while Roosevelt "felt . . . that the Soviet Union was legitimately entitled to obtain full and legitimate security at the termination of the war," this security was to come about, not by means of territorial concessions, but by the complete dismantling of the German war machine and the inception of a comprehensive system of collective security. That is, Soviet security was to be insured by a thorough-going American hegemony. Stalin evidently understood this implication of the Charter. In the course of his talks with Eden he is reported to have said, "I thought that the Atlantic Charter was directed against those people who were trying to establish world dominion. It now looks as if the Atlantic Charter was directed against the U.S.S.R." And indeed it was, insofar as the Soviet Union stood in the way of the realization of the American peace.

Moreover, if the controversy is dealt with only on the level of the letter of the Charter, it remains unintelligible. What was really involved was a clash of two variant concepts of the peace to come at the close of the war. The Soviets as well as the British envisioned a peace constructed along the lines of balance of power and territorial security. The British in particular looked upon the coming peace as possible only by means of a cooperative coalition, a coalition founded on a mutual compromise of interests and a definitive settlement based on such a compromise. Simply to refuse to consider such a settlement would be to run the risk "that cooperation between Great Britain and Russia and between the United States and Russia both during and after the war may be seriously endangered." The British peace, then, could only come about by virtue of productive collaboration by the Allies in the postwar period, a collaboration built on tripartite agreements. But the idea of definite tripartite agreements was alien to the American concept of peace—collaboration was unnecessary. What was necessary was American supremacy, and the diligent prevention of encroachment upon this supremacy.

American opposition carried the day. The Anglo-Soviet treaty of May 26, 1942, was marked by the absence of any territorial provisions. But resistance to nonrecognition of 1941 Soviet frontiers on the basis of the Atlantic Charter continued unabated. As late as October 11, 1943, Churchill wrote to Eden, noting that while "we affirm the principles of the Atlantic Charter . . . [we are aware] that Russia's accession thereto is based upon the frontiers of June 22, 1941. We also take note of the historic frontiers of Russia before the two wars of aggression waged by Germany in 1914 and 1939." In the face of resistance of this sort, it was plain that a new ploy was necessary to counter it. This new ploy was the unconditional-surrender announcement which clearly established a ban on all territorial settlements prior to the termination of the war, thereby giving Roosevelt an effective means for dismissing further Soviet demands. But more than this, unconditional surrender provided Roosevelt with the necessary pretext for his refusal to recognize Soviet territorial gains in the course of its westward march in 1944 and 1945. Such a pretext was necessary for the realization of the American peace.

Postwar scholarship has recognized the role of unconditional surrender in establishing a ban on territorial settlement, but the ban has been viewed as a tactical ploy in the course of coalition warfare: It was feared that, if the principle of territorial settlement prior to peace was ever accorded validity, the coalition would be weakened by the introduction among its members of mutual suspicions and by efforts by various members to intrigue in order to obtain commitments with regard to territory at the expense of other members. The validity of this interpretation is placed in precarious straits by Stalin's interpretation of the ban principle a year prior to the Casablanca Conference: "It is very important for us to know whether we shall have to fight at the peace conference in order to get our western frontiers." The ban evidently increased Soviet suspicions of American intentions.

The argument that American intransigence in the winter and spring of 1942 and the unconditional-surrender announcement a year later were elicited in the main by the threat posed by Soviet demands for recognition of her 1941 frontiers is admittedly weak. Taken alone, the explicit demand made by Stalin in December, 1941, comprised no real threat to the vision of an American peace. But why then the intransigence? Why the clear division between American and British thought on the matter? The answer lies in the fact that official American thought informed Stalin's demand with a meaning quite alien to the British view. In a memorandum to Roosevelt dated February 4, 1942, Hull gave frank expression to this American view of the matter—an interpretation with which Roosevelt subsequently registered his approval:

It is believed that the assent at the present time to *any* . . . territorial demands . . . would result in only a temporary improvement of the relations between the Soviet Union and Great Britain. If the British Government, with the tacit approval of this government, should abandon the principle of no territorial commitments prior to the Peace conference, it would be placed in a difficult position to resist additional Soviet demands . . . which would certainly follow whenever the Soviet Government would find itself in a favorable bargaining position. There is no doubt that the Soviet Government has tremendous ambitions with regard to Europe. . . . It would seem that it is preferable to take a firm attitude now, rather than to retreat and to be compelled to take a firm attitude later when our position had been weakened. . . .

Thus, while ostensibly "harmless" and security-oriented, the Soviet demands were seen by American officials as a prelude to ever greater demands aimed at making Russia "the dominating power of Eastern Europe if not of the whole continent." It is clear, then, that the Soviet Union was considered from the outset a direct threat to American hegemony, a threat best handled by means of American strength and American refusal to enter into any settlement that might entail concessions to the Soviets. If the United States ever conceded territory to the Soviets it would be hard pressed to force their withdrawal; the force necessary to effect such a withdrawal would be aggressive and therefore legally unjustifiable. But, if no formal concessions were made, any forced Soviet withdrawal from the territory held at the close of the war would be eminently justifiable. Such action could be construed as the implementation of the ideals expressed in the Atlantic Charter. The role of unconditional surrender was simply to close the door on all concessions and thereby preserve American hegemony. Without it such hegemony would have ceased to be a tenable approach to the postwar world.

It may be objected that Roosevelt did make concessions to the Soviets in two salient instances, thereby breaking his record of consistent intransigence and laying waste to the idea of hegemony implemented by the unconditional-surrender policy. The first of these instances was the Anglo-Soviet plan for carving out spheres of influence in Eastern and Southeastern Europe, which Roosevelt approved after its proposal in 1944. But if the record is carefully checked it is clear that Roosevelt gave his assent only with great reluctance—a reluctance based officially on unconditional surrender. And it is of primary significance that what Roosevelt approved was a temporary scheme, to expire in three months, that was grounded solely on immediate military circumstances; any implication of a permanent political settlement was absent from the agreement. (It is clear from Churchill's testimony that by 1944 he had adopted the American assessment of Soviet ambitions. He dissented from the American strategy, however, suggesting that the only way of blunting these ambitions would be by gaining a permanent political settlement with the Soviets that would preclude full realization of their ambitions. Otherwise, he warned, the boundaries of military occupation would harden into permanent political frontiers. Evidently he gave little credence to the idea that American strength could force a general Soviet withdrawal at the close of the war.) Therefore, the Balkan settlement of 1944 is no stumbling block to the interpretation advanced above. Indeed, Churchill's dissatisfaction with the form of the final agreement reinforces this view.

The second instance that challenges this interpretation is the agreement reached at Yalta. But if one subjects the general agreement to a careful reading, this challenge is rendered more apparent than real. The agreement reached delineated temporary boundaries based on the military situation. (Robert Sherwood provides corroboration in his observation that "at Yalta, Roosevelt was adhering to the basic formula of unconditional surrender.")

The foregoing is admittedly fragmentary. There is much regarding *what* unconditional surrender was and *why* it was that has not been discussed. But this is unavoidable; no essay of this length could attempt a comprehensive study of the policy and retain a modicum of adequacy. What I have attempted is to place unconditional surrender within the framework of a logical outgrowth of its historical context—in terms of being both an explicit expression of the total-victory motif and a necessary extension of a basic trend of thought regarding the postwar peace. In the preface I alluded to the idea that the answer to the question *why* might help understand *what* came of the policy. Therefore, the question of consequences should be considered in light of the conclusions reached in refuting the two myths.

The traditional criticism of unconditional surrender has been the assertion that the policy prolonged the war by virtue of the fact that it gave the Germans no real alternative other than a desperate fight to the end. A modification of this criticism maintains that, while the policy itself did not elicit the "consolidation of resistance into one of desperation," the use made of the policy by German propagandists did. Postwar scholarship has for the most part abandoned this line of thought; the question of whether or not the policy did in fact lengthen the war has no definitive answer—it is simply a moot point. In rendering this judgment, historians have assumed one very significant premise: that total victory was the only outcome that was acceptable to the Allies. It is evident that, had a negotiated or compromise peace been acceptable, the war would have been shorter. The fact that the question as to the policy's effect on the war's length has been tacitly declared unanswerable implies that the policy represented no real break with basic Anglo-American thought about the war. Why then the myth?

Another outcome often attributed to the unconditional-surrender policy—the main criticism leveled by postwar scholarship—has been the advent of Soviet hegemony in Eastern and Central Europe. Sumner Welles gave expression to this idea when he stated that unconditional surrender "was a decision dictated by the President's conviction that as Commander-in-Chief his paramount obligation was to permit nothing to jeopardize the winning of the war. Yet with the advantage hindsight gives us, it seems fair to say that it was this decision that was largely responsible for the division of the world today into two warring camps." This analysis in turn recalls Baldwin's invective: by following the policy implicit in unconditional surrender, "we substituted one enemy for another; and today's enemy, Soviet Russia, is more threatening than the old." I concur. Unconditional surrender and the world view it implemented did contribute in large measure to postwar Soviet hegemony in Eastern and Central Europe. And this is the supreme irony of the matter. The policy helped lead to the very outcome it was aimed at preventing.

This is not to vindicate the assessment of Welles and Baldwin in particular and a good portion of postwar scholarship in general. My agreement with the general outlines of their criticism is a qualified one. Unconditional surrender per se was not responsible for the shape of the postwar world. It was the continuation into the postwar period of the pattern of thought implicit in the policy that finalized what the policy itself had only created in tentative fashion. Unconditional surrender led to a flow of Soviet military might into Eastern and Central Europe unfettered by any prior territorial agreement. But adherence to the basic world view that had given birth to the policy led to the consolidation of the military line of advance into a hard and fast political division.

From 1945 into the 1950's the United States stubbornly refused to negotiate a settlement with the Soviets. Instead we adopted a policy of "aggressive containment" whose revisionist aspects were so blatant that even as vehement an opponent of Soviet expansion as Winston Churchill was led to the conclusion that the United States' strength was being marshaled to secure the unconditional surrender of the Soviet Union rather than to facilitate a "suitable division of interests in Europe." Settlement short of recognition of American hegemony was still alien to American thought.

The unconditional-surrender policy provided the embryo of the Cold War. But another policy founded on the same vision gave it birth. And this is the real tragedy: While condemning the policy of unconditional surrender, the authors of the Cold War persisted in operating under the same assumptions that had necessitated it.

Implicit in the foregoing is a theory of history, a theory that sees history, not as a temporal succession of unconnected events, but as *continuity.* This is the conception I have brought to bear on this treatment of unconditional surrender—an attempt to see the policy as part of a continuity, as a concrete extension of a world view that predated it and still animates a great deal of American thought today.

9   The Future of Asia

Lin Yutang

Did the Second World War witness the continuation of old-style Western imperialism? "Yes and no," answered the widely regarded Chinese writer Lin Yutang. His Between Tears and Laughter *was a bitter wartime*

From **Between Tears and Laughter** by Lin Yutang (New York: John Day Co., 1943), pp. 110–21. Reprinted by permission of the author.

*condemnation of Allied policy in Asia. Yutang argued that the failure of
America and Great Britain to provide real military aid to China was
intentional, that it was the natural result of their determination, on racist
grounds, to prevent the emergence of the peoples of Asia. This plan was
cloaked in vague promises about "self-determination" and China's
postwar role as a great power. Yutang insisted that, even though the
Americans may have believed such rhetoric, it must not be taken for
reality.*

Unfortunately, God will not temper the wind. Poor lamb, you'd better grow
your wool fast.

I see nothing but starvation and chaos and bloodshed in Asia. I know our
policy in Asia will grow into a disaster, with mounting confusion before the war
is over. In the war councils of today, there is a blind spot, and that spot is Asia.
The same absent-mindedness that characterized the situation suggested in
General Arnold's speech at Madison Square Garden on March 6, 1943, will
continue to characterize the Allied policy in Asia. As we refuse to think about
postwar problems now, so we refuse to think about Asia until the war is won.
General Arnold said, "Six weeks ago at Casablanca . . . I headed for the Far East.
Before departure, President Roosevelt expressed himself briefly, 'China's ports
are closed, the Japanese hold the Burma Road. How can we increase the air
tonnage carried in? How can we build a larger combat force?' " I thought that
President Roosevelt had known that China's ports were closed a year before
Casablanca. Thoughtfulness of this type really resembles forgetfulness. I thought
this must have occurred to anyone who ever spent a minute's thought on the
strategy of fighting Japan from China. How could the most obvious fact on the
map of the Orient be forgotten, and why up to now is there no plan, and *no
wish for a plan*, for China's partnership even in the war against Japan?

Meanwhile, General Arnold in the same speech made it amply clear that
increase of air transport will be difficult, for supplying the China-India front
means taking planes out of the other fronts. There will be more planes sent to
China as a gesture to pacify the American public, so that the public will be lulled
into silence, but the basic policy will be unchanged. Everything, we shall be told,
will depend upon the reopening of the Burma Road, but we are awfully sorry we
cannot spare the British Navy to land troops at Rangoon. The difficult we do
immediately, the impossible a little later on. China belongs to the impossible.
And we adore the Chinese.

A hurricane will blow. President Roosevelt announces the intention to use
China as a base to invade Japan—the only logical base, but between that
announcement of intention and actual planning, there will be another time lag of
years. Events will happen and the complex situation will become more complex
still, while we say that nothing in the Far East matters until Hitler is defeated.
The public realizes now that the cutting off of the Burma Road meant the
isolation of China and agrees that London was stupid in not permitting Chinese
troops to come into Burma and defend her own vital line, but the public will not

admit the stupidity of continuing the present policy of dilly-dallying until either Kunming or Calcutta falls. For Japan was listening when President Roosevelt declared China as the only base for invasion of Japan. Besides, the Japanese know the map of the Orient pretty well, even if the others don't.

Meanwhile, where is the mechanism for concerted Allied action in Asia? General Doolittle bombed Japan in spite of the request of the Government of China that it be delayed a month in order to give time for strengthening the Chinese ground defense of her air bases near Kinhwa. The biggest air base in all Asia with underground concrete hangars was needlessly sacrificed. General Wavell started unilaterally the march toward Akyab without consulting Chungking. Where is the mechanism for concerted action? And why must China's role in 1943 be decided at Casablanca without her representation? And so we must go deeper to the root of the matter.

The Chinese people as a whole are now convinced that the blockade of supplies for China is political and not military. If any doubt in Chinese minds existed, it was completely dispelled by Winston Churchill's speech of March 21, 1943. The situation had clarified, England was feeling confident and strong. On March 17, four days before, the British Prime Minister had made it emphatically clear that "the administration of British colonies"—including India, Burma, the Malay States, the Straits Settlements, and Hong Kong—"must continue to be the sole responsibility of Great Britain." Now he made it plainer than ever that Asia was to be kept down as a system of colonies. The defeat of Hitler was to be the "grand climax of the war," after which only would begin a "new task," the war with Japan and reconquest of Asia. Then and then only, with China kept isolated for years—perhaps till after 1945—would begin the "rescue of China" from the predicament into which the London government had deliberately and according to purpose thrown China by ordering the Burma Road closed a second time. A "rescued" China then would not be a "leading victorious power." In fact, there will be no "leading" or "great victorious" Asiatic "power" at all at the end of the war, so that the nest of White Imperialism will be safe. A "Council of Asia" will be set up, with "our Dutch Allies" and presumably the French participating. We may be quite sure that at this "Council of Asia" the ruler of the greatest number of Asiatic colonies will naturally have the greatest representation, for the maintenance of "law, justice, and humanity."

Now everything fits into a pattern. The blockade of supplies for China since 1939 can be understood. The closing of the Burma Road and the weakening of China can be understood. The refusal to let China have an air force of her own can be perfectly understood. From the point of view of imperialist strategy, it is superb and masterly. The Empire of Queen Victoria had no better premier and no more devoted servant, with greater sagacity, stronger courage, more far-sighted vision, and a better political genius.

But why this scare about China and about Asia at all? Asia is frightening the Anglo-Saxon powers. By all principles of justice, she need not, but by all principles of power politics, she does frighten them a great deal. The future of Asia at the peace table and after the war seems to me amazingly simple, if we follow the principles of justice. On the other hand, I admit the same problem looks as complicated as that of Middle Europe by all the known principles of power politics. In fact, it can look so complicated that it makes a true partnership of China at the Allied War Council impossible. By bungling, Asian politics can be made complicated enough to look like, and actually become, a nightmare.

Fear, I am told, is one of the greatest driving powers of mankind. Ladies are afraid of mice, diplomats are afraid of birdies, and I am afraid of diplomats. So why shouldn't the diplomats be scared of a mighty Asia? Professor Spykman of Yale, for instance, is terribly afraid of a strong and united China and of a united and strong federated Europe, and I am terribly afraid of Professor Nicholas John Spykman.

What have we got in Asia as we picture the peace ahead of us? Japan has been the upsetting factor. But Japan as a menace will have been eliminated after the war. What then have we got in Asia to settle? There is China, a great pacific power, indoctrinated with principles of human, democratic, peaceful living that are very close to the American temperament. There is India, determined to achieve her freedom, which is nobody's business to interfere with, led by a political party as strong, as truly national in character, and as well organized as the Chinese Kuomintang, and by as wise, capable, patriotic, inspiring, democratic leaders as Chiang Kai-shek. China and India have lived as neighbors without one war in the past four thousand years.

There is no background of racial hatreds, suspicions, wars, or heritage of national antagonisms such as we find in Europe, and the peoples of Asia as a whole are by nature not half as aggressive as the Europeans. Russia will not fight China, nor will China fight Russia. To the Chinese and to the Americans, the future of Asia is simple. There is no problem for the United States, because the United States will let the Philippines go. Other people's jewels don't keep you awake if you have no greed in your heart. No insoluble problems exist if the Christian powers will let Malaya, the Dutch Indies, Siam, Indo-China, Burma, and India go. All of them aspire to self-government, and all of them will give trouble to Europe not when they are masters, but only when they are to be exploited as slaves. The moment you covet any of their territories and their tin and rubber, however, your conscience will irresistibly compel you to station troops there to prevent communal strife and bloodshed, and then all your troubles begin. But whose bloodshed? Will the Javanese or the Indians or the Burmese threaten the United States or England? Will not blood be shed because the westerners will wrangle and fight for their tin and rubber?

On such a simple basis, it is possible to take China into immediate and equal partnership in the war, laying plans together and fighting together and dreaming together for some future better world. Americans want to kill the Japs, and the Chinese want to kill the Japs. America hasn't got a Hong Kong or a Dutch Indies to worry about, and China hasn't got a worry about Indo-China, or Siam, or Burma. China wants to recover her own territory, and does not want others' territory. America wants no territory at all, not even Kulangsu, my childhood home. So let's get together and just kill the Japs as fast as we can, and we don't have to worry if we lick the Japs too soon or defeat Hirohito before we defeat Hitler. Some may want to bomb the Japanese Emperor's palace, and others may not. But these are minor and inconsequential issues that need not make us look beneath the bed before going to sleep at night.

That is the simple picture, a picture of achievable human justice and of a fair prospect of lasting peace in Asia, at least as fair a prospect as there has been in South America since the downfall of the Spanish and Portuguese Empires. For peace is possible in Asia. Peace is possible in North America and South America. Peace is possible in Africa.

Peace is not possible only in Europe. And peace in Asia will become impossible only when Asia assumes the European pattern of balance of power. Of all the five continents of the earth, only Europe has not yet learned to live at peace. Europe is the focus of infection of this earth, and imperialism is the toxin by which it spreads until the whole world is so sick, so sick.

Now for some good old confusion as some of our Allied leaders will have it. If you knew the whole story you would not eat a meal in peace, or sleep a wink at night. If I had to look beneath the bed every night, I wouldn't want to live. But there are people whose minds are otherwise constituted. Not one thug, but possibly three or four, are hiding beneath the diplomats' beds every night. There are great humbugs and they beget little humbugs and they will dance attendance on us all our life, if we will believe the diplomats, until we ourselves get into the diplomats' proper frame of mind.

I have said that facts are always complicated and first principles are the only things we can be certain about. Let's now leave the principles and go after the facts.

The first feeling is one of terrible uncertainty, for we cannot be certain of one knowable fact. What are Russia's intentions? What are China's intentions? As diplomats, we should be prepared for the worst. If China becomes independent and strong, will that not set a bad example for India? Are you so sure China has no imperialist designs? Do not be too sure, if China has an air force of her own, and especially if Japan is completely eliminated. So let's see to it that she will not have even a baby air force of her own when peace comes, and perhaps it is even wise not to knock out Japan completely. What precautions will the white powers have to take in Asia so that the white man will not be completely driven out of the continent? Besides, what will happen if by any mishap we defeat Japan too early, before Hitler is liquidated and before Europe's troubles are solved? Will not American influence predominate in Asia as in North Africa at present? Will not the Dutch Indies and Burma be left very much to themselves, and a little truculent when we settle with Hitler? What will happen to Singapore and to Hong Kong when the Japanese evacuate? . . .

The problem of the colonies is extremely complex. Must one really decide now whether Britain is to keep India, Burma, Malay, Hong Kong? Either "yes" or "no" to this question is very awkward. And if the British must keep their colonies, how are we to force the Dutch to give up theirs? Is it not better for war morale in this War for Freedom if we do not talk about the problem of the colonies until the war is won, when a fighting morale will no longer be necessary?

As a matter of fact, China and England are already heading for conflict. Churchill has made it amply clear and definite that he is not "grovelling," and that the "administration of British colonies" will be the "sole responsibility" of Britain, which is to tell America to keep her hands off. On the other hand, Chiang Kai-shek has made it equally definite and clear that China does not covet others' territory, but wants all her own territory back. These two policies must come to a clash around Hong Kong. China wishes to negotiate on Kowloon, a leased territory opposite Hong Kong, like other leased territories in Shanghai and Tientsin. England refuses to open negotiations. It is thought that dilly-dallying is the best way of treating the problem until it explodes by itself. I have no doubt that if Britain does not return Hong Kong to China, this problem of Hong Kong alone will burst the Peace Conference. I know that the Chinese people are willing to go to war with England over Hong Kong, even if the Chinese government won't. Chinese people have freely expressed the opinion that five million of our soldiers have not died to keep the British in Hong Kong, the booty of the Opium War, and possibly the second brightest jewel in the English Crown.

But really the picture is more complicated than you think. There is Russia, the great bugbear of the democracies. Everything is global nowadays, and we have to think globally. Russia refuses to declare war on Japan, and she knows what she is doing. Japan will be her trump card, and she will not want to play it, but keep it in her hand. What if Russia combines with Hitler and Japan? And what if it is to Russia's advantage to keep Japan in the war while she dictates what she wants to Europe? The thought occurs to us that if Russia can court Japan, why should not some other ally do the same, because after all Hitler is our immediate enemy? . . . Besides, if Russia wants to keep Japan to knock us out, why shouldn't we keep Japan to knock out Russia? Will not the elimination of Japan enhance Russia's power in the East? . . . Will China not double-cross us and negotiate with Japan? No, that is one thing certain at least, thank God! China is honest and dependable, and therefore let's ignore her. . . . She'll have to take what we choose to give her. . . . If Russia would only say something—it keeps one on tenterhooks! Besides, there is the possibility that Russia may combine with China and India and control the geopoliticians' Eurasian "Heartland" and half of the world's population. That will be the geopolitician's nightmare come true! Oh, why doesn't Russia say something?

And so like Alice in Wonderland,
the fears grow bigger and
bigger even as the tones
fall lower and lower
until the fears
themselves take
on the shape of
a mouse's tail—
the ugly, filthy
thing. Anyway
look, Russia
is such
a big
power
China
also
is go-
ing
to be
a big
pow-
er
you
can-
not
af-
ford
to
let
Ind-
ia
go
.

.

.

But above all, China herself is the biggest problem. The deeper tendencies of power-political thinking, or statesmanlike foresight according to power politics, already pose an insoluble difficulty. As Professor Spykman warns us, "A modern, vitalized and militarized China of 450,000,000 people is going to be a threat not only to Japan, but also to the position of the Western Powers in the Asiatic Mediterranean." "The preservation of the balance of power will then be necessary not only because of our interest in strategic raw materials [rubber and tin] but because of what unbalanced power in this region could do to the rest of the world." Hence, according to Professor Spykman, in order to set up such a highly desirable balance of power in the Far East, "the United States will have to adopt a similar protective policy toward Japan" as she adopts toward England. However, we are caught at present in the contradictory and illogical position of helping China, our potential enemy, to crush Japan, our potential friend in the Far East. This is confusion worse confounded. Hence we must help China to be strong enough not to be completely knocked out of the war, but not strong enough to stand on her feet after the war and challenge others, while we must crush Japan enough to win the war and not crush her enough so that she cannot revive and recover her power.

If further confusion is desired, I can offer some. Even Professor Spykman's proposal of planning for a half-strong and half-weak China and a half-strong and half-weak Japan does not insure complete security. That these two nations may be so cunningly manipulated that they will keep on fighting each other and exhausting each other for the West's benefit is conceded. It is conceivable, however, that decades from now, Japan and China may one day stupidly wake up to the Professor's clever trick, and realize that they have been set upon one another by the Yale Professor. Nothing so unites two enemies as the knowledge that they have been the common victim of a third mischievous party. By the time Professor Spykman's high politics prevail in the postwar world, nations will so groan in disillusionment and the spirit of true world co-operation will be such a forgotten thing that economic and political autarchy will be the basic policy of every nation.

The combination of two half-strong nations may nevertheless produce one fully strong power. In fact, writers who insist on Anglo-American domination of the Pacific areas are proceeding upon this theory. They must see to it that no rapprochement between Japan and China will ever be permitted. This, however, can only be done by putting China under military surveillance. On the other hand, China will equally demand putting England under military surveillance because a rapprochement between England and Germany is much more likely than a rapprochement between Japan and China. It is China's business to see that England and Germany do not get together, because every time that happens, a military Germany is resurrected and another World War is produced. China has as much right to demand security in Europe as England has to demand security in the Far East. . . . The Chinese are courteous, but not fools. They do not play power politics, but when others play it they understand it very well.

Such are the necessary and inevitable consequences of thinking on lines suggested by our power-politicians. These are they who pride themselves on "realism" and call us, the people, who believe in the other simple picture of the future of Asia, deluded fools or visionaries. That is what the picture of the future of Asia looks like in terms of power politics, when we transfer our power-political thinking to Asia.

Such may be the "facts" the diplomats are referring to when they say they "know" them, or they may not. One thing is certain, viz., that none of the above "facts" are known or knowable. In the dark, anything that moves may be a mouse's tail. In any case, these are facts which are yet to be produced as consequences of our own acts and created by our own choice. They are not the objective facts of physical science, and should not share the same scientific prestige. But it is exactly on this type of facts that diplomatic thinking is based, diplomatic fears are generated, and the gall of diplomatic courage is being ruined. It is on the basis of such unknown and unknowable facts that the policy has been established that China must be kept away from any Allied War Council, must be given no air force of her own, and Japan must not be defeated too early, and that a year and a half have elapsed after Pearl Harbor without the Allies coming to a formulated co-ordinated strategic plan for fighting Japan. It is on the basis of such generated fears that we are prevented from fighting together and dreaming together for a better world.

The illiterate shepherds of Asia Minor two thousand years ago heard or related that "Good will toward men" had something to do with "Peace on earth," but the twentieth-century man has advanced scientifically so far that he cannot see the connection, and has descended into confusion. Did Confucius not warn us, "A nation without faith cannot stand"? The same is true of the world.

Unit VIII

Legacies of the Second World War

That the Second World War wrought great changes may be a truism, since any event of that magnitude will have large effects. It may also be that there existed even deeper causes and more basic explanations for the upheavals in human life that are associated with World War II. Had there been no war the atom still might have been split, the British Empire would probably have disintegrated, America and the Soviet Union undoubtedly would have become super-powers. Nevertheless, speculation of this sort remains speculation, for the war did take place, bringing misery to millions, moments of sublime glory to a few, and profoundly influencing the lives of all who survived.

What of those survivors? What legacies did the Second World War bestow on those who lived through it—and on those who, born later, did not experience the war but are now living with the changes it produced? Anyone who attempts to deal with these questions must be wary of confusing causes and effects and of the very idea of the cause-effect relationship. All of the issues treated in this volume—total war, the Second Front, strategic bombing, war crimes, the problems of coalition diplomacy, for example—were deeply influenced by historical developments predating the Second World War. And, of course, few if any issues resulting from the war are presently being dealt with for the reasons that produced them originally. Still, the war was a laboratory for change; or, to use more appropriate language, it was a breeder reactor in which changes of tremendous consequence received supercharges. The hypervelocity of change has not slowed noticeably since.

Documents

1 Memorandum by the Secretary of the Treasury to President Roosevelt

Henry Morgenthau, Jr.

Secretary of the Treasury Morgenthau was a determined advocate of harsh punishment for Nazi Germany. He had arranged to present at the Quebec Conference in November, 1944, the so-called "Morgenthau Plan' which proposed dismantling German industrial capacity and dividing the country into small pastoral states. Roosevelt and Churchill had approved this policy of vengeance only to back down shortly afterward. But Morgenthau and many others (including the Russians) persisted in the view that the total destruction of German economic power was essential to a lasting peace. Despite the prolonged attempts to devise the wisest scheme, the current status of Germany remains one of the most tortuous legacies of the war.

[Washington,] January 10, 1945

During the last few months we have been giving further study to the problem of what to do with Germany after her defeat.

We are more convinced than ever that if we really mean to deprive Germany of the ability to make war again within a few years it is absolutely essential that she be deprived of her chemical, metallurgical and electrical industries. We don't think that this alone will guarantee peace, but that it is one of the steps we must take now.

We base this conclusion on the following premises, which seem to us unassailable:

(1) The German people have the will to try it again.

(2) Programs for democracy, re-education and kindness cannot destroy this will within any brief time.

"Memorandum by the Secretary of the Treasury (Morganthau) to President Roosevelt, January 10, 1945," from **Foreign Relations of the United States, 1945,** III (Washington, D.C.: U.S. Government Printing Office, 1968), pp. 376–77.

(3) Heavy industry is the core of Germany's warmaking potential.

Nearly all Americans grant the first point. A few, such as Dorothy Thompson, appear to disagree with the second; but all that we know and have learned recently—our experience with war prisoners, for instance—seems to argue against them. As to the third, America's own accomplishments in four years seem to us a shining lesson of what an equally versatile people can do. Our industry was converted from the world's greatest peacetime producer in 1940 to the world's greatest producer of military weapons in 1944. The Germans are versatile. Leave them the necessary heavy industry to build on and they can work as fast and as effectively as we.

The more I think of this problem, and the more I hear and read discussions of it, the clearer it seems to me that the real motive of most of those who oppose a weak Germany is not any actual disagreement on these three. points. On the contrary, it is simply an expression of fear of Russia and communism. It is the twenty-year-old idea of a "bulwark against Bolshevism"—which was one of the factors that brought this present war down on us.

Because the people who hold this view are unwilling (for reasons which, no doubt, they regard as statesmanlike) to come out in the open and lay the real issue on the table, all sorts of smoke screens are thrown up to support the proposition that Germany must be rebuilt. Examples are:

(a) The fallacy that Europe needs a strong industrial Germany.
(b) The contention that recurring reparations (which would require immediate reconstruction of the German economy) are necessary so that Germany may be made to pay for the destruction she has caused.
(c) The naïve belief that the removal or destruction of all German war materials and the German armament industry would in itself prevent Germany from waging another war.
(d) The illogical assumption that a "soft" peace would facilitate the growth of democracy in Germany.
(e) The fallacy that making Germany a predominantly agricultural country, with light industries but no heavy industries, would mean starving Germans.

We can submit to you studies which in our opinion will demonstrate that these propositions and others leading to the same conclusions are false.

This thing needs to be dragged out into the open. I feel so deeply about it that I speak strongly. If we don't face it I am just as sure as I can be that we are going to let a lot of hollow and hypocritical propaganda lead us into recreating a strong Germany and making a foe. of Russia. I shudder for the sake of our children to think of what will follow.

There is nothing that I can think of that can do more at this moment to engender trust or distrust between the United States and Russia than the position this Government takes on the German problem.

P.S.: I have given a copy of this to Ed Stettinius.

2   President Roosevelt's Press Conference

It was generally assumed that the United Nations would deal with the various international problems—both political and economic—arising from the war. Unhappily, as is suggested by the following excerpt from the President's press conference of April 5, 1945, national leaders had given little thought to how the UN would settle boundary claims, mandates, and other divisive matters. Implicit in Roosevelt's comments was the view that effective action by the United Nations depended on continued great-power cooperation. The faith that the UN could work miracles may have been one of the dubious legacies of the Second World War.

The President: . . . It seems obvious that we will be more or less responsible for security in all the Pacific waters. As you take a look at the different places captured by us, from Guadalcanal, the north coast of New Guinea, and then the Marianas and other islands gradually to the southern Philippines, and then into Luzon and north to Iwo Jima, it seems obvious the only danger is from Japanese forces; and they must be prevented, in the same way Germany is prevented, from setting up a military force which would start off again on a chapter of aggression.

So that means the main bases have to be taken away from them. They have to be policed externally and internally. And as a part of the western Pacific situation, it is necessary to throw them out of any of their mandated ports, which they immediately violated almost as soon as they were mandated, by fortifying these islands. . . .

Q. Mr. President, on the question of the Japanese mandates that you say will be taken away from them, who will be the controlling government in those mandates, the United States?

The President: I would say the United Nations. Or—it might be called—the world, which has been much abused now, will have a chance to prevent any more abuse. . . .

Q. Mr. President, do you think we will have a chance to talk with you again on other subjects before you go, such as the three-to-one vote? . . .

The President: As a matter of fact, this plea for votes was done in a very quiet way.

Stalin said to me—and this is the essence of it—"You know there are two parts of Russia that have been completely devastated. Every building is gone, every farm house, and there are millions of people living in these territories—and it is very important from the point of view of humanity—and we thought, as a gesture, they ought to be given something as a result of this coming victory.

"Extracts from President Roosevelt's Press Conference, April 5, 1945," from **Foreign Relations of the United States, 1945,** I (Washington, D.C.: U.S. Government Printing Office, 1967), pp. 196–98.

They have had very little civilization. One is the Ukraine, and the other is White Russia. We all felt—not any of us coming from there in the government—we think it would be grand to give them a vote in the Assembly. In these two sections, millions have been killed, and we think it would be very heartening—would help to build them up—if we could get them a vote in the Assembly."

He asked me what I thought.

I said to Stalin, "Are you going to make that request of the Assembly?"

He said, "I think we should."

I said, "I think it would be all right—I don't know how the Assembly will vote."

He said, "Would you favor it?"

I said, "Yes, largely on sentimental grounds. If I were on the delegation—which I am not—I would probably vote 'yes.'"

That has not come out in any paper.

He said, "That would be the Soviet Union, plus White Russia, plus the Ukraine."

Then I said, "By the way, if the Conference in San Francisco should give you three votes in the Assembly—if you get three votes—I do not know what would happen if I don't put in a plea for three votes in the States." And I said, "I would make the plea for three votes and insist on it."

It is not really of any great importance. It is an investigatory body only. I told Stettinius to forget it. I am not awfully keen for three votes in the Assembly. It is the little fellow who needs the vote in the Assembly. This business about the number of votes in the Assembly does not make a great deal of difference.

Q. They don't decide anything, do they?

The President: No.

By the way, this is all off the record.

3   The Potsdam Declaration

The Potsdam Conference of July 17-August 2, 1945, was notable for several reasons. It was the final wartime summit meeting. It brought together the veteran negotiator, Stalin, and two "new boys," President Harry S. Truman and Clement Attlee, who replaced Churchill as British Prime Minister after the conference began. Potsdam produced a

From **Foreign Relations of the United States: The Conferences of Berlin (Potsdam), 1945** (Washington, D.C.: U.S. Government Printing Office, 1960), pp. 363–64.

*statement of principles to guide the Allies in the occupation of Germany;
but successful conversion of principles into accomplishment demands a
spirit of tolerance and solidarity that probably no longer existed at that
time.*

The Principles to Govern the Treatment of Germany in the Initial Control
Period.

Political Principles
   1. In accordance with the Agreement on Control Machinery in Germany,
supreme authority in Germany is exercised, on instructions from their respective
Governments, by the Commanders-in-Chief of the armed forces of the United
States, the United Kingdom, the Union of Soviet Socialist Republics, and the
French Republic, each in his own zone of occupation, and also jointly, in
matters affecting Germany as a whole, in their capacity as members of the
Control Council.
   2. So far as is practicable, there shall be uniformity of treatment of the
German population throughout Germany.
   3. The purposes of the occupation of Germany by which the Control
Council shall be guided are:
   (i) The complete disarmament and demilitarization of Germany and the
   elimination or control of all German industry that could be used for military
   production. . . .
   (ii) To convince the German people that they have suffered a total military
   defeat and that they cannot escape responsibility for what they have brought
   upon themselves. . . .
   (iii) To destroy the National Socialist Party and its affiliated and supervised
   organizations, to dissolve all Nazi institutions. . . .
   (iv) To prepare for the eventual reconstruction of German political life on a
   democratic basis and for eventual peaceful cooperation in international life
   by Germany.
   4. All Nazi laws which provided the basis of the Hitler regime or
established discriminations on grounds of race, creed, or political opinion shall
be abolished. No such discriminations, whether legal, administrative or
otherwise, shall be tolerated.
   5. War criminals and those who have participated in planning or carrying
out Nazi enterprises involving or resulting in atrocities or war crimes shall be
arrested and brought to judgment. . . .
   6. All members of the Nazi Party who have been more than nominal
participants in its activities and all other persons hostile to Allied purposes shall
be removed from public and semi-public office, and from positions of
responsibility in important private undertakings. . . .
   7. German education shall be so controlled as completely to eliminate Nazi
and militarist doctrines and to make possible the successful development of
democratic ideas.

8. The judicial system will be reorganized in accordance with the principles of democracy, of justice under law, and of equal rights for all citizens without distinction of race, nationality or religion.

9. The administration in Germany should be directed towards the decentralization of the political structure and the development of local responsibility.... For the time being, no central German Government shall be established....

10. Subject to the necessity for maintaining military security, freedom of speech, press and religion shall be permitted, and religious institutions shall be respected. Subject likewise to the maintenance of military security, the formation of free trade unions shall be permitted.

Economic Principles

11. In order to eliminate Germany's war potential, the production of arms, ammunition and implements of war as well as all types of aircraft and sea-going ships shall be prohibited and prevented. Production of metals, chemicals, machinery and other items that are directly necessary to a war economy shall be rigidly controlled and restricted to Germany's approved post-war peace-time needs....

12. At the earliest practicable date, the German economy shall be decentralized for the purpose of eliminating the present excessive concentration of economic power as exemplified in particular by cartels, syndicates, trusts and other monopolistic arrangements.

13. In organizing the German economy, primary emphasis shall be given to the development of agriculture and peaceful domestic industries.

14. During the period of occupation Germany shall be treated as a single economic unit....

15. Allied controls shall be imposed upon the German economy but only to the extent necessary:

(a) to carry out programs of industrial disarmament, demilitarization, of reparations, and of approved exports and imports.

(b) to assure the production and maintenance of goods and services required to meet the needs of the occupying forces and displaced persons in Germany and essential to maintain in Germany average living standards not exceeding the average of the standards of living of European countries....

4   Thirtieth Meeting of the Council of Foreign Ministers, September 30, 1945

Attlee, Stalin, and Truman agreed at Potsdam to establish a Council of Foreign Ministers, to be composed of representatives from the "Big Three," plus France and China. It was believed that this body would deal with ongoing matters of particular concern to the great powers and could—by periodic meetings—maintain an atmosphere of openness and harmony. Just the reverse resulted. The Council became bogged down in bitter wrangling and the parliamentary trivia that characterized the opening stages of the Cold War. Indeed, the following extract from the U.S. delegation minutes of the first meeting in London suggests that "Cold War rhetoric" was the C.F.M.'s sole contribution to history.

Bidault: Shall we continue the discussion of the protocol? The Protocol Committee has met and has reported an important quantity of matter. It is in one language—I shall translate.

Molotov: But I must draw your attention to the fact that we have proposed to begin the discussion of the Soviet proposal.

Byrnes: But, Mr. Chairman, I understood that we proposed that we begin with the Committee proposal; therefore I propose that we begin the Committee proposal. I understand that the protocol has been proposed—I understood that the Committee proposal was to be considered before that of any individual member of the Council.

Molotov: In view of the fact that the proposal of the Soviet Delegation has been deferred more than once, the Soviet Delegation are unable to participate in the discussion of the other question until its proposal has been given consideration.

Bidault: What is the wish of the Council?

Byrnes: Mr. Chairman, I think there must be a misunderstanding. We have a Protocol Committee; every Delegation has a member on it. My information is that the Committee has a report. If the Committee has a report, certainly the report of the Committee should be considered in preference to a request by any one Delegation.

Molotov: Unfortunately, for my part I am not able to make any other suggestion.

Bidault: Does any member of the conference wish to make any other suggestion?

Byrnes: Yes, Mr. Chairman. I wonder if there is not some misunderstanding. This Committee, on which the Soviet Delegation has a

From "United States Delegation Minutes of the Thirtieth Meeting of the Council of Foreign Ministers, London, September 30, 1945," from **Foreign Relations of the United States, 1945,** II (Washington, D.C.: U.S. Government Printing Office, 1967), pp. 493–502.

representative, just like all the other Delegations, has been considering the protocol and has agreed upon some proposal, and, if possible, would not my friend be agreeable to hearing the Committee; then, if any of us objects to anything in it, we must all of us agree that that Delegation could have a hearing.—Mr. Chairman, I only have learned now, have understood now what the motion is. And I am told that what Mr. Molotov's motion is, is that instead of considering the protocol, we should consider the proposal that he made with reference to peace treaties, and I know that this afternoon I agreed that tonight it should be discussed. But I certainly did not mean that it had right of way or preference over the report of the Committee. I suggest that we hear the protocol, and if there are any changes, we can give it back to the Committee. Then they can go to work, and then we can discuss the other matter.

Molotov: Before discussing the results of the work done by the Protocol Committee, the Soviet Delegation finds it necessary to again acquaint itself with the result of the meeting of the Protocol Committee. At the present—at this moment—the Soviet Delegation are not ready to discuss the results of the meeting of the Protocol Committee as they must acquaint themselves with the report. . . .

Byrnes: Mr. Chairman, I am informed by our representative on the Protocol Committee that there is no difference in the text submitted by the Soviet Delegation and that already reported by the Committee, except a few unimportant things, and that there is agreement among all the members of the text of the general protocol affecting all five.

Molotov: In this case, I suggest that we first consider the general protocol, provided it is ready, then pass to the proposal made by the Soviet Delegation. . . .

Bevin: Mr. Chairman, I don't know what was referred to the Committee; we did not know what was in the Soviet draft. We adjourned in order to consider the Soviet draft. We agreed that the whole protocol should be examined with the Soviet Delegation draft, and now it is said that only one part of it is referred to the Protocol Committee. Now that I have seen the Soviet Delegation's draft which it referred, I am afraid I was somewhat dismayed. I agreed, Mr. Chairman, to the reference of the Protocol, because I was told it was ready, but I understood from Mr. Molotov that the other drafts covering the remainder would be ready in time, and that the whole thing was to be considered by the Committee.

Molotov: The Soviet Delegation can only agree to the protocol affecting all five being discussed by the Protocol Committee consisting of the five of them. The protocol affecting four should be discussed by a protocol committee of four, and so on. The Soviet Delegation will not agree to any other procedure.

Byrnes: Mr. Chairman,———

Molotov: At our general meeting the Soviet Delegation will no longer participate in the discussion—in the plenary session—of questions other than general questions. And if my colleagues disagree with this, then I suggest that the meeting be closed. There is no use our wasting time in empty talk.

Bidault: I do not think of indulging in empty talk, although we do talk much, and my recollection of what happened during the preceding meetings are not exactly so exciting as what has been said. The French Delegation is quite willing to listen to anything any Delegation has to say with the hope of avoiding having wasted all the time we have been talking in common together. . . .

Molotov: I have another suggestion to make, Mr. Chairman. It goes without saying that the Soviet Delegation will not agree to sign the general protocol unless the proposal made by the Soviet Delegation is accepted.

Byrnes: Mr. Chairman, I will ask my good friend what difference would there be if he agreed to sign yesterday and to sign today?

Molotov: We have already stated not for the first time that we withdraw our vote from the decision of September the 11th, and that means that this decision has ceased to exist as a decision, it is cancelled. It is obvious that if anyone withdraws his voice from a decision, this decision ceases to exist as a decision. That is plain. It could not be otherwise. We know very well that the Soviet Delegation considers the decision of September the 11th to be a mistake, and how is it possible for us after this to sign a protocol which embodies that statement? And we cannot do that, and you cannot compel us to do that, just as no one can compel anyone to say what one does not agree to. This could not be otherwise and no collective work would be possible otherwise, and any other interpretation will only mean that we do not realize what the Council of Foreign Ministers constitutes and it is high time we realized that. All the decisions contained in the protocol are only those decisions which have been agreed to by all. It could not be otherwise, and no one can make another agree to a decision to which he does not agree. We hold that the decision of September the 11th is incorrect, and we have withdrawn our vote from the decision, and we cannot sign the protocol which would contain that decision. No one of you could do that, unless he agrees. I have finished.

Bidault: Does this mean that Mr. Molotov does not wish to sign the general protocol or that he asks that the text of our protocol should be altered?

Molotov: I want to say that unless an additional decision is accepted to the effect that the decision of September 11 concerning procedure is cancelled, we shall not sign any protocol. If you disagree to this then no protocols are needed. That is all.

Byrnes: Mr. Chairman, I don't think my friend would want to insist on that suggestion. I have in my hands the Russian text that he distributed this afternoon. That text shows the text of the decision of September 11.

Molotov: That will remain.

Byrnes: There ought to be no difficulty in showing just what the facts were—that on a certain day, I don't know the day, but it was about the sixteenth meeting, after we had had about sixteen meetings, that the Soviet representative said he thought he made a mistake in agreeing to the decision on September the 11th, and he would no longer adhere to it.

Molotov: That's right.

Byrnes: Of course in our procedure the thing that I thought the Soviet representative would do would be to move to rescind or repeal the resolution of

September 11, but he did not make that motion. If such a motion were made even now, it would be for the Council to act on the motion, and the records show what occurred. All that I am saying is that the protocol ought to show just what occurred, and if it did, there could be no reason for objection by anybody, because everybody knows the position taken by the Soviet representative now. I thought he would move to cancel or repeal it or in some way have the records show it, other than by a mere statement.

Molotov: That is what I want to say—that an error has been made and should be corrected, and the decision revoked. Otherwise, we shall not sign any protocol. Or else the incorrect item should be excluded, and no special decision would be required. Or else the decision adopted on September 11 should be deleted, and in this case no special decision revoking it would be required. I will not suggest that we exclude anything from the protocol, but unless the mistake has been put right, the Soviet Delegation will sign no protocol. No one can compel the Soviet Delegation to sign what the Soviet Delegation does not agree to, and says so openly. That ought to be clear.

Byrnes: Mr. Chairman, when a council adopts a resolution, acts upon it for sixteen meetings, it cannot be excluded from the record, but that does not preclude the records showing exactly what occurred and the record should show, at some place, that on September 22 the Soviet representative informed the Council that he had made a mistake in agreeing to the resolution of September 11, and that the assent of the Soviet Delegation to that decision was withdrawn. If he wants a statement of that kind, that is the fact. . . .

Byrnes: Is the statement of the Soviet representative not only that he make a statement, but unless the Council revokes the decision, he will sign no protocol?

Molotov: That is right.

Byrnes: Then you will sign no protocol?

Molotov: I am prepared to stop with that.

Byrnes: How about the communiqué?

Molotov: Then there will be no communiqué. There is no use working on it. Unless there is a protocol, there can be no communiqué, because the communiqué must reflect the protocol.

Byrnes: I thought the communiqué might record the record of the meetings, what had been done, even though we did not have a protocol. I would like to know the views of the other members of the Council.

Molotov: Unless there is a protocol, we shall not participate, and not be a party to anything.

Byrnes: Then, Mr. Chairman, we find out we have no protocol, and no communiqué. . . .

Bidault: What now?

Molotov: He who is busy should go home tomorrow.

Bidault: What are the views of the other members of the Council, who are also busy?

Bevin: I should like for the sake of our own Government to record the action of September 22, Mr. Molotov's having said he made an error, and the fact that the peace treaties could not be discussed after that go on the record of this meeting. I should also like that it go on the record of this meeting that I suggested this, and asked in what manner we should deal with the peace treaties in the light of that decision. And that having suggested this, we were met with an ultimatum that we had to agree to this or we could not go on. Had that suggestion been considered for a few minutes, we might have gotten over this difficulty.

Molotov: I have a statement to make on this subject:

"At the general meeting of the Council of Foreign Ministers composed of five Ministers the Soviet Delegation cannot participate in discussions of questions relating to the peace treaties with Italy, Rumania, Bulgaria, Hungary, and Finland, because this procedure does not conform with the decision of Berlin."

Bidault: In the name of the French Delegation I beg to ask the Soviet Delegation what is exactly the character of this statement? Is it meant for the whole Council, or for any other use?

Molotov: I have made this statement at the meeting of the Council of Foreign Ministers, and I ask that this statement be recorded in the protocol.

Byrnes: What protocol?

Molotov: In the minutes of this particular meeting.

Bidault: In that case I am obliged to say that the French Delegation adheres to the decision of the 11th of September. France, being situated in Europe, considers that nothing connected with European affairs can be settled without France. I also ask that this be recorded in the minutes.

I wonder what we should do now? I wonder whether after the discussion it might not be useful to think it over a little longer and adjourn, and have a meeting tomorrow before the departures that have been announced by several members actually take place. Anyway, the French Delegation does not feel sleepy, but it is indicated that we shorten a discussion which is not useful and may be harmful.

Byrnes: Mr. Chairman, I only want to say that this proposal to establish the Council of Foreign Ministers was proposed by the United States at the Berlin meeting of the Heads of Governments. Remembering the unfortunate experiences following the last war it was our firmest hope that we might avoid them, and that this Council might be the machinery to enable us to avoid the pitfalls of 1919. In our opinion it was the vehicle that would promote the establishment of a lasting peace on this earth. We believed that it could do the spadework, and that, meeting as friends, we could adjust difficulties, and then call in nations that had fought, suffered, and died in this war, and have them join in our work in order that they agree to the results of our efforts.

Because of that in the last few days I have urged that there would be an agreement to call a conference in order to give the nations of the world a chance to come and see what we had agreed upon before they were asked to sign on the dotted line. We have signed the armistice terms, Great Britain, the Soviet Republics, and the United States—when we signed them, we signed some of them in behalf of the other nations of the world, and the others were signed by the three Governments in the interests of other nations. That had to be done because while hostilities were on, all nations could not be expected to sign the terms of surrender. When it comes to framing the peace that would be a just peace, and no peace is a lasting peace unless it is a just peace, when it comes to that kind of peace, the nations in whose behalf we signed the armistice terms are entitled to be heard and to be present when the treaties are signed.

I hope that we could agree to call such a conference and give hope to all the peoples of the world who love liberty and love freedom. My proposal, although offered with the understanding that if it could be agreed to, I would agree to the proposal of Mr. Molotov—but I could not secure his approval. I must say that I am disappointed because we sought only to bring to the conference table our friends and our allies, not our enemies. At Berlin the Heads of Governments never dreamed of having a paper so narrowly interpreted that it would work against the interests of our own friends. If tonight we could send word to the world that those of us who represent the larger powers were going to do the spadework on the treaty and then all people were going to be invited in to say what kind of a world we were going to have in the future, there would be happiness in millions of homes. To help in this work we have come three thousand miles across the ocean with the hope we might contribute in some part to the accomplishment of our objectives. We were disappointed, but we shall not lose our interest in the affairs of the world. We shall continue to exercise all of our efforts, use all the power that we have, to help bring about a just and enduring peace on this earth.

Molotov: The Soviet Delegation holds the view that if there is an agreement with another government, this agreement should be carried out. And the Soviet Government feels that to depart from such a practice would mean undermining the prestige of such decisions and would do harm to the governments with whom the agreements have been signed. The Berlin agreement was accepted by the three Governments, and voluntarily accepted. This agreement is intended to insure peace, and why does it happen that only the Soviet Government is defending its Government's decision, whereas other governments ignore the fact that such a decision has been adopted? Why do these other governments not regard themselves as bound to defend the decision of their governments? In order that other United Nations may believe our decisions and agreements, they should be carried out. If we do not respect these decisions ourselves, then nobody will respect them.

In the course of this war our three Governments—I am referring to Great Britain, the United States of America, and the Soviet Union, have held conferences and have adopted a number of major decisions. It was not immediately that we sometimes arrived at decision; there were sometimes disagreements on certain questions. Then we used to defer them until our differences had been settled, but once these difficulties were settled, and decisions were taken between the three Governments, we, each of our Governments, felt it their duty, and a matter of honor, to defend these decisions both in deed and in word, and to carry them out.

The Soviet Delegation prefers no new claims before our colleagues. The only thing that the Soviet Delegation prefers is that the decisions adopted by us in common and voluntarily should be carried out. Does that mean to ask for too much? Could we do otherwise? The Soviet Delegation is now compelled to come out in defense of the Berlin decision alone. The representatives of other Governments who participated in the conference at Berlin treat lightly these decisions and do not feel themselves bound by these decisions, but the Soviet Delegation feels that it defends a just cause and that it can defend this attitude with assurance, as this attitude is not only the attitude of our own, but also is an attitude which is recorded in the decision by the three Powers. . . .

If we carried out the decisions and agreements which we signed, then our word will be trusted, both within our states and outside of them, but if we do not carry them out, then no one will trust us. It is impossible to imagine a sadder situation for the course of the maintenance of a lasting peace than this. As long as the agreement exists the Soviet Government will carry it out honestly and constantly, and the Soviet Government will regard it as their duty and obligation to carry out these agreements—as their duty and their obligation to their own people as well as to other allied nations. Only along this course shall we work for the sake of lasting peace in the world. I have finished.

Byrnes: I cannot refrain from saying a word with reference to the Berlin Agreement. That Agreement, in providing for the discharge of the duties of the Council members, said that it would be composed of the members representing those states which were signatories to the terms of surrender imposed upon the enemy states concerned. It said further that as regards the peace settlement with Italy, France should be regarded as a signatory of the terms of surrender for Italy. And then the Berlin Agreement provided that other members would be invited to participate when matters directly concerning them are under discussion. Pursuant to that language this Council met, and on September 11 the Governments of the Soviet Union, the United Kingdom, and the United States adopted a resolution which reads, according to the Russian text handed me this afternoon, as follows: I first read the English text of the agreement.

"All five members of the Council should have the right to attend all meetings and take part in all discussions, but in matters concerning peace settlements members whose Governments have not been signatories to the relative terms of surrender should not be entitled to vote."

That was not only an invitation which was authorized by the Berlin Agreement—it was a solemn agreement on the part of the Governments at this table. It was entered into by the Foreign Ministers of five Governments; it was lived up to for sixteen meetings. I agree with what Mr. Molotov says—I quote his words of a few moments ago, "If we carry out the agreements we make, our word will be trusted, but if we do not carry them out, no one will trust us." I speak with regret, but I cannot refrain from speaking when my Government is charged with not living up to the Berlin Agreement.

Mr. Chairman, does any one know of any reason why this Council should continue longer? . . .

5   The Playing Fields of Malvern

Angus Calder

A very different though related legacy of the Second World War was the emergence of science from the obscurity of the laboratory into the full glare of public awareness. Scientific contributions to the war efforts of the contending nations had been invaluable; thus the importance of science—and of scientists—was for the first time fully recognized in the Second World War. With recognition came responsibility and also, as the following selection from Angus Calder's intriguing study of Britain during the war intimates, the potential for power.

The First World War had proved that "scientific research" and "national defence" were now synonyms. Britain's rulers had found that her industry had lagged so far behind in the application of science that she had depended on Germany for countless drugs, for magnetos, for tungsten, for smelted zinc. In 1915 the Government's Department of Scientific and Industrial Research (D.S.I.R.) had been established, to encourage and assist co-operative research organizations in individual industries, to give grants to students and postgraduates, and to control its own laboratories, research stations and research boards.

This work had continued on a modest scale between the two wars, and D.S.I.R. laboratories did important work in the Second in such matters as the construction of concrete runways, the preservation of food, and advanced aerodynamics (where Government research establishments provided the theoretical backbone for the achievements of British aircraft design). But whereas the First World War had confirmed the importance of scientific research, the Second established the importance of the scientist and his questioning, irreverent outlook.

It had seemed by no means certain at the outset that this transformation would happen. In 1938, it had been the initiative of the then President of the Royal Society which had prodded the Government into crystallizing the idea of a central register of men with administrative, executive—and scientific—qualifications. In practice, administrative experience had proved to be a highly elusive entity, and after the register had tried to cope with a surge of amiable muddlers who believed themselves equipped to direct great enterprises, it had settled down to its main work, directing scientists and engineers where they were most needed. In the autumn of 1939 the universities had been emptied suddenly of many of their most brilliant men, who had largely

From **The People's War: Britain 1939–1945** by Angus Calder, pp. 457–72. Copyright © 1969 by Angus Calder. Reprinted by permission of Pantheon Books, a Division of Random House, Inc.

gravitated to radar. But a serious dearth of further technically qualified recruits, especially for telecommunications, had soon emerged, so that in July 1940, all people qualified as engineers, chemists, physicists and quantity surveyors had been required to put their names on the register.

However, it seemed clear to many that not all the available talent was being used, and that much of it was being misused. Years before, a brilliant group of scientists had set up a small dining club, called the "Tots and Quots" (*quot hominies, tot sententiae*) to mark their diversity of viewpoints. Amongst these men, now malcontent, were Solly Zuckerman and J.D. Bernal. At one of their meetings in the summer of 1940, Allen Lane, the founder of Penguin Books, was present, and suggested that their bitter criticisms of the inadequate mobilization of science for the war effort should be published in his series of "Specials." The book took a fortnight for its twenty-five authors to put together, and within a month, anonymously, it was on the bookstalls. It is a most important document, as Zuckerman, Bernal, and others who helped with its writing, found jobs of key national importance where they put their ideas into practice.

Science in War complained roundly that "A large proportion of the scientific brains in this country are not being used at all and, due to defects of organization, most of those that are being used are not working at anything like their possible efficiency." Scientific method, the authors argued, must be applied in every field of battle and every corner of the war economy. Their point was not that scientists should be used as consultants merely—indeed, the trouble was that this was the limited role to which business and the civil service assigned them at the moment. They must be brought right into the crucial discussions of policy; they must be there when decisions were made. The book predicted "a revolution in strategy far greater than that introduced by Napolean" when scientists were directly involved in warfare; and subsequent events showed that this arrogance was justified. Scorn was poured on the "verbalism" of the arts graduates trained in classics and the humanities who still dominated British public life. The authors quoted an editorial from the famous journal *Nature* which pointed out that at the Civil Defence Camouflage Establishment, "Of sixty-five technical officers, all but four are either professional artists or, at the time of recruitment, were students at art schools. Not one member of the establishment is a qualified biologist." But only a biologist could advise on the principles underlying visual concealment or deception. Paint was, therefore, splashed on with ignorant abandon. "An extravagant example of this foolishness was the decoration of the cooling towers of a large works to represent a grove of tall trees. It should scarcely be necessary to point out that the result of light and shade is such as absolutely to kill this piece of stage scenery at bombing range."

And beyond the obvious applications of science, the authors pleaded for the use of applied psychology in the forces, for the involvement of social scientists is the assessment of morale and the construction of propaganda, and for "scientific management" in industry, gloomily remarking of the seven-day week recently introduced into war factories that "The ministers responsible were probably acting in ignorance rather than deliberately sabotaging the war effort." Lo and behold, these things came to pass.

For *Science in War* was pushing at a door which was already half open, and which would soon be torn off its hinges by the pressure of events. Scientists, even in their role as consultants, had already shown themselves capable of influencing events. As Zuckerman points out, the original suggestion that radar should be explored had come from Watson Watt himself; and when Peierls and Frisch early in 1940 had shown that it was possible to exploit nuclear fission in the development of a bomb with unprecedented destructive potential, there had been no staff requirement for such a weapon. The Tizard Committee itself had in effect drawn scientists into the process of decision making at the most crucial level (though during the war Sir Henry Tizard himself experienced the other edge of the blade when, as a member of the Air Council, he was involved in the inspection of various designs of W.A.A.F. underwear). The position which Tizard's arch rival, Lindemann, now occupied in the counsels of Churchill was more than a portent—it was already an important political fact. And the famous clash of opinions between the two men, in which Lindemann, in 1942, was victorious, illustrated the uncomfortable truth that when the scientist became involved in Government, his claim to objectivity was jeopardized by the ambience of top-level politics.

The story of the arguments between the humourless, vain and often cruel Lindemann and the gentlemanly, witty, balanced Tizard has often been told in such a way as to exaggerate their differences over specific questions of policy. Where the use of the R.A.F. was concerned, their disagreement in effect boiled down to one of emphasis; though it was Blackett's view that Lindemann was fanatical, besotted with the idea that "any diversion of aircraft production and supply to the anti-submarine campaign, to army cooperation or even to fighter defence—in fact, to anything but bombing" would be "a disastrous mistake." . . .

The whole controversy, then and since, has illustrated the degree to which major strategic decisions, in the middle of the war, might be influenced by academic scientists working in secret. The same penetration had been achieved by experts in other fields. It will be remembered that the distinguished Scientific Food Committee had proposed, after Dunkirk, a rock-bottom but adequate "basal diet" which had been spurned. The official historian of food policy suggests that the committee's weakness stemmed from its remoteness from the practical work of the administrators who would have had to implement such a diet. ". . . It was only possible for scientists to influence food policy if they were behind the scenes and privy to the innermost counsels of the Ministries of Food and Agriculture." They soon were; the same historian later points out that by mid-1941 "the influence of scientific advice could be said to penetrate to every corner of ministry activity."

Still more striking was the permeation of all three services with boffins which is summed up by the phrase "operational research." *Science in War* provides a definition. "The waging of warfare represents a series of human operations carried out for more or less definite ends. Seeing whether these operations actually yield the results expected from them should be a matter of direct scientific analysis. There had been some work of this kind done in the

First World War, but the term "operational research" and the attitude which it represented became widely current only in the Second. . . .

The marriage of the military mind with scientific common sense was far from complete when the war ended. This was not always because the boffins themselves were naive about war. Blackett said in 1958 that "During nearly twenty years of my lifetime of sixty years, I have been either training for war, fighting wars, or studying and thinking about them. In between, I became an experimental atomic physicist." He had served in the navy in the First World War, when Lindemann had been a daring experimental pilot and Tizard had served in the Royal Flying Corps.

But the immediate background from which most of the boffins came was the university laboratory, where they had been great men in their own fields (and had known it), and had been used to judging others by different standards from those of rank and seniority which applied in the civil service and the armed forces. They were the only outsiders whom it proved impossible for Whitehall to digest into its traditional way of doing things. After all, in their scientific work, if the youngest of their colleagues had a good idea, it was still a good idea. . . .

The nickname "Sunday Soviets," so hypertypical of the period, serves as a text for a further point about the arrival of science in the corridors of power. While the older generation of boffins—Lindemann, Tizard, A.V. Hill—were generally right-wing in politics, the young men who had made their reputations in the 1930s were often ardent Marxists. That old-fashioned radical H.G. Wells had satirized this new strain of scientists as "the Martians." *Science in War* interspersed its more specific criticisms with general assaults on capitalism and traditionalism. Amongst other unthinkable feats, the war hoisted a Communist boffin, J.D. Bernal, into the highlands of the military establishment.

Science, by tradition, was pacific and internationalist. Now political anti-Nazism went hand in hand with annoyance at the disruption of their work to break down traditional inhibitions among British scientists. The dictators had broadcast to the world their contempt for intellectual standards by the persecution of Jewish and left-wing scientists—many of whom were now doing vital work in Britain. From the wall of Rowe's room, a photograph of Goering looked down, with much inspirational force, on the Sunday Soviets.

Yet scientists who had seen the free passage of ideas between the nations as an essential basis for achievement could not always settle down happily into the atmosphere of ultra-security imposed by total war. The atom bomb troubled the peace of mind of some, at least, of those who pressed the work on it forward. Britain's greatest nuclear physicist, Sir James Chadwick, told two American scientists, "I wish I could tell you that the bomb is not going to work, but I am ninety per cent certain that it will."

And in the case of the atomic bomb, the limits of the influence of scientists were illustrated. Niels Bohr, the great Danish nuclear scientist, was smuggled out of Europe in a high-speed Mosquito (nearly perishing from lack of oxygen en route). He was flown, first to Britain, then to America, to assist in the development of the bomb. In 1944, he tried desperately to convince Roosevelt and Churchill that international control of this terrible new force was essential from the outset, and that the Russians must be brought in. He had struck up a curious friendship with Sir John Anderson, who had done research work on the chemistry of uranium before the First World War. Anderson, convinced by Bohr's arguments, pressed on Churchill that "no plans for world organization which ignore the potentialities of Tube Alloys can be worth the paper on which they are written." Churchill peppered Anderson's minute with disapproving remarks and "wrote at the end simply 'I do not agree.' " He continued to keep Tube Alloys a secret, not only from Stalin, but from the Labour members of the cabinet. . . .

Total war against a totalitarian state had a logic of its own, a logic, one might say, of the *Catch 22* variety, which overrode qualms. If Germany got the atom bomb first, the results would be unthinkable. The allies must anticipate the Germans and possess a weapon such as Hitler would use if he could. And when the time came, there was only one way to justify the labour and the money, or, for that matter, to find out if and how the bomb worked. That was, to use it.

It is argued sometimes that research undertaken for war purposes (for "defence," in the terminology of 1984) indirectly benefits peaceful industries and serves mankind; which, of course, begs the question whether it was necessary to bomb Hiroshima to find out about nuclear power for electricity. Sir Solly Zuckerman, who went on to become Chief Scientific Adviser to a post-war British Government, concedes that "a state of war can stimulate the scientist to great feats of the imagination and to great practical achievement." He goes on to point out that when scientists "abandoned, or slowed down, the basic researches they had been carrying out in peacetime" to devote themselves to the demands of war, "most of them enjoyed resources on a scale they had never dreamt of in peace . . . But I do not know," he adds, "of any of these wartime researches yielding results as far-reaching as those which had been revealed in years of peace . . . The fundamental scientific discoveries on which the great technical achievements of the Second World War were based were made well before the war." And he might have added that those discoveries, directly or indirectly, had belonged jointly to scientists of more than one of the combatant nations.

For the moment, in spite of everything, the public optimism of men of science served to colour the millenarian visions of the war years. Just before the war, the British Association for the Advancement of Science had bowed to the pressure of enthusiasts, "Wellsian" and "Martian," and had set up a new division for "Social and International Relations of Science." One of the prime movers had been the veteran scientific publicist and educationalist, Sir Richard Gregory, who was president of the B.A. during the war. In September 1941, the new division sponsored a conference on "Science and World Order," in London, where scientists from twenty-two nations met to "demonstrate the common purpose of men of science in ensuring a post-war order in which the maximum benefits of science will be secured for all people." It lasted for three days. There was a huge demand for tickets, the B.B.C. publicized the conference at home and abroad, and it was filmed by the Ministry of Information. The speakers included Herbert Morrison, as well as an impressive array of Fellows of the

Royal Society. But "perhaps its most notable feature was the audience. Young men in flannels and hatless girls outnumbered the die-hards of science, to applaud the suggestion of Professor A.V. Hill . . . that scientific advisory bodies should be established for each department of the cabinet." There were messages from Churchill and the King, and all present enthusiastically endorsed a Seven Part Scientific Charter, replete with noble aims, which stressed the need for freedom of speech and for international interchange of ideas. The ultra-Tory *National Review* fulminated against "papers read by the group of socialist partisans and their cortège of political cheapjacks. . . ." Though Hill was a Conservative M.P. as well as a former member of the Tizard Committee, it was correct in identifying the conference as yet another distasteful manifestation of the left-wing idealism which provided the Spirit of the Age.

As scientists themselves progressed through a maze of appointments and committees towards some real authority, the rapprochement of science and society had its parallels at the level of research itself. Operational research could not stop short at analysing the performance of machines; it was inevitably concerned with the people who handled them.

The authors of *Science in War* regarded "social science" as a complement to their own work in physics, biology and chemistry. In the early 1930s, a group of progressive experts and businessmen had set up Political and Economic Planning (P.E.P.) which continued to publish influential reports on industrial and social questions during the war. A P.E.P. broadsheet of 1934 had spoken of the need to make heard in the circles of Government the views of "those on whose service technical civilization depends—the administrators, the managers, the engineers, scientists, teachers and technicians." One of P.E.P.'s early members had been Julian Huxley, whose contention that political planning should "always be in touch with scientifically ascertained fact" sums up part of its credo.

In 1937, Huxley had been one of the sponsors of a new social survey organization, Mass Observation, a name often seen in these pages. It did more than any other body to popularize "social science" in the weeklies and illustrated papers. Its enthusiastic "observers" all over the country were instructed to watch their fellow humans with the closeness, and detachment, of an anthropologist or biologist. Also in the late 1930s, the Gallup Poll had made its first appearance in Britain.

Yet survey techniques had been so little understood in higher administrative circles that when, in October 1939, the War Cabinet had pondered the introduction of rationing, its chosen method of ascertaining public opinion had been to ask the then Minister of Labour to make "soundings" among bodies "representative of public opinion." Of nineteen contacts, only two had been actively hostile, and inquiries on Fleet Street had elicited what had seemed to the cabinet the "significant fact" that rationing was not in the forefront of the public mind. The old notion that public opinion was an aggregation of the views held by pressure groups and journalists still survived; and the fact that the decision then taken actually accorded with wider public opinion was merely good luck. . . .

The Second World War made it imperative that the Government should find the best ways of selling to people the commodities and attitudes which it thought were good for them. Information had to be collected to find out if propaganda had been effective. Further propaganda must be produced, tailored ever more closely to the prejudices of the public. The Ministry of Information had three thousand staff at its peak, excluding postal censorship workers, and other Government departments employed seventeen hundred people on "information" work in January 1944. The advertising industry, one might say, was nationalized for the duration.

On one level, this was good "People's War" activity; how sublimely democratic that Government departments should worry constantly about their relationship with ordinary people. But the overall effect, of course, was quite the opposite. Having found out what people thought and how they behaved, the rulers of the country could manipulate them more efficiently, while simultaneously conforming themselves to the lowest common denominator of public opinion. The old gentlemanly notion that the Government was doing all right if the habitues of London clubs approved of it was superseded by the obsession of politicians with the opinion polls and their increasing use of the soft sell, the below the belt advertisement and what Daniel Boorstin calls the "pseudo event." Ancient superstitions were still very much alive when the war ended, and the contemporary assessments of the 1945 General Election result have considerable antiquarian charm. But the straws were there in the wind, and the largest of them was Woolton's success as Minister of Food. After the war, which had given him much useful experience, he undertook the first sustained and methodical exercise in image building known to British politics, as organizer of the Conservative Central Office. . . .

Of course, the motivations which have led to the acceptance of "scientific management" have been very similar. The First World War, by bringing British management close to collapse, had stimulated interest in such techniques as F.W. Taylor had pioneered in the U.S.A. Their advance between the war had been slow; Britain had no institution to compare to the Harvard Business School, and only three universities had small departments teaching management. But the considerable American invasion of British industry had created colonies of modernity. General Motors, Ford, Goodyear, Monsanto, Proctor and Gamble, Hoover and Remington Rand had bought British businesses or built their own factories. At the same time, the balance of the British economy had been shifting towards the newer and lighter forms of engineering, and within the engineering industry itself the old skilled jobs were being increasingly broken down to semi-skilled level. To maintain a smooth and peaceful flow of work through increasingly large factories of increasingly interdependent workers, skilled management was essential. In 1939, its practitioners had remained rare in Britain. The war made them the heroes of the hour, the demigods of a new ideology. . . .

6   Letter to President Harry S Truman

Dwight D. Eisenhower

The physical destruction wrought by the war was staggering. In Europe, for example, millions of dwellings had been destroyed; factories lay in ruins; communications were totally disrupted; and many countries' transportation systems, essential to the distribution of food and fuel, were paralyzed. The effects in terms of human suffering were tremendous, especially for one particular group—the displaced persons who had lost homes, livelihoods, and countries. What to do with the "DP's," stateless persons for the most part, was one of the most formidable problems bequeathed by the war.

18 September 1945

Dear Mr. President:

During my absence from this Headquarters, receipt of your letter concerning the problem of displaced persons was acknowledged. I was then on a trip during which I made an inspection of a number of the installations in which we have displaced persons. This letter deals primarily with my own observations and will be supplemented, either immediately or in the near future, by a more extensive report comprehending the findings of subordinate commanders and staffs and of a special Jewish investigator.

As to the seriousness of the problem, there is not the slightest doubt. The hopelessness of the ordinary displaced person comes about from fear of the future, which involves questions, always of international politics, and from the practical impossibility of participating, at this time, in any useful occupation.

To speak very briefly about the psychological attitude of these people, I give you a few impressions gained by direct conversations with them. A very large percentage of the persons from the Baltic States, as well as from Poland and Rumania, definitely do *not* want to return to their own countries *at this time*. Although such a return represents the height of their ultimate ambitions, they constantly state, "We cannot go back until there is a change in the political situation—otherwise we will all be killed". They state that the governments of all these states will persecute them to the point of death, although they insist that they bitterly opposed German domination of their respective states just as they opposed domination by any other government.

With respect to the Jews, I found that most want to go to Palestine. I note in your letter that you have already instituted action in the hope of making this possible. All of these matters are, of course, distinctly outside any military

"Dwight D. Eisenhower to President Harry S Truman, September 18, 1945." Official File Number 127-A, Harry S Truman Papers, Truman Library, Independence, Missouri.

responsibility or authority, and there is nothing whatsoever that I or my subordinates would be justified in promising or intimating in regard to them. However, the matter draws practical importance for us out of the possibility that caring for displaced persons may be a long-time job. Since I assume that most countries would be unwilling to absorb masses of these people as citizens in their respective countries, the only alternative is that of hoping they will gradually voluntarily disperse in the areas of Western Europe and try to establish themselves in a self-sustaining life. To this end we encourage everybody to go out and get a job if he possibly can, and have been trying to explore the possibilities of agriculture and small business in the hopes of establishing small colonies of these people near their present locations. One great difficulty is that they do not desire to look upon their present location as any form of permanent home. They prefer to sit and wait rather than to attempt, as they say, "forcing themselves into a population where they would never be welcome".

With regard to actual living conditions; I personally visited five camps, two of which were exclusively Jewish and a third largely so. Two of the camps were villages taken from the Germans. Two others were city suburbs which had been taken over and occupied, one by the Jews, one by the Poles. In one camp, which was Jewish, I found conditions less than satisfactory, but found also that the camp and local authorities were taking over additional houses in the immediate vicinity, throwing the Germans out of these houses in order to provide more and better accommodations for the displaced persons. You will understand that to provision these people adequately they must be housed in the same general vicinity; an impossible administrative problem would be presented if they were scattered indiscriminately throughout the German population. All feeding of displaced persons is under military or UNRRA control, whereas, with few exceptions, the German population has to look out for itself. You will understand, also, that when we speak of "camp" we do not mean either a tent camp or one made of huts. Speaking generally, every displaced person is in a permanent building of some sort, either an ordinary dwelling or building that was once used for other purposes. In the camp where I found conditions unsatisfactory, there were still guards on the entrance and passes were required for visits to any distant spot. This practice is stopped, but the Jewish leaders within the camp itself insisted that some form of control was necessary in order, as they said, that "all of us do not get a bad name." I found no instances of displaced persons still living in the old "horror" camps.

In one camp we have experienced, on the part of a considerable minority of the displaced persons, a distinct lack of cooperation. I am still reporting on evidence given me by these people themselves. The most simple of sanitary regulations were constantly violated to a degree that in some instances could be termed nothing less than revolting, although this has much improved. The voluntary police begged me to permit them to have arms. Upon my flat refusal to entertain such an idea I received the reply, "We have some very mean men here and they can get us all in trouble". However, I am certain that since these people are completely dependent upon us for food, the necessary standard of conduct can be maintained without any resort to harsh methods.

At no place did I find any timidity on the part of any officer to throw a German out of a house in order to give better accommodations to displaced persons, but as before mentioned, problems of feeding, distribution and medical care for this completely helpless group, make it imperative that they be sufficiently concentrated in order that these services can be performed. In those instances where I believe officers have over-emphasized the administrative difficulties, vigorous steps are being taken and improvement will be prompt.

When it is realized that the Army in this area has been faced with the most difficult types of redeployment problems; has had to preserve law and order; furnish a multitude of services for itself and for the thousands of people it employs, and on top of this has had this question of displaced persons with unusual demands upon transportation, housing, fuel, food, medical care and security, you can well understand that there have been undeniable instances of inefficiency. Commanders of all grades are engaged in seeking these out and I am confident that if you could compare conditions now with what they were three months ago, you would realize that your Army here has done an admirable and almost unbelievable job in this respect.

Respectfully,
Dwight D. Eisenhower

7   The Long Telegram

George F. Kennan

By February, 1946, relations between the United States and the Soviet Union had deteriorated to the point of open hostility. At this time, when the Truman administration was groping toward new definitions of American foreign policy, the following analysis of Russian conduct by George Kennan, Minister of the U.S. Embassy in Moscow, burst like a thunderclap over official Washington. Kennan's "long telegram" was an important event in the history of the Cold War.

February 22, 1946, 9 p.m.

Answer to Dept's 284, Feb 3 involves questions so intricate, so delicate, so strange to our form of thought, and so important to analysis of our international

From **Foreign Relations of the United States, 1946** (Washington, D.C.: U.S. Government Printing Office, 1970), pp. 696–709.

environment that I cannot compress answers into single brief message without yielding to what I feel would be dangerous degree of over-simplification. I hope, therefore, Dept will bear with me if I submit in answer to this question five parts, subjects of which will be roughly as follows:

(One)   Basic features of post-war Soviet outlook.

(Two)   Background of this outlook.

(Three)   Its projection in practical policy on official level.

(Four)   Its projection on unofficial level.

(Five)   Practical deductions from standpoint of US policy.

I apologize in advance for this burdening of telegraphic channel; but questions involved are of such urgent importance, particularly in view of recent events, that our answers to them, if they deserve attention at all, seem to me to deserve it at once. . . .

Part One: Basic Features of Post-War Soviet Outlook, As Put Forward by Official Propaganda Machine

(A) USSR still lives in antagonistic "capitalist encirclement" with which in the long run there can be no permanent peaceful coexistence. As stated by Stalin in 1927 to a delegation of American workers: "In course of further development of international revolution there will emerge two centers of world significance: a socialist center, drawing to itself the countries which tend toward socialism, and a capitalist center, drawing to itself the countries that incline toward capitalism. Battle between these two centers for command of world economy will decide fate of capitalism and of communism in entire world."

(B) Capitalist world is beset with internal conflicts, inherent in nature of capitalist society. These conflicts are insoluble by means of peaceful compromise. Greatest of them is that between England and US.

(C) Internal conflicts of capitalism inevitably generate wars. Wars thus generated may be of two kinds: intra-capitalist wars between two capitalist states, and wars of intervention against socialist world. Smart capitalists, vainly seeking escape from inner conflicts of capitalism, incline toward latter.

(D) Intervention against USSR, while it would be disastrous to those who undertook it, would cause renewed delay in progress of Soviet socialism and must therefore be forestalled at all costs.

(E) Conflicts between capitalist states, though likewise fraught with danger for USSR, nevertheless hold out great possibilities for advancement of socialist cause, particularly if USSR remains militarily powerful, ideologically monolithic and faithful to its present brilliant leadership.

(F) It must be borne in mind that capitalist world is not all bad. In addition to hopelessly reactionary and bourgeois elements, it includes (one) certain wholly enlightened and positive elements united in acceptable communistic parties and (two) certain other elements (now described for tactical reasons as progressive or democratic) whose reactions, aspirations and activities happen to be "objectively" favorable to interest of USSR. These last must be encouraged and utilized for Soviet purposes.

(G) Among negative elements of bourgeois-capitalist society, most dangerous of all are those whom Lenin called false friends of the people, namely moderate-socialist or social-democratic leaders (in other words, non-communist left-wing). These are more dangerous than out-and-out reactionaries, for latter at least march under their true colors, whereas moderate left-wing leaders confuse people by employing devices of socialism to serve interests of reactionary capital.

So much for premises. To what deductions do they lead from standpoint of Soviet policy? To following:

(A) Everything must be done to advance relative strength of USSR as factor in international society. Conversely, no opportunity must be missed to reduce strength and influence, collectively as well as individually, of capitalist powers.

(B) Soviet efforts, and those of Russia's friends abroad, must be directed toward deepening and exploiting of differences and conflicts between capitalist powers. If these eventually deepen into an "imperialist" war, this war must be turned into revolutionary upheavals within the various capitalist countries.

(C) "Democratic-progressive" elements abroad are to be utilized to maximum to bring pressure to bear on capitalist governments along lines agreeable to Soviet interests.

(D) Relentless battle must be waged against socialist and social-democratic leaders abroad.

Part Two: Background of Outlook

Before examining ramifications of this party line in practice there are certain aspects of it to which I wish to draw attention.

First, it does not represent natural outlook of Russian people. Latter are, by and large, friendly to outside world, eager for experience of it, eager to measure against it talents they are conscious of possessing, eager above all to live in peace and enjoy fruits of their own labor. Party line only represents thesis which official propaganda machine puts forward with great skill and persistence to a public often remarkably resistant in the stronghold of its innermost thoughts. But party line is binding for outlook and conduct of people who make up apparatus of power—party, secret police and government—and it is exclusively with these that we have to deal.

Second, please note that premises on which this party line is based are for most part simply not true. Experience has shown that peaceful and mutually profitable coexistence of capitalist and socialist states is entirely possible. Basic internal conflicts in advanced countries are no longer primarily those arising out of capitalist ownership of means of production, but are ones arising from advanced urbanism and industrialism as such, which Russia has thus far been spared not by socialism but only by her own backwardness. Internal rivalries of capitalism do not always generate wars; and not all wars are attributable to this cause. To speak of possibility of intervention against USSR today, after elimination of Germany and Japan and after example of recent war, is sheerest nonsense. If not provoked by forces of intolerance and subversion "capitalist" world of today is quite capable of living at peace with itself and with Russia. Finally, no sane person has reason to doubt sincerity of moderate socialist leaders in western countries. Nor is it fair to deny success of their efforts to improve conditions for working population whenever, as in Scandinavia, they have been given chance to show what they could do.

Falseness of these premises, every one of which pre-dates recent war, was amply demonstrated by that conflict itself. Anglo-American differences did not turn out to be major differences of western world. Capitalist countries, other than those of Axis, showed no disposition to solve their differences by joining in crusade against USSR. Instead of imperialist war turning into civil wars and revolution, USSR found itself obliged to fight side by side with capitalist powers for an avowed community of aims.

Nevertheless, all these theses, however baseless and disproven, are being boldly put forward again today. What does this indicate? It indicates that Soviet party line is not based on any objective analysis of situation beyond Russia's borders; that it has, indeed, little to do with conditions outside of Russia; that it arises mainly from basic inner-Russian necessities which existed before recent war and exist today.

At bottom of Kremlin's neurotic view of world affairs is traditional and instinctive Russian sense of insecurity. Originally, this was insecurity of a peaceful agricultural people trying to live on vast exposed plain in neighborhood of fierce nomadic peoples. To this was added, as Russia came into contact with economically advanced west, fear of more competent, more powerful, more highly organized societies in that area. But this latter type of insecurity was one which afflicted rather Russian rulers than Russian people; for Russian rulers have invariably sensed that their rule was relatively archaic in form, fragile and artificial in its psychological foundation, unable to stand comparison or contact with political systems of western countries. For this reason they have always feared foreign penetration, feared direct contact between western world and their own, feared what would happen if Russians learned truth about world without or if foreigners learned truth about world within. And they have learned to seek security only in patient but deadly struggle for total destruction of rival power, never in compacts and compromises with it.

It was no coincidence that Marxism, which had smouldered ineffectively for half a century in Western Europe, caught hold and blazed for first time in Russia. Only in this land which had never known a friendly neighbor or indeed any tolerant equilibrium of separate powers, either internal or international, could a doctrine thrive which viewed economic conflicts of society as insoluble by peaceful means. After establishment of Bolshevist regime, Marxist dogma, rendered even more truculent and intolerant by Lenin's interpretation, became a perfect vehicle for sense of insecurity with which Bolsheviks, even more than previous Russian rulers, were afflicted. In this dogma, with its basic altruism of purpose, they found justification for their instinctive fear of outside world, for the dictatorship without which they did not know how to rule, for cruelties they did not dare not to inflict, for sacrifices they felt bound to demand. In the name of Marxism they sacrificed every single ethical value in their methods and tactics.

Today they cannot dispense with it. It is fig leaf of their moral and intellectual respectability. Without it they would stand before history, at best, as only the last of that long succession of cruel and wasteful Russian rulers who have relentlessly forced country on to ever new heights of military power in order to guarantee external security of their internally weak regimes. This is why Soviet purposes must always be solemnly clothed in trappings of Marxism, and why no one should underrate importance of dogma in Soviet affairs. Thus Soviet leaders are driven necessities of their own past and present position to put forward a dogma which (*) outside world as evil, hostile and menacing, but as bearing within itself germs of creeping disease and destined to be wracked with growing internal convulsions until it is given final coup de grace by rising power of socialism and yields to new and better world. This thesis provides justification for that increase of military and police power of Russian state, for that isolation of Russian population from outside world, and for that fluid and constant pressure to extend limits of Russian police power which are together the natural and instinctive urges of Russian rulers. Basically this is only the steady advance of uneasy Russian nationalism, a centuries old movement in which conceptions of offense and defense are inextricably confused. But in new guise of international Marxism, with its honeyed promises to a desperate and war torn outside world, it is more dangerous and insidious than ever before.

It should not be thought from above that Soviet party line is necessarily disingenuous and insincere on part of all those who put it forward many of them are too ignorant of outside world and mentally too dependent to question (*) self-hypnotism, and who have no difficulty making themselves believe what they find it comforting and convenient to believe. Finally we have the unsolved mystery as to who, if anyone, in this great land actually receives accurate and unbiased information about outside world. In atmosphere of oriental secretiveness and conspiracy which pervade this government, possibilities for distorting or poisoning sources and currents of information are infinite. The very disrespect of Russians for objective truth—indeed, their disbelief in its existence—leads them to view all stated facts as instruments for furtherance of one ulterior purpose or another. There is good reason to suspect that this government is actually a conspiracy within a conspiracy; and I for one am reluctant to believe that Stalin himself receives anything like an objective picture of outside world. Here there is ample scope for the type of subtle intrigue at which Russians are past masters. Inability of foreign governments to place their case squarely before Russian policy makers—extent to which they are delivered up in their relations with Russia to good graces of obscure and unknown advisers whom they never see and cannot influence—this to my mind is most disquieting feature of diplomacy in Moscow, and one which western statesmen would do well to keep in mind if they would understand nature of difficulties encountered here.

Part Three: Projection of Soviet Outlook in Practical Policy on Official Level
We have now seen nature and background of Soviet program. What may we expect by way of its practical implementation?

Soviet policy, as Department implies in its query under reference, is conducted on two planes: (one) official plane represented by actions undertaken officially in name of Soviet Government; and (two) subterranean plane of actions undertaken by agencies for which Soviet Government does not admit responsibility.

Policy promulgated on both planes will be calculated to serve basic policies (A) to (D) outlined in part one. Actions taken on different planes will differ considerably, but will dovetail into each other in purpose, timing and effect.

On official plane we must look for following:

(A) Internal policy devoted to increasing in every way strength and prestige of Soviet state: intensive military-industrialization; maximum development of armed forces; great displays to impress outsiders; continued secretiveness about internal matters, designed to conceal weaknesses and to keep opponents in dark.

(B) Wherever it is considered timely and promising, efforts will be made to advance official limits of Soviet power. For the moment, these efforts are restricted to certain neighboring points conceived of here as being of immediate strategic necessity, such as Northern Iran, Turkey, possibly Bornholm. However, other points may at any time come into question, if and as concealed Soviet political power is extended to new areas. Thus a "friendly" Persian Government might be asked to grant Russia a port on Persian Gulf. Should Spain fall under communist control, question of Soviet base at Gibraltar Strait might be activated. But such claims will appear on official level only when unofficial preparation is complete.

(C) Russians will participate officially in international organizations where they see opportunity of extending Soviet power or of inhibiting or diluting power of others. Moscow sees in UNO not the mechanism for a permanent and stable world society founded on mutual interest and aims of all nations, but an arena in which aims just mentioned can be favorably pursued. As long as UNO is considered here to serve this purpose, Soviets will remain with it. But if at any time they come to conclusion that it is serving to embarass or frustrate their aims for power expansion and if they see better prospects for pursuit of these aims along other lines, they will not hesitate to abandon UNO. This would imply, however, that they felt themselves strong enough to split unity of other nations by their withdrawal, to render UNO ineffective as a threat to their aims or security, and to replace it with an international weapon more effective from their viewpoint. Thus Soviet attitude toward UNO will depend largely on loyalty of other nations to it, and on degree of vigor, decisiveness and cohesion with which these nations defend in UNO the peaceful and hopeful concept of international life, which that organization represents to our way of thinking. I reiterate, Moscow has no abstract devotion to UNO ideals. Its attitude to that organization will remain essentially pragmatic and tactical.

(D) Toward colonial areas and backward or dependent peoples, Soviet policy, even on official plane, will be directed toward weakening of power and influence and contacts of advanced western nations, on theory that in so far as this policy is successful, there will be created a vacuum which will favor communist-Soviet penetration. Soviet pressure for participation in trusteeship arrangements thus represents, in my opinion, a desire to be in a position to complicate and inhibit exertion of western influence at such points rather than to provide major channel for exerting of Soviet power. Latter motive is not lacking, but for this Soviets prefer to rely on other channels than official trusteeship arrangements. Thus we may expect to find Soviets asking for admission everywhere to trusteeship or similar arrangements and using levers thus acquired to weaken western influence among such peoples.

(E) Russians will strive energetically to develop Soviet representation in, and official ties with, countries in which they sense strong possibilities of opposition to western centers of power. This applies to such widely separated points as Germany, Argentina, Middle Eastern countries, etc.

(F) In international economic matters, Soviet policy will really be dominated by pursuit of autarchy for Soviet Union and Soviet-dominated adjacent areas taken together. That, however, will be underlying policy. As far as official line is concerned, position is not yet clear. Soviet Government has shown strange reticence since termination hostilities on subject foreign trade. If large scale long term credits should be forthcoming, I believe Soviet Government may eventually again do lip service, as it did in nineteen-thirties to desirability of building up international economic exchanges in general. Otherwise I think it possible Soviet foreign trade may be restricted largely to Soviets own security sphere, including occupied areas in Germany, and that a cold official shoulder may be turned to principle of general economic collaboration among nations.

(G) With respect to cultural collaboration, lip service will likewise be rendered to desirability of deepening cultural contacts between peoples, but this will not in practice be interpreted in any way which could weaken security position of Soviet peoples. Actual manifestations of Soviet policy in this respect will be restricted to arid channels of closely shepherded official visits and functions, with super-abundance of vodka and speeches and dearth of permanent effects.

(H) Beyond this, Soviet official relations will take what might be called "correct" course with individual foreign governments, with great stress being laid on prestige of Soviet Union and its representatives and with punctilious attention to protocol, as distinct from good manners.

Part Four: . . . What We May Expect by Way of Implementation of Basic Soviet Policies on Unofficial . . . Plane, . . . for Which Soviet Government Accepts No Responsibility

Agencies utilized for promulgation of policies on this plane are following:

One. Inner central core of communist parties in other countries. While many of persons who compose this category may also appear and act in unrelated public capacities, they are in reality working closely together as an underground operating directorate of world communism, a concealed Comintern tightly coordinated and directed by Moscow. It is important to remember that this inner core is actually working on underground lines, despite legality of parties with which it is associated.

Two.   Rank and file of communist parties. Note distinction is drawn between these and persons defined in paragraph one. This distinction has become much sharper in recent years. Whereas formerly foreign communist parties represented a curious (and from Moscow's standpoint often inconvenient) mixture of conspiracy and legitimate activity, now the conspiratorial element has been neatly concentrated in inner circle and ordered underground, while rank and file—no longer even taken into confidence about realities of movement—are thrust forward as bona fide internal partisans of certain political tendencies within their respective countries, genuinely innocent of conspiratorial connection with foreign states. Only in certain countries where communists are numerically strong do they now regularly appear and act as a body. As a rule they are used to penetrate, and to influence or dominate, as case may be, other organizations less likely to be suspected of being tools of Soviet Government, with a view to accomplishing their purposes through (*) organizations, rather than by direct action as a separate political party.

Three.   A wide variety of national associations or bodies which can be dominated or influenced by such penetration. These include: labor unions, youth leagues, womens organizations, racial societies, religious societies, social organizations, cultural groups, liberal magazines, publishing houses, etc.

Four.   International organizations which can be similarly penetrated through influence over various national components. Labor, youth and womens organizations are prominent among them. Particular, almost vital, importance is attached in this connection to international labor movement. In this, Moscow sees possibility of sidetracking western governments in world affairs and building up international lobby capable of compelling governments to take actions favorable to Soviet interests in various countries and of paralyzing actions disagreeable to USSR.

Five.   Russian Orthodox Church, with its foreign branches, and through it the Eastern Orthodox Church in general.

Six.   Pan-Slav movement and other movements (Azerbaijan, Armenian, Turcoman, etc.) based on racial groups within Soviet Union.

Seven.   Governments or governing groups willing to lend themselves to Soviet purposes in one degree or another, such as present Bulgarian and Yugoslav governments, North Persian regime, Chinese Communists, etc. Not only propaganda machines but actual policies of these regimes can be placed extensively at disposal of USSR.

It may be expected that component parts of this far-flung apparatus will be utilized, in accordance with their individual suitability, as follows:

(A) To undermine general political and strategic potential of major western powers. Efforts will be made in such countries to disrupt national self confidence, to hamstring measures of national defense, to increase social and industrial unrest, to stimulate all forms of disunity. All persons with grievances, whether economic or racial, will be urged to seek redress not in mediation and compromise, but in defiant violent struggle for destruction of other elements of society. Here poor will be set against rich, black against white, young against old, newcomers against established residents, etc.

(B) On unofficial plane particularly violent efforts will be made to weaken power and influence of western powers of colonial, backward, or dependent peoples. On this level, no holds will be barred. Mistakes and weaknesses of western colonial administration will be mercilessly exposed and exploited. Liberal opinion in western countries will be mobilized to weaken colonial policies. Resentment among dependent peoples will be stimulated. And while latter are being encouraged to seek independence of western powers, Soviet dominated puppet political machines will be undergoing preparation to take over domestic power in respective colonial areas when independence is achieved.

(C) Where individual governments stand in path of Soviet purposes pressure will be brought for their removal from office. This can happen where governments directly oppose Soviet foreign policy aims (Turkey, Iran), where they seal their territories off against Communist penetration (Switzerland, Portugal), or where they compete too strongly, like Labor Government in England, for moral domination among elements which it is important for Communists to dominate. Sométimes, two of these elements are present in a single case. Then Communist opposition becomes particularly shrill and savage.

(D) In foreign countries Communists will, as a rule, work toward destruction of all forms of personal independence, economic, political or moral. Their system can handle only individuals who have been brought into complete dependence on higher power. Thus, persons who are financially independent—such as individual businessmen, estate owners, successful farmers, artisans and all those who exercise local leadership or have local prestige, such as popular local clergymen or political figures, are anathema. It is not by chance that even in USSR local officials are kept constantly on move from one job to another. . . .

(E) Everything possible will be done to set major western powers against each other. Anti-British talk will be plugged among Americans, anti-American talk among British. Continentals, including Germans, will be taught to abhor both Anglo-Saxon powers. Where suspicions exist, they will be fanned; where not, ignited. No effort will be spared to discredit and combat all efforts which threaten to lead to any sort of unity or cohesion among other (*) from which Russia might be excluded. Thus, all forms of international organization not amenable to communist penetration and control, whether it be the Catholic (*) international economic concerns, or the international fraternity of royalty and aristocracy, must expect to find themselves under fire from many, and often (*)

(F) In general, all Soviet efforts on unofficial international plane will be negative and destructive in character, designed to tear down sources of strength beyond reach of Soviet control. This is only in line with basic Soviet instinct that there can be no compromise with rival power and that constructive work can start only when communist power is dominant. But behind all this will be applied insistent, unceasing pressure for penetration and command of key positions in administration and especially in police apparatus of foreign countries. The Soviet regime is a police regime par excellence, reared in the dim half world of Tsarist police intrigue, accustomed to think primarily in terms of police power. This should never be lost sight of in gauging Soviet motives.

Part Five: [Practical Deductions from Standpoint of US Policy]

In summary, we have here a political force committed fanatically to the belief that with US there can be no permanent modus vivendi, that it is desirable and necessary that the internal harmony of our society be disrupted, our traditional way of life be destroyed, the international authority of our state be broken, if Soviet power is to be secure. This political force has complete power of disposition over energies of one of world's greatest peoples and resources of world's richest national territory, and is borne along by deep and powerful currents of Russian nationalism. In addition, it has an elaborate and far flung apparatus for exertion of its influence in other countries, an apparatus of amazing flexibility and versatility, managed by people whose experience and skill in underground methods are presumably without parallel in history. Finally, it is seemingly inaccessible to considerations of reality in its basic reactions. For it, the vast fund of objective fact about human society is not, as with us, the measure against which outlook is constantly being tested and re-formed, but a grab bag from which individual items are selected arbitrarily and tendenciously to bolster an outlook already preconceived. This is admittedly not a pleasant picture. Problem of how to cope with this force is undoubtedly greatest task our diplomacy has ever faced and probably greatest it will ever have to face. It should be point of departure from which our political general staff work at present juncture should proceed. It should be approached with same thoroughness and care as solution of major strategic problem in war, and if necessary, with no smaller outlay in planning effort. I cannot attempt to suggest all answers here. But I would like to record my conviction that problem is within our power to solve—and that without recourse to any general military conflict. And in support of this conviction there are certain observations of a more encouraging nature I should like to make:

(One) Soviet power, unlike that of Hitlerite Germany, is neither schematic nor adventuristic. It does not work by fixed plans. It does not take unnecessary risks. Impervious to logic of reason, and it is highly sensitive to logic of force. For this reason it can easily withdraw—and usually does—when strong resistance is encountered at any point. Thus, if the adversary has sufficient force and makes clear his readiness to use it, he rarely has to do so. If situations are properly handled there need be no prestige engaging showdowns.

(Two) Gauged against western world as a whole, Soviets are still by far the weaker force. Thus, their success will really depend on degree of cohesion, firmness and vigor which western world can muster. And this is factor which it is within our power to influence.

(Three) Success of Soviet system, as form of internal power, is not yet finally proven. It has yet to be demonstrated that it can survive supreme text of successive transfer of power from one individual or group to another. Lenin's death was first such transfer, and its effects wracked Soviet state for 15 years after Stalin's death or retirement will be second. But even this will not be final test. Soviet internal system will now be subjected, by virtue of recent territorial expansions, to series of additional strains which once proved severe tax on Tsardom. We here are convinced that never since termination of civil war have mass of Russian people been emotionally farther removed from doctrines of communist party than they are today. In Russia, party has now become a great and—for the moment—highly successful apparatus of dictatorial administration, but it has ceased to be a source of emotional inspiration. Thus, internal soundness and permanence of movement need not yet be regarded as assured.

(Four) All Soviet propaganda beyond Soviet security sphere is basically negative and destructive. It should therefore be relatively easy to combat it by any intelligent and really constructive program.

For these reasons I think we may approach calmly and with good heart problem of how to deal with Russia. As to how this approach should be made, I only wish to advance, by way of conclusion, following comments:

(One) Our first step must be to apprehend, and recognize for what it is, the nature of the movement with which we are dealing. We must study it with same courage, detachment, objectivity, and same determination not to be emotionally provoked or unseated by it, with which doctor studies unruly and unreasonable individual.

(Two) We must see that our public is educated to realities of Russian situation. I cannot over-emphasize importance of this. Press cannot do this alone. It must be done mainly by government, which is necessarily more experienced and better informed on practical problems involved. In this we need not be deterred by *ugliness* of picture. I am convinced that there would be far less hysterical anti-Sovietism in our country today if realities of this situation were better understood by our people. There is nothing as dangerous or as terrifying as the unknown. It may also be argued that to reveal more information on our difficulties with Russia would reflect unfavorably on Russian American relations. I feel that if there is any real risk here involved, it is one which we should have courage to face, and sooner the better. But I cannot see what we would be risking. Our stake in this country, even coming on heels of tremendous demonstrations of our friendship for Russian people, is remarkably small. We have here no investments to guard, no actual trade to lose, virtually no citizens to protect, few cultural contacts to preserve. Our only stake lies in what we hope rather than what we have; and I am convinced we have better chance of realizing those hopes if our public is enlightened and if our dealings with Russians are placed entirely on realistic and matter of fact basis.

(Three) Much depends on health and vigor of our own society. World communism is like malignant parasite which feeds only on diseased tissue. This is point at which domestic and foreign policies meet. Every courageous and incisive measure to solve internal problems of our own society, to improve self confidence, discipline, morale and community spirit of our own people, is a diplomatic victory over Moscow worth a thousand diplomatic notes and joint communiqués. If we cannot abandon fatalism and indifference in face of deficiencies of our own society, Moscow will profit—Moscow cannot help profiting by them in its foreign policies.

(Four) We must formulate and put forward for other nations a much more positive and constructive picture of sort of world we would like to see than we have put forward in past. It is not enough to urge people to develop political processes similar to our own. Many foreign peoples, in Europe at least, are tired and frightened by experiences of past, and are less interested in abstract freedom than in security. They are seeking guidance rather than responsibilities. We should be better able than Russians to give them this. And unless we do, Russians certainly will.

(Five)   Finally we must have courage and self confidence to cling to our own methods and conceptions of human society. After all, the greatest danger that can befall us in coping with this problem of Soviet Communism, is that we shall allow ourselves to become like those with whom we are coping.

KENNAN

Essays

8 Psychological Effects of the Atomic Bomb in Hiroshima: The Theme of Death

Robert Jay Lifton

Of all the changes and problems begotten by the Second World War, none has received more attention than the effects of the atomic bomb. The postwar period is, after all, thought of primarily as the "atomic era." Interest in the atomic bomb has focused on the physical, political, and diplomatic questions. Robert Jay Lifton has observed that "little attention has been paid to psychological and social elements, though these might well be said to be at present the most vivid legacies of the first atomic bomb." Lifton's brilliant study goes far toward correcting this deficiency and is, on most counts, a stimulating and thoughtful effort.

Hiroshima commands our attention now, eighteen years after its exposure to the atomic bomb, perhaps even more insistently than when the event actually occurred. We are compelled by the universal threat of nuclear weapons to study the impact of such weapons upon their first human victims, ever mindful of the relevance of this question to our own future and to all of human survival.

Much research has already been done concerning the physical consequences of the Hiroshima and Nagasaki disasters, particularly in relation to their unique feature of delayed radiation effects. But little attention has been paid to psychological and social elements, though these might well be said to be at present the most vivid legacies of the first atomic bomb.

My own interest in these problems developed during two years of research, conducted in Tokyo and Kyoto from 1960-1962, on the relationship of the individual character and historical change in Japanese youth. I was struck by the significance which the encounter with nuclear weapons had for the Japanese as a

"The Psychological Effects of the Atomic Bomb in Hiroshima: The Theme of Death" by Robert Jay Lifton. From **Daedalus: Themes in Transition** (Summer 1963), pp. 263–311. Reprinted by permission of **Daedalus,** Journal of the American Academy of Arts and Sciences, Boston, Massachusetts.

whole, even for young Japanese who could hardly remember the event. Also involved in my undertaking a study in Hiroshima was concern with the psychological aspects of war and peace, as well as previous interest in the behavior of individuals and groups under extreme conditions.

I began the work in April of 1962, first through two brief visits to Hiroshima, followed by four and a half months of residence there. My approach was primarily that of individual interviews with two groups of atomic bomb survivors: thirty-three chosen at random from the more than ninety-thousand survivors (or *hibakusha*), listed at the Hiroshima University Research Institute for Nuclear Medicine and Biology; and an additional group of forty-two survivors specially selected because of their prominence in dealing with A-bomb problems or their capacity to articulate their experiences. Included among the latter were physicians, university professors, city officials, politicians, writers and poets, and leaders of survivor organizations and peace movements.

Hibakusha (pronounced hi-bak'-sha) is a coined word which is by no means an exact equivalent of "survivor" (or "survivors"), but means, literally, "explosion-affected person" (or persons), and conveys in feeling a little more than merely having encountered the bomb, and a little less than having experienced definite physical injury from it. According to official definition, the category of *hibakusha* includes four groups of people considered to have had possible exposure to significant amounts of radiation: those who at the time of the bomb were within the city limits then defined for Hiroshima, an area extending from the bomb's hypocenter to a distance of 4000, and in some places up to 5000, meters; those who were not in the city at the time, but within fourteen days entered a designated area extending to about 2000 meters from the hypocenter; those who were engaged in some form of aid to, or disposal of, bomb victims at various stations which were set up; and those who were *in utero* and whose mothers fit into any of the first three groups. In addition to these interviews with *hibakusha*, I sought out all those in Hiroshima (mostly Japanese, but also Americans and Europeans) who could tell me anything about the complex array of group emotions and social problems which had arisen in the city over the seventeen years that had elapsed since the disaster.

I was aware of the delicacy of my situation as an American psychiatrist conducting this study, and I relied heavily upon the continuous support and assistance of Japanese groups within the Hiroshima community, so that all meetings and interviews were arranged through their introductions. In the case of the randomly selected group, my first contact with each survivor was made through a personal visit to the home, in the company of a Japanese social worker from Hiroshima University. My previous experience in Japan—including the ability to speak a certain amount of Japanese—was helpful in eliciting the many forms of cooperation so crucial for the work. Perhaps of greatest importance was my conveying to both colleagues and research subjects a sense of my personal motivation in undertaking the work, the hope that a systematic study of this kind might clarify important problems often spoken about loosely, and thereby in a small way contribute to the mastery of nuclear weapons and the avoidance of their use.

Interviews generally lasted about two hours; I tried to see each research subject twice, though I saw some three or four times, and others just once. I tape-recorded all sessions with subjects of the randomly selected group, and did so with many of those in the special group as well, always with the subject's consent. Interviews were conducted in Japanese, and a research assistant was always present to interpret. After making an initial appraisal of the problems involved, I decided to focus my questions upon three general dimensions of the problem: first, the recollection of the experience itself and its inner meaning seventeen years later; second, residual concerns and fears, especially those related to delayed radiation effects; and third, the survivor's sense of self and society, or of special group identity. Subjects were encouraged to associate freely to these topics and to any feelings or ideas stimulated by them. And in gathering these data, I sought always to evaluate to what degree exposure to the atomic bomb in Hiroshima resembles psychological and social patterns common to all disasters, as described in the general literature on disaster, and in what ways it might be a unique experience. What follows is a composite description of some of the basic trends I have observed.

The Experience Recalled

The degree to which one anticipates a disaster has important bearing upon the way in which one responds, and the predominant tone in the descriptions I heard was that of extreme surprise and unpreparedness. Since it was wartime, people did of course expect conventional bombing; there had been regularly occurring air-raid warnings because of planes passing over Hiroshima, though only an occasional stray bomb had actually been dropped on the city. American planes did drop leaflets warning Hiroshima inhabitants that their city was going to be demolished and urging them to evacuate from it. But very few people appear to have seen these leaflets, and those who did tended to ignore them as enemy propaganda. Nor did these leaflets make any mention of an atomic bomb or any other special weapon. Many wondered at Hiroshima's relatively untouched state, despite its obviously strategic significance as a major staging area for Japan's military operations in China and Southeast Asia. There was general apprehension, the feeling that there was something dangerous about Hiroshima's strangely intact condition, that the Americans must be preparing something extraordinarily big for the city (though this latter thought could have been partly a retrospective construction). At 8:15 A.M. on August 6, 1945, the moment the bomb fell, most people were in a particularly relaxed state, since, following a brief air-raid warning, the all-clear had just been sounded. People were unprepared, then, because of a false sense of immediate security; because of the psychological sense of invulnerability all people tend to possess, even in the face of danger; and because of the total inability of anyone to anticipate a weapon of such unprecedented dimensions.

It was only those at some distance from the bomb's hypocenter who could clearly distinguish the sequence of the great flash of light in the sky accompanied by the lacerating heat of the fireball, then the sound and force of the blast, and the impressive multicolored "mushroom cloud" rising above the city. Two thousand meters is generally considered to be a critical radius for high mortality (from heat, blast, and radiation), for susceptibility to delayed radiation effects, and for near-total destruction of buildings and other structures. But many were killed outside of this radius, and indeed the number of deaths from the bomb—variously estimated from 63,000 to 240,000 or more—is still unknown. Falling in the center of a flat city made up largely of wooden residential and commercial structures, the bomb is reported to have destroyed or so badly damaged, through blast and fire, more than two-thirds of all buildings within 500 meters—an area roughly encompassing the city limits—that all of Hiroshima became immediately involved in the atomic disaster. Those within the 2000-meter radius could not clearly recall their initial perceptions; many simply remember what they thought to be a flash—or else a sudden sensation of heat—followed by an indeterminate period of unconsciousness; others recall only being thrown across a room or knocked down, then finding themselves pinned under debris of buildings.

The most striking psychological feature of this immediate experience was the sense of a sudden and absolute shift from normal existence to an overwhelming encounter with death. This is described by a young shopkeeper's assistant, who was thirteen years old at the time the bomb fell, and 1400 meters from the hypocenter:

> I was a little ill . . . so I stayed at home that day. . . . There had been an air-raid warning and then an all-clear. I felt relieved and lay down on the bed with my younger brother. . . . Then it happened. It came very suddenly. . . . It felt something like an electric short—a bluish sparkling light. . . . There was a noise, and I felt great heat—even inside of the house. When I came to, I was underneath the destroyed house. . . . I didn't know anything about the atomic bomb so I thought that some bomb had fallen directly upon me . . . and then when I felt that our house had been directly hit, I became furious. . . . There were roof tiles and walls—everything black—entirely covering me. So I screamed for help. . . . And from all around I heard moans and screaming, and then I felt a kind of danger to myself. . . . I thought that I too was going to die in that way. I felt this way at that moment because I was absolutely unable to do anything at all by my own power. . . . I didn't know where I was or what I was under. . . . I couldn't hear voices of my family. I didn't know how I could be rescued. I felt I was going to suffocate and then die, without knowing exactly what had happened to me. This was the kind of expectation I had. . . .

I stress this sudden encounter with death because I believe that it initiates, from this first moment of contact with the atomic bomb, an emotional theme within the victim which remains with him indefinitely: the sense of a more or less permanent encounter with death.

This early impact enveloped the city in an aura of weirdness and unreality,

as recalled by an elderly electrician, who at the time of the bomb was in his mid-forties, working at a railroad junction 5000 meters from the hypocenter.

> I was setting up a pole . . . near a switch in the railroad tracks. . . . I heard a tremendous noise. There was a flash. . . a kind of flash I had never seen before which I can't describe. . . . My face felt hot and I put my hands over my eyes and rushed under a locomotive that was nearby. I crawled in between the wheels and then there was an enormous boom and the locomotive shook. I was frightened, so I crawled out. . . . I couldn't tell what happened. . . . For about five minutes I saw nobody, and then I saw someone coming out from an air-raid shelter who told me that the youngest one of our workers had been injured by falling piles . . . so I put the injured man on the back of my bicycle and tried to take him to the dispensary. Then I saw that almost all of the people in that area were crowded into the dispensary, and since there was also a hospital nearby, I went there. But that too was already full. . . . So the only thing to do was to go into [the center of] Hiroshima. But I couldn't move my bicycle because of all the people coming out from Hiroshima and blocking the way. . . . I saw that they were all naked and I wondered what was the matter with them. . . . When we spoke to people, they said that they had been hit by something they didn't understand. . . . We were desperately looking for a doctor or a hospital but we couldn't seem to have any success. . . . We walked toward Hiroshima, still carrying our tools. . . . Then in Hiroshima there was no place either—it had become an empty field—so I carried him to a place near our company office where injured people were lying inside, asking for water. But there was no water and there was no way to help them and I myself didn't know what kind of treatment I should give to this man or to the others. I had to let them die right before my eyes. . . . By then we were cut off from escape, because the fire was beginning to spread out and we couldn't move—we were together with the dead people in the building—only we were not really inside of the building because the building itself had been destroyed, so that we were really outdoors, and we spent the night there. . . .

This rote and essentially ineffectual behavior was characteristic of many during the first few hours, in those situations where any attempt at all could be made to maintain a group cooperative effort; people were generally more effective in helping members of their immediate families, or in saving themselves. This same electrician, an unusually conscientious man, kept at his post at the railroad over a period of several weeks, leaving only for brief periods to take care of his family. Again his description of the scene of death and near-death takes on a dreamlike quality:

> There were dead bodies everywhere. . . . There was practically no room for me to put my feet on the floor. . . . At that time I couldn't figure out the reason why all these people were suffering, or what illness it was that had struck them down. . . . I was the only person taking care of the place as all of

the rest of the people had gone. . . . Other people came in looking for food or to use the toilet. . . . There was no one to sell tickets in the station, nothing . . . and since trains weren't running I didn't have much work to do. . . . There was no light at all and we were just like sleepwalkers. . . .

And a middle-age teacher, who was also on the outskirts of the city about 5000 meters from the hypocenter, describes his awe at the destruction he witnessed:

I climbed Hijiyama Mountain and looked down. I saw that Hiroshima had disappeared. . . . I was shocked by the sight. . . . What I felt then and still feel now I just can't explain with words. Of course I saw many dreadful scenes after that—but that experience, looking down and finding nothing left of Hiroshima—was so shocking that I simply can't express what I felt. I could see Koi [a suburb at the opposite end of the city] and a few buildings standing. . . . But Hiroshima didn't exist—that was mainly what I saw—Hiroshima just didn't exist.

And a young university professor 2500 meters from the hypocenter at the time, sums up these feelings of weird, awesome unreality in a frequently-expressed image of hell:

Everything I saw made a deep impression—a park nearby covered with dead bodies waiting to be cremated . . . very badly injured people evacuated in my direction. . . . The most impressive thing I saw was some girls, very young girls, not only with their clothes torn off but with their skin peeled off as well. . . . My immediate thought was that this was like the hell I had always read about. . . . I had never seen anything which resembled it before, but I thought that should there be a hell, this was it—the Buddhist hell, where, we were taught, people who could not attain salvation always went. . . . And I imagined that all of these people I was seeing were in the hell I had read about.

But human beings are unable to remain open to emotional experience of this intensity for any length of time, and very quickly—sometimes within minutes—there began to occur what we may term psychic closing-off; that is, people simply ceased to feel.

For instance, a male social worker, then in his twenties and in military service in Hiroshima, was temporarily on leave at his home just outside of the city; he rushed back into the city soon after the bomb fell, in accordance with his military duty, only to find that his unit had been entirely wiped out. A certain amount of military order was quickly re-established, and a policy of immediate mass cremation of dead bodies was instituted in order to prevent widespread disease, and in accordance with Japanese custom. As a noncommissioned officer and one of the few able-bodied men left, he was put in

charge of this work of disposing of corpses, which he found he could accomplish with little difficulty:

> After a while they became just like objects or goods that we handled in a very businesslike way. . . . Of course I didn't regard them simply as pieces of wood—they were dead bodies—but if we had been sentimental, we couldn't have done the work. . . . We had no emotions. . . . Because of the succession of experiences I had been through I was temporarily without feeling. . . . At times I went about the work with great energy, realizing that no one but myself could do it.

He contrasted his own feelings with the terror experienced by an outsider just entering the disaster area:

> Everything at that time was part of an extraordinary situation. . . . For instance, I remember that on the ninth or tenth of August, it was an extremely dark night. . . . I saw blue phosphorescent flames rising from the dead bodies—and there were plenty of them. These were quite different from the orange flames coming from the burning buildings. . . . These blue phosphorescent flames are what we Japanese look upon as spirits rising from dead bodies—in former days we called them fireballs. —And yet at that time I had no sense of fear, not a bit, but merely thought, "those dead bodies are still burning." . . . But to people who had just come from the outside, those flames looked very strange. . . . One of those nights I met a soldier who had just returned to the city, and I walked along with him. . . . He noticed these unusual fireballs and asked me what they were. I told him that they were the flames coming from dead bodies. The soldier suddenly became extremely frightened, fell down on the ground, and was unable to move. . . . Yet I at that time had a state of mind in which I feared nothing. Though if I were to see those flames now I might be quite frightened. . . .

Relatively few people were involved in the disposal of dead bodies, but virtually all those I interviewed nonetheless experienced a similar form of psychic closing-off in response to what they saw and felt, and particularly in response to their over-all exposure to death. Thus, many told how horrified they were when they first encountered corpses in strange array, or extremely disfigured faces, but how, after a period of time as they saw more and more of these, they felt nothing. Psychic closing-off would last sometimes for a few hours, and sometimes for days or even months and merge into longer-term feelings of depression and despair.

But even the profound and unconscious defensive maneuvers involved in psychic closing-off were ultimately unable to afford full protection to the survivor from the painful sights and stimuli impinging upon him. It was, moreover, a defense not devoid of its own psychological cost. Thus, the same social worker, in a later interview, questioned his own use of the word "businesslike" to describe his attitude toward dead bodies, and emphasized the pity and sympathy he felt while handling the remains of men from his unit and the pains he took to console family members who came for these remains; he even recalled feeling frightened at night when passing the spot where he worked at cremation by day. He was in effect telling me not only that his psychic closing-off was imperfect, but that he was horrified—felt ashamed and guilty—at having behaved in a way which he now thought callous. For he had indulged in activities which were ordinarily, for him, strongly taboo, and had done so with an energy, perhaps even an enthusiasm, which must have mobilized within him primitive emotions of a frightening nature.

The middle-aged teacher who had expressed such awe at the disappearance of Hiroshima reveals the way in which feelings of shame and guilt, and especially shame and guilt toward the dead, interfere with psychic closing-off and painfully assert themselves.

I went to look for my family. Somehow I became a pitiless person, because if I had pity, I would not have been able to walk through the city, to walk over those dead bodies. The most impressive thing was the expression in people's eyes—bodies badly injured which had turned black—their eyes looking for someone to come and help them. They looked at me and knew that I was stronger than they. . . . I was looking for my family and looking carefully at everyone I met to see if he or she was a family member—but the eyes—the emptiness—the helpless expression—were something I will never forget. . . . I often had to go to the same place more than once. I would wish that the same family would not still be there. . . . I saw disappointment in their eyes. They looked at me with great expectation, staring right through me. It was very hard to be stared at by those eyes. . . .

He felt, in other words, accused by the eyes of the anonymous dead and dying, of wrongdoing and transgression (a sense of guilt) for not helping them, for letting them die, for "selfishly" remaining alive and strong; and "exposed" and "seen through" by the same eyes for these identical failings (a sense of shame).

There were also many episodes of more focused guilt toward specific family members whom one was unable to help, and for whose death one felt responsible. For instance, the shopkeeper's assistant mentioned earlier was finally rescued from the debris of his destroyed house by his mother, but she was too weakened by her own injuries to be able to walk very far with him. Soon they were surrounded by fire, and he (a boy of thirteen) did not feel he had the strength to sustain her weight, and became convinced that they would both die unless he took some other action. So he put her down and ran for help, but the neighbor he summoned could not get through to the woman because of the flames, and the boy learned shortly afterward that his mother died in precisely the place he had left her. His lasting sense of guilt was reflected in his frequent experience, from that time onward, of hearing his mother's voice ringing in his ears calling for help.

A middle-aged businessman related a similarly guilt-stimulating sequence. His work had taken him briefly to the south of Japan and he had returned to Hiroshima during the early morning hours of August 6. Having been up all night, he was not too responsive when his twelve-year-old son came into his room to ask his father to remove a nail from his shoe so that he could put it on and go off to school. The father, wishing to get the job quickly over, placed a piece of leather above the tip of the nail and promised he would take the whole nail out when the boy returned in the afternoon. As in the case of many youngsters who were sent to factories to do "voluntary labor" as a substitute for their schoolwork, the boy's body was never found—and the father, after a desperately fruitless search for his son throughout the city, was left with the lingering self-accusation that the nail he had failed to remove might have impeded the boy's escape from the fire.

Most survivors focus upon one incident, one sight, or one particular *ultimate horror* with which they strongly identify themselves, and which left them with a profound sense of pity, guilt, and shame. Thus, the social worker describes an event which he feels affected him even more than his crematory activities:

> On the evening of August 6th, the city was so hot from the fire that I could not easily enter it, but I finally managed to do so by taking a path along the river. As I walked along the bank near the present Yokogawa Bridge, I saw the bodies of a mother and her child. . . . That is, I thought I saw dead bodies, but the child was still alive—still breathing, though with difficulty. . . . I filled the cover of my lunch box with water and gave it to the child but it was so weak it could not drink. I knew that people were frequently passing that spot . . . and I hoped that one of these people would take the child, as I had to go back to my own unit. Of course I helped many people all through that day . . . but the image of this child stayed on my mind and remains as a strong impression even now. . . . Later when I was again in that same area I hoped that I might be able to find the child . . . and I looked for it among all the dead children collected at a place nearby. . . . Even before the war I had planned to go into social work, but this experience led me to go into my present work with children—as the memory of that mother and child by Yokogawa Bridge has never left me, especially since the child was still alive when I saw it.

These expressions of ultimate horror can be related to direct personal experience of loss (for instance, the businessman who had failed to remove the nail from his son's shoe remained preoccupied with pathetic children staring imploringly at him), as well as to enduring individual emotional themes. Most of them involved women and children, universal symbols of purity and vulnerability, particularly in Japanese culture. And, inevitably, the ultimate horror was directly related to death or dying.

Contamination and Disease

Survivors told me of three rumors which circulated widely in Hiroshima just after the bomb. The first was that for a period of seventy-five years Hiroshima would be uninhabitable—no one would be able to live there. This rumor was a direct expression of the *fear of deadly and protracted contamination from a mysterious poison believed to have been emitted by the frightening new weapon*. (As one survivor put it, "The ordinary people spoke of poison; the intellectuals spoke of radiation.")

Even more frequently expressed, and I believe with greater emotion, was a second rumor: trees and grass would never again grow in Hiroshima; from that day on the city would be unable to sustain vegetation of any kind. This seemed to suggest *an ultimate form of desolation even beyond that of human death*: nature was drying up altogether, the ultimate source of life was being extinguished—a form of symbolism particularly powerful in Japanese culture with its focus upon natural aesthetics and its view of nature as both enveloping and energizing all of human life.

The third rumor, less frequently mentioned to me but one which also had wide currency in various versions, was that all those who had been exposed to the bomb in Hiroshima would be dead within three years. This more naked death symbolism was directly related to the appearance of frightening symptoms of toxic radiation effects. For almost immediately after the bomb and during the following days and weeks, people began to experience, and notice in others, symptoms of a strange form of illness: nausea, vomiting, and loss of appetite; diarrhea with large amounts of blood in the stools; fever and weakness; purple spots on various parts of the body from bleeding into the skin (purpura); inflammation and ulceration of the mouth, throat, and gums (oropharyngeal lesions and gingivitis); bleeding from the mouth, gums, nose, throat, rectum, and urinary tract (hemorrhagic manifestations); loss of hair from the scalp and other parts of the body (depilation); extremely low white blood cell counts when these were taken (leucopenia); and in many cases a progressive course until death. These symptoms and fatalities aroused in the minds of the people of Hiroshima a special terror, *an image of a weapon which not only kills and destroys on a colossal scale but also leaves behind in the bodies of those exposed to it deadly influences which may emerge at any time and strike down their victims*. This image was made particularly vivid by the delayed appearance of these radiation effects, two to four weeks after the bomb fell, sometimes in people who had previously seemed to be in perfect health.

The shopkeeper's assistant, both of whose parents were killed by the bomb, describes his reactions to the death of two additional close family members from these toxic radiation effects:

My grandmother was taking care of my younger brother on the 14th of August when I left, and when I returned on the 15th, she had many spots all over her body. Two or three days later she died. . . . My younger brother, who . . . was just a [five-month-old] baby, was without breast milk—so we fed him thin rice gruel. . . . But on the 10th of October he suddenly began to look very ill, though I had not then noticed any spots on his body. . . . Then on the next day he began to look a little better, and I thought he was going to survive. I was very pleased, as he was the only family member I had left, and I took him to a doctor—but on the way to the doctor he died. And at that time we found that there were two large spots on his bottom. . . . I heard it said that all these people would die within three years . . . so I thought, "sooner or later I too will die." . . . I felt very weak and very lonely—with no hope at all . . . and since I had seen so many people's eyebrows falling out, their hair falling out, bleeding from their teeth—I found myself always nervously touching my hair like this [he demonstrated by rubbing his head] . . . . I never knew when some sign of the disease would show itself. . . . And living in the countryside then with my relatives, people who came to visit would tell us these things, and then the villagers also talked about them—telling stories of this man or that man who visited us a few days ago, returned to Hiroshima, and died within a week. . . . I couldn't tell whether these stories were true or not, but I believed them then. And I also heard that when the *hibakusha* came to evacuate to the village where I was, they died there one by one. . . . This loneliness, and the fear. . . . The physical fear . . . has been with me always. . . . It is not something temporary, as I still have it now. . . .

Here we find a link between this early sense of ubiquitous death from radiation effects, and later anxieties about death and illness.

In a similar tone, a middle-aged writer describes his daughter's sudden illness and death:

My daughter was working with her classmates at a place a thousand meters from the hypocenter. . . . I was able to meet her the next day at a friend's house. She had no burns and only minor external wounds, so I took her with me to my country house. She was quite all right for a while but on the 4th of September she suddenly became sick. . . . The symptoms of her disease were different from those of a normal disease. . . . She had spots all over her body. . . . Her hair began to fall out. She vomited small clumps of blood many times. Finally she began to bleed all over her mouth. And at times her fever was very high. I felt this was a very strange and horrible disease. . . . We didn't know what it was. I thought it was a kind of epidemic—something like cholera. So I told the rest of my family not to touch her and to disinfect all utensils and everything she used. . . . We were afraid of it and even the doctor didn't know what it was. . . . After ten days of agony and torture she died on September 14th. . . . I thought it was very cruel that my daughter, who had nothing to do with the war, had to be killed in this way. . . .

Survivors were thus affected not only by the fact of people dying around them but by the way in which they died: a gruesome form of rapid bodily deterioration which seemed unrelated to more usual and "decent" forms of death.

We have seen how these initial physical fears could readily turn into lifetime bodily concerns. And during the years that followed, these fears and concerns became greatly magnified by another development: the growing awareness among the people of Hiroshima that medical studies were demonstrating an abnormally high rate of leukemia among survivors of the atomic bomb. The increased incidence was first noted in 1948, and reached a peak between 1950 and 1952; it has been greatest in those exposed closest to the hypocenter, so that for those within 1000 meters the increase of leukemia has been between ten and fifty times the normal. Since 1952 the rate has diminished, but it is still higher than in nonexposed populations, and fears which have been aroused remain strong. While symptoms of leukemia are not exactly the same as those of acute radiation effects, the two conditions share enough in common—the dreaded "purple spots" and other forms of hemorrhage, laboratory findings of abnormalities of the blood, progressive weakness and fever and (inevitably in leukemia, and often enough in acute irradiation) ultimate death—that these tend to merge, psychologically speaking, into a diffuse fear of bodily annihilation and death.

Moreover, Hiroshima survivors are aware of the general concern and controversy about genetic effects of the atomic bomb, and most express fear about possible harmful effects upon subsequent generations—a very serious emotional concern anywhere, but particularly so in an East Asian culture which stresses family lineage and the continuity of generations as man's central purpose in life and (at least symbolically) his means of achieving immortality. The Hiroshima people know that radiation *can* produce congenital abnormalities (as has been widely demonstrated in laboratory animals); and abnormalities have frequently been reported among the offspring of survivors—sometimes in very lurid journalistic terms, sometimes in more restrained medical reports. Actually, systematic studies of the problem have so far revealed no higher incidence of abnormalities in survivors' offspring than in those of controlled populations, so that scientific findings regarding genetic effects have been essentially negative. However, there has been one uncomfortably positive genetic finding, that of disturbances in sex ratio of offspring: men exposed to a significant degree of radiation tend to have relatively fewer daughters, while exposed women tend to have fewer sons, because, it is believed, of sex-linked lethal mutations involving the X chromosome—a finding whose significance is difficult to evaluate. Moreover, there are Japanese physicians who believe that there has been an increase in various forms of internal (and therefore invisible) congenital abnormalities in children of survivors, despite the absence so far of convincing scientific evidence.

Another factor here is the definite damage from radiation experienced by children exposed *in utero*, including many stillbirths and abortions as well as a high incidence of microcephaly with and without mental retardation (occurring almost exclusively in pregnancies which had not advanced beyond four months). This is, of course, a direct effect of radiation upon sensitive, rapidly growing fetal tissues, and, scientifically speaking, has nothing to do with genetic problems. But ordinary people often fail to make this distinction; to them the birth of children with abnormally small heads and retarded minds was often looked upon as still another example of the bomb's awesome capacity to inflict a physical curse upon its victims and their offspring.

There are also other areas of concern regarding delayed radiation effects. There has been a definite increase in cataracts and related eye conditions, which was not stressed to me by survivors as so great a source of emotional concern as the other problems mentioned, but has been nonetheless far from negligible. There is accumulating evidence that the incidence of various forms of cancer has increased among survivors. There has also been evidence of impairment in the growth and development of children, though contested by some on the grounds of inadequately accounting for social and economic factors. And there is a large group of divergent conditions—including anemias and liver and blood diseases, endocrine and skin disorders, impairment of central nervous sytem (particularly midbrain) function, and premature aging—which have been attributed by various investigators to radiation effects, but have not shown increased incidence in large-scale studies involving control populations. Even more difficult to evaluate is a frequently reported borderline condition of general weakness and debilitation also believed—by a very large number of survivors and by some physicians as well—to be caused by delayed radiation effects.

These fears about general health and genetic effects have inevitably affected marriage arrangements (which are usually made in Japan by families with the help of a go-between), in which survivors are frequently thought to encounter discrimination, particularly when involved in arrangements with families outside of Hiroshima.

A company employee in his thirties, who was 2000 meters from the bomb's hypocenter when it fell, described to me virtually all of these bodily and genetic concerns in a voice that betrayed considerable anxiety:

> Even when I have an illness which is not at all serious—as for instance when I had very mild liver trouble—I have fears about its cause. Of course, if it is just an ordinary condition there is nothing to worry about, but if it has a direct connection to radioactivity, then I might not be able to expect to recover. At such times I feel myself very delicate. . . . This happened two or three years ago. I was working very hard and drinking a great deal of *sake* at night in connection with business appointments and I also had to make many strenuous trips. So my condition might have been partly related to my using up so much energy in all of these things. . . . The whole thing is not fully clear to me. . . . But the results of statistical study show that those who were exposed to the bomb are more likely to have illnesses—not only of the liver, but various kinds of new growth, such as cancer or blood diseases. My blood was examined several times but no special changes were

discovered. . . . When my marriage arrangements were made, we discussed all these things in a direct fashion. Everyone knows that there are some effects, but in my case it was the eleventh year after the bomb, and I discussed my physical condition during all of that time. From that, and also from the fact that I was exposed to the bomb while inside of a building and taken immediately to the suburbs, and then remained quite a while outside of the city—judging from all of these facts, it was concluded that there was very little to fear concerning my condition. . . . But in general, there is a great concern that people who were exposed to the bomb might become ill five or ten years later or at any time in the future. . . . Also, when my children were born, I found myself worrying about things that ordinary people don't worry about, such as the possibility that they might inherit some terrible disease from me. . . . I heard that the likelihood of our giving birth to deformed children is greater than in the case of ordinary people . . . and at that time my white blood cell count was rather low. . . . I felt fatigue in the summertime and had a blood count done three or four times. . . . I was afraid it could be related to the bomb, and was greatly worried. . . . Then, after the child was born, even though he wasn't a deformed child, I still worried that something might happen to him afterward. . . . With the second child too I was not entirely free of such worries. . . . I am still not sure what might happen and I worry that the effects of radioactivity might be lingering in some way. . . .

Here we see a young man carrying on effectively in his life, essentially healthy, with normal children, and yet continually plagued by underlying anxieties—about his general health, then about marriage arrangements, and then in relationship to the birth of each of his children. Each hurdle is passed, but there is little relief; like many survivors, he experiences an inner sense of being doomed for posterity.

And a young clerk, also exposed about 2000 meters from the hypocenter, but having the additional disadvantage of retaining a keloid scar resulting from facial burns, expresses similar emotions in still stronger fashion:

Frankly speaking even now I have fear. . . . Even today people die in the hospitals from A-bomb disease, and when I hear about this I worry that I too might sooner or later have the same thing happen to me. . . . I have a special feeling that I am different from ordinary people . . . that I have the marks of wounds—as if I were a cripple. . . . I imagine a person who has an arm or a leg missing might feel the same way. . . . It is not a matter of lacking something externally, but rather something like a handicap—something mental which does not show—the feeling that I am mentally different from ordinary people . . . so when I hear about people who die from A-bomb disease or who have operations because of this illness, then I feel that I am the same kind of person as they. . . .

The survivor's identification with the dead and the maimed initiates a vicious circle on the psychosomatic plane of existence: he is likely to associate the mildest everyday injury or sickness with possible radiation effects; and anything he relates to radiation effects becomes associated with death. The process is accentuated by the strong Japanese cultural focus upon bodily symptoms as expressions of anxiety and conflict. Thus the all-encompassing term "A-bomb sickness" or "A-bomb disease" (*genbakushō*) has evolved, referring on the one hand to such fatal conditions as the early acute radiation effects and later cases of leukemia; and on the other hand to the vague borderline area of fatigue, general weakness, sensitivity to hot weather, suspected anemia, susceptibility to colds or stomach trouble, and general nervousness—all of which are frequent complaints of survivors, and which many associate with radiation effects. Not only does the expression "A-bomb disease" have wide popular currency, but it has frequently been used by local physicians as a convenient category for a condition otherwise hard to classify, and at the same time as a means of making it possible for the patient to derive certain medical and economic benefits.

These benefits also loom large in the picture. Doctors and survivors—as well as politicians and city officials—are caught in a conflict between humanitarian provision for medical need, and the dangers (expressed to me particularly by Japanese physicians) of encouraging the development in survivors of hypochondriasis, general weakness, and dependency—or what is sometimes called "A-bomb neurosis." During the years immediately after the war, when medical care was most needed, very little adequate treatment was available, as the national medical law providing for survivors was not enacted until 1957. But since that time, a series of laws and amendments have been passed with increasingly comprehensive medical coverage, particularly for those in the "special survivors" group (those nearest the hypocenter at the time of the bomb and those who have shown evidence of medical conditions considered to be related to A-bomb effects). In the last few years the category of "special survivors" has been steadily enlarged: distance from the hypocenter, as a criterion for eligibility, has been extended from 2000 to 3000 meters; and qualifying illnesses—originally limited to such conditions as leukemia, ophthalmic diseases, and various blood and liver disorders, all of which were considered to be related to radiation effects—have been extended to include illnesses not considered to be necessarily directly caused by radiation but possibly aggravated by the over-all atomic bomb experience, such as cancer, heart disease, endocrine and kidney disorders, arteriosclerosis, hypertension, and others.

Maximum medical and economic benefits, however, can be obtained only by those "certified" (through a special medical procedure) to have illnesses specifically related to the atomic bomb; but some physicians believe that this "certification"—which can be sometimes given for such minor conditions as ordinary anemia (as well as for more serious illnesses)—tends to stamp one psychologically as a lifetime A-bomb patient. The rationale of these laws is to provide maximum help for survivors and to give them the benefit of the doubt about matters which are not entirely scientifically resolved. But there remains a great deal of controversy over them. In addition to those (not only among doctors, but also among city officials, ordinary people, and even survivors themselves) who feel that the laws foster an exaggerated preoccupation with atomic bomb effects, there are other survivors who criticize them as being still insufficiently comprehensive, as having overly complicated categories and sub-categories which in the end deny full care for certain conditions.

My own impression in studying this problem is that since "A-bomb disease" is at this historical juncture as much a spiritual as a physical condition (as our young clerk made so clear)—and one which touches at every point upon the problem of death—it is difficult for any law or medical program to provide a cure.

The general psychological atmosphere in Hiroshima—and particularly that generated by the effects of the mass media—also has great bearing upon these psychosomatic problems. As one would expect, the whole subject of the atomic bomb and its delayed radiation effects has been continuous front-page news—from 1945-1952 within the limits of the restrictions upon publicizing these matters imposed by the American Occupation, and without such restrictions thereafter. Confronted with a subject so emotionally charged for the people of Hiroshima—its intensity constantly reinforced by world events and particularly by nuclear weapons testing—newspapers in Hiroshima and elsewhere in Japan have dealt with it dramatically, particularly in circulating the concept of "A-bomb disease." Mass media are caught in a moral dilemma in some ways similar to that I have already described for physicians, city officials, and survivors themselves: there is on the one hand the urge to give full publicity to the horrors of nuclear weapons through vivid description of effects and suspected effects of atomic bomb radiation—thereby serving warning to the world and also expressing a form of sympathy to survivors through recognition of their plight—and on the other hand the growing awareness that lurid reports of illness and death have a profoundly disturbing effect upon survivors. Responsible media have struggled to reconcile these conflicting moral pressures and achieve balanced treatment of an unprecedentedly difficult problem; others have been guided mainly by commercial considerations. In any case, the people of Hiroshima have been constantly confronted with frightening descriptions of patients dying in the "A-bomb Hospital" (a medical center built specifically for the treatment of conditions related to the bomb) of "A-bomb disease." In the majority of cases the relationship of the fatal condition to delayed radiation effects is equivocal, but this is usually not made clear, nor does it in any way lessen the enormous impact of these reports upon individual survivors. Also furthering this impact have been the activities of peace movements and various ideological and political groups—ranging from those whose universalistic dedication to peace and opposition to nuclear weapons testing lead them to circulate the effects of the bomb on a humanistic basis, to others who seek narrower political goals from the unique Hiroshima atmosphere.

What I wish to stress is the manner in which these diverse passions—compounded of moral concern, sympathetic identification, various forms of fear, hostility, political conviction, personal ambition, and journalistic sensationalism—interact with the psychosomatic preoccupations of survivors. But I would also emphasize that these passions are by no means simply manufactured ones; they are the inevitable expression of the impact of a disaster of this magnitude upon basic human conflicts and anxieties. And whatever the medical exaggerations, they are built upon an underlying lethal reality of acute and delayed radiation effects, and upon the genuine possibility of still-undiscovered forms of bodily harm.

Yet, in bodily terms or otherwise, human beings vary greatly in their capacity to absorb an experience of this kind. And one's feelings of health or invalidism—as well as one's symbolic attitude toward the bomb—have much to do with individual emotions and life-patterns. This is made clear by a middle-aged female artist who experienced the bomb just 1500 meters from the hypocenter, and during subsequent years suffered continuously from a variety of bodily symptoms of indefinite origin, as well as from general unhappiness in marital and family relationships:

> It looks as though marriage and the normal life one leads with marriage is good for the health. . . . Among A-bomb victims, those who are married and well established with their families have fewer complaints. Of course, even those who are settled in their families remember the incident. But on the whole they are much better off and feel better . . . their attitude is *"shōganai"* [it can't be helped]. "It is useless to look back on old memories," they keep saying. They are simply interested in their immediate problems of marriage and everyday life. They look forward rather than backward. . . . Those without families, on the other hand, keep remembering everything. Clinging to their memories, they keep repeating the experience. . . . They curse the whole world—including what happened in the past and what is happening now. Some of them even say, "I hope that atomic bombs will be dropped again and then the whole world will suffer the same way I am suffering now."

This kind of hostility is likely to occur together with psychosomatic complaints, and particularly in those people who feel that their life has been blighted by the atomic bomb—those who lost close family members or who in one way or another feel themselves unable to recover from the experience. The cosmic nature of the emotion—its curse upon (and in some cases wish for total annihilation of) the whole world—resembles in some ways the retaliatory emotions of hurt children. But it contains additional elements of personal recollection: the experience of "world-destruction" at the time of the bomb. And it is a projection into the future: the even greater world-destruction one can envisage as a consequence of a repetition of the use of nuclear weapons.

Unwanted Identity

It is clear by now that exposure to the atomic bomb changed the survivor's status as a human being, in his own eyes as well as in others'. Both through his immediate experience and its consequences over the years, he became a member of a new group; he assumed the identity of the *hibakusha*, of one who has undergone the atomic bomb. When I asked survivors to associate freely to the word *hibakusha*, and to explain their feelings about it, they invariably conveyed to me the sense of having been compelled to take on this special category of existence, by which they felt permanently bound, however they might wish to free themselves from it. The shopkeeper's assistant expresses this in simple terms characteristic for many:

> Well . . . because I am a *hibakusha* . . . how shall I say it—I wish others would not look at me with special eyes . . . perhaps *hibakusha* are mentally—or both physically and mentally—different from others . . . but I myself do not want to be treated in any special way because I am a *hibakusha*. . . .

To be a *hibakusha* thus separates one from the rest of humankind. It means, as expressed by a young female clerical worker left with a keloid from her atomic bomb exposure at 1600 meters, a sense of having been forsaken.

> I don't like people to use that word [*hibakusha*] . . . . Of course there are some who, through being considered *hibakusha*, want to receive special coddling (*amaeru*). . . . But I like to stand up as an individual. When I was younger they used to call us "atomic bomb maidens.". . . More recently they call us *hibakusha*. . . . I don't like this special view of us. . . . Usually, when people refer to young girls, they will say girls or daughters, or some person's daughter . . . but to refer to us as atomic bomb maidens is a way of discrimination. . . . It is a way of abandoning us. . . .

What she is saying, and what many said to me in different ways, is that the experience, with all of its consequences, is so profound that it can virtually become the person; others then see one *only* as a *hibakusha* bearing the taint of death, and therefore, in the deepest sense, they turn away. And even the special attentions—the various forms of emotional succor—which the survivor may be tempted to seek, cannot be satisfying because such succor is ultimately perceived as unauthentic.

A European priest, one of the relatively few non-Japanese *hibakusha*, expresses these sentiments gently but sardonically:

> I always say—if everyone looks at me because I received the Nobel Prize, that's okay, but if my only virtue is that I was a thousand meters from the atomic bomb center and I'm still alive—I don't want to be famous for that.

Hibakusha look upon themselves as underprivileged in other ways too. Not only are they literally a minority group (one-fifth of the city's population), but they are generally considered to be at the lower socioeconomic levels of society, and have even at times been compared to the *burakumin*, or outcast group. For once it was realized that Hiroshima was not permanently contaminated after all, not only did the survivors attempt to rebuild their homes, but hordes of outsiders—some from overseas areas, some from the industrial Osaka region, some of them black marketeers and members of gangs who saw special opportunity beckoning: all of them both physically and culturally more vigorous than the atomic-bombed, traditionalistic Hiroshima population—poured into the city, and became perhaps the main beneficiaries of the economic boom which later developed. Survivors have encountered discrimination not only in marriage but also in employment, as it was felt that they could not work as hard as ordinary people and tended to need more time off because of illness and fatigue. Of course, survivors nonetheless regularly work and marry; but they often do so with a sense of having, as *hibakusha*, impaired capacity for both. They strongly resent the popular image of the *hibakusha* which accentuates their limitations, but at the same time accept much of it as their own self-image. Thus, concerning occupational competition, older survivors often feel that they have lacked the over-all energy to assimilate their economic, spiritual, and possibly physical blows sufficiently to be the equal of ordinary people; and young survivors, even if they feel themselves to possess normal energy, often fear that being identified by others as a *hibakusha* might similarly interfere with their occupational standing. Concerning marriage, the sense of impairment can include the need to have one's A-bomb experience more or less "cleared" by a go-between (as we have seen); fears about having abnormal children, or sometimes about the ability to have children at all; and occasionally, in males, diminished sexual potency (thought of as organic but probably psychogenic).

However well or poorly a survivor is functioning in his life, the word *hibakusha* evokes an image of the dead and the dying. The young clerk, for instance, when he hears the word, thinks either of the experience itself (". . . Although I wasn't myself too badly injured I saw many people who were . . . and I think . . . of the look on their faces . . . camps full of these people, their breasts burned and red. . . .") or, as we have already heard him describe, of the aftereffects: "when I hear about people who die from A-bomb disease or who have operations because of this illness, then I feel that I am the same kind of person as they. . . ."

We are again confronted with the survivor's intimate identification with the dead; we find, in fact, that it tends to pervade the entire *hibakusha* identity. *For survivors seem not only to have experienced the atomic disaster, but to have imbibed it and incorporated it into their beings, including all of its elements of horror, evil, and particularly of death.* They feel compelled virtually to merge with those who died. And they judge, and indeed judge harshly, their own behavior and that of other survivors on the basis of the degree of respect it demonstrates toward the dead. They condemn, for instance, the widespread tendency (which, as Japanese, they are at the same time attracted to) of making the anniversary of the bomb an occasion for a gay festival—because they see this as an insult to the dead. Similarly they are extraordinarily suspicious of all individual and group attempts to take any form of action in relationship to the atomic bomb experience, even when done for the apparent purpose of helping survivors or furthering international peace. And they are, if anything, more critical of a survivor prominent in such programs than they are of "outsiders," constantly accusing such a person of "selling his name," "selling the bomb," or "selling Hiroshima." The causes for their suspiciousness are many, including a pervasive Japanese cultural tendency to be critical of the man who shows unconventional initiative (as expressed in the popular saying "A nail which sticks out will be hammered down"), as well as an awareness of how readily the Hiroshima situation can be "used" by ambitious leaders. But there is an ultimate inner feeling that any such activities and programs are "impure," that they violate the sanctity of the dead. For in relationship to the atomic bomb disaster, it is only the dead who, in the eyes of survivors, remain pure; and any self- or group-assertion can readily be seen as an insult to the dead.

Finally, this imposed identity of the atomic bomb survivor is greatly affected by his historical perceptions (whether clear or fragmentary) of the original experience, including its bearing upon the present world situation. The dominant emotion here is the sense of having been made into "guinea pigs," not only because of being studied by research groups (particularly American research groups) interested in determining the effects of delayed radiation, but more fundamentally because of having been victimized by the first "experiment" (a word many of them use in referring to the event) with nuclear weapons. They are affected by a realization, articulated in various ways, that they have experienced something ultimate in man-made disasters; and at the same time by the feeling that the world's continuing development and testing of the offending weapons deprives their experience of meaning. Thus, while frequently suspicious of organized campaigns against nuclear testing, they almost invariably experience anxiety and rage when such testing is conducted, recall the horrors they have been through, and express bitter frustration at the world's unwillingness to heed their warnings. And we have seen how this anger can at times be converted into thoughts of cosmic retaliation. There remains, of course, a residuum of hostility toward America and Americans for having dropped the bomb, but such hostility has been tempered over the years and softened by Japanese cultural restraints—except, as we have also seen, in individuals who experienced personal losses and blows to self-esteem from which they have been unable to recover. More than in relation to the dropping of the bomb itself (which many said they could understand as a product, however horrible, of war), survivors tend to express hostility in response to what they feel to be callousness toward their plight, or toward those who died, and also toward nuclear weapons testing. Thus, in singling out President Truman as an object of hatred, as some do, it is not only for his having ordered that the bomb be used but also for being assertively unapologetic about having done so.

Survivors tend to be strongly ambivalent about serving as symbols for the rest of the world, and this ambivalence is expressed in Hiroshima's excruciating conflict about whether or not to tear down the so-called "A-Bomb Dome" (or "Peace Dome")—the prominent ruins of a dome-shaped exhibition hall located almost directly at the hypocenter. The dome has so far been permitted to stand as a reminder of the experience, and its picture has been featured in countless books and pamphlets dealing, from every point of view, with the A-bomb problem. Three different sets of attitudes on the question were expressed to me. The first: Let it remain permanently so that people (especially outsiders) will remember what we have been through and take steps to prevent repetitions of such disasters. The second: Tear it down for any of the following reasons: it does no good, as no one pays any attention to it; we should adopt the Buddhist attitude of resignation toward the experience; the dome is inauthentic, does not adequately convey what we really experienced, and is not in fact directly at the hypocenter; it is too painful a reminder for *us* (*hibakusha*) to have to look at every day (perhaps the most strongly felt objection); and, we should look ahead to the future rather than back to the unpleasant past. And the third: Let it neither be permitted to stand indefinitely nor torn down, but instead left as it is until it begins to crumble of its own, and then simply removed—a rather ingenious (and perhaps characteristically Japanese) compromise solution to the dilemma, which the city administration has proposed. Most survivors simultaneously feel various conflicting elements of the first and second sets of attitudes, and sometimes of all three. The inner conflict is something like this: For the sake of the dead and of our own sense of worth, we must give our experience significance by enabling it to serve wider moral purposes; but to do so—to be living symbols of massive death—is not only unbearably painful but also tends ultimately to be insincere and to insult, rather than comfort, the dead.

Beyond Hiroshima

We return to the question we raised at the beginning: Does Hiroshima follow the standard patterns delineated for other disasters, or is it—in an experiential sense—a new order of event? We must say first that the usual emotional patterns of disaster are very much present in what I have already described. One can break down the experience into the usual sequence of anticipation, impact, and aftermath; one can recognize such standard individual psychological features as various forms of denial, the "illusion of centrality" (or feeling of each that he was at the very center of the disaster's path), the apathy of the "disaster syndrome" resulting from the sudden loss of the sense of safety and even omnipotence with which we usually conduct our lives, and the conflict between self-preservation and wider human responsibility which culminates in feelings of guilt and shame; even some of the later social and psychological conflicts in the affected population are familiar. Yet we have also seen convincing evidence that the Hiroshima experience no less in the psychological than in the physical sphere, transcends in many important ways that of the ordinary disaster. I shall try to suggest what I think are some of the important ways in which this is true. And when these special psychological qualities of the experience of the atomic bomb have been more fully elaborated—beyond the preliminary outlines of this paper—I believe that they will, in turn, shed light on general disaster patterns, and, of greater importance, on human nature and its vicissitudes at our present historical juncture. We may then come to see Hiroshima for what it was and is: both a direct continuation of the long and checkered history of human struggle, and at the same time a plunge into a new and tragic dimension.

The first of these psychological elements is one we have already referred to, the continuous encounter with death. When we consider the sequence of this encounter—its turbulent onset at the moment the bomb fell, its shocking reappearance in association with delayed radiation effects, and its prolonged expression in the group identity of the doomed and near-dead—we are struck by the fact that it is an interminable encounter. There is, psychologically speaking, no end point, no resolution. This continuous and unresolvable encounter with death, then, is a unique feature of the atomic bomb disaster. Its significance for the individual survivor varies greatly, according to such factors as previous character traits, distance from the hypocenter at the time the bomb fell, fatalities in his immediate family, and many other features of his bomb experience and subsequent life pattern. There is little doubt that most survivors lead reasonably effective personal, family, and occupational lives. But each retains, in greater or lesser degree, emotional elements of this special relationship to death.

In the light of the Hiroshima experience we should also consider the possibility that in other disasters or extreme situations there may also be more significant inner encounters with death, immediate or longer-term, than we have heretofore supposed. Psychiatrists and social scientists investigating these matters are hampered by the same factors which interfere with everyone else's approach to the subject: first, by our inability to imagine death, which deprives us, as psychiatrists, of our usual reliance upon empathy and leaves us always at several psychological removes from experiential understanding; and second, by the elaborate circle of denial—the profound inner need of human beings to make believe that they will never die—in which we too are enclosed. But these universal psychological barriers to thought about death become much greater in relation to a nuclear disaster, where the enormity of the scale of killing and the impersonal nature of the technology are still further impediments to comprehension. No wonder, then, that the world resists full knowledge of the Hiroshima and Nagasaki experiences, and expends relatively little energy in comprehending their full significance. And beyond Hiroshima, these same impediments tragically block and distort our perceptions of the general consequences of nuclear weapons. They also raise an important question relevant for the continuous debate about the desirability of preparedness for possible nuclear attacks: If the human imagination is so limited in its capacity to deal with death, and particularly death on a vast scale, can individuals ever be significantly "prepared" for a nuclear disaster?

The Hiroshima experience thus compels us, particularly as psychiatrists, to give more thought to psychic perceptions of death and dying. Here I would particularly stress the psychological importance of identification with the dead—not merely the identification with a particular loved one, as in the case of an ordinary mourning experience, but rather, as we have observed in atomic bomb survivors, a lasting sense of affiliation with death itself. This affiliation creates in turn an enduring element, both within, and standing in judgment of, the self—a process closely related to the experience of shame. Also of great importance is the *style of dying*, real or symbolic, the way in which one anticipates death and the significance with which one can relate oneself to this anticipation. Among those I interviewed in Hiroshima, many found solace in the characteristically Japanese (partially Buddhist) attitude of resignation, but virtually none was able to build a framework of meaning around their overwhelming immersion in death. However philosophically they might accept the horrors of war, they had an underlying sense of having been victimized and experimented upon by a horrible device, all to no avail in a world which has derived no profit from their sufferings.

And this sense of purposeless death suggests the second special feature of the atomic disaster: *a vast breakdown of faith in the larger human matrix supporting each individual life, and therefore a loss of faith (or trust) in the structure of existence.* This is partly due to the original exposure to death and destruction on such an extraordinary scale, an "end-of-the-world" experience resembling the actualization of the wildest psychotic delusion; partly due to the shame and guilt patterns which, initiated during the experience itself, turned into longer-lasting preoccupations with human selfishness (preoccupations expressed to me by a large number of survivors); and partly due to the persisting sense of having encountered an ultimate form of *man-made* destruction. Phrased in another way, the atomic bomb destroyed the complex equilibrium which ordinarily mediates and integrates the great variety of cultural patterns and individual emotions which maintain any society, large or small. One must, of course, take into account here the disruption accompanying the extensive social change which has occurred all over Japan immediately following World War II; and one must also recognize the impressive re-emergence of Hiroshima as an actively functioning city. Nonetheless, this profound loss of confidence in human social ties remains within survivors as a derivative of the atomic bomb experience.

A third psychological feature of particular importance in the Hiroshima disaster is that which I have called *psychic closing-off*. Resembling the psychological defense of denial, and the behavioral state of apathy, psychic closing-off is nonetheless a distinctive pattern of response to overwhelmingly threatening stimuli. Within a matter of moments, as we have seen in the examples cited, a person may not only cease to react to these threatening stimuli but in so doing, equally suddenly violate the most profound values and taboos of his culture and his personal life. Though a highly adaptive response—and indeed very often a means of emotional self-preservation—it can vary in its proportions to the extent at times of almost resembling a psychotic mechanism. Since psychic closing-off, at least in the form it took in Hiroshima, is specifically related to the problem of death, it raises the question of the degree to which various forms of psychosis might also be responses to the symbolic fear of death or bodily annihilation.

The psychic closing-off created by the Hiroshima disaster is not limited to the victims themselves, but extends to those who, like myself, attempt to study the event. Thus, although I had had previous research experience with people who had been exposed to extreme situations, I found that at the beginning of my work in Hiroshima the completion of each interview would leave me profoundly shocked and emotionally spent. But as the work progressed and I heard more and more of these accounts, their effects upon me greatly lessened. My awareness of my scientific function—my listening carefully for specific kinds of information and constantly formulating categories of response—enhanced the psychic closing-off necessary to me for the task of conducting the research (necessary also for a wide variety of human efforts which deal with problems in which death is a factor). It is this vast ramification of psychic closing-off, rather than the phenomenon itself, that is unique to nuclear disaster, so much so that all who become in any way involved in the problem find themselves facing a near-automatic tendency to seal themselves off from what is most disturbing in the evidence at hand.

Finally, there is the question of *psychological mastery of the nuclear disaster experience*. Central to this problem is the task of dealing with feelings of shame and guilt of the most profound nature: the sense that one has, however unwittingly, participated in this total human breakdown in which, in Martin Buber's words, "the human order of being is injured." That such feelings of self-condemnation—much like those usually termed "existential guilt"—should be experienced by the *victims* of a nuclear disaster is perhaps the most extreme of its many tragic ironies. Faced with the task of dealing with this form of guilt, with the problem of re-establishing trust in the human order, and with the continuing sense of encounter with death, the survivor of a nuclear disaster needs nothing less than a new identity in order to come to terms with his post-disaster world. And once more extending the principle beyond the victim's experience, it may not be too much to say that those who permit themselves to confront the consequences of such a disaster, past or future, are also significantly changed in the process. Since these consequences now inhabit our world, more effective approaches to the problem of human survival may well depend upon our ability to grasp the nature of the fundamentally new relationship to existence which we all share.

9 THE EUROPEAN SURRENDER

John Ney

The catch phrase "Coca Cola imperialism" (or variants thereof) has now come to rival even "living under the threat of nuclear annihilation" as the most popular superficial summation of postwar international affairs. That American business practices, cultural idioms, and typically American products have exerted tremendous influence abroad is beyond question. But why this wholesale export of an American "life style" has occurred, why other peoples have embraced these values so readily, and what the ultimate effects will be are still debated. Certainly, the Second World War was an important factor. It served as an object lesson, for only America seemed to emerge from the war with its political and social values intact and with the strength of its economic system vindicated. However, some writers, including John Ney, argue that the Americanization of the world, and certainly of Europe, began long before the Second World War. The following selections from Ney's book indirectly raise several important and ironic questions about the slaughter that was World War II. If Ney and others are correct—if Frenchmen, Germans, Poles, and Russians sooner or later are to become Americans in all but name—then one may ask, "why was the war fought?" Or, phrased differently, was it worth fighting?

Even after taking into consideration the inevitable time lag between change and its recognition, the realization of American control in Europe seems extraordinarily tardy. Indeed, such recognition has only become acute in the last few years, but now it is not a challenge from America that Europeans have to cope with—or *will* have to cope with, to put it more severely—but the fact that the battle is over and the European sword long since broken over the European knee.

Perhaps there is always a delay between fact and its admission, in which case it is not surprising that eventual recognition of any fact should begin, as it has concerning American control in Europe, with the surface of the animal. It is not unhealthy in itself to draw attention, as American and European commentators alike have done, to the amount of American capital in Europe, the hordes of American businessmen, the transformation of Europe's economic and commercial and social life, and so on. What is disturbing is the inability, once that is done, to distinguish between the symptoms of a change and the forces which brought the change about.

After all, American businessmen and tourists did not arrive in Europe by accident. Nor were they successful in having their own way by accident. They represented—and continue to represent—the exploitation of very definite American rights, rights which were won long before they were born, and of which they are almost invariably ignorant. Not practically ignorant, for they have enough wit to see that they have a superior position and to use it to reap its rewards, but technically ignorant in that they are not familiar with the historical development of the rights which created the position.

When did the historical development start? One is tempted to peg it at the American Revolution, but no less an authority than Henry Adams would put it even further back in time. In writing in *The Education of Henry Adams* of America becoming a formal world power in 1898 as a result of the war with Spain, he said: "The sense of solidarity counts for much in one's contentment, but the sense of winning one's game counts for more; and in London, in 1898, the scene was singularly interesting to the last survivor of the Legation of 1861. He thought himself perhaps the only person living who could get full enjoyment of the drama. He carried every scene of it, in a century and a half since the Stamp Act, quite alive in his mind—all the interminable disputes of his disputatious ancestors as far back as the year 1750—as well as his own insignificance in the Civil War, every step in which had the object of bringing England into an American system. . . . After two hundred years of stupid and greedy blundering, which no argument and no violence affected, the people of England learned this lesson just at the moment when Hay would otherwise have faced a flood of the old anxieties. . . . the sudden appearance of Germany as the grizzly terror which in twenty years effected what Adamses had tried for two hundred in vain—frightened England into America's arms—seemed as melodramatic as any plot of Napoleon the Great. He could feel only the sense of satisfaction at seeing the diplomatic triumph of all his family, since the breed existed, at last realized under his own eyes for the advantage of his oldest and closest ally [Hay]. . . . He could see that the family work of a hundred and fifty years fell at once into the grand perspective of true empire-building."

No one should fail to recognize it as a remarkable passage, least of all a contemporary American proconsul. Adams had the background, the access to state documents, the years of intimacy with national figures, the high native intelligence—the authority, finally—to talk of "bringing England into an American system," of England flapping into "America's arms," of "triumph," of "true empire-building," and make refutation difficult if not impossible.

It is not surprising that such statements would have seemed delirious to the Englishmen who passed Adams on the streets of London in 1898; or farfetched to most Americans of the age; or incomprehensible to Charles de Gaulle's father or Jean-Jacques Servan-Schreiber's grandfather. But it is remarkable that they are not articles of faith in our own day. Although the book in which they appear has been sanctified as one of the world's great autobiographies for over forty years and read by armies of students and scholars, the flat statements in which

America is defined as the realization of formidably naked ambition—and the passage quoted above is only one among a great many—have been curiously passed over.

Adams claims that the colonial gentlemen who set the American Revolution in motion were well aware of its implications. They understood that if they won, they had to keep on winning; that if they were too advanced for England, they were going to be much too advanced for the rest of the world; and that the victorious little country was not going to exist in a vacuum—it was going to end up running the world unless it was superseded, not by a more powerful country but by a more sophisticated system. Which was unlikely, because England in 1775 represented the best the rest of the world could put up, the crowned champion of a tournament which had started with the Reformation. (And significantly for the future, a tournament in which Russia had not distinguished itself.) If the tender United States had superseded England as Fortune's darling, there was no need to worry about those already passed over. They had to bow in time as England had bowed: there wasn't even any hurry.

If there has been an American conquest, does it follow that there has been a European surrender? And even if there has been a surrender, isn't the conquest of more importance than the surrender? At first, one tends to say "Not necessarily" to the first question and "Yes" to the second. But then one remembers that no conquest is ever complete without a surrender on the part of the conquered, and the American conquest of Europe is complete. The Normans were successful in England because the native Britons finally gave up and accepted them; the Moors were unsuccessful in Spain because the Spaniards didn't. Aztec legend prophesied the arrival of conquerors from the sea, so Cortez and his men had eventual surrender guaranteed before they landed.

Without surrender, ultimate colonization is impossible, as in the case of Vietnam, a relatively weak country which will *not* surrender and thus cannot be colonized. The choice between surrender and resistance is not dictated by manpower, material resources, or any other surface indicator, but is a psychological-sexual state of mind. Surrender is essentially the admission that something is lacking and that there is a willingness to take a chance on the conqueror being able to supply it. (The lack is the difference between the lives of the conquered and the conquering: what is left when the second is subtracted from the first, according to the arithmetical values of the conquered—not, of course, of the conquering.) Personified, surrender is the restless, lonely woman who lives by herself on a remote farm and keeps her restlessness from herself until the day she gazes, D. H. Lawrence fashion, from the rear porch onto the bare, sinewy back of the mysterious, self-sufficient drifter splitting wood for a meal. Her sigh, which carries clearly across the sunbaked yard, lets them both know that there is nothing left for her but to bow to him.

American conquest in Europe has been subtle and religious rather than coarse and military—in comparison to the Normans in England, the Spanish in the New World, and the Americans themselves on their own continent and in

Asia—but the rules remain the same in that the conquest did not become a reality until Europe surrendered by admitting its lack and its need.

The surrender entailed the offering up of the material as well as the psychological, and in 1900 Europe was filled with the accumulation of centuries. From the valley of the Loire to the mouth of the Danube endless attics and storerooms were crammed with ancient uniforms, letters, furniture, paintings and forgotten dolls (the painted cheeks still bright under the gray dust); the libraries were loaded with unread books; the cluttered palaces reeled under the sheer weight of possessions . . . all faded, all worthless. But the living were still fabulously alive. Colette's Léa was a ravishing, vital woman; her enormous lover, Speleïeff, had trememdous presence; the women's dresses were gorgeous, tantalizing; the men stroked their moustaches with assurance; the soft air at Auteuil rang with real laughter: ". . . a fetching hat, a hat that turned up on one side only, trimmed like a single sail to the wind . . . her swan neck rising from a pleatless collar, a white and rounded neck like the bole of a birch tree."

It may be said that the Europeans blew all that to pieces by themselves in the First World War, that it was destroyed before it was "surrendered" to the Americans and the new way of life. But it may also be claimed that the First World War was a fit of pique brought on by an unspoken presentiment of death—as a ruined man will throw away what is left of his money rather than let his creditors have it.

In support, I recall Feliks Topolski, who had served with General Anders's Polish forces in World War II, telling me a compelling story about a vast collection of refugees in central Europe who had slowly drifted into the mountains to avoid the advancing armies. They finally ended up in an uninhabited valley, a hundred thousand pitiable wretches without food, their clothes in rags, all hope gone. They composed themselves for death and were already dropping like flies when the American army discovered their existence and ordered them saved. The enormous field kitchens were backed up into the ghastly valley, the six-by-six trucks loaded with warm clothing pulled up the narrow roads, and the individual soldiers went toward them with candy bars and K-rations proffered. But, in a strange moment for the western world, the tottering wrecks didn't reach out for sustenance. "They had given themselves up for lost," said Topolski. "They had seen that death, after all, was the end for which Europe had been yearning since 1914, and they had accepted it. Physical salvation was a very unwelcome distraction, and they didn't want it at all." Resistance could not last long, of course. "Such ghosts, without control of their future, had to accept deliverance. Not only because there was so very little choice, I suppose, between death and the American way of life, but also because nothing was theirs to decide any more. They had abandoned themselves to the mercies of Providence, and if Providence chose to send them K-rations instead of sweet sleep they had to obey. But in the moment of refusal it was very apparent that their desire—and that had to have been the desire from 1914, too—had been for annihilation, for an end to all and everything."

It is not so changed today. Watching the unguarded faces of Europeans in public places, one often senses that the human spirit is unwillingly present.

There is a somber indifference to life in the present, and the implication that such life is only temporary; and Death, the preferred companion who is so barely offstage that the atmosphere is charged with his seductive appeal, seems not to have arrived recently but to have been there for a very long time. Death still seems to hang as heavy and as real in Europe as he does in the paintings of Breughel and Bosch. He is the anthropomorphic Death of plague and pestilence, a lively personality who was unaccountably left behind when the immigrants sailed across the Atlantic. Indeed, his absence from the New World heart may be the basis of all differences between Americans and Europeans.

Whatever the reason, though, the surrender had to become more conscious after World War I. What was left after 1918, and even after 1945, could not have been given up without a certain knowledge. The old religion, the old ways, the old prides . . . all were formally abandoned, and the lips—dry and cool, but also parted and receptive—were correctly offered. Technically, the surrender was an acceptance of the situation as it really was. Europe admitted that it, too, found unabashed materialism more attractive than anything else. Pressed, it admitted that the old life had always been inferior. The picturesque peasant, the elongated aristocrat, the demonic artist, the country restaurant with sunshine playing through thick-leafed plane trees, the glorious chateau, the quiet square, the wonderful music, the Catholic and Protestant marvels, the nubile women . . . none of it had been enough. It was medieval, old-fashioned, slightly shameful, almost a fraud. Subtracted from the American way, it revealed an imposing lack; and when Europe felt the lack so keenly that life became unbearable, there was no choice except to embrace the American to get at the secret of his complacence. That embrace was the true moment of conquest, the moment of surrender at which conqueror and conquered assumed their official identities. . . .

* * *

In this book, what used to be called the "point of departure" has been the assumption that all Europe is Americanized and going to become more so. (Students of the present as past will note that if the phrase "point of departure," once as sensually pleasing to the American tongue as the current "charisma," "viable," and "confrontation," had been written of as mortal twenty years ago, public incredulity would have been as great as if "dialogue" were similarly treated today.) The surrender is complete. On the basis of visible evidence and experience, it would seem to be a valid assumption.

With a clearer understanding now of what underlies newspaper features, a report such as Tad Szulc's in the *New York Times* (part of which was quoted earlier in the section on England) assumes genuine meaning:

"From the Iberian Peninsula to Scandinavia and from the British Isles to Italy, Western Europe is becoming Americanized in its consumer habits. Western Europe imports a steadily growing volume of United States goods, along with industrial licenses, capital, techniques and managerial talent to reproduce American products.

"It consumes in increasing quantity foods packaged the American way and bought at the 'super-marchés' and 'super-mercados.' It spends 'les weekends' at 'les picnics' and 'campings.' It dresses its children in Levi's and cowboy shirts and it uses credit cards more and more. It smokes American cigarettes, for taste and for status, and it watches 'The Man from U.N.C.L.E.' (as 'El Agente de Cipol' in Spain and as 'Agents Très Spéciaux' in France) on television, as it drinks a pop-top can of locally brewed Schlitz beer.

"This process of everyday Americanization in Western Europe is directly related to the mounting influx of United States private capital—an estimated $10-billion in new investments since 1958—and management. Jean-Jacques Servan-Schreiber . . . has concluded in . . . 'The American Challenge' that an Americanized Europe will become the world's third industrial force after the United States and the Soviet Union. A survey by correspondents of the *New York Times* in 10 European capitals and a recent leisurely tour of Western Europe have produced the picture of a multilingual and multicultural European society that is Americanizing itself along strikingly uniform lines. . . .

"The critics of American policy do not take out their anti-Washington attitudes on American products. In Rome a correspondent reported that Coca-Cola (known in Italy as Koka) 'is sold at most Communist rallies.' Elsewhere, the United States finds itself berated for Vietnam or for rioting in Newark or Detroit while its critics smoke Kent cigarettes—produced locally under license, imported or smuggled—and drink Coke, 7-Up or Fanta, a popular orange soft drink produced by the Coca-Cola concern. The soft drink symbolizes, in a sense, this phenomenon of Americanization. The European landscape is fairly covered with billboards and posters advertising in various languages 'the pause that refreshes.' European airwaves carry the message of Pepsi Cola and whether Europeans think young or old they have to live with American jingles translated from English into their own languages. Trucks with posters proclaiming 'Tutto va meglio con Coca-Cola' speed down the Italian highways from Naples to Milan, and there is no intimate little bar between the Adriatic coast and the Aosta valley where a thirsty Italian or a foreign tourist may not find his Koka or Pepsi. What this avidity for American-brand soft drinks, bottled by local companies, does to wine consumption in Europe, is impossible to measure. The producers in the main European wine-drinking countries—France, Italy, Spain, Portugal, Greece and Germany—deplore the fact that people sometimes seem to prefer a sweet carbonated drink to the nobility of wine. But they have not produced comprehensive statistics.

"Perhaps the clearest explanation for the momentum of this advancing revolution in Made-in-America tastes, habits and manners lies in the sentiment that Europeans are Americanizing themselves not out of any conscious identification with the United States, but simply because American ways and products 'are the best,' or are the most fashionable. A Spanish Government official explained that he smoked American cigarettes because 'they taste better' (most Spaniards stick to their own 'black' cigarettes) and that he had just purchased an American washing machine for his wife because it was 'the best thing on the market.' The American cigarette, in demand since the liberation days of World War II, tends to be overwhelmingly a status item. With a pack of 'legal' American cigarettes selling between the postdevaluation equivalent of 42 American cents in Spain and 85 cents in Britain, it is not infrequent for Europeans to carry two packs—the American brand for smoking in public and the local brand for when they are alone. In most countries, smuggled American cigarettes cost one-half the official price. At least one American brand, Kent, is manufactured in Switzerland for 'legal' European consumption. The same advertising techniques exist here as in the United States. Hence there is 'Marlboro country' in Europe.

"Such intense propagandizing of other American products ranging from detergents to cosmetics is a leitmotif of European merchandising. . . . American-imported goods usually cost more than similar local products. Custom duties, often designed to discourage luxury items, make it so. Locally produced American brand name products have to be competitive with the local name goods. Canned juices or soups produced in Europe by large American companies often undersell the independent domestic producer because of the volume in which the United States owned corporations deal.

"Fundamentally, the correspondents found, the phenomenon of Americanization is fed by the rising living standard in Western Europe. The postwar economic and sociological changes in Europe—larger family incomes, women increasingly at work, the gradual disappearance of the household servant and the creation of mass-consumer markets—have made traditional American solutions to daily problems not only desirable but also necessary. The sociological change in the European home has created an immense market for refrigerators, blenders and dishwashers, as well as for frozen and canned foods. Until not long ago, these precooked foods were regarded as 'barbaric American inventions,' but now even servants press their employers to open a can of Campbell's soup (very popular in Europe) instead of preparing soup the old-fashioned way.

"Supermarkets, indistinguishable from the American kind and complete with piped-in music and air-conditioning, have wrought their own revolution in food tastes, merchandising and frozen foods, started in the United States, forced European producers and packagers to modernize. Even American ideas such as paper napkins and plates, once frowned on, have made their appearance. Ten years ago, it would have been unthinkable for the proud Spaniard to do the family shopping, but today he pushes his shopping cart down the aisle of a 'super mercado' with no loss of dignity. Therefore, Señor Rodriguez (Mr. Smith of Spain) may fill his cart with frozen fish, a novelty here, a bottle of Scotch, College Inn vegetable juice from the United States and a box of Ajax detergent.

"In most European cities, the Americanization includes the 'lavamats' and 'laundromatos,' now an accepted institution. As personal checking accounts are becoming increasingly popular—and as downtown traffic jams mount—even Madrid and Lisbon have provided drive-in banking services. The development of these and other American tastes in Western Europe stems from a variety of sources. But the correspondents believe that the lengthy postwar presence of United States military personnel—notably in West Germany but also in France,

Italy and Britain—played a major role in introducing American products and ideas to Europe. American tourists and American movies, television and publications are another constant fountainhead of United States influence.

"Since it is generally assumed in Europe that the process of Americanization will keep gaining, rather than losing momentum . . . the steadily mounting presence of American tourists in Western Europe is certain to accelerate the process, because the tourists set in motion a chain reaction. To attract dollar-bearing tourists, the European city fathers and hotel and store owners are busy developing styles and facilities attractive to the visitors. But once the European customer discovers these facilities, he often seeks them himself. The beginning of 'jumbo' trans-Atlantic flights in the nineteen-seventies is expected to increase the American tourist presence and, therefore, to heighten the socioeconomic and cultural cross-fertilization that has been operating in the last decade.

"Inevitably, a social or cultural synthesis implies a two-way traffic. The American visiting Europe does go home with new ideas and they may range from the sudden discovery that a Chateau Mouton Rothschild wine or a Spanish Riscal merits being served in an American home to the notion that there may be something to be said for the European obsession with bidets. It may also go deeper and encourage an American who toured the Louvre to return home and visit New York's Metropolitan Museum or Washington's National Gallery. Yet, the visible trend today is for the everyday-American influence to assert itself to a much greater extent in Europe than for European ways to make an impact on America. As an Italian intellectual remarked recently, the 'Western wind is blowing stronger.' "

The obvious could not be put more simply, but it is not invalid because it is either obvious or simple. (Or because it appeared in November, 1967. If anything, the surface Americanization has increased since then.) As was pointed out earlier, once the psychological basis of the surrender and the colonization is comprehended, the physical results can be understood and appreciated. The accumulated data then assumes multidimensional meaning, and, within limits, can be informative and helpful. . . .

America may collapse, but until it does, Americanization will continue. The collapse is problematical, the Americanization is a current fact. Also, as pointed out, it is doubtful that the decline of America, whether from internal collapse or external attack, would spell the end of the Americanization process. Modern Europe could not have come into being if America had never been, so the consumer-society Europe of the future, east or west, does not depend on continued American existence any more than European Christianity in the Dark Ages depended on the continued existence of Rome. If America is overturned, Russia might fill the power vacuum by taking over: but unless Russia substitutes some other idea-method for the American philosophy of increasing material consumption as the apex of human evolution, America would rule from the grave. And what other idea-method could be substituted? One can hardly think of another, and the D.C.'s notion that Americanization would disappear with America begins to seem untenable.

Perhaps he had a presentiment of that himself when he claimed earlier, to Jim and Milo and me, in the Alcron bar, that it makes no difference that Russia has achieved such actual (as distinguished from theoretical) Americanization as it has without using American capital and American supervisors. "We have the independence the west Europeans say they want, but what difference does it make?" he had asked. "Resistance to Americanism in the east may continue on several levels—the inertial incompetence is the most important—but the idea itself is triumphant. Even if we could become more proficient at produce-and-consume than you, it would not be real resistance, but merely the extension of America through the American idea. . . . What difference does it make where it comes from? The reality is whether America-as-idea has taken over. And to what degree. Not whether America-as-idea comes from Russia, or America, or Germany . . . or even from Albania."

He had contradicted that view with his summary of his *report*, but in later sessions he had returned to his earlier position: "Tipping is now allowed in the Soviet Union again," he said. "After fifty years—isn't that the handwriting on the wall?" And: "We have such hopeful people. They think that because they can say the CIA runs half the countries in the world and would like to run the other half, they have solved the problem. When you tell them, 'No, that isn't important. What matters is that the American Negro has a higher per capita income than an Englishman, to say nothing of an east European,' or, 'The United States is widening its lead in science research and application over Europe, again to say nothing of east Europe,' they only take out their notebooks confidently and tell you that the new U.S. immigration laws have ended the 'brain drain' from west Europe, so the United States can't go on. Of course the United States can't go on, but not for those ridiculous reasons. What can you do with such people?"

"Make Americans out of them" Jim Carter would have said, and that solution seems unavoidable. Whether the United States goes on as a political-economic entity or disappears, Americanism—the dedication to produce-and-consume—will last until the millenium, provided it is not unhorsed by a greater idea or a universal catastrophe. Barring the last two possibilities, there would seem to be no appeal from the ultimate Americanization of the world whether under the auspices of Americans or their disciples. . . .